Y0-CCH-195

American Public Finance

American Public Finance

Seventh Edition

WILLIAM J. SHULTZ, LL.B. Ph.D.
Bernard M. Baruch School of Business and Public Administration, the City College of New York

C. LOWELL HARRISS, Ph.D.
Professor of Economics, Columbia University

PRENTICE-HALL, INC.
Englewood Cliffs, N.J.

1959

L. C. Cat. Card No.: 59-9045

Printed in the United States of America
02873

Preface

The mature man-of-affairs today knows from experience that taxation, government spending, and public debt policy have a larger place in our economic life than ever before. Today's students will find the need for an understanding of public finance ever more persistent as they gradually assume the responsibilities that lie ahead—responsibilities for their own individual family affairs, for the businesses and professions in which they work, for local government and other civic matters, and for state, national, and even worldwide affairs.

This revision of AMERICAN PUBLIC FINANCE, like its six predecessors, is designed to provide the necessary understanding or, more accurately, to build a basic foundation for dealing with the problems of public finance. No volume written today can meet all the needs of those who will deal with issues of the future. Yet without the foundation which is laid here, no one can expect to deal adequately with the fiscal problems of today or to prepare himself for meeting certain of the developing and inescapable challenges of a changing world.

This revision reflects both the sweeping change of modern life and the persistence of underlying fiscal problems and principles. Much of the volume may, at first glance, seem familiar to those who used the sixth edition. The general framework is largely unaltered. Increased emphasis on budgeting and somewhat less space given to nontax revenues will be obvious. Otherwise, the structure is changed only in detail. Content, however, has been altered throughout. In many cases material of the preceding edition has been condensed and not infrequently deleted to make room for new developments in fiscal theory and practice. The two chapters on Fiscal Policy have been completely rewritten to take account of progress in this field of thought and the experience of the last two post-war cycles. Questions and problems have been added for each chapter, and the use of tables and charts has been increased. Nevertheless, realistic recognition of the needs which the book is to serve has led us to reduce the length somewhat.

In our efforts to make this book as good as possible we have been aided directly by scores of professors of economics, government officials, tax practitioners, scholars, and students. For special help on this volume we wish to thank Dr. Robert T. Patterson of the American Institute for Economic Research, and Professors Morris Beck of Rutgers University, H. K. Allen of the University of Illinois, Randall S. Stout of Pennsylvania State University, and Paul E. Alyea of the University of Alabama.

W.J.S.
C.L.H.

New York City

Table of Contents

Introduction 1

Why Study Public Finance? 2
Public Finance as a Study 3

Public Finance and related studies, 3. Methodology of Public Finance, 4. The bias of special interests, 6.

Recent Trends 7

PART ONE. GOVERNMENT EXPENDITURE

1. Growth, Agencies, and Purposes of American Government Expenditure 10

Growth 11

War and threats of war, 12. National growth and urbanization, 12. Expansion and quality improvement of government functions, 14. Rising price levels, 15. Business fluctuations, 16. Special interest pressure groups, 16.

Agencies 17
Purposes 19
Purposes of Federal Expenditure 21

National defense, 22. Veterans' service and benefits, 24. International affairs and foreign aid, 24. Natural resources and transportation, 24. Agricultural aid, 25. Welfare and other "social expenditures," 25. Interest, 26. General government, 26.

2. Growth, Agencies and Purposes of American Government Expenditure (Concluded) 28

Purposes of State Expenditure 28

General functions, 28. Capital outlays, 30.

Purposes of Local Expenditure 30

Cities, 33. Counties, 33. Special districts, 35.

Expenditure for Public Education 35

Why treat education as a government function?, 36. Growth, 37. School finance, 38. Government-supported colleges, 40. Probable trends in educational expenditure, 41. Libraries, 41.

Expenditure for Highways, Streets, and Airports 42

Provision of highways as a government function, 42. Development of highway expenditure, 42. Airport expenditure, 44. Probable trends, 44.

Social Welfare Expenditure 45

Emergency relief after 1930, 45. Old Age and Survivors Insurance, 46. Unemployment insurance, 47. Welfare grants, 48. Government employee pension funds, 48. Probable trends, 48.

3. Scope of Government Expenditure 52

Political Theories 52

Individualistic doctrine, 53. Collectivistic doctrine, 54. Critique, 55.

Economic Considerations 56

Productivity of government expenditure, 56. Transfer expenditures, 59. Doctrine of "comparative social benefits," 59. Fiscal policy objectives, 62. Alleviating poverty, 62. Subsides to high-fixed-cost industries, 63. Projects too large for private investment, 64. Limits of government expenditure, 64. Commitments to spend, 66. Compulsion or inducement by other governments, 66. Measures of government expenditure, 67.

Conclusion 68

4. Economics of Government Expenditure 70

Benefits of Government Expenditure 70

Social benefit and supplementary individual benefit, 70. Nonprofit nature of social benefit, 71. Indivisibility of social benefit, 72.

Economic Effects 73

Normal government expenditure and economic growth, 73. Normal government expenditure and national income, 75. Normal government expenditure and the economic pattern, 76. Financial effects of normal expenditure, 78. Fostering particular industries, 79.

Government Expenditure and Incentives 81

Effects on the Distribution of Income 82

5. Efficiency in Government Expenditure 84

Concept of Government Efficiency 84

Government Reorganization 87

Redistribution of functions among government units, 87. Administrative reorganization of the federal government, 89. Administrative reorganization of state government, 89. Administrative reorganization of local government, 90. Financial organization, 90.

Central Supervision and Control of Local Finances 92

State prescription of local accounting systems, 93. State inspection of local accounts, 93. State prescription of local budget systems, 93. State control of local finances, 94.

Personnel Management 95

Policy-determining and administrative officials, 95. "Civil service" appointment of subordinate employees, 96. Quality of civil service personnel, 97. Supervision of government personnel, 99. State supervision of local employees, 99.

Expert Effort to Improve Operating Methods 100

Nonofficial Promotion of Government Economy 101

Taxpayers associations, 101. Bureaus of municipal research, 102. Professional administrators' associations, 102. Other economy pressure groups, 103.

6. Government Budgeting and Accounting 104

Government Budgets 104

The period covered by a budget, 105. Scope of the budget, 105. Essentials of budgetary procedure, 108. The formulating agency, 108. Formulation procedure, 109. The preliminary budget, 111. Enactment of a budget, 115. Supplementary budgetary authorization, 119. Execution of a budget, 121. Opportunities for improvement, 123.

Government Accounting 125

Basic principles, 125. Elements of progress, 127.

Part Two. Principles of Taxation

7. Constitutional Aspects of Taxation 132

General Legal Principles 132

Power to enact tax statutes, 133. Inherent, designated, and delegated powers of taxation, 134.

Application of Constitutional Limitations to Tax Statutes . . . 135

Doctrine of "subject and measure," 136.

Constitutional Law of Federal Taxation 137

"General welfare" limitation, 138. Prohibition against export taxes, 138. Limitation on levy of direct taxes, 139. Limitation on levy of indirect taxes, 140. "State instrumentalities" limitation, 140. "Due process of law" limitation, 140. The Tenth Amendment, 141. Provisions to check avoidance and evasion, 141. Conclusions, 141.

Federal Constitutional Limitations on State and Local Tax Powers 142

Prohibition against export and tonnage taxes, 142. Supremacy of treaties over state tax powers, 142. Prohibition against impairment of the obligation of contracts, 143. Prohibition of discrimination against citizens of other states, 143. "Due process of law" limitation, 143. "Equal protection of the laws" limitation, 147. "Federal instrumentalities" limitation, 147. Interstate and foreign commerce limitations, 149. Freedom of religion, speech, and the press, 150.

State Constitutional Limitations on State and Local Tax Powers 150

Types of limitations, 150. Evaluation, 151.

8. Shifting and Incidence of Taxes 153

Basic Factors in Tax Shifting 154

Incidence of Special Commodity Taxes 156

Tax imposed upon producers—competitive conditions, 156. Tax imposed upon producers—monopoly, oligopoly, and monopolistic competition, 160. Special circumstances of demand and supply affecting incidence, 161. Tax imposed upon distributors, 163. Tax on commodities and services used in business, 163. Special short-term factors in commodity tax incidence, 163. Secondary incidence of commodity taxes, 164.

Incidence of a General Commodity Tax 165

Incidence of Periodic Taxes on Durable Properties 167

Incidence of a special property tax, 167. Capitalization, 170.

Incidence of Taxes on Net Income 172

Taxes on personal compensation, 172. Taxes on business profits, 173. Taxes on rents and interest, 176.

Shifting of Taxes Levied by Limited Jurisdictions 176

Commodity taxes, 177. Business taxes, 177.

9. Distributive and Regulatory Aspects of Taxation 179

Distribution of Tax Burdens among Individuals 180

Benefit doctrines, 180. Privilege doctrine, 182. State-partnership doctrines, 183. Objective ability doctrines, 183. Subjective sacrifice doctrines, 184. Neutrality Doctrine: Reasonable Classification, 185. Incentives, 186. Creation or use of income as a guide to personal distribution, 186. Burdensomeless taxes, 187. Critique, 188.

Distribution of Tax Burdens among Economic and Social Classes 189

Taxation and equality of economic opportunity, 189. Critique, 190.

Tax Exemptions 191

Minimum exemptions, 191. Social exemptions, 193.

Progressive Taxation 194

Theory, 194. Accomplishment of tax progression, 196. Effectiveness of progression, 198. Limits to progression, 198.

Regulatory Taxation 199

Controlling consumption, 200. Controlling production and distribution, 200. Controlling business structure and conduct, 201. Conclusion, 201.

10. Revenue, Legislative, and Administrative Considerations . . 204

Revenue Considerations 204

Inherent productivity, 204. Stability, 205. Elasticity, 205. Diversity of revenue sources, 206.

Enacting Tax Laws 207

Originating tax bills, 207. House action, 207. Senate action, 208. Final action, 209. Evaluation, 209. Enactment of state and local taxes, 209.

The Administrative Problem 210

Tax avoidance, 211. Tax evasion, 211.

Administrative Principles 212

Certainty, 212. Familiarity, 214. Convenience, 215. Economy, 216. Tax consciousness, 218.

Administrative Organization 219

Federal tax organization, 219. State tax organization, 220. Local tax organization, 222. Centralization of state and local tax administration, 222. Administrative personnel, 223.

Administrative Technique 224

Assessment technique, 224. Tax penalties, 227. Tax liens, 227. Improvement, 228.

PART THREE. FEDERAL, STATE, AND LOCAL REVENUES

11. The American Tax System 232

Combined Federal, State, and Local Tax Collections 232

Over-all growth, 232. The tax burden, 234. Political distribution of tax collections, 236. Relative importance of sources, 236.

The Federal Tax System 237

1917–1939, 237. 1940 to the present, 239.

State Tax Systems 241
Local Tax Revenues 244
Social and economic distribution of tax burdens 244

12. Personal Income Taxes 249

The Federal Tax 249

History, 249.

State and Local Personal Income Taxes 250

Current status, 251.

Constitutional Law of Personal Income Taxation 252
Jurisdictional Basis for Personal Income Taxation 252

The Income Concept 254

General concepts, 254. Nonmoney ("psychic") income, 256. Tax-exempt receipts, 257. Business cost and expense deductions, 258. Personal expense deductions, 259. Treatment of capital gains and losses, 261. Pros and cons of taxing capital gains, 262. Special favorable treatment of capital gains, 265. Treatment of capital losses, 266. Current status of capital gains and loss taxation, 266. Critique, 267.

13. Personal Income Taxes (Concluded) 269

Personal Income Tax Rate Schedules 269

Personal exemptions, 269. Application of progression, 270. Limits to progression, 272. The tax rate and family incomes, 275. Timing of income realization, 277.

Administration 278

"Pay-as-you-go" collection of the federal tax, 278. Tax return simplification, 279. Information-at-source, 280. Audit, check, and review, 280. State and local administration, 282. Penalties, 283. Evasion and avoidance, 283.

Economic and Distributional Considerations 286

Poll Taxes 288

14. Taxes on Business 291

History of Federal Business Taxes 292

The Federal Corporation Income Tax 293

Taxable income, 293. Rates, 300. Supplementary rates on undistributed corporate profits, 301. Excess profits taxes, 302. "Rationalization" of corporation and personal income taxes, 303.

Social Security Payroll Taxes 305

The OASI payroll taxes, 305. Problems of the OASI payroll taxes, 306. Unemployment insurance payroll taxes, 306.

Pension Fund Taxation 308

State Corporation Organization and Entrance Taxes 308

Annual State Corporation Taxes 309

Capital stock taxes, 309. Corporation income taxes, 310. Allocation, 311.

State Taxes on Public Utilities 313

Gross earnings taxes, 314. Other taxes on public utilities, 315. Critique, 315.

15. Taxes on Business (Concluded) 318

State Bank Taxes 318

State Taxation of Insurance Companies 319

Present status, 319.

Severance Taxes 320

Business License Taxes 321
Taxes on Racing 322
Chain-Store Taxes 323
General Unincorporated Business Tax 324
Value-Added Taxation 324
Constitutional Law of Business Taxation 325

Federal business taxes, 326. State business taxes, 326.

Administrative Considerations 327

Intrastate uniformity, 328.

Economic Considerations 328

Incidence of business net income taxes, 329. Incidence of other business taxes, 330. Distributive considerations, 331. Business taxation and the pattern of economic development, 332. Taxation and business location, 333. Business taxation and economic progress, 335.

16. Commodity, Sales, and Related Excise Taxes 337

Customs (Tariff) Duties 337

Economics of the protective tariff, 338. Rate structure, 339. Rate determination, 340.

Federal Commodity, Service, and Transfer Excises 341
State and Local Taxes on Specific Commodities and Services . 343

Constitutional considerations, 343. Liquor and beverage taxes, 343. Tobacco products taxes, 344. Other state commodity and service taxes, 344.

State General Sales Taxes 344

Scope, 344. Rates and minimum exemptions, 345.

Administration of Commodity and Sales Taxes 346

The tax base in relation to administration, 346. Point of collection, 347. Manner of collection, 348. Enforcement and evasion, 348.

Economic and Distributive Considerations 349

Shifting and incidence, 350. Distributive effects, 351. "Regulatory" excises, 352.

Future of Consumption Taxes 353

17. Motor Vehicle and Fuel Taxes 356

Motor Vehicle License Taxes 356

Bases, 357. Rates, 360. Reciprocity, 360. Administration, 360.

Motor Vehicle Fuel Taxes 361

Scope, 361. Rates, 361. Administration, 361.

Economic Considerations 362

Incidence, 362. Distribution of the burden, 363. Highway user taxes in relation to street-highway costs and use, 363.

18. Property Taxes 367

Basis 368

Classes of taxable property, 368. Exemptions, 369. Jurisdiction to tax, 372. "Taxable value," 373.

Assessment of Ordinary Property 374

Assessment organization, 374. Rural realty, 376. Urban realty, 377. Personalty, 379. Underassessment and unequal assessment, 381.

Assessment of Special Classes of Property 384

Mineral and timber lands, 384. Railroad and public utility properties, 384.

19. Property Taxes (Concluded). 387

Review 387

Organization, 387. Procedure, 387.

Equalization 388

Procedure, 389.

Rate Structure 389

Determination, 390. Limitations, 391.

Collection 392

Time and manner, 392. Delinquency and remedies, 393.

Property Tax Reform—the Classified Property Tax 394

Classified taxation of realty, 394. Classified taxation of tangible personalty, 395. Classified taxation of intangibles, 395. Recording taxes, 396. Critique, 396.

Property Tax Reform—Abolition of the Personalty Tax 397

Property Tax Reform—the Land Value Tax 398

Economic Considerations 400

Incidence, 400. Distributional considerations, 402. Effects on consumption, saving, and investment, 403.

The Future of the Property Tax 405

20. Inheritance, Estate, and Gift Taxes 407

Federal Estate Tax 407

State Death Taxes 408

Current status, 409. State jurisdiction to tax, 410.

The Taxable Estate 411

Elements of the gross estate or share, 411. Deductions, 413. The marital deduction, 413. Time of valuation, 414.

Personal Exemptions and Rates 414

Minimum exemptions, 415. Relationship discrimination in inheritance tax rate schedules, 415. Progressive rate schedules, 416. The federal estate tax credit for state death taxes, 417. Tax rates on property of nonresident decedents, 418.

Administration 418

Special problems, 419. Time of payment, 419.

Economic Considerations 420

Effects on capital accumulation and business development, 420. Encouragement of trust and estate liquidity, 422. Philanthropic bequests, 422. Distributive theories, 422. Reduction of large fortunes, 424.

Gift Taxes 425

The federal gift tax, 425. State gift taxes, 426.

Integration of the Death and Gift Taxes 427

21. Enterprise, Service, and Sovereign Revenues 429

Government Enterprises 429

General considerations, 429. Scope of government enterprises, 430. The "relative efficiency" issue, 431. Prices versus rates, 433. Profit or deficit policy of government enterprises, 433. Setting government enterprise charges, 434. Incorporation of government enterprises, 436. Federal enterprises, 437. The postal system, 438. Power enterprises, 439. State enterprises, 440. Municipal enterprises, 441. Toll road, 441.

Public Domain and Other Properties 442

Investment Income 444

Fees and License Charges 445

Service fees, 446. License charges, 447. Revenue considerations, 448.

Special Assessments 449

Nature, 449. Assessment, 450. Conclusion, 451.

Excess Condemnation 452

Sovereign Revenues 453

PART FOUR. INTERGOVERNMENTAL FISCAL RELATIONS

22. State-Local and Intercommunity Fiscal Relationships . . . 458

Basic Principles 459

State-Local Distribution of Functions 460

Shift of extra-local functions, 460. Local revenue deficiency and functional shifting, 462.

Separation of Revenue Sources 462

Shared Taxes 463

Bases of distribution, 464. Critique, 465.

Supplementary Local Rates 466

State-Local Grants-in-Aid 466

State control, 467. Bases for distribution: supplementation, stimulation, equalization, 468. State aid and government efficiency, 471. Treatment of cities, 472.

Extension of Local Taxing Authority 472
City-Suburb Fiscal Relationships 473

23. Interstate, Federal-State, and International Fiscal Relationships 476

Interstate Fiscal Relationships 476

Double taxation, 477. Interstate tax uniformity, 479. Interstate tax competition, 480. Tax barriers to interstate commerce, 481.

Federal-State Fiscal Relationships 481

Separation of revenue sources, 483. Shared taxes, 484. Supplementary state rates, 486. State credits against federal taxes, 486. Deductibility of state taxes from federal tax base, 487. Grants-in-aid, 487. Conclusion, 492.

International Fiscal Relationships 493

Part Five. Government Borrowing and Indebtedness

24. History and Status of American Government Debt 498

The Federal Debt 499

1790–1917, 499. 1917–1930, 499. 1931–1940, 501. 1940–1945, 502. Postwar debt policy, 504.

State and Local Debt 508

Nineteenth century—state, 508. Nineteenth century—local, 509. 1900–1932, 510. 1933–1940, 510. Since 1940, 511.

25. Principles of Government Borrowing 513

Law of American Government Borrowing 513

Constitutional limitations on state borrowing, 514. Constitutional and statutory limitations on local borrowing, 515. Central control of local borrowing, 517.

Purposes of Government Borrowing 517

War loans, 518. Other emergency borrowing, 520. Borrowing to finance government enterprises, 521. Borrowing to finance ordinary capital construction, 521. Borrowing to smooth budgetary irregularities, 525. Borrowing for refinancing, 525. Borrowing to pay bonuses, 526. Supplementary nonfiscal reasons for borrowing, 526.

The Government Bond Market 527

Normal buying motivations, 527. Normal marketing procedure, 527. "Patriotic" loans, 529. Forced loans, 530.

Yield on Government Bonds 530

Zero yield, 533.

Burden of Government Debt 534

26. Government Debt Management 537

Maturities of Government Loans 537

Perpetual loans, 538. Long-term loans—"callable-term" provision, 538. Long-term loans—maturity period, 539. Intermediate loans, 540. Short-term loans, 540. "Moneyness" as related to debt maturity, 541.

Redemption Provisions and Other Security Elements 542

Default, 542. "Credit" bonds, 544. Sinking-fund bonds, 544. Serial bonds, 545. Other elements of security, 546. "Revenue" (government-enterprise) bonds, 547.

Tax Exemption and Other "Bonus" Incidents 548

Basis and extent of tax-exempt bonds, 548. Fiscal and social effects of tax-exempt bonds, 548. Abolition of tax-exempt bonds, 551. Bondholder redemption option, 551. Other bonus features, 552.

Control of Interest Rates and Bond Prices 553

Short-term stabilization, 553. Long-run control of interest rates, 554.

Reduction of the National Debt 555

Part Six. Fiscal Policy

27. Fiscal Economics 561

National Income Theory 561

National income, 561. The "Multiplier," 563. The savings-investment relationship, 563. Cumulative change: cyclical ups and downs, 565. Employment and prices in national income expansion and contraction, 566. Fiscal operations and national income, 566. National income models, "gaps," and fiscal action, 567. Creeping inflation, 568.

Government Expenditure 569

Domestic expenditure, 569. Expenditure abroad, 570.

Taxation 570

Absorption of purchasing power, 571. Effect on propensities to spend and to save, 572. Effects on investment, 573. Effect on incentives to work and to operate businesses economically, 573. Conclusion, 574.

Borrowing and Debt Retirement 575

Absorption of funds that would otherwise be spent, 575. Absorption of funds being saved or already saved, 575. Borrowing that results in creation of money (deposits created by bank lending), 576. Debt reduction, 576. Debt and currency, 577.

Conclusion 578

Tax-financed expenditures—balanced budget financing, 578. Deficit financing, 578. Surplus financing, 579. Budget balance over the long run, 579. Interrelation of Fiscal and Monetary Economics: debt management, 579. Compatibility of growth and stability, 580.

28. Fiscal Policy 581

Development of the Fiscal Policy Concept 581

Objectives of Fiscal Policy 583

Full employment and avoidance of inflation, 583. Combating chronic economic stagnation, 584. Combating chronic inflation, 584. Pragmatic stabilization, 585. Economic growth, 585. Conflicts in objectives, 586.

Conditions for Effective Use 587

Economic forecasting, 587. Legislative, administrative, and popular understanding, 588. Administrative discretion on timing, 589. Coordination with other policies, 590.

Economic Control through Expenditure Policy 591

Timing of regular expenditure, 591. Programmed public works, 591. Automatically stabilizing expenditure, 594.

Economic Control through Taxation 595

Automatically stabilizing taxes, 597. Administrative tax rate discretion, 597. Formula tax rate flexibility, 598. "Control" taxes and tax features, 598.

Economic Control through Debt Policy 599

State and Local Government Policy 600

Effectiveness of Built-in Stabilizers 601

Critique 602

Appendix—History of Public Finance 605

Bibliography 609

Index 617

Tables and Charts

Tables

1–1. American Government Expenditure, Selected Years 1890–1958 . . 11
1–2. Percentage Distribution of Government Expenditure by Disbursing Agencies, Selected Years 1890–1958 17
1–3. Functional Distribution of American Government Expenditure, 1929, 1938, 1942, 1953, and 1957 20
1–4. Federal Expenditure, Selected Years 1922–1959 23
2–1. Purposes of State Expenditure, Selected Years 1913–1958 . . . 29
2–2. Local Expenditures, Tabulated by Functions, 1957 31
2–3. Purposes of City Expenditure, Selected Years 1905–1957 32
2–4. Purposes of County Expenditure, Selected Years 1902–1957 . . 34
2–5. Factors in Public School Expenditure, Selected Years 1890–1958 . 38
2–6. Old Age and Survivors Insurance. Illustrative Monthly Benefits Under Law in Effect in 1959 47
4–1. Government Expenditures for Factors of Production, 1939 and 1957 76
7–1. Tax "Situs" for Property Interests 146
11–1. American Tax Revenues, Selected Years 1890–1959 233
11–2. Combined American Tax Collections, 1958 235
11–3. Federal Internal Revenue Receipts, Selected Fiscal Years 1930–1959 238
11–4. Sources of State Tax Revenue, Selected Years, 1915–1958 . . . 242
11–5. Per Capita Tax Collections in Selected States, 1958 243
11–6. Estimated Distribution of Taxes by Income Classes, 1954 . . . 246
13–1. Estimated Number of Taxable Returns, Income, and Taxes, 1958 . 274
14–1. Receipts and Deductions of Corporations Filing Federal Income Tax Returns for Period July, 1955–June, 1956 294
16–1. Selected Federal Sales Tax and Excise Rates and Yields, 1959 . . 341
20–1. Federal Estate Tax Rates, Amount of Tax, and Credit for State Tax 408
20–2. Gross Estate, Deductions, and Tax: Estate Tax Returns Filed in 1955, Including Nontaxable Estates 412
21–1. Federal Business-Type Activities, Selected Assets and Liabilities, 1958 438

22–1. State Financial Aid to Local Governments, Selected Years 1902–1958 463
22–2. State Financial Aid to Local Governments, by Function, 1957 . . 467
23–1. Federal Grants to States and Local Units, Selected Years 1915–1959 488
24–1. American Government Debt, Selected Years 1790–1958 500
24–2. Federal Debt Outstanding June 30, 1958 505
24–3. Estimated Ownership of Federal Debt, February, 1946, and October, 1958 506
24–4. Local Debt (Net), Selected Years 1912–1957 511
26–1. Ownership of Tax-Exempt Securities, 1950 and 1957 549

Charts

1–1. Government Expenditures as Percentages of Gross National Product, 1929–1958 14
1–2. American Government Expenditure, by Disbursing Agencies, 1890–1958 18
1–3. Expenditure for Selected Nondefense Functions, 1952 to 1957 . . 19
11–1. American Tax Revenues, 1890–1959 234
11–2. State and Local Taxes, Per Capita, in Dollars of 1958 Purchasing Power, 1902–1958 236
11–3. Sources of American Tax Revenues, 1958 237
11–4. Sources of Federal Internal Tax Revenue, 1940–1959 240
11–5. Sources of State Tax Revenue, Selected Years 1915–1958 . . . 241
12–1. Receipts and Deductions Reported on Personal Income Tax Returns, 1955 260
13–1. Federal Personal Income Tax Bracket Rates, Selected Years, 1929 to 1959 272
13–2. Proportion of Taxable Income of Married Couple, No Children, Absorbed by Federal Personal Income Tax, Selected Years 1929 to 1959 273
14–1. Federal Corporation Income Tax Rates, Calendar Years 1913–1959 300
24–1. American Government Debt, 1870–1940 501
24–2. American Government Debt, 1940–1958 504
24–3. State and Local Debt per Capita in Dollars of 1958 Purchasing Power, 1902–1958 511

Introduction

"PUBLIC FINANCE" is not a precise term. "Public" as an adjective may describe not only the activities of a government, but those of a utility or a charitable association. "Finance" covers all types of monetary transactions —of individuals, banks, business corporations, and government units. Yet a century of popular usage in England and the United States has given the two words "Public Finance" a precise connotation. "Public Finance" is the study of the facts, principles, techniques, and effects of obtaining and spending funds by government bodies and of managing government debt.

The subject matter of Public Finance has not been strictly delimited. Occasionally, scholars arbitrarily annex special topics to the general body of fiscal[1] thought. Others just as arbitrarily exclude some topic which is logically an element of fiscal knowledge. In this respect, Public Finance resembles other living and growing bodies of human knowledge. The trend of our times is to broaden the scope of what is included in Public Finance. The reason is obvious—government activity plays a larger role than before, and financing that enhanced activity raises ever broader problems.

Three divisions of the subject have long been recognized: (1) government[2] expenditures, (2) government borrowing and indebtedness, and (3) sources of government revenue, of which the most important is taxation. Some writers add a fourth general division, "fiscal administration." In our analysis, administrative techniques associated with public expenditure are discussed under that heading, and tax administration is handled as a subdivision of taxation. Interrelations of federal, state, and local finances are treated as a separate fourth division of our study. Finally, the effects of government finance upon national income, employment, and the gen-

[1] The "fisc" is the public treasury. "Fiscal" is the adjective corresponding to the noun-term "Public Finance." It covers the expenditure as well as the obtaining of government funds.

[2] Throughout this volume, "government" is used in preference to "public" as an adjective applied to the activities of governments—federal, state, or local. The authors would prefer the term "Government Finance" to "Public Finance" but defer to general usage.

eral level of prices have become so far-reaching that they receive separate analysis under the heading "fiscal policy."

WHY STUDY PUBLIC FINANCE?

Today, more than ever before, the average citizen needs to understand Public Finance. It intimately affects most issues of public policy. Fiscal factors now exert a major influence on economic and social development and on many important forms of personal activity—for example:

(1) National defense is a primary consideration, here and abroad. Its costs are responsible for the real "bite" in today's taxes.

(2) On the average, Americans work over three months out of every twelve to support the federal, state, and local governments—taxes absorb roughly one-fourth of the income we would otherwise have available for spending. With this money, however, we "buy" many of the most important elements of our mode of living—national defense, local police protection, education, highways and streets, our legal system, Social Security, and many intangible services. Are we getting the most value with respect to (a) the scope of government services performed and (b) the efficiency with which they are performed? Are we spending on some wrong things? Is waste in government extensive? What can be done to reduce it?

(3) The purchasing power of the dollar—the vital issue of whether we shall have a stable currency or the evils of deflation or inflation—depends in substantial part upon federal finance, upon budgetary surplus or deficit, and the management of the federal debt.

(4) Fiscal policies have an important influence on the level of employment. One reason is that government purchases account for the employment of millions and that the seven million federal, state and local employees (exclusive of the military services) are buyers of consumer goods. In addition, federal fiscal policy is a major factor in determining whether millions of workers will stand in breadlines or receive overtime pay.

(5) The pace of economic growth and of our ability to raise our standard of living hinges to an important extent upon both the creative activities of governments at all levels and the discouragements which taxes impose on private initiative.

Here are but five of a long list of ways in which government spending, borrowing, and taxing influence our living. Wisdom in fiscal policy means better living for all; unsound fiscal practices, adopted through legislative and popular ignorance, can check progress and even cause retrogression. Every man and woman today needs an understanding of the principles and applications of Public Finance to discharge competently the responsibilities of citizenship.

College students have a special "bread-and-butter" interest in the study of Public Finance. Many will seek careers in government service; for them Public Finance is a storehouse of tools they will subsequently use. Many college students will become lawyers and accountants. A good proportion of these will have to advise clients on tax matters, one of the more lucrative parts of professional practice today. College students who enter business will never be free of tax problems, and some will join that growing group of corporation employees who specialize in the complex and highly important work of tax compliance. Many young men and women will eventually be involved with a variety of fiscal issues, from service in the local community to exacting and profitable transactions with government agencies.

PUBLIC FINANCE AS A STUDY

As a study of principles, of cause-and-effect relationships, Public Finance is a social science. Yet it is more. As an exposition of techniques, of practical methods of raising and spending governmental funds, it is a political art.

Public Finance and related studies. Public Finance relies heavily upon other social sciences. Economics contributes first premises for study of the shifting and the effect of taxes, and the effects of government spending, taxing, and borrowing—particularly those of the federal government—upon the nation's economy. Social Psychology and Sociology provide the derivation of some principles of tax administration and illuminate areas and problems of expenditure. From Political Science, Public Finance draws heavily; the analyses of government functions, of revenue raising, of expenditure and debt control, and of the interrelation of federal, state, and local financial functions—all have roots in Political Science. History and Statistics supply evidence to support or contradict various fiscal propositions. Notions of equity which influence decisions about spending (aid to the poor) or taxing (how much more to tax one person than another) draw upon Ethics.

Even as a political art, Public Finance is not independent of allied fields of study. Since the powers of governments to spend, borrow, and tax are limited by constitutional and statutory restrictions, principles of law, and particularly of constitutional law, are an important background for the study of Public Finance. Moreover, one cannot know taxation in actual operation without knowing something about tax law. Understanding of accountancy is essential to the study of government units as going concerns and of the significance of some tax provisions for business. Knowledge of business finance and business administration is essential to appreciate the virtues and disadvantages of taxes levied upon various types of business activity. Government spending involves issues of engineering (what is the most economical highway construction for particular traffic loads?), medicine (public health), personnel management, aesthetics, military strategy, astronomy (rocket flight to the moon), and a myriad of other subjects of varying importance and complexity.

Clearly, Public Finance is not a single, compact, self-sufficient branch of human knowledge. Rather, it is in the best sense a synthetic subject, drawing upon several allied sciences and arts. This very diversity adds to its interest. Public Finance achieves its unity through the homogeneity of its subject matter—the financial aspects of the activities of government bodies.

Public Finance is commonly studied as a branch of Economics, but until recently this circumstance was more an accident of tradition than a reasoned conclusion. The Physiocrats, Adam Smith, and the English economists of the early nineteenth century were active critics of Mercantilism, a doctrine of government supervision and regulation. In their inquiries into the virtues and vices of various government activities, they considered the fiscal aspects of government activity in general. So far-reaching was their influence that later students viewed Public Finance as an integral element of Economics. Conceivably, had the outstanding British study of the problems of Public Finance a century or so ago been made by students of government organization instead of Economics, we might today study Public Finance as a branch of Political Science, as is to some extent the case in continental Europe. During the past two decades, however, the subject of how the fiscal operations of governments influence the national income has come strongly to the fore. This development has markedly reintegrated Public Finance with Economics, so that today Public Finance is one of the most important, most practically alive, branches of Economics. Still, this predominance of focus should not blind students to the important elements of Political Science, Law, Sociology, and other sciences and arts embodied in Public Finance.

Methodology of Public Finance. As a *political art,* Public Finance is an exposition of a technique—a way to get things done. It presents judgments, conclusions, and maxims on particular issues of practice and procedure, which may be taken as a guide and standard by legislators, administrative officials, and students of public affairs. Budgetary procedures and other expenditure controls are recommended. Debt management is analyzed. Techniques of tax administration are submitted. These technical conclusions may be used by officials and students of public affairs. As judgments, conclusions, and maxims, they are not arbitrary, a priori propositions, for they have evolved from careful inquiry. Only after extensive comparative research, for example, was it possible to conclude that state assessment of extensive public utility properties is preferable to local assessment, and why. Only through intimate understanding of the mechanics of legislative procedure can tax and expenditure laws be appreciated as delicate balances of political, social, and economic pressures.

Were society nonprogressive, a fixed fiscal technique or procedure might be continuously effective and valuable. But where changes are rapid, as in our generation, a fixed technique or procedure may soon become outmoded, valueless, even dangerous. The development of state aid, of income tax collection at source, of stratospheric income tax rates, required procedures and critiques that our grandfathers would never have recognized. If the elements which constitute the art of Public Finance are to remain pertinent to actual government needs and circumstances, they must be ceaselessly expanded, modified, and supplemented by scientific inquiry. We should no more rest content with fiscal techniques previously acquired than with bygone engineering or medical techniques.

What is the methodology of Public Finance as a *science?* Nineteenth-century writers debated the respective merits of the deductive or the inductive method of inquiry. But this controversy has subsided and its echoes are silent. For Public Finance as for most other fields of knowledge, deduction and induction are both essential.

Inductive fiscal inquiry may be descriptive, historical, or statistical.

Description, notably the case-study approach, was until recent years the primary inductive tool of Public Finance. Comprehensive information—or even data sufficient to permit application of sampling techniques—was lacking for most fiscal topics. Students of Public Finance were limited to detailed examination of individual cases where facts could be had. Such a case analysis of fiscal activity in Wisconsin or Boston might be used to support some general proposition of Public Finance—but there could be no assurance that Wisconsin or Boston provided a typical instance. As ever more individual case studies have become available, however, limited generalizations and working hypotheses, expressed in terms of possibility and occasionally high probability, have been formulated.

Statistical data on many phases of Public Finance have accumulated rapidly. Federal, state, and local bureaus, and various research agencies, now publish voluminous figures. Various statistical procedures enable us to marshal and use these figures to discover pertinent generalizations. Statistical data are so complete that definite conclusions can often be formulated. The tabulation of state and local tax revenues, for example, conclusively establishes the growth in relative importance of the gasoline tax and motor vehicle license charge. In other cases, the conclusion derived from a statistical calculation cannot be stated as absolute, but it may be put forward tentatively as a probability or as an indication of a trend.

Descriptive and statistical analysis of current problems can be supplemented, within limits, by historical research. Every appropriation bill, every tax or government loan statute, is in the nature of an experiment. Its results, favorable or unfavorable, appear in the course of time and may be noted in official or unofficial studies and reports. This record of past experiences is comparable to a series of experiments, with continual variation in controlling factors; as the series grows fuller and the variations cover more and more of the important factors involved, perhaps specific cause-

and-effect relationships may be isolated and established as generalizations. The federal Treasury's unhappy experience with bond issues during the Civil War, as contrasted with the successful marketing of the World War I Liberty Loans, for instance, is an eloquent commentary on the importance of marshaling and firing patriotic sentiment to create a popular market for war loans.

But historical instances and analogies must be used with supreme care. The student of Public Finance must remain aware that *post hoc non est propter hoc*—that the accident of historical occurrence does not, solely of itself, establish causality. Contributing factors in the historical case may be absent in the present, or vice versa. Too often the hasty scholar or the willful propagandist forgets that "circumstances alter cases," and improperly draws parallels between past and present events. The failure of state income taxes prior to 1911, for example, is not an argument against the present-day levy of state income taxes, for improved administrative techniques have been developed which make possible today what failed fifty years ago.

Inductive inquiry, whether historical, descriptive, or statistical, is likely to give a series of disconnected conclusions, hardly to be considered a system or science. These scattered truths must be coordinated and related by *deductive reasoning*, and a background must be built up by correlating them with the allied social sciences and arts.

Syllogistic reasoning, progressing from generalizations to particular circumstances, is a fundamental feature of the deductive method. Thus, given the legal generalization that the states may not levy taxes on the acts of importation or exportation, it can be concluded that a particular state may not levy a license tax on importers and exporters.

Hard work and skill in collecting facts and rigorous thinking are the tools of Public Finance as a science. If we use them intelligently and industriously, we shall progress toward better solutions of vital and tough problems. Of course, we cannot expect the precision of engineering nor the miracles of chemistry. Yet study will enable us to predict with some confidence the results of alternative fiscal courses and thus make better choices. To this extent, certainly, we reason scientifically.

The bias of special interests. Taxes and government expenditure are of great concern to individuals and to groups. To protect and advance their interests, they must often persuade a legislative body or the public generally. The need for such persuasion has led to some excellent study, careful collection of facts, and competent analysis. On the other hand, bias and actual misrepresentation also appear; some of it is obvious, but much more is difficult to detect and evaluate. The student of Public Finance, whether the occupant of the White House or a youth in college, must consider these special interest appeals, if only because they often contain facts and argument essential for balanced judgment. They will rarely be adequate in themselves, however. A common weakness of many that have real merit is a failure to consider the *whole* set of issues involved.

The wisest solution of social problems is the selection of the best, or least bad, alternative or combination of alternatives. Too often taxes are condemned, or expenditures praised, in special interest appeals, without regard to whether a better source of revenue is available or a better use of funds possible. Such narrow approaches are dangerous: they oversimplify and mislead, and they distract attention from the more basic problem—examination of all the relevant alternatives, their merits and weaknesses.

RECENT TRENDS

Tremendous strides have been made in the study of Public Finance in recent years. The legacy of World War I was partly responsible, but more important was the depression of the 1930's. The depression made it harder for taxpayers to pay taxes and for governments to collect them just when the demands for increased expenditures were rising. Stimulation of intensive, though not always brilliant, study of tax, spending, and borrowing problems resulted. As tax rates rose and new taxes were imposed, more concern was felt about the economic and social effects. The New Deal's extension of the activities of government during the 1930's gave rise to much serious study of the government's financial problems.

The country's failure to achieve reasonably full employment intensified the discussion. Some observers felt that the government was doing too much; for example, taxes were alleged to be so high that investment was discouraged. Others argued that the government should expand its activities, especially borrowing and spending. To some economists it seemed that *the* problem of Public Finance was how to get full employment. These arguments will be analyzed later. The point here is that the elements of Public Finance were discussed more widely and with increasing thoroughness and understanding. Problems of social welfare, of the relations of government and business, of the operation of the monetary system, and of many other broad subjects were studied in part as problems of Public Finance.

World War II intensified scholarly and popular interest in fiscal matters. Military considerations dominated our *productive* economy, and the exigencies of federal taxation and borrowing, our *financial* economy. Highly competent persons from all walks of life concentrated their best thought on Public Finance, though poorly-informed and biased pleaders also raised their voices. Peace did not bring a return to fiscal "normalcy." Local and state problems pressed with growing urgency. Peace slid into "cold war," accentuated by the Korean struggle. It became evident that federal spending, taxing, and borrowing would continue at levels without any prior peacetime precedent. Supposedly temporary expedients of war finance had to be reviewed as possible long-term elements of the fiscal system. Once again, as many times before, Public Finance had to shift its focus and encompass new horizons.

PROBLEMS

1. How do taxation and government spending affect the college student? The small business? The person retired?

2. Identify five issues of national policy and five of local government policy which actively involve (a) government spending and (b) taxation.

3. Discuss with an accountant and an attorney how taxes are concerned in the problems with which they deal.

4. Find examples of arguments for (a) tax reduction and (b) increases in public spending which do not take account of the full range of relevant considerations.

5. "A knowledge of economics is necessary, but not sufficient, for understanding Public Finance." Discuss.

PART ONE

Government Expenditure

DURING the late 1950's, the federal, state, and local governments of the United States have been spending nearly $130 billion annually gross—$730 per capita per year. This total, which exceeds what the country spends on food and clothing, compares with $28 per capita in 1913 and $139 in 1940.

Our task in Part One is to ascertain the facts about the *growth* of American government expenditures to this level and about the current *purposes* of this expenditure, to analyze the *principles* of government spending, and to study the techniques of *controlling* and *budgeting* governmental expenditure.

CHAPTER 1

Growth, Agencies, and Purposes of American Government Expenditure

How much, and for what, do American governments—federal, state, and local—spend each year? To what extent, and why, are expenditures increasing? Is the growth at a rate higher than that at which the whole economy is expanding?

Questions such as these are primarily factual. Fortunately, reliable figures are now collected and published. Federal expenditures are presented in considerable detail in the annual *Reports of the Secretary of the Treasury* and *The Budget of the United States Government*. Data on state and city expenditures, functionally classified, are published annually by the federal Bureau of the Census in its *State Finances* and *City Finances* series. It also compiles figures on expenditures of other localities using carefully selected sample data. Convenient annual summaries of expenditures are presented by the Tax Foundation and the Tax Institute, in the Department of Commerce's *Statistical Abstract,* and in a growing number of publications. All federal agencies, most states and their agencies, and many localities publish detailed accounts of spending. Although data are not always complete, the explanations not always clear, and the classifications not always as illuminating as the student desires, the information available is much more satisfactory now than in the past.[1] Moreover, each year brings more analysis of both the theory and the practice of government spending. Intelligent evaluation is not easy, but it is more nearly possible than ever before.

[1] Nevertheless, there are difficult problems of agreeing upon what, for the problem at hand, should be considered "spending": C. L. Harriss, "Government Expenditure: Significant Issues of Definition," *Journal of Finance,* Dec., 1954, pp. 351–364. Wide differences in reports on amounts of spending can result from choice of what to include. For example, federal "payments to the public" in 1958 were $83.3 billion, but "budget expenditures" were $71.9 billion—no small difference.

TABLE 1–1

American Government Expenditure, Selected Years 1890–1958

Year	*Amounts (in billions)*[1]	*Amounts (in billions) in Dollars of 1958 Purchasing Power*[2]	*Per Capita*	*Per Capita in Dollars of 1958 Purchasing Power*[2]	*Per Cent of Gross National Product*[3]
1890.........	$ .9	$ 3	$ 14	$ 48	7
1903.........	1.6	5	20	57	7
1913.........	2.7	9	28	95	8
1919.........	21.1	29	201	270	33
1923.........	8.3	14	75	130	14
1929.........	10.2	17	85	140	10
1932.........	12.8	27	103	220	22
1936.........	15.9	33	125	270	19
1940.........	19.5	40	149	300	19
1944.........	104.9	172	782	1230	50
1947.........	53.3	64	372	430	20
1950.........	66.2	79	446	520	23
1955.........	108.7	122	660	730	28
1957.........	124.4	126	720	730	29
1958[4]........	128.0	128	730	730	31

[1] Includes Social Security expenditures, outlays financed by borrowing, all postal costs, and expenses of government utilities.

[2] The Bureau of Labor Statistics Consumer Price Index (linked with earlier indexes for years before 1913) is used in adjusting for changes in the value of the dollar. Such adjustments are necessarily imperfect. Nevertheless, the estimates here, as rounded, give a reasonably accurate indication of the order of magnitudes involved.

[3] If government spending were expressed as a percentage of National Income or of Net National Product, the percentages would be larger.

[4] Estimated.

SOURCES: This table and predecessors in earlier editions include data from a variety of sources. Most derive from tables which appear in *Statistical Abstract of the United States, 1958* and *Historical Statistics of the United States, 1789–1945, A Supplement to the Statistical Abstract of the United States.*

GROWTH[2]

As indicated in Table 1–1, combined federal, state, and local expenditures have grown tremendously. This growth has occurred not only in absolute amount but also in relation to population and national income. In the past 45 years, American government expenditure increased 26-fold on a per capita basis, almost fourfold in relation to gross national product.

Six major reasons for this astonishing rise will now be examined.

[2] See S. Fabricant, *The Trend of Government Activity in the United States Since 1900* (National Bureau of Economic Research, New York, 1952); M. S. Kendrick, *A Century and a Half of Federal Expenditures* (National Bureau of Economic Research, 1955); A. M. Soloway, "Growth of Government Over the Past 50 Years: An Analytical Review," *Federal Expenditure Policy for Economic Growth and Stability* (Washington, 1957), pp. 19–59.

War and threats of war. "The warfare world, not the welfare state," accounts for most of today's government expenditure and for most of the increase during the past 50 years. Immediate costs of hostilities are only part of the total cost of war. Interest on war debt continues for decades. As the years pass, pensions and other forms of aid to veterans increase, partly because of political pressure. The Civil War cost over $15 billion. By 1959 the still incomplete bill for the few months of fighting in the Spanish War was over $4 billion. World War I costs, also still incomplete, exceed $60 billion. The direct costs of World War II already approach *half a trillion* dollars, with the final cost certain to be much higher.

Each war has left federal spending on a new, lasting, higher level. Partly responsible for these increases has been the price inflation associated with war. However, much of the increase must be attributed to expenditures directly resulting from the war—costs of carrying the war debt, veterans' aid, and maintenance of an enlarged defense establishment.

The current uneasy peace compels the United States to maintain its military establishment upon a semiwartime basis. Direct military expenditures, exclusive of hang-over costs of World War II but including expenditures on atomic energy, NATO, and other foreign purposes classified by the President as "direct military," were budgeted at $47 billion for 1959. This was around 60 per cent of the total cost of federal government and over 40 per cent of combined federal, state, and local government expenditures. Military costs rise as weapons, communications and transport equipment, and the other constituents of defense become more intricate and require more advanced training. Still higher defense outlays seem inevitable as new and more costly weapons replace those made obsolete by our developing science.

A new major item of peacetime spending—foreign aid—entered the federal budget after World War II. To some extent, particularly with respect to Point Four appropriations, such aid was motivated by humanitarian considerations. The chief stimulus of our foreign aid grants, however, has been military. These grants are intended to win us allies, and to strengthen these allies, in the "cold war." They are to help ward off war, if that is possible; if not, to prepare us to wage it more effectively.

States have occasionally made direct military contributions by equipping regiments of the National Guard subsequently incorporated into the federal military forces. State bonuses to World War II veterans have exceeded $3 billion. Indirectly, war may also affect state and local expenditure. During each World War, federal demands for materials and services compelled states and localities to postpone all but the most indispensible construction. When the wars ended, the state and local governments then started ambitious programs of capital outlays at a time when costs were inflated as a result of war financing.

National growth and urbanization. The population of the United States increased by 85 million between 1910 and 1959. This growth led to a *spreading* of population into hitherto thinly-settled areas and to *concentration* of population in already-settled areas. Both effects of population growth add to the cost of government.

Where population spreads into new areas, new government spending units—school districts, road districts, drainage districts, villages, and towns—must be organized to provide government services. Concentration of population in already-settled areas, particularly urbanization, also increases government expenditure. Higher per capita cost of city government as compared with rural government is accounted for partly by higher wage and cost levels and partly by the larger number and better quality of service functions which cities provide. Unlike farm families, each urban family cannot provide its own water or garbage disposal system and is not likely to provide food and lodging for its needy members. Increasing population density necessitates special remedial activities, such as juvenile recreation programs, that ward off social disadvantages of urban and suburban growth rather than confer added social benefits. Metropolitan crowding breeds problems of sanitation, crime, social welfare, air pollution, and traffic which are less pressing in the countryside and in small communities. Per capita expenditures in 1957 for police in cities of over 500,000 were $17 compared with $8 in cities of from 10,000 to 25,000. Fire department costs per capita were one-third greater.[3]

But density of population also produces government economies. A legislature for a population of millions costs little more than one for a population of thousands. It may cost no more to construct a motor highway at a low per capita cost through a densely populated state than through a sparsely settled region. Many government services such as forest-fire prevention are performed at relatively constant cost, irrespective of the number of individuals benefited. Furthermore, economies of mass production are applicable to some government functions. In the purchase of standardized supplies and use of mechanical equipment, New York City can effect economies impossible to several hundred small cities having the same aggregate population.

There is also the factor of *economic growth.* An industrial civilization calls upon its government agencies for many services not required by an agricultural civilization. Industry having produced the automobile, an improved highway system required the expenditure of billions of dollars. Metropolises, developed by commerce and industry, magnified the possibilities and ramifications of social delinquency, and state and local governments had to develop new agencies of social welfare and a new penology to meet the situation. Labor difficulties grew up with industry, and the

[3] Careful statistical analysis indicates that local government spending per capita is associated not so much with population size of cities as with density. H. E. Brazer, "Factors Affecting City Expenditures," *NTA . . . Proceedings . . . 1957*, pp. 437–443.

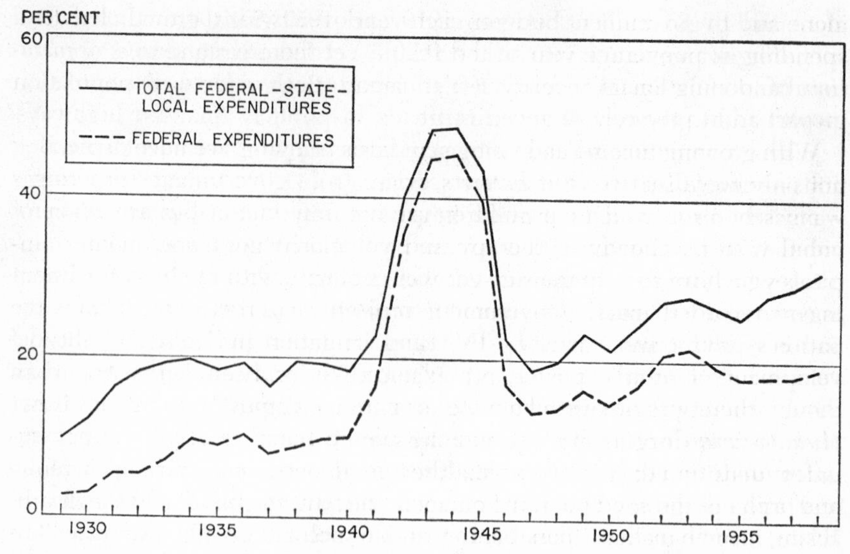

CHART 1–1. Government Expenditures as Percentages of Gross National Product, 1929–1958.

public looked to government to create and supervise ameliorative projects —workers' compensation, public employment agencies, unemployment insurance, the National Labor Relations Board, and other labor supervisory bodies. Monopolistic trends and financial malpractices established the need for the Federal Trade Commission, the Securities Exchange Commission, the Interstate Commerce Commission, and the various state railroad and public utility commissions.

Economic progress and increasing population involve higher government expenditure, but they also result in higher national income. Were the scope of government activity to remain the same while economic and population growth continued apace, the cost of government activity, measured as a percentage of national income, would probably diminish. But, as we shall see, the scope expands.

Expansion and quality improvement of government functions. The addition of new functions has expanded American government expenditure over and above the increase compelled by national growth. Less than a century ago, Herbert Spencer described the role of the State as that of "passive policeman"—a protector of the peace, a guardian of domestic law and order. But today American government activities range from medical and economic aid in distant lands to the replanting of deforested hillsides and the provision of social insurance. The "New Deal" legislation of the 1930's committed the federal government and the states to many functions which were originally denounced as "socialistic" but which now are inextricable parts of the American economic system. Social Security benefits alone add to government budgets each year over twice the total of federal spending in an average year of the 1920's. Yet there is no serious demand for abandoning Social Security. For transportation we have chosen to shift in part from privately financed railroads to publicly financed highways.

With growing income and rising standards of living, we have demanded not only *more* services but *better* services from government—superhighways, schools in which our children are not only taught but are also provided with psychological therapy and vocational guidance, mental hospitals which try to help the sick get well, libraries with facilities for listening to recorded music. Government projects undertaken to expand the nation's productive capacity—TVA and irrigation projects, and the development of atomic power, for example—have been authorized even though there was no overwhelming economic compulsion to initiate them. *Humanitarian* urging has opened the public purse to assist the nation's unfortunate and the nation's unfit—the unemployed, many farmers, widows and orphans, the aged poor, the maimed, the halt, the blind, and the insane. Rising income makes it possible to provide such aid on a higher scale. The federal and state governments have added to their costs by expanding and strengthening their controls over various aspects of business activity. In part these expenditures may result from economic growth, but in part they constitute new responsibilities undertaken in response to changing popular views of the scope of government functions. As interdependence increases, the scope of the *general public* interest also expands. Undoubtedly, the American people have come to use their governments to accomplish more and broader objectives. Performing these added functions requires larger expenditure. It is hard to judge how many of the 400 or more broad types of functions now performed by American governments are new since 1913. Some are, and many have been subdivided and elaborated. Meanwhile, few functions of earlier times have been dropped.

Rising price levels. Another major cause of the rising cost of government is that the dollar "isn't what it used to be." Whenever commodity prices and salary levels increase, each dollar appropriated for government expenditure buys less and less. To maintain activities at the level of prior years, governments must increase their monetary appropriations. When the general price level is declining, a given level of government service may be maintained at lower cost. But largely because of war, price and wage levels have risen far more during periods of expansion than they have receded during business slumps. Hence, governments must pay more than in the past for purchases and compensation to achieve any given service accomplishment.

Statistically, the effect of changing price levels upon government costs can be discounted somewhat by stating expenditures in terms of dollars of constant purchasing power. This is done in Table 1–1. Note that the absolute increase of total government expenditures from 1890 to 1929 was

1100 per cent, whereas the "true" increase in dollars of constant purchasing power was under 600 per cent. Between 1940 and 1958 dollar spending rose over 500 per cent, but in terms of purchasing power the increase was 300 per cent.

Business fluctuations. In the past, broad cyclical fluctuations of business activity have operated as a one-way ladder for government expenditure. Legislators are infected with the general optimism that accompanies boom times, and thoughts of government progress and expansion capture their imaginations. Congress, the state assemblies, county and town boards, and city and village councils vote new functions and enlarge existing ones. Taxpayers offer little objection, because the combination of prosperity, rising property values, and increasing incomes make taxpaying less difficult; the functions may seem worthwhile, perhaps badly overdue.

When recession comes, the new functions are found to be "frozen" into the system. There may be attempts at "economy," but rarely do they restore the old level of government costs. Moreover, it is now accepted that government must undertake relief functions associated with business recession. These relief functions may carry the recession cost of government above even the prior prosperity level, as in the 1930's. And then these depression relief functions in turn may freeze into the government structure and continue after the most pressing need has passed.

Special interest pressure groups. Influencing Congress, a state legislature, or a municipal council to vote an appropriation desired by some group—funds for a federal census of manufacturing helpful to business, an appropriation to sustain the price of butter to benefit dairy farmers, or funds for a more liberal teachers' pension system—has become, to an increasing extent, an organized procedure. The hope of getting benefits at the expense of others *can* be achieved by use of government. Any group interested in having public money appropriated to some particular purpose usually has a trade or professional association to act for it, or quickly organizes one. Representatives of the association lobby on behalf of the appropriation; they present the case for it at legislative committee hearings; they interview individual legislators to persuade them personally of the merits of the appropriation. The association presses its members to write or telegraph to key legislators, and to persuade relatives and friends to do the same, in support of the appropriation.

Such pressure-group tactics prove effective. Legislators are supposed to base their judgments on considerations of the "general good," not on demands of special groups which may sometimes run counter to the general interest. But skillful presentations by group lobbyists may make the group interest appear to be the general interest, particularly when there is no organized group to present counterarguments. Moreover, when the desk of a legislator is buried deep under cards, letters, and telegrams from members of the interested group who are his constituents and whose votes may be crucial to his future political career, he cannot fail to be impressed and his judgment is influenced.

Appropriations sought by interested groups may or may not serve the general public interest. The group pressures, however, certainly account for some of the increase in public expenditures through government.

Note that the factors cited to explain the growth of spending do not include either a drop in efficiency or a rise in graft. Although conclusive proof is hardly possible, efficiency is probably higher, and graft lower, than in the past. Expenditure growth has not, on balance, resulted from deterioration in the quality of public service—quite the contrary.

AGENCIES

American government functions are divided among three major classes of political units—the federal government, the states, and the 102,300 local units.[4] For the most part, the activities of these bodies complement each other, each class presumably performing the functions for which it is best fitted. Obvious examples of this arrangement are the federal government's control of currency and foreign relations, and its maintenance of a navy. Local units provide fire protection and sanitary facilities. One class of government sometimes supplements an activity primarily administered by another. States have assumed part of the cost of education and of highway maintenance, once exclusively local; the Federal Bureau of Investigation supplements local protection of life and property. Occasionally two government bodies cover the same function, with consequent overlapping.

Neither functions nor expenditures are distributed in any fixed proportion among the three classes of government units. Prior to the middle 1930's, federal expenditures dominated

TABLE 1–2

Percentage Distribution of Government Expenditure by Disbursing Agencies, Selected Years 1890–1958

Year	*Federal*	*State*	*Local*
1890.......	36	10	55
1903.......	32	13	56
1913.......	27	14	60
1919.......	88	3	10
1923.......	37	14	49
1929.......	27	18	55
1933.......	36	19	45
1936.......	53	15	33
1940.......	49	20	31
1944.......	91	4	4
1948.......	68	16	17
1950.......	62	19	19
1955.......	65	16	19
1958[1]......	63	17	20

[1] Estimated from various sources, including federal budget data.

Derived from National Industrial Conference Board, *The Economic Almanac for 1950; Summary of Governmental Finances in 1957.*

[4] In 1957, there were 3,047 counties, 17,183 municipalities, 17,198 townships, 50,446 school districts, and 14,405 special districts.

the national total only during emergencies. At other times, as shown in Table 1–2, the federal proportion was from one-fourth to one-third. During the 1920's, local governments spent one-half or more of the total. But this proportion will probably never be repeated. The expansion of federal expenditures as a result of war and national defense needs will dominate the proportions of American government expenditure in the foreseeable future. States, too, have expanded their functions much more rapidly than localities; indeed, through shifting of functions and the development of state aid, states help bear costs of expenditures that were once exclusively local. States, once relatively unimportant as disbursing agencies, seem likely to assume a more important role in the future.

In 1957, *state* spending per capita averaged $135, of which $44 went for aid to localities and $34 for capital outlay. Variations were wide. Five states spent over $200 per capita—Nevada leading with $252, whereas Delaware and Louisiana spent around $215. Seven states spent about $100 per capita—Nebraska (the lowest) $99, Illinois $102, New Jersey $113. Almost one out of four states spent about $20 per capita on capital outlay —Mississippi, Missouri, and Pennsylvania, for example; Connecticut, how-

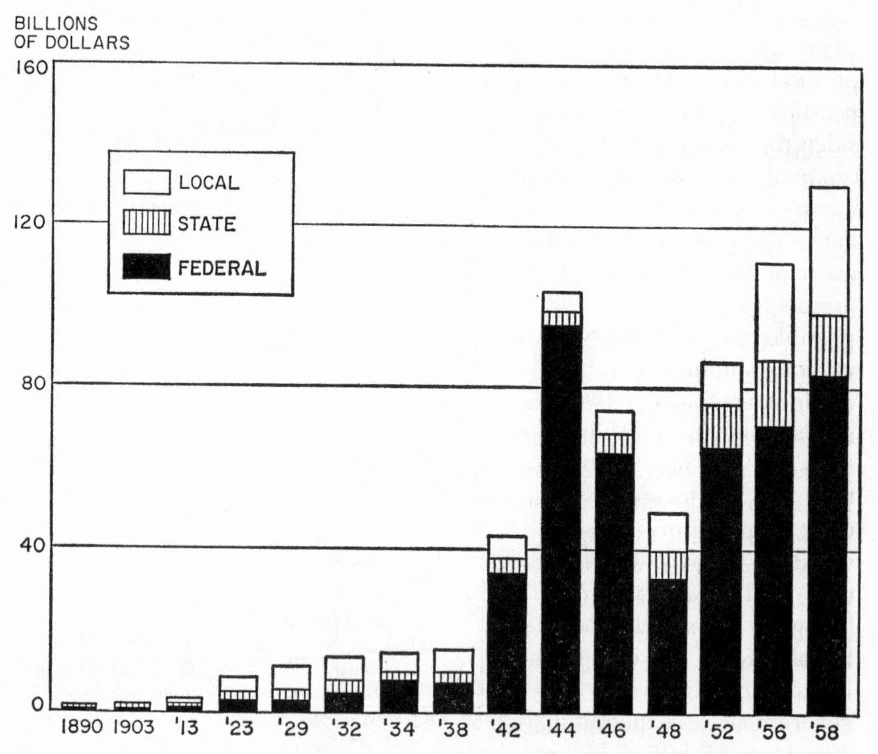

CHART 1–2. American Government Expenditure, by Disbursing Agencies, 1890–1958.

ever, spent $93 and California and several others around $40 per capita on capital projects.

City expenditures also vary widely from the $130 per capita average of 1957. Boston spent $400 per capita, New York City $300, whereas Chicago and Lincoln, Nebraska, spent around $110. These figures, however, have only limited value, because of the differences in responsibilities assigned to city governments. New York and Boston make large outlays for schools, whereas in Chicago and many other cities school costs are met by special districts with separate budgets. County expenditures also vary greatly per capita.

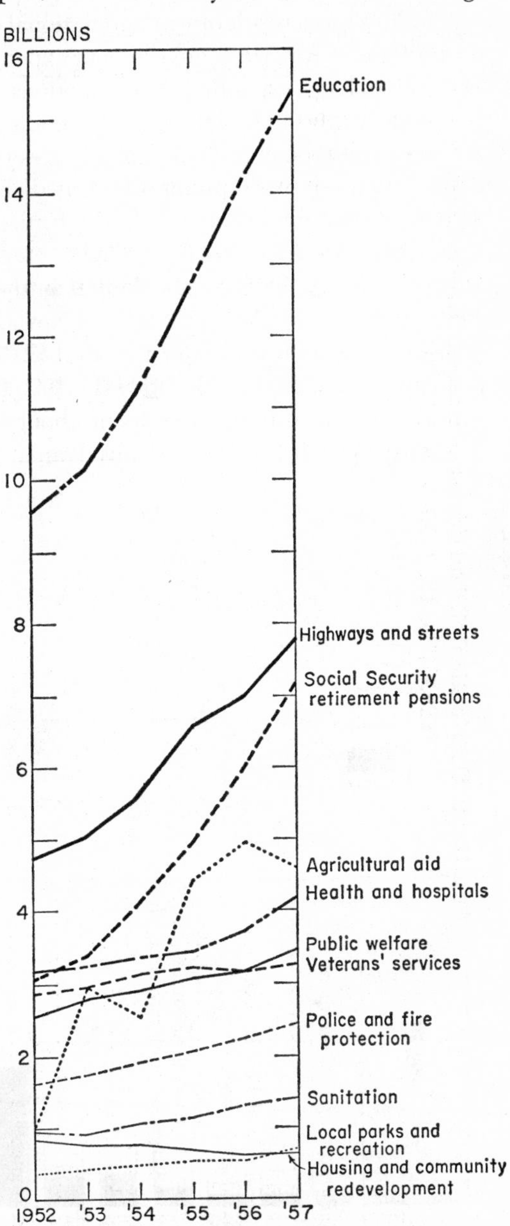

CHART 1–3. Expenditure for Selected Nondefense Functions, 1952 to 1957.

PURPOSES

To understand the purposes of American public expenditures, one must consider the outlays of all government units together. Because of different ways the data are presented and because of grants from one government to another, it is not possible to be absolutely certain of groupings. The broad outlines are clear, however, and are shown in Table 1–3.

As of 1929, one-fifth of the total of American government expenditure was devoted to schools. Construction and maintenance of highways and streets, and national defense ranked next in importance. Nine years later, government expenditures were over $5 billion higher; four-fifths of the difference

TABLE 1–3

Functional Distribution of American Government Expenditure, 1929, 1938, 1942, 1953, and 1957[1]

(Amounts in billions)

Purpose of Disbursement	1929 Amount	1929 Per Cent	1938 Amount	1938 Per Cent	1942 Amount	1942 Per Cent	1953 Amount	1953 Per Cent	1957 Amount	1957 Per Cent
Education	$ 2.5	19	$ 2.4	13	$ 2.5	6	$ 8.0	8	$ 15.5	13
Highways and streets	1.9	15	1.7	9	1.6	4	4.6	5	7.9	7
Social welfare and health			5.2	27	4.8	11	7.8	8	16.5	14
National defense and veterans[2]			1.6	9	27.4	61	58.1	58	50.0	42
Protection[3]	6.0	46	.7	4	.8	2	1.1	1	2.4	2
Agriculture and natural resources			1.1	6	1.4	3	5.7	6	6.6[4]	5
General government and miscellaneous			3.3	17	1.5	3	4.3	4	6.0	5
Sanitation	a	a	.2	a	.2	a	.9	1	1.4	1
Local parks and recreation	a	a	.1	a	.1	a	.4	a	.6	1
Nonhighway transportation	a	a	a	a	a	a	a	a	1.5	1
Interest	1.5	11	1.6	9	1.8	4	6.9	7	8.5	8
Trust funds and enterprises[5]	a	a	.3	1	1.3	3	.6	1	—.4	a
Debt retirement[6]	1.1	9	.7	4	1.1	2	.5		3.0	2
Total	$13.0	100	$18.9	100	$44.6	100	$98.9	100	$119.5	100

[a] Less than $50,000,000, or one-half of one per cent, or not available.

[1] Includes capital outlays and expenditures financed by borrowing. The concept of expenditure differs in various ways from that in Table 1–1. Postal outlays paid for by charges, most expenses of liquor monopolies and other enterprise-type functions, and retirement and certain other trust fund outlays are not included here. Minor differences in classifications mar the comparability from year to year, but not significantly.

[2] Includes varying amounts of foreign aid—$0.8 billion in 1957.

[3] Police and fire.

[4] Includes $0.6 billion housing and community development.

[5] Excludes spending from Social Security trust funds; such amounts are included under "social welfare and health." Enterprise expenditures are the difference between receipts and outlays.

[6] Gross retirement, not the difference between retirement and new borrowing.

SOURCES: 1929 figures from National Industrial Conference Board, *Cost of Government in the United States, 1929–1930*. 1938 figures from U.S. Treasury, *Bulletin*, August, 1939. Later years from U.S. Bureau of the Census, *Summary of Governmental Finances in the United States* Series. Because of rounding, details will not necessarily add to totals.

was accounted for by the expansion of social welfare and relief. Less was spent for schools and for highways and streets in 1938 than in 1929, so that the relative importance of these two functions had declined considerably.

Beginning in 1941, national defense spending soared and has ever since dominated American government expenditure. Welfare outlays dropped in relative importance. The expansion of Social Security, however, has led to huge growth in payments to persons who have retired. Meanwhile, education has resumed its position as the major nondefense expenditure. The growth of public debt as a result of war and huge state-local construction programs has produced annual interest costs of substantial size. Chart 1–3 shows recent trends.

Costs of each function are not distributed pro rata among the levels of government—federal, state, and local. Education is primarily a local function, but state outlays for school purposes have become important. On the other hand, practically all of the expenditure for national defense is federal. States account for most highway spending, localities for streets.

PURPOSES OF FEDERAL EXPENDITURE[5]

Article I, Sec. 8, of the federal Constitution grants the federal government, through Congress, certain specified powers—provision for the national defense, conduct of diplomatic relations with other nations, control of immigration and naturalization, regulation of foreign and interstate trade, and control of the monetary system. Nowhere is there mention of any power to construct internal improvements, or to aid agriculture, commerce, industry, or the merchant marine, or to relieve the distress caused by business depression, or to construct lighthouses, or to engage in any of the multitude of "service" functions which the federal government performs today. And the Tenth Amendment provides that: "The powers not delegated to the United States by the Constitution, nor prohibited by it to the States, are reserved to the States respectively, or to the people." But Article I, Sec. 8, also gives Congress power "To lay and collect taxes, duties, imposts, and excises, to pay the debts and provide for the common defense and general welfare of the United States." The construction of that "general welfare clause" was fiercely contested during the first fifty years of the country's history.[6] Should it be construed strictly, and the role of the federal

[5] Detailed and extremely valuable information on the expenditures of the federal government is to be found in the published reports of hearings before Congressional committees, especially the hearings before the Appropriations Committees.

[6] The issue turned upon the comma after the word "excises." Was it intended to mark off an independent clause, so that Congress was given power "to pay the debts and provide for the common defense and general welfare"? Or, in consonance with eighteenth-century writing style, was it casual, so that the grant of power should read, "To lay and collect taxes, etc. (in order) to pay the debts and provide for the common defense and general welfare"? Under the first construction, a real "general welfare" power is granted; under the second, a limitation is placed on federal tax powers. The records of the Constitutional Convention would indicate that the second, narrower construction was in the minds of the delegates.

government be limited to that of arbiter between the states and as international "front" for the union? Or should it be construed liberally, and the way thus opened for practically unlimited federal activity? Historical authority supported the case for the "strict constructionists." That of the "loose constructionists" rested on popular approval—and gained the ultimate victory.

Although federal powers to regulate private activity come constantly under the eyes of the courts, federal activities and expenditures are relatively free from judicial interference. An individual or other plaintiff rarely has an interest so affected by the expenditure of public funds that he may invoke the judgment of the courts—unless the activity for which the funds are expended regulates or otherwise limits his personal or business rights.

Except during the 1930's, expenditures for war, to meet the threat of war, and as a consequence of war, have always dominated federal spending. The pattern of federal civil expenditure has been a widely changing one. Until the middle of the nineteenth century the civil functions of the federal government were held to a minimum. Thereafter they expanded unevenly but rapidly and culminated in the "New Deal" program of the mid-1930's. Eighteen depression-free years, the demands of a military economy, and a changed political atmosphere have narrowed only slightly the area of federal civil operation, which continues much broader than even the most visionary imaginings of the 1920's.

National defense. World War II military expenditures reached a peak of $91 billion in 1945. Defense spending then dropped rapidly to around $13 billion in 1950, when fighting broke out in Korea. This evidence of the Communist threat led to a large and expensive rearmament program, one costing 13 per cent of the national income. The only thing likely to check an apparent upward trend is an improvement in international relations.

Defense expenditures cover a bewildering array of procurements. The following breakdown of $46 billion of defense outlays for 1960 gives some idea of the relative importance of different items of military spending:

Pay and allowances for military personnel—$11.9 billion.

Operation and maintenance, including such details as operation of West Point and Annapolis, other training facilities, purchase of gasoline and spare parts for equipment, medical care—$10.4 billion.

Major procurement, including the production of naval ships, aircraft, tanks, and ordnance—$13.9 billion.

Military construction, including camps and other facilities within the United States and abroad—$1.7 billion.

Research and development—$3.4 billion.

Atomic energy—$2.7 billion.

Military assistance abroad—$1.9 billion.

TABLE 1–4

Federal Expenditure, Selected Years 1922–1959

Purpose of Expenditure	"Normalcy" 1926	Depression 1932	"New Deal" 1936	War 1944	Postwar 1949	Postwar 1959
	Amounts (in millions)					
Farm aid	a	$ 443	$ 938	$ 912	$ 2,512	$ 6,392
Public works and natural resources[1]	a	450	730	433	2,157	4,251
Relief and welfare	...	500	2,292	17	1,563	4,345
Social security[2]	...	...	28	862	939	10,686
Other civil payments	$ 610	755	611	2,849	1,872	5,325
Total civil	$ 610	$2,148	$4,599	$ 5,073	$ 9,043	$30,999
National defense	595	702	912	87,039	12,907	46,845
Veterans' aid	742	985	2,351[b]	629	6,726	5,162
Foreign aid (nonmilitary)	...	...	...	...	6,053	1,441
Interest	832	599	749	2,609	5,445	7,578
Total	$2,779	$4,434	$8,611	$95,350	$40,174	$92,025
	Percentage Distribution					
Farm aid	a	10	11	1	6	7
Public works and natural resources	a	10	8	a	5	5
Relief and welfare	...	11	27	...	4	5
Social security	...	...	a	1	2	12
Other civil payments	22	17	7	3	5	6
Total civil	22	48	53	5	22	34
National defense	22	16	11	91	32	51
Veterans' aid	27	22	27[b]	1	17	6
Foreign aid (nonmilitary)	...	...	...	...	15	2
Interest	30	13	9	3	13	8
Total	100	100	100	100	100	100

[a] Relatively small amounts included with "Other civil payments."
[b] Includes $1.7 billion bonus payment.
[1] Includes highway grants to states.
[2] Includes retirement and insurance benefit payments under the Social Security system but *not* additions to Social Security trust funds or unemployment insurance.

SOURCES: U.S. Secretary of the Treasury, *Annual Report*, for various years; *The 1959 Federal Budget Midyear Review*. All data for fiscal years. Due to rounding, details will not necessarily add to totals.

Some extravagance, some avoidable waste, are unquestionably involved in these staggering outlays.[7] For the most part, however, by practical standards the spending is probably done with about as much efficiency as one can reasonably expect. Yet greater value for these huge sums must be a continuing goal of national policy. The major problem lies not in better

[7] One of the greatest of avoidable wastes has been the failure to hold on to highly and expensively trained personnel. In 1958, fortunately, Congress voted new compensation scales which are designed to aid the retention of experienced officers and enlisted men.

"housekeeping," nor in tighter pricing of procurement, but in selecting the right things on which to spend.

Veterans' service and benefits. Aid to veterans reached a peak of $7.3 billion in 1947, when the program for schooling and vocational rehabilitation was in full operation. The annual figure is now over $5 billion, plus retirement pay of $600 million. More than half goes for pensions for disabled veterans and survivors of deceased servicemen. Appropriations will probably increase as the number of aging veterans seeking aid grows, as the deaths of veterans lengthen the list of pension-drawing survivors, and as Congress continues to liberalize aid. Some economies could result from the reduction of hospital services given for disabilities that are not connected with military service.

International affairs and foreign aid. The foreign service costs $200 million a year. Information, student exchange, and related programs cost over $100 million.

Partly for humanitarian considerations, partly to secure and strengthen allies in a war-threatened era, between 1948 and 1953 the United States advanced some $30 billions in loans and gifts to other countries, including our former enemies, Germany and Japan. The initial step was the Marshall Plan, under which some $13 billions went to the war-weakened countries of Europe to assist their economic rehabilitation. When in 1950 it became evident that this country had to unite with other lands to check the encroachments of Communist Russia, the United States committed itself to making contributions under the Mutual Security Program to build up the military strength of the European members of the alliance. By 1959 these Mutual Security grants had totaled nearly $20 billion. Finally, beginning in 1950, the United States began making Point Four grants to underdeveloped countries to assist their economic progress.

These foreign aid contributions remain highly controversial. Are we getting good value for the $3 billion a year in military aid, including almost $1 billion for Korea, Nationalist China, and Vietnam? Would larger amounts be an efficient way to strengthen the free world's defense?

Is our $1 billion of aid to underdeveloped areas achieving reasonably good results for them? and for us? Might accomplishments be enhanced by different kinds of administration? by greater reliance on private business? As we shift from gifts to loans, can we not economically provide more dollars, counting on repayment later? For some countries, "trade not aid" may offer the most promising solution. Some, however, have little to sell. And generally, the poor areas of the world seek more help than the American taxpayer is willing to provide. The resulting disputes are likely to continue to influence both domestic politics and foreign relations. Rational balancing of considerations is very difficult.

Natural resources and transportation. Federal spending under the category of "natural resources"—a mixture of outlays for current operations and for new construction, excluding highways—is currently $1.5 billion a year. This does not include atomic energy, for since 1955 the federal budget has classified atomic energy development as a military, instead of a natural resource, expenditure. Flood control, irrigation, national forests and parks, and multipurpose river projects like the Tennessee Valley Authority, the St. Lawrence, and other river developments, account for most of this outlay. Over 300 specific projects in the 1959 budget include something for most Congressional districts, including new farm land to add to agricultural surpluses. Highways, airports and ship and plane navigational aids, and ship and inland waterway subsidies in 1959 will cost well over $3.5 billion. The postal deficit will be about $600 million despite rate increases.

Agricultural aid. When agriculture was the biggest single industry in the country, federal agricultural aid beyond selling and giving land was almost nonexistent. Now that farming produces less than 5 per cent of the net national income, farmers are major beneficiaries of the federal government; $60 billion in farm aid from 1932–59 has by no means solved the farmers' problems, for annual aid is now over $6.4 billion (two-fifths as much as *all* state-local spending on education!). Agricultural research and related services cost about $270 million a year. Financing rural electrification and telephones comes to nearly $380 million, in the form of loans to be repaid. The biggest and most unpredictable item of farm aid is the program of crop price support, including soil conservation and soil bank payments, which are designed to raise prices by reducing output.

The farm programs are varied and complex. For specified crops representing about half of all farm marketings, the Department of Agriculture sets "support" prices at a per cent of "parity" as defined by Congress.[8] Whenever the market price of one of the designated products falls below the support price, various federal agencies acquire part of the crop at the latter price, or guarantee private crop loans on which the farmer can default, turning the crop over to the government. Export subsidies and subsidies for processing various farm products for special uses also help to sustain prices for certain crops.

The whole farm aid policy arouses much well-justified criticism. Probably no item of federal spending serves the general public, including most farmers, so poorly per dollar spent. The costs will continue until policies more realistically adapted to modern conditions become effective.

Welfare and other "social expenditures."[9] In the 1930's, as part of the "New Deal," the federal government assumed an important group of social functions. One of them—relief of the unemployed through public work

[8] The parity price for a bushel of wheat, for example, has the buying power that the price of a bushel of wheat had in a past base period.

[9] This section does not include Old Age and Survivors Insurance or unemployment benefits financed by payroll taxes. The huge increase shown in Table 1–4 for Social Security is chiefly OASI.

projects and relief grants to local governments—disappeared in the 1940's. The others have continued on an expanding scale. Currently the federal government spends over $4.3 billion under the heading "Labor and Welfare." Half is for grants to the states for aid to the aged, to families with dependent children, to the blind, and to the disabled. Public health outlays exceed $300 million. Somewhat over $200 million is distributed among a variety of agencies for research. Grants to states for administering unemployment insurance, training of workers, and employment exchanges cost $300 million. Urban renewal and housing aids, not counting loans for college housing, receive over $150 million plus large amounts of financing help in the form of loans. Agricultural surpluses costing about $250 million are donated for distribution to families on welfare.

Interest. Interest on the federal debt will be $8 billion in 1960 and is more likely to increase than to fall. A rise in the *rate* of interest is not improbable, and some growth in the debt itself will result from the combined effects of the recession of 1958, which reduced tax yields, and of the upward trend of spending.

General government. The remaining categories of federal spending, commonly classified under the heading of "general government," total less than $1.5 billion. Some of the outlays comprising this remainder are as follows:

	Millions
The President, White House staff, and Bureau of the Budget	$ 14
Congress	112
The judicial system	46
Tax collection	378
Debt management and other financial activities	130
Property and records management	275
Prisons, alien control, Federal Bureau of Investigation, etc.	197
Weather services	41
District of Columbia, territories, and possessions	95
Central personnel management and personnel costs	108

They are what critics often have in mind when they complain of federal "extravagance" and demand "slashes" in spending. Unquestionably appropriations could be reduced by eliminating this or that service, but most of the present services can justify themselves on the basis of their contribution to the general welfare. Some improvements in operating efficiency are doubtless possible. Yet they would hardly dent the over-all total of federal spending. If the cost of federal government is to be cut substantially, reductions must come from the spending categories previously listed.

PROBLEMS

1. What factors account for the growth of American government spending? How are they interrelated?

2. Give examples of improvement in the quality of government service over the last quarter-century. What services today are poorer than in the past? Why?

3. Explain why states have become relatively more, and localities relatively less, important spending agencies since 1890.

4. Examine the economic issues involved in reducing benefits to farmers by $2 billion and using the money to aid underdeveloped lands.

5. Describe the provisions in the federal Constitution that bear upon government spending.

6. Study the material issued by one or more of the pressure groups seeking a change in government spending.

7. Is there *general public* interest in subsidies to farmers? Why? Would your answer be different if the financing did not burden low income consumers and taxpayers?

8. "Since 1953 it has *not* been the warfare world that has raised the cost of government." Comment. What does account for the recent increases?

CHAPTER 2

Growth, Agencies, and Purposes of American Government Expenditure (Concluded)

PURPOSES OF STATE EXPENDITURE

AFTER early and generally disastrous experiences with canal construction, railroad aid, and bank aid, states tended during the nineteenth century to reduce their activities to a minimum. Agriculture was given some small assistance. State officials administered, often badly, the school funds obtained from the sale of "school lands." A few state hospitals and asylums were maintained. Otherwise, at the turn of the century, most of the states confined themselves to the bare "overhead" functions of government.

General functions. Between 1900 and 1958, state spending per capita increased from $2 to $150. Allowing for the drop in the purchasing power of the dollar, this was still a 25-fold increase. What is the explanation? During the past half-century, the scope of state activity has broadened startlingly. The states are masters of revenue sources denied to local governments; consequently the states have had to supplement, and in some cases take over, functions once the exclusive responsibility of local units. Advent of the automobile necessitated paved *highways* beyond the capacity of local governments to construct and maintain. At first, the states contributed to local highway activity by grants-in-aid, but most of them have assumed sole responsibility for arterial highways.

In *education*, too, state contributions have risen. From 1900 on, educational grants for school purposes assumed ever larger importance; all indications point to still further expansion of state activity in this field. California and Delaware have made education completely a state function; several other states pay for a standard minimum education, the local districts being responsible only for any excess over the minimum. Elsewhere, school authorities are campaigning either for similar state assumption of

TABLE 2–1

Purposes of State Expenditure, Selected Years 1913–1958

Purpose of Disbursement (Current and Capital)	1913	1923	1931	1938	1947	1958
Amounts (in millions)						
General government ...	$ 44	$ 84	$ 148	$ 165	$ 234	$ 578
Protection to person and property	26	55	89	131	171	674
Development and conservation of natural resources	...	52	84	97	207	890
Health, sanitation[1]	7	24	40	46	107	2,170
Highways[2]	26	384	998	1,033	861	6,674
Social welfare (excl. unemployment aid)[2]	94	198	309	1,369	1,845	2,949
Education[2]	140	382	632	927	1,639	7,325
Miscellaneous[2]	12	69	82	107	860	1,899
Net total: current	$317	$ 895	$1,447	$3,180	$5,924	$17,632
Net total: capital	31	352	935	695	949	5,924
Net total: total	$348	$1,247	$2,382	$3,875	$6,873	$23,159
Interest	14	50	111	126	63	396
Public enterprises	21	13	16	224	6	869
Trust fund[3]	...	...	...	...	1,067	3,675
Percentage Distribution of Total Expenditure[4]						
General government ...	13	6	6	4	4	3
Protection to person and property	7	4	4	3	3	3
Development and conservation of natural resources	...	4	3	2	3	4
Health, sanitation	2	2	2	1	2	9
Highways	8	30	40	26	14	28
Social welfare (excl. unemployment aid)	27	16	12	34	31	13
Education	40	30	26	23	28	31
Miscellaneous	3	6	3	3	14	8
Interest	...	4	5	4	1	2
Total	100	100	100	100	100	100
Capital (included in functions) ...	9	30	39	18	14	25

[1] State hospital expenditures, included under Health and Sanitation in 1957, under Social Welfare in earlier years.

[2] Includes grants to local governments.

[3] Primarily unemployment benefits and workmen's compensation.

[4] Percentages do not take account of expenditures on public enterprises and for trust funds.

Because of rounding, items do not necessarily add to totals.

SOURCE: U.S. Bureau of the Census, *State Finances* series.

the school functions or for larger state grants. On their *universities* alone, states now spend more than they did on all functions thirty years ago.

Hospitalization for the tubercular and mentally ill has long been primarily a state function. Before the depression of the 1930's, however, state governments left relief activities largely to localities. The depression forced most states to engage heavily in relief activities. The Social Security Act of 1935 imposed new expenditure obligations upon the states. (1) To take advantage of the credit allowed in the federal payroll tax, all states passed *unemployment insurance* laws; benefit payments under these laws were over $2 billion in 1958, an all-time high. (2) All states established systems for assisting four categories of the poor—(a) the aged, (b) families with dependent children, (c) the blind, and (d) the permanently and totally disabled; over half the cost comes from the federal government.

The ranking of the various state functions, measured by relative expenditures, has shifted from period to period, as indicated in Table 2–1.

Individual states vary widely as to the relative support they give to individual functions. In 1957, for example, New York was spending about 13 per cent of its state budget on highways, whereas the proportion in Nebraska was around 37 per cent. New Mexico spent 40 per cent of the current state budget on education, Rhode Island 13 per cent. In six states interest on debt was a minute item; in Maryland and Massachusetts it was 4 per cent of total state expenditures. One state alone, New York, accounted for more than one-fifth of the total state outlays for mental hospitals.

Capital outlays. In 1913, capital outlays were less than 10 per cent of the total of state expenditure; today, at over $7 billion, they are 20 per cent of a vastly greater total. One function alone, highways, accounts for four-fifths of state capital outlay. In many states, years of depression and wartime neglect, growing population, and higher standards of acceptable service have created tremendous need for more and better hospitals, corrective institutions, highways, recreational facilities, university and office buildings, and public housing. State funds for school construction, now generally small, will probably increase.

PURPOSES OF LOCAL EXPENDITURE

Local government functions, more than state or federal activities (except the postal system), tangibly touch every man, woman, and child. School districts and municipalities are still primarily responsible for education. Cities, counties, and towns spend heavily on streets and roads. The policeman or sheriff who represents "law and order," the fireman, the visiting nurse and the health clinic, the public park, the water-supply system—all are manifestations of local government.

Local expenditures for 1957, classified by functions and by the classes of

TABLE 2–2

Local Expenditures, Tabulated by Functions, 1957

Purpose of Disbursement	*County*	*City*	*Town-ship*	*School District*	*Special District*	*Total*
			Amount (millions)			
General government	$ 586	$ 504	$ 91	...	...	$ 1,181
Public safety	214	1,736	130	...	$ 13	2,093
Health, sanitation	869	1,800	84	...	137	2,890
Streets, highways and other transportation	1,174	1,551	323	...	311	3,358
Social welfare	1,106	487	72	...	...	1,666
Education	666	1,368	370	$9,638	...	12,042
Housing, community, and natural resource development	119	247	...	...	308	673
Miscellaneous	577	1,278	105	...	57	2,017
Interest	88	512	47	232	201	1,080
Total	$5,399	$9,483	$1,222	$9,870	$1,026	$26,700
Capital	$1,065	$3,323	$ 252	$2,244	$ 597	$ 7,481
			Percentage Distribution by Functions			
General government	11	5	7	...	...	4
Public safety	4	18	11	...	1	8
Health, sanitation	16	19	7	...	14	11
Streets, highways and other transportation	21	16	26	...	30	12
Social welfare	20	5	6	...	...	6
Education	12	15	30	98	...	45
Housing, community, and natural resource development	2	3	...	...	30	3
Miscellaneous	11	14	9	...	6	8
Interest	2	5	4	2	20	4
Total	100	100	100	100	100	100
Capital (included in functions)	19	35	21	23	58	28
			Percentage Distribution by Class of Government			
Public safety	10	83	6	...	1	100
Health, sanitation	30	62	3	...	5	100
Streets, highways and other transportation	35	46	10	...	9	100
Social welfare	67	29	4	...	...	100
Education	5	11	3	80	...	100
Housing, community, and natural resource development	18	37	...	...	45	100
Capital	14	45	3	30	8	100
Total	20	35	5	37	4	100

SOURCE: U.S. Bureau of the Census, *Summary of Governmental Finances in 1957*.

TABLE 2–3

Purposes of City Expenditure, Selected Years 1905–1957

Purpose of Disbursement (Current and Capital)	*City Population over 30,000*[1]			*City Population over 100,000*[2]		*City Population over 25,000*[3]	
	1905	1913	1923	1930	1938	1947	1957
			Amounts (in millions)				
General government	$ 34	$ 67	$ 125	$ 180	$ 184	$ 212	$ 348
Public safety	88	127	285	366	360	612	1,370
Health, sanitation	52	89	215	280	202	495	1,450
Streets	100	161	325	518	259	321	887
Social welfare and corrections	22	40	88	156	523	271	483
Education[4]	125	199	701	777	732	600	1,312
Recreation	22	45	75	110	94	110	374
Miscellaneous	6	22	61	99	120	209	857
Interest	53	110	228	341	207	125	256
Total	$502	$860	$2,103	$2,827	$2,681	$2,955	$7,337
Capital	$142	$227	$ 537	$ 748	$ 377	$ 313	$1,707
Enterprises and trust funds[5]	69	124	261	335	454	255	400
			Percentage Distribution				
General government	7	8	6	6	7	8	5
Public safety	19	15	14	13	13	21	19
Health, sanitation	11	10	10	10	8	17	20
Streets	20	19	16	18	9	11	12
Social welfare and corrections	4	5	4	5	19	9	7
Education	25	23	33	27	27	20	18
Recreation	4	5	4	4	4	4	5
Miscellaneous	1	3	3	4	4	7	12
Interest	11	13	11	12	8	4	3
Total	100	100	100	100	100	100	100
Capital expenditure	28	27	25	26	14	11	23

[1] Cities with populations over 30,000: 154 in 1905, 199 in 1913, 248 in 1923.
[2] Cities with populations over 100,000: 94.
[3] Cities with populations over 25,000: 397 in 1947, and 481 in 1957, based on 1950 census.
[4] School expenditures in some cities are not attributed to the city governments, but to independent school districts occupying the same areas as these cities.
[5] Includes net deficits from utilities, plus net expenditures from trust funds not offset by special receipts.
Because of rounding, details do not necessarily add to totals.
SOURCE: U.S. Bureau of the Census, *City Finances* series.

local governments making them, are shown in Table 2–2.[1] Education is far and away the major local government function. The $12 billion of local

[1] These figures include expenditures of funds received from states. Thus there is double counting in Tables 2–1 and 2–2.

school expenditure in 1957 accounted for two-fifths of local spending in that year. School districts are responsible for over three-fourths of local school finances. By the measure of expenditures, construction and maintenance of streets and highways, and provision for public health and sanitation are next in order of importance among local functions.

The $9.5 billion expenditure of cities in 1957 was more than one-third of the total for all local governments. The $10 billion spent by school districts accounted for over another third. Townships have little functional importance outside of New England, but special districts have been growing in financial importance, partly because of their role in public housing.

Cities. Table 2–3 shows the expenditures of cities, including the spending on schools in only a portion of cases. (Special school boards do this spending in many cities.) Again, education is the biggest single item, although police and fire protection combined as public safety are higher; so, in combination, are health and sanitation. One item of municipal expenditure that might abruptly assume major proportions is public welfare. During the middle 1930's this was the largest item in the budget of many communities; this could happen again should recession produce prolonged unemployment. Very few cities could meet the relief needs for which they are presumably responsible. The strain of relief costs on municipal budgets was severe in some cities during even the mild recession of 1958.

Cities are continually cutting new streets or improving existing ones, constructing schools, hospitals, libraries, parks, prisons, and other public buildings, building water and sewer systems. Capital outlays normally run between a quarter and a third of total city budgets. New York City's capital budget of $500 million, which does not include all construction spending, is one-tenth as large as capital outlays of all states combined. Yet there are few, if any, cities which have built enough since 1945 to meet the needs accumulated in the depression and war and to keep up with population growth and rising standards. Slum clearance and "urban renewal," traffic congestion and transit, airports and recreational facilities, all seem likely to put increasing demands on cities for capital outlays.

Counties. Variety in size, population, and functions of counties is extraordinarily great. Obviously, Daggett County in Utah, with its 400 inhabitants, and Cook County in Illinois, with its 4.5 million, are vastly different. New England counties are little more than judicial districts. Elsewhere, counties are important civic units—they support schools, build roads, maintain hospitals, asylums, and jails, and coordinate and supervise the administrative and fiscal activities of the smaller government units within their area. The aggregate figures presented in Table 2–4 conceal a vital dissimilarity of government activity.

General administrative expenses, including county judiciaries and the maintenance of official records, account for about 10 per cent of total county expenditures. Counties are the primary highway and road units in

TABLE 2–4

Purposes of County Expenditure, Selected Years 1902–1957

Purpose of Disbursement	1902	1913	1932	1946	1957[a]
	Amounts (in millions)				
General government	$ 71	$102	$251	$ 316	$ 586
Protection to person and property	7	15	44	64	214
Health, sanitation	2	3	33	172	869
Highways	29	56	236	356	1,145
Social welfare and corrections	20	38	182	489	1,106
Education	34	58	182	108	666
Miscellaneous	2	6	53	132	725
Total current service expenditure	$165	$278	$981	$1,637	$5,311
Interest	$ 10	$ 17	$119	$ 52	$ 88
Capital outlays	22	90	311	118	1,065
	Percentage Distribution of Current Service Expenditure				
General government	44	37	26	19	
Protection to person and property	4	6	4	4	
Health, sanitation	1	1	3	11	
Highways	17	20	24	22	a
Social welfare and corrections	12	14	19	30	
Education	21	21	19	7	
Recreation	. . .	. . .	1	1	
Miscellaneous	1	2	5	7	
Total	100	100	100	100	

[a] Figures for 1957 are classified by *total,* instead of *current service,* spending. See Table 2–2 for percentages of total expenditures.

SOURCES: U.S. Bureau of the Census, *Wealth, Debt and Taxation,* 1902 and 1913; *Financial Statistics of State and Local Governments,* 1932; *County Finances,* 1946; *Summary of Governmental Finances in 1957.*

many states; where the state government has taken over the arterial highway system, the counties remain responsible for the "market" and "feeder" roads. Roads absorb one-fifth of all county spending.

County operation of schools is rare, but except in New England the counties are often the agencies for distributing state school-aid to the rural school districts and have some general supervisory authority. They sometimes levy special school taxes, distributing the receipts among the districts on an equalizing basis. Social welfare activities have been among the most rapidly growing of county functions. Poor relief, free hospitalization, child aid, and similar social welfare services, which cities provide for urban populations, are performed by counties for rural populations and in some cases for town and city dwellers as well.

As population spreads out from cities, towns, and villages, the county is in some cases becoming a relatively more important governmental unit. Here and there the public uses it to fill various gaps in arrangements for providing services. To date, however, the trend has not developed proportions of major significance.

Special districts.[2] Special districts or "authorities" have been set up in many states to provide special services to the residents of special areas. These special districts are of two types: (1) those which provide such government services as street lighting or police and fire protection to areas or groups within larger units, such as concentrated settlements in sparsely settled areas, and (2) superdistricts, covering areas of two or more regular government units, which administer a centralized service—multitown fire or water supply, for example—more efficiently and more cheaply than could the individual units. In 1957, the 14,405 special districts were for the following functions:

Fire	2,624	Irrigation and water conservation.	564
Highways	782	Cemeteries	1,107
Health and hospitals	568	Urban water supply	787
Sanitation	451	Libraries	322
Nonhighway transportation	134	Flood control	209
Housing	969	Multipurpose	879
Drainage	2,132	Parks and recreation	316
Soil conservation	2,285	Other	276

Most of these districts have the power to levy taxes. The rest rely on special assessments and income from sale of services. A tabulation of special district expenditures which does not quite cover all "authorities" totals $1.7 billion a year.

Although special districts have existed in some states almost as long as the states themselves, their widespread development is a comparatively recent development. Information as to their activities and expenditures and the machinery for their effective control are both inadequate.

EXPENDITURE FOR PUBLIC EDUCATION[3]

The tradition of a free, generous public school system is one of the most cherished elements of our American civilization. It was a revolutionary concept when introduced by the colony of Massachusetts in the middle of

[2] No separate analysis is made of school district expenditures. They are included in the general discussion of educational expenditures later in this chapter. For a recent analysis, see J. C. Bollens, *Special District Governments in the United States* (University of California Press, Berkeley, 1957).

[3] See Tax Institute, *Financing Education in the Public Schools* (The Institute, Princeton, 1956).

the seventeenth century. General popular recognition of the value of a free educational system, particularly the extension of such a system to include tax-supported secondary schools, was slow in developing. Not until the middle of the nineteenth century could the tradition be said to have been definitely established. Since then, education has been much the largest non-military item of government spending. Since 1900, government spending on schools has risen from 1.5 to 4 per cent of net national income.

Education could have been left to private enterprise, with some assistance from charity, as is still predominantly the case with medical care. There are private and church-sponsored schools now. Government might have used its powers of coercion to compel attendance, as it does today; tax-supported grants to families unable to pay the costs could have met the needs of lower income families. Quality standards might have been enforced by regulation and testing. But such were not the choices which—for reasons wise or unwise—our forefathers made.

Why treat education as a governmental function? If people want education badly enough to pay taxes for it, why will they not pay for it in free markets? Why do we rely so heavily upon government and the political process to provide education? There are a variety of reasons. Most fundamental, perhaps, is the fact that everyone is affected by the quality of the people around him. What each person makes of his own capacities affects others—his children, of course, but also his neighbors, those with whom he works, and even those far away with whom he has indirect but essential economic relations. In our interdependent economy each person's economic life depends not only upon his own productive capacity but also upon that of all others. The more skilled and productive the masses, as well as the leaders, the higher the standard of living for all. Economic growth requires higher skills, possessed ever more broadly. Clearly, there is a general, as well as an individual, interest in what people become through what they are taught.

This general interest includes capacity for citizenship. The higher the quality of citizens, the better, we believe, the benefits all can gain from democracy. And ignorance, through political action, may lead to avoidable errors, causing everyone to suffer. Moreover, today we see vividly new dimensions to the general interest—national defense, a truly inherent function of government which requires, as never before, the most advanced skills of modern civilization, in science, diplomacy, persuasion, ability to teach, and organization and management. In addition, national defense requires that the public as a whole have a large and growing body of skills—not everyone the same skills but as many as possible with abilities that can come only from good education of many types.

The individual, in pursuing his own interests in education, cannot be expected to take adequate account of the general public interest. The consumer, moreover, is incompetent to judge the product. He cannot know the value of education for him until he has it. The child obviously cannot make rational choice. Many parents, too, would be unable to make wise decisions on this matter. Here is an area of life where compulsion has a crucial and proper part to play—compulsion democratically and competently controlled.

Financing of schools by taxes also rests on economic factors. Even if there were no school taxes, some parents would not be able to pay for the education of their children. Some would not be willing to do so on an adequate scale. Burdening a parent with heavy school costs during a fraction of his working life would create serious payment difficulties. In many communities, not only rural ones, there are too few children to make more than one or two schools at each level economically feasible. Consequently, there has been overwhelming reason for treating schools in most areas as a "natural monopoly."[4] Finally, as an economic reason, the quantity of education provided without a price to the user, per hour or day, does not give rise to the problems of controlling the quantity demanded that would arise if, say, steak or transportation had no price. Absence of price as a rationing factor is not critical in education.

The choice of government as the agency to operate schools has not rested on calculated analysis of the merits of government in relation to possible alternative agencies for getting the best quality education reasonably possible. Today this is hardly an issue. We are committed to public schools. The problem is how to improve them in a framework of government.

Growth. In 1870, public education expenditures amounted to $63 million. Ninety years later, in 1960, the total may exceed $17 billion. From 1902 to 1958, the expenditure per capita in dollars of constant purchasing power rose almost 700 per cent. As shown by data in Table 2–5, several factors, in addition to the general rise in prices, have contributed to the growth. (1) As the country's population grew, the number of school-age children has increased, doubling in less than two generations. (2) Since the proportion attending school also rose, enrollment has tripled (the rise in the short period of 1952 to 1958 was 8 million). (3) The length of the average school term was increased from 135 days to 179 days. (4) A larger proportion of children have stayed on longer in school, swelling enrollment where costs per pupil are highest. In 1958, almost 25 per cent of all pupils attending public school were in high school, as against 2 per cent in 1890. The education offered is much more expensive and, despite exceptions, the quality is higher. The number of pupils per teacher has dropped almost one-fourth since 1900. Just after World War I, only one out of five teachers had as much as two years of education beyond high school. Today, three

[4] Businesses do a great deal of employee training. In a society in which employees are free to shift jobs, there is general advantage in providing a set of schools open to all, even for basic technical training, rather than relying upon what businesses will provide. Their efforts are logically devoted to more specific training for the jobs in their own plants.

TABLE 2–5

Factors in Public School Expenditure, Selected Years 1890–1958[1]

Items	1890	1940	1950	1954	1958 Estimate
Children 5 to 17 years of age					
Number[2]	18.5	29.8	30.8	34.5	41
Per cent of population	30	23	20	22	23
Pupils enrolled					
Number[2]	12.7	24.6	25.1	28.8	34
Per cent of children 5 to 17	69	85	82	84	83
High-school students					
Number[2]	.2	6.4	5.7	6.3	8.5
Per cent of pupils enrolled	2	26	23	20	25
School term (days)	135	175	178	179	180
Average days attended	86	152	158	159	160
Total expenditures[2, 3]	$141	$2,344	$5,802	$9,092	$16,000
Expenditures per capita[3] . . .	$ 2	$ 18	$ 38	$ 57	$ 90
Expenditures per pupil in average attendance[3]	$ 17	$ 106	$ 209	$ 351	$ 470
Average teacher's salary	$252	$1,441	$3,010	$3,825	$ 4,700

[1] This table does not include approximately one-seventh of the total number of children attending school in this country, parochial and other private schools being excluded.

[2] In millions.

[3] Includes outlays for new construction.

SOURCE: U. S. Office of Education, *Biennial Survey of Education in the United States* series. Figures for 1958 are authors' estimates based on a variety of sources.

out of four have at least four years of college. Salaries have risen. Better and more costly buildings and equipment are provided.

School finance. Public education in the United States has from the beginning been primarily a local responsibility, discharged as a rule by special school districts.[5] By 1900, however, the system of exclusive local responsibility for school finance had begun to break down. Divergence between the educational needs and the taxable resources of individual districts became pronounced and demanded remedy. A wealthy community might be able to provide excellent educational facilities with a modest school tax, whereas a confiscatory rate in a neighboring poor district would finance only meager schooling. State financial help developed, but slowly.

During the 1920's, state equalization of educational opportunity replaced the casual and frequently ill-considered distribution of state school aid, as discussed in Chapter 24. State participation in education was furthered by the financial difficulties of many local districts during the

[5] In the nineteenth century, federal and state governments made large land grants and special money grants which were often tragically mismanaged. Lands were sold for less than their real value, deeds were improperly recorded or not recorded at all, proceeds of land sales vanished without record, bad loans were made, officials absconded with funds. In only a few states did the local school districts receive any substantial lasting benefit from these funds.

1930's. Educators developed a new standard—the state government should furnish, or guarantee through state aid, a minimum school program in all districts of the state. Local districts should be responsible only for supplements over this minimum.

Response to the appeal for state school funds has varied widely. Today states pay about 50 per cent of the total costs of the nation's public schools. Highest proportions are around 90 per cent—in Delaware and New Mexico—and 80 per cent in North Carolina. Most Southern states are above the national average. On the other hand, state funds form only about 5 per cent of combined school revenues in Nebraska.

But even if equalization of educational opportunity were accomplished *within each state,* there would still remain a wide variance between states. School expenditure per capita in 1957 was $40 in Arkansas and Mississippi, whereas New York spent $84, California $98, and Arizona and Wyoming around $90. Spending per pupil is generally highest where per capita incomes are highest, and lowest where incomes are lowest. Yet in terms of the income of their people, some states with low expenditures have been making greater efforts for their schools than some of the states with high expenditures. Lack of resources, more than lack of effort, accounts for many of the poorest of the nation's school systems.[6]

Proposals that the public use the federal government, as well as states and localities, to help pay for education have been gaining supporters. Advocates argue that the increase in productivity that comes from better education, the number of vital issues in which there is a large amount of common national interest, the importance of education for national defense, and the extensive migration of population give all areas an interest in the education offered in all other parts of the country. In general, states with low expenditures on education have relatively high rates of emigration. Indisputable evidence of Russian scientific accomplishment has increased the conviction of many Americans that, to get enough action soon enough to secure our safety, we must act on a national scale. Opponents of federal financing argue that the federal government is too hard pressed for funds and that every person with capacity to pay federal taxes is subject to state-local taxing authority; that federal aid would lead to federal dictation of the methods and content of education; that after-tax income differentials among states are far less serious than only a few years ago; that difficult problems of racial segregation and religious liberty would be aggravated; that the inevitable reduction of state sovereignty and local initiative would weaken desirable elements of our political structure.

In addition to grants of public lands, the federal government has for many years made small sums available for agriculture and home extension

[6] Nearly 6 million children are educated in parochial and other private schools, and the number grows about 300,000 a year. In general, governments pay none of the costs of such education, although some benefit is accorded in the form of tax exemptions.

education, vocational rehabilitation, and a few other programs. In the 1930's—except for WPA and PWA aid on special projects, student assistance through the National Youth Administration, and the establishment of the school-lunch program—little was done to enlarge federal aid to schools. During and since World War II, federal aid has been given to meet the special needs of some war production and military-base centers. Temporary indirect aid has been given in paying for education of veterans, and in loans for dormitories.

Many suggestions for federal financial help for schools have been before Congress. The Eisenhower administration has favored, but not vigorously, some support for school construction. It also endorsed scholarships and various aids (largely beyond high school), especially for study of subjects with defense implications. The National Education Association strongly favors federal financial grants to be concentrated in poorer areas. Congress voted in 1958 to set up new systems of grants to states to finance the strengthening of instruction in science, mathematics, and modern foreign languages; states or localities must match federal funds, dollar for dollar. In addition, loans to nonprofit, private schools are authorized for the same purposes. Several programs of research, testing, and guidance are to receive aid, including plans to encourage the unusually able student. College students may apply for a new type of loan, and so may graduate students, especially those interested in college teaching. For the next few years the total annual federal expenditure for education will probably range around $200 million. The effects, however, will be greater than this total may suggest, because of the efforts of states and localities to adapt their schools and colleges to qualify for federal funds.

Government-supported colleges. Colleges and universities supported by governments, primarily by states but to a growing extent by municipalities as well, account for about half of the country's higher education expenditure and half of the student body. Roughly 15 per cent of the $2 billion gross cost of these government-supported colleges in 1958 came from student fees, gifts, and endowment earnings, a bit more from dormitory and other charges. Taxes and borrowings accounted for 70 per cent.[7] In dollars of constant purchasing power, state-local per capita spending on institutions of higher learning has increased 20-fold since 1902.

There is strong pressure on states and localities to spend still more on higher education. Several arguments are advanced in support of such action. (1) Most important is the great increase in the number of those who will inevitably seek to enter college. There are more young people, more families can afford college, more jobs require advanced education, and more people recognize the contribution a liberal education can make to the quality of life. (2) Private institutions, which traditionally have relied

[7] For a good analysis, see H. K. Allen, *State Public Finance and State Institutions of Higher Education in the United States* (Columbia University Press, New York, 1952).

heavily upon endowments and tuition, cannot expand to perform even as big a fraction of the job as they do today. (3) Salaries, a large item of college costs, must rise substantially if any large recruitment of competent staff is to succeed. (4) Large additions of buildings and equipment must be made at high price levels.

Probable trends in educational expenditure. All indications point to a continued rise in school expenditures. Prices creep up, and the main item of cost—salaries—must rise substantially in most school systems if quality of instruction is not to deteriorate. The number of children to be educated will grow 12 million or so by 1970.[8] The average child is spending more years in school. Wide improvement must be made in the material features of many school systems, especially—but by no means exclusively—in the Southern states, in areas where rural teaching standards are still pitifully low, and in mushrooming suburbs. Large shifts of population, which occur as new industrial establishments develop in previously sparsely settled areas, create the need for entire new school systems. In some of the Southern states, even before the Supreme Court's decisions against segregation, there was growing pressure to raise outlays for Negro education, which have averaged less than the expenditures for white students.

The costs of meeting the requirements of even modest standards are tremendous. There is widespread agreement that accomplishments of the better school systems leave much to be desired. Even in communities with the most advanced schooling, standards of desired educational achievement are constantly being raised. Money alone will not assure good education. Yet the chances of getting good schools are greater the more we spend. Unfortunately, really good education is expensive.[9] But it is also a great bargain. In terms of dollars and cents alone, large additions to our educational outlays will yield generously by enlarging our human capacity to produce.

Libraries. Tax-supported libraries are an integral part of the American system of public education. Provision of libraries is chiefly a function of local government, with total outlays now running only a little over $150 million a year. In most cities, buildings, equipment, and salaries have not kept pace with rising population, demand for service, and the general price level. The lag has probably been greater than in the case of schools, where public interest has been more concentrated. A system of federal

[8] Only 20 years ago population experts forecast long-run stabilization of school-age population somewhat under 25 million, that is, no more growth. Our postwar difficulties have been accentuated because school authorities planned on this basis. Predictions, even by experts, can be wrong.

[9] Continued efforts will undoubtedly disclose more ways to use existing staff and plant more efficiently. New teaching aids, such as TV, offer opportunities of doing a better job more economically. See R. A. Freeman, *School Needs in the Decade Ahead* (The Institute for Social Science Research, Washington, 1958).

financial grants to improve libraries in localities under 10,000 was getting started in 1958.

EXPENDITURE FOR HIGHWAYS, STREETS, AND AIRPORTS

Everyone every day uses, at least indirectly, streets and highways provided by government. Some of us use them a great deal. The 3 million miles of highways, roads, and streets that web this country range from some of the finest in the world to some not much better than the dirt roads that were the rule around 1900 when the auto started the modern highway system. Although the tens of billions of dollars that have been poured into streets and highways in recent decades have made our modern economy possible, they have not been adequate for today's needs. Spending for highways, roads, and streets is bound to rise.

Provision of highways as a government function. Transportation facilities are vital to economic development. Upon their availability and relative cost depend effective utilization of scattered natural resources, the extent to which an economy can specialize in production, and the cost of distribution. Expenditures on transportation facilities are *strategic* contributions to economic progress. They could have been left to private enterprise—corporate-built toll roads, corporate-owned railroads, corporate airports—and to some extent they were. Our first highways were private toll roads, and our railroad system was left entirely to corporate development. However, the great web of local roads, of incalculable economic and social importance, could not be constructed and operated by private enterprise on any basis that would produce profit. Thus, local governments took responsibility and made them free. Transportation at lower cost became possible. Production specialization was stimulated, and prices fell. Monopoly was discouraged, since cheaper access to markets brought more sellers.

When the automobile made necessary a highway system beyond nineteenth-century imaginings, it also created two new sources of revenue—the auto license charge and the gasoline tax—well adapted to financing the creation of such a system. A fiscal foundation was thus established for the state governments to participate on a major scale in providing highway facilities.

Two important responsibilities of the federal government—provision of postal services and of national defense—require transportation capacity beyond what might be provided privately. At least, federal activity in financing highways has been justified in part by such needs, especially those of defense.

Development of highway expenditure. Local governments, chiefly counties, bore the entire cost of public roads during the nineteenth century. They relied upon statute labor for much of the work. Instead of collecting taxes and paying for road labor, localities called upon freeholders to work for a specified number of days on the roads. At the appointed time men brought their plows, barrows, scrapers, and rollers, and in leisurely, neighborly fashion put their local roads into condition for the season. As late as 1889, eight states levied no taxes for road purposes. By 1904, roads and highways were universally financed either by property taxes or by labor obligations which could be paid in cash. The cheapness of constructing and maintaining dirt roads and the continued use of statute labor kept the nation's highway bill low. In 1902, total state-local street and highway expenditures of $175 million were, in today's dollars, about $6 per capita.

Expenditures mounted rapidly with the building of the surfaced roads required by automobile traffic. In 1913, the state and local governments spent about $400 million on streets and highways. In 1927, the bill approximated $1.8 billion, or, in today's dollars, about $24 per capita.

Building arterial primary roads for interurban traffic, a task which involved expensive grading and surfacing, went beyond both the duty and capacity of local governments. The states believed at first that they could solve the financial problem by supplying aid—supplementing local appropriations by state funds. New Jersey provided a system of state road aid in 1891, Massachusetts in 1892. However, the local construction of primary roads led to piecemeal and uncoordinated highway building. Width, surfacing, and solidity would change at each county or town border, with consequent reduction of the utility of the highways for through travel. The states themselves then undertook the construction and maintenance of arterial highways and main market roads. Massachusetts was the first to initiate such a program. State highway control spread rapidly, and an increasing mileage of roadways was incorporated into the state systems. Today, one-sixth of the country's roadways are state highways, and another substantial fraction of county roads are state-controlled. States bear only a tiny part of the cost of city and town streets. Nearly 3,000 miles of state highways charge tolls and are, in general, self-financing.

In 1904, state highway expenditure was $26 million, plus $4 million in grants. The corresponding figures for 1957 were $4.9 billion and $1.1 billion.

When in 1916 the federal government began to contribute toward highway construction, it limited its appropriations to the improvement of post roads, matching state spending on a limited basis. Federal highway aid subsequently came to be viewed as a major factor in developing a continental system of motor highways, rather than a minor expenditure to aid the postal service. When World War II started, the federal government was spending about $200 million annually on highways, not counting large amounts of relief and recovery funds used for construction and maintenance of highways, streets, bridges, and allied purposes. After a slow postwar start, federal aid for highways rose far above prewar levels. In 1956, Congress adopted a mammoth new program under which the federal government assumes 90 to 95 per cent of the cost of 41,000 miles of "interstate and defense" highways. Original cost estimates of $28 billion over a decade have proved much too low. Total spending, plus that for continuing grants of about half the expenditure on primary and secondary roads, will probably exceed $50 billion by 1972. The new program provides some federal aid ($200 million in 1959) for urban highways. States and localities remain substantially, or entirely, responsible for construction and maintenance of most street and highway mileage.

Airport expenditure. The growth of air transport raised the question of whether nonmilitary airport construction and operation should be financed by operators and users of planes, as railroad and bus companies finance their terminals, or by governments, probably with varying amounts of subsidy and control. The decision was to subsidize air transport. Federal aid to localities, bypassing the states, began in 1938. Through World War II most funds for construction of 1,100 civil airports came from the federal government as depression public works aid or as a war cost. Modest grants to localities on a year-to-year basis from 1946 to 1955 helped finance new fields and extend older ones. The rate of development, however, lagged behind the increase in air travel and size of planes. A new program approved by Congress in 1955 emphasizes longer-range planning and provides for increased federal spending to aid localities. Needs are growing. Jet planes, for example, require longer runways. Crowded skies increase the need for better control systems, and federal spending for construction and operation of these facilities is rising rapidly. The $400 million of federal aid allotted to this purpose in 1959 is more than twice the 1957 total.

Ownership and control of airports remain chiefly with local governments. Revenues seldom cover full cost of operation, including return on investment and a property-tax equivalent. Airlines and owners of private planes, of course, oppose higher user charges. Consequently, public spending continues to subsidize air travel.

Probable trends.[10] Highway expenditures will certainly rise. Pressure for better facilities will continue to come from auto and truck users and manufacturers, the oil, rubber, and cement industries, and construction firms. One may debate whether highway mileage is reasonably adequate today, but there is no doubt that in a few years we shall need more. Even clearer already is the need for *better* highways as represented by better surfaces, more lanes, more safety, more beauty, elimination of railroad grade crossings, easier curves, more exits, and many other improvements. Movement of population from cities to suburbs, new housing developments, and relief of traffic congestion will require much street expenditure by metropolitan areas. Cities have hardly begun to meet the need for "off street" parking facilities. All of this new construction, and the added maintenance it entails, must be undertaken at a higher level of costs than we have ever

[10] Chapter 17 continues the discussion of street-highway finance.

before known. Somewhat like education outlay, however, this can be a highly constructive aid to general economic development. If wisely made, it will reward us generously by reducing costs of production and distribution and providing a source of pleasanter and safer consumer enjoyment.

SOCIAL WELFARE EXPENDITURE

The past quarter-century has seen a revolution in the public attitude toward social welfare, with expenditures in this area now greater than those on schools. Previously, the care of persons financially unable to provide for themselves was viewed as the responsibility of their families, with charity aiding where family resources could not suffice, and with local governments helping in extreme cases. Three tendencies, however, have combined to alter this view: (1) Growing humanitarian sentiment fosters the idea that the misery of any is the responsibility of all. Only through government can everyone be forced to share in discharging this general social responsibility. (2) There is spreading acceptance of the view that society as a whole suffers when some undergo hardship and misery. It is to the self-interest of the entire public to prevent and alleviate hardship and misery. (3) Urbanization has both accentuated the social ills resulting from population concentration and weakened the family as a self-sufficient social unit. And there is a fourth factor—the political power of those seeking help.[11]

Early welfare expenditures of American governments consisted primarily of "indoor relief" of the extreme poor—local poorhouses. Some states authorized their local units to provide a limited amount of "outdoor relief" —money allowances or grants of food and clothing to needy individuals or families living in their own homes. Such local relief could not come close to meeting the problem, however, even in its milder form during the 1920's.

State welfare expenditures were still more limited and were directed to more specialized objectives—institutional care of "categorical" groups such as the insane, the blind, the crippled, deaf-mutes, and other defectives. During the 1920's, there was some development of state expenditure for mothers' aid and assistance to dependent children.

Federal welfare contributions prior to the 1930's were indirect. Yet in 1929 no less than twenty-one federal agencies, including the Children's Bureau created in 1912, were interested in the nation's social work.

Emergency relief after 1930. The tide of misery that flowed in the wake of increasing unemployment after 1929 overwhelmed the private charities and soon outran the relief capacities of local government units, which were hamstrung by declining tax collections and weakened credit standing. Pub-

[11] Two other points deserve mention. One is the public's willingness to use the coercive power of government more generally than in the past. The other is development of administrative capacity to make huge programs feasible.

lic opinion swung to the view that the higher levels of government must do more to meet this social emergency. New York was the first state to act. In 1931, it provided an initial $20 million for unemployment relief. New Jersey and Pennsylvania soon took similar steps. By 1933, more than half of the states were expending state funds on relief.

Pressure for federal relief led to the provision in 1932 of RFC advances to the states to assist them in furnishing relief and "work relief." As misery deepened, demands for direct federal relief expenditure multiplied. In 1933, provision of relief was established as a major federal function, and so continued until World War II. The federal program embraced two elements—grants to state and local units for relief, and "work-relief" appropriations to provide temporarily for "employables" without jobs.

Old Age and Survivors Insurance. The Social Security Act of 1935 made social welfare a permanent major function of federal and state governments. It created two broad *insurance* programs, one for retired workers and survivors of deceased employees and one for the temporarily unemployed. It also made the federal and state governments partners in a *welfare* program providing aid to several categories of needy persons.

The Old Age and Survivors Insurance system, or OASI, is a national program which in 1959, after several extensions, covers almost all employees and the self-employed.[12] The system provides for two types of benefits—pensions and survivors' allowances. The benefit is paid when a covered individual retires after 65 (62 for women, in some cases). The amount is dependent upon payroll tax payments made to his account during his period of coverage and upon whether he has a dependent wife.[13] Survivors' benefits also depend on the payroll taxes paid to the insured's account and whether there are dependent children. Table 2–6 gives some examples of benefit payments. A totally and permanently disabled worker over 50 also receives a monthly benefit. For a tenth or more of his life the typical American is likely to get much of his living from OASI. And in every month of his working life he will pay several dollars toward the cost of the system.

OASI benefits, fully tax exempt, are paid as a matter of right, without regard to the financial position of the recipient. To receive the pension, however, the applicant must have retired—that is, have no work in covered employment yielding more than $1,200 a year. (This limitation has been relaxed to permit appreciably larger earnings in some cases, and it does not apply if the insured is 72 or older.) As of 1959, approximately 12 million *persons* were receiving retirement pensions averaging $70 a month; 3 mil-

[12] Some state-local government employees, clergy, doctors, and casual laborers are not covered. Federal government civilian employees and the military, having their own system, are outside OASI. Railroad workers have a special, and more generous, system. It is financed by its own payroll taxes.

[13] The Social Security payroll taxes are described in Chapter 14.

lion were surviving widows or parents. These OASI benefits by themselves will rarely provide a decent living to their recipients. As supplements to other resources, however, they can represent the difference between a difficult old age or widowhood and one that is financially comfortable. In relation to contributions present benefits are generous. To date the number receiving benefits has been only a small fraction of the number paying taxes. As time passes and those drawing benefits increase greatly, the total system expenditures will rise to, perhaps, $20 billion a year by 1985—or more, if Congress continues to liberalize benefit scales at frequent intervals.

Unemployment insurance. Unemployment insurance is administered by the states and is paid for by taxes on employers. States were, in fact, compelled to impose this tax under a credit arrangement.[14] Federal rules set minimum standards of coverage, which permit exclusion of many persons covered by OASI. States, for example, may deny coverage to employees of firms with under eight workers, but few are so restrictive. The

TABLE 2–6

Old Age and Survivors Insurance. Illustrative Monthly Benefits Under Law in Effect in 1959

Average Monthly Wage	*Retired Worker (no Wife)*	*Retired Worker and Wife*	*Aged Widow*	*Widow and One Child*	*Widow and Three or more Children*
$100	$ 59	$ 89	$44	$ 89	$ 89
200	84	126	63	126	162
300	105	158	79	158	240

self-employed are not within the system. Since each state has its own rules for determining benefits, variation in payment scales is wide. Holding a job for long enough to earn around $300 entitles an employee, after a "waiting period" of some two weeks, to unemployment benefits when he is discharged or laid off. He must register with the state employment agency for referral to "suitable" jobs, but he has great freedom in rejecting job offers without losing his benefit. As a rule, his weekly benefit check varies from $25 to $35. It continues, ordinarily, for 20 to 26 weeks in any one year or until he obtains employment. For most persons these benefits are too small to make idling attractive, even though there is unquestionably some abuse. A second or third earner in a family, for example, may rather welcome periods of compensated unemployment.

In 1959, some 45 million employees, out of a total labor force of about 68 million (including government employees), were covered by unemployment insurance. During the recession of 1958, over 3 million persons received unemployment benefits at one time. The average weekly payment

[14] This is explained in Chapter 23. The federal government operates a separate system for railroad employees.

was $31. Congress in 1958 voted to make loans to states to continue benefits up to 39 weeks in a year, but few states were willing to go into debt for this purpose.

Welfare grants. Federal law, as noted earlier, provides *aid to the states*, on a matching basis, for four important types of aid—to the needy aged, to poor families with dependent children, to the blind, and to the totally and permanently disabled. State and local welfare programs were greatly stimulated. As of early 1959, about 2.5 million needy aged were receiving average monthly grants of $61, and nearly 750,000 families with 2.1 million children were getting an average of $27 per month per child. The costs of these two programs were $230 million a month, with more than half coming from federal funds. Almost 110,000 blind and 320,000 disabled received average monthly aid of $67 and $60 respectively, at a total monthly cost of around $25 million. In addition, some food from farm surplus stocks helped in many cases.

State and local provision for needy persons who do not fall in the four categories for which there are federal welfare grants is very seldom adequate. In the spring of 1958, 430,000 recipients, generally family groups, received public assistance outside of the Social Security program; their benefits averaged $61 a month at a cost of some $26 million monthly to states and localities.

Government employee pension funds. One growing item of public expenditure is contributions to pension funds for civil servants. Nearly all government units, from the federal government down to the smallest village, now have pension systems for their employees. Most plans involve joint contributions by the employing government and the employee. The contributions are paid into special trust funds, invested in government bonds.

When these pension systems were established, the relationship between benefit payments and contributions was presumably calculated on actuarial bases. Because of actions to meet rising living costs, benefits have generally proved to be more generous than warranted by contributions. Therefore, in addition to the $2.5 billion currently being paid by governments into these pension funds, liability is accruing which will have to be covered by special appropriations in the future. Recent steps to bring state-local employees under OASI have imposed some temporary costs on governments and have required readjustment of established plans.

Probable trends. Over the long run, total social insurance and welfare expenditures will multiply if only because millions will claim OASI benefits. In the near future, the fact that will most influence such spending will be the general level of economic activity. When employment drops, OASI, unemployment insurance benefits, and relief all rise—but perhaps not enough. As had been predicted, even a recession as mild as that in 1958 showed that existing provisions for unemployment insurance often failed to meet real needs. Local governments, with state aid as established, proved incapable of financing "adequate" relief where unemployment was heavy. Thus, demands for more nearly "adequate" standards are to be expected. But what is *sufficient* aid? There can be no absolute standards of adequacy of relief, pensions, or unemployment aid, any more than there can be absolute standards of provision for public education or for police protection. Still, just as standards for all other public functions have risen with the years, so it is certain that there will be continuing pressure to make programs more generous or less inadequate.[15] Yet we are already committed to a large increase in taxes to pay for OASI benefits on the present scale. We can afford more for various welfare and social insurance programs, but we should try to put money where it can do the most good. What, we should ask, are the unachieved goals? What is the most efficient way of reaching them?

Even with a continuation of great prosperity, spending for the truly needy will place substantial burdens on governments if reasonably humane standards are met. Fifteen years of booming business failed to eliminate "spot" poverty—the family whose breadwinner had deserted or suffered prolonged illness, those too old or unable to work, those whose productive capacity is not adequate to earn enough to support a family, and many without money enough to move to areas of greater opportunity and get established there. This hard core of serious poverty calls for a variety of policies. It needs more than larger appropriations to pay bigger benefits. It requires, among other things, skilled social work, which can often do much to help individuals and families become self-supporting. The personal service involved is expensive. If it is good service, however, the rewards amply justify the cost—not only the better life of the people involved, and their children, but also for society in the eventual reduction in need to pay welfare and, even more, in the addition of productive workers. Modern society is learning how, and is becoming prosperous enough, to aid constructively an increasing portion of the distressingly large number of human beings whose lives have drained rather than contributed to the community. Here is one of the great horizons for public spending.

Expenditures on *public health* will probably grow. Traditionally, state and local governments have provided some hospital service for the very poor, the mentally ill, and persons with tuberculosis; the federal government has supported hospitals for veterans. Certain protective and preventive functions have also been performed by governments. To bring up to reasonably high standards the hospital, sanitation, and other facilities required for performing these generally accepted functions will require

[15] The rapid growth of private pension plans may reduce the pressure for raising OASI benefit scales. See Chapter 14.

many billions of dollars. Various plans have been presented to Congress for increasing public spending for health—funds for more research, for building hospitals, for training doctors and dentists, for giving more medical aid to the very poor, and for putting a large part of the payment for medical, dental, and hospital services on a compulsory insurance basis. Although adoption of compulsory health insurance seems unlikely, there will doubtless be a general trend toward increasing both the quantity and the quality of medical aid provided by government expenditure. Humanitarian arguments are strongly supported by the high degree of common individual and group self-interest in improving standards of physical and mental well-being.

It is also probable that public expenditures for *housing* for low income groups will grow. Such spending may be kept outside regular budgets by using special "authorities" and corporations. Aid to housing may also be given indirectly in the form of property tax reduction and government subsidy of borrowing. Considerable experience with "public housing" has been gained in the last quarter-century, enough to indicate that policies and attitudes formed in the 1930's are not always best today. The attempt to deal with two different problems—housing and poverty—in a single program has brought many disappointments. Possibly, the most efficient way to deal with what are indeed serious problems of housing would be to concentrate on improving housing. The most efficient way to deal with poverty is likely to focus on what will help the poor—the poorest first, and all the poor, not a select few. However, the dominant political support is still for housing subsidies which attempt to deal with both problems in the same program.

Welfare expenditures are likely to rise for another reason. They invite the formation of *pressure groups* of recipients of the public bounty. The aged have been marshaled in support of various proposals for expanded pensions; in Colorado their influence has been strong enough to commit the state to a very expensive pension program; they are a power in California politics. A tremendous urge of self-interest motivates the participants in such pressure groups, yet they are able to appeal to legislatures and the voting public under the banner of altruistic idealism. Their arguments may have some basis, but as a rule there is one great weakness—they fail to compare the merits of their case with those of other groups, including taxpayers. Seldom will they succeed in getting all they ask for, but complete failure may be almost as rare. Government spending obligations will tend to rise as a result.

Finally, if the price level continues to rise, OASI and other benefits will undoubtedly be adjusted upward. Government, unlike private, insurance companies, can raise benefit scales—and taxes—to meet needs growing out of inflation.

PROBLEMS

1. Account for the growth of state spending since World War I.

2. "Larger spending on schools, highways, and even welfare would bring returns substantially greater than the cost." Discuss. What kind of evidence would help in judging the issues involved?

3. Examine the arguments for and against federal financial aid for public schools.

4. Study the arrangements in your locality for providing relief to the needy.

5. Discuss the problems involved in deciding how much a state ought to spend on education. Do the problems of a locality differ? How?

6. You are advisor to the governor of your state. Some additional funds are available for spending on a permanent basis. Write a memorandum comparing the relative merits of spending on (a) schools, (b) highways, (c) public health, and (d) aid for the aged.

7. "We cannot hope to keep OASI and old-age assistance costs within reasonable limits unless we adjust benefits to what the recipient has contributed, *not* to need." Discuss.

CHAPTER 3

Scope of Government Expenditure

SHOULD the federal government expend funds on more atomic submarines —or to dredge a Mississippi River channel—or to subsidize wheat farmers? Should a state government pay for judges' salaries—or for motor highways —or for unemployment insurance? Should a county spend for schools—or for poor relief—or for swamp drainage? Should a city hire and pay firemen —or construct a water-supply system—or provide a children's playground? To what extent, if any, is it wise to raise the real income of the lower 5 or 50 per cent of the public?

Questions such as these are ever-recurrent, constantly debated, vital political issues. They are facets of the fundamental query: What are the proper functions of government? And the many attempts to frame a categorical theory of government functions have failed to produce general agreement.

POLITICAL THEORIES

Political thought ranges between two poles. One is the Anarchist State; government would be practically nonexistent, and all necessary economic and social controls would be exercised by competition in free markets and by voluntary groupings of individuals. In the second, the Communist State, government would exercise all ownership and operation of productive property, be the source of all economic enterprise, and say how the total national income would be distributed. Less extreme than the anarchist ideal were the laissez-faire, individualistic doctrines which until recent years dominated English and American writings on Public Finance. Less extreme than the communist principles is the body of "collectivistic" proposals for government intervention and activity in fields "touched with a public interest." Between the extremes are a multitude of blended or compromise theories, generally vague and often resting on economic rather than political grounds.

Individualistic doctrine. In many of their aspects, governments must be agencies that coerce individual citizens. Unfortunately, government coercion is directed by fallible human beings. Often it is wise and just. Sometimes it is stupid and abusive. Adam Smith, writing his *Wealth of Nations* in 1776, was acutely aware of the blundering coercion by the governments of his day. He and most early nineteenth-century writers on Public Finance who were influenced by him held that in general the State should act only as a "passive policeman," guaranteeing to each individual the fullest freedom for the exercise of his faculties compatible with the equal freedom of all others and protection from outside enemies. Such limited government use of force to prevent one person from coercing or hurting others would prevent abuse and help create conditions in which the people could develop their capacities. When, said these writers, the State presumed to do more, when it presumed to participate positively in the development of human nature or of human capacity and character, it defeated itself and retarded the development of the "fullest life."

Free public education was frowned upon as being outside the proper sphere of the State's activities. Roads and canals could be constructed better by private corporations. Government expenditures for social welfare were condemned. As one English parliamentarian wrote in 1830:

> Every particle of expense that is incurred beyond what necessity absolutely requires for the preservation of the social order for protection against foreign attack is an unjust and oppressive imposition upon the public.[1]

But the march of events overwhelmed these conservative doctrines. In particular, the industrialization of England and western Europe produced frightful social conditions that could not be glossed over by the self-righteous generalities of Individualism. No sooner had individualistic conservatives finished dogmatizing about the limits of State action than their dogmas were set aside in favor of necessity or expediency.

Later writers of the English and French schools of political thought discarded the rigid yardstick of their predecessors. They compromised between social conservatism and the progress of the times by classifying government functions as primary and secondary. The primary functions were military and civil protection and the civil administration of government. All other activities—support of the schools, building and maintaining roads, public improvements, social welfare activity—were classified as secondary. Expenditure on the primary activities of government was justifiable *per se.* Expenditure on the secondary activities was to be looked upon askance. If a great public benefit was clearly and unmistakably discernible, then expenditure on secondary activities might be approved, but

[1] Sir Harry Parnell, *On Financial Reform* (London, 1830), p. 118.

approval could be accorded only if such benefit were established beyond reasonable doubt. Along with free education one of the first major exceptions was made for communication and transportation. Such services provided by governments cheaply or freely were recognized as valuable in enlarging the opportunity of the individual, in stimulating specialization and the division of labor, in breaking down local monopoly, and in raising the general level of social well-being.

Collectivistic doctrine. At the ultimate extreme of communist doctrine would be the propositions that all economic and many noneconomic activities involve some public interest, and that the State should absorb and embrace all, or nearly all, human effort. Given the wish that is father to the thought, some element of "public interest" or "social benefit" can be discerned in practically every activity. After all, the "public," or some part of it, has an "interest" in every element of manufacture, in every merchandising procedure, in every standardized or individualized service rendered.

Extreme Communism, like Anarchism, is rarely advocated. But just as a selection of moderated anarchist principles could be erected into the practical political philosophy of Individualism, so a moderated Communism—or "Collectivism," as its proponents prefer to call it—can be developed into a practical political agenda. In piecemeal fashion, this collectivist doctrine has had incidental but growing acceptance in the United States.

Education was accepted as a government function, at least by some writers, as far back as colonial times. A passion for "internal improvements" during the first third of the nineteenth century led the states to construct highways and canals; later the states assisted railroad and banking development. Free hospitalization, maternity assistance, old-age pensions, and unemployment insurance are expansions upon earlier, rudimentary poor relief. Agricultural aid has assumed protean forms. Group disasters are now held to be matters of public concern, and the relief of the victims through governmental agency a social obligation. The federal government has become directly or indirectly a major purveyor of credit. TVA is discussed as a forerunner of still greater regional development projects. Federal responsibility for maintaining employment was assumed by Congress in 1946.

Through the establishment of regulatory authorities—the Interstate Commerce Commission, the Federal Trade Commission, the Securities and Exchange Commission, and other federal bodies, a horde of state public utility commissions, boxing commissions, racing commissions, and innumerable municipal departments and commissioners of markets, plumbing, elevator inspection, etc.—the protective function has expanded from its earlier, simple soldier-policeman status to a widely embracing guardianship of the individual in his personal and business capacities. The development of atomic energy and foreign aid are both leading government into new and important activities. Moreover, war has come to involve the entire economy and to require specialized and intricate equipment. Considerations of national defense have consequently forced the government to take a larger and more direct interest in the details of industrial capacity, in scientific research, and perhaps in education.

Critique. The doctrines of Individualism and Collectivism are susceptible of neither unquestioned proof nor disproof. What government activity cannot be either condemned or approved, depending upon the principle used as first premise? A writer who believes with the individualists that "the least government is the best government" will condemn government expenditures for unemployment relief or the regulation of security issues. Another, who believes that it is a matter of "public interest" to maintain the physical condition and morale of the unemployed and to protect the untutored investor, will just as obviously approve such expenditures. Fear that government may become tyrannical, that officials will be overbearing, that inefficiency and stupidity are likely when decisions are made politically, lead to a "least government" conclusion. On the other hand, confidence in the high quality of government personnel and the efficiency of elections as a device for expressing potential choices, or distrust of private business as shortsighted and unresponsive to true consumer-employee-investor interest, become bases for supporting widened scope of government activity.

Political philosophy, we must conclude, provides no conclusive guide for determining the best scope of government expenditure.[2] Bases for arguments may be obtained, but where the first premises are bare credos, the arguments must remain inconclusive. Today there is no serious dispute that some costly functions are inherently governmental, notably national defense, preservation of law and order, and foreign relations. But what others? Views differ. Popular opinion during the past fifty years has swung from its earlier individualistic attitude to an increasingly collectivistic acceptance of broadened government service. President Cleveland could, with general approval, veto an appropriation of $25,000 to buy seed corn for Texas farmers ruined by drought, with the statement, "I veto this appropriation because there is no warrant in the Constitution of the United States for taking the funds which are raised from the taxes and giving them from one man to another, and I further veto it in order to teach the lesson that while the people support the government, the government does not support the people." Today most of us accept federal appropriations for farm aid as a matter of course. Likewise as a matter of course, most of us accept federal expenditures on antitrust investigation, state provision of recreational areas, and municipal expenditures to operate incinerators.

[2] For a brilliant presentation of the contrary view, see H. C. Simons, *An Economic Policy for a Free Society* (University of Chicago Press, Chicago, 1948), Chapter 1. An excellent study, by a political scientist and an economist working jointly, is that of R. A. Dahl and C. E. Lindblom, *Politics, Economics, and Welfare* (Harper & Bros., New York, 1953).

One factor in this evolution of popular opinion has been the improving caliber of government personnel. The elected or politically appointed officials who were often amateurs with regard to their administrative responsibilities have been largely replaced by civil service "career men" with tested ability and eventually long experience. A minority may develop into bureaucratic deadwood, but the public justly assumes that the proven abilities of the majority enable governments to undertake successfully functions that would have been grossly mismanaged in times past.

It must not be concluded that Collectivist principle today has a clear field. There are many current adherents to Individualistic doctrine—though their modern individualism would have seemed arrant social radicalism to the nineteenth-century conservatives. Our present-day critics of the extension of the scope of government activity argue that it threatens not only economic efficiency but also, and more important, fundamental human freedoms. When government with its powers of coercion controls a large part of the nation's economic life, individuals and voluntary groups are likely to find their freedom of action and thought first restricted, then eventually destroyed. Government has a vital role in preserving and protecting liberty and freedom. The expansion of government, however, may bring destruction and perversion of freedoms that are essential for the good life now and for social progress for the future.

ECONOMIC CONSIDERATIONS

The last few years have witnessed a revival and expansion of economic analysis of government spending. Perhaps more has been done in clarifying than in solving problems. Before looking at the present state of thinking, however, we must note one important point: Assuming that the public has chosen to use government as the agency for achieving an objective, expenditure is not always the only method available. Compulsion using the police or some other power, tax exemption, guaranties and insurance involving little or no spending, and other devices are to varying degrees practical alternatives to spending. Wise selection of method requires consideration of facts peculiar to each situation. These are not limited to the economic considerations we now discuss.

Productivity of government expenditure. Is government activity unproductive? Critics contend that the State takes from its citizens funds which otherwise would be used to buy food, to build houses, to manufacture shoes and ships and sealing wax. The funds are spent for interest on public debt, salaries, and materials used by the various administrative departments. By this process funds which might have been devoted to "productive" use may be diverted to "nonproductive" activity. If so, this economic argument bolsters the political argument, already noted, that the sphere of government activity should be restricted to a minimum.

The controversy turns upon the definition of the term "productive." If the term is limited to the production of tangible commodities, much government activity will certainly appear less "productive" than much business activity. Although some government spending results in material products —atomic bombs, highways, schoolhouses—immaterial services predominate—judicial process, military, police and fire protection, education, social relief, and public utility regulation. But Economics no longer identifies "productive" with "material." All nondetrimental and nonparasitic activities which satisfy material or immaterial wants are "productive." The actor is "productive" just as is the bricklayer; a member of a commission, or a teacher, is no less creative than a manufacturer of spools.[3]

The productivity of government and private activities should be judged by the same broad standards. A major difficulty arises, however, from the large coercive element in government expenditure. In his private activities, an individual will not pay more for an item than he thinks it is worth to him. As a member of a community, however, he may be forced to buy through his government things which seem of less value than their cost. Thus, when a private industry uses resources, it is presumably reacting to the wishes of the community as expressed freely through the purchases, at profit-yielding prices, by its customers of its products made with these resources; otherwise, its chances of survival are slight. When government uses scarce resources, however, it may be getting them by the use of its coercive powers in ways unrelated to the free and presumably informed wishes of the community. Does the resulting allocation of resources give the public less of what it wants than would allocation by the private economy operating in free markets? Our political processes have so many imperfections that there is no justification for believing that specific decisions on spending and taxing represent careful and intelligent balancing of views. Often there is a substantial minority opposed. If I do not like this year's auto styles, I am free not to buy a new car. Do I have similar freedom not to "buy" a new street if the city council has voted to use my taxes in this way? *The fear that the allocation by government coercion is less good than*

[3] National Income figures generally consider government activity as "productive," with reservations on which all economists are not yet in agreement. Government employees are usually *assumed* to "produce" an amount equal in value to what they are paid. The Department of Commerce now treats interest on government debt as a "transfer" item, not income created by government-owned capital; the reason is that most of the debt is now war rather than "capital" debt. Welfare and veterans' payments, among many others, are treated as transfer rather than productive items because no service is rendered currently for the payment. One of the major problems is whether government services provided to business (and paid for by taxes rather than specific charges) should be counted as final products or as items whose value is used by business and thus incorporated in the products of business. The material goods and services purchased and consumed by governments are counted as products of business, not government; it is assumed that the value obtained through use by government is equal to cost. Obviously, the treatment in national income computation does not *prove* either that the outlays are productive or, if they are, to what extent.

the allocation by free markets underlies much of the criticism of the expansion of government activity.

Yet government spending may be *more* productive than private. The system of free markets does not adequately evaluate all alternatives. General social costs and general social benefits are rarely taken into account by the individual purchaser, whether a person or a giant corporation. The individual in deciding in free markets the worth to himself of a particular item does not have to weigh the value of the use of the same resources for national defense or for medical research or for education. Consequently, the sum of the actions of individuals in free markets would not take account of the social benefit from alternative use of resources in national defense, in medical research, or in education. The allocation of resources by free markets weighs only the alternatives of competing purchasing powers, not alternatives of relative social need, and these two are frequently not identical.[4]

There are some cases—not many—in which government provision of a service without specific charge can lead to a clear saving of resources and to an increase in the net benefit to the community. Free use of streets and sidewalks is an example. The manpower required to collect a charge from users and the resources needed to prevent evasion would probably be very much greater than those needed to collect an equal amount in taxes. Moreover, the annoyance, inconvenience, and loss of utility to the users might be great if a charge were made for each use. Provision of the service free by the government and payment by taxes will be *more productive* than provision by a private business.

A government function, like a private enterprise, may prove detrimental. Bad legislative or administrative judgment may result in a project which not only fails to produce the desired result but which directly or indirectly injures individuals or the community. Should a faulty dam crumble, a city would lose its water supply and a countryside would be flooded. And sometimes a sinecure government position, preserved as a "political plum," may be purely wasteful and without discernible benefit to anyone but the incumbent. The use of government funds to buy food for destruction to keep farm prices high is widely condemned as detrimental to the country as a whole. But these wasteful activities are exceptions. Normally, the service resulting from a government expenditure benefits some, many, most, or all citizens. Schools serve both the children who attend and the social structure of which they are component parts. A playground which promotes the health and protects the moral character of city children has produced values far above any monetary measure.

[4] The term "neighborhood effects" helps indicate what is involved. The typical example of social cost is smoke. A business whose furnaces belch smoke into the air thereby creates a nuisance and imposes real, and sometimes financial, costs on others, burdens which it need not include in its own accounts. An agency concerned for the whole community would—or might—consider such costs.

Questions may be raised on the "productivity" of military and naval preparations. Are not such activities "unproductive"? Is not war the supreme example of "unproductive," detrimental government expenditure? War to preserve the nation is tragic, but preferable to subjugation. If large peacetime expenditures prevent war by discouraging potential enemies or if they hasten victory, they may be the most "productive" of all the nation's outlays. Whether the hundreds of billions of dollars spent upon defense and war are to be accounted supremely beneficial, or whether they are to be considered massive waste, depends upon the individual's guess about what his world would be like if an enemy had won a past war or if we stood today with little to defend ourselves.

Transfer expenditures. A major issue in deciding the scope of government spending today is the extent of the use to be made of transfer expenditures. Billions are spent by governments, not to acquire goods and services for the general public, but to transfer purchasing power from one group to another. The recipient gives no services in return. Examples are relief, OASI and unemployment insurance benefits, farm aid, and to varying degree veterans' benefits and interest on government debt. Presumably the spending does serve a public purpose. Still, per dollar spent, the outlay is not productive to the same extent as expenditure which induces the output of goods and services for the public. Where transfer spending is involved, government determines not *what* the money will be used to buy but *who* will make the decision, that is, the recipient instead of the taxpayer. The economic results of enlarging or reducing the scope of transfer spending are likely to be much different from a change of comparable size in productive spending.

Doctrine of "comparative social benefit." To establish that government expenditure is "productive," or at least that it effects a transfer which benefits the recipient, does not settle the issue of the best scope of government spending. Some basic questions are still unanswered. Should any specified activity be undertaken by a government, or should it be performed by individuals freely through private business or philanthropy? Should government assume or enlarge a particular function though it thereby deprive individuals of funds which they would otherwise have devoted to some other purpose? Economics has sought answers, at least in theory, in the doctrine of "comparative social benefit."

The argument runs as follows: Governments are agencies through which society makes certain expenditures—those producing a general social benefit.[5] Such social benefit will be derived from any undertaking "touched with a public interest." What activities are "touched with a public interest"? Here again is the ever-present individualist-collectivist issue. Assuming some degree of "public interest" in what governments do, the money to

[5] Some qualifications apply, implicitly at least. It is assumed, for example, that the benefit will not be provided efficiently by the operation of the private economy.

pay the cost must come from the people. In the long run, assuming that public borrowings are all repaid and ignoring possibilities under special conditions, government expenditures reduce the funds available for individual expenditure and saving—if my income tax is increased to help pay for a reclamation project, or if my property tax is raised to provide for an expanded school system, I am left with less money to buy clothes or to spend on amusements or to invest. Is the social benefit derived from the government's expenditures greater or less than the personal benefit which the original holders would have derived from the use of these funds? If greater, the government expenditure is justified. If less, the function must be condemned. This principle of comparative social benefit, or "maximum social advantage," becomes the measuring rod of government activity.

In principle, the "social benefit" concept can be refined further by applying to it the principle of marginal utility. As a government service is increased, the marginal utility or "marginal social benefit" of each additional increment of the service declines. Yearly provision by a city of 10,000 gallons of water per resident—barely sufficient to cover minimum requirements—would be absolutely essential. Provision of 50,000 gallons per person, permitting liberal use, would produce some additional social benefit, but not proportionately as much as the initial 10,000 gallons. More than 100,000 gallons per person might be of no use whatsoever. Any single government function is subject to the law of diminishing utility. So also is the sum total of government functions. If a government unit serving an unchanged population is spending $200 million a year where formerly it spent only $100 million, surely it is a fair assumption that some at least of the additional services provided by the extra $100 million are less vital, less valuable, to the community than the services provided by the original $100 million. The activities or functions involved in transfer spending present an especially difficult problem. To the recipient of a higher OASI or welfare payment, the gain is worth every dollar received. But how much of this is *social* benefit? Perhaps the gain to the community is only a small fraction of the individual benefit.

Inevitably, as the marginal utility of successive increments of government service tends to diminish, the marginal value to the taxpayers of the heavier taxation necessitated by the greater expenditure increases. Marginal social cost of the service rises, this cost being the sacrifice of the taxpaying members of society. Higher taxes cut the net income of the taxpayers, reduce savings and personal expenditures, and enhance appreciation of the marginal personal satisfactions to be obtained by those savings and expenditures. The sacrifice imposed on a taxpayer by successive increases of his tax burden increases more than proportionately. Should the cumulation of tax increases push his remaining income below the level of material subsistence, he might well feel that the last increment of taxation was intolerable, although in actual amount it was no greater than an earlier increment that had seemed only inconvenient.

According to the "marginalists," the benefit of the last increment of government expenditure on any function should be measured against the marginal benefit of individual expenditure or saving of a like amount. The establishment or enlargement of a government function is justified only when the social benefit of the final dollar spent upon it outweighs the sacrifice imposed upon the taxpayer who surrendered that dollar. If the taxpayers would suffer less from the deprivation of an additional $50,000 than the public would gain from its expenditure by the government, then it should be appropriated. If the balance lies the other way, the government function is without justification.

The "marginal" doctrine can be applied, at least in principle, not only to government expenditures as a whole but also to particular functions. Shall a particular $50,000 that can be included in a municipal budget be appropriated for schools, or street lighting, or parks, or poor relief? Or to which function shall an obligatory $50,000 budget cut be applied? Look at the marginal social benefit produced by each particular function and add or subtract your $50,000 according to the maximum advantage derived from its application.

The social-benefit concept of government expenditure, particularly in its marginal utility form, may be expressed in terms having a deceptive air of definiteness and finality. But even if the propriety of any proposed government activity can be determined definitely, how shall its marginal social benefit actually be measured? What yardstick can scale the social benefit of the last $10,000 spent by a government on boll weevil elimination, or medical research, or printing the *Statistical Abstract*, or paving a street, or distributing poor relief? What scale will weigh the respective merits of $50,000 spent on special school classes for mentally deficient children as against $50,000 spent on a traffic signal system to reduce street accidents?

Not only is there no way to calculate the marginal social benefit of a government expenditure, but there is no measure for the social or personal sacrifice involved in the corresponding tax payment. Psychologists have yet to develop a yardstick for individual satisfactions, let alone a measure of composite monetary appreciation. What unit can be used to measure the sacrifice imposed upon my wife by foregoing a new dress, or upon me by foregoing a motor trip, because of the increased income or property tax that the expansion of some government function causes me to pay? Furthermore, with the disutility of what tax payment shall the marginal social benefit of a public expenditure be compared? One tax system could wring the bulk of government revenue from the lowest income groups, reducing their expenditures for necessities, driving them to submarginal standards. Another tax system could skim the revenue in question from higher-level incomes, checking saving and possibly capital investment, and reducing the consumption of luxuries. Patently, the different tax systems will create variant social and personal disutilities for the tax payment in question—different intensities of sacrifice are involved when taxes compel the poor to restrict their expenditure on necessities and when they cause the rich to forego certain luxuries or reduce their saving.

Students of Public Finance must put aside the doctrine of "comparative social benefit," with or without its "marginal utility" refinements, except as a highly suggestive general principle. It rests upon a series of quantitative concepts which, at least with present statistics, cannot be given quantitative expression. Valid conclusions with respect to any particular government function can seldom, if ever, be derived from it. Its practical value, which can be substantial, however, lies in forcing the student, the voter, and the public official to *compare alternatives* and to look at the "margin" rather than the total or the average, that is, to think about a little more or less—here in spending, or there in taxes. This need is especially important where, as in government activity, beneficiaries of spending are sometimes different from those who must pay. Bias is inevitable. One possible way to help overcome it, to increase the rationality of decision-making, is to focus on practical alternatives.

Fiscal policy objectives. Economists emphasize what are generally called "fiscal policy" criteria for deciding on the scope of government spending. The depression of the 1930's generated widespread agreement that government policy should be directed toward helping achieve and maintain prosperity. Expenditures could play a vital role in such policy. War and postwar inflation have created worry about rising prices and a broad, but perhaps not universal, consensus that government policy should operate to keep prices stable at a "reasonable" level. Here again government expenditures may be crucial. As we shall discover later, economic theory shows how government spending, taxing, and borrowing may stimulate business or inflate prices. This theory, however, is of limited value in defining the scope of government expenditure because many other private and public policies have equal or greater effect. Only when the economist can relate a spending program to monetary, tax, and other programs can he properly use his theory to advise on the scope of government expenditure needed to produce full employment or to check inflation. Undoubtedly, however, the criterion of achieving and maintaining prosperity without inflation has become a major contribution of economic theory to guiding government spending.

Alleviating poverty. There are economic, as well as social and humane, advantages to raising the real income of the poor. The productive, the transfer, and the economic stabilization spending of government can all help reduce poverty. In fact, more or less of the justification for many spending programs whose scope is in question rests on the belief that the poor will benefit. But the economist, endorsing the end, may not be satisfied with the means proposed.

He will ask, "What is the most efficient way of achieving the goal?" An expenditure program for the masses, financed by taxes on those masses, may do nothing to alleviate poverty, even though it does change the pattern of the poor's consumption. Perhaps the result is "better" for them than they would freely choose. Who knows?[6]

The economist may be able to enlighten the discussion. He will, for example, emphasize the difference between spending to help the poor which redistributes income—such as relief—and that which can lead to the increase of income—such as expenditure on education and public health. What is helpful in meeting short-run needs of the poor may do little to accomplish the long-run goal of reducing the causes of poverty. Some kinds of government spending do raise individual and national productivity. The economist will also direct attention to another basic issue—the relative merits of alternative methods of achieving an objective. Two examples will illustrate. If reduction of farm poverty is the goal, expenditure that raises prices of farm crops is inefficient because most poor farmers have little to sell. If we seek to aid the aged poor, a broad system of grants to the aged is an inefficient method because it spreads available funds over a group which includes many with little, and some with no, need and thereby reduces the amounts available for those who are poorest.

Subsidies to high-fixed-cost industries. Economic theory has developed a case for one special type of government expenditure—the industrial subsidy—which so far has had little application but may become significant in the future. If an industry requires heavy capital investment and hence must operate with high fixed costs, a price that will give a reasonable return on the capital investment may so restrict sales that plants large enough to enjoy maximum technical economies cannot be utilized fully. This is particularly likely to be true if there is monopolistic or oligopolistic control of the industry, so that prices can be "administered" at a level which enlarges profit but which reduces the quantity sold. A government subsidy to an industry with such a cost structure—railroads for example—could permit and, if properly planned, induce it to lower its charges, stimulate usage, and reduce total cost per unit.

Conceivably, the resulting increase in the country's real social income through broader consumption of the industry's products at lower prices could be far greater than the reduction of social income through the taxes needed to pay the subsidy. The theoretical possibility of such a net gain has been established. The reasoning is abstruse, however, and has not yet

[6] In general, however, are not adults better judges of their own wants than they are, as voters, of the wants of others? This question raises directly the individualist-collectivist controversy.

appealed to legislators. The practical problems, moreover, are formidable.[7]

Projects too large for private investment. We should also note briefly one case in which economic theory may help decide on the wisdom of an expenditure to be judged primarily by economic rather than social or military criteria. Some projects—usually regional developments such as TVA—may require so much capital and such extensive use of the power of eminent domain and may involve so many other governments—national, state, or local—that private business cannot or will not go ahead on a big enough scale to use resources most efficiently. In some cases the issue may take a slightly different form; namely, that government, being a continuing organization, can take a longer view than any private body; only by acting through government, it is sometimes argued, can the community give adequate weight to the needs of the distant future.

Very few projects of such huge size or remote maturity arise in a single generation. What may seem to be examples are likely to be amenable to private development with government cooperation, such as granting power of eminent domain to privately financed railroads or to slum-clearance housing projects. Our larger corporations are about as permanent as government; many carry on activities vastly greater in dollar terms than any but the four or five largest federal departments. In some cases, greater efforts of government to assure the security of private investment would bring out the capital necessary.

Limits of government expenditure. Some writers have suggested that, regardless of social benefit, a government's functions are limited by its economic background—the wealth and income of the nation or region. A community cannot for any long period divert to education, highways, and parks so much of the income of its residents that they are left without the wherewithal for food, clothing, and shelter. A national government cannot divert resources to national defense, postal services, and foreign aid beyond the point where an insufficiency of the material necessities of private living results.

There are communities throughout the United States so poor that the most crushing tax levies could not produce enough revenue to finance what are generally considered minimum standards of education and other essential government functions. However, this situation does not necessarily limit the government functions performed *for* the community. They may be taken over by a central government with greater resources at its command, or the local unit may be assisted by state aid.

As applied to national or state governments, the theory of an absolute economic limitation upon government functions requires several qualifications. If many more billions of dollars were absorbed by taxes and if

[7] For discussion, see H. R. Bowen, *Toward Social Economy* (Rinehart & Co., New York, 1948), especially Chapter 17; and R. W. Harbeson, "A Critique of Marginal Cost Pricing," *Land Economics*, Feb., 1955, pp. 54–74.

these same billions were paid out within the same community as transfer expenditures, the area's power to produce and consume would be undiminished—except for possible adverse effects on incentives, which might be significant. Transfers outside the area, however, do reduce its economic power. The analysis of limits to transfer expenditures is rather different from the analysis applicable to spending that directly absorbs output and resources. How do recipients use the money? How do taxpayers react to taxes that do not produce public goods and services?

When a government activity replaces or anticipates a private activity, the resources and income which would have been applied to that activity can be diverted to the government without reducing the economic standards of the area. Residents of a city are no poorer if the city takes over a toll bridge, opens it to free passage, and collects from the taxpayers the same amount that was formerly paid as tolls; in fact, their real income may rise because they get more use out of the bridge when there is no toll. To the extent that federal funds spent on Department of Commerce reports save business firms from paying the same or greater amounts to private research agencies, the taxing and the spending offset each other with no net subtraction from the country's income.

Even apart from these qualifications, when the theory of limits is applied to national governments it is too elastic to have much meaning except in war or other emergency periods. Experiences abroad during two World Wars show that a people can be held to a low diet for several years, their clothing requirements can be reduced to mere body covering, and they can be compelled to forego amenities of civilized living, while the government commands men and resources for military purposes. Under such circumstances, a real economic limit of government activity—the reservation of such a minimal fraction of the national income as is necessary to purchase the wherewithal to maintain the producing elements of the civilian population at functioning efficiency—may be reached.

In an economy like that of the United States, however, the economic limit of government expenditures is almost impossible to predict. When there are large quantities of idle or partially idle resources, increased government spending may draw on them and expand the national income, so that no reduction of production for private consumption occurs. A few bottlenecks, however, can seriously limit such expansion. The ultimate proportion of this country's production resources that could be absorbed by a government economy would depend upon the direction of the spending, the way the funds were raised, the ability and willingness of the community to work more efficiently and longer hours, the seriousness of bottlenecks in production, the amount of producers' and consumers' capital that could for a time be drawn upon, and other factors. The experience of World War II and the postwar years has proved that the limits of government expenditure are far higher than generally assumed in the 1930's.[8]

Fiscal writers sometimes observe that, unlike individuals, governments tailor their revenue systems to fit their expenditure programs. Administrative officials and legislators first map out a program of accomplishment. Next, the cost of such a program is calculated. The final step is to adjust the revenue system so that it will provide the necessary funds. When revenues are inadequate, borrowing can fill the gap.

While there is truth in this reasoning, the exceptions are more common than a generation ago. Localities often operate under tax-limit laws. Their governing officials may heartily wish to expand some function, spend more—but the tax limit is strict. *Revenues most certainly condition current expenditures for local units.* Even the federal and state governments, unchecked by tax-law limitations, are not free to engage in every expenditure which may occur to legislators imbued with the idea that a government first determines expenditures and then raises revenue sufficient to cover the costs. Congressional willingness at times to restrain defense expenditures in the face of a disturbing international situation is eloquent witness to the restraint that revenue considerations can impose on spending.

Commitments to spend. Any government may at times find itself committed legally, morally, or economically to an expenditure program over which it has little control but which it might reject if it were completely free to act. Thus, one generation or one administration may incur debt requiring interest payments for long periods; or a social insurance program may establish a benefit payment schedule that becomes a binding commitment on the future. Physical assets may not be properly maintained, resulting in a backlog of rehabilitation expense. Salary scales and functions may be written into constitutions or contracts that are most difficult to change. As a practical matter, a continuing society is apt to find that at any one time its units of government have little choice about much of their spending—the commitments are inescapable short of drastic legal, social, or economic change.

Compulsion or inducement by other governments. Localities find the scope of their spending dictated in part by the state. The dictation may be absolute, but more often it is a minimum which the locality is free to exceed. In addition, states often provide inducements for localities to spend, the state agreeing to pay part of the cost of a program. Similarly, the federal government offers inducements—which sometimes are in fact compulsions—for states to undertake a function or to extend one already being performed. One level of government, in other words, can have a considerable voice in determining the scope of spending at another level. Nor is it unrealistic to say that our biggest expenditure, national defense,

[8] The issue of an absolute economic limit to government expenditure should be distinguished from that of whether high government expenditures may not have a detrimental effect upon the economy or whether taxes, as such, create limits.

is influenced more by decisions in Moscow than by forces which we can control.

Measures of government expenditure. To compare government spending in the economic life of several countries[9] or states, or to compare the relative roles of government activity within some political unit over a span of time, we must have (a) a uniform concept of expenditure or at least details that permit adjustment for changes in the concept and (b) some common base for comparison. Problems arising in the definition of "government expenditure" include the following: treatment of the expenses of partly or entirely self-supporting enterprise-type activities; transfer as contrasted with more productive spending; borrowing and debt retirement; the use of conscription or other nonmarket acquisition of resources, or compulsion on private activity; tax exemption as a substitute for spending; cash or accrual accounting; intergovernmental payments; the use of government procurement as a device for influencing private business; and doubtless other considerations. The concept that is best will depend upon the purpose of the comparison. Breakdowns of data now available in this country permit numerous adjustments desirable for one or another purpose, but difficulties remain—and there are unsuspected pitfalls for the unwary.

Income is generally the most useful base against which to measure.[10] A comparison of (a) the ordinary government expenditure total minus transfers with (b) the income of the area, will reflect more or less accurately the division of effort between the government and the private sectors.

Estimates of the national income of the United States and of most other countries are now available. Imperfections of the basic data and sometimes questionable statistical procedures reduce the apparent validity of some estimates. But where continuing series of annual figures have been calculated by a uniform method, they have some comparative value. For whatever the comparison is worth, government expenditures of different countries, or government expenditures of any particular country over a period of years, may be compared with national income. The ratios so obtained are useful for showing, in broad outline and subject to various qualifications, the relative development of government activity as between countries, and the developing relation of government to private activity for a particular country over a period of years. Recently, the national income of the United States has been subdivided by states. Little progress has yet been made in estimating income for smaller political units.

[9] C. L. Harriss, "Government Expenditures: International Comparisons," *Les Effets Économiques des Dépenses Publiques* (Institut International de Finance Publiques, Les Éditions de l'Épargne, Paris, 1958), pp. 93–107. For data, see United Nations, *Yearbook of National Accounts Statistics* (Columbia University Press, New York, 1958).

[10] Measurements going back to the years for which income data are not available are probably best confined to the proportion of the labor force producing for government.

Expenditures of state and local governments may be measured against population. Figures on per capita government spending for various functions are often revealing. Comparisons among states and localities can start at no better place than per capita spending, related perhaps to income if possible.

CONCLUSION

Political philosophy and economic theory give only limited help in defining the best scope of government expenditure. As groups, economists and political theorists supply arguments to both sides of many controversies. Yet there are costly functions which by general agreement government *must* perform—education, defense, service of its debt, preservation of law and order. The problem that arises over such functions is deciding *how much* to do.

Practical politics reflecting unreasoned popular opinion or actually molding such opinion, rather than political or economic theory, supply the explanation of the current functions of any government unit. Enthusiasts for some cause organize as a group, propagandize to gain popular support or at least a latent popular sympathy, establish a lobby at the state or national capital, persuade, threaten, wheedle, cajole, and tyrannize a sufficient number of legislators into voting their project. Or a less idealistic group, seeing some indirect but substantial benefit for themselves if a government will undertake a function, creates a high-principled social reason for it, employs a professional lobbyist, and negotiates the voting of the new function. Unless the proposed project will injure some definite group, the legislature probably hears only one side of the case, authorizes the new function, and votes an appropriation. *One of the very greatest obstacles to true economy in government is the lack of reliable criteria for deciding what spending should be increased and what reduced.*

PROBLEMS

1. Distinguish between functions which are inherently governmental and those which may wisely, but not necessarily, be performed by government.

2. What, if any, freedoms might be gained and lost if government were to undertake a substantial range of functions now performed in the private sectors of the economy?

3. Discuss the merits and weaknesses of the political process as compared with the market process of allocating economic resources.

4. "This endless drain of government spending will surely weaken the productive strength of the economy." Comment.

5. Discuss the practical usefulness of the doctrine of comparative social benefit.

6. "Economics offers surprisingly few guides to the proper scope of government spending." "To judge the advisability of this new spending proposal, we must look to the economic effects." Criticize these two statements.

7. "After taking account of the functions the state compels us to perform, the limits it puts on our revenue-raising power, and the programs established in the past, we have found virtually no real freedom to decide what we shall do next year." Discuss this paraphrase of a mayor's statement.

8. Would you judge that urban redevelopment is a desirable function of government? Why? If so, is there enough national interest to justify federal sharing of the expense? Why? Would you apply the same arguments to farm aid?

9. "Government spending to provide services is productive. Transfers are not. The factors governing the proper scope of the two are very different indeed." Discuss.

CHAPTER 4

Economics of Government Expenditure[1]

WHEN the governments of a country spend $130 billion or more a year gross, as ours do, economic life is affected profoundly. Individuals and groups derive benefits which would not otherwise have been theirs. Some industries profit from the governments' activity; others suffer from the diversion of private purchasing power. Price levels feel the influences. The flow of funds for private investment is modified. Distribution of wealth and income and the nature and direction of economic growth are influenced.

Reaction and interaction of government expenditure extend through the entire economic and social structure of a country in an infinite series of ramifications. This endless web of cause and effect cannot be examined in detail. We can, however, study a few broad aspects of the problem.

BENEFITS OF GOVERNMENT EXPENDITURE

Ineffective though the concept of "social benefit" may be as a standard of propriety for government functions, it is useful in analyzing the economic character of government expenditure. Without having solved the individualist-collectivist controversy, we may assume that some element of social benefit—some factor of "public interest"—underlies or can be read into every government expenditure.

Social benefit and supplementary individual benefit. When a city employs firemen and maintains fire-fighting apparatus, its interest in preventing Jim Smith's house or John Doe's factory from burning, or saving them after they have caught fire, is secondary; the social loss which results from destruction of property—anybody's property—is the primary concern. When a school district provides instruction for Smith's or Doe's children,

[1] Exclusive of the influence of government expenditure upon the level of prices and employment, considered in Part Six, which deals with Fiscal Policy.

the dollar-and-cents value these children derive—which their parents might purchase from private schools—is subordinate to the social benefit of an educated population. When the federal government subsidizes the construction and operation of American ships, it is expending funds for the military and intangible values embodied in a national merchant marine; the decision does not—or should not—turn upon the benefits which some individuals incidentally derive.

It is almost impossible to conceive of a government function that does not benefit certain individuals as well as promote the general social welfare. Smith and Doe benefit individually from their city's expenditure on fire protection. Likewise they benefit individually from the education given to their children. Even defense expenditures may carry a superimposed individual benefit—the manufacturers and workers making military equipment may earn more than if the public spent the money privately. But these individual benefits are a by-product, supplementary to the basic general benefit.[2] Only the social purpose involved, the group benefit, justifies government expenditure.

Nonprofit nature of social benefit. Let us assume—though there are some who would argue the point—that the by-product *individual* benefits inherent in some government activities could be provided, and adequately provided, by private enterprise operating on the profit incentive. Private detective agencies could offer some individuals and business concerns the protective services now supplied by the public police. For the children whose parents could pay the necessary tuition charges, private schools could more than supplant the public school system.

But there is no business profit to be derived from *social* benefit, which is the primary basis of any government function but only a by-product consideration for private business enterprise. No individual or syndicate, by charging a price to consumers who are willing to pay, could make a profit from the maintenance of military and naval armaments. No individual or consortium could have desire or reason to operate a judiciary system. Private schools are concerned with the education of their own pupils, not the community. The manufacturer of railway equipment labors to create a market for his output and to profit from its sale; that the use of his equipment will promote transportation and commerce and contribute to the economic development of the nation is incidental. Private business enterprise cannot be counted upon to develop adequately a social benefit function which yields it no profit and which can never be more than incidental to the individual services it sells. Such is not the job of business. The natural indifference of private business enterprise to the *social-benefit* by-products

[2] Even in the cases of relief payments to the unemployed, the blind, the aged, and other needy individuals, or aid to farmers, the normal primary purpose of the expenditure is not the individual benefit to the recipient but the general public benefit involved in relieving broad social and economic pressures.

of its activities is the reason why particular activities markedly "touched with a public interest" must be performed by government. In other words, because of the inherent nonprofit nature of social benefit, the community cannot count upon private enterprise to undertake the social benefit activities it desires. It turns to the political or government process to perform these activities.

Indivisibility of social benefit. When *individual* benefit does accrue from some government activity, it can sometimes be divided into units and charged to the recipient. A municipal water system can make frontage or meter charges; the postal service can charge rates collected through the sale of stamps; courts and judicial officers can set fees for particular services; motor highway systems can be financed in part by motor vehicle license charges, gasoline taxes, and tolls.

But the primary *social* benefit from a government function is indivisible. Though the value may be tremendous—the preservation of society itself—it cannot be separated into parts and sold to the beneficiaries as can food and clothing. The individual cannot be allowed a choice about how much he will "enjoy" or pay for; his decision would not take adequate account of the interests of others, for he would have no reason to pay for benefits for them. What has been called "the pure case" is that in which the amount one person or group enjoys does not influence the amount available for others. The establishment of rules for living together is one example, the services of a lighthouse a second. National defense is still a third. The amount of defense I get this year from federal spending does not reduce the amount available to my neighbor, or the man across the country. Expenditure on federal courts is almost as clear a case. It helps establish federal law for the country, a joint service of incalculable value not only to the 180 million Americans of today but also to the unnumbered millions of their descendants. However, the court time one litigant requires does affect the access of others to the judicial process. Here, then, the pure-case rule does not apply completely or exclusively. This condition is typical of government activity in the modern world. But it does not alter the fact that indivisible social benefit exists and is, or ought to be, the justification for government spending which results from the use of the power to coerce.[3]

For those benefits of government activity that are indivisible, it is folly to argue that taxes should be so levied as to apportion the costs of such functions among individuals according to their individual shares in the collective benefit.[4] Supplementary individual benefits may be isolated, and fees and charges may assess some part or all of these by-product values to the beneficiaries. But the costs of the collective social benefit can be han-

[3] For a more complete analysis see E. R. Rolph, *The Theory of Fiscal Economics* (University of California Press, Berkeley, 1954), Chapter 2.

[4] Chapter 10 discusses the benefit principle of taxation.

dled only as a collective obligation upon the community, to be apportioned among its members by whatever tax standard or standards enjoy current approbation.[5]

ECONOMIC EFFECTS

Full consideration of the effects of government activity must take into account not only the expenditure but also the methods of financing this activity—taxation and borrowing. Governments, through their expenditures, confer benefits upon the collective community and frequently upon particular groups. Through taxation and borrowing they deprive the same or other groups of purchasing power which might otherwise be devoted to private consumption or production.

More often in the past than at present, observations on the economics of government activity were based exclusively upon one aspect—either on the spending or on the taxing function. Mercantilist writers argued that the State in its operations gave employment to thousands who had no other employment and provided many manufacturers with a market for their goods. Government expenditures were an unmixed blessing, contributing to prosperity, injuring none and benefiting all. Louis XVI of France, reproached for lavish outlays on his château while his people were starving, is said to have replied gravely and sincerely that that was the very reason for expending his funds with open hands—so that they would come into the possession of the people and ease their misery. Obviously, such views ignored taxing activities.

English economists of the laissez-faire school, on the other hand, tended to ignore the results of government expenditure and studied the reduction of private purchasing power by taxation. According to their reasoning, funds which otherwise would have been devoted to production disappeared into government coffers, the initiative of entrepreneurs was discouraged, and economic progress retarded.

Today we recognize that both the obtaining and the spending of government funds have important effects. For purposes of study, however, we must often separate the two. One point at which they are considered together is in the discussion of Fiscal Policy in Part Six.

Normal government expenditure and economic growth.[6] One of the

[5] One economic function of price is to restrict consumption of items requiring scarce resources. For some government functions a charge or "price" that will restrict consumption is appropriate. For the great majority of government services, however, society does not want the individual to be able to determine the amount he uses or to let the charge determine his use.

[6] The term "normal" applied to government spending is used in this chapter as excluding (1) extraordinary war and national emergency spending, and (2) spending undertaken for its secondary effects on national income, employment, and prices rather than for the immediate functional purpose. The economics of such "abnormal" government spending is covered in Part Six.

main concerns of economists today is economic growth. This contrasts with their preoccupation prior to World War II with the issues of efficient allocation of scarce resources and how to achieve full employment. Increasing attention is being paid to government spending as a factor contributing significantly to economic growth and offsetting the tendency of taxes to retard efficient economic development.

Categories of government spending that contribute most to economic growth are those for (1) education, (2) research, (3) highways and some other types of government capital facilities, (4) public health, and (5) aid to the efficient operation of markets, such as provided by antimonopoly programs, employment exchanges, and information services.

Government expenditure on education ranks at the top of the list of contributors to economic growth. The training of our citizenry is the bedrock foundation upon which all aspects of economic progress rest.

Advancement of knowledge through research—not merely in the natural sciences but also in the social sciences—must be listed high among the factors that stimulate economic growth. For many decades government has promoted research of various kinds, particularly through state universities. Research spending has risen dramatically since 1940. The objectives of most government-sponsored research are primarily military, but the benefits extend far beyond military applications—witness current industrial and medical utilizations of atomic research. One advantage that government-sponsored research has over private is that, except for secret military projects, results are often made freely available for further private development without patent restrictions. Increasing amounts are also going for research in medicine, agriculture, traffic control, forestry, and other nonmilitary subjects which for one reason or another concern governments. Improvement of cities, diplomacy, juvenile delinquency, monetary and tax systems, and scores of other problems call for far more knowledge. The better that society deals with them, the healthier and faster its economic growth. We are not likely to get the study we badly need unless we vote public funds, although in some cases the actual study may be conducted more effectively by universities or nonofficial agencies than by the government that pays the bill.

Government capital outlays, such as TVA and other river developments, water and sewage systems, courthouses and recreational facilities, implement economic growth. Although in some cases private enterprise might have accomplished the same results, many valuable projects would not be undertaken privately on an adequate scale. The total benefit includes a large social element; there is insufficient private benefit to support profit-producing charges on a scale to pay for as much development as justified. Not all "pork barrel" development outlays, however, aid economic growth. The social benefit derived from some fails to offset the check to economic growth resulting from the taxes that finance them.

We may think of the *highway system* as an opportunity for week-end and vacation pleasure driving. It serves this purpose, of course, but more important to our economy is its role in business transport. By creating this highway system, the federal, state, and local governments have made a major contribution to economic growth. Federal subsidies to aviation and state and local expenditures on airports are a smaller-scale promotion of the same objective.

Preservation of our human resources through *public health programs* conserves and improves one of our most important economic assets. Government spending can add to the productive life and efficiency of the labor force. Crucial elements of such programs offer no opportunity for the profit necessary to interest private enterprise on an adequate scale.

The efficiency of the exchange process—of markets in the broadest sense—has much to do with economic advance. The public can use government to forestall abuse of market power, for example, monopoly. The prevention of deception in financial and product markets is an appropriate function of government. Aid to communication can serve the general public interest, as the founders of the postal system recognized. Knowledge to assist consumer choice can help raise real income in the basic sense. Efficiency in private business and personal life often requires information which free, profit-seeking enterprises will not supply adequately but which government can provide. Relatively small amounts spent on government employment exchanges will yield a general economic return out of all relation to the sums spent. They reduce the wastes of unemployment that exist because would-be employers and would-be employees cannot always get in touch with each other promptly. They cut to some extent the wastes that result when people are employed in jobs that do not correspond to their aptitudes and interests. Government spending to help raise the efficiency of private economic decision-making may not be large. It can, however, contribute greatly to real economic progress.

Normal government expenditure and national income. As indicated in the last chapter, government, like other productive agencies, creates valuable goods and services. They are part of the Gross National Product. The income received by the schoolteachers, firemen, mailcarriers, and others who perform these services is part of the National Income. The expenditure we make through government for goods and services that are the fruits of production, like the spending we do in the markets of private business, is the income of those who provide the goods and services. Two decades ago, critics of the widening scope of government activity sometimes argued that the flow of funds to governments and the subsequent disbursement reduced national income. The development of national income theory and accounting, however, has helped reduce the prevalence of this false view.

It is true that the treatment of some taxes and some government spending in the computation of national income does not satisfy all informed students, but the matters in dispute are not important here. We can be satisfied with three central points: every salary paid to a government employee is income just as fully as any salary paid by a business concern; every government payment for materials or services constitutes gross income to the seller; transfers, however, though part of the disposable income of the recipient, are not part of national income because the recipient has rendered no productive service in return. It is often helpful to think of taxation and government spending as a *detour* for income, to emphasize that what goes to government does not enter a blind alley.

TABLE 4–1

Government Expenditures for Factors of Production, 1939 and 1957

	Percentages					
	1939			1957		
	Total	*Federal*	*State and Local*	*Total*	*Federal*	*State and Local*
Wages and salaries	44	38	45	30	23	39
Interest	7	7	6	7	8	3
Transfer payments and grants	15	25	14	15	19	10
Purchases from businesses	31	20	40	48	50	49
Subsidies less net current surplus of government enterprises	3	10	–5	[a]	[a]	–[a]
Total	100	100	100	100	100	100

[a] Less than one-half of one per cent. Subsidies to farmers are classed as transfer payments.

SOURCES: *Survey of Current Business* and *Summary of Governmental Finances in 1957*. Differences in the classifications of the data for 1957 have required estimates which are subject to a small margin of error. Because of rounding, details will not necessarily add to totals.

Normal government expenditure and the economic pattern.[7] The "detour" analogy must not be interpreted to mean that government expenditure is a passive element in the economy. On the contrary, every government expenditure has some effect upon the country's economic pattern or structure, on the allocation of its material and human resources.

In analyzing the influences of government expenditure on the economic pattern, the distinction between (a) "exhaustive" or "resource-using" and

[7] This discussion deals only with redistribution of consumption and production *among economic groups* caused by the use of tax funds for government spending. It does not consider redistribution *over periods of time* produced by spending financed by borrowing. These are covered in Part Five.

(b) "transfer" expenditures is useful. The former[8] are those that absorb materials or personnel that would otherwise be available for nongovernment use—fuel purchased for a public building or a woman hired to teach school. "Transfer" payments, we recall, are those for which the recipient provides no goods and renders no service. As indicated in Table 4–1, "resource-using" expenditures account for the great bulk of government payments.

"Resource-using" expenditures obviously exercise a marked effect upon the economic pattern. Government purchases of tangible materials and commodities change the balance of market supply and demand and hence the pattern of production and prices.[9] When a government unit purchases granite for a public building, or concrete to build a highway, or tin for a stockpile against a war emergency, it pays with funds obtained from taxpayers. These taxpayers would unquestionably have utilized these funds for quite different purchases—more or better clothing, or travel, personal luxuries, or the million and one things that individuals buy, but rarely including granite or concrete or tin. The incidence of government expenditure for materials and commodities is a factor of great importance in shaping the economy. However, some government spending replaces private spending; in other words, at least part of the public would buy some of the services privately if government did not make them available. Thus the net resource use due to government spending, compared with what would exist if the government did not perform the functions it has undertaken, is less than the gross figures would suggest.[10]

Government salary and wage payments command personnel that would otherwise be available for private employment. It is true that the funds drawn from the rest of the community by taxation are spent by the government employees who receive them in pretty much the same way as they would have been spent by their original possessors. The *location* of the spending, however, may be different. For example, capital cities and military-base areas have more retail business than if government salary payments were not made in the locality. Some foreign lands now get a welcome supply of dollars from the spending of U.S. military personnel.

[8] Economists have no standard term for the kind of government spending that uses up resources. Sometimes the term "cost" is used, with "noncost" applying to transfer spending.

[9] There can be a multitude of special effects resulting from the *way* in which funds are spent. Governments sometimes limit their purchases to special markets such as a local community, or to goods produced by unionized labor, or to plants meeting special requirements. The Walsh-Healey Public Contracts Act, for example, gives the Secretary of Labor power to specify the minimum wages that must be paid by firms selling to the federal government. Beginning in 1957 a strict set of "voluntary" restrictions on the import of oil were enforced in part by federal refusal to buy petroleum products from companies failing to comply with "requests." Standards for humane slaughter voted by Congress in 1958 are made effective by federal limitation of its purchases to companies which meet the requirements.

[10] Mr. J. Heilbrun has called this point to the authors' attention.

Many government employees, of course, work at jobs quite different from those at which private spending would have placed them. The utilization of human capacity is certainly changed by government demand.

Government "transfer" expenditures do not use up "inputs" of materials or labor. A veteran getting a government benefit does not have to render current services for the payment; his present productive capacity is not absorbed like that of the schoolteacher or civil service clerk. Since there is no diversion of materials or labor, it might appear that "transfer" expenditures would not affect the economic pattern. This conclusion overlooks the important consideration that the beneficiaries of a "transfer" payment and the taxpayers who provide the funds may belong to widely different economic groups, so that their utilizations of the funds will vary. Payment of interest on government debt held by banks and insurance companies, or the retirement of such debt, with funds drawn from business and individual taxpayers changes the uses that would be made of these funds. Families who receive welfare aid spend their allowances differently than would the taxpayers who foot the bill. Government subsidy payments to maintain a group of prices—such as wheat or cotton—or to hold down certain prices—such as wartime food subsidies—are a type of "transfer" expenditure that influences the general price pattern out of all proportion to the amounts involved. "Transfer" expenditures transform the economic structure even though they do not contribute to the net "burden" of government in the sense of absorbing resources which cannot then be used elsewhere.

Financial effects of normal government expenditure. Normal public expenditures, financed by taxation and a moderate amount of borrowing, have little effect on the volume of credit and currency, or on the *general* price level. Purchasing power diverted from private hands by tax payments and bond issues is returned to the market through government expenditures. Government activities absorb labor and material which otherwise might have gone into private production, but this is counterbalanced by the restriction of private purchases through taxation and borrowing. Just as the shift of purchasing power from private hands to government units stimulates some industries and represses others, so it probably raises somewhat the prices of materials and skills used by the government and weakens other prices. Relative prices change, but not the general price level.

In some cases, however, a relatively small expenditure by government, or the mere promise to spend under certain conditions, can have a considerable influence on the direction and even the level of private financial activity. A government guarantee or insurance of a loan can promote a much larger amount of private financing. The volume of new housing built and paid for by private credit depends partly upon the terms of Federal

Housing Administration insurance of mortgages. The amounts banks lend to business depend a little on the payments the Small Business Administration will make to support the loan. Federal finances are now so large and complex, so intimately tied in with the whole monetary system, that one cannot clearly disentangle the purely "expenditure" effects. Federal use of funds in ways now considered "normal" have both short-run and long-run effects on the financial system. It is impossible to determine, however, whether the net results realistically attributable to spending are in fact great over the long run—though they certainly are significant in the short run as the Treasury builds up huge temporary deposits in the commercial banking system and then spends them.[11]

Fostering particular industries.[12] Even in normal times, some businesses exist mainly by reason of government expenditure. Those producing specialized armaments are the outstanding example; today a change in the level of armament spending, or a shift from one type of weapon to another, can have a big effect on certain industries and even regions. But, in addition to maintaining occasional lines of activity by "normal" purchases, a government may make special purchases to help an industry in exceptional difficulties. Buying of certain minerals in the late 1950's provides examples. A government may also, as a public function—for some particular social benefit—*subsidize* an industry. Examples are subsidies to aviation, shipbuilding, and shipping. Local governments sometimes raise and pay a flat sum, or make a gift of suitable buildings, to induce a business enterprise to establish itself in the community. Furthermore, benefits not designed as subsidies may accrue to particular businesses as a result of certain government expenditures. Public provision of highways, for example, aids bus and truck operators.

Social benefit can be imputed to a subsidy that enables an industry essential to the national welfare to survive during a period of development —the airlines, for example—or while it maintains idle standby capacity for emergency defense use. It is argued in support of shipping subsidies that a merchant marine is a prime national asset in wartime. High operating costs because of strict safety standards and high labor rates, and subsidies which many foreign shipping lines receive from their governments,

[11] If federal investments in the initial capital of such agencies as the farm credit institutions, the Reconstruction Finance Corporation, the Home Loan Banks, the Federal National Mortgage Association, and the Federal Deposit Insurance Corporation be considered expenditures, it might be argued that these outlays have had far-reaching effects upon the pattern of American long-term and short-term credit. The long-run financial consequences of these investments, however, should not be viewed as results of the particular expenditure transactions involved. Rather, they flow from the financial functions made possible by the government's investments.

[12] This section does not consider special favors that take the form of tax exemption, aid to farmers, or housing subsidies.

make it normally impossible for American lines to meet the charges set by their foreign competitors and cover costs. So the federal government covers the losses of the American lines and adds a return on the capital invested, counting the existence of a merchant marine as compensation.[13]

Whether federal subsidies of this character are worth what they cost is an open question. The greatest difficulty, probably, is that no one can say for certain how much on balance any subsidy improves national security or accelerates progress.[14] The open subsidy in the form of an outright grant of money has one clear advantage over indirect aids such as tax exemption or interest rate concessions and favored terms in procurement contracts—the open subsidy can be seen. The public can at least learn what it is sacrificing. Groups seeking favors, however, often prefer to conceal the full cost of what they will receive. Thus they tend to avoid asking for direct expenditure subsidies.

Three other federal policies represent efforts of government to use its spending power to help particular industries not because of what they produce but because of their size or location. (1) Small businesses facing the competition of large and established firms often find survival difficult. Yet the public interest is served by the creation of new businesses that can eventually prosper and also by the growth of existing small firms which have a promising future. Pressure for federal help to small business has led to some action. All sorts of advice and guidance paid for by government are now available—including help in obtaining federal procurement contracts. In addition, loans from the Treasury, often supplementing those of banks, are being given in increasing, though hardly large, amounts. The net cost of these loans to taxpayers will probably prove insignificant. (2) Some areas have been depressed, especially in relation to the rest of the economy. To help them, the federal government in its own buying gives a slight preference to suppliers in these regions. In locating its offices and other establishments, it also favors such areas. (3) Firms setting up branches in any of a large number of foreign lands can get federal insurance, for which they pay, against certain special risks of doing business abroad. Again, the net cost to the Treasury will probably be slight.

A theoretical justification can be made, as we saw in Chapter 3, for subsidies to permit price reductions that will stimulate use of productive capacity which would otherwise be idle. In spite of the practical difficulties, the

[13] U.S. shipping firms in the postwar period got indirect help from government spending. Congress requires that half of the cargoes of relief and recovery goods supplied by our government must go in ships registered in this country even though the freight rates are above those of other lines.

[14] One subsidy, the grant of free public lands to railroads, yielded the government a good profit (even ignoring the rise in value of land retained by the government); until 1946, the government received as discounts on its rail shipments a total much in excess of the value of the land it gave.

possibilities of increasing the community's total real income by some such action seem sufficiently promising to justify sympathetic study.

Local bounties to encourage settlement of business enterprises are suspect. The gain of the community which thus attracts an enterprise may be offset by the loss of whatever other community would otherwise have had it. Suicidal rivalry in such bounty-granting is a logical outcome of the practice. The country may benefit little, and the taxpayers of one set of communities have bought the distress of another. Worse yet, the practice encourages the development of migratory parasitic firms which stay long enough to collect their bounty and then move on to some other "sucker" community. Yet the practice seems on a slight increase, with effort to avoid the mistakes of the past. The chief form of subsidy now offered (ignoring tax exemption) is the provision of buildings at favorable rentals. Far more common is the use of public funds to publicize the area, to put in special sewers, streets, and other facilities, and generally to engage in commercial development. Often the community or some regional organization works with utilities, railroads, and other private groups to build up industry. Modest expenditures of public funds in these last-mentioned ways sometime bring good results.

GOVERNMENT EXPENDITURE AND INCENTIVES

Critics of particular public expenditures sometimes argue that business and individual incentives are dulled by the spending (as well as by taxes to raise the revenue). Expansion of social insurance and welfare expenditure, it is claimed, makes it unnecessary for individuals to work as hard and be as frugal as they would if they had to rely on themselves. The business spending of private electric utilities or railroads may decline because of public spending on new power projects or on waterways and highways. Maximum pressure to reduce costs and speed technical progress may never be required if the government steps in and spends to support a listless industry. A unit of government which can count on aid from another if it seems unable to finance its own spending will not have maximum incentives to self-reliance.

These charges are undoubtedly valid to some extent. The net effect will depend upon the conditions of each case. But the argument is not completely one-sided. Government spending is at times conditioned to *add* incentives—grants-in-aid that require matching by other governments are perhaps the most important example today. Federal and state expenditures on agricultural research have spurred many forms of farming. Government highway spending helped make automobile manufacture and its many attendant industries a major factor in the American economy. Government statistics provide the foundation for much market research and for other vital business functions.

EFFECTS ON THE DISTRIBUTION OF INCOME

If a government limited its functions to the provision of a judiciary structure and the protection of life and property, and financed its expenditures by taxes resting primarily upon those who derived individual benefit, the pre-existing distribution of wealth and income would be undisturbed. Suppose, however, that this government obtained its income from consumption excises. Low income groups would pay the major part of the cost. Such an arrangement would augment any previous inequality of income. Finally, the government might devote a major proportion of its expenditures to social welfare functions whose supplementary individual benefits went to the poorer groups and obtain its revenues from sharply progressive personal taxes bearing heavily on the most prosperous. Such government finance would reduce income inequality, perhaps sharply.

Both American and foreign nineteenth-century fiscal policies may have accentuated inequality in the distribution of wealth and income. For a half-century at least, the tendency has been in the opposite direction. Expansion of the educational program, the growing scope of state and local social welfare activity, veterans' benefits, the development of social insurance—all are aspects of State action which, over and above such elements of "social benefit" as may be read into them, contribute directly more to the welfare of the poor than to the rich.

Today there is no doubt that government spending raises significantly the incomes of the poor. It does so unevenly and somewhat crudely. But poverty measured in terms of real consumption is distinctly less than if present spending programs did not exist. What other groups benefit or suffer from government spending, ignoring taxes to pay the costs? Some farmers, some people because they are old, some veterans, and some smaller groups gain more than the general public. Beyond this, however, it is difficult to say much that is useful about the relative benefits of public spending to different groups. Moreover, since every individual and family belongs to many groups—urban or rural, young or old, well or poorly educated, veteran or nonveteran, religious or nonreligious, creditor or debtor, motorist or nonmotorist, healthy or sick, high or low income—clear grouping, as required for analysis, is apt to ignore vital interrelations. The great, inherent difficulties of study of this problem are far from solution. Moreover, to consider the total effects of government finance—taxation as well as spending—is even more formidable except for one broad, but highly important, generalization: Taxes bear with especial severity on high-income groups and spending provides relatively most to the poor.

A final difficulty is that we have no way to know what private spending is replaced. If there were no public schools, for example, one family might spend $500 on private schools and another only $300. When government provides them equal educational facilities, is there a significant difference in the effects of public spending on the distribution of real income? In a sense there certainly is, but we have no knowledge of the magnitudes.

PROBLEMS

1. Distinguish between individual and social benefit from government spending. What would be the problems of trying to measure each?

2. Show why spending that is well worth its cost to the public might not be done by profit-seeking business.

3. "The government spending that contributes most to economic growth is that made by states and localities rather than that by the federal government." Discuss, taking account of the differences in magnitudes involved.

4. Try to find examples of spending by your locality and your state which contributes to economic growth by expanding knowledge.

5. Show how transfer, as well as resource-using, expenditures can change the pattern of the economy.

6. What would be the arguments for and against the federal government trying to channel its normal spending into (a) industries and (b) regions which are at least somewhat depressed?

7. "Government spending to raise the price of farm products hurts the very poor." Is this statement true? What significance does your answer have for your appraisal of the spending involved?

8. ". . . it should be clear as crystal that the marginal dollar of government spending has greater social utility than the marginal pay-envelope dollar." Discuss.

CHAPTER 5

Efficiency in Government Expenditure

CRITICS commonly denounce governments as extravagant, wasteful, and spotted with graft. Greater efficiency and honesty are demanded. Some such arguments have probably been made as long as taxes have burdened men. Recently the chorus of complaints has become louder. And for good reason! Government spending is so vastly greater than in the past that any given percentage of waste is much more serious and can amount to large sums indeed. Achieving economy in government is a public problem of tremendous importance. We deal with "big money" here, and it will remain big because obstacles to solution of the problems are complex and far more difficult, fundamentally, than is generally recognized.

Two essentially different problems must be distinguished. Only one involves the really large amounts, but the other, too, is important. (1) The big issues in government spending are those which deal with (a) whether to undertake a program and (b) the scale on which to perform it. Shall we have national defense, or fire protection or state aid for localities? If we answer "Yes," in each case there is then the question of "how much." The decisions reached determine the general magnitude of expenditure. (2) Yet, having decided on an objective, there are different ways of seeking to achieve it. Some are cheaper than others. Occasionally the differences in cost are large, although as a rule they are small in relation to the total that *must* be spent to conduct the program on the scale decided.

CONCEPT OF GOVERNMENT EFFICIENCY[1]

Why should achieving efficiency in government be so difficult?

At the very heart of the problem is the fact that "efficiency in govern-

[1] A pathbreaking study of the concept of efficiency and the attempt to apply it in an important case is R. N. McKean, *Efficiency in Government Through Systems Analysis* (John Wiley & Sons, Inc., New York, 1958). The volume contains a good bibliography.

ment" is a concept that is hard to define. Why not merely apply business standards of efficiency? Can we not determine the methods used by the most successful private businesses and adapt them to government—and, perhaps, note the methods used by the least successful concerns and see that governments do not use such methods? In a few instances the answer is "Yes"—when governments do about the same things as business concerns, such as buying gasoline or paper clips, writing checks, and keeping certain records. More often the answer must be "No," since most of the costly activities of government are most emphatically *not* business. The major reason government does them is that they are not things business can or will do well. The experience of highly efficient General Motors, for example, may guide a federal agency to better packing of spare parts; it would not be much help in deciding how many planes to order for protection against a potential enemy.

The businessman generally measures results and costs in the same terms —dollars. The most efficient method will be the one which gives the biggest excess of dollar returns over dollar costs. For government, however, few of the most important results can be measured in dollars. Costs can be so measured, but not results, because the social benefits of government services are not sold and no way exists to measure their worth. The cost of an extra hundred fighter planes, of a thousand new books for a library, or of a score of new beds in a hospital can be measured in dollars, but not their benefits. Obviously, then, to determine whether or not a government expenditure should be increased must rest on nonbusiness judgments. Such judgments are necessarily less grounded in measurable fact than business judgments.

The fact that the results of government spending are not measured in immediate dollar terms, as are those of business, helps account for the feeling sometimes encountered that "economy in government" can be achieved by mere "not spending," by slashing budgets. Sometimes the elimination of a government function may be sound economy. Sometimes an "across the board" budget reduction for a department may compel it to overhaul its procedures and prune out wasteful elements. Often, however, arbitrary budget reductions would lower rather than promote efficiency. At times, true economy requires spending more to get a better quality of service, or a new service whose value, as nearly as reasonable men can determine, exceeds the cost.[2] In some cases, true economy will temporarily require spending more to lay the foundations for less spending later.

Yet the common assumption that the cost of government is higher than needed for the services we get rests on solid foundation. The following are

[2] In 1940, for example, it became tragically obvious that failure to spend more on armaments earlier had been a grievous mistake. The postwar armament cuts did not look so wise when fighting began in Korea.

a few major reasons why considerable waste will prevail *unless* special means of prevention are adopted:

(1) Interest groups press for a certain program beyond the scale that will benefit the general public because the share of the cost which the advocates must bear is less than the gains they expect. Consequently, there is a bias toward carrying programs farther than is in the broad *public* interest.

(2) Objectives are often poorly defined. What, *really*, is the purpose of this farm program, that air base, the hospital expansion? Without a clear notion of the goal being sought, selection of the best means of trying to reach it is well-nigh impossible.

(3) Government officials are not under the insistent pressures to economize that face most businessmen. There is no bankruptcy for failure, no diminution of profit for general laxity, little or no reward for economy. On the contrary, the ordinary government official has an incentive to enlarge his department's spending, since his opportunity for advancement may depend in part upon the growth of his "empire."

(4) The political process, and elections especially, are not highly efficient in revealing what people want in relation to what they will pay for. (a) Government spending decisions rest with men who want to be re-elected. Increased spending of someone else's money is one way to get votes. (b) Opposition to taxes *per se* may grow beyond rational bounds. The public may fail to do what is economical merely because payment would require more of those hated taxes.

(5) Unlike a business, there is often no individual in a government hierarchy to make decisions or to get prompt, decisive, and effective action. Where government decision-making rests with a group such as a general staff, a city council, or a legislature, the press of many interests is likely to result in compromises and concessions. These are the essence of politics, but not always the epitome of administrative efficiency.

(6) Men may be appointed, or elected, to key positions with little or no capacity for the job. Civil service provisions produce reasonably competent and experienced personnel, but do not attract or favor creative executive ability.

(7) Military spending, currently the most substantial item, must be shrouded in secrecy. This secrecy severely limits the possibility of vigorous and intelligent outside scrutiny.

(8) Billions of dollars are spent, especially by the military, for very highly technical items or projects. Competent examination of proposals, and critical judgment on their execution, by legislators and the public is often close to impossible.

(9) Capital accounting and the "time perspective"—valuing future costs and benefits—in government have defects which make efficient capital investment exceptionally difficult.

More rational planning of programs, more efficient government operation, elimination of waste, and promotion of economy do not ordinarily develop spontaneously within the administrative structures of government. They usually require special provision. In this and the following chapter we shall examine various procedures for controlling government operations in the interest of efficiency and economy—government reorganization, supervision and control of local finances, improvement of personnel management, government accounting, government budgeting, and the accomplishments of nonofficial organizations in promoting government efficiency and economy.

GOVERNMENT REORGANIZATION

Governments grow like old English houses—a wing added here, an extension there, up-to-date plumbing put into this section, another shut off and allowed quietly to crumble away. Such growth is picturesque rather than efficient, and in government the results are overlapping duties, wasteful duplication, and divided responsibility.

Redistribution of functions among government units. Any inquiry into government efficiency should begin with the query, "Is the present distribution of functions among our governments the most effective and economical that could be planned?" The answer would be "No."

Take the case of the *town* and the *township*. This unit was developed in colonial New England to govern a village and its surrounding territory, and it served well the rudimentary government needs of that frontier society. As New Englanders migrated westward, they carried with them the township government. And so it has persisted in almost half the states. But today, outside New England, it is an artificial unit frequently without a population center and as a rule fit for no good government purpose—it is too small and inexpertly staffed. In most states, were town functions shifted to the counties or to the state government, they would be better and more cheaply administered and their costs would be more fairly distributed.

Is the present arrangement of *school districts* the most efficient organization for providing education? For many years educators have urged rational reorganization and consolidation of school districts. With improvement in transportation facilities, the radius of school attendance has far exceeded the limits which originally determined the areas of most school districts. In many instances, fewer and larger school units supply better educational facilities at lower cost. Much has already been accomplished along these lines. Between 1942 and 1957 consolidations reduced the number of school districts by over 50 per cent. Yet there are still thousands with less than 50 pupils each.

County organization has been much criticized. Through consolidation, small or sparsely-settled counties in many states could cut their costs of government substantially, but political considerations so far have blocked most efforts toward such consolidation. The state or special districts, it is argued, could handle much more economically such traditional county functions as road maintenance, drainage, and poor relief. On the other hand, some new activities—the maintenance of airports, the administration of certain elements of agricultural aid—might be better managed by the counties than by the government units now carrying them.

Special districts of all sorts have been established to handle particular functions. Too often the motive has been avoidance of tax or debt limits which hampered pre-existing government units, but in some cases the new agency is the only feasible device for extending operations beyond unduly narrow local jurisdictions. Sometimes the special district illustrates popular government at its best; the people involved handle their own affairs and pay the bills. Sometimes the special district is government at its worst; graft-ridden political organizations provide poor service at high cost. More often special districts are wasteful for reasons inherent in the system: units are too small to operate with reasonable efficiency, to employ well-trained people and to buy the best equipment and use it intensively; there is no effective machinery for standardization and coordination of service; overlapping and extreme complexity create wasteful duplication and make popular control practically impossible. In general, government efficiency would be enhanced by the drastic reduction in the number of special districts—but the number grew by 74 per cent from 1942 to 1957.[3]

Because of the planlessness of our state and local government system, millions of dollars are wasted, and, probably more serious, the quality of both vital public services and enriching amenities suffers. But no single formula—a general shifting of town and village functions to counties, a transfer of county and other local functions to the state, a uniform creation of special districts of one type or another—will cure the evil. In some cases, further centralization is indicated in spite of the plea for "local home rule." Only larger units can afford the specialized personnel and equipment needed to provide some services at a truly high quality level. Vast improvements in methods of transportation and communication have removed much of the original justification for small units. New needs of metropolitan areas cannot be met except by action on a scale that involves a region which includes many now independent localities. But centralization is not a panacea. For every state the units best fitted to administer the functions in question must be determined separately on the basis of public services

[3] There is a current trend to develop "authorities" to undertake the building and operation of revenue-producing facilities such as toll roads and airports. As a rule they are more nearly instrumentalities of existing governments than autonomous units. Although subject to some of the same criticisms as special districts, they appear in general to operate in a more business-like manner, but often with little public control.

rendered, area and population to be served, and taxable resources. Nor should one forget that the roots of democracy grow where the individual can participate in government.

Although to determine what organization of government units will handle public functions most efficiently is supremely difficult, it is often only a first step toward effecting reform. Political parties and individual officeholders who feel that they have a vested interest in the current political structure oppose reorganization. And in public inertia and indifference to the drab appeal of economy or efficiency they have a powerful ally. A sweeping plan for the general reorganization of local government in any state would prick so many private interests and rouse so many personal enemies that despite, or more probably because of, its merits, it would almost certainly be defeated in the legislature or at the polls. Authorities experienced in piloting government reform measures advise a "go slow" policy. Proponents of reform, their ultimate goal clearly in mind, should accomplish their program piecemeal—one part this year, one part next—choosing the most favorable course of campaign and keeping their enemies well divided.

Administrative reorganization of the federal government. Our federal government grew to mammoth size without much regard for coordination or efficiency. By the 1920's, the need for reorganization was generally recognized. President Hoover made some progress in reorganization, but the vast expansion of government activities in the 1930's gave rise to many new agencies and problems. Several important steps were taken before World War II vastly complicated the problem by leading to the creation of still another host of new agencies and functions.

During the 1940's and 1950's, serious study of the administrative reorganization of the federal government—most notably by groups headed by Herbert Hoover—plus conscientious efforts to improve operating efficiency led to substantial change. It is still too early to appraise the results. They have not brought the savings which some advocates expected, but many expectations were grossly exaggerated. The reorganization has taken place at a time when many other developments were also in process, so that results cannot be isolated. Where the problems are much the most important, in the Department of Defense, the evaluation of accomplishment in relation to potentiality is certain to leave many doubts. Opposition of some officials, and on occasion the pressure of groups served by an agency, have blocked some recommended changes. The mammoth size of the federal government and the inevitable shifting of its responsibilities mean that continuous efforts must be made to keep organization harmonious and as efficient as possible.

Administrative reorganization of state government. State government functions changed little during the nineteenth century, and the machinery of state government which had been adequate at the beginning of the century was still effective at its close. But the expansion of state activities and functions since 1900 has strained the antiquated state administrative organization. Pressure for administrative reorganization in the interest of greater efficiency and economy has developed, and well over half of the states have cleaned administrative house in the last four decades. The years since World War II in particular have brought extensive study and action.[4]

The state reorganizations so far effected have not all followed what seem to be the best general principles. Where the reorganization is accomplished by constitutional amendment so that it can extend to the entire state government, a well-integrated structure of government can be established with responsibility centering upon the governor. Some of the statutory reorganizations, however, able to touch only partially the prerogatives of constitutionally elected administrative officials, have accomplished only a partial integration of organization and responsibilities. In several states, however, statutory reorganization has gone no further than centralizing such fiscal procedures as budgeting, general accounting, expenditure control, centralized purchasing, and sometimes personnel supervision under the governor.

The results of these reorganizations are not always easy to ascertain, since resulting economies depend to a considerable extent on the attitude of the succeeding administration. Moreover, quality of service is not easily measured.

Administrative reorganization of local government. An important feature of municipal government reform has been the campaign to centralize all administrative functions of city government in a salaried *city manager*. As of 1959, almost 1,600 localities, under conditions set by state laws, had adopted "manager" government. A trained executive, hired for his ability rather than elected for political considerations, is thus placed in charge of the affairs of city government. Relatively permanent tenure, more conducive to efficiency and effective management than the periodic rotations of elected officials, is assured to the administrative head of the government. A man with technical qualifications for managing the "business" of a city is given that responsibility.

Administrative reorganization of other units of local government must in most cases wait upon the consolidation and reshifting of their functions. In some of the more populous counties, however, the governments are enterprises of such magnitude that, irrespective of other reforms, they demand the best possible administrative structure. "Manager" government is applicable to counties where wealth and population are concentrated. To date, less than 20 counties have adopted this reform.

Financial organization. Inquiries into local finances frequently uncover

[4] Developments are well summarized biennially in *The Book of the States* (The Council of State Governments, Chicago).

cases of treasurers or other financial officials of small government units who "keep their accounts in their heads," or "put receipts into one pocket and pay bills out of the other, and keep track of things that way." Such rudimentary financial management may be effective if the amounts involved are small and the man is honest and intelligent. But for any unit spending more than a few thousand dollars a year, such hit-or-miss methods would obviously result in hopelessly tangled finances.

Separate units should be responsible for the collection of funds, for the custody of funds and for payments on government account, for budgetary procedure, and for checking government payments. These may be set up as separate bureaus within a department or as separate departments. The federal government and most of the state and large city governments have adopted this element of financial management. Tax collection is one of the functions of a "revenue bureau" or a "tax commission" or a "division of taxes and revenue." Funds so collected are received by a "treasurer" who is responsible for their custody and makes payments from them; usually he is also responsible for the issue of bonds and all debt-service payments. A "budget bureau" formulates the budget. And a "comptroller," "auditor," or "accounting office," among other functions, checks expenditure warrants and supervises the accounting procedure of all government departments. Counties, towns, small municipalities, and special districts, however, still loosely intermingle the four functions and the offices responsible for them.

Of itself, the creation of separate administrative units for the four functions is but an initial step toward efficient financial management. To the department or division primarily associated with each function must be assigned all the elements of that function. Tax collection is still uncentralized in many states—gasoline taxes and auto license charges are collected by the highway department, corporation taxes by the secretary of state, bank taxes by the banking commission, and so forth—with consequent unevenness of fiscal administration.

Officials charged with financial functions are too often burdened with supplementary unrelated activities, or, worse still, a major financial function is attached as a supplementary responsibility to some other office. Counties often combine the offices of sheriff and tax-collector, or treasurer and road commissioner. For some government units, budget-making is still an ex officio function of officials charged primarily with other functions. Sound financial management requires a strict separation of each of the financial functions from other government activities.

Most authorities recommend that the financial functions of a state or municipal government be assigned to bureaus unified under a single Department of Finance, rather than be divided among independent departments. But the official responsible for the final post-audit should under any circumstances be independent from the other financial offices and free from executive control. His responsibility is to the legislature. A separate organization for tax administration may be desirable to assure this function the full consideration it deserves. Some authorities recommend that the budget agency be independent and answerable only to the executive.

Should financial officials—tax commissioners, treasurers, comptrollers, auditors, budget directors—be appointed or elected? Critical opinion would seem to be overwhelmingly in favor of appointment for financial officers, with the possible exception of comptrollers and auditors. Voters cannot judge the technical fitness of candidates for such positions. To make these offices the footballs of politics is to open the door to incompetence, corruption, and mismanagement. The election of comptrollers and auditors is advocated on the ground that since these officials must check upon the activities of all other administrative divisions, they must be independent of executive pressure. But, with the present state and municipal electoral machinery, the election of such officials usually means their cooperation with a party machine.[5] Most states have provided for an independent audit of local government accounts by making it a state function.

CENTRAL SUPERVISION AND CONTROL OF LOCAL FINANCES

Thousands of interested observers constantly watch the fiscal operations of the federal government, of the state governments, and of the larger cities. While inefficiency and even graft in these units are far from unknown, there is a fair probability that sooner or later serious deficiencies will be uncovered and exposed to a pitiless publicity. County, town, and village governments, however, often function in relative obscurity. Waste and even graft may color their operations without ever coming to public attention. For any one locality the loss may be small, but it may aggregate millions for all local governments in a state.

It is too much to hope that a progressive political leader will step forward in each local government throughout the country to place its finances on a sound basis and provide some means for keeping them on that basis. In the case of the minor local governments, fiscal reform on a widespread basis can be aided immensely by pressure from above.

Constitutional or statutory limitations on borrowing and tax rates are a rudimentary and often ineffective attempt to prevent local extravagance.[6] Many states have gone further and prescribed uniform local accounting

[5] In the choice between the two evils, open executive responsibility for comptrollers seems preferable to a concealed responsibility to party machines. To preserve the independence of the auditor or other official who makes the final post-audit of expenditures, his term of office may be longer than that of the appointing executive or his appointment may be vested in a legislative committee.

[6] Limitations on local borrowing and indebtedness are considered in Chapter 24. Limitations on local tax rates are considered in Chapter 19.

and budgetary systems, state supervision of local accounts, and even actual state supervision or control of local finances.

State prescription of local accounting systems. Compulsory uniform accounting systems for one or more classes of local units have been authorized in about half of the states, and optional systems prepared by state agencies are available in many more.

"Uniform accounting" is an elastic concept in reference to the varying problems of municipalities but can be accomplished with fair success in counties, whose administration is more standardized. Early attempts to force well-meant but arbitrary record systems on all government units of a given class frequently failed of fullest success, sometimes because of defects in the proposed system, more usually because of opposition by local officials. Supervisory agencies now emphasize education of local officials and cooperation with them as vital elements in the approach to accounting uniformity.

Experience in the states which have prescribed local accounting systems indicates that a *simple* basic procedure is the most important of all requirements. Small units would derive no benefit from many of the accounting refinements necessary for larger, more complicated governments; their officials would properly resent the added responsibility and labor. Using a simple basic procedure, successively more refined accounting systems for superior classes of government units can be built up with no sacrifice of comparable uniformity. Moreover, all that should be prescribed is a minimum; any unit should be free and encouraged to adopt refinements. State assistance is usually essential to the successful installation of prescribed local accounting systems.

State inspection of local accounts. All states except Georgia provide for some form of state inspection of local accounts to assure conformity of the financial and budgeting policies of local units, and of their accounting methods and controls, with statutory requirements. Such state inspection does not preclude audit of local accounts by independent professional accountants, which may also serve other, more constructive purposes.

The most elementary but most effective element in state inspection of local accounts is periodic or occasional examination of their accounts by state auditors. In nearly half the states, both county and municipal accounts are subject to examination; other states limit such examination to the accounts of specified classes of local governments. Greatly facilitating state inspection is the requirement that local governments make periodic reports of their financial status to some state agency. Most states require both counties and municipal governments to make such reports; a few limit the requirement to one class of government.

State prescription of local budget systems. Still another check upon local financial procedures is the statutory prescription of local budgeting procedure and forms. To guide legislative action in this field, the National

Municipal League in 1928 published a Model Municipal Budget Law. At present almost all states require local preparation of budgets, and over half of the states require such preparation to be in accord with state-established procedure.

The purpose is to erect a first line of defense against local deficits and to avoid local extravagance by correlating anticipated revenue and expenditure. Under these local budget laws, local units may not set tax rates or pass other revenue measures until they have prepared an estimate of expenditures. Statutory rules prescribe the estimating of revenues and expenditure by regulating procedures to be adopted respecting surpluses or deficits, tax yields, tax delinquencies, offsets for uncollectible revenue, reserve accounts, illegal expenditure, emergency appropriations, and other fundamental elements of budgetary technique. A common provision is that local budgets must be adopted before the fiscal year begins, so that there will be no budgetary hiatus. Another is that a prior-year deficit must be included as an expense item in the current-year budget. Tax delinquency notes must be paid off during a one- to three-year period in order to forestall accumulation of floating debt. Some provision is generally made for a simple pre-audit procedure or other administrative check on the execution of the local budgets.

Prescribed local budget systems, like prescribed local accounting systems, must start with a supremely simple basic formula for the smallest units of government. Refinements and variations to meet the special conditions in larger or more complicated units are built up from this foundation.

Local units generally require state assistance in adjusting themselves to smooth working of the prescribed system. Some state agency should prepare standard forms to conform with the statute. Periodic check by a state agency of the local budgetary procedures is helpful, possibly even necessary, in effecting the purposes of the law, not so much to judge the wisdom of the expenditure or revenue provisions as to ensure that they conform with the rules established by the state authority.

State control of local finances. Several important local functions have long been subject to a considerable degree of state supervision and even control. Public education is the leading example. All states require that regular and often comprehensive reports be made to state departments of education, and about two-thirds of the states maintain staffs of educational inspectors. In the highway field, state highway commissions, state departments of public works, or state engineering departments exercise a varying degree of supervision over local road construction and maintenance. Most states subject local charitable institutions to inspection. In the administration of public health work and funds provided under the Social Security Act, the states have assumed a very large measure of control. In fact, as far as public health and social security work are concerned, the counties and municipalities in some states are little more than administrative districts for a semistate function. And finally, as will be discussed later, state supervision is an important factor in effective local tax administration.

A number of states have also embarked upon a much broader program of controlling local expenditures. Indiana took the initiative in 1919, when the legislature vested the State Board of Tax Commissioners with absolute power of supervision and control over the finances of all local governments. Every proposed tax levy and bond issue had to be submitted to this board for ratification or disapproval. This stringent system of central control was dropped by Indiana in 1932, but five years later was resurrected by Iowa, with the review function exercised by deputies of an ex officio board of state officials. Without attempting the universality which was the essence of the Indiana Plan, several other states have made partial approaches to state control of local finances.[7]

PERSONNEL MANAGEMENT

The ultimate determinant of the character and efficiency of government activity is the caliber of the 8,200,000 civilians and the 2,800,000 persons in the armed forces who perform public services.[8] Able men will accomplish results under any government setup. And the most thoroughgoing administrative reorganization is of no avail if the officeholders and employees are knaves and fools. As more responsibility has been put on government, the importance of getting top quality personnel has increased. Since the great bulk of nonmilitary spending, and much military spending, is on personnel, the need for effective personnel policies is absolutely vital.

Policy-determining and administrative officials. A first point of attack is the election of administrative officials. When state treasurers, city commissioners of sanitation, county superintendents of the poor, or township tax assessors are elected by popular vote, the corps of public officials is made up primarily of politicians and vote-getters. By the law of probability, some will also be good administrators. But their ability in the offices to which they are elected is incidental. Once in office they must devote time and attention to maintaining political footholds and preparing for subsequent elections; their official duties are all too likely to be neglected or referred to subordinates. The operations of their departments suffer from less than top quality direction. Moreover, elected officials are responsible to

[7] In Colorado, for example, the State Tax Commission must approve an increase in local levies of more than 5 per cent. In North Carolina, a state Local Government Commission reviews proposed local bond issues.

[8] In early 1959, civilian employment in the federal government was 2,200,000, compared with a war peak of 3,600,000; about 525,000 were in the postal service. School employees made up 40 per cent of the 6,000,000 state and local government employees; one-sixth of the state and local government employees were employed on a part-time basis only. State-local employment increases about 200,000 a year.

the political machine which backed their nomination and election—and which will determine their future careers.

A partial cure for this evil is the "short ballot." Only policy-determining representatives—the members of the legislative body and the chief executive—are elected. Administrative officials are appointed by the chief executive and are directly and solely responsible to him, as in the federal government. Although internal reorganizations of state and city governments during the past three decades have usually embraced this reform, scores of thousands of elective offices have still to be made appointive. But the transformation will be difficult. It will be under attack not only from the political machines whose control of state and local government is endangered, but also from an electorate induced to see the reform as an attack on democratic principles.

A distinction must be drawn between policy-determining officials and the subordinate employees who perform the routine of the government functions to which political policy applies. The former, as indicated, should be appointed by the chief executive and be responsible to him. Although it is highly desirable that they understand the functions they are to supervise, they need not be technical experts in their fields.

"Civil service" appointment of subordinate employees. The case is far different with subordinate officials and the rank and file of government employees. Their function is not to develop policy but to accomplish work. Their qualifications should relate to ability in their positions, and they should continue in their positions so that they can acquire the efficiency that comes with continued experience. To apply to these subordinate officials and employees the Jacksonian principle, "To the victor belong the spoils," to make appointment to these positions the reward of political affiliation, would produce a government personnel whose major qualification was political facility. Uncertain tenure of office would kill incentive toward efficient service as well as discourage many competent people from ever applying for government jobs.

A "merit system" whereby public employees are appointed and promoted on the basis of competitive examinations and supervisors' ratings, and centralization of personnel management, are the two prime requisites for the efficient conduct of modern government. In the federal government today, only a small number of posts are outside the "competitive service," the technical term for the merit system; even key subordinates in positions with considerable policy-making influence have tenure.

State civil service reform has made less progress. Fewer than half of the states have what may be properly termed comprehensive merit systems, but all states make some use of merit systems, limited at times, however, to positions where receipt of federal funds depended upon the reform. About 1,000 cities, nearly 200 counties, and a few special districts operate under some form of merit system for all or part of their services. Generally, however, the patronage system is still entrenched in municipal and other local government. Even when there is a merit system, loopholes can be, and are, created to permit rewarding of the party faithful. The condition of selection can include generous allowance for "personality" or other intangibles. Jobs may be classified as "temporary," and hence outside the merit system rules, but last indefinitely.

Administration of local "merit" personnel management has taken two forms. In Massachusetts and New Jersey, for example, a single state agency serves all cities. Such service is compulsory in the former state and voluntary in the latter. In most states with local civil service development, each city has its own agency. Most of these local civil service boards consist of three or more members whose terms overlap and who are removable only for cause. This has proved the best arrangement in cities where the spoils motive is still strong. City-manager cities find most effective a personnel director immediately responsible to the manager.

Quality of civil service personnel. Placing the civil service on a merit basis can assure a minimum of competence, reduce turnover, and eliminate serious graft. But much more is needed to produce a government personnel of high competence, able to fulfill its responsibilities efficiently and economically. Among the factors that influence the quality of civil service personnel are the following:

(1) *Compensation.* Salaries should be high enough to attract men and women of ability equal to the requirements of the various positions. The fact that there are commonly more applicants for civil service positions than there are positions should not be taken as an indication that government pay schedules are ample. Job specifications are often set lower than really appropriate, and many applicants for civil service positions are not well qualified for the real requirements of the positions. Actually many government units have not kept their salary schedules, particularly those for higher-level positions, in line with rising prices and business compensation levels. Less than 5 per cent of all full-time government employees were being paid $7,200 or more in 1957. Half of all state employees got less than $3,500 a year, city workers a little more. And even after pay increases of 1958, half of all federal employees were receiving less than $5,000, and scarcely a handful got over $12,000. The "fringe" benefits—pensions, long vacations, sick leave, shorter work week—that formerly were a special attraction of civil service employment are now matched or surpassed by private industry.

(2) *Security.* Job tenure, freedom from the fear of future unemployment, has always been one of the major attractions of civil service for a certain type of personality—a type, incidentally, that usually makes an excellent subordinate but not always a good executive. Today large areas of private business offer fully as much job security to their employees as does government. Moreover, some of the security of government employment is illusory,

as federal experience since World War II has illustrated. Congress or the executive may eliminate a function or cut an agency, or reorganization of one sort or another may require staff reductions. In such cases an employee's status as a permanent civil servant does not protect him, although such status guides the order of dismissal. Furthermore, security of federal jobs has also been cut by new rules on "security" risks. Top officials have wide authority to discharge employees for "security" reasons regardless of years of service and quality of work.

(3) *Incentives.* Government employees, like all of us, do better if they have incentives. Good work should be rewarded with more pay, prestige, and responsibility. Poor work should be penalized. It is difficult, however, to organize much government service so that individual achievement can be appropriately rewarded. Because of the departmentalization of government services and the prevalence of seniority rule, most civil service employees can look forward, whatever their merit, only to creeping promotion, except for two extraneous eventualities—their particular departments may expand rapidly or they may succeed in transferring to some newly-created agency.

(4) *Morale.* The European civil servant, even in the lower ranks, enjoys an element of social prestige which is one of the attractions of the service. Not so in this country. Reiterated public complaints about graft, waste, incompetence, and sheer laziness on the part of government employees, complaints validly applied to only a minority, cast a cloud on all the staff. In the federal service especially, morale and efficiency were badly hurt a few years ago by sweeping charges of disloyalty and immorality that are utterly unfair to the group as a whole. Indiscriminate criticism can rob an entire civil service of its pride, with unfortunate effects on the character of its work and disastrous effects on recruitment of capable new members.

(5) *Dismissal.* Getting rid of an incompetent individual who has gained tenure is extremely difficult. For very good reasons the laws provide safeguards against discharge without "cause." But "cause" is very difficult to establish. Consequently, a government employee's work must be impossibly bad before it is cause for dismissal. Even then, hearings and cautious procedure may take months and absorb endless hours of official effort. As a consequence, incompetents who would be soon weeded out of a private business organization stay on and on in government service.

(6) *Recruitment and promotion.* Heretofore recruiting for the civil service has been passive; governments have been content to depend on applicants who responded to the announcement of positions open. The deterrents to government employment just listed make more aggressive seeking of new government personnel advisable. The Hoover Commission recommended more vigorous federal recruitment. It is needed just as badly

by state and local units. Especially serious is the problem of obtaining competent personnel for scientific, professional, technical, and administrative positions.[9] At present these positions are often filled by promotions from lower ranks, with relatively little outside recruitment. This procedure has some advantages in that the capacities of the promoted employees are fully known in advance, and it provides the incentive of promotional opportunity to the lower ranks. Its disadvantage is that special qualifications needed for some of these positions may not be possessed by any of the subordinates in line for the promotion. A better balance must be found between promotion from within and securing superior individuals from the outside. A surprising number of governments refuse to consider nonresident applicants. Such limitation of scope for recruitment is sheer waste.

Supervision of government personnel. In recent years government has learned, with business, that personnel management is an art that requires expert attention. Personnel programs cannot be left to the diverse interests and capacities of various department heads. The government personnel function has been generally centralized in "personnel boards" or "directors." The usual functions of these boards or directors are: (1) making job analyses, classifying positions according to duties and employee requirements, and recommending corresponding rates of pay; (2) testing qualifications of applicants for employment; (3) establishing standard practices in regard to transfers, promotions, hours, vacations, sick leaves, and the like; (4) preparing, installing, and supervising systems of service ratings for promotion; (5) regulating layoff and re-employment; and (6) deciding cases of discipline and dismissal. Unfortunately, too much government personnel practice has lagged behind that of the more progressive businesses. Yet there are examples which show that real progress is possible and suggest methods of proceeding.

State supervision of local employees. There is growing supervision by state agencies of certain classes of local employees—particularly those in education, highway, and health and welfare departments. The most notable example is the setting of minimum standards for teaching positions, or certifying the eligibility of teachers. Similar techniques, including the setting of job specifications, are spreading to other departments. Increasingly, state departments charge themselves with training local employees in their special fields. The federal government exercises some control over state personnel administering Social Security funds.

[9] At least one leading state has tried systematically to learn from potential employees what is needed to make state employment more attractive. Some of the improvement indicated is easy–giving job examinations at night or on Saturdays. Many things, however, require legislative action. Such action is more easily obtained if evidence of the need can be presented. One advantage of establishing new government authorities rather than using existing agencies for carrying out some program is that the authority can pay the salaries and make the other efforts needed to get technical personnel. A regular agency is bound by rules applying generally throughout the government.

EXPERT EFFORT TO IMPROVE OPERATING METHODS

Governments have "production management" problems just as do businesses. In some respects the problems are similar. Businesses have been studying how to manage more efficiently, and some of the best experts in business management have been called in by national governments, states, and cities to examine certain phases of government operations.

The studies have revealed many opportunities for improvement—to do the same job more cheaply or to improve the quality without proportionate increase in cost. Analyses have shown, for example: (1) how more mechanization is economical, and in what specific ways; (2) where reliance upon outside contractors offers savings, especially in the long run;[10] (3) how filing and record-keeping can be simplified and made more effective; (4) ways to make better use of office space and to reduce costs of building maintenance; (5) how reform of purchasing methods can reduce prices paid; (6) the opportunities for developing and using cost accounting, with the computation of "standard costs" to guide operations; (7) how to search out the best methods being used and then to transfer them where appropriate, for example, from one regional office to the others; (8) ways to improve personnel management, including suggestion systems and incentive plans; (9) the uses of capital budgeting projected further into the future; (10) substitution of less for more expensive personnel in certain jobs; (11) planning the flow of work to make fuller use of personnel and equipment all the time; (12) renting, buying, and caring for public property more efficiently.[11] Some, but by no means all, of the improvements are applications of successful business methods.

Progress, although not rapid, has been made in putting the recommendations into practice. Bureaucratic and official inertia, dwindling of public enthusiasm, inadequacy of appropriations, legislative reluctance to approve change, and, sometimes, weaknesses in the proposals themselves, all help explain delay. If one were to identify each individual aspect of government operations and find where in this country or abroad it is being performed best, a very impressive list of efficient operations would result. Then, if over the next few years every governmental agency, large and

[10] Private firms often have more experience, better equipment, and more highly specialized personnel for particular kinds of operations than is possible within even a large governmental unit. The issue, therefore, is not merely the relative efficiency of government and private business—though that may be a factor—but whether, for the job to be done, there is a better means than the government can provide. Small communities, for example, may get cheaper management of the water or sewage system by hiring a firm which specializes in such work. Even the largest can get all but routine construction done considerably cheaper by use of private engineers and builders than by relying upon the government's own labor force. Associations of civil service employees, however, press for greater reliance upon government agencies.

[11] See Municipal Finance Officers Association, *Public Property Management* (The Association, Chicago, 1957).

small, would apply the improvements appropriate to it that have proved highly successful somewhere, Americans would get considerably better value in government.

Large governments can afford to employ a permanent staff of specialists in management methods, though outside advice is often needed. The federal government has made a start, and at least eleven states have special units—California's with a staff of over 30.[12] New York City has a City Administrator with a small staff. States can wisely develop agencies not only for their own purposes but also to aid localities.

NONOFFICIAL PROMOTION OF GOVERNMENT ECONOMY

Although institutional mechanisms such as those studied in this and the next chapter help the fight for governmental economy, they are but tools and must be directed and kept in repair by outside forces. One is the taxpayer. Rarely, however, does the individual taxpayer have the inclination, the time, the technical understanding, and the political or public influence to act as a guardian of his own and other taxpayers' interests. But what is beyond the capacities of an individual may be accomplished by many taxpayers acting together as a pressure group. And programs of administrative improvement that would be beyond the power of state and local officials acting as individuals may be undertaken by state, regional, and national associations of such officials.

Taxpayers associations. Outstanding among the economy pressure groups are the taxpayers associations.[13] Hundreds of such groups have been established since 1920, but the mortality has been high and only a few score, including many of the 38 state associations, are now truly effective.

Taxpayers associations are supported by voluntary contributions from their members. A paid secretary is employed to attend budget hearings, analyze expenditure and taxation projects, probe into the less obvious workings of government, publicize the policies and findings of the association, and lobby in the interest of public economy. A few of the larger state associations maintain permanent research staffs and make extended studies of the finances of their state and local governments. Some have

[12] For a concise discussion see R. T. Daland and R. Wickham, "States Seek Efficiency," *National Municipal Review,* Apr., 1958, pp. 166–170.

[13] The National Tax Association, organized in 1907, is not to be confused with the taxpayers associations described in the text above. This association, through its annual conferences, provides a forum where tax administrators, tax scholars, tax attorneys and accountants, and business tax officers can exchange views and information. By concentrating the attention of its members on desirable fiscal reforms it has proved a force for fiscal progress in the United States. The published reports of the proceedings of its annual conferences and the files of its *National Tax Journal* constitute an invaluable library of fiscal information. A summary of activities of taxpayers associations appears each month in the *National Municipal Review.*

built up an effective structure of county and municipal subcommittees or subassociations which, with the advice and assistance of the central organization, work on problems of local finance. Most associations focus on government expenditures and seek to prevent extravagance and graft. Increasingly, however, they are also giving attention to revenue measures.

Bureaus of municipal research. Efficiency in city government is promoted by a special type of civic pressure group—the bureau of municipal research. The first of these organizations was formed in New York City in 1906. It stated the following objectives, which have since become established as the program for the 60 or more bureaus of municipal research subsequently organized in other communities:

(1) to promote efficient and economical government;
(2) to promote adoption of scientific methods of accounting and reporting details of municipal business, with a view to facilitating the work of public officials;
(3) to secure constructive publicity in matters relating to municipal problems;
(4) to collect, classify, analyze, correlate, interpret, and publish facts on the administration of municipal government.

Most bureaus of municipal research are independent organizations financed by voluntary contributions. A few receive their support from community chests, some operate as departments of chambers of commerce or boards of trade, and some are financed by the treasuries of the cities they serve. Like taxpayers associations, their main effort is to cooperate with the elected and appointed officials of their communities. Only in extreme cases do they appeal to public opinion against these officials. By giving city voters unbiased facts and through adroit use of publicity, they have contributed profoundly during the past fifty years to the improvement of municipal government.

Professional administrators' associations. Mutuality of interests on the part of officials engaged in identical or similar public activities has stimulated the formation of a number of national "public professional" associations. One of the oldest and most active is the Municipal Finance Officers Association of the United States and Canada, which was formed in 1906. A score or more of such associations are now in existence—among them, to mention but a few, the International City Managers Association, the National Association of Purchasing Agents, the National Association of Assessing Officers, the American Public Health Association, the American Society of Municipal Engineers, the International Association of Chiefs of Police, the International Association of Public Works Officials.

Annual conventions provide members with a pleasant opportunity to meet other individuals "who speak the same language." But to an increasing degree, these associations are becoming agencies of improvement, reform, and progress. Individuals and committees conduct serious research into topics of interest to the membership, and the resulting reports frequently become milestones of accomplishment. Their recommendations for improving government operations in their special fields carry substantial weight. No brief account can begin to do justice to the progress these groups are making for better government.[14]

Other economy pressure groups. Government inefficiency adds to the tax burdens of business. So the state and national business associations, among their other activities, keep a watchful eye on government expenditures and are active in promoting public economy. In this group are the National Association of Manufacturers, the United States Chamber of Commerce, the American Bankers Association, the National Association of Real Estate Boards, as well as the state chambers of commerce, the state manufacturers' and merchants' associations, and the state and local real estate boards. Too frequently, however, such groups, as well as taxpayers associations, take the narrow view that "not spending" and "economy" are the same. Real economy requires careful study to see where the public interest requires an increase in spending and where a reduction is desirable. Parsimony may be the greatest extravagance.

The League of Women Voters has done praiseworthy work in fostering the study of government activities by its 110,000 members. Its local units and state federations frequently exercise considerable influence toward better government at state and local levels. Many communities have "town clubs," "civic associations," or "service clubs," whose members keep themselves informed on local government activity and constitute themselves watchdogs of the public interest.

PROBLEMS

1. How does the problem of getting efficiency in government require analysis of both programs and management?

2. What would you expect to happen if governments refused to pay salaries for top officials roughly comparable to those paid in the private economy?

3. What government reorganization has taken place in your state since World War II? In your locality?

4. When does economy in government require larger spending?

5. In what ways can state supervision of local finances aid localities?

6. "The introduction of business methods in government will not overcome some of the greatest obstacles to achieving efficiency, but it can make a substantial contribution." Discuss. Try to find what your state and locality are doing to apply new methods of operation.

[14] *The Municipal Yearbook for 1958* (International City Managers Association, Chicago, 1958), for example, has 50 pages listing selected model ordinances on over 50 types of city problems. This annual volume contains a wealth of information on local government and its finance.

CHAPTER 6

Government Budgeting and Accounting[1]

Two key instruments for helping to achieve economical and good government are modern budgeting and accounting.

GOVERNMENT BUDGETS[2]

Government budgeting, using the term in its broadest sense, is not new. Even if vaguely and haphazardly, every government body has had to plan its activities, and its personnel and material needs, in order to reconcile its expenditure plans with its revenue possibilities. However unscientific, this determination is in its essence budgetary. But "government budgeting" has come to be applied to a definite and increasingly systematic procedure for planning and controlling government expenditures for the sake of balance, efficiency, economy, and adjustment to revenue possibilities. A budget is a tool, a means to an end, or in fact a group of related ends, for budgeting serves a variety of purposes. Some involve allocation of scarce resources. One allocation problem arises in deciding the total that should be spent through government, that is, the choice of government as contrasted with private use of resources. A second is the choice of alternatives among major functions—national defense vs. public health vs. agriculture

[1] This chapter does not deal with the influence of budgeting on the general level of economic activity and prices. This issue is discussed in Part Six.

[2] More complete discussions, together with references to other sources, are to be found in Jesse Burkhead, *Government Budgeting* (John Wiley & Sons, Inc., New York, 1956); Arthur Smithies, *The Budgetary Process in the United States* (McGraw-Hill Book Co., Inc., New York, 1955); and Lewis H. Kimmel, *Federal Budget and Fiscal Policy 1789–1958* (Brookings Institution, Washington, 1959). A valuable specialized study is F. C. Mosher, *Program Budgeting* (Public Administration Service, Chicago, 1954). See also United Nations, *Budgetary Structure and Classification of Government Accounts* (Columbia University Press, New York, 1951); and *A Manual for Economic and Functional Classification of Government Transactions* (Columbia University Press, New York, 1958).

vs. more efficient transportation. Another purpose of budgeting involves the choice of general methods of achieving an objective that has been determined—providing a level of educational opportunity, for example. Finally, there are the managerial problems of so planning and controlling details of spending to maximize efficiency.

The growth of government finance has made the federal budget something of a "plan" for a big section of the nation's economy; its elements affect every other part. Federal budgets offer the possibility that federal finances can reflect carefully reasoned planning of the federal government's use of its unquestioned power to raise or lower the level of employment and prices; we discuss these issues in Chapters 27 and 28. Our concern here is with the other aspects of budgeting.

Finally, we note a striking contrast between budgeting in this country and in many others. Abroad, including Canada, the budget as presented by the cabinet to the legislative body becomes law without modification, except as the executive approves. Otherwise the government falls.

The period covered by a budget. Since budgets must be approved by legislatures, the budgetary period of any government unit is determined by the timing and frequency of its legislative sessions. One legislature cannot make the decisions of its successors—at least we operate on this principle. Consequently, budgets look no farther ahead than the period controlled by the legislature. Forty-three states have biennial sessions; hence, their budgets are for two-year periods. The legislative bodies of the federal government, five states, and most local units meet annually, so they have one-year budgetary periods.[3] The opening and closing dates are determined by the fiscal year of the government unit. A few government bodies employ the calendar year. Some odd datings are found—years beginning October 1 in Alabama, April 1 in New York, Washington, and Wyoming, and September 1 in Texas. Most states and local governments and the federal government use July 1–June 30 fiscal years.

Two reasons—one obsolete, one still valid—dictate the arrangement of fiscal years. The obsolete reason is that state and local governments used to rely predominantly on property-tax revenues, which were collected in the fall when farmers had cash from their crops. Thus, a government with a fiscal year beginning on January 1 would have had to wait nine months for most of its current-year revenue, whereas one with a July–June fiscal year obtained funds early in its operating year. The second reason, which applies today, is that legislatures convene in January. Thus they have six months to debate budgets, which then go into effect shortly after adoption.

Scope of the budget. A budget should be "universal," that is, it should embrace every item of receipt and expenditure. A budget document serves

[3] In some cases, including the federal government, appropriations approved in one year's budget may not actually be spent until later years.

several purposes. Data adequate for one purpose will be incomplete or unnecessary for another. A truly comprehensive presentation has the great merit of permitting flexibility, of enabling one to include, exclude, rearrange, and otherwise organize information to deal with each type of problem, including the biggest and the broadest. American government budgets rarely achieve this ideal in practice. Honest doubt about how to handle some things, a desire to make totals appear smaller, and mere oversight lead to omission of items.

Until 1932, special fund transactions were not included in the federal budget, and only since 1945 have all major government corporations been included. Even when included, important receipt and expenditure items may be offset against each other—postal receipts and costs, for example—so that only net differences appear in the budget figures as ordinarily presented. Other items may be relegated to special exhibits, better treatment than complete omission but not fully informative. State budgets frequently fail to include some capital outlays, the expenditures of state institutions maintained by special charges or property-tax levies, and unemployment insurance taxes and benefits. City budgets, too, often do not include debt-financed capital expenditures—but later they may include the interest and debt retirement as current expense; occasionally they exclude operating expenses of public enterprises.

Baffling problems arise over capital outlays and debt repayment. It has been argued that *capital* expenditures cannot be incorporated in the regular budget because of their irregularity. Sometimes the proposal is advanced that capital expenditures should be set up in an independent "budget" to be financed expressly by borrowing. Both suggestions at times result from the political cowardice that courts public plaudits with expenditures for improvements but would like to avoid presenting the tax bill. In the first place, not all capital expenditures need be financed by borrowing. A substantial part should be financed by taxation, as pointed out in Chapter 25, so this argument for excluding them from the general budget fails. In the second place, despite the irregularity of individual capital projects, those of a large government unit can often be so planned that the annual capital outlay presents no insuperable budgetary difficulties. A government budget should cover capital as well as current expenditures, though distinguishing between them. The budget should indicate clearly those expenditures which will provide services over a long period, as contrasted with those for current operations. Otherwise the public is apt to spend too little on projects that require taxes now for something whose major worth appears gradually. However, when capital items are financed by borrowing, budgets must avoid double counting; the outlays for the project itself and the debt repayment later must both be recorded, but only one of the two entries should be treated as an expenditure.

Estimates of depreciation of capital items not covered by maintenance are needed for a clear picture of full economic cost of government in any period. Yet budgets give little, if any, guidance for estimating to what extent highways, schools, or water works wear out each year.

The federal government includes construction outlays and other capital expenditures—$4 billion or more a year for nondefense construction—in its budget as current expense but with no offset for depreciation. Several states, and many localities, include important construction outlays in their regular budgets. Some, however, have separate capital budgets, and a few have long-term capital programs of at least a tentative nature.

Special funds, established by legislative enactment and supported by designated tax sources or rates, are one of the greatest obstacles to inclusive budgeting. Social security benefits and the payroll taxes financing them are the largest items to escape budget totals. But innumerable other special funds exist. A county may operate with a "general fund" and as many as a dozen special and independent funds—one for school aid, one for poor relief, one for libraries, one for road maintenance, and so forth. When functions are so pigeonholed, the budget of the general functions is a distorted document, one which presents only a fractional financial picture of past and projected activities. Or, although presenting figures, it may give little indication of the actual control which the legislature can exercise. In 1954, for example, *half* of all state tax collections were earmarked.[4]

How should the receipts and payments of *trust funds,* such as those for employee pensions, the receipts and payments of the *revolving funds* used in some defense procurements, and applications of the large federal holdings of foreign currencies acquired from sale of surpluses abroad, be incorporated in the federal budget? The full details should be presented in some way, but there is no general agreement on how. Special exhibits, perhaps, might solve the problem.

Institutions supported by special tax levies and *government enterprises* require special treatment. Such agencies frequently incur either deficits or surpluses, which in the long run involve payments from or payments to the general treasury. The postal deficit, for example, must be taken into account every year. Finances of public enterprises are too closely bound up with the general finances of the government units with which they are associated to be excluded altogether from the budgets of these units. Budgets of public utilities and government institutions which have earning capacity are best set up as detailed supplementary schedules, with the net deficit or net surplus incorporated in the general budget.

Special revenues earmarked to particular offices or departments also

[4] For a concise analysis of earmarking and a state-by-state description of practices, see Tax Foundation, *Earmarked State Taxes* (The Foundation, New York, 1955). Much earmarking grew up because legislatures felt that new taxes could be imposed more easily if the public believed that some desired function would clearly benefit.

warp the budgetary picture. A sheriff's office, for example, may report only the excess of expenditures over fees received. Or a city department of markets may make no return of license revenues and the expenditures covered by them. Such agencies seem to operate on an economical basis, drawing little on the general revenue. Yet this apparent economy may mask flagrant squandering of earmarked revenues. For effective budgeting, all incidental and special departmental revenues must be included.

Essentials of budgetary procedure. The complex budgetary routines of large governments and the simple financial planning of small units are based on certain essentials. The first requirement is a decision on what is to be attempted, the goals or objectives to be obtained. This step, however, is now taken largely outside of what is ordinarily considered the budgetary process. Yet since it is in fact the most important, modern principles of budgeting put heavy emphasis on the role of budgetary procedure in helping decide on the ends of public policy. There is next the choice of methods of achieving the objectives. When these two major decisions have been made, a more familiar three-step pattern can be followed: (1) the formulation of a financial plan, (2) the enactment of legislation to effect the plan, and (3) the execution of the plan.

The formulating agency. Government budgets are sometimes formulated by the executive, sometimes by a board of administrative officials or of administrative officials and members of the legislature, sometimes by a committee of the legislative body. "Executive" budgets, those prepared originally by an agency of the executive, are generally superseding the other types except for small local units. The federal budget is prepared by the Bureau of the Budget, an agency directly responsible to the President. Over 40 states[5] and a growing number of cities also have executive budgets. Budget boards, whose members are usually administrative department heads acting ex officio, formulate the budget in a few states; in several, the governor appoints special members who have no other administrative duties. In a few cases, both administrative heads of the government and representatives of the legislature are included in the budget boards. Many cities have either the administrative type or combined administrative-legislative boards to formulate their budgets. A few cities still leave budget formulation to a legislative committee. "Legislative" budgets are quite common among counties and subordinate units of local government.

The executive budget is generally superior to the board and legislative budgets. The president, governor, mayor, or other executive officer is ordinarily in the best situation to collect the information necessary for formulating the budget. He alone is in a position to look at the financial situation as a whole. But for the state and local governments still laboring

[5] The *Book of the States, cit. supra,* summarizes existing procedures and new developments.

under administrative decentralization, a budget board composed ex officio of the administrative department heads is the most effective, if not the only, way to bring together all the necessary information. Where there is an executive budget, the American principle of separation of powers may properly lead the executive to accept without major change the requests for funds made by the legislature and the judiciary for their own operations.

A governor, or mayor, or budget board cannot, of course, either engage in or directly supervise (a) the detailed clerical work of collecting departmental estimates or (b) the more responsible task of studying and revising these estimates. Budget compilation is itself a complete function, worthy of a separate department or bureau. In the absence of administrative centralization of executive functions, a budget bureau responsible to the executive and independent of other government affiliations would seem to be most effective. Such a bureau becomes the instrument by which the executive may effect his budget program. The budget of the federal government is compiled by such a bureau, as are the budgets of over a dozen states and of several large cities. If the department of finance is well integrated, one of its bureaus may handle budget formulation. One requisite of the executive budget—the undivided responsibility of the executive—is lost, however, unless the department is completely subservient to the executive. A third possibility arises when the budget is formulated by a board. The labor of compilation may be performed by a permanent budget staff attached to the board.

High competence in the staff of the budget-formulating agency is of utmost importance. The fiction that the executive makes all important decisions about his budget is just that—a fiction. He can really study and decide only a handful of the crucial issues. The budget director and his staff exercise the major part of the executive's budgetary authority, especially in decisions at lower levels. The job involves more than the preparation of an accounting work-sheet. The chief responsibility is to make judgments, to decide among alternatives. Whether or not the decisions are well made depends upon the caliber and working conditions of the budget staff. Their training and capacity should extend far beyond accounting, for they must know the significance of the contents of the accounts if they are to make wise decisions about what is to be approved and what to be rejected. They should know enough of the objectives, technical details, and operations subject to their review to be able to pass informed and imaginative judgments on requests from government divisions. The quality of a budget staff has a decisive effect on the quality of its operations.

Formulation procedure. Budget formulation for a large city or state government usually begins nine months or more in advance of the fiscal year, or biennium, to which it will apply. Department heads must work out their estimates; the formulating agency must collate, adjust, and incorporate the estimates into a unified budgetary proposal; and the legislative body must pass upon the proposal. Federal budget preparation starts 15 months before the beginning of the fiscal year to which the budget applies.

The first step is usually taken by the budget bureau or equivalent agency, which calls upon all departments for their estimates on the forthcoming budgetary period. The department heads, in consultation with department specialists who may work only on budget problems, estimate forthcoming expenditures and incidental receipts according to a prearranged uniform accounting classification and enter the figures under the appropriate keyed headings. Entries are made in detail, only identical material items or position grades being grouped. The forms used may, but typically do not, require an estimate of what might be accomplished with more or less money. An agency has an inducement to seek more than it expects, to give budget examiners room for cutting.

Revenue-collecting departments must also present their forecast of receipts. Such estimates are bound to be plagued by uncertainty.[6] Some taxes are relatively stable in their yields, and past collections ordinarily offer a fair guide to estimates on future receipts. For example, unless a major boom or collapse occurs, property tax assessments remain fairly stable or change in a way that can be foreseen, so that localities can usually estimate the yield to a surprisingly close figure. Forecasts of personal income and business tax receipts, which involve forecasts of the general and the regional economy, are frequently wide of the mark because of unexpected changes in national income. Sales tax estimates can also be far enough off to affect the net totals of a budget surplus or deficit appreciably. Estate and inheritance tax yields, which can be influenced tremendously by the chance grouping of the deaths of rich individuals, are especially liable to error. Some grants to be received from other governments are definite in amount, but some—and also shared taxes—are uncertain when the final budget decisions must be made.

Departmental expenditure estimates, together with estimates of probable revenues, are returned to the budget bureau. There they are consolidated into a single document. Almost invariably, the expenditure estimates exceed the revenue estimates, and the process of "balancing the budget" ensues. In some cases, major policy issues are involved; in the federal government, the Cabinet and the National Security Council are usually called into consultation by the President. In a small municipality, the mayor calls in his department heads and presents them the problem of paring their estimates. In a larger government unit, examiners comb through the original estimates to pick out possible savings, presumably

[6] For an account of the problems and one state's solutions, see R. S. Herman, *Revenue Estimating in New York State Government* (State of New York, Albany, 1952).

solely with an eye to efficiency and economy, often in practice reflecting the personal judgments and prejudices of the individual examiners.

Continuation of an existing expenditure is much easier than any change that involves increase, regardless of merit. All too often the person who really decides knows very little about the true facts and alternatives. One or more members of the staff of the Bureau of the Budget are assigned to specialize on the affairs of each major federal agency; their continuing and intimate contact provides some of the competence needed for intelligent review of the titanic federal departmental requests. Later come conferences between the budget director and the department heads, protests that the original estimates were irreducible minima, bickerings and the most earnest analysis, and recalculations. And up to the last minute, important items may depend upon difficult issues of either tax or spending policy on which the mayor, governor, or president is reluctant to decide. This is highly significant in the case of military spending and international affairs; changing techniques of defense and uncertainties of world politics have for several years led to much indecision on items of major expense until the absolutely final deadline.

The preliminary budget. The budgetary document prepared by the formulating agency is commonly called the "preliminary" budget. For a village or small school district, it may be presented in its entirety on a few typewritten pages. The 1960 preliminary federal budget, however, was a volume of 1,000 large and closely-printed pages containing thousands of detail tables. New York City and several states produce volumes that are even bulkier and heavier than the federal one. New York City's has weighed 33 pounds.

The preliminary budget should be in a form which meets the needs of the legislature and also of those members of the public who wish to examine proposals and perhaps appear at public hearings. The federal budget should also be easily usable by persons studying the relation between federal finance and national income. The federal government and many others have made good progress in presenting budget data more effectively. No one presentation will best serve all purposes, and hence different classifications of the same data are desirable.

Federal "spending" figures show actual outlays or disbursements primarily on the basis of checks issued, but this is not the basis on which Congress acts. Action takes the form of granting three basic types of "new obligational authority":

(1) *Appropriations* are legal authorizations to make payments from the Treasury.

(2) *Contract authorizations* give an agency the power to make a contract to spend money; the actual payment must be authorized later by an appropriation.

(3) *Authorizations to expend from debt receipts* (a) permit the Treasury to make borrowed funds available to an agency or enterprise, often in exchange for its notes, or (b) authorize a government corporation to borrow directly from the public and spend the proceeds, or (c) allow cancellation of notes issued by a government enterprise and held by the Treasury so that the enterprise may borrow again from the Treasury and spend.

The total of new obligational authority granted in any one year may be substantially greater or less than disbursements, and carry-overs of unused but still valid authority are usually one-third or more of the total to be spent. Some authority to spend is never used. Congress can always cancel spending authority carried over from earlier years, but there is widespread opinion that review of past actions is less thorough than it ought to be.[7]

Government budgets are formulated on a mixed "cash" and "accrual" basis. In the so-called "administrative" or "conventional" government budget, anticipated receipts and most disbursements are attributed to the fiscal year in which they are to be paid. Some expenditures, however, are charged to the year when they became legal obligations. Thus, interest on federal savings bonds is budgeted each year on the basis of the bonds outstanding, although the greater part of each year's allotment will not be paid out until much later when the bonds, plus accrued interest, are redeemed. A special tabulation, however, serves economists and businessmen who use the federal preliminary budget for forecasting. They want a picture of the "cash flows" it will produce—what funds government will actually draw from the national economy during the fiscal year, and what funds it will put back into the income stream. The 1960 budget, for example, shows cash receipts at $93.5 billion and cash outlays at $92.9 billion, compared with $77.1 billion and $77.0 billion in the budget as ordinarily presented. An important source of difference is the treatment of Social Security transactions. Tax receipts are treated as current expenditure—but outside the conventional budget totals—when paid into trust funds, and benefits paid are not counted as spending. At present, payroll taxes and benefits are about equal.

Many preliminary budgets are formulated on a departmental "materials-and-salary-line" or "line-item" basis. The proposed expenditures for each department are listed as salaries for so many clerks, janitors, and other personnel classifications, and as purchases of office supplies, automobiles, and other materials, without indication of what the personnel will be doing or what the purchased items will be used for. If the functional activities of each department are fairly simple and well understood, as they are for

[7] A law passed in 1958 requires more detailed accounting of unspent appropriations carried over from prior years. It will presumably facilitate the review and cancellation of amounts whose expenditure does not now seem wise and the postponement of new appropriations until the funds already authorized are committed.

most small government units, this basis of listing the budgetary details apprises the legislature and public fully on the *functional purposes* of the proposed appropriations. However, it gives no indication of whether the amount to be spent is appropriate—whether the cost per unit of service to be accomplished is as low as reasonably possible and whether the amount of the service to be performed is best. The line-item system gives reasonably good assurance that the amount paid per pencil is not excessive. It gives no basis for judging the more important questions: Is the number of pencils, or clerks, the best number to do the job? How much of this job ought to be done? The absolute impossibility of knowing what detailed conditions will prevail a year ahead means that a line-item budget is certain to become obsolete. To provide enough money, it will provide more than is needed for some conditions that develop. Or if it provides only for what can be foreseen, it will be inadequate in some cases.

For large government units, each of whose departments may engage in a wide range of activities and which may have particular activities shared by a number of departments or agencies, a "materials-and-salary-line" budget is far from adequate. Such government units should have their budgets formulated on a "functional" basis—health, defense, justice—with salaries and purchases grouped by specific purposes or activities.

Subdivision should then be organized on a performance basis. Performance budgeting emphasizes what a government *does,* not what it *buys*—not the amount of fuel and labor for building operation but the amount of space maintained. It focuses on accomplishment rather than the means to accomplishment. Sometimes this is easy, but more often the difficulties are so formidable that several years will be required to shift from older bases. A few cities, led by Richmond, Virginia, a decade ago, and an occasional state, have progressed toward performance-basis presentation. Because of its truly superior nature, rapid extension is desirable.

The federal budget now presents the same totals for each agency with two entirely different breakdowns—one by program, the other by object. In addition, work-load data appear, an important move toward performance-basis presentation. For example, the 1960 Internal Revenue Service budget estimates show nine *functions* or programs—such as rulings, planning, etc.; collections; audit of tax returns; tax fraud and special investigations; legal services; taxpayer conferences and appeals. The total spending is $366 million. This same total is also classified by twelve *objects* of spending—such as personal services; transportation of things; printing; equipment; refunds. The *work-load* presentation of one program, collection of revenue, shows the number of returns to be filed, tax computations to be made and verified, refunds and credits to be made, notices to be mailed, taxpayer delinquent accounts closed, and delinquency investigations. There is also a terse textual description of each function. There is no indication of what might be accomplished with more money or what would be lost if the appropriation were reduced.[8]

Preliminary budgets should be prepared in at least three sections. The first should be a *summary* of past and proposed expenditures, and of past and proposed revenues. This will give the legislators an over-all picture to guide them in their study of details. It will be the only part of the budget document that most of the public will ever look at. An executive "budget message," or some other analytical statement, giving the why's and where-fore's of all significant budgetary provisions, can be incorporated in this summary section. Charts can visualize important trends and proportions. Some government units, as a matter of improving public understanding, publish and distribute these budget summaries in pamphlet form. The federal *Budget in Brief* is excellent. A summary of major proposals rejected and of the reasons for rejection is desirable but, to the authors' knowledge, is never provided.

A second part of the preliminary budget should contain the *schedules* of the proposed expenditures and of the actual expenditures of the preceding year or biennium. These, with the explanation of what they are to accomplish, are the vital body of the preliminary budget. Since the legislature must pass upon these items in formulating its appropriation bill, the statement of proposed expenditures should be explicit, not in minute detail but in relation to responsibility. The statement should not be limited to figures. The reasons—"justifications" in budgetary terminology—ought also to be presented.

The third part should indicate the *proposed methods of raising funds*. As with expenditure schedules, revenue operations of the preceding year or biennium should be placed beside the proposals for the coming period.

A fourth section will often be desirable. It will present special exhibits, analyses, and tabulations. These can aid in making decisions even though they are not the bases for appropriations or revenue action. The 1960 federal budget, for example, has a 50-page part on trust funds and in addition 12 special analyses—such as, receipts and payments to the public; federal credit programs; federal activities in public works and other construction;

[8] In this country's second largest budget, that of New York City, some progress has been made in describing what is to be done. For example, Budget Examination, to receive $730,000 in 1958, is described as follows: "Prepares the departmental Expense Budget and performs all work, examinations and recommendations thereto; performs research into departmental activities; reports on departmental requests for transfers of funds; undertakes fiscal, procedural and organizational surveys; directs the installation of performance standards and directs the adoption of work-load data on program achievements and costs; makes surveys of wage and salary problems as they affect the Career and Salary Plan and investigates wages, hours, etc., for positions excluded from the Plan." Again there is no indication of what any part of the job costs or how much is accomplished. For a few departments, however, work-load data do appear. For example, the Tax Department's $8,300 to be spent on photostat operators' salaries will result in 40,000 documents photostated. The Municipal Finance Officers Association has a series of studies on the use of performance budgeting.

federal aid to state and local governments; federal research and development programs; and comparison of budget receipts and expenditures by function for a ten-year period. There is, for any large government, no end to the special analyses which at one time or another can be useful to the public, the legislature, and the executive. One year it may be the reasons for not expanding the police force, the next may explain why assistants were provided for teachers, the third may go into detail about reasons for reallocating outlays for public health.[9]

In the federal and state budgets, for the formulation of which experienced staffs are available, details and varied classification are possible. Budgetary presentation in detail may even be desirable, though actual appropriations should be in more general terms that give officials freedom for use of judgment in management. The tendency of the last generation has been to make budgets too detailed as to objects of expenditure while ignoring both function and performance. What is essential is that the legislature be able to view spending proposals as both (a) a schedule of expenditures which are made to perform various *functions* and (b) a schedule of *disbursements* to be made by a set of government departments. Government departments are not always organized on strictly functional lines, and a complicated cross classification may be necessary to show the budget figures in both relations. However, the greater the detail, the longer the time required for preparation and review—and the greater the amount of obsolescence to be expected.

Where uniform budgets are required of local governments, it is essential that they be simple. Many local officials called upon to formulate such budgets have too little experience to be able to prepare refined accounts. Efforts that can be made should be focused on what is most important, the ends to be accomplished, and the relative effectiveness of alternative means—and not upon the number of clerks employed or families on relief.

Enactment of a budget. Once a preliminary budget has been formulated, it is transmitted to the legislative body. There it may be referred either to a standing committee on finances or appropriations, or to the legislative body sitting as a committee of the whole. The committee should call administrative officers and get their frank opinions even when the executive has rejected a department's requests. Otherwise legislators and the public have no way to learn the views of persons closest to a job. Interested individuals and organizations ought to be given opportunity to express their views on both spending and taxes. On the basis of its considerations, the committee prepares and introduces an appropriation bill.

Congressional procedure can be taken as reflecting on a magnified scale the general legislative handling of budgets. The President's Budget goes

[9] Perhaps every year one out of three departments should be permitted to "appeal" without restraint over the budget bureau and one out of three required to show what would happen if its spending were reduced by a tenth.

to Congress in January. First consideration is given by the House of Representatives, where the requests for funds are drafted into appropriation bills and referred to the Committee on Appropriations. This committee and its Senate counterpart are divided into subcommittees.[10] Hearings begin ordinarily in private with a defense of the general request by the department head; then follow justifications, by subordinate officials, of detailed requests. Questioning by committee members is often intelligent, searching, and extensive. Congress is at its strongest relative to the executive branch when considering appropriations. Since both parties are always represented on the committees, dissenting voices are usually raised. Attention may center on trivial or major issues. Persons defending requests for funds—especially any increases—are often subjected to exhaustive, and perhaps unpleasant, questioning and are required to justify policies and actions that otherwise receive little public airing. In these hearings one can see the tremendous significance of the power to control the public purse. Evidence is at times submitted either verbally or in writing by persons outside the government. After editing and deletion of secret evidence, testimony at hearings is printed and made public. Unfortunately, the mass of detail is so great that no Congressman can be expected to read it. The hearings may also cover appropriation bills submitted by members of the House independently of the executive. Generally, however, anything not in the executive budget faces an uphill fight in Congress.

One unnecessary weakness of the federal budget system—true also of state and local procedures—appears at this point. Congress has provided itself with inadequate professional technical aid. Staffs to aid the appropriation committees in reviewing, checking, and ferreting out budgetary facts are small. No matter how competent the Bureau of the Budget, it is an agency of the executive, and neither does nor is expected to criticize Presidential requests. Consequently, members of Congress are almost entirely on their own to learn what is being done and proposed. Their time is far too limited to do the thorough job that is needed. A permanent first-rate Congressional Budgetary staff would probably save hundreds of times its cost.

No satisfactory answer has yet been found to another persistent question confronting appropriation subcommittees. To what extent should such subcommittees use their powers to redirect or modify established policies of the government? Most such policies—foreign affairs, highway development, aid for veterans—require funds for their execution. Since funds are ordinarily limited, some body must allocate the limited funds available among the various uses. The process of allocation, however, requires judgment. And the formation and exercise of judgment will almost always lead to the examination and evaluation of the policies themselves. How far

[10] There is a strong tendency for subcommittees to be made up of Congressmen with special interests in the work of the department whose appropriations they decide.

should an appropriations committee go in this direction? Should it do more than try to insure efficient execution of an established policy? When there will not be funds enough to permit full and efficient execution of all policies, should it act as arbiter? What are its qualifications for this function? If it believes a policy unwise, should it withhold funds despite the decision of the legislature in adopting the policy? To what extent can it assume that in adopting each policy the legislature took adequate account of the general budgetary situation? These questions raise fundamental problems of government for which, unfortunately, there are as yet no generally accepted solutions.

Appropriation subcommittees make their recommendations together with an explanatory report to the full appropriations committee, which, as a rule, endorses them and sends each individual bill to the floor of Congress. In the House, the time allowed for general debate is fixed rigidly by the leaders of the two parties, who then allocate their respective shares of the total time. After general debate each section of an appropriation bill is considered briefly. Although amendments may be proposed under narrowly restricted conditions, they have almost no chance of being adopted except in the unlikely event that the spokesman for the majority party endorses them. After passage by the House, the bill goes to the Senate.

Here, committee and subcommittee procedure is generally similar to that of the House, except that an effort is made to minimize the duplication of testimony already given. Debate on the floor of the Senate is not limited as in the case of House debate. The final Senate bill usually differs from the House version, almost invariably providing larger totals. Interests dissatisfied with what the House provided can concentrate their efforts on Senators. A conference committee, composed as a rule of members of the Senate and House appropriation subcommittees, is appointed to compromise the differences.

Occasionally, irrelevant material is attached as a rider which the President must accept if his administration is to get funds. Some governors and mayors—but not the President—have power to veto individual items of an appropriation bill.[11]

Congressional rules provide that appropriation bills may not contain substantive legislation, but Congress may attach conditions to the spending of funds and thus, in effect, add new law.[12] It should be noted also that

[11] There is no prospect that the Constitution will be amended to give the President the item veto, as requested by President Eisenhower in 1959. Such power would greatly increase the relative strength of the executive. Power to veto riders to appropriation bills might, however, be granted and would undoubtedly be desirable.

[12] For example, the 1958 authorization for the Agricultural Marketing Service provides "That no part of the funds herein appropriated shall be available for any expense incident to ascertaining, collating, or publishing a report stating the intention of farmers as to the acreage to be planted in cotton, or for estimates of apple production for other than the commercial crop."

when Congress passes legislation providing for some function and authorizing appropriations for it, a separate vote of funds is necessary to provide the funds in question—and such appropriation is by no means always made.

Final determination of a budget, both appropriations and revenues, is a legislative matter. It must, therefore, be within the discretion of the legislature and its committees. But the broad purposes of the budget are lost if individuals in the legislature or its committees can modify tax or appropriation bills to suit their pleasure or introduce separate appropriation and revenue bills at will. Legislatures, it has been argued, should be allowed to reduce, but not increase, budget items. To strengthen their position as critic of executive proposals for appropriations, perhaps they should abdicate their function of initiating appropriation legislation. These principles have been incorporated in the budget laws or constitutions of several states and are included in a number of city charters.

Such provision gives the executive an element of legislative power in that he can determine the maximum extent of a government's activities for the budgetary period. For this reason, attempts to limit legislative action on appropriation bills have been strenuously opposed. Legislative power to modify executive budgetary proposals has tended to remain untrammeled, but limitations have been placed on the character and form of special appropriation bills. Some state legislatures may not consider such bills until both houses have passed upon the governor's budget bill. Special appropriation bills may be required to embody specific provision for raising the revenue necessary to cover the proposed expenditure.

Congress, some state legislatures, and many local legislative bodies have sought a short cut through the weary detail of budgetary authorization by voting "permanent" or "continuing" appropriations for specified departments or functions. These "permanent" appropriations are set up in a special budget or special section of the general budget to which little further consideration is given. Unless an increase in such an appropriation is desired, it goes through year after year unchanged. Such practice is all right where the items involved are truly stable, such as interest payments, tax refunds required by law, or salaries established by constitutional provision. There is also considerable justification where "permanent" appropriations constitute minima for important institutions whose functions might be jeopardized by arbitrary budgetary cuts or by a budgetary hiatus resulting from a legislative deadlock. But "permanent" appropriations are a negation of sound budgetary principle in other cases. On the one hand, such appropriations may "freeze" departments that should continue to develop but cannot because the legislature declines to reopen an appropriation. On the other hand, a declining function covered by a continuing appropriation invites use of funds made available where they are less useful than elsewhere—in government or the taxpayers' pockets.

Legislatures may authorize expenditures either by specific appropriations for the detailed items of each department's activity or by large lump sums for each department. *Detailed appropriations* strait-jacket departmental activity, particularly when the budgetary period is biennial, as in most states. They deprive the agency head, who ought to be responsible, of opportunity to use his judgment to manage as changing conditions indicate to be best.[13] Detailed appropriations also become mandatory appropriations which the executive cannot reduce, even when reduction is desirable. So vital did this point become during the depression that several state legislatures authorized the governor to reduce the detailed appropriations they had previously voted. There is another defect in a system in which funds are voted in detail. Budget officers get substantial power to decide how an agency will operate, for they in fact often determine how many clerks of a specific grade or how much equipment the agency will have. Yet the typical budget officer is not qualified to make good management decisions. Nor is he responsible for results.

Lumped appropriations, on the other hand, may constitute blank checks which virtually place the administrative branches of the government above legislative control. Congressional practice varies. Some minor elements are specified. More often a lump sum is voted an agency. There is then, however, an implicit understanding that money will be spent according to the pattern indicated by the agency's spokesmen in their "justification" to Congress of the request for appropriations. Any significant departure can bring trouble at the hearings for the next year. Some agencies are now permitted to make limited shifts of funds from one use to another, ordinarily on condition that the Committee on Appropriations is notified.

No one standard can be fixed to determine the extent to which budgetary appropriations should be detailed or lumped. The longer a budgetary period, the less detail should be specified. If the executive exercises strict supervision over the execution of the budget, the legislature may be justified in making lumped appropriations for each department. Such current expenditures as the salaries of departmental personnel which continue more or less unchanged from year to year, can safely be lumped. Much depends upon the relative integrity and managerial competence of legislators and administrative officials. One inherent weakness of detailed appropriations is that the leeway which is absolutely necessary in a world of change often does not really have to be used. But if the appropriation is available, it will frequently be spent.

Supplementary budgetary authorization. At its best, the formulation of a budget involves much guesswork. When the time for actual expenditure

[13] In fact, however, some flexibility can be obtained by violating the spirit of the law. Employees can be assigned to jobs quite different from those suggested by their titles. A study in New York City found that in 1952 "Sanitation Man Class 'B' and 'C' (cleaners and sweepers)" were acting as auto mechanics, photographers, telephone operators, and investigators.

comes around—9 to 21 months later for governments with one-year budgetary periods, 21 to 33 months later for those units with two-year periods—circumstances may have so altered that original allotments are insufficient or excessive. Tax collections may be far different from forecasts because of changes in business conditions.

Appropriation deficiencies are handled in three ways. The simplest is to introduce a special "deficiency appropriation" bill if the legislature is in session, or to call a special session if the emergency is sufficiently critical. The practice is generally frowned upon, both because of the expense and trouble of special sessions and because the voting of deficiency bills at regular sessions opens wide the door to departmental flouting of the regular budget and to "pork-barrel" legislation.[14] But there is no alternative when a government is faced with an emergency which could not have been anticipated. Congress, certainly, cannot be expected to foresee the changes in economic, military, and foreign affairs which may occur in the modern world.

The second method, found in over half the states, is the inclusion in the regular budget of a special supplementary or contingent fund administered by the executive, comptroller, or some board, often with some participation by members of the legislative finance committee. Departmental deficiencies, if approved, are covered from the supplementary fund.

The third and most common technique, except at the federal level, is to transfer funds between departments. The deficiencies in some parts of a government unit may be fairly closely balanced by excesses developed by others. Transfers solve both problems simultaneously. Approval of the executive, the comptroller, or some other high official or board is generally required for such transfers.

Excesses, like deficiencies, must be expected. The most common arrangement is that any excess of appropriations over actual expenditures at the end of a budgetary period simply lapses. Waste undoubtedly results from this practice. Near the end of the fiscal year officials rush to spend money. One reason is that they can hope to accomplish something with the money even if they do not get the best possible value. Another reason is that failure to spend would indicate that the appropriations had not been needed. The legislature would then have good reason to vote less for the next year when the need for the money may be substantial. Sometimes, such excesses are transferred to a special debt-retirement fund or to reserves for later use. Frequently, they are transferred to cover other departmental deficiencies.

A few states, particularly in the South, make appropriations conditional upon availability of revenue. Should available funds be insufficient to

[14] A legislature can preserve its members' "pork-barrel" projects by making the gesture of cutting their funds in the basic appropriation bill, but leaving the authorizations still operative. The administrative agencies continue the projects. As expected, funds for these projects are exhausted before the close of the budgetary period. A deficiency appropriation, passed without public scrutiny, restores the earlier cut.

cover original appropriations, the governor or budget bureau is authorized to reduce certain classes of appropriations. In Alabama the governor must reduce all appropriations pro rata. A sliding-scale arrangement of applying graded cuts to different classes of appropriations has been worked out for West Virginia. In some other states—Idaho, for example—the governor or budget director has power to reduce particular appropriations that may seem excessive.

Execution of a budget. If, after a budget had been voted, the departments ignored the schedules drawn up for them and spent solely at their own discretion, all the labor of budget formulation, all the legislative scrutiny of appropriation proposals, would count for little. Departmental expenditures must be under continuous check by the executive. Both he and the administrative officials must be held accountable to the legislature. The instruments for such control are the pre-audit, the allotment, and the post-audit.

Most government expenditures are made by checks drawn by the treasurer of the unit, upon authorization or "warrants" prepared by the departments. Sound procedure requires that an intervening official, usually called a "comptroller" or "controller," scrutinize all warrants to determine their legal propriety and legislative authorization before the money is paid out. For the federal government, pre-audit is done by the individual spending agency under rules worked out in cooperation with the General Accounting Office under the Comptroller-General. About half of the states and some of the larger cities have established comptrollers' offices for pre-audit work. In many of the other states and municipalities, however, some pre-auditing is done by the auditor's office or by the department of finance.

Government auditing differs from business auditing in that it looks primarily to (1) statutory requirements governing revenues and (2) statutory authority for expenditure items rather than to the honesty and expediency of the payments. Procedures for handling tax and other revenues must be adapted to the provisions of the law, funds carefully accounted for, and amounts due but not collected shown clearly. In the course of time, many legislatures have so hedged departmental expenditure with restrictions that pitfalls lurk on every side.[15] A pre-audit of departmental expenditures

[15] Some of the numerous legislative provisions limiting most federal expenditure procedure are the following: purchases and contracts for supplies or services must be made after advertising and allowing sufficient time for the submission of bids, unless immediate delivery or performance is required by the public exigency; American materials and manufactured goods must be purchased for public use, unless the head of a department or establishment finds it inconsistent with the public interest, or the cost unreasonable; no advance of public money shall be made in any case whatever; it is obligatory upon government departments to purchase articles manufactured by the federal prison industries when they are available, before making similar purchases elsewhere; all printing, except such classes of work as shall be excepted by the Joint Committee on Printing, must be done at the Government Printing Office; no employee of the Pinkerton Detective Agency, or similar agency, shall be employed in any government service; no appropriated money may be used for compensation of any publicity

before payments are actually made is a valuable safeguard to departmental officials who otherwise might innocently find themselves making improper payments. But pre-audit slows action. Moreover, pre-audit officials have at times interpreted their function as giving them a right to check upon the expediency of details of expenditure. Such policy is a perversion of the purposes of the pre-audit and more likely to impair efficiency than to accomplish true economy.

While checking upon the statutory authorization for expenditures, the pre-audit official can maintain a running account of each department's payments and determine whether it is keeping within its budgetary allowance. The executive can use pre-audit summaries to maintain current supervision over all department expenditures. During depression and war, large amounts of federal spending were exempted from pre-audit requirements to speed action.

Some state and city governments divide the budgetary appropriations to each department into quarterly or monthly "allotments." Before a department can obtain its allotment for the period, it must submit to the budget office a quarterly or monthly estimate of anticipated expenditures. Although the departments are not rigidly bound to these plans, the executive head must authorize any serious departures. In this way, not only are the departments kept within their appropriation limits, but the executive can harmonize expenditures to minimize temporary borrowings in anticipation of tax revenues. As soon as a Congressional appropriation becomes law, the department concerned submits to the Bureau of the Budget a request for apportionment of the money, usually by quarters. The Bureau can modify the proposed plan and can require the establishment of reserves for emergencies. It cannot actually prohibit the spending of appropriated funds, but the President has some discretion to hold up the use of appropriations. Each department allots its total to its various internal units. As money is committed and disbursed, detailed reporting sends accurate information up channels.

At the end of a budgetary period, the legislature should receive assurance that the administrative agencies have made their expenditures in accordance with appropriation laws. Such assurance should take the form of a post-audit made by a qualified agency independent of the executive

---

expert unless specifically appropriated for that purpose, nor shall any appropriated funds be used to compensate or pay the expenses of accountants or other experts in inaugurating new or changing old methods of transacting the business of the United States; no site may be purchased for the purpose of erecting a public building until the written opinion of the Attorney-General shall be had in favor of the validity of the title, nor until consent of the state legislature has been given; leases may not be let for other than cash rentals. During World War II many temporary exceptions were made. The complete list of provisions is published by the General Accounting Office in its series *Prohibitory Statutes*.

and reported to an appropriate legislative committee. Yet less than half the states have legislative post-audit systems.

In many states, the State Auditor's or State Comptroller's office makes the post-audits for the small local units. In other cases, the county board or city council may employ private accountants to make the audit. The federal government, state governments, and large local units assign the function to a special official—a comptroller or auditor. Unfortunately, since he is often charged with pre-audit and other accounting functions as well, his responsibilities to the executive and to the legislature are confused. Post-audit systems tend to place overmuch concern on detail. Adequate control of detail is, of course, important; but it does not require that as much of the record be scrutinized as is usual. It can be achieved by a well-designed accounting and pre-audit system supplemented by post-audit of a small, scientifically selected sample of actual cases. If the auditing agency were relieved of more detail, it might then devote greater effort to the evaluation of the efficiency, as well as the legality, of the spending actually made. Most governments greatly need careful study of what has been done, study that focuses on managerial efficiency judged by results. Such study ought to be made by a staff independent of the executive, reporting to the legislature and the public. The best auditors do something of this sort but never, it is safe to say, as much as is reasonably possible. The General Accounting Office, fortunately, is increasing its efforts in this direction. The annual report of its activities and its recommendations for improvements in operating procedures is, on the one hand, encouraging and, on the other, depressing, as one contemplates so much that ought to have been done years ago.

Opportunities for improvement.[16] The discussion to this point has indicated several ways to improve budgeting. Of course, what is appropriate for one unit of government may not suit many others. In all cases, however, there is need for a process that will aid (1) in making choices about (a) programs and major policies—for example, the amount of policing or tax collection—and (b) the choice among possible alternatives of achieving each broad objective—new clinic buildings or larger staffs using present facilities to improve public health—and (2) in controlling what is done so that actual operations will be as efficient as possible. Clearly, these needs are not the same. The budget process that serves one purpose well can be deficient for others.

The big problems involve the major policy decisions and to a lesser extent the choice of methods of executing them. And it is in this area that budget systems are weakest. At all levels of government, budgets as now

[16] For revealing discussion, see *Improving Federal Budgeting and Appropriations: Hearings . . . [House] Committee on Government Operations* (Washington, 1957).

prepared tell us little, really, about what is a reasonable cost of providing a unit of a service. They do even less in helping us to decide—or even forcing us to consider explicitly—the fundamental question, "In view of the cost of different services, how much of each should we seek?" The general move toward functional budgeting, plus the increase in attention given to performance, are in the right direction, but they have done only part of the job.

At the federal level, and to varying extent in the states and perhaps some localities, we need closer coordination of the appropriations groups with those in charge of substantive legislation which determines what general policies are to be pursued. Congress can now adopt programs which require spending, without explicit consideration by those most familiar with budgetary problems. Two other reforms would have general application. One is long-range budgeting. The present system focusing on one year is both inadequate and unnecessary. A five-year "look ahead" in general terms is a reasonable goal. The second is to shift the emphasis from consideration of *changes* from year to year to the entire program each year. The present system favors current activities unduly, to the relative disadvantage of new possibilities.

The emphasis on executive control of the budget may have gone too far. Legislative bodies could at least do more to seek and utilize information. In localities and states, the council or legislature tends to be restricted to the data which the executive supplies. Yet this is not necessarily all that is needed for wise judgment. Congress, too, is limited unduly to what material the administration supplies. There ought to be ways to maintain discipline and order in the executive branch, while providing the legislature and the public with such information as that on which the executive budget officers acted adversely. Any legislature's influence will depend upon the processes it develops for constructive participation. More efforts should be made for a judicious mixture of penetrating legislative analysis of policy and careful study of detail. The former is most important, and now least well done.

The mixing of management and budgeting has also been excessive. There *is* unending need for better management in government. Yet this is a job in itself and not best handled as a part of the budget process. The two cannot be separated entirely, but they are not the same. The primary emphasis of budgeting should not be whether an agency is working efficiently—which is the concern of management. The deeper issue involves which functions ought to be undertaken and to what extent.

Finally, at the federal level there is a widely recognized need for better integration of the parts into the whole. Two objectives would be served. One is the better balance of parts relative to each other. The second is the integration of government finance into the needs of the economy.

GOVERNMENT ACCOUNTING[17]

Accounting systems for business have been compared to instrument boards, reporting in visual, coordinated form the financial result of internal operations, so that the owners and creditors of a concern can know how much of an enterprise it is, the costs of its outputs, and where, how fast, and how safely it is going. Administrative officials, the legislature, the bondholders, and the taxpayers of a government unit also need to know its financial position and to have a quantitative picture of its operations, including the costs of the services it provides. Guides to management and aids to economic analysis—to say nothing of protections against malfeasance and misfeasance—are needed. A technique of government accounting is just as essential to efficient government as business accounting is to sound private enterprise.

Some procedure of recording government transactions has always developed whenever and wherever governments have operated. But a mere tally of receipts and payments hardly constitutes an accounting *system* and fails utterly to perform most of the functions possible under an effective procedure of accounts. Principles of accounting appropriate to major government needs have been formulated. The task of today is to develop administrative machinery for the use of this technique, to continue to improve it, and to persuade legislatures and administrative officials to adopt the improved procedure.

Basic principles. Unlike business accounting, which solves its problems on the basis of experience, reason, and experiment, much of the procedure of government accounting is determined by law. Government accounting must operate within the framework of laws which create arbitrary "funds," which earmark taxes and other revenues to particular expenditures, which establish specific reporting and budgeting classifications, and which otherwise dictate accounting procedures. Within this framework, sound accounting principles derived from business fields, or evolved by reason and testing, may be applied. When the law and sound accounting principles conflict, which they frequently do, the law rules—until amended.

The units of government accounting are the "funds" established by constitutional provision, by statute, and by executive order. As defined by the National Committee on Governmental Accounting, a fund is "a sum of money or other resources segregated for the purpose of carrying on specific activities or attaining certain objectives in accordance with special regulations, restrictions, or limitations."[18] Plural "fund" accounting is neces-

[17] A volume which treats the general issues and also contains a bibliography is Irving Tenner, *Municipal and Government Accounting* (Prentice-Hall, Inc., Englewood Cliffs, N.J., 3rd ed., 1955).

[18] National Committee on Governmental Accounting, *Municipal Accounting and Auditing* (The Committee, Chicago, 1951), p. 234.

sary for large government units because any single accounting system that provided a good basis for certain classes of activities would not be suited to others. Each fund is an independent accounting entity. Only for reporting purposes is there any combining or aggregating of the accounts of separate funds.

For effective budgetary control and for intergovernment uniformity in financial reports, the accounting authorities recommend eight classes of funds:[19]

1. General
2. Special revenue
3. Working capital
4. Special assessment
5. Bond
6. Sinking
7. Trust and agency
8. Utility or other enterprise

Unfortunately, ignorant and indifferent legislation, instead of consolidating and unifying government finances under a minimum number of funds falling within the classification above, has spawned funds in indiscriminate fashion. The result is at once confusion and rigidity, often hiding the true picture of government operations and blocking efforts toward economy and efficiency.

Proper classification is of course an essential of good government accounting. As with commercial accounts, there should be separation into balance sheet and operating accounts. The latter are subdivided into revenue and expenditure accounts. Revenue accounts should be further classified by sources to facilitate budgetary estimating, to help control revenues, and to picture the distribution of tax burdens. Expenditure accounts are set up by departments with subclassifications according to budget-defined objects—personal services, contractual services, materials, supplies, etc. Uniform keying of the various subaccounts within the departmental classifications permits a later reporting by function of the total expenditures of the government unit.

Double-entry recording of operations is as essential to government accounting as to business accounting. Memorandum tallies offer no protection against omission or error and provide no instrument for control.

Government *operating accounts* have for the most part been reported primarily on a *cash* basis, revenues and other receipts being noted as collected, expenditures being entered as payments are actually made. Although cash accounting provides a record of completed transactions and permits of auditing control, it contributes little to budgetary control and to understanding the most truly significant financial changes. *Accrual* accounting, on the other hand, pictures obligations incurred but not yet liquidated and receipts due but not yet realized. Budgetary management is facilitated by accrual accounting, since appropriations can be entered

[19] National Committee on Governmental Accounting, *A Standard Classification of Municipal Accounts* (The Committee, Chicago, 1953).

upon authorization and subsequently reduced by reversible encumbrance accounts for orders placed and by voucher records for actual payments. Likewise, the revenues that finance these expenditures appear as receivables on their legal receipt dates. Discrepancies between revenues due and actual receipts can be covered by creation of reserves for delinquent and uncollectible items. The Hoover Commission on Organization of the Executive Branch of the Government recommended more federal use of accrual accounting. It would facilitate control of appropriations for which commitments have been made but the funds not yet spent, and commitments to spend not yet covered by appropriations. The progress toward accrual accounting at the federal level has been slower than in some states and localities.

Traditional government accounting does not use *balance sheets* in the normal business sense. Sometimes the only assets shown are cash, bank deposits, and bonds owned, yet the government may own assets of huge value—natural resources, buildings, highways, water systems, taxes due but unpaid. Liabilities shown may consist only of some accounts payable and public debt accrued, while unfunded liabilities such as accrued pension obligations are ignored. More progressive governments, however, include as assets (a) taxes receivable and other estimated revenues less allowance for uncollectible amounts and (b) accounts receivable. They include as liabilities appropriations for the year minus amounts already used or committed. The exclusion of fixed assets is explained by the fact that they are not resources which the government expects to use to meet its liabilities or which earn income. Long-term debt is excluded because it is a charge on future revenues, not an obligation which must be met out of resources now on hand.

Separate sets of accounts cover fixed assets, debt, various funds, and the relations between funds. The fixed asset accounts show acquisitions and retirements but not depreciation. The failure to account for depreciation (net above maintenance) understates the full economic costs of the services provided during the period.

Elements of progress. Prior to the 1920's the government accounting goal was generally to obtain some application of business accounting procedures to the casual confusion of government record-keeping, even though the procedures of business and government accounting diverge at many points. More recently, a well integrated art of government accounting, adapted to the peculiarities of government transactions, has been developed. But there is still room for refining many techniques, and the possibilities of improving their application to particular situations are endless.

Many constitutional provisions and statutes run counter to sound accounting principles. Various departments, commissions, and bureaus have virtual financial autonomy under old laws, and they jealously cherish their prerogatives and oppose being drawn into general accounting systems.

Independent funds based on special tax rates, fees, and other revenue items are found embedded in departments or attached to institutions; again there is resistance to the elimination of these special funds and their earmarked revenues and the carrying of revenue and expenditure into the general accounts. Progress has been made along this second avenue of reform, but the task ahead, particularly in the field of local government accounting, is still tremendous.

Once the way has been cleared for introducing sound government accounting systems, a great labor of education must begin. In small units, some official or clerk must literally be taught the elements of government bookkeeping to maintain whatever accounting system is installed. Larger units must include in their staffs a trained government accountant or even an accounting department. Courses on government accounting are now offered in some colleges. Where local units are required or invited to install accounting systems prepared by a state agency, provision for instruction in the operation of the system is usual. Businesses selling or renting accounting equipment give help not only in the mechanics of its use but also in the introduction and development of new systems. Professional accounting groups have assisted in the practical application of better methods, but very few governments yet do much in utilizing the methods that have been developed. The National Committee on Governmental Accounting, although opposing attempts to allow for depreciation in computing operating expense and balance-sheet totals, specifically endorses the inclusion of depreciation in cost accounting.

Accounting to control inventory efficiently can be done better than is generally the case. Fortunately, the Department of Defense has made good progress in handling its vastly complex job of inventory accounting. Finally, governments are learning that more complete mechanization of accounting often permits cheaper operation while giving improved results.

PROBLEMS

1. Show how the kind of budget document that is needed for one purpose of budgeting may not serve others effectively.

2. "Budgeting involves estimates of an uncertain future. But because of the influence of accountants, budgets . . . are prepared in a degree of detail that is quite unwarranted. . . ." Discuss this quotation from Smithies. In doing so, examine one or more budget documents.

3. "When [the legislature] consents to the Executive making the budget, it will have surrendered the most important part of a representative government. . . ." Discuss.

4. Explain the difference between object, functional, and performance presentation in a budget.

5. What kinds of budgetary presentation are likely to assist in program formulation? Why?

6. Outline an ideal system of legislative review of an executive budget and discuss the obstacles to the operation of such a system.

7. ". . . the purpose of governmental accounting is to produce financial information in a form that is readily useful to all of the parties concerned." What are the various uses and what kind of information is needed to serve them?

8. What are the arguments for and against capital budgeting and capital accounting in government?

9. Give the reasons for and against putting the responsibility for improving the management of government in the budget agency.

10. Examine the hearings before a Congressional committee on appropriations.

PART TWO

Principles of Taxation

Before we can study intelligently the specific taxes that compose the American tax system, we must familiarize ourselves with a body of general principles. These principles relate to four aspects of taxation: (1) the constitutional law which establishes the legal framework within which the American tax system must operate; (2) the shifting and incidence of various types of taxes—i.e., the economic considerations that frequently enable those who pay a particular tax to pass it on to others; (3) the distributive aspects of taxation—i.e., a discussion of how the burden of particular taxes and of the tax system as a whole should be shared among individuals and groups; and (4) the vitally important revenue and administrative aspects of taxation.

CHAPTER 7

Constitutional Aspects of Taxation

TAXES are levied through the agency of laws enacted by legislative bodies. Congressional power to enact tax laws is prescribed by the federal Constitution. Each state legislature is limited in its taxing power by the federal Constitution and by its own state constitution. The taxing powers of local governments are granted by state constitutions and statutes and are subject to the limitations of the federal Constitution, the state constitutions, and the state statutes.

Courts have the final word upon the constitutionality of a tax statute. Federal courts pass on the validity of a federal, state, or local tax law under federal constitutional limitations. State courts determine whether a state or local tax conforms with the limitations of a state constitution. No matter how desirable from an economic, social, or administrative viewpoint, a tax may not be levied if it is held to contravene constitutional limitations. Understanding American tax problems, therefore, involves an understanding of the relevant constitutional principles.[1]

GENERAL LEGAL PRINCIPLES

Certain basic legal principles of tax levy, more fundamental even than constitutional prescriptions or limitations, derive from the very character of government itself, or from the common law which antedates all American constitutions. A brief survey of these basic legal principles must precede an analysis of constitutional tax law.

[1] Most of the vast amount of litigation over taxes concerns, not constitutional issues, but rather the meaning and administration of laws whose constitutionality is clear. The reviews published by the leading law schools contain notes and articles on tax law, and the quarterly *Tax Law Review* is devoted entirely to taxation. Legal articles of greatest significance are summarized in *Legal Periodical Digest.* Tax "services" such as those published by Prentice-Hall, Inc., provide current and comprehensive information on tax law.

Power to enact tax statutes. Unless forbidden by express or implied constitutional provision, tax laws may be enacted under two sovereign government powers—the *taxing power* and the *police power.* Both powers are "inherent"—part and parcel of the concept of "the State" and inseparable from it.

Definitions of the *taxing power* in judicial decisions and in treatises on constitutional and tax law are in substantial agreement despite their diverse wordings. By definition, the tax power is the State's sovereign power to exact contributions from persons[2] or to make levies upon property. Such power, however, is subject to three inherent limitations: (1) The revenue derived must be applied to "public purposes," (2) the persons or property taxed must be within the jurisdiction of the State, and (3) the exaction must be "reasonably apportioned" among the persons or property subject to the tax.

In the absence of constitutional limitations, the legislature's powers to set tax rates are generally held to be absolute. Confiscatory rates would not invalidate a tax otherwise valid. This principle ordinarily applies also to those license taxes on special occupations which are clearly exercises of the tax power rather than of the police power. Some state courts, however, will not permit the use of the tax power in a manner that amounts to a prohibition of a useful or legitimate occupation.

The *police power* may be defined as the power of a sovereign State to control persons and property within its jurisdiction in the interest of the general welfare. License fees levied to finance the cost of regulating a particular industry or occupation are based on the police power. Legal authorization for certain taxes producing a net revenue may also be partly found in the states' police power. It may, for instance, be desirable to restrict the performance of an act inherently harmless but injurious to the public welfare if done too frequently. Instead of arbitrarily limiting the number of persons who may perform the act or the number of times it may be performed, a tax may be levied upon the performance of the act, and the desired result be indirectly effected. The liquor-license charges levied in most states can thus be justified as an exercise of both the police and the taxing powers. A number of state oleomargarine levies intended to discourage the competition of this food with butter found their support in the police power rather than the tax power. In 1940, Kentucky enacted a chain-store levy based explicitly on the state's police power, since a conflict of interpretations between federal and state courts made it impossible under the state's tax power to enact a chain-store tax that would be sustained in both courts.

Governments may also derive the right to levy certain taxes from specific powers other than the tax power and the police power. The Supreme

[2] Including corporations which, according to legal fiction, are "persons," though not "citizens."

Court has stated specifically that Congress may use the taxing power to enforce another power granted to the government. For example, Congress may levy customs duties as an exercise not only of the Constitutional grant of this particular tax power but also of the power to regulate foreign commerce. Congress may impose a prohibitory tax on state banknotes as an incident of its power to regulate the currency.

Inherent, designated, and delegated powers of taxation. The tax power having been described as an "inherent" power of "sovereign" governments, it is pertinent to inquire what American governments are "sovereign."

When the thirteen colonies threw off British sovereignty, they acquired the status of independent sovereign states, confirmed by the Treaty of 1783. As each new state entered the federal union, it acquired a standing co-equal with those already members and itself became sovereign. Therefore, all states are clothed with full sovereignty, including the "inherent" power of taxation. Checks to the exercise of their tax powers are the self-imposed limitations of their state constitutions and the limitations of the federal Constitution, which they accepted by ratification.

The federal government owes its existence to the federal Constitution. Such elements of sovereignty as it possesses were directly or by implication bestowed upon it by constitutional provision. Tax power is not "inherent" in such a limited sovereignty. Rather, like all the other powers of the federal government, its tax powers are designated by the federal Constitution.

A local government is merely an instrumentality of a state government; it lacks independent sovereign status. It has only those attributes of sovereignty delegated to it by the state law under which it is organized. Among the powers delegated to local governments are their powers to tax. By immemorial custom in some states, the creation of a local government carries with it the delegation of tax powers. The constitutions of other states provide that the creation of a local government implies a delegation of tax powers. Still other state constitutions require that such delegation be specifically expressed in the statute organizing a local government or a class of local governments.

Sometimes it is said that legislatures "delegate" certain tax powers to such administrative bodies as tax commissions, but this is a mistaken view. Sovereign tax power is a legislative attribute. Unless there is specific constitutional authorization, the legislature cannot delegate the determination of tax bases and tax rates to any other branch of the government. The limitation rests on a solid foundation—the long struggle for democracy in which legislative control of the purse has been crucial. The most the legislature can do toward investing another branch of the government with tax powers is to authorize an official body to promulgate administrative rules and regulations and to organize assessment and collection machinery. The discretion so granted administrative officials, however, is sometimes extensive.

APPLICATION OF CONSTITUTIONAL LIMITATIONS TO TAX STATUTES

Judicial determination of the constitutionality of tax statutes is partly a procedure of strictly syllogistic reasoning, partly an application of authoritarian rules and judicial prejudice. Logical deduction governs the application of a construed constitutional rule to a construed tax statute. The constitutional rule is the first premise of a syllogism. Second premise is the statute in issue. Given these two elements, the conclusion of validity or invalidity is the product of mechanical logic.

But before the courts can apply this routine reasoning, they must construe the meaning of the constitutional provision which the taxpayer insists is a bar to the tax being contested. Next they must construe the meaning of the tax statute. Logic is no guide when the issue is one of construction. Rather, the two determinants are the legal principle of *stare decisis*—the acceptance of prior judgments on the same point—and the personal convictions of the individual judges who sit on the issue.

As new judges with new personal convictions enter the federal and state courts or as current incumbents change their convictions, the constructions of constitutional phrases and tax statutes change. Outright reversals of the opinions of earlier courts are rare. But frequently only lip service is paid to the principle of *stare decisis*. Judicial acumen can usually find a basis for distinguishing the law at issue from a similar law covered by an earlier decision.

When other resources fail, a high court wishing to hand down a decision in conflict with an established line of law without reversing earlier decisions may create a "legal fiction"—it may establish an analogy for the case before it and decide the issue on the basis of the analogy. Once established, a legal fiction by the doctrine of *stare decisis* becomes an integral part of the body of ruling law. Legal fictions—"as if" procedures of judicial reasoning—are found in all fields of law. Outstanding among the legal fictions of tax law are the doctrines of "subject and measure," "*situs*," the "personality" of corporations, and the "benefit" character of "privilege" legislation, considered later.

Constitutional tax law embodies definite elements of persistence and consistence despite the arbitrary personal factors which enter. Slow turnover of judicial personnel ensures a generation of life to much of the constitutional tax law established in recent years. And the present courts must build their interpretations upon the foundation of older constitutional tax law. This older body of tax law may not determine the conclusions which the courts reach today, but it does determine the reasoning employed.

Doctrine of "subject and measure." During the 1900's, the federal Supreme Court wished to liberalize the application of some constitutional limitations to new forms of taxation without reversing earlier opinions. To this end it established the legal fiction of "subject and measure."

The *subject* of a tax is the class of persons, category of property, act, privilege, or other circumstance[3] upon which a tax is levied or the existence of which gives rise to tax liability—or which "generates" the tax. Thus, "male persons over the age of 21" may be the subject of a poll tax. A death tax may be construed to have as its subject either the "act" or the "privilege" of transferring property by bequest, inheritance, or otherwise at the death of the owner. "Income" or "the franchise or privilege of doing business within the state as a corporation" may be construed as the subject of a state corporation income tax—with markedly different constitutional results according to the subject ascribed to the tax.

The *measure* of a tax is the unit to which the rate of the tax is applied. For a poll tax the measure would be "per person." For a property tax it would be the value of the taxable property stated in units of $100 or $1,000. Measure of a motor vehicle license tax might be the horsepower of the taxed car, its value, the mileage operated, or the width of the tires. Capital stock or assets employed in the taxing state, or the income earned within the taxing state, may be the measure of a state privilege tax on out-of-state corporations.

Having established the fiction of a distinction between subject and measure in taxation, the Supreme Court was for a while inclined to hold that if the subject of a tax was within federal constitutional limitations, the measure need not be in harmony with these limitations. Since measure determines the economic character of a tax, this doctrine promised to free federal and state taxation from most of the limiting constructions evolved by earlier courts. But in 1910, the Supreme Court wavered. In determining whether a state tax conformed with the limitations of the federal Constitution, the Court indicated that the measure would have to be taken into consideration. For the decade following, the Court tacked about in uncertainty and threw much of the body of tax law into extreme confusion.

During the 1920's the Supreme Court seemed to be evolving a new doctrine—the measure of a state or local tax as well as its subject must conform to all the limitations of the federal Constitution. Sometimes the Court expressed this principle by declaring that both the substance and the form

[3] In economic discussion, two other terms, "base" and "object," are used which overlap and combine the legal concepts of "subject" and "measure." The base or object of a tax is the economic element which gives immediate rise to tax liability. Thus, property is the base or object of a property tax, corporation income or corporation capital stock of a corporation tax, estates or inheritances of a death tax, sales or sales receipts of a sales tax.

of state and local taxes must be in harmony with federal constitutional limitations. The rule was applied severely. No distinction was drawn between tax laws that discriminated against nontaxable elements and uniform taxes that incidentally applied to such elements. On two points, however, the Supreme Court refused to make consistent application of its measure-conformity rule. Federal and state death taxes were upheld even though their measures included the value of tax-exempt bonds owned by the decedent. Furthermore, if a special tax was specifically stated to be "in lieu" of property taxes, and if the burden thereby imposed was no greater than the burden of the alternative property tax, the Court was likewise willing to overlook "nontaxable" elements.

In the 1930's, the Court validated some taxes where the measure of a tax included but did not discriminate against "nontaxable" elements. Although later decisions in conflict with this principle created new confusion, a 1940 decision reaffirmed the authority of a state to "levy a tax on a legitimate subject, such as a franchise, measured by net assets or net income, including tax-exempt federal instrumentalities or their income."[4] The most recent decisions show the Court supporting its earlier position that if a tax is based on a constitutionally acceptable subject, considerable latitude will be allowed in its measure. A 1955 case reiterated the significance of the distinction between a state tax on corporate assets including federal bonds —invalid—and a tax on stockholders or depositors measured by such assets—valid.

CONSTITUTIONAL LAW OF FEDERAL TAXATION

Under the Constitution the federal government enjoys only those tax powers designated in that document. These designated tax powers, however, are very broad, for in Art. I, Sec. 8, Congress is given power "to lay and collect taxes, duties, imposts, and excises"—a selection of terms covering practically every sort of exaction that could go under the popular idea of "taxation."

Five specific limitations circumscribe this generous designation of tax powers: (1) The purpose of any federal tax must be "to pay the debts and provide for the common defense and general welfare of the United States"; (2) no tax or duty may be laid on articles exported from any state; (3) except for taxes on income, direct taxes must be apportioned among the states according to population; (4) indirect taxes must be uniform; and (5) the provision of the Fifth Amendment that no person "shall be deprived of life, liberty or property without due process of law" is sometimes construed as a limitation on federal tax powers. Furthermore, from the general constitutional principle of mutual independence of the federal

[4] *Tradesmen's National Bank* v. *Oklahoma*, 309 U.S. (1940) 560.

and state governments, the rule that the federal government may not tax the property, the agencies, or the instrumentalities of an essential function of a state government has been developed. The Court has not yet passed on the issue of whether Congress, like state and local taxing bodies, is prevented from imposing taxes that infringe upon the freedoms of speech, press, and religion guaranteed by the Constitution.

"General welfare" limitation. The vague qualification that federal taxes should "provide for the . . . general welfare of the United States" could have been construed to mean anything or nothing. Actually, it has been applied to but two issues in federal taxation—to earmarked taxes and to regulatory taxes.

When the revenue from a federal tax goes into the general Treasury fund, the Court will pursue no inquiry into the general character of federal expenditures. But if the receipts of a particular tax are earmarked to a particular function, activity, or expenditure, the Court may then inquire whether that function is truly "for the general welfare." And should the Court decide in the negative, as it did in the case of the crop reduction payments under the AAA program, any tax earmarked to that function—in that case, the processing taxes—must be declared invalid. Sufficient general welfare inheres in Social Security payments, however, to support a payroll tax inferentially dedicated to such payments.

A levy primarily to discourage or regulate some private activity and productive of no substantial revenue is deemed not levied "for the general welfare." Should the regulation involved be authorized elsewhere in the Constitution, the tax may be sustained as an exercise of this other power. Thus, a prohibitory tax on state bank notes can be sustained as an exercise of the federal government's currency powers—and a protective tariff as an exercise of the federal government's power to regulate foreign commerce. Where no other power can be adduced in support of the tax, it must fail. But the Court generally takes a very liberal attitude in construing regulatory taxes as revenue rather than control measures. For example, the prohibitive firearms tax has been upheld as a revenue measure; the Court sustained as revenue measures the tax on marijuana designed to restrict traffic to legitimate channels and the registration fee on wagering intended to help states control criminal action beyond the direct reach of the power of Congress.

Prohibition against export taxes. The constitutional provision forbidding Congress to levy an export duty is clear and precise. Complicating its application, however, is the difficulty of determining which taxes are export duties and which are not. A tax specifically levied on the business of exporting or on commodities exported or made or held for export would come under the prohibition. But the federal courts have further held that a tax which bears "directly and closely" on the "process of exporting" is in substance an export duty. Under this construction, a tax on the bills of lading of exported articles, a tax on marine insurance policies covering exported articles, and an excise tax on sporting goods sold to foreign customers have all been held unconstitutional. An income tax applying to net income derived from an export business does not come under the prohibition.

Limitation on levy of direct taxes. According to the Constitution, "no capitation, or other direct, tax shall be laid, unless it shall be apportioned among the several states which shall be included within this union according to their respective numbers." This provision clearly applies to the levy of a poll tax or a property tax by the federal government. On the basis of the population count, were the federal government to impose a billion dollar real estate tax, approximately $95 million would have to be apportioned to New York, approximately $10 million to Arkansas. New York, which has a high per capita average for property values, need impose only a three mill levy to collect its quota. Arkansas, much poorer in property values per capita, would have to impose a levy of more than ten mills. The unfairness of such distribution of a federal tax is patent. From a practical point of view then, the clause outlaws a federal property tax and presumably a federal capital levy.

So long as a definite poll or property tax is not involved, the federal courts have been inclined to construe the term "direct tax" narrowly. The Supreme Court has said:

> While taxes levied upon or collected from persons because of their general ownership of property may be taken to be direct, this court has consistently held, almost from the foundation of the government, that a tax imposed upon a particular use of property or the exercise of a single power over property incidental to ownership, is an excise which need not be apportioned.[5]

In 1895, however, the Court held a federal income tax to be in effect a tax on the property producing the income, and thus to constitute a direct tax. On this argument the 1894 federal income tax was held unconstitutional in the famous *Pollock* v. *Farmers Loan and Trust Co.* decision because it was not apportioned among the states according to population.[6] With the ratification of the Sixteenth Amendment in 1913, eliminating the necessity of apportionment in the case of "taxes on incomes, from whatever source derived," this limitation on the levy of federal income taxes was removed. Subsequently, however, in the leading case of *Eisner* v. *Macomber,* it was decided that stock dividends were not "income," and hence did not come under the Sixteenth Amendment.[7]

[5] *Bromley* v. *McCaughn,* 280 U.S. (1929) 124.

[6] 157 U. S. (1895) 429, 158 U. S. (1895) 601.

[7] 252 U.S. (1920) 189. The tendency is to limit this restriction. A dividend of preferred stock to a common-stock holder is taxable—*Helvering* v. *Gowran,* 301 U.S. (1937) 676.

Limitation on levy of indirect taxes. The constitutional provision that "all duties, imposts and excises shall be uniform throughout the United States" has been specifically stated to require geographic uniformity only. What is more, the requirement is limited to geographic uniformity in law as contrasted to geographic uniformity in effect. A federal tax may be levied on a subject, such as tobacco manufacturing, which exists only in certain states. And exemptions and rate differences may be incorporated in a federal tax without bringing it under this limitation.

"State instrumentalities" limitation. Nowhere does the federal Constitution specifically forbid the federal government to tax state functions or state instrumentalities. Judicial implication created this prohibition in the *Knowlton* v. *Moore*[7a] decision as a corollary to the corresponding rule, also established by judicial construction in *Collector* v. *Day*,[7b] that the states could not tax the functions or instrumentalities of the federal government. According to long-established interpretation of the courts, a federal tax could not be levied upon the compensation of state and local officers and employees engaged in the exercise of essential government functions, or upon state and local bonds or the interest thereon. Sales to or by a state or local government in connection with any essential government function were also protected from federal taxation. But all salaries, payments, and receipts were subject to federal taxation where a state or local government acted in a "proprietary" capacity or where it incidentally supervised or regulated some private activity.

The Supreme Court, however, reversed itself upon the constitutionality of the application of the federal income tax to state and local salaries generally. In 1938 the Court upheld federal taxation of salaries paid by the Port of New York Authority, not on the ground that the Authority was a proprietary agency but on the position that the federal tax was nondiscriminatory. A year later, in the key *Graves* v. *O'Keefe*[8] decision, the Court faced the issue squarely, overruled *Collector* v. *Day*, and extended the federal income tax to all state and local salaries. Still undecided is the issue whether the federal income tax can be extended to the interest on state and local bonds, but by implication such extension should now be warranted. However, as long as the federal income tax statute specifically excludes such interest, a test case cannot be pressed for Supreme Court decision. In general, the *Graves* v. *O'Keefe* decision lays the foundation for general elimination of the "state instrumentalities" limitation except as a guard against discriminatory taxation directed against the independent sovereignty of the states.

"Due process of law" limitation. The federal courts have made little use of the "due process of law" clause in the Fifth Amendment as a limitation

[7a] 178 U.S. (1900) 41.
[7b] 11 Wall. (1871) 113.
[8] 306 U.S. (1939) 466.

on federal tax powers, although taxpayers have made many attempts to invoke it. This clause (which has no "equal protection" feature) stands as protection against a tax classification or discrimination so palpably arbitrary and unreasonable as to seem a confiscation of property rather than an exercise of the tax power. Retroactive application of a tax would be forbidden under this clause when, at the time of the transaction which occasioned the tax, the taxpayer could not have understood or foreseen the nature of the tax burden imposed. Compelling the inclusion of a gift made before death in the taxable estate with no opportunity for rebuttal has fallen under the ban of this provision. But income tax changes can be made retroactive, at least to the beginning of the calendar year of the change.

The Tenth Amendment. The Tenth Amendment to the Constitution reserves to the states or to the people all powers not delegated to the United States nor prohibited by it by the States. It does not, however, restrict the federal government's power to levy taxes as taxes, even though there may be incidental regulatory effects that perhaps go beyond the powers delegated to the federal government.

Provisions to check avoidance and evasion. The Supreme Court has gone far in upholding provisions that, though apparently extreme and perhaps of doubtful constitutionality if considered by themselves alone, operate to prevent tax avoidance and evasion, that is, "protect the revenue." To tax a gift made in contemplation of death as part of the estate, even though there is no transfer *at* death, is constitutional as a "permissible classification of an appropriate subject of taxation." To look beyond legal technicalities of property law to the apparent economic substance is proper and necessary; the "niceties of the art of conveyancing" must be disregarded.[9] Congress need not be bound by the law of property as defined by the various states. The growth of a person's "net worth" will be accepted, in the absence of proof to the contrary, as evidence that he received income above what may have been reported for tax purposes.

Conclusions. The Constitution clearly grants the federal government very wide taxing powers. In recent decades the Supreme Court has time and time again interpreted these powers broadly. Long-established but restrictive precedents have been overruled. New issues have been decided in the government's favor. Constitutional limits remain, of course, but it is highly improbable that they will prevent Congress from making any fundamental use of the taxing power that it is apt to desire, either to raise revenue or for regulation within a range even broader than has generally been considered permissible. As a corollary, the citizen must look to Congress itself for basic protection from arbitrary or unwise tax policy, not to the courts.

[9] *Helvering* v. *Hallock,* 309 U.S. (1940) 106; *Helvering* v. *Clifford,* 309 U.S. (1940) 331.

FEDERAL CONSTITUTIONAL LIMITATIONS ON STATE AND LOCAL TAX POWERS

Under our federal government, since the states are primary sovereign bodies they inherently possess full tax powers. The Constitution neither designates nor specifies the tax powers they may exercise. Instead, it assumes that they enjoy full taxing power and establishes certain restrictions on this power.

In all, the federal Constitution imposes ten limitations on state and local tax powers. Two are specifically stated as restrictions on the taxing power: (1) The states may not levy import or export duties, and (2) the states may not levy tonnage taxes without the consent of Congress. Five are general restrictions on state powers and apply only incidentally to tax powers: (3) Federal treaties are a part of the supreme law of the land; (4) the states may not pass laws impairing the obligation of contract; (5) the citizens of each state are entitled to all the privileges and immunities of citizens in the several states; (6) no state shall deprive any person of life, liberty, or property without due process of law; and (7) no state shall deny to any person within its jurisdiction the equal protection of the laws. The last three restrictions—(8) the states may not tax property or instrumentalities of the federal government, (9) the states may not tax interstate commerce, and (10) states and their subdivisions may not impose taxes infringing upon liberties guaranteed by the Constitution—are not to be found in any specific wording of the Constitution but are the offspring of judicial implication.

Relatively few cases have turned upon the first five or the last of these limitations. But the other four have given rise to a flood of litigation in the course of which the courts have shifted their position several times.

Prohibition against export and tonnage taxes. In all respects, the constitutional prohibition against the levy of export taxes by the states (Art. I, Sec. 10) corresponds with the similar prohibition against the federal levy of export taxes. States may not tax directly or indirectly the business of exporting or exported commodities, except where the export movement has not yet begun. A state franchise tax measured by gross income may include in the measure income from handling goods for export. If some of the income of an exporting concern is derived from intrastate operations, a general income tax may apply to its net income.

A tonnage duty is a tax upon vessels, according to their size or capacity, for the privilege of entering or leaving a port or navigating the waters of a state. A state tax of this character is strictly forbidden by the federal Constitution, but there is no limitation on the levy by states of tonnage fees, property taxes, or other taxes on vessels.

Supremacy of treaties over state tax powers. Treaties concluded by the federal government take precedence over state law. To date, few state tax problems involving treaty limitations have arisen. Should the federal government enter into a treaty with another country providing for reciprocal nondiscrimination as to taxation or property rights, that treaty would override any provisions of state tax laws to the contrary.

Prohibition against impairment of the obligation of contracts. State tax powers are affected in two ways by the provision of the Constitution that no state shall pass any law impairing the obligation of contracts.[10] Having once issued a tax-exempt bond, a state may not subsequently attempt to tax that bond under a property tax or tax the interest on the bond under an income tax. The original issue with its exemption privilege constitutes a contract which may not be abrogated by legislative action. Similar protection is accorded to any other exemption from state or local taxation of a contractual character. Furthermore, if a local government floats a bond issue under a statute requiring the levy of a tax sufficient to cover the debt service, that tax levy may not be repealed subsequently, and so long as the bond issue is outstanding the legislature may not eliminate the requirement of the tax levy.

Prohibition of discrimination against citizens of other states. According to the Constitution, the citizens of each state shall be entitled to all the privileges and immunities of citizens in the several states. States are thereby prevented from discriminating in their tax laws against citizens of other states, whether resident or nonresident. Peddlers from other states may not be taxed more heavily than resident merchants merely because of nonresidency, nor may the property of nonresidents be valued at a rate higher than that of residents, nor may a special death-tax rate place a heavier tax burden on the estates of nonresident decedents than on the estates of resident decedents. Corporations, lacking "citizenship," are not protected by this provision; the states are free to levy different and heavier taxes on foreign corporations than they levy on domestic[11] corporations.[12]

"Due process of law" limitation. One clause of the Fourteenth Amendment provides that no state shall deprive any person of his life, liberty, or property "without due process of law." In its application to taxation, many lawyers are inclined to regard this broad language as a blanket injunction against excessive exercise of state tax powers. As Judge Cooley said, "In tax cases, especially those carried to the Supreme Court of the United States, it is customary, it seems, to add to other constitutional objections,

10 This does not mean, of course, that a state is prohibited from imposing taxes which in effect make it impossible for its citizens to fulfill the terms of their private contracts.

11 A "domestic" corporation is, from the viewpoint of a taxing state, a corporation organized in that state. A "foreign" corporation is, from the viewpoint of a taxing state, a corporation organized in any other state of the United States. The term "alien corporation," used in later chapters of this volume, is reserved for corporations organized in countries other than the United States.

12 But see below with respect to cases on the "equal protection of the laws" limitation as applied to the taxation of foreign corporations.

for good measure, the contention that the tax law violates the due process of law provision."[13] This "due process of law" clause has three specific applications to state tax statutes: (1) It constitutes an injunction against the levy of a tax beyond the territorial jurisdiction of the state or local taxing government; (2) it may be interposed to check extreme or confiscatory state or local taxes; (3) it prohibits a state from utilizing any forms of assessment or review which are essentially arbitrary, unjust, or unfair or which deny the taxpayer a fair opportunity to assert his substantive rights before a proper judicial tribunal.

An injunction prohibiting a taxing government from levying a tax beyond its territorial jurisdiction assumes that the subject matter of a tax always has a determinable geographical location. But taxes are levied on all sorts of intangible elements—on acts, on privileges, on legal rights—having no physical existence, much less location. To meet this difficulty, the courts have created the legal fiction of *situs*—namely, legal location. The *situs* of the subject matter of any tax is wherever a court of competent jurisdiction says it is. And since physical laws are no bar to legal paradoxes, a taxable item may have more than one *situs*, may be legally situated in more than one tax jurisdiction, and hence may be subject to more than one tax.

A person has a taxable *situs* at his domicile. Income may have a double *situs*—in the state where it is earned or accrues and in the state of recipient's domicile. Even income derived from real property in another state may be taxed by the state of the recipient's domicile. An act or activity has a taxable *situs* wherever any essential element is performed. A legal privilege is taxable only by the state which grants it. A corporation's capital stock has a taxable *situs* in the state wherein it is organized as well as in the state of the share-owner's domicile, and so much of the capital stock as is employed in business in other states has an additional taxable *situs* in such states.

During the nineteenth century, the courts were inclined to ascribe taxable *situs* to any state or district which extended protection to, exercised control over, or could show some interest in the item taxed. Instances of multiple *situs* were common, but the prevailing localization of property interests and the states' simple tax systems made multiple taxation rare. The problem attracted little interest outside of tax circles. But as absentee ownership of property and absentee conduct of business increased, as corporate development introduced new complexities of property interests, and as the states extended the scope of their taxes, instances of burdensome multiple taxation became numerous. Protest grew widespread, and the courts turned ear to it. The turning point was the case of *Union Refrig-*

[13] T. M. Cooley, *The Law of Taxation* (Callaghan and Co., Chicago, 4th ed., 1924), Vol. I, p. 331.

erator Transit Co. v. *Kentucky*,[14] wherein the Supreme Court discarded the old fiction of *mobilia sequuntur personam*, and gave one *situs*—the state wherein it was located—to tangible personal property permanently used in business. In casual and unsystematic fashion, the Supreme Court during the next thirty years outlawed many forms of double taxation of property interest. During the 1920's and 1930's, in particular, judicial construction swept the field of death taxes clear of double taxation.

On no occasion, however, did the Court hold that the Fourteenth Amendment implicitly prohibited double *situs* and hence double taxation; in each instance, the Court itself construed the existence or nonexistence of more than one taxable *situs*. Thus, the door was held open for the Court to reinstate double taxation, if ever its views changed, without any fundamental reversal of basic principles. Such a change in the viewpoint has occurred. The Court now holds the view that where two or more states exercise substantial control over an element of property, income, or business, including the owner of the property or business, and the recipients of the income, all the states involved have a taxing power over the element in question. Thus, in 1942, common stock in an estate was held to have a tax *situs* in two states—one in the state of the decedent's domicile and one in the state where the corporation received its charter. In 1947 intangible property in trust was held to have a tax *situs* in the state in which the trustee resided, regardless of the fact that the trust itself was located, and the beneficiaries resided, in another state which would also have jurisdiction to impose property tax. The present status of tax *situs* for property interests is indicated in Table 7–1.

Further issues of territorial jurisdiction and of the application of the "due process of law" clause in the Fourteenth Amendment surround the question of when a foreign corporation is so "doing business" in a state as to be subject to its tax laws. Although the cases on this issue are confusing, some general rules have been established. Isolated acts performed by a corporation within a state do not constitute such "doing business" as to confer taxing jurisdiction upon the state. Incidental acts unconnected with the main purpose for which the corporation was organized likewise fail to confer taxing jurisdiction. Furthermore, unless a foreign corporation is organized and active as a holding company, mere ownership of property does not bring it within the jurisdiction of the taxing state.

"Due process of law" is rarely invoked in defense against *confiscatory* state or local taxes. As the Supreme Court stated, "When the power to tax exists, the extent of the burden is a matter for the discretion of the lawmakers . . . even if the tax should destroy a business, it would not be made invalid or require compensation upon that ground alone."[15] One of

[14] 199 U.S. (1905) 194.
[15] *Fox* v. *Standard Oil Co. of N.J.*, 292 U.S. (1935) 40.

TABLE 7–1

Tax "Situs" for Property Interests

Property Interest	*Domicile of Owner or Creditor*	*Domicile of Obligor or Debtor*	*Location of Property*	*Special Business Use Location*
Real property interests			X	
Tangible personalty:				
Permanent location			X	
Temporary location	X		X	
Indeterminate location	X			
Intangible personalty:				
Money	X		X	X
Bank deposits	X			X
Open book accounts	X			X
Negotiable instruments	X			X
Corporation bonds	X	X[1]		X
Corporation shares	X	X		X
Mortgages	X		X	
Trust corpus	X	Trustee	X	

[1] Except for death tax purposes.

the rare instances where the Supreme Court condemns a state or local tax as "confiscatory" occurs when a new tax, embodying some element of discrimination, applies to a binding commitment made before the new tax was imposed and when it could not have been anticipated. When a special tax peculiarly heavy upon foreign corporations was levied after a "foreign" railroad had made heavy investments in a state, the Court held the tax "confiscatory" and outlawed by the "due process" clause. Similarly, death taxes cannot be applied retroactively to dispositions of property tax-free when made. Wherever possible, however, the courts try to avoid construing a tax as retroactive.

For all taxes involving a valuation to determine the tax basis—property taxes, income taxes where an administrative body assesses the taxable income, and corporate excess taxes—the procedural protection of the "due process of law" limitation is important. There must be a formal act of assessment consisting of a description of the subject matter of the assessment, its inclusion in the tax list, and the determination of its value; furthermore, the assessment must be made a matter of record to inform the taxpayer of both the fact and the amount of his assessment. Finally, the taxpayer must be notified of the assessment, and he must have an opportunity to appear before some agency of review and present his case against the assessment, and the practical possibilities of his compliance must be considered.

"Equal protection of the laws" limitation. In the same sentence of the Fourteenth Amendment which includes the "due process of law" limitation is to be found the provision that no state shall "deny to any person within its jurisdiction the equal protection of the laws." This clause forbids arbitrary or hostile discrimination based on no reasonable distinction. The federal courts are generally loath to condemn any state or local tax law as arbitrary or hostile; if reason can possibly be found for a tax classification, it will usually be upheld. But many inconsistent decisions stand on the books. Discriminations which have been held to invalidate state or local taxes are: a gross-receipts tax on taxicabs operated by corporations with no corresponding tax on taxicabs privately operated; a provision that a gift made less than six years prior to a donor's death should be presumed conclusively to have been made in contemplation of death and hence be subject to a death tax; intentional and systematic overassessment of a parcel of property as compared with surrounding properties; impositions on foreign corporations in excess of taxes levied on comparable domestic corporations; chain-store taxes discriminating between intracounty and intercounty chains or levied in the form of a gross income tax; and a higher license fee on nonresident than on resident fishermen. Examples of alleged discriminations held not to be objectionable are: a tax on the distributing house of a group of chain stores which does not apply to the depots maintained by large department stores; a progressive tax on a series of stores owned by one individual, claimed to be aimed directly at chain stores; motor vehicle license charges higher on public carriers than on private carriers; exemption from an electric power tax of private power plants and power used for irrigation pumping; taxation of "other moneyed capital" at a lower rate than state bank shares; a tax on residents' deposits in out-of-state banks five times higher than on their deposits in local banks; and heavier assessment ratios on railroad property than on other property.

"Federal instrumentalities" limitation. Judicial construction rather than the federal Constitution forbids the state to tax federal agencies or instrumentalities. In *McCulloch* v. *Maryland,* Chief Justice Marshall argued:

> That the power to tax involves the power to destroy; that the power to destroy may defeat and render useless the power to create; that there is a plain repugnance, in conferring on one government a power to control the constitutional measures of another, which other, with respect to those very measures, is declared to be the supreme power over that which exercises the control, are propositions not to be denied. . . . The states have no power, by taxation or otherwise, to retard, impede, burden, or in any manner control, the operations of the constitutional laws enacted by Congress to carry into execution the powers vested in the general government.[16]

[16] 4 Wheat. (1819) 431, 436. In 1928, however, the Court said, "The power to tax is not the power to destroy while this Court sits"—*Panhandle Oil Co.* v. *Knox,* 277 U.S. (1928) 218.

Marshall's comments of 1819 expressed a proposition of constitutional law that still sets limits to state and local tax powers. Unless Congress specifically authorizes the application, a state or local tax, no matter how reasonable or nondiscriminatory it may be, is invalid to the extent that it applies to federal property, federal agents, or federal instrumentalities.

But though the doctrine is established, there remains in issue the construction to be placed upon the concept of "federal instrumentalities." For a long while the courts steadily widened this concept, hampering state and local tax powers at an irritating number of points. Recently, however, the Supreme Court has considerably narrowed its construction of "federal instrumentalities." State tax laws do not apply within federal military posts and reservations. Since the Indians are the wards of the federal government, their properties are free of state taxes.[17] States may not tax federal bonds, nor may the interest on such bonds be brought under a state income tax.[18] States may tax the federal government's contractual payments to outside individuals or organizations, or subject to state sales tax any items purchased by a contractor for sale to the federal government on a "cost plus" basis contract. Moreover, three 1958 decisions uphold state-local taxation of real and personal property owned by the federal government but being used by private firms in carrying out contracts with the United States. However, states cannot apply taxes to the Atomic Energy Commission's management of a town (like Oak Ridge) owned by the federal government. Prior to 1939, federal salaries could not be subjected to state income taxes, but in that year two Supreme Court decisions and the federal Public Salary Tax Act fully cleared the way for this tax element. National banks are federal instrumentalities, and the states may tax them only within the limits prescribed by federal statute.

In spite of the recent more liberal interpretations of the "federal instrumentalities" limitation, it continues to be an awkward restriction on state and local tax powers, productive of inequitable discriminations and loopholes for evasion. Most economists hold that the prohibition should be against *discriminatory* taxation of federal instrumentalities, not against *all* state and local taxation. A simple federal statute giving consent to nondiscriminatory taxation of federal agencies and instrumentalities could in all probability accomplish such reform. Congress did this very thing in connection with state and local taxation of national banks and federal employees. Possibly, such a statute might contain a reciprocal clause—permission to tax federal instrumentalities would be extended to all states

[17] Earnings derived from leases on Indian land were long held to be beyond state taxing power, but in line with its policy of limiting the federal and state instrumentalities restrictions, the Supreme Court overruled its earlier decisions and made such income taxable. In the absence of specific Congressional exemption, property held in trust by the federal government for Indians may be subject to state death tax.

[18] But a corporation franchise tax may include interest on federal bonds in its measure if no purposed discrimination is involved.

that granted the federal government corresponding permission with respect to state instrumentalities. By this expedient, the way would be paved for removal of an awkward impediment to uniform federal and state taxation.

Interstate and foreign commerce limitations. State governments are constitutionally forbidden to levy import, export, or tonnage duties. But state taxation of interstate or foreign commerce is not otherwise explicitly prohibited. From the doctrine of the division of federal and state powers, however, the federal courts have implied extensive limitations upon state powers to tax foreign and interstate commerce. For a long while judicial construction expanded the scope of these implied limitations. Then the Court began to relax somewhat the severity of many earlier rulings. Nevertheless, its position is still not entirely clear.

As the law now stands, any state or local tax which *directly or indirectly effects a discrimination* against interstate or foreign commerce as a business[19] or against goods brought in from another state or country,[20] is unconstitutional. Furthermore, there are limitations to the application even of nondiscriminating uniform taxes to interstate business and to property used in interstate commerce. Commodities in interstate commerce not yet arrived at their final destination, and commodities in foreign commerce unsold by the importer or still in their original packages, may not be taxed by the states. Once such goods have come "to rest," even temporarily, at any stage in the distributive process, or any time after a sale within the state has been consummated, they may be taxed. Goods bought by a consumer from a seller in another state, and held or stored for use, are subject to state taxation.[21]

A state may not tax the gross receipts of an individual or a corporation when a portion of such receipts are derived from interstate sales or other interstate business activities, according to earlier cases.[22] Such gross-receipts taxes are permissible when they include provision for allocation so that double taxation of interstate business cannot occur. However, a tax on gross receipts or measured by gross receipts is invalid if it burdens or interferes with interstate commerce without necessarily discriminating against it.[23] Unless net income is derived exclusively from interstate activity, it is held to be too far removed from interstate business activity for a state income tax thereon to constitute a burden on interstate or foreign

[19] A recent decision invalidated a local license tax which in fact discriminated against out-of-state wholesalers. Also prohibited is a tax on out-of-state businesses for the privilege of soliciting business in the state.

[20] Under the Twenty-First Amendment, this restriction does not apply to state liquor taxes.

[21] But a sales tax, as distinguished from a use tax, does not apply if the sale is made outside the state.

[22] An exception is made when the gross receipts tax is in lieu of a property tax.

[23] But a state may impose nondiscriminatory taxes on vehicles engaged exclusively in interstate commerce.

commerce. Intrastate business activities of foreign corporations may be taxed on the basis of allocated income or capital stock. Even if the corporation is engaged in interstate commerce exclusively, the Court held in 1959, net profit, reasonably allocated, may be taxed by a state in which the firm sells. A divided Court upheld a franchise tax on a pipeline company doing only an interstate business; the tax was justified as compensating the state for protecting such necessary local activities as keeping the pipeline in repair; the tax was measured by the value of the capital employed in the state but was not in lieu of property tax.

The shifting attitude of the Court has created annoying uncertainty.[24] In 1959, however, the Court swept away more of the remaining commerce-clause restraints on state taxing power. Only time will reveal what restrictions remain in fact.

Freedom of religion, speech, and the press. The Supreme Court has faced the issue of whether a state or any of its subdivisions may impose a charge —tax or fee—for the enjoyment of a right granted by the federal Constitution. A unanimous Court in 1936 held invalid a Louisiana license tax on the privilege of selling advertising space by newspapers with circulation over 20,000 as a restriction on freedom of the press as well as a violation of due process. In a series of cases involving Jehovah's Witnesses, a divided court held that local license taxes on the sale of literature, even though nondiscriminatory, could not be applied to sellers of religious books and tracts. Such a tax was held to infringe the constitutionally guaranteed freedoms of religion, speech, and the press.

STATE CONSTITUTIONAL LIMITATIONS ON STATE AND LOCAL TAX POWERS[25]

When state and local governments enact tax laws they must consider not only federal but state constitutional limitations. A very few states impose no constitutional restrictions on state or local taxing power, allowing the legislature full discretion in the enactment of tax statutes. At the other extreme there are a few, such as Arkansas and Louisiana, which impose extreme restrictions, limiting very narrowly the power of the legislature and of local governments. The variety of limiting provisions is so great that only a listing of some of the more typical forms is possible here.

Types of limitations. One common set of limits applies to the way tax laws are enacted and to the general use of the taxing power. For example, constitutions often require that taxes be levied only by general laws and

[24] A leading tax attorney discusses the situation as it stood in 1958 in J. R. Hellerstein, "Recent Developments in Commerce Clause Limitations on State Taxation," *Tax Executive*, Jan., 1958, pp. 117–140.

[25] See G. D. Morrow, "State Constitutional Limitations on the Taxing Authority of State Legislatures," *Nat. Tax Journal*, June, 1956, pp. 126–133.

for public purposes; that no taxes be imposed for corporate, religious, or other special interest groups, with railroads and utilities sometimes singled out; that the taxing power cannot be relinquished or contracted away. Several constitutions specify that revenue bills must originate in the lower house and receive a prescribed proportion of votes. Initiative and referendum provisions are prescribed in some cases.

Most states have some form of "equality and uniformity" provision.

Limitations on the rates of one or more taxes appear in over half the state constitutions. The most common apply to property taxes, but income and excise tax rate limits can also be found. Some types of taxes are specifically forbidden—poll taxes and personal income taxes, for example. There are many provisions governing the kind of tax that may be imposed, especially the exemptions under the property tax, but also sometimes details of income taxes or of a tax that is in lieu of some other. Some constitutions make certain taxes mandatory or require, more generally, that taxes must be imposed for the support of state government, debt service, and schools.

Tax earmarking is now found in the majority of constitutions. In Michigan and Colorado most revenue, in fact, is earmarked for one or another purpose—highways, old-age pensions, schools, localities, debt service. Constitutions often spell out exemption provisions, mandates governing the manner of tax administration, and the taxing authority to be given localities.

Evaluation. Most of these provisions are strikingly different from the kind found in the federal Constitution. The justifications advanced for the various state limitations are, of course, widely varied. Some rest upon reasonable interpretations of lessons to be learned from history—the desirability of restraint upon use of the taxing power, for example. Very many more, however, are the result of conditions and attitudes that were essentially temporary, or at least far less likely to be permanent than is a constitution. Without question, most state constitutions contain altogether too much detail on tax matters.

Thoughtful men may differ on just exactly what kind of provisions belong in written constitutions and what should be left to statutes and judicial interpretation. But the preponderance of opinion would agree that a constitution is *no* place to embody details about the kind of tax structure to be developed, nor the rates to be imposed, nor the uses of particular funds. Conditions change so much that the best arrangement at one time can be utterly obsolete a generation later. Changes in economic structure, the level of prices, the taxes imposed by the federal government or neighboring states, the administrative capacity of states, the role of local government, and the use of tax funds are some of the developments which have already made well-meant decisions of our fathers—and the successes of narrow pressure groups—needless burdens today.

PROBLEMS

1. Indicate the provisions regarding federal taxation which you believe should be in the Constitution. Give reasons. What, if any, of the existing provisions seem undesirable? Why?

2. Do the same as in Problem 1 for provisions in the federal Constitution bearing upon state taxation.

3. Compare the tax provisions in the constitution of your state with those in the constitution of some other state.

4. "The Constitution deprives Congress of no taxing power it should really wish to use." Discuss.

5. "Both the 'due process' and the 'interstate commerce' limitations on state taxing power give the courts excessive influence, for it is the courts which finally decide, not the people or their representatives." Discuss.

6. Select five of the provisions in the federal Constitution limiting taxing power and discuss what appears to be their economic significance.

7. "We must protect our children by inserting in our state constitution provisions which will prevent future legislatures from voting high or unfair taxes." Examine the reasons for and against this statement, assuming that you are writing in 1933. Indicate the type of limits that might get substantial support and then try to imagine the results in 1960 of the existence of such limits.

8. In what sense can the police power be used to impose taxes?

CHAPTER 8

Shifting and Incidence of Taxes

IT is common knowledge that when a government collects a gasoline tax of four cents a gallon from motor-fuel wholesalers, it is not these distributors who bear the burden. They charge the tax to the service stations, and these in turn pass it on to the motorist. Very likely, the gasoline pump bears a notice which states the net price of gasoline per gallon, the tax to be added, and the total price that the motorist must pay.

We take it for granted that a cigarette tax and a liquor tax are passed on to consumers, though there may be some question as to whether the ultimate price of the taxed items rises by exactly the amount of the tax, by more, or by less. But what, if any, are the effects on prices of property taxes, of personal income taxes, of taxes on business earnings, of the federal tariff, of an inheritance tax? To what extent can these taxes be shifted by the original payers to others in the economy, thus transferring tax burdens from those who pay the collector to persons who have no direct contact with tax administration? To what extent do these taxes add to the costs of the original payers, yet permit no corresponding expansion of gross income through price adjustments, so that the original payers find their net income reduced?

In short, who ultimately bears the burden of the various taxes imposed by the federal, state, and local governments?

This question has challenged the keenest thought of economists. Multiplied taxes and rising tax rates, which make tax burdens ever heavier, create need for unbiased thinking. Although there may be wide confusion in the popular mind on how taxes may be shifted and whom they ultimately burden, economists are in substantial agreement on important broad, basic principles, though not on all details.[1]

[1] The major remaining controversies turn rather on the conditions assumed than on the economic reasoning involved. Perhaps the best example will be found in E. R. Rolph, *Theory of Fiscal Economics* (University of California Press, Berkeley, 1954), where rigorous analysis, but based on restrictive assumptions, leads to the general

Two new terms require definition. *Shifting*[2] a tax means the transfer of its burden by the original payer to someone else. The prices of the goods or services sold by the original payer may increase by the amount of the tax, thus shifting it *forward* to consumers. Or the prices paid for purchases —the prices of raw materials, the rent of land and buildings, the interest on borrowings, the wages of employees—may be reduced, thus shifting the tax *backward* to the producers of raw materials, to the landlord, to the creditor, or to the employees.

Incidence is the ultimate resting of a tax upon some individuals or class who cannot shift it further. A tax may possibly be shifted but once from the original taxpayers, in which case the incidence is upon the group who have received the transferred burden. Or the process of shifting may proceed through a long chain of economic relationships, with fractions of the tax clinging along the chain until there is no immediate connection between the original taxpayers and those who collectively bear the tax; in this case the incidence of the tax has become diffused.

A third concept is also important: the *effect* of a tax—that is, the consequences that follow from its imposition and shifting. For many problems it is not enough to know who ultimately pays a tax. It is also necessary to know what happens as a result of the tax—how it influences individual and group action during the shifting and after the tax comes to rest.

BASIC FACTORS IN TAX SHIFTING[3]

Whether a tax can be substantially shifted depends on (1) the nature of the tax, (2) the economic environment under which it is levied,[4] and (3)

---

conclusion that taxes are shifted backward to a far greater extent than most economists believe. R. A. Musgrave prefers to treat incidence by comparing the substitution of one tax for another and examining the results; "On Incidence," *Journal of Political Economy*, Aug., 1953, pp. 306–323. For an interesting study of a particular industry, see R. P. Collier, "Some Empirical Evidence of Tax Incidence," *National Tax Journal*, Mar., 1958, pp. 35–55.

[2] In some discussions "escape," "evasion," and "avoidance" are used as synonyms for "shifting." Each of these terms, however, has a distinctly different meaning and is used with such meaning elsewhere in our study. The term "impact" is used to indicate the point at which the tax originally falls or is imposed.

[3] The analysis in this chapter ignores the effect of the deductibility of one tax that is sometimes allowed in computing another tax, a factor that is occasionally of considerable significance. The question of what types of taxes can be shifted is often begged, and the issue confused, by use of the terms "direct tax" and "indirect tax." These terms were first developed by the Physiocrats–"direct" for nonshifted taxes, "indirect" for shifted levies. Adam Smith used them loosely according to distinctions in assessment methods–"direct" for taxes assessed according to income or property, "indirect" for taxes assessed in proportion to expenditures. Subsequent writers have twisted and turned the words to a confusing variety of meanings. Some authors consider "direct taxes" the periodic taxes on persons or property, and "indirect taxes" the nonrepeated impositions on commodities. Other writers have used the terms to distinguish between taxes on objects as against taxes on events, between taxes on possession as against taxes

the taxpayers' practices in taking advantage of any possibility of shifting. The relation of the first two factors to the problem of tax shifting constitutes the subject matter of this chapter. As to the third factor, one can say (a) that there will be enough scattered cases in which the taxpayer will not take full advantage of his ability to shift a tax to yield puzzling examples of exceptions, but (b) that fundamental economic pressures are strong enough to keep the exceptions small and temporary relative to the situation as a whole.

Any specific conclusion about tax shifting rests upon many assumptions that are generally not made explicit. Assumptions about the extent to which resources are being utilized, monetary conditions, the nature of the industries involved, custom and the legal system, and the expected permanency of the tax are some of the many possible examples. The analysis that follows, which generally assumes full employment and stable monetary conditions, contains some illustrations of the effects of changing particular assumptions. Hundreds of other illustrations could be cited. Yet few would be of more than minor importance. However, in analyzing any practical problem, the student must take great care in making his assumptions. Some that are given little attention here may be crucial in specific situations.

Two generalizations on the relation between the nature of a tax and the possibility of shifting it may be stated at the start:

1. A tax cannot be shifted when it is purely personal—when, like a general poll tax or an inheritance tax, it has *no* relation to any business dealings of the taxpayers. This is so because taxes can be shifted only through business relations, through the prices (including wages and rents) charged for goods and services.[5] These price changes are in turn determined by changes in market conditions (demand or supply of the commodity or service involved). And a personal tax cannot determine market conditions, since it is not part of any business relationship. Once the person liable has paid the tax, of course, his economic behavior is affected; others may suffer or benefit, but this takes us beyond the realm of shifting to that of economic effects.

---

on consumption, between taxes on production as against taxes on consumption, between taxes on income as against taxes on expenditure. American law uses the two terms in a special sense divorced from all economic considerations. Such confused and contradictory usage has robbed the terms "direct" and "indirect" of any value they might possibly have had in fiscal economics. Accordingly, they are not employed in this study.

[4] A special case under this heading occurs where an earmarked tax is spent for a purpose that affects the basis of the tax. Thus the building of motor highways with revenues derived from gasoline taxation increases the demand for gasoline and affects its price over and above the price effect of the shifting of the tax. Such a situation is rare, and no further analysis is given to it.

[5] Shifting within the family and charity present cases which are in a sense exceptions. If my income tax rises, for example, I may cut down my philanthropies or my help to members of my family. What I do in such a situation is not what is ordinarily termed shifting the tax.

2. A tax upon "economic surplus" cannot be shifted. "Economic surplus" may be defined as "that part of a payment or accretion of purchasing power which is not necessary either to maintain the service of a factor of production, or to its necessary or desirable increase." Included in this concept are net economic rent, net profits above normal interest and "necessary" payment for risk, and such windfall receipts as inheritances, gambling gains, and some capital gains. Net economic rent and net profit above the allowance for normal and necessary interest and risk do not determine prices or costs, but are determined by them. Inheritances and gambling gains have nothing to do with business procedure. Hence, a tax confined to these elements cannot work itself either forward or backward into prices or costs.[6]

INCIDENCE OF SPECIAL COMMODITY TAXES[7]

Taxes on products and services are now common in this country. They are widely varied, of course. A few are heavy enough to present problems of shifting and incidence that are of practical significance.

A special commodity tax—one upon a particular commodity or class of commodities such as gasoline—may be imposed upon the manufacturers or some class of distributors of the commodity. In the price and cost adjustments that result from the imposition of the tax, the burden may be borne by the enterprises that initially pay the tax; or it may be shifted forward to distributing enterprises and to consumers; or it may be shifted backward to labor employed by the taxpaying enterprises or to the suppliers of materials and services used by them; or the price and cost adjustment may involve a combination of these various shifts of tax burden. Initial adjustments may differ from long-term adjustments.

Tax imposed upon producers—competitive conditions. A commodity tax, at a flat amount per unit, or one proportional to price, is in effect an added cost of production. Under purely competitive conditions, no single competing producer can raise his prices above the established market price in order to compensate for the tax. Therefore the tax must be absorbed initially by the producers. Obviously, then, the profit from inframarginal output (all output with unit costs *below* those of the marginal output) is reduced by the tax; the "normal" profit of marginal output is either reduced to a subnormal level or converted to loss.

Producers can minimize the resulting profit reduction or loss by reducing

[6] Two important qualifications should be noted: (1) In practice, the part of such a receipt that is true economic surplus will be extremely difficult to isolate, and (2) for the economy as a whole, the total of such surpluses is probably small.

[7] For an excellent study, see J. F. Due, *Theory of Incidence of Sales Taxation* (Columbia University Press, New York, 1942).

output;[8] high cost elements of their production that prior to the tax had yielded only a "normal" profit are discontinued. Furthermore, some producers, sooner or later, will discontinue production entirely, at least with respect to the taxed commodity. Thus, the output of the taxed commodity declines. Whether this reduction occurs soon after the imposition of the tax or is laggard depends, among other things, on whether the plant, equipment, materials, and personnel used for its production can be readily retired or shifted to other fields of production.

Reduction of output leads to upward pressure on the market price.[9] A smaller quantity of the commodity flows to meet a demand which we assume is unchanged. The price is accordingly bid up to a point where it eventually provides a "normal" profit to the productive capacity that is now marginal. The decline in production then ceases. If the demand for the commodity is relatively inelastic, the price rises, perhaps considerably, with but slight reduction in output. If the demand schedule is relatively elastic, the cutback in production is proportionately greater than the price rise. The supply of labor and of materials used in production of a taxed

[8] The diagram below illustrates the reaction of a competitive producer to imposition of a special commodity tax:

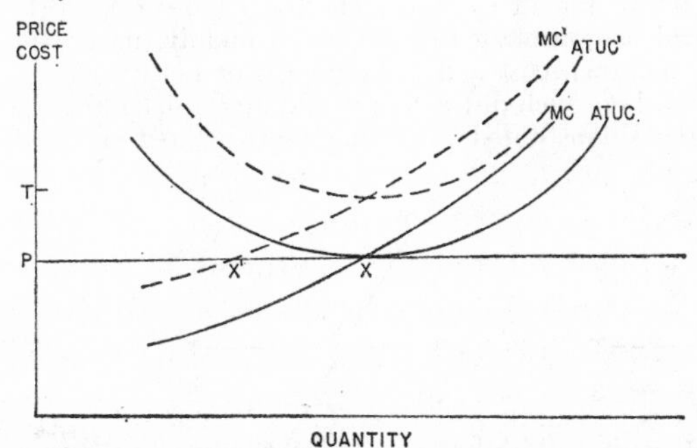

Prior to imposition of the tax, the producer has achieved equilibrium. His marginal cost schedule, MC, and his average total-unit-cost schedule, ATUC, coincide at point X on the competitive-market price schedule, P. Accordingly, he sells quantity X at price P, just covering all costs, including a normal return on his investment.

An excise tax of PT per unit is imposed. The producer's marginal and average total-unit-cost schedules rise correspondingly. ATUC′ is his new average total-unit-cost schedule and MC′ his new marginal cost schedule. Since, under competitive price theory, this producer cannot raise his selling price above the market price, P, he must accept a loss. He can minimize his loss by eliminating output X—X′, for which marginal cost, including tax, is higher than P. At output X′, the cost of the marginal units, including tax, is just covered by competitive market price, P.

The discussion of the process is sometimes in terms of "marginal producers" who enter or leave the industry. Nevertheless, it is both more accurate formally and more realistic to think in terms of the addition or subtraction of productive capacity at the margin, changes which will be made by producers who remain in business.

[9] The drop in demand for productive factors will not in fact be matched exactly as to types of materials, plant, and labor by the government spending of the tax proceeds. Therefore, as indicated later, one must expect in the short run some backward shifting of tax to owners of productive capacity which cannot transfer readily to other uses.

commodity is likely to be relatively more inelastic in the short run than in the long run. Therefore, a special commodity tax tends to be more susceptible to backward shifting in the short run than in the long run.

How will the price rise compare with the size of the tax rise?

If the taxed commodity was produced at *constant* cost,[10] relative elasticity of demand would be the exclusive determinant of the long-term reaction of price and output to the imposition of the tax. In the case of commodities produced at *increasing* cost, the cutback of production would lop off a higher-cost output. The new equilibrium price would therefore be somewhat lower than the original price plus the tax; the resulting reduction of the number of units sold would of course be somewhat less than if the price had to rise by the full amount of the tax. If the commodity was produced at *decreasing* cost (not consistent with the conditions of pure competition), the smaller output would have to be sold at a price higher than the original price plus the tax, in order to cover costs, because the unit costs of production are higher with the smaller output.[11]

[10] That is, the cost of production per unit was constant for all amounts of the commodity within the range of the decrease in volume resulting from the addition of the tax to the original price. Throughout, unless noted to the contrary, cost as used here includes normal return for all capital, including payment for risk and opportunities sacrificed. To avoid complicating the discussion unduly, no attempt is made to distinguish between marginal cost and average cost or between long-run and short-run cost at every point where such distinction would be formally appropriate.

[11] The three propositions stated above may be illustrated by the following diagrams:

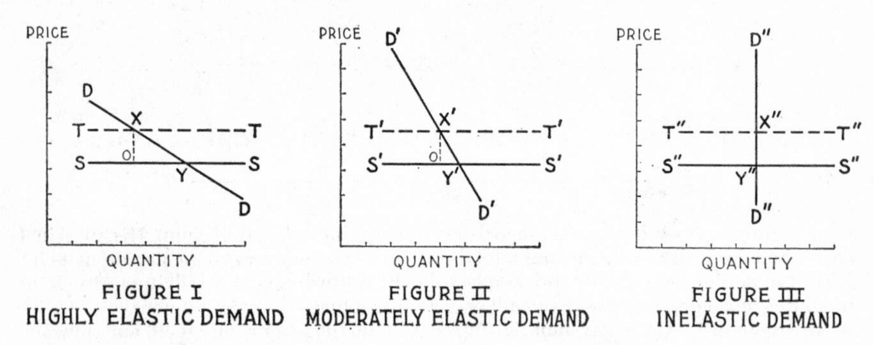

FIGURE I
HIGHLY ELASTIC DEMAND

FIGURE II
MODERATELY ELASTIC DEMAND

FIGURE III
INELASTIC DEMAND

Without being precisely accurate, we can say that demand for the commodity represented in Figure I, indicated by the line DD, is elastic—as the price per unit falls, purchases increase rapidly. Demand for the commodity represented in Figure II has some elasticity, but not so much as in the preceding case. In Figure III, demand for the commodity represented is absolutely inelastic—line D″D″ is vertical and no change in unit price can cause purchases of the commodity to increase or decrease in amount.

Lines SS, S′S′, and S″S″ represent the original supply conditions of the three commodities before the imposition of the tax. The amount of each commodity purchased at these original supply prices is indicated by the points Y, Y′, and Y″. Lines TT, T′T′, and T″T″ represent the prices which must be paid, after imposition of the tax, to provide "normal" profit to the new marginal producers of the commodities. The amount of each commodity purchased at the increased price is indicated by the points X, X′, and X″.

The cutback of output results in reduction of demand for the materials, labor, and other factors that enter production of the taxed commodity. According to the relative elasticities of supply and demand of each of these production factors, their prices tend to be reduced. This tendency may be viewed as a special aspect of a cost decline in an increasing-cost production. We probably do better, however, to consider it a backward shifting of part of the commodity tax.

Thus when a producer of some specially taxed commodity says, "Of course I add the tax to my price," he is aware of only one element of the incidence of the tax. He is neglecting the repercussions of the tax on

---

The horizontal distances *O*Y and *O′*Y′ indicate the reductions of purchases which result in the first two cases from the addition of the tax to the original price. Note that the horizontal distance *O*Y is greatest in Figure I, which represents a commodity with a highly elastic demand. In Figure III, representing a commodity with an absolutely inelastic demand, there is no horizontal difference whatsoever between X″ and Y″.

The effect upon the cost of production and price of a commodity of imposing a special tax on such commodity, assuming elastic demand for the commodity and production at constant cost, at increasing cost, and at decreasing cost, may be illustrated as follows:

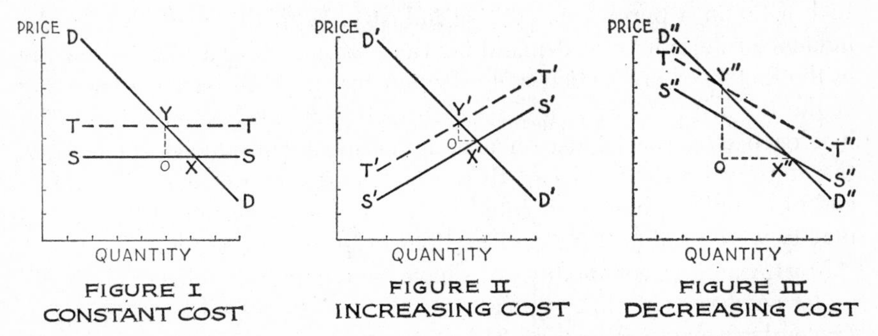

FIGURE I CONSTANT COST FIGURE II INCREASING COST FIGURE III DECREASING COST

The slanting lines DD, D′D′, and D″D″ represent elastic demand for a commodity in the range of the adjustment.

In Figure I, the supply of the taxed commodity is produced at constant cost (line SS, representing the series of original supply prices for all amounts of the commodity, is horizontal), and purchases and supply balance at price X. The addition of the tax to the series of original supply prices for all amounts (line TT being higher than line SS by the amount of the tax) results in a decrease of purchases equal to *O*X, but the vertical difference *O*Y between points Y and X is exactly the vertical difference between lines SS and TT—the new price is higher by exactly the amount of the tax.

In Figure II, the supply of the taxed commodity is produced at increasing cost (line S′S′, representing the series of original supply prices for all amounts of the commodity, slants upward to the right), and purchases and supply balance at price X′. As in the preceding case, the addition of the tax to the series of original supply prices results in reduced purchases. Because of the slant of the lines S′S′ and T′T′, the vertical distance *O′*Y′ between points X′ and Y′ is less than the vertical distance between lines S′S′ and T′T′—the new price is higher by less than the amount of the tax.

In Figure III, where line S″S″ represents the series of original supply prices of a commodity produced at decreasing cost (the slant of line S″S″ is downward to the right), the contrary slant of lines S″S″ and T″T″ causes the vertical distance *O″*Y″ between points X″ and Y″ to be greater than the vertical distance between lines S″S″ and T″T″—the new price is higher by more than the amount of the tax.

quantity demanded, output, and costs of production and distribution. The incidence of a special tax on a competitively produced commodity is not in one direction, but in several—including, possibly, reduced profit (or induced loss) for the producing firms, a higher price for consumers, lower materials prices paid to the suppliers of the industry, and in the form of lower wages for labor. In what proportions these four principal groups, and perhaps others, will share the burden of the tax will depend upon the relative elasticity or inelasticity of their supply and demand.

Tax imposed upon producers—monopoly, oligopoly, and monopolistic competition. To analyze the other extreme—monopoly—we postulate that a producer so circumstanced sells his output at a price which yields a maximum over-all profit. The monopolist has absolute control over his product so that, if a special tax is imposed upon it, he can immediately adjust the price and output to accommodate his changed cost circumstances.

Assuming that a monopolist was previously charging optimum price, the best price increase that he could make in adjusting to a special commodity tax would be somewhat less than would result from imposition of such a tax in a purely competitive industry. With this qualification, the influence of elasticity of demand for the product and elasticity of supply of the factors of production will influence forward and backward shifting of the tax as in the case of a competitively produced commodity.[12] The incidence of a special tax on a monopolistically produced commodity, therefore, is on the producer, the consumers, the producer's labor force, and his suppliers, but to a greater extent on the producer than if the commodity were produced under conditions of pure competition.

Most American commodity taxes have been imposed on items produced under conditions of oligopoly (a few sellers) or monopolistic competition (several sellers of products which, although not identical, are close substitutes). In such cases the producers commonly have considerable control over the prices of their products. Where the group is small and all face the same tax, they can in fact act as a unit without a formal agreement that would violate antitrust laws. They have the power to raise their selling prices immediately upon imposition of a tax, and as a rule they do so. They are less capable than a single monopolistic producer of accurately judging optimum prices, however, and they may react by increasing their prices by the full amount of the tax. The resulting prices tend to be higher than

[12] The diagram on page 161 illustrates the reaction of a monopoly producer to imposition of a special commodity tax.

Prior to imposition of the tax, the producer has achieved optimum volume and pricing. He has set his volume at X, at which output his marginal revenue, MR, and marginal cost, MC, schedules coincide. On the basis of the demand schedule for his commodity, D(AR), the monopoly producer sets his price at P. At this price, the market just absorbs volume X of the product. The producer's unit cost is C, determined by production of X units at the average total-unit-cost schedule, ATUC. His unit monopoly profit is CP, and his total monopoly profit is the rectangle CCPP.

the optimum or most profitable prices; the volume of sales will fall below the total that is best for all producers combined. A process of trial-and-error adjustment is likely to result, with the ultimate solution far from certain. If there are few producers, the final result may closely resemble that under monopoly, with the producers absorbing more than a nominal amount of the tax. If there are numerous producers, the tax, as under pure competition, will tend eventually to be shifted for the most part forward to consumers.

Special circumstances of demand and supply affecting incidence. Two distinct commodities may be so nearly identical that from the point of view of consumers they are very close competitors—for example oleomargarine and butter, and domestic goods which compete with imported goods. So long as the prices of the two commodities are approximately the same or bear a reasonable relation to quality differences, both commodities will maintain their positions on the market. If a tax is levied on one of these commodities and the sellers seek to add the tax to the price, consumer demand will shift from the taxed to the untaxed commodity.

What effect this shift of purchases will have on the prices of the two *competing* commodities will depend upon the character of their supply. Where both are produced at constant or decreasing cost, the taxed commodity will be driven completely off the market unless it succeeds in

A tax, T, is imposed and the producer's marginal cost schedule is raised to MC′ and his average total-unit-cost schedule to ATUC′. MC′ and MR coincide at volume X′ instead of at volume X. ATUC′ establishes that volume X′ must be produced at C′ unit cost, higher than D by the amount of the tax. The optimum price for this smaller volume

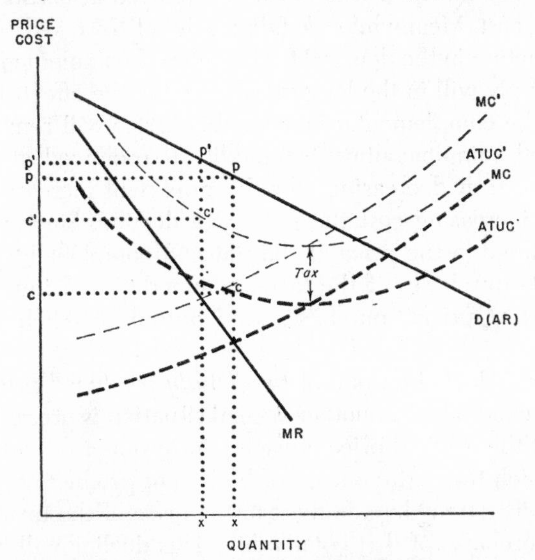

of production, according to D(AR), is P′—only slightly higher than P. The producer's new total monopoly profit—rectangle C′C′P′P′—is considerably less than his former total monopoly profit—the rectangle CCPP.

tapping a specialty demand, since it can never regain price equality with the other. If the two commodities are produced at constant cost, the untaxed commodity will take over its rival's market without any change in price. In the exceptional case of two commodities produced at decreasing cost, the untaxed commodity will be able to take over its rival's market at a lowered price.

But a tax levied on one of the competing commodities where both are produced at increasing cost will not necessarily force it altogether off the market. Although part of its market will go to its untaxed rival, the increased output will raise the cost of production and hence the price of the untaxed commodity. At the same time, the reduction in output will lower the production cost of the taxed commodity and thus the price at which it can be placed upon the market. At the point where the cost increase of the untaxed commodity and cost decrease of the taxed item together equal the amount of the tax, a new price equilibrium for the two commodities will be established, higher than the original price but not higher by the full amount of the tax. Thus a tax on one of two competing commodities produced at increasing cost is shifted to the consumers, partly through a price increase of the taxed item, partly through a related price increase in its untaxed rival.

A tax laid on one of two *complementary* commodities—items such as typewriters and typewriter ribbons whose consumption is necessarily joint—presents a second special case. Purchases of the taxed commodity will fall off in accordance with the elasticity of its demand, and the effect upon its price will depend upon whether it is produced at constant, increasing, or decreasing cost. Meanwhile the fall in sales of the taxed commodity will lead to a reduction in the demand for its untaxed complement. The circumstances of supply will in the long run determine the effect of this reduced demand for the complementary commodity. Price will remain unchanged if the untaxed complementary commodity is produced at constant cost. If it is produced at decreasing cost the price will increase. Should it be produced at increasing cost the price will decline. Since the demand is joint, any change in the price of the untaxed complementary commodity further affects purchases of the taxed commodity and involves still more readjustments of prices, purchases, and output to reach a new market equilibrium.

When a tax is levied on one of two *jointly produced* products, such as gasoline and residual oils, another special situation is presented. It may be assumed that the original price of each joint product has adjusted itself to a point at which the entire output of both joint products is consumed. An attempt to shift the tax by adding it to the price of the taxed product will reduce the purchases of that commodity. This decline will in turn cause a reduction in the outputs of both the taxed commodity and its untaxed joint product. Such a reduction in the output of the untaxed commodity, unaccompanied by a change in demand, will give the producers the opportunity to raise the price to the point where the lower purchases at the higher price will just equal the output reduction that results from a drop in purchases of the taxed commodity. Thus a tax on one of two commodities jointly produced, besides its effect on the price of the taxed item, increases the price of the untaxed by-product, the degree of increase depending upon relative elasticities of demands and supplies of the two commodities.

Tax imposed upon distributors. If a special tax on a commodity is imposed upon some class of its distributors—the wholesalers or the retailers—the ultimate incidence is much the same as if the tax were imposed on the manufacturer or primary producer.

However, because of the practically universal system of distributor pricing by markup, even the most competitive distributors tend to react to a commodity tax as though they operated under imperfect competition. They generally add the full amount of the tax to their prices. Consumer purchases, of course, fall off in response to the increased price. The distributors pass this reduction in quantity sold back to their suppliers. The contraction of operations forced upon the producers sets in motion cost adjustments and backward shifting tendencies that eventually modify the retail price increase and redistribute the burden of the tax among consumers, suppliers, labor, and the producers themselves. The distributors who actually pay the tax also shoulder part of its burden, since their profit is reduced somewhat as a result of a drop in the quantity of the taxed commodity sold.

Tax on commodities and services used in business. Many commodity taxes fall on things purchased by businesses to use in further production. Prices of the later stage products and services rise. Federal taxes on business machines and telephone services, state taxes on purchases of equipment and insurance, raise the costs (and prices) of the output of most businesses. The end effects are widely diffused.

Special short-term factors in commodity tax incidence. The adjustment of price and output resulting from the imposition of a commodity tax is by no means frictionless. Although the general outlines of the long-run process are reasonably clear, for shorter or longer periods after the imposition of a tax many different conditions affect the results, often in ways not easily predictable.

A drop in sales resulting from an increase of retail prices to absorb a tax tends to be effected without friction and without lag. The readjustment of output, however, is not so smooth a process. Producers often find it impossible to convert their capital equipment rapidly to other lines of production. Both dealers and producers think in terms of "maintaining their markets," and they may seek means—sometimes even those contrary to their true economic advantage—to avoid losing these markets because of a reduction in purchases consequent upon a price rise following the imposition of a tax.

The time required for the shifting of productive capacity varies widely. For some firms the period of readjustment may be short. In the case of an expanding industry the growth trend may quickly take up the slack in sales and production caused by adding the tax to price. When productive activity is not readily transferable to other lines, however, readjustments of supply take a longer time, since they are accomplished by the deterioration of the equipment of the industry and the failure of new capital to enter it because profits are below normal.

Business cycle trends are also important in determining the ease and rapidity of a commodity tax shift. In a boom period, with consumer demand high, a special commodity tax can be readily shifted forward in higher prices. In fact, it may provide an excuse for a greater (pyramided) price increase. A tax imposed during a recession, on the contrary, tends to remain on the industry longer because of the difficulty of shifting productive capacity and the inability of the seller to get a higher price from consumers. Some concealed forward shifting may develop, however, in the form of a smaller price decline than would otherwise occur. Backward shifting to employees and suppliers will be easiest during recession because there are likely to be few alternative employers and buyers.

The typical firm sells more than one product and has only a general notion of the cost and demand schedule of each. If all items are not taxed alike and if overhead costs are more than nominal, the output and price adjustment of a taxed article may fall anywhere within a fairly wide range. Prices may sometimes rise quickly by more than the tax as sellers try to cover their overhead costs with a smaller volume of sales.[13] Contractual agreements or tradition may hinder shifting. The quality of the product may be changed. New techniques of production may develop to increase productivity, and the tax may keep the price from falling rather than cause it to rise. Speculative buying and selling may for a time result from a new tax rate or the anticipation of its imposition. The tax rate itself makes a difference. Rates of 75 per cent or higher as found in the British purchase tax after World War II will have results which differ in kind as well as amount from the results of, say, federal manufacturers' taxes of 10 per cent in this country. These and many other conditions reduce the certainty with which the economist can predict actual shifting in the short run.

Secondary incidence of commodity taxes. Where the elasticity of demand for a commodity is high, consumer expenditures on this commodity will be lower after the imposition of a tax than before. The purchasing power

[13] In other words, pricing on an *average cost* rather than a marginal cost basis may in fact be the seller's policy. Even though the optimum theoretical adjustment cannot be reached by average rather than marginal determination, the average method may seem the more practicable and the more popular.

thus released will be available for expenditure on other commodities and will tend to strengthen demand for them. Conversely, if the demand for a commodity is highly inelastic, the imposition of a tax will cause consumers to spend more on that commodity than formerly. Demand for other commodities will weaken.

Meanwhile, as purchases of the taxed commodity fall, the capital and equipment released from this line of production move to other, and presumably untaxed, lines. Since the influx of capital operates to increase the output of the untaxed commodities, if demand factors remain unchanged, the prices of these untaxed commodities tend to decline. But, as was noted above, depending on the relative elasticity of the demand for a taxed commodity, the imposition of a tax may either strengthen or weaken demand for other untaxed commodities. Higher demand for untaxed commodities offsets the tendency of an increased supply to lower prices; weakened demand does the opposite.

These secondary effects of a tax imposed on a particular commodity involve such varied relationships of supply and demand and operate so circuitously that they may have to be ignored in considering the practical economic effects of taxes on particular commodities.

One highly important conclusion about community welfare can be drawn here. A set of commodity taxes that changes relative prices can be presumed to reduce consumer well-being, because buyers will be induced to shift their consumption from items they wanted more intensively at the margin to others for which their desire is smaller.[14]

INCIDENCE OF A GENERAL COMMODITY TAX

A universal tax on all commodities, a comprehensive manufacturers' excise or a retail sales tax, for example, may for some purposes be considered a series of individual taxes on particular commodities. Starting with this premise, assuming that the government spends all it collects and that monetary conditions are unchanged, and applying the principles already developed, we would arrive at the conclusions that the tax would hardly reduce purchases of necessities for which demand is relatively inelastic, that purchases of seminecessities having more elastic demand schedules would fall off slightly, and that purchases of semiluxuries and certain luxuries for which demand is highly elastic might decline sharply. Final prices for many commodities would be higher than before—in some

[14] Conceivably excises might in some instances so modify the price pattern as to increase general welfare. As a rule, however, consumer well-being would be better maintained if the revenue sought were obtained through personal income taxation and consumers were left free to adjust the patterns of their consumption. See M. Friedman, "The Welfare Effects of an Income Tax and an Excise Tax," *Journal of Political Economy*, Feb., 1952, pp. 25–33.

instances by more than the amount of the tax, in others by less.[15] Taking into account the fact that the consumption of necessities outweighs the consumption of luxuries, we should conclude that a general commodity tax, while reducing the *volume* of purchases, would increase somewhat the total of consumption *expenditure* and reduce saving.

Of course, many families with small incomes normally spend all they get. A general commodity tax cannot increase their consumption expenditures; it can only reduce the volume of commodities and services they buy. In effect, it reduces their real income.

Although the line of reasoning is different, somewhat the same conclusion is reached for consumers in the middle-income range. Each individual divides his income between consumption expenditure and savings in proportions dictated by his personal tastes and his general economic status. But for many middle-income individuals, saving may be reduced less easily than consumption because of mortgage and other fixed commitments. A general commodity tax, instead of increasing the monetary amount of their consumption expenditures and so reducing their savings, is likely to reduce their commodity purchases somewhat. Of course, among the tens of millions of consumers in the middle-income range there will be every conceivable response. The long-run reactions will differ from those following closely upon the imposition of the tax. As knowledge about consumer spending accumulates, we shall become better able to judge the probable effects of mass reaction to broad-based consumption taxes. In general, however, the tax will reduce total consumption and modify its basic character.[16]

Only among the small numbers of families whose consumption expenditure is not conditioned primarily by income considerations, do we find the total of commodity purchases and its distribution relatively unaffected by a general commodity tax. On the general market, however, the expenditures of this group are completely overshadowed by the expenditures of the masses, including many highly prosperous families which spend to the limit of their income.

We may conclude that a general commodity tax will raise commodity

[15] The total effect on the price level will depend upon monetary developments. If services are not taxed, the pattern of consumption spending will probably shift to include more use of services, less of commodities.

[16] A general commodity tax reduces the value which the individual, and hence the consuming public generally, derives from money spent on consumption purchases. Money laid out for savings and investments, however, may retain its original value. Hence, such a tax will cause consumers to decrease their consumption and increase their savings until the increasing utility of the former and the decreasing utility of the latter strike a new equilibrium. Some families might increase their savings in the face of a general commodity tax, thereby reducing their commodity purchases by more than the amount of the tax and altering their consumption demand schedules even more than was indicated in the text. This effect would be particularly noticeable if the general commodity tax was of an emergency character and its duration was expected to be short; for the period of the tax there would exist incentive for the middle-income group to hold down expenditures and increase savings.

prices and reduce the total of consumer purchases. Purchases of necessities, for which demand is relatively inelastic, may be reduced but slightly. But demand for semiluxuries and luxuries will suffer doubly. A distinct change in the consumption pattern of the community may ensue. What effect this magnified falling-off of demand for luxuries will have on their prices will depend upon whether they are produced at constant, increasing, or diminishing cost. Obviously, the final results will also depend upon what the government buys with the added tax revenue, and upon over-all economic conditions at the time of the tax change.

Moreover, since some items of consumer expenditure would probably be exempt—rentals, medical services, tuition fees—there would tend to be a shift of consumer demand to such items. Their output would increase and so would their price, if increasing cost conditions prevail. And so on! The possible complexities can become very great, especially if the tax rate is high.

INCIDENCE OF PERIODIC TAXES ON DURABLE PROPERTIES[17]

Durable properties and property rights—land, buildings, machinery, furniture, mortgages, corporate and municipal securities—may be taxed periodically. Such a tax cannot, of course, be paid in kind out of the property itself. If the property produces a periodic monetary income such as rent or interest, or contributes to the earning of business profit, the tax may be paid out of this income. If the property yields its services directly to the owner without his receiving them in monetary form, as does an owner-occupied dwelling or an automobile maintained for pleasure driving, the tax must be paid out of the owner's other income.

Possibilities of shifting a periodic tax on durable property differ, depending upon: (1) whether the tax is universal on all properties or limited to a specific class of properties, (2) whether the taxed property is held for personal use or is rented or employed in some business connection, and (3) whether the property is reproducible or nonreproducible.

Incidence of a special property tax. In no way can an owner shift a special annual tax imposed on a class of property commonly held for *personal* use—on pleasure automobiles or on owner-occupied dwelling houses. His personal ownership involves no business relationship that will enable him to shift the tax forward or backward to someone else.

Even when the taxed property is *rented* to a tenant instead of being held

[17] We do not discuss periodic fixed-sum taxes such as annual license taxes on businesses. Although these are common, they are generally at low rates. They are a form of fixed cost which is independent of the firm's output. Total earnings must be large enough to cover such levies in the long run. In the short run, however, such taxes should not enter the price-output decision-making process, because they do not affect the variable costs over which the firm has control.

for personal use, the owner cannot immediately shift the tax by increasing the rental charge. Under normal circumstances this rental charge, like any other price, is established by the interaction of demand and supply of such properties in existence. Neither the demand for such properties nor their supply is immediately affected by the tax. Hence, the tax cannot immediately affect the rental charge—unless, of course, the pre-tax rent was less than the maximum the landlord could have obtained and the tax prompts him to take fuller advantage of his position.

In tracing the long-term effect of special periodic taxes on rented properties, we must distinguish between reproducible and nonreproducible properties. Included under the heading reproducible properties are buildings, machines, and all other durable items which, after they become unusable, can be replaced by identical or similar properties created by human effort. Land,[18] many other natural resources, patent rights, and historic buildings are examples of nonreproducible properties.

Let us assume that the supply of land suitable for given uses and the supply of other nonreproducible properties are fixed. A periodic tax on these properties may reduce the net rents derived from them and hence, as we shall see later, reduce their capitalized values. But no matter how long the tax lasts, it cannot alter supply nor affect demand. Barring unusual contractual relationships, the long-term effect and the immediate effect of the tax remain the same—the tax is not shifted.[19]

But if a durable property subject to renting is reproducible—office space or an apartment—a special periodic tax upon it will eventually affect the quantity provided. Since the net rental return from the property is reduced

[18] In economic treatises, land is generally considered nonreproducible, but this is not strictly true. Arable land comparable with existing parcels can be produced at the expense of cutting timber, draining swamps, irrigating arid regions, and applying fertilizer to infertile ground. Building sites comparable with existing parcels can often be created by grading or filling in uneven lots and by constructing streets and transit facilities. The distinction between land and reproducible capital properties is therefore relative rather than absolute. This consideration must be borne in mind as a qualification of the conclusions developed above. This caution is even more important if the argument is extended to other natural resources.

[19] If the theory of rents, instead of the theory of supply and demand, is used as a first premise, the same conclusion can be reached with respect to a tax on rented land. The rent chargeable for any parcel of land is determined by the excess of its productivity over marginal land. Since the value of land, speculative variations aside, is the capitalization of its annual net rental, marginal land has no value to be subjected to taxation. If the landlords of supramarginal land attempt to add their taxes to their rental charges, the resulting gross rentals will exceed the differential productivity of their parcels of land over marginal land. Tenants will desert supramarginal properties for marginal land. To win them back, the landlords must reduce rentals to their old level, absorbing the tax themselves.

Or, more briefly, the nonshiftability of a tax on rented land can be argued on the basis of the "economic surplus" doctrine. The value of a parcel of rented land is normally a capitalization of its net rental. A tax on the land, therefore, is equivalent to a tax on its rent. Net rent is an "economic surplus." A tax on "economic surplus" cannot be shifted. Hence, a tax on rented land cannot be shifted.

by the amount of the tax, it becomes less profitable than properties not subject to periodic taxation. Investment capital henceforth avoids the taxed property and seeks other, more remunerative placement. Old properties wear out and are not replaced. Or if demand for the properties in question is growing, fewer new properties are produced to meet the increased demand. Under the circumstances, bids for the properties must rise—prospective tenants must eventually offer higher rentals. At last, the increased rentals cover the tax, and the net income derived from the taxed rented properties represents a rate of return equal to that yielded by other, untaxed investments. Through the higher rental, the tax has finally been shifted by landlords to tenants.

Time allowance for this shifting process depends upon five factors: (1) the average life of the properties involved, (2) whether the current supply was all newly created or whether there was an appreciable number on the point of disappearing from the market, (3) whether demand for the properties is markedly inelastic or relatively elastic, (4) whether demand is decreasing, static, or increasing, and (5) whether some of the tax may for a time be shifted backward to specialized labor and capital. Depending upon the combination of these factors, the process of shifting periodic property taxes from landlords to tenants may take a relatively long or short interval. In a rapidly growing community, a new house tax might be shifted into rents within the space of a year. In a community which had achieved full growth and had a good supply of new houses, a house tax might not become fully embodied in rents for twenty or thirty years. The foregoing principles constitute a hypothetical norm rather than a description of the actual shifting that occurs.

When property subject to a special periodic tax is used for *business* purposes, however, all or part of the tax may be incorporated into the prices of articles or services produced through the use of a taxed property. All firms in the industry, presumably, must pay the tax. It is a cost which must be covered if productive capacity is to be preserved. Marginal plant, however, will not support higher costs and will be abandoned or not replaced. Investment will tend to shift to nontaxed properties. Prices of commodities produced by use of the taxed property will rise because of the resulting reduction of output, though not necessarily by an amount exactly covering the tax. Although "business" may write the tax checks to the government, the consumers of the firms' products shoulder the burden. The full results of the tax on commodity prices, however, will not be felt immediately because of the lag in withdrawing marginal property from production. If the analysis of the shifting of a special property tax is pushed further, it reveals that the shift of some capital to untaxed uses will reduce the yields available in such uses. The owners of investments in such lines will find their incomes declining. There are so many other factors also relevant, however, that such analysis must be heavily qualified.

Capitalization. A parcel of land or other durable property yields a continuous stream of services to an owner who employs it for his personal wants or a continuous sequence of rent receipts to a landlord who leases it to a tenant. Partly offsetting these gross service or rental receipts are recurrent costs of repairs and allowances for depreciation or obsolescence. Through the process of capitalization, the remaining net service or rental values determine the capital value of the parcel of land or item of property. At any time, the value of a piece of land or a durable property is the sum of this year's net service or rental receipts, plus next year's net service or rental receipts discounted at the current rate of return on capital to allow for postponement, and so on to the point where the discount for postponement practically balances the value of a year's net services or rentals. To summarize the result of this calculation, the value of a durable property is the capitalization of its annual net yield at the current rate of return on capital. In other words, it is the dollar amount which, if invested at the prevailing interest rate, will bring the same net dollar income as the property.[20]

Whenever or for such time as a special tax on a durable property cannot be shifted, it obviously diminishes the possible *net* services or rentals. And the capitalized value of these annual net services or rentals—or, in other words, the capital value of the property in question—is proportionately reduced. To the extent that a special periodic tax on land and other durable properties is not shifted, it is capitalized as a reduction in the present value of the land and properties.[21] Tax capitalization is permanent in the case of properties held personally, and of land and nonreproducible properties, where a periodic tax can never be shifted. In the case of reproducible properties, where the impossibility of shifting the tax is temporary, the tax capitalization is likewise temporary and diminishes as the time approaches for complete shifting of the tax.

When a property subjected to a nonshiftable periodic tax is sold, the purchaser naturally takes the tax into consideration in the price he offers. In calculating the net value of the services or rentals he will obtain from the property, he deducts the amount of the tax. Insofar as the price he offers is based upon a capitalization of the net services or rentals of the property, his offer will be lower by the capitalized amount of the tax. Thus,

[20] The formula for determining the capital value of an asset with perpetual life is

$$\text{Price} = \frac{\text{Expected permanent annual income}}{\text{Rate of Interest}}$$

A piece of land expected to bring, net, $1,000 a year permanently will, if the going rate of interest in the market is 5 per cent, have a capital value of $20,000. In other words, $20,000 is the amount which if invested under conditions prevailing at the time will net as much as the land. A more complete illustration appears in note 22.

[21] A government *subsidy* to the owner or user of land, such as provided some farmers, has the opposite effect. To the extent that it is believed to be permanent, it will be reflected in the price of the land. The owner of the land when the subsidy becomes effective gets the capitalized value. Future operators receive no benefit.

the purchaser "buys himself free" of a nonshiftable tax. The current and capitalized future burdens of the tax fall exclusively upon the owner at the time the tax was imposed.[22] The smaller the area imposing a tax, the greater the chances of capitalization. Alternatives in other jurisdictions are easier to utilize.

The same forces operate in the pricing of outstanding common stock of corporations. If business income tax rates rise, any part of the tax not shifted to consumers will reduce the net income for stockholders. Anyone buying shares will offer a price which reflects the lower net earnings. He will get, presumably, the same rate of return on his investment. The tax

[22] A hypothetical example is offered to illustrate the principles of shifting and capitalizing special taxes on rented properties. We assume that the market rate of interest appropriate to the uncertainties involved in real estate ownership is 5 per cent.

A rented residence is worth $30,000–$15,000 for the lot and $15,000 for the house. The rent has been $1,800 a year. The landlord has paid $300 a year on a ten-mill property tax, so that his net rent has been $1,500 a year or 5 per cent on his investment. Now the tax rate is doubled, and the landlord has to pay an additional $300 a year. Eventually he is able to shift the $150 house tax to the tenant, in accordance with principles stated in the text. But the $150 tax on the land value he must bear himself. The situation is presented in the following tabulation:

	Ten-Mill Tax Rate			Twenty-Mill Tax Rate		
	House	*Lot*	*Total*	*House*	*Lot*	*Total*
Value of property ...	$15,000	$15,000	$30,000	$15,000	?	?
Rent	900	900	1,800	1,050	$900	$1,950
Taxes	150	150	300	300	300	600
Net rent	$ 750	$ 750	$ 1,500	$ 750	$600	$1,350

A prospective purchaser checks over the values and rents of the property. He is willing to pay $15,000 for the house, because the $1,050 house rent will give him, after taxes, a net rent of $750 a year, or 5 per cent on his investment. But he will not pay $15,000 for the lot, since the net rent, after taxes, of $600 would represent only 3 per cent on the investment. He sets a price of $12,857 for the lot. With the tax assessment brought down to that figure, and the tax correspondingly reduced, he will net $643 a year, or 5 per cent on the $12,857 purchase price for the lot. The capitalization situation is shown in the next tabulation:

	Twenty-Mill Tax Rate Before Capitalization			Twenty-Mill Tax Rate After Capitalization		
	House	*Lot*	*Total*	*House*	*Lot*	*Total*
Value of property ...	$15,000	?	?	$15,000	$12,857	$27,857
Rent	1,050	$900	$1,950	1,050	900	1,950
Taxes	300	300	600	300	257	557
Net rent	$ 750	$600	$1,350	$ 750	$ 643	$ 1,393

does not burden him. It is a form of capital levy on the person who owned the shares when the rate increase went into effect.

INCIDENCE OF TAXES ON NET INCOME

Income taxes currently overshadow commodity and property taxes. The big "shifting" question, then, is "Who eventually pays the personal income tax?" The usual reply is that such taxes are not shifted. Like most easy generalizations, this one is not strictly accurate. Thus, a general income tax applied to pure net income can rarely be shifted. But if the tax is not general, or if "net income" as determined under the tax law does not coincide with "economic net income," possibilities of tax shifting enter.

Taxes on personal compensation. A tax on wages and salaries can be shifted only if it affects either the demand for, or the supply of, labor. Demand for labor would be affected if the taxing government spent more or less of the funds obtained by the tax than the taxpayers would have, if they had retained these funds. To simplify the analysis, we shall assume equivalent spending by the government and the taxpayer, so that demand for labor is unaffected. Thus, the tax can be considered as affecting only the supply of labor. Conclusions derived from such analysis can be suitably modified where there is reason to believe that government spending and taxpayer spending of the amount of the tax would differ.

The Physiocrats and the early Classical economists argued that wages and salaries tend to a minimum-of-subsistence level. A tax on wages and salaries, by forcing their "real" value below this minimum of subsistence, would raise the death rate because of starvation, misery, and epidemics. The supply of labor would thus be reduced in the face of an undiminished demand. Employers' competition for labor would cause wages and salaries to be bid up until their purchasing power, exclusive of the tax, once again reached a minimum-of-subsistence level. In the long run, a tax on wages and salaries would thus be shifted to employers.

Since modern income taxes generally include a minimum exemption, however, they will not impinge upon minimum-of-subsistence incomes, and the old argument cannot apply. But even where an exceptional type of income tax, like the payroll taxes imposed to finance Social Security programs, includes no minimum exemption, we may not conclude that the part deducted from the employee's pay is shifted to employers. In few lines of employment today are wages at a minimum-of-subsistence level. Rising productivity, custom, public opinion, and the collective bargaining power of labor have resulted in wage levels embodying varying standards of comfort, and public relief and charity prevent obvious starvation of the unemployed. Although standard-of-comfort wage levels are not altered easily, they provide a margin upon which taxes can encroach. A moderate payroll or income tax generally comes out of this margin between labor's income and its minimum of subsistence and is borne by the wage- and salary-earners.[23]

There may be occupations that are not covered by a broad wage and salary tax. This used to be true of Social Security taxes. Tax-free occupations—including leisure and self-employment—then compete for labor with those taxed. Total inducements, chiefly but not entirely wage rates, after deduction for tax liability tend toward equality. Wage rates before deduction for tax liability tend to rise in the taxed occupation, but employers, to meet the higher cost, must charge more; the higher prices will cut the quantities of commodities sold. The tax is passed on to consumers (and some unemployment may follow). Moreover, since labor is not the only factor of production, shifts to laborsaving methods tend to follow; wage rates, in free markets, would then fall somewhat. In the case of Social Security, however, the close relation of tax to benefit should tend to remove any differential in attractiveness of taxed and untaxed employment that makes possible the shifting of the tax to consumers.

The part of the Social Security tax that is measured by wages and salaries but that is imposed upon the employer would be largely shifted to employees under perfectly competitive conditions. Under real market conditions, however, such shifting is apt to be slow and incomplete. In the meantime, owners of business and consumers bear part of the burden.

Taxes on business profits.[24] Net business profits were once defined by the economic theorist as an "economic surplus." As so defined, they are determined by prices and costs, without in turn exerting any effect on prices and costs. To the extent that this is true, a general tax that reduces only net business profits can be shifted neither forward to prices nor backward to cost factors.

The same general conclusion is also reached by using another argument. In any line of business where competition is truly effective, prices establish themselves at or close to the production costs of the marginal firms (or marginal capacity). At the margin, costs are covered but there is no profit. Since the tax does not enter into the prices charged for these price-determining marginal outputs, it cannot affect the prices charged for the supramarginal production where costs are less. A general business profits tax,

[23] In collective bargaining, union representatives may argue that an increased tax on wages necessitates a pay rise. It is doubtful whether this argument has any appreciable effect on wage negotiations, which turn primarily on the bargaining strength and adroitness of the union, and on the capacity of the employer to meet pay increases. One conceivable exception exists when an employer is working on a cost-plus contract —perhaps for a government. The tax argument is a convenient rationalization when it is available, but hardly a deciding factor.

[24] For an excellent summary of the theory and problems of the incidence of taxes on business profits, see M. H. Gillim, *The Incidence of the Excess Profits Tax* (Columbia University Press, New York, 1945). See also R. Goode, *The Corporation Income Tax* (John Wiley & Sons, Inc., New York, 1951), especially pp. 44–73.

or a general net income tax applying to business profits, is not shifted *if* it falls *only* on profits after all economic costs have been covered.

The definition of "profits" implied in the theory just summarized, however, is much narrower than the definition used by business and by the tax laws. There are important items which the economist recognizes as costs but which are not considered costs by accountants and tax laws. The latter, therefore, include as "profits" more than the "economic surplus" or the "noncost" items of the economist.

The major differences concern: (1) the normal return that could be obtained on the equity of the owners in the business, (2) the payment that must be offered to induce investors to assume the risks inherent in business in an uncertain world, and (3) the payment for innovation (if it is considered separate from the others). Most businesses can get some or a great deal of their capital funds by borrowing on bonds or mortgages; they can get the use of capital goods by leasing them. The interest and rentals they pay are treated as costs by the economist, the accountant, and the tax collector. However, businesses must also have some equity capital, funds put in by owner as direct investment, by purchase of stock, or by reinvestment of earnings. These funds could earn income if invested in other forms. They will not be put into the equity of the business unless the owners expect a net return equal to at least what they could obtain elsewhere—a normal rate of interest. Moreover, the equity investment must absorb any losses, and there is always some risk of loss, often great risk. Since equity funds are essential for business and since their investment involves risks and forces owners to sacrifice the chances of obtaining interest, businesses can expect to get capital funds only if a return equal to normal interest plus payment for risk is offered. This return, usually termed "profit," is an essential economic cost. Only the amounts above it are "economic surplus."

American taxes on "business profits" do not allow a normal return on equity investment and payment for risk as a deductible cost. The profits taxes, therefore, are imposed on essential items of cost, but not on all items of cost. Interest paid and the rental paid on leased capital goods are not subjected to business profits tax. Investors can be expected to make equity funds available only if the expected return *after* tax equals the expected return from nontaxed investments. The tax thus becomes a part of the cost of getting capital. As a cost, it must be covered by selling price if the business is to be established or to continue to provide the commodity or service. It is shifted to the consumer. Such shifting is impersonal, indirect, and largely concealed, perhaps even from the business manager himself. He may not consciously include business income tax in his planning. But he must offer investors a net return which he can earn only if he can charge consumers prices that in effect include tax.

The broad process of equalizing the net returns on taxed and untaxed income from property will tend to reduce the yields in untaxed areas. The flow of investment funds away from the taxed toward the untaxed opportunities—from common stock to bonds—will result in lower yields from the untaxed forms than would otherwise be the case. Though it may not seem realistic to say that some of the taxes on business profit are thus shifted to those property owners who invest in bonds, there will be some such effect.

Some firms of course earn for short periods, and occasionally for long periods, higher returns on invested capital than are needed to attract new investment. Such returns are an "economic surplus," in the true sense. A tax falling on them will not be a cost that must be covered in price. The firm presumably gets as much profit as possible, and the tax in no way increases its ability to charge more or pay less for factors of production. The tax rests on the owners.

Taxes on business profits may also fall on owners rather than on consumers where the capital has been invested before the tax (or increased rates) became effective. If the investment cannot be shifted promptly to nontaxed forms, a tax on current yield will tend to fall on present owners until they can reduce their investment enough to cut output to the point where a higher price can be charged. For some time many railroads have not earned enough to attract equity funds from the sale of new stock, yet they have paid taxes on "profits." The taxes fall primarily on owners.

If a corporation has preferred stock as well as common stock, an unshifted profits tax will not affect the preferred-stock holders so long as profits after taxes still suffice to pay the preferred dividend. The tax will rest entirely on the common-stock owners.

Should a particular line of business—liquor manufacturing or distributing, for example—be subjected to a substantial *special* profits tax, another possibility of shifting enters. The average return on capital invested in the business is reduced by the tax, presumably below the level for other, untaxed business activities. New and replacement capital will be deterred from flowing into this business, forcing its contraction—or, at least, it will not expand as rapidly as those lines of business attracting new capital. Output will either be reduced or held below what would have been the normal expansion. Eventually this check on output, in the face of an unchanged demand for the product, will force prices upward until the tax is covered or, if supply factors are less elastic than demand, will force down rents or wages. The tax will be shifted either forward or backward.

A monopolist or a quasi-monopolist who is not subject to public control has the power to establish prices which produce a maximum "monopoly profit." Any higher as well as any lower schedule of prices would produce lower profits. Any raising or lowering of an optimum schedule of prices with a view to "passing on" a special profits tax would defeat its purpose, since such action would reduce profits.

In but two situations may a tax on a monopolist's profits be shifted.

Should a monopoly enterprise, prior to the imposition of a profits tax, have failed to bring its prices up to the maximum profit level, the tax may lead to an increase in prices. Between the margin of the prior price level and the optimum level, a price increase to cover taxes will not reduce profits. Similarly, if a public utility regulatory commission should treat a profits tax as a cost factor to be taken into account when determining rates—and this is now the general practice—the imposition of a profits tax might result in higher rates without reducing company profits.

Taxes on rents and interest. A special tax on the true net investment return from some particular class of property or property right—on certain net rents, or "true" interest on certain types of monetary investment—will have the same effects as a special periodic tax on the property producing the return. Where the property is reproducible, or where mere monetary investment is involved, the lowered rate of return will discourage the investment of new funds. The amount of the taxed property or investment capital will decrease until the diminished quantity, in the face of an unchanged demand, produces an enhanced gross rent or gross interest sufficient to cover the tax. Thus, a tax on rents on buildings and other improvements will eventually be shifted to tenants, and a tax on the interest on certain investments will eventually be shifted to the borrowers. A special tax imposed on net land rents and on the returns from nonreproducible properties is normally not shiftable, since it usually cannot affect the supply of the land or properties in question; it will be capitalized into lower prices for the land or properties.

A general tax applying to all *income* from property will be neither shifted nor capitalized, except as the supply of saving may be affected. With returns from all properties and all investments equally reduced, capital will not be diverted from any one field and into others, and the supply of any type of property or of investment capital in any field will not be changed.[25] Capital values will also remain unchanged, since the rate of capitalization declines identically with the returns on capital investment.

SHIFTING OF TAXES LEVIED BY LIMITED JURISDICTIONS

Many commodity and business taxes are freely shifted by the initial taxpayers to their customers, but this generalization is subject to a very important qualification peculiar to the United States. Except for federal taxes, American taxes are not universal in their application. State A's capital stock tax applies only to corporations organized or operating in State A.

[25] In practice, the benefits of "liquidity" would probably not be taxed. Consequently, some qualifications of the text statement may be necessary as some increase in hoarding should be expected. This change might tend slightly to raise the pre-tax earning of capital. Some reduction in saving might also result, increasing slightly the costs of borrowing by businesses and buyers of residences.

State B's manufacturers' excise applies only to commodities manufactured or sold in State B. Concerns in other parts of the country are not subject to the capital stock tax of State A, and commodities produced or sold in other states are not subject to the manufacturers' excise of State B.

As a rule retailers in the different states are not in active competition with each other. Hence, these variations in state or local taxes rarely affect retail marketing positions, except as competition of mail-order firms may force local business to absorb local taxes. But manufacturers and, to a lesser extent, wholesalers, extractive businesses, and such service industries as finance, advertising, transportation, insurance, and "tourism," may compete in a national market. Shoes made by a St. Louis manufacturer who had to pay a normally shiftable turnover tax may compete in New York stores with shoes made by a Lynn manufacturer who paid nonshiftable corporate excess and income taxes. A Pennsylvania machine manufacturer who paid a capital stock tax may be bidding for New Jersey customers against a New York machine manufacturer who paid no such tax. Because forms and rates of taxes levied on competing businesses and commodities vary as between states, the rules of tax incidence discussed earlier do not always apply in full detail to American state and local taxes.

Commodity taxes. When one state taxes the production of an article which competes with identical articles manufactured in other states imposing no corresponding tax, the situation would appear to be a clear case of the levy of a commodity tax on similar but competing commodities. But such is not the case. Here there is no problem of increasing the output of a competing untaxed commodity to replace part or all of the output of the commodity driven from the market by the tax. Consequently, there is no variation in the production cost of the untaxed commodity to affect the sales prices of both the taxed and the untaxed commodities. Instead, if but one state or district taxes the production of a certain commodity, the producers in the taxed district must bear the tax as a reduction of their profits. If the tax drives them out of business, other producers with presumably the same schedule of unit costs operating in untaxed regions will replace them. This substitution will have no long-term effect on the price of the commodity unless there are distinct production cost differentials between the taxing and the nontaxing states.

Business taxes. When competing businesses located in different districts or states are subjected to varying forms and rates of business taxes, the resulting discriminations and inequalities may bar the complete shifting of taxes which, if applied to all competing firms, might be shiftable. A manufacturing firm located in State A and subjected to a heavier combination of ordinarily shiftable taxes than a competitor in State B cannot include the taxes in the prices charged without losing part or all of its market to its competitor in State B. It must absorb the taxes as a reduction of net profits, regardless of arguments for the ordinary shiftability of such taxes.

Should an excess of unshiftable state or local taxes drive a firm out of business, there need be no reduction in the supply of the commodities or services to force the price upward. He can be replaced by a producer located in a state or locality with lighter taxes who bears no excess of unshiftable taxes.

PROBLEMS

1. Show how commodity tax shifting may be different in the long run than in the short. (*Hint:* Both demand and supply are likely to be more elastic over a period of years than over a few months.)

2. Why is a business relationship necessary for tax shifting?

3. Assume, as in fact occurred, that corporation profits after tax were as high, relative to invested capital, after several years of high tax rates as when rates were lower. Discuss the significance for the theory of tax shifting.

4. Show how a flat-rate tax on all commodities and services will cause some prices to change relatively more than others. Under what conditions might the price of some of the taxed commodities drop?

5. "There is really only one important tax whose incidence is clear, the tax on personal income." Discuss.

6. Explain the process of tax capitalization.

7. How may a tax be shifted backward?

8. Can a state in effect impose a tax on consumers or stockholders in other states? What conditions will tend to impede the shifting of a state's taxes to outsiders?

CHAPTER 9

Distributive[1] *and Regulatory Aspects of Taxation*

ONE of the greatest, inescapable, and basically divisive issues of modern society is how the heavy costs of government are to be shared. Under a flat-rate poll tax every individual would pay the same amount. Any other system of taxation requires some individuals to pay, directly or indirectly, heavier taxes than others. Distribution of the burden among individuals and social and economic groups is determined by the character of the tax system. Are there any ultimate principles for such distribution of tax burdens whereby different tax systems can be approved or condemned? What, if any, are the principles of justice or equity in taxation? What are the economic effects of one distribution of taxes compared with another?

Discussions of principles of tax distribution are often one-sided denunciations or defenses of particular taxes. The resultant conclusions are of little value; they rest on a misunderstanding of the place of tax distribution principles. These principles apply not to particular taxes but only to *systems* of taxes. A general sales tax, standing by itself, might be difficult to justify. But a moderate sales tax could work in acceptably with a progressive income tax embodying a large minimum exemption and with rates already very high. The distributional effect of any one tax may be balanced by that of other taxes in the system. Individual taxes may be validly praised or condemned for their effect on the distribution of the burden of a tax system, but not for the distribution of their own exclusive burden. In selecting taxes the objective is to choose the best of the alternatives available. If heavy use is already being made of a "good" tax, the best alternative may

[1] The term "distributive" as applied to taxation refers to the apportionment of taxes among individual taxpayers and groups. This meaning is entirely different from that used in marketing and in business generally. This chapter and most fiscal literature approach the problem of the distribution of taxes in terms of probable incidence after immediate shifting, but without regard to the effects on national income studied in **Part Six.**

be moderate use of a "poorer" tax rather than more intensive use of the "good" one.

DISTRIBUTION OF TAX BURDENS AMONG INDIVIDUALS[2]

Taxes fall on persons, not on things. Legally, of course, a tax may be on property, a sale, or a business. But the ultimate burden is personal, reducing someone's income or the net value of his property or raising the prices he must pay. Numerous doctrines and considerations dealing with the distribution of tax burdens among individuals—and groups—must be considered.

Benefit doctrines. The *benefit* doctrine is that each individual should be taxed in proportion to the benefits he derives from government functions. The chief reason is a belief that such treatment is fair, but two others have some merit. A tax so based will not impair incentive, and it will encourage economy in decisions on government spending. The doctrine has two branches: (1) the cost-of-service theory, and (2) the value-of-service theory.

Underlying the *cost-of-service* theory is the thought that each individual should be compelled by taxation to pay the cost of the services performed for him by the government.[3] Government functions would be conducted on the principle of government enterprises; through taxes, each individual would be assessed the cost of the services performed for him. But what is then the basis for apportioning government costs among the individuals benefited? There is little basis except possibly for enterprise services, such as the postal system, transit, water, and a few regulatory activities. How can my individual responsibility for America's World War II costs be determined? How can responsibility for the costs of a child's education be allocated to the child itself, to its parents who may or may not wish their offspring educated, to his future employers who want a trained employee, to the general community which is better off for an educated populace, and to all the others who have an interest in the promotion of popular education? Even at the university level, where some charges are often imposed, there is question of how broadly the benefit of training extends over the whole public rather than being confined to the student.

According to the *value-of-service* theory, an individual should share in

[2] For most of us, the family is the basic economic unit, not the individual. The discussion of distribution of tax burdens might be more realistic if it specifically referred to families as well as to individuals. The extra wordage, however, would be cumbersome.

[3] Why, then, not perform the function in the market and let everyone buy freely, paying a price to cover cost, as for bread or shoes? The main answer is that *compulsion* can serve a useful purpose, that the community may wisely force people to accept and pay for things it is socially desirable that they receive but which many would not purchase on their own behalf (such as old-age pensions or education).

the costs of government in proportion to the value of the benefits he derives. Here, too, there is the difficulty of measuring the extent to which each person benefits from government activities. Value-of-service doctrine advocates have, however, proposed various standards. Those who conceive protection to be the sole function of government have argued that the individual benefit from protection varies in proportion to the property owned. To such writers, a single general property tax has seemed the best means of distributing tax burdens equitably—it is a sort of insurance premium. Other writers have contended that since each individual benefits from government activities to the extent that he eats, drinks, and otherwise enjoys life in a material manner, a tax based on private expenditure, a retail sales tax, would be most just.

Quid pro quo doctrines were natural as long as protection was the major function of government. It could reasonably be argued that protection bore some relation to property or expenditures, even though now we look upon individual benefit from a protective function as an incidental by-product of the more important indivisible social benefit. Today, general public welfare is the major objective of many government activities, and individual benefits are recognized as incidental. Benefit doctrines no longer find *general* application because of the subordination of individual benefit.

The benefit principle does play an important part in the theory of fees, special assessments, tolls, and government enterprise charges. Furthermore, it still finds some application to taxation. In fact, as increased government spending tends to bring measurable benefits to distinguishable individuals or groups, there is more interest in the benefit criterion.[4] It is sometimes possible to isolate classes of individuals or of property, marked by distinguishing characteristics, which derive special benefit from broad groups of government activities. Taxes on such a class may be justified by the special benefits bestowed upon it by the government. Use of local taxes on real estate to pay for fire protection and other services for the property is an example. Motorists, distinguished by their ownership of motor cars and use of motor fuels, derive a special benefit from government expenditures on highway construction and maintenance. Two "benefit" taxes can, therefore, be imposed upon them—the motor vehicle license tax and the motor fuel tax. Heavy trucks contribute more than light trucks to highway wear and tear and they can therefore be compelled to pay more. Certain other expenditures—poor relief payments, veterans' benefits, and farmers' subsidies, for example—also provide marked special benefits for distinguishable groups of individuals. To make this benefit the basis for

[4] When at least part of the benefit is received by someone in another governmental unit, there is an unusually strong reason for trying to impose a benefit-based tax. The outsider will then contribute to cost of government, and he is willing to do so because of the benefit he gets.

special taxes on these groups, however, would clearly defeat the social purposes of the expenditure. The benefit principle has been used to justify that part of the Social Security payroll tax imposed on the employee. Some government activities may be said to be of special benefit to business enterprise rather than of general economic benefit to individuals as such. On this argument, of very slight validity at best, general business taxes may be considered to have a "benefit" justification.

Differences in the quality of local government rest partly upon geographical applications of the benefit principle. Benefit principles also have a part in deciding which level of government will pay for a service. One argument for making a function a local rather than a state or national responsibility is that those who benefit will pay and will vary their spending according to the worth of the service to them. Moreover, certain constitutional restrictions on jurisdiction to tax rest in part upon judicial belief that tax proceeds ought to be available for benefiting the person taxed.

Privilege doctrine. A variant of the benefit doctrines goes under the name of the *privilege* theory. Privileges granted by governments—to inherit property or to do business as a corporation, for example—confer special benefits that could not be enjoyed except for the government's grant of *permission*. The privilege doctrine holds that these special benefits warrant special taxes. Many yardsticks, among them property used in connection with the privilege or net or gross income resulting from its exercise, may be used to measure the benefits presumably derived from the exercise of the privilege. The privilege doctrine resembles the value-of-service doctrine somewhat, except that the taxpayer's special benefit is presumed to derive not from any government activity or service, but from the permission to do something not otherwise legally permissible.

Isolating the group benefiting initially from a legal privilege in order to impose a special tax upon it involves little administrative difficulty. If the privilege consists of doing an act which would otherwise be without legal sanction, the tax can be levied on each performance of the act, as with death taxes levied on property passing by bequest or inheritance. If the privilege is one of assuming a condition not otherwise permissible, as in doing business in a corporate form, the tax can be imposed on the occasion of each renewal of the privilege.

The basic weakness of the privilege doctrine is its underlying assumption that the permission to perform certain acts or assume certain conditions confers a special benefit. Actually, the State is all-sovereign and except for self-imposed constitutional limitations has the power to prohibit every act and every condition. Every act or condition not specifically prohibited might be considered specially permitted. To do business in an unincorporated form is a legal privilege, just as it is to do business in an incorporated form. To dispose of property by gift or sale is as much subject to government permission as to dispose of it by inheritance or bequest. When every act and every condition may be considered the exercise of a legal privilege, what special economic benefit is inherent in any particular legal privilege to justify its being made the basis of a special tax?

Another weakness of the privilege doctrine is that it rests on the implicit assumption that the value of the privilege stays with the initial recipient. Under the pressure of competition, however, the benefits of privileges granted businesses will tend to be passed to consumers, employees, or suppliers. When thus shifted, the benefit cannot be singled out for special taxation. A final weakness of this doctrine is that many of the legal privileges granted by government result in broad social benefit. To penalize them by special taxes would lead to restricted use. The general welfare would suffer.

In spite of the weaknesses of the privilege doctrine as an over-all distributional basis for taxation, it has a prominent place as the constitutional foundation for a number of state taxes.

State-partnership doctrines. Still another variant of the benefit theory—the *State-partnership* doctrine—is sometimes offered as special justification for business taxes, though not as a general standard of tax distribution. In support of business taxes it may be argued that business can be transacted in security and safety only because of the protection accorded by the State. Furthermore, the State provides and enforces laws which facilitate business intercourse. The State is therefore an active partner in every business enterprise and should receive its partnership share in any profits, preferably in taxes on net income. Yet, clearly, the idea of partnership between the government and individuals is a fiction, not a practical reality. The State-partnership doctrine can at most be but a supplementary argument buttressing a tax which finds its major justification under some other doctrine.[5]

Objective ability doctrines. "Ability to pay" is probably the doctrine of tax distribution most often cited today. Does it mean more than merely that taxes are to be imposed on those whose cash or other resources make them able to raise the money demanded? It does. Yet it is one of the vaguest concepts used in determining major public policy. Behind the *ability* doctrine is the principle that government costs are incurred for general social purposes and are an obligation of society rather than of particular individuals. This obligation must be distributed among the individuals composing the social unit in a manner which takes account of hardship and seeks to reduce it. Such a distinction results when each individual contributes according to his "ability" or "faculty." Adam Smith made the ability doctrine the first of his four canons of taxation:

[5] For disapproval of this curt dismissal of the State-partnership doctrine, and a positive argument for the theory, see P. Studenski, "Toward A Theory of Business Taxation," in *Journal of Political Economy,* Vol. XLVIII, Oct., 1940, pp. 630–631.

I. The subjects of every state ought to contribute toward the support of the government, as nearly as possible in proportion to their respective abilities; that is, in proportion to the revenue which they respectively enjoy under the protection of the state.[6]

Most fiscal writers hold that the ability concept can be applied properly only to individuals, that a business concern as such has no independent, impersonal "tax-paying ability." But the argument has been developed that business units possess an impersonal tax "ability" measured by net income or by the relation of net income to capital; this argument is used in attempts to justify proportional corporation income tax and progressive excess profits taxes.

"Ability" is a vague term and has been given many interpretations. Colonial America held the individual to be the norm of "ability," and on this standard, a poll tax was considered essentially equitable. Jean Bodin and many later writers considered property the best criterion of taxpaying "ability." Property yields, individual expenditures, individual incomes, and savings have at various times been proposed as ideal criteria of "ability." Income is popularly accepted today as a major standard of "ability." So, too, are "windfall" receipts, such as certain inheritances and gifts.

Each of the proposed objective measures of "ability," including the income standard, suffers from the same shortcoming—it fails actually to *measure* "ability." If one individual has twice as much property or in the course of a year spends twice as much, or receives twice as much income, or saves twice as much as a second individual, does the first individual have exactly twice as much "ability" as the second individual? Or is the proportion somewhat more than double, or somewhat less? None of the objective ability doctrines can answer these questions. Yet they *must* be answered in applying the doctrine. Whether the tax burden should be proportional, regressive, or progressive in relation to property, expenditure, savings, or income cannot be settled on objective grounds.

In a certain negative sense, however, there may be an objective application of the ability principle. The amount needed to support a socially endorsed minimum standard of living can be calculated. Below this figure there would be no "ability to pay." Above it, however, objective guides are not evident.

Subjective sacrifice doctrines. John Stuart Mill[7] propounded the *subjective sacrifice* doctrine, a refinement upon the objective ability doctrine. He argued that income, property, savings, or any other measuring rod of taxpaying "ability" has a diminishing utility to its possessor. Consequently, a rich man's payment of a given sum in taxes entails less sacrifice than the

[6] Adam Smith, *The Wealth of Nations,* Book V, Chapter 2.

[7] John Stuart Mill, *Political Economy* (London, 1848), Book V, Chapter 2, sec. 2. This doctrine is probably what the "man in the street" means by "ability to pay."

poor man's payment of an equal amount. Some writers argue that the tax legislator's ideal should be *equal* sacrifice on all taxpayers. Others argue for *proportional* sacrifice. Still a third school of economists insists upon *minimum or least social* sacrifice as the ideal.

But if any subjective sacrifice theory—the equal sacrifice principle, the proportional sacrifice principle, or the least sacrifice principle—is to provide a clear standard for tax burden distribution, the formula for the diminishing utility of wealth or income must be known. And as yet, the "law" of the diminishing utility of wealth or income has not been inductively established, even though the principle seems logical.[8] Since every fiscal economist is free to choose his own formula, agreement is rare. According to the particular formula of diminishing utility chosen, the equal sacrifice principle can lead to regressive, proportional, or progressive taxation; proportional sacrifice may produce proportional or progressive taxation; and progressive taxation or outright confiscation of all wealth above a given figure may be an outcome of the least sacrifice principle.

Neutrality doctrine: reasonable classification. If fairness and equity are goals of tax policy, can we look to jurisprudence, where the same goals are prominent, to get help in learning what they mean and perhaps something about how to achieve them? We can—a little. Equity, we find, relates differences in treatment to reasonable or relevant bases or sources. Equal treatment is not always equitable—and neither is unequal treatment. The crucial factor in deciding whether inequality is equitable is the adequacy or relevance of the element which accounts for the difference. For example, in determining how a total tax load ought to be shared, color of hair is not relevant, but size of income may be. What about age? height? place of residence? type and source of income? Opinions may differ, but final decisions ought to rest on careful and explicit consideration of the issues.

The underlying presumption is that individuals and businesses in essentially similar circumstances should receive the same tax treatment. As far as they are concerned, taxes should be *neutral*. However, individuals or businesses differently circumstanced can, and perhaps should, be taxed differently. If so, the differences in burden ought to be reasonably related to the conditions that account for them. If the tax differential modifies the original relationship or difference, any departure from neutrality ought to rest upon some rational basis, not arbitrary or capricious factors.

This apparently negative neutrality doctrine seems to tell us more what *not* to do than what to do. It gives no indication of the normal standard, what might be called the basic starting point. Yet it does have positive

[8] A fundamental assumption, often not made explicit, of subjective sacrifice doctrines is that all individuals have equal capacity to enjoy income, that tastes and desires have the same relative intensity for all. Denial of this assumption involves giving up the claim that a system of progression in taxes which does not take account of differences in taste can give equality of sacrifice.

value. It performs the helpful service of alerting us to the fact that taxes can and do upset pre-existing economic relationships between individuals and businesses and that the sources of the changes may, or may not, be reasonably related to the results. Present personal income taxes do discriminate in favor of home-owners and against those who rent apartments or houses. Corporation income taxes do discriminate against businesses financed entirely by equity capital and favor those financed by debt. The neutrality doctrine does not pretend to provide a basis for deciding whether the results are desirable. It does not attempt to offer a complete guide to tax burden distribution.

What is the standard of being "similarly circumstanced" that would warrant identical tax treatment? Are two family heads "similarly circumstanced" if they have the same incomes but spend different amounts, or if they spend the same but have different incomes, or if they have the same incomes and spend the same but have different family obligations and distribute their spending among different objectives? The list could be extended indefinitely! With the great variety of business structure and operation, *what* circumstances are properly the basis for *how much* difference in taxes? Neutrality gives us no answer. Yet we *are* ahead if the neutrality doctrine has forced us to agree that an actual distribution of taxes rests on considerations that are not relevant or appropriate to the result. To have identified trouble is no small gain.

Incentives. Today, much more than in the past, the public must be concerned with the relation of the distribution of taxes to incentives. Total tax burdens are so heavy that the way they are distributed can have a significant effect on the willingness and ability to work, save, and assume risk. What seems "just," or desirable on some proper grounds, may either reinforce or undermine the chances of achieving other goals which are also important. These latter goals may constitute even more highly rated ends of the economy than those of tax distribution. The troublesome conflicts are predominantly the result of high tax rates, for low rates will not influence incentives enough to cause concern. It is when income tax rates soar to 91 per cent—being justified on the grounds that such an extreme is needed to distribute a big total burden fairly—that incentives are inevitably affected.

Creation or use of income as a guide to personal distribution. A person's tax may be adjusted (a) to what he produces or (b) to what he consumes. His production and that of his property are measured by his income; his consumption is measured by his spending. A tax on income relates the burden to what one *contributes* to the economy. A tax on spending relates the burden to what one *takes out* of the economy, to the amount one uses up. Is there any significant difference in the fairness or rationality of two systems, one of which distributes burden according to what each person puts into the stream of production, the other according to what he draws out? Putting the issue in this unusual way, a leading British economist has urged reconsideration of traditional thinking about tax distribution—in both developed and underdeveloped lands. He argues that on grounds of fairness as well as of economic effects, society would be wise to increase the emphasis on "taking out" rather than "putting in" as the basis for differentiating tax burdens.[9]

Burdensomeless taxes. A tax that brings revenue without imposing a burden—what a dream! The dream in one sense is impossible, for anyone who pays a tax would be better off if he were free of the burden. Yet there are three realistic situations in which decisions about the distribution of taxes can take account of the peculiar nature of things, peculiarities which in a sense do remove the burden as far as concerns the general public.

As shown in Chapter 8, some taxes tend to be capitalized. Such a tax in effect is a perpetual charge on the person who owned the property when the tax was originally imposed and its permanence recognized. Upon such original owner, the burden of the tax is not the single-year amount; it is the capitalization effect at the time the tax is imposed. Consequently, a tax which seems modest may be very heavy upon the owner of the property at the time the tax is imposed. But it is no burden on the person who buys later—his buying price is proportionately less. To reduce the tax later would involve giving a windfall to new owners. It follows, therefore, that a tax which can be fully capitalized and has existed perhaps thirty to fifty years constitutes no present burden. Even though initially "unjust" by one or another of the standards of tax equity, it may have become a levy that in a significant sense burdens no one. The more recent the imposition or rate increase, the greater is the probability that it has burdened present owners.

The second case is that in which the tax falls on a true economic surplus—payments which exceed those necessary to make a factor of production available. We might, for example, get a service if we were to pay only the costs of making it available, say $15,000. However, because of the relation of demand and supply the market price is $20,000. The $5,000 is a surplus in the sense used here. A tax on this $5,000 burdens the taxpayer, of course, but it taxes only the extra income which the peculiar good fortune of his position would have given him. Society recoups through taxes what it paid extra in prices, and the supply of the service will continue. So the community as a whole, in a sense, is not burdened. The more of its total taxes an economy can get from recipients of such surpluses, the less the burden that must be distributed among others. The possibility of imposing such taxes does exist—taxes on increments in pure land rent, for example. It is

[9] N. Kaldor, *An Expenditure Tax* (G. Allen & Unwin, Ltd., London, 1955). Mr. Kaldor is generally sympathetic to the policies of the Labour party.

doubtful, however, that an economy can in fact hope to single out economic surplus to bear much of its total revenue burden.

The third possibility is the shifting of a tax to persons in another jurisdiction. One locality or state may succeed in getting consumers or property owners elsewhere to bear some of its burden. Again, the possibility will rarely be large. The justification in principle is far less than the attraction of expediency.

Critique. Although everyone seems agreed that taxes should be "just," there is no unanimous popular acceptance of any one standard of "justice" to the exclusion of others. The "man in the street" may agree that taxes should be levied according to benefits received, and also according to the taxpayer's ability, and also according to sacrifices imposed, and also to avoid serious damage to incentives—though widely different conclusions may be drawn from each of these premises. He will agree that persons in essentially similar circumstances should be treated alike, but he is apt to have little idea of how to decide which circumstances are similar and which are sufficiently different to warrant different tax treatment.

Another set of arbitrary assertions enters—the measures of benefit, ability, or sacrifice. Is wealth the best measure? or income? or consumption expenditure? or savings? or some other element? Is any consideration to be given to relative abilities and efforts expended in procuring a given income, or to the nature of the satisfaction derived from different kinds of expenditure?

Still another kind of problem arises in comparing the "justice" of a tax measure with the "justice" of the economic effects it produces. How far should one go in trying to take account of such related consequences? Finally, allowance must be made for the administration of the tax. A tax that promises to yield the desired goal of justice may fail utterly because of bad administration.

If the right combination of factor and measure is used in building up the argument, almost any tax system can be proved "just." By using a different combination of factor and measure, however, the same tax system can be proved utterly unjust. The situation might seem ludicrous if popular aspiration for "justice in taxation" did not play into the hands of self-seeking interests. Unions press for taxes on high income groups, arguing "ability to pay." Lobbyists for independent retailers argue that chain stores have special elements of "ability" which warrant their being subjected to prohibitive chain-store taxes. Railroads argue, under the cost-of-service doctrine, that highway users should bear street and highway costs, rather than the general community of which the railroad is a part. Real estate owners, claiming they are unjustly burdened, urge sales taxes. With the various group interests seeking to shift tax burdens onto "the other fellow," "justice" and "injustice" have become mumbo-jumbo words to conjure support or provoke opposition from a blind and bewildered public opinion.

DISTRIBUTION OF TAX BURDENS AMONG ECONOMIC AND SOCIAL CLASSES

Since taxes and tax systems do discriminate between social groups as well as between individuals, should this discrimination motivate the framing of tax systems—should a tax be levied for its "social regulatory" effects? Should the State use its taxing power to eliminate or reduce inequalities of wealth and income? A scattered line of scholars outside Classical tradition have answered "Yes." In the fifteenth century the Florentine scholar Guicciardini wrote:

> Since we are all citizens of the same state and each the equal of the other, there can be no true equality or justice in taxation unless the taxes reduce us all to the same economic level. . . . If, then, we introduce the progressive principle (with sufficient severity) we shall become truly equal as we reasonably ought to be.[10]

The German economist Wagner gave this socio-political theory of taxation more precise expression in the nineteenth century:

> Taxation, in addition to serving the purely financial purpose of providing sufficient revenue, should be employed for the purpose of bringing about a different distribution of wealth from that which would result from the working of free competition upon the basis of the present social order.[11]

Equalization doctrines frequently seek to ally themselves with one or another of the "justice" principles already analyzed—some writers even avoid the term "equalization" and present the principle under the name of "social justice." Fundamentally, there can be no alliance between principles of "justice" in the distribution of individual tax burdens and the doctrine of utilizing the tax power to achieve extrinsic social or group aims. The lines of argument run in different planes, and can fuse only by assumption.

Taxation and equality of economic opportunity. Unequal distribution of economic power means that some members of society have greater economic opportunities than others. Some find it easier to survive the competitive testing of markets than others, not because they contribute more but because they start with advantages which the possession of property inevitably gives. Moreover, other things being equal, the greater a person's wealth and income, the easier for him to acquire more. Accumulation feeds upon itself. Opportunity becomes less and less equal.

There are economists and social philosophers who believe that maximum economic progress and the building of a better society require the diffusion rather than the concentration of power. They hold that the greater the

[10] Quoted in E. R. A. Seligman, *Progressive Taxation in Theory and Practice* (American Economic Association, 2nd ed., 1908), p. 135.

[11] A. Wagner, *Finanzwissenschaft* (Leipzig, 1880), Vol. 1, sec. 27, quoted in E. D. Fagan and C. W. Macy, *Public Finance* (Longmans, Green & Co., New York, 1934), p. 179.

equality of opportunity and the pressure of competition, the more will society be able to derive the best from all its members; that inequality breeds oppression and exploitation; that the basic security of society is endangered if extremes of wealth and income are not checked and reasonably equal chances given everyone. They would use taxation as one instrument to equalize economic opportunity.

Progressive taxation can be an important, though by no means a sufficient, method of checking the tendency toward cumulative economic inequality and of assuring more nearly equal opportunity. In other words, without progression in taxes the functioning of the economy would be threatened by cumulative inequality. More dangerous, perhaps, political freedoms and highly prized social values might not long survive the concentration of wealth and economic power which would result from the inevitable inequality of ability, training, inheritance, and scruples.[12]

Critique. The practical problems of formulating an equalizing tax system are formidable. Tax power, under the equalization doctrine, becomes a weapon in group conflict. And the conflicts are many—between the consumer and the strong labor union, between the farmer and the consumer, between the employer and the employee, between the investor and other elements in the economy, as well as between rich and poor. If one accepts the goal of equalization, one is apt to find others employing the principle in ways that seem highly dangerous or unfair. The use of the coercive power of government to "equalize" may be both a curse and a blessing.

To state that a tax system should have a social or class aim is, like the statement that it should be "just," an arbitrary assertion. And to deny that a tax may properly have such an aim is no less arbitrary. The scholar as a scientist can neither approve nor condemn the equalization doctrine. He can try to point out its probable consequences, good and bad. He can record its prevalence and the extent to which it influences tax legislation. If he supports a preference for one set of results to another, he is acting like a human being, but he is not being a scientist.

Our problem today, however, is not *whether* taxes will affect individuals and groups unequally. With taxes now around $650 a year per capita and amounting to well over one-fourth of the national income, it is impossible that everyone pay the same amount. Today's problems are *how* unequal shall taxes be and what should be the basis for differences of treatment.

Nor is there any serious dispute over the issue of levying taxes to further social ends. Taxes are so heavy that they must vitally affect individuals, groups, regions, industries. Here again the practical problem is to devise the best, or least bad, combination of taxes from the viewpoint of relative burdens on various economic and social groups. This principle is accepted

[12] The leading modern American exponent of these views was H. C. Simons. See his *Personal Income Taxation* (University of Chicago Press, Chicago, 1938), pp. 1–40. He vigorously advocated other measures to preserve competition and opportunity.

by special pleaders as well as by more objective students. The special pleader's argument is that his interest is identical with that of the community as a whole; favorable treatment of him by the tax law (at the expense of others, although this phase of the argument tends to be omitted) will promote the welfare of the entire community. The student of Public Finance, and the legislator who must vote tax measures, have the obligation to take a more objective point of view.

TAX EXEMPTIONS

Tax exemptions may be grouped into five classes according to the motivations behind them:

(1) Constitutional exemptions, necessitated by the federal and state constitutional limitations on tax legislation;
(2) Economic exemptions, like those to encourage the settlement or development of new enterprises;
(3) Distributive exemptions in the interests of "tax justice"—minimum personal exemptions, and exemptions to eliminate overlapping double taxation;
(4) Exemptions to accomplish social ends;
(5) Administrative exemptions.

The first class was considered in Chapter 7, the second will be covered in Chapter 18. Administrative exemptions are discussed in Chapter 10. Here, we shall consider minimum and social exemptions that affect the distribution of tax loads.

Minimum exemptions. In taxes levied on individuals, minimum exemptions always appear desirable. Underlying this feeling is the realization that the extremely poor pay taxes not merely at the cost of some luxuries or savings but at the cost of the necessities of life.

Classical economists would have limited minimum tax exemptions to a minimum-of-subsistence level. They approved only those exemptions covering the lowest income which would keep the recipients alive and in strength. Were basic subsistence taxed, they argued, the sickness and death resulting from the diminished incomes of the poor would, by reducing the working population, force wages up and shift the tax to employers. Today we take a broader view. A moderate standard of living rather than the minimum of subsistence should be the measure for tax exemptions. The socially desirable standard is one which includes moderate comforts for even the poorest classes. Individuals who just manage to achieve this standard should not have their circumstances worsened by a tax.[13] Such individuals, argue proponents of the ability and sacrifice doc-

[13] World War II saw the federal personal income tax exemption for many persons go below this level. When the cost of living changes during periods of general inflation or deflation, the number of dollars needed to provide any given minimum of subsistence or standard of comfort also changes. In practice, however, Congress and state legislatures have taken little explicit account of this fact.

trines of taxation, are without "taxpaying ability." In fact, a considerable burden of commodity, business, and property taxes is shifted into prices of consumer goods and services, where it bears with relative severity on the lowest income groups; hence there is all the more reason for exemptions in personal taxes to counterbalance somewhat this maldistribution of tax burdens.[14]

Minimum exemptions take three forms: (1) lump-sum, (2) continuing, and (3) vanishing. Under a *lump-sum* exemption, should the income, estate, or other taxable element exceed the exempted amount even by a small sum, the entire amount is subject to the tax. If an income tax exemption is fixed at $1,000, a $999 income would be tax free while a $1,001 income would be entirely taxable. This form is inequitable and is rarely found.

Continuing exemptions allow the full amount of exemption, regardless of the size of the income, estate, or other taxable element. If the $1,000 income tax exemption is continuing, a $1,000,000 income as well as one of $1,500 would be permitted the full exemption. When the rate schedule of a tax is progressive, a continuing exemption in effect reduces the taxable income—or estate, or inheritance, or other tax base—of the taxpayer's top bracket subject to his highest rate. Consequently, in terms of *tax rate* and hence amount of tax saved, the value of the exemption to the taxpayer rises with his tax base; the federal personal income tax exemption of $600 saves about $120 of tax to a taxpayer with less than $2,000 taxable income and about $540 to one with over $200,000. Allowing minimum exemptions to large taxpayers is no part of the principle of minimum exemptions and reduces the tax yield. Despite this disadvantage, however, the continuing exemption is the characteristic form in America.[15]

A *vanishing* exemption avoids the disadvantages of both the lump-sum and the continuing exemptions. It diminishes as the tax base increases over the exemption figure. In an income tax with a $1,000 exemption vanishing at a dollar-for-dollar rate, a $1,000 income would be entirely exempt, one of $1,500 would enjoy a $500 exemption, while an income of $2,000 would be fully taxable. Unlike the lump-sum exemption, the vanishing exemption

[14] A moderate minimum exemption greatly simplifies the administration of many taxes. Since costs of assessment and collection for a tax on incomes or estates of a few hundred dollars would often be greater than the revenue, common sense dictates their exemption. Exemptions advisable for administrative reasons are, in general, higher than those approved on distributive grounds. The administrative argument for exemptions is best viewed as a supplement to the distributional argument.

[15] Iowa, Kentucky, Minnesota, and Wisconsin, in their income taxes, grant fixed-amount deductions from the tax instead of exemptions of taxable income. Thus, if a rate schedule begins with 3 per cent and rises to 10 per cent, the deduction from the amount may be $30 for all income levels. The fixed-amount deduction is a sort of continuing exemption whose ratio to marginal income remains constant instead of increasing.

does not involve a sudden, heavy tax imposition. Moreover, it grants no exemption to the upper-bracket groups.

Special groups can be helped by extra income tax exemptions—the blind, the aged, military personnel—but a tax exemption is a very crude method of granting such assistance. It gives no help to those with greatest need because they have too little income to be liable to tax; it affords the greatest aid to persons with large incomes, who need it least.

Social exemptions. State and local property taxes commonly exempt the property of religious, charitable, educational, and similar institutions. If the institution is incorporated, it is also freed from special corporation taxes. Bequests and gifts to such institutions are generally exempted from death and income taxation. The federal income tax exempts a large group of religious, educational, scientific, charitable, hospital, labor, veteran, civic, mutual, fraternal, agricultural, and other organizations from the income tax; gifts and bequests to these institutions are generally not subject to federal gift and estate tax.

Several reasons justify these social exemptions. Since most of these institutions do not earn any true profit, they are, on this score, without tax-paying ability. Then, too, it is argued that their work is of social value to the community; to compel them to curtail these services for the sake of tax revenue would be unwise and perhaps stupidly expensive because valuable activities could not, or would not, be replaced. Furthermore, these institutions often perform services which state or local governments would otherwise have to undertake. Compel them by taxation to forego such performance, and the government would be putting money into one pocket by taking it out of the other.

But the policy of liberal social exemptions has not altogether escaped criticism. Critics have objected that an exemption of religious property is in effect a subsidy to churches—forbidden by many state constitutions. Exemption of income-producing property owned by religious, charitable, and educational institutions has also been protested, often effectively. Although such income may be utilized for social ends, the property itself is an economic asset and should, the argument runs, contribute its quota to the upkeep of the governments which make its economic use possible. This last argument has most force where a large institution engrosses so great a proportion of the property in a small taxing district that a disproportionate burden is imposed on the remaining property.

As corporation income tax rates have grown to be a major item of business expense, there has been increasing complaint about the competitive advantage of tax-exempt cooperatives and ordinary business activities run by exempt institutions. If a college runs a macaroni factory as an investment, why exempt the factory earnings? If business is to be taxed, why not all business? Since World War II, the law and its administration have reduced, in some cases eliminated, the federal income tax advantage of cooperatives and of businesses owned by an institution itself exempt.

PROGRESSIVE TAXATION

We emphasized earlier that choice of a principle of tax justice—benefit, or ability, or sacrifice—and selection of a broad measure of that principle—property, or income, or expenditure, or savings, or some other element—leaves still unsettled the question of how this measure should be employed in framing a schedule of tax rates. Should the tax be *proportional*—should it constitute a fixed proportion of the taxpayer's property, income, expenditure, or savings? Should the tax be *progressive*, with successively higher rates on larger units of the measure? Should it be *regressive*, with rates decreasing for successively larger units of the measure? And if the tax is to be either progressive or regressive, what should be the formula?

Theory.[16] What theories or principles support progressive taxation? Nineteenth-century proponents of the benefit doctrine of taxation usually argued for either a regressive or proportional distribution of the general burden. The argument for regression was based upon the observations that a government's social expenditures benefited the poor more than the rich and that government protection was more the prevention of exploitation of the poorer by the richer class than vice versa. Proportional distribution of tax burdens was defended upon the generalization that the protective activities of government concerned property rather than individuals, and hence a tax burden proportional to individual property holdings paralleled the distribution of government benefits. A few writers, however, argued that the benefit principle of taxation dictated a progressive tax burden. Government expenditures, they said, went largely to protect the property and persons of the rich from the poor, and many government expenditures were of particular benefit to the rich.

During the nineteenth century, a French radical and a conservative American economist advanced the "compensatory" argument for progression.[17] Walker's justifications were: (1) "The undoubted fact that differences of property and income are due, in no small degree, to the failure of the state in its duty of protecting men against violence and fraud," and (2) "differences in wealth are in a measure due to the acts of the state itself, having no political purpose, as treaties of commerce, tariffs, currency legislation, embargoes, non-intercourse acts, wars, etc."

[16] Valuable surveys are E. D. Fagan, "Recent and Contemporary Theories of Progressive Taxation," *Journal of Political Economy*, Vol. 46, 1938, p. 457; and W. J. Blum and H. Kalven, *The Uneasy Case for Progressive Taxation* (University of Chicago Press, Chicago, 1953).

[17] C. A. Royer, *Théorie de l'impôt ou la dîme sociale* (Paris, 1862). F. A. Walker, *Political Economy* (New York, 1883), pp. 489–490; in the 1888 third edition of this work these passages were omitted.

But the ability and sacrifice doctrines present the strongest arguments for progression. According to many adherents of these doctrines, since the principle of diminishing utility applies to ownership of wealth and receipt of income, taxpaying ability increases more rapidly than does the increase of wealth or income. A poor man's property represents necessities, and all his income is expended on such items. As wealth and income increase, the proportions devoted to necessities and seminecessities grow smaller and smaller. The surplus over and above, which measures taxpaying ability most truly, mounts more rapidly than the basic wealth or income.[18]

In the 1930's, quite another line of argument was used to support tax progression—that it would help stabilize the economy. Chapter 27 discusses this argument.

Progressive taxation is of course the keystone of the equalization doctrines of taxation. But the acceptance of these doctrines in their extreme form would lead to a progression so steep as to be confiscatory on large fortunes and incomes, since there would be no conclusive reason for stopping equalization short of complete individual (or family) equality.

Arguments against progression, above certain modest amounts, take different forms. (1) Proportional taxation will take enough more from the high than from the low income groups to meet reasonable humanitarian needs, such as financing the transfer of real income to help the poor. In other words, progression is not needed to take much more from the prosperous than from the poor. (2) A person who has worked hard should receive the fruits of his efforts, or at least not be penalized excessively. Is it not unfair, critics ask, to put progressively heavier burdens on those who do most for society, as measured by what the public will freely pay? (3) Most of the nonroutine administrative problems of income and death taxes result from the existence of progressive rates. As we shall see in later chapters, attempts to shift income or wealth from one tax bracket to another create troublesome problems of enforcement. These would disappear with the end of progression. (4) Moreover, such attempts lead to distortions of personal and business life. Economic activity is channeled into lines that would not otherwise represent the taxpayer's best judgment of what is economically wise. (5) Injustice results from differences in the ability of taxpayers to escape high rates, legally or illegally. (6) The schedule of rates may be steeper than can be reasonably justified by the decline in the marginal utility of money. If so (one can hardly prove the point one way or the other), a policy adopted to treat different income groups equally by

[18] It is interesting to note that the sacrifice argument for progressive taxation was compactly stated in the Institutes of Manu, supposed to date from the twelfth century B.C.:

"To make the burden of taxes equal, it should be made to press with equal severity upon every individual. This is not effected by a mere numerical proportion. The man who is taxed to the amount of one-tenth of an income of 100 rupees per annum, is taxed far more severely than the man who is taxed an equal proportion of an income of 1,000 rupees."

taking account of the differences in the marginal utility of income, discriminates in fact against those in the upper ranges. (7) Incentives to effort and risk-taking may be damaged, and the ability to accumulate capital will be curtailed. Among the adverse results would be a reduction in the ability of small and closely-owned businesses to grow. (8) The total revenue obtainable from the progressive portion of a high rate schedule is surprisingly small.

The case for progression may, or may not, seem "uneasy," but it rests rather more on intuition than some of us like. Instinctively, we endorse it, but without being able to prove the point. Some of the doubts held by many scholars today result from extremes to which law-makers have gone. Thus, it is not so much progression that disturbs more and more serious observers as the extent to which it has been carried here and in some foreign lands.

Accomplishment of tax progression. How can progressive tax burdens be imposed? The obvious way is by applying progressive rates to a personal tax base. But is this the only way? Not necessarily, for a little tax progression might be secured by a judicious selection of nonpersonal taxes such as commodity taxes on luxuries of the high income groups, and by the use of continuing exemptions.[19]

Total Income	*Taxable Income*	*Tax*	*Tax as Per Cent of Total Income*
$ 2,000	$ 0	$ 0	.0
2,500	500	100	4.0
3,000	1,000	200	6.7
4,000	2,000	400	10.0
5,000	3,000	600	12.0
10,000	8,000	1,600	16.0
100,000	98,000	19,600	19.6

Since ownership of business is held by groups with above-average wealth, nonshiftable business taxes which reduce business profits will rest more heavily on the prosperous than on the poor. Consequently, a corporation income tax with a proportional rate will, to the extent that it is not shifted, impose a crudely progressive burden, with painful exceptions, upon individual incomes. Homestead exemptions introduce a moderate, irregular amount of progression into the property tax.

Income and death taxes having progressive rate schedules will impose progressive burdens. But progression applied to the rate schedules of commodity taxes can do very little. (Try to imagine a rate on cigarettes or beer that would impose a progressive burden on consumers.) Nor will

[19] How a continuing exemption in a tax with a proportional rate can produce progression is illustrated by the following example of a 20 per cent income tax with a $2,000 exemption. As the tax base—income, for example—increases above the exemption, the amount exempted is an ever-smaller fraction of the whole and the tax rate applies to a growing proportion of the whole.

a progressive rate schedule in a business tax produce a progressive burden upon any group of individuals. All relation between burden and base disappears if the tax is shifted. And in the case of a nonshifted business tax, there is no assurance of any consistent relationship between the business base involved and the private circumstances of the owners of the taxed business. Progressive business taxes may accomplish various regulatory ends, but they are a mistaken means to any distributive end.

Personal tax schedules can be made progressive in three ways. Instead of stating the tax as a percentage rate, it can be stated in *fixed amounts per unit of the base*. An income tax might thus be levied as $1 for incomes up to $100, $3 for incomes between $100 and $200, $6 for incomes between $200 and $300, and so forth. For broad income brackets this method would involve regression within the limits of each bracket. This criticism does not apply if the income brackets are very narrow, as they are on the simplified federal personal income tax return where liability is stated in this way.

Where the rate of a personal tax is stated as a percentage, its progression may be either lump-sum or by brackets. *Lump-sum* progression, sometimes called "totality progression," is accomplished by applying each successively higher rate to the entire tax base. In an income tax, incomes up to $1,000 might be taxed 15 per cent, incomes between $1,000 and $2,000 might be taxed 18 per cent on the entire income, incomes between $2,000 and $3,000 might be taxed 20 per cent on the entire income, and so forth.[20]

For *bracket* progression, each successively higher rate is applied only to that portion of the income coming within the tax bracket. Thus, the income tax might be 15 per cent on incomes up to $1,000, 15 per cent on the first $1,000 of incomes between $1,000 and $2,000 and 20 per cent on the excess, whereas incomes between $2,000 and $3,000 might be taxed 15 per cent on the first $1,000, 20 per cent on the next $1,000, and 25 per cent on the excess of the income over $2,000. With rate schedules otherwise comparable, lump-sum progression imposes the heavier burden because the high rates apply to the whole rather than to a fraction of large incomes or estates. In the United States, bracket progression is the rule.

The effect of any given schedule of progressive rates will depend upon the general level of incomes and property values. Let us assume that prices and incomes double. The man now receiving $8,000 can buy no more than when he got $4,000. With progressive income tax rates, however, his tax may be substantially more than twice what it was. Falling prices yield the opposite result. A schedule of progressive rates that is appropriate at one

[20] A "notch" provision is required in connection with lump-sum progression, so that in certain income ranges the tax does not cause a higher pre-tax income to be lower after tax than another income that was smaller before tax. Thus, if the rate on $1,000 is 10 per cent and the rate on all incomes of from $1,001 to $2,000 is 15 per cent, without a notch provision, the tax on $1,000 would be $100, leaving $900 after tax, and the tax on $1,001 would be $150.15, leaving $850.85 after tax. The usual method is to impose special rates on incomes in the notch.

time will presumably not be appropriate after any considerable inflation or deflation.

Effectiveness of progression. The rate schedule of a progressive tax does not indicate the *effective* progression.

(1) Bracket progression, as already indicated, produces an effective progression lower than the sequence of bracket rates because only fractions of the taxable base are subject to the higher bracket rates.

(2) In the case of the personal income tax, certain types of income—interest on tax-exempt bonds, and a large proportion of oil-well yields, for example—are exempt, and another type—capital gains—is taxed at a special low rate. These types of income are received to a disproportionate extent by individuals in the higher income brackets.

(3) Charitable donations and bequests, which reduce the tax due, are relatively more important for upper than for lower income and wealth groups.

(4) Income and death tax liability can often be substantially reduced by readjustments of an individual's affairs. Laws permit what is now a long list of such opportunities; several will be described in later chapters.

The 1955 federal burden on a taxable income of $1,000,000 was nominally around 86 per cent for a married man. Yet, in fact, the average effective rate on reported incomes over $1,000,000 was about 40 per cent of net income including exempt capital gains but not including tax exempt interest. There can be, and generally is, a significant difference between the *nominal* progression of an income or death tax and its *effective* progression.

Limits to progression. How high can progressive tax rates go? Theoretically, bracket progression can impose rates up to 100 per cent—that is, to complete confiscation of the excess of incomes or estates over specified levels. In practice, several considerations indicate that progression should stop far short of 100 per cent:

(1) The higher the top level rates of a progressive tax, the greater is the incentive to minimize the tax by all legal means—and some that are illegal—devisable by able "taxperts." Personal and business decisions are distorted for tax reasons. Pressure for emasculating the law grows. The highest rates of the federal personal income tax tend to be self-defeating by their very severity.

(2) The total taxable income embodied in the excess of incomes over $500,000, or over $100,000, or even over $50,000, is trifling compared with the country's total income base or with the revenue needs of the federal government. Semiconfiscatory rates on high income brackets may be imposed for social reasons, but they yield rather little revenue. (The top rates may, in fact, yield no revenue on balance after allowance is made for the extra use of avoidance devices they stimulate.) The same is true of very high top-bracket estate or inheritance tax rates.

(3) Income and death taxes with nearly confiscatory top bracket rates may exercise injurious influences on economic development. They tend to dry up important sources of funds for new capital growth, and they may weaken the incentives to effort and efficiency that contribute to economic progress.

We cannot give any categorical answer to the question of how high progressive tax rates can safely go. We can only say that personal income tax progression carried to the top rates of the present federal tax produces a number of adverse economic effects. These must be weighed against the distributional arguments for sharp progression. The revenue significance is slight; stopping the present federal rate schedule at 50 per cent would cut the yield of the tax by only 3 per cent.

Some support has been mustered for a constitutional amendment limiting the top federal peacetime income and estate tax rates to 25 per cent. Several state legislatures have endorsed the principle. The proposal finds little support among fiscal scholars. Such a limit would force Congress to turn to alternative revenue sources which would generally be regarded by economists as less desirable than the higher income and death tax rates.

REGULATORY TAXATION

Broadly speaking, every tax which touches business relationships is "regulatory." A tax which raises the price of a commodity deters its sale and hence its production; the sale and production of commodities that compete directly or indirectly may be affected beneficially. A tax which imposes a discriminating burden on any type of business or class of business organization upsets the competitive equilibrium. Special exemptions in any tax constitute a sort of bounty to the exemptees and alter the business pattern.

Fiscal scholars have always recognized that taxes and exemptions modify the economic structure. The controversy is not over the fact of modification, but over whether it should be deliberate. Since all taxes have nonrevenue results, the selection from among the possible alternative bases and rate structures cannot be wise unless it takes account of all results.

Occasionally in the past—the protective tariff is a case in point—and with increasing frequency in recent times, legislators have enacted taxes primarily or even exclusively for their regulatory effects. The objectives of these deliberately regulatory taxes or exemptions may be classified as: (1) to control certain elements of consumption, (2) to control certain elements of production or distribution, and (3) to control business conduct.[21] In some foreign countries we find cases of bachelor taxes and other levies specially devised to encourage marriage or otherwise control the social

[21] Excluded from this discussion, but covered in Part Six, is the issue of regulation through taxation of the general level of economic activity.

system, but this type of tax control has not so far appeared in American legislation, except possibly in some uses of poll and franchise taxes.

Controlling consumption. Consumption of commodities and services can be controlled by taxation in two ways: (1) Purchase of harmful commodities may be discouraged by discriminatory taxes, and (2) socially desirable consumption can be stimulated by suitable exemptions, such as the exemption of food from some general sales taxes or of private hospitals and schools from property taxes.

The federal tax system offers several interesting examples of regulatory taxes which produce hardly any revenue but which discourage the sale of harmful items. Opium manufactured for smoking purposes is taxed $300 per pound; sales of marihuana for nonmedicinal purposes are taxed $100 per ounce. Sales of machine guns and certain firearms to unlicensed parties are taxed $200 per transfer. Payment of these taxes would make the prices of narcotics and firearms practically prohibitory. Nonpayment gives the federal government, which does not possess police powers enabling it to forbid manufacture and sale of these items, power to prosecute for tax evasion.

The so-called "sumptuary" taxes, like the federal tobacco and liquor excises, represent a partial approach to consumption control through taxation. Here, the regulatory objective is not to prohibit consumption of articles deemed obnoxious to public morals,[22] but rather to penalize their purchase by making them more expensive. The entire idea of "sumptuary" excises is self-contradictory. If they effectually reduce consumption of the taxed articles they must fail as revenue producers, whereas if they succeed as revenue producers they have failed as consumption controllers. This self-contradiction has not interfered with the persistence of the idea.[23]

Controlling production and distribution. Prohibition of harmful commodities, practices, and services can be accomplished by taxing the producer as well as the product. The federal opium and firearms excises are

[22] Only a trifling number of people could be found today who consider smoking immoral; the disapprovers of liquor drinking are more numerous, but still a minority of the population. Nonetheless, the tradition has persisted, at least for fiscal purposes, that tobacco and alcoholic liquor pander to the weaknesses of the flesh and that indulgence in them should be penalized. The term "sumptuary" has the same base as "sumptuous."

[23] Oleomargarine taxes, once imposed by the federal government and many states, represent another perversion of the regulatory principle as applied to consumption of harmful articles. In the 1860's, dairy farmers found that oleomargarine, made from animal fats and vegetable oils, was beginning to offer serious competition to butter. They claimed that its consumption was harmful. Actually it is but slightly, if at all, inferior to butter in nutritional and other health elements. But Congress, moved by the bloc of votes represented by the dairy farmers, taxed oleomargarine two cents a pound. Subsequently the rate was set at ten cents a pound, if margarine was colored to resemble butter, one quarter cent a pound if it was not colored. In addition, as many as 18 states superimposed state margarine taxes of 5, 10, and 15 cents. The federal tax was dropped in 1950; many state levies have also been repealed.

further enforced by heavy license taxes on the manufacturers, exemptions being allowed to those who produce under regulation exclusively for authorized uses. A federal tax of two cents per hundred is imposed on white phosphorous matches, not because they are harmful to the users, but because the process of their manufacture is injurious to workers. Somewhat analogous to this match tax were the attempts in 1916 and 1918, held to be unconstitutional, to end child labor by taxing products of such labor when they entered interstate commerce. One of the most famous prohibitory taxes is the 10 per cent federal levy on state banknote circulation, imposed in 1865; the injury to be avoided in this case was the weakness of a currency system which included the notes of poorly regulated state banks.

Tariffs are in essence commodity taxes on one group of items, imported articles, while a competing group—domestic articles—are tax free. As with the other regulatory levies, the "success" of a "protective" tariff may be measured by its failure to produce revenue. Chain-store taxes, discussed in Chapter 15, are designed to handicap chain stores in their competition with independent dealers.

Regulation of production or distribution can also be accomplished by a discriminatory (1) exemption or (2) rate variation in an otherwise nonregulatory tax. Some states authorize local governments to exempt the property of newly established enterprises for a term of years as a means of attracting such enterprises. The general exemptions of educational, charitable, and other nonprofit institutions from various forms of taxation can also be considered a regulatory discrimination to encourage them.

Controlling business structure and conduct. A tax may also be used to restrain some practices of business in general or to encourage others. According to arrangements for consolidated returns and taxation of intercorporate dividends under a corporation income tax, the development of holding companies may be either impeded or fostered. The undistributed profits tax of 1936, repealed in 1939, by checking the accumulation of corporate earnings and making corporations more dependent upon the general capital market for the financing of expansion, tended to reduce the power of corporate management.

Special federal tax concessions to owners of oil wells and some mines are intended to encourage exploration and extraction. The lowered unemployment payroll tax rates on firms with relatively stable employment records are designed partly to induce business to stabilize employment. During World War II, one of the major devices used to enforce wage and salary controls was the rule that firms granting increases without prior government approval would not be permitted to deduct wage and salary payments in computing income subject to tax.

Conclusion. Many fiscal scholars have condemned regulatory taxation as perverting the true purpose of taxation—revenue—and as interfering with the conformity of taxes to the principles of fiscal justice. Moreover, they argue, economic regulation through taxation demands a degree of wisdom which neither lawmakers nor tax administrators possess.

Such sweeping condemnation rests on weak logical grounds. Although revenue is unquestionably the primary purpose of most taxes, to state that it is the one and only true purpose is mere arbitrary assertion. Justice in imposing taxes is not necessarily affronted by regulatory taxes, since if they are successes as regulatory measures they will yield little or no revenue and hence work little or no fiscal injustice. And economic regulation, if it is to be undertaken, may require for its accomplishment by taxation no greater legislative or administrative wisdom than the use of more direct means. Furthermore,

> The taxing power can be easily demonstrated to have many advantages over "ordering and forbidding devices" that are conventionally employed by the police state. It does not ordinarily imply a vast bureaucracy; it leaves the specific decisions in the hands of private entrepreneurs; it is largely automatic and immediately effective. Its sanctions strike at the very sinews of economic power—the payment of money. The taxing power, however, is of course neither the exclusive technique available to the modern state, nor one suitable for all ends of policy, but it is one that must be skillfully blended with all the other powers and instrumentalities of government in effectuating common objectives.[24]

A regulatory tax is but a means to an end, and it must be judged in part by that end. If a practice acknowledged to be bad, such as the indiscriminate sale of narcotics, cannot be stopped by direct prohibition because of constitutional limitations on the federal government but can be checked by a tax, what reasonable objection can be raised against such a tax? If educational and charitable institutions can be stimulated by tax exemption, why not exempt them? Where the objective is a special group disadvantage won at the expense of the general welfare, as in the case of oleomargarine and chain-store taxes, then the taxes that accomplish such an end are to be condemned just as any more direct means to accomplish such a purpose would have to be condemned. Where there is dispute as to the goal, as with the issue of high depletion deductions to stimulate mineral production, any tax measures directed toward such goals are open to debate.

Two separate issues arise. One is whether the end itself is desirable, and if so to what extent. The second is whether the tax measure is the most efficient means of achieving the end. A tax provision may get results but at an excessive cost. Often the serious investigator encounters great difficulty in learning what the cost of a regulatory tax feature really is, in the short run and the long. Moreover, a special problem in achieving regulatory ends arises when the taxes used also yield revenue. The treasury welcomes the revenue and wants to hold on to the source. The interests of regulation may then be sacrificed to the pressures for revenue.

[24] Temporary National Economic Committee, *Taxation of Corporate Enterprise* (Monograph No. 9, Washington, 1941), p. 115.

PROBLEMS

1. Devise a scale of personal income tax rates which you believe to be fair. Defend your position.

2. Give the arguments for and against greater use of the benefit principle in raising government revenue.

3. Comment on McCulloch's famous statement that when you abandon proportionality in taxation, "you are at sea without rudder or compass, and there is no amount of injustice and folly you may not commit."

4. "If one is not convinced that the marginal utility of income declines as the amount of income received increases, one has no solid basis for justifying progression in the tax system." Discuss.

5. Indicate the factors which seem reasonable as a basis for determining differences in the amount of tax individuals pay.

6. How might a tax be effective but not efficient as a regulatory measure?

7. Show how it is not necessary to have progressive rates (a) to raise substantially more revenue from a rich man than from one of modest income, and (b) to get progression in the personal income tax considered as a whole.

8. Would progressive rates on corporation income impose progressive burdens on taxpayers? Why? What evidence would help in answering this question?

CHAPTER 10

Revenue, Legislative, and Administrative Considerations

TAX statutes exist to produce revenue. The best possible tax by legal, economic, and distributive standards—if there were such a tax—would have no place on the statute books if it yielded no revenue. And many a tax subjected to the scholars' barrages of criticism is levied and collected year after year because it pours a stream of dollars into local, state, or federal treasuries.

Besides an anlysis of revenue considerations, this chapter deals with the practical issues of tax enactment and tax administration.

REVENUE CONSIDERATIONS[1]

Yield is determined partly by the inherent character of a tax, partly by outside circumstances.

Inherent productivity. Some taxes produce billions of dollars a year, others only a few thousands. These differences in productivity depend upon the tax base, the rate schedule, the related economic effects of the tax, and its administrative aspects.

Obviously the broader the *base* of a tax, the greater its revenue possibilities. With property values in the United States measured by the hundreds of billions, a general property tax even at moderate rates is certain to produce large revenues. So, too, with a gross income or general sales tax and a general net income tax. A tobacco products or gasoline tax, involving an item of general consumption, can likewise produce billions. But a tax on a comparatively narrow base—club dues or yacht sales—can yield only a trifle.

Any *exemption* which narrows the tax base naturally reduces produc-

[1] Revenue adequacy is a problem of the system as a whole and is discussed in Part Six.

tivity. Personal exemptions in an income tax slice a substantial fraction from potential yield. From one-fourth to one-third of potential retail sales tax revenue is sacrificed by exempting foodstuffs.

Within limits, the higher the tax *rate* the greater its yield. But taxes are subject to the rule of diminishing productivity. Each tax rate increase is likely to produce less of a growth in yield than the preceding rate increase of the same size. Particularly is this true of business and personal taxes, where incentives to avoidance and evasion multiply as the tax rate increases. Optimum rates for municipal and state taxes may be low because escape—by removal into other lower-taxing areas—is open to some taxpayers.

A tax which lowers the level of general business activity may reduce the over-all productivity of a tax system, even though the particular tax in question has a positive yield. A tax on a commodity having highly elastic demand, or on one of two competing commodities or lines of business, is likely to fail as a revenue producer because of the consequent decline of consumption and production.

Finally, taxes differ widely in the acuteness of their *administrative problems*. A stamp tax on legal documents is practically self-administering, whereas no organization or technical adroitness has succeeded in taxing stocks and bonds effectively under the property tax.

Stability. With a given rate schedule, the yield of a tax based upon net income fluctuates far more as business fluctuates than do revenues from taxes based on property values, on gross income, or on sales. Yields from taxes on necessities are more stable than yields from taxes on luxuries.

Stability has traditionally been considered a desirable element in the revenue system. More recently the belief has grown that the federal government should palliate depression by operating on a "cyclical budget," with deficit financing during periods of declining business and debt retirement during prosperity. From this viewpoint, the instability of federal income tax yields becomes a virtue. For state and local governments, however, the situation is different. Their financial security depends substantially upon their maintaining a close balance of receipts and expenditures. Consistent revenue inflow is essential to effective state and local budgeting. And any such government is in desperate plight if its income falls off sharply just when recession requires extra expenditures for relief. Desirable though net income taxes may be in most respects, a state should not build its revenue system exclusively, or even preponderantly, around such taxes without making provision for significant revenue fluctuations. A number of states buttress their corporation income taxes by alternative capital stock or gross income schedules in order to establish minimum tax liability. Stabilization reserves are even more desirable—but rare.

Elasticity. Elasticity to meet changing budgetary needs must be combined with the stability of a revenue system. Emergencies or an enlarged scope of government activity may necessitate added revenue. Or, more rarely, a reduction of expenditures may pave the way for revenue reduction.

Rate variation can make the yield of most nonregulatory taxes elastic. Raise the rates and the yield will be higher; lower the rates and the yield will be reduced—but not proportionately. The principle of diminishing productivity must be taken into account. As the rate or rate schedule of any tax is pushed higher, its upward elasticity diminishes. Beyond the point of optimum productivity, further upward elasticity disappears altogether. Unfortunately, we have little concrete evidence to prove what rate of a tax is the optimum. Elasticity may also be lost where outside restrictions, established by constitutional or higher legislative authority, such as those in many states on property taxes which limit the rate which the taxing authority may impose.

Taxes whose rates are determined by regulatory rather than fiscal considerations are likely to be inelastic. This inelasticity is of little importance if the revenue yield is small. But when a regulatory tax is also a major revenue producer, such inelasticity may have unfortunate consequences.

Tax systems, as distinguished from individual taxes, are usually broadly elastic. When additional revenue is desirable, new taxes can be enacted. Some taxes can be dropped when an emergency is over. As a rule, however, "emergency" taxes develop into permanent elements of the tax system and the "elasticity" they represent operates in only one direction—upward. Because they have already been pushed to such extremes, however, tax systems the world over have less potential upward elasticity than before World War II. The uncultivated fields of potential taxation are not hopefully fertile.

Diversity of revenue sources. Upon occasion, theorists have proposed some single tax—a land increment, income, or sales tax—to produce all the revenue needed by a government. A single tax, they argue, would simplify considerations of individual or social distribution and would make the economic effects easier to calculate and control.

But no one tax, within the margins of its productivity, could cover all the current revenue requirements of American governments. The extremely high rates necessary if major dependence were placed on some one tax would be bad in themselves because they would aggravate the distorting effects that taxes produce. Two levies with modest rates would be less likely to undermine the bases of economic efficiency than dependence on either tax alone.

A set of taxes upon various aspects of personal capacity and economic behavior, rather than one single tax, is desirable for nonrevenue reasons. No one tax is free from serious defects, and complete reliance on any one might produce more glaring conflicts with ideas of justice or economic wisdom than use of several taxes. Niceties of distributive justice may be accomplished best through combinations of taxes. Special economic objectives may require particular taxes for their accomplishment. And public opinion, irrationally perhaps, will accept through a multitude of taxes a burden it would denounce as "confiscatory" if imposed by one tax.

ENACTING TAX LAWS

The process of enacting tax laws has become increasingly important during the past quarter-century. Previously, except during World War I, there were relatively few taxes, rates by current standards were low, and changes were infrequent. Framing a workable revenue law rarely presented serious legislative perplexities. Today, however, national, state, and even local governments impose many more kinds of taxes and at higher rates which magnify all the problems. Taxes and their enactment have become major political issues. We shall examine how federal tax laws are framed and passed,[2] and then comment briefly on state and local procedures.

Originating tax bills. The federal Constitution provides that federal revenue measures must originate in the House of Representatives. In practice, however, the President or the Treasury often initiates revenue recommendations. Sometimes these executive proposals are made in great detail, other times in broad terms only. Members of the House are free to propose tax bills. Scores are introduced each session but only those with strong party support have any chance of serious consideration. Senators can propose modifications to tax bills passed by the House.

House action. Congressional consideration of a revenue measure begins with the powerful Committee on Ways and Means of the House of Representatives. Its 25 members, divided by party in roughly the proportions of the House membership, ordinarily conduct public hearings on the President's revenue suggestions and other tax proposals given consideration by the political leaders. The Secretary of the Treasury is invited to open these hearings. After he presents the executive's proposals in broad terms, other Treasury officials follow with more detailed discussion. Then members of the public and of Congress who have sought permission present their arguments.

The Committee chairman has almost complete power in scheduling topics to be considered and in allotting time to witnesses. Treasury spokesmen may be allotted several days. From them the Committee receives carefully prepared analyses of Treasury policy, and supporting data, covering the whole range of the tax proposals before the Committee. "Outside"

[2] The best comprehensive description of federal tax enactment procedure is R. Blough, *The Federal Taxing Process* (Prentice-Hall, Inc., Englewood Cliffs, N.J., 1951), Part II. An excellent account of pressure-group action is W. L. Cary, "Pressure Groups and the Increasing Erosion of the Revenue Laws," *Federal Tax Policy for Economic Growth and Stability* (Washington, 1955), pp. 260–275.

witnesses may be assigned from 15 minutes to half an hour, with additional time possibly to answer questions put by members of the Committee. With relatively few exceptions their testimony is of the "special interest" variety. There is seldom a representative of consumers or of the general public as such. The biased interest of most of the "outside" witnesses results in presentations made vigorously, sometimes with a high degree of competence but not necessarily in the best public interest. In fact, argument tends to be greater than information, and misinformation presented plausibly and persuasively may overbalance facts and logical argument. These witnesses almost invariably advocate measures that would reduce revenue and seldom propose specific ways to offset such revenue loss.

As the testimony piles up, running perhaps to thousands of printed pages, Committee members may discuss among themselves and decide how they will vote on specific issues. Decisions are made in closed "executive sessions." For expert assistance the Committee can draw on the technical staff of the Joint Committee on Internal Revenue Taxation (this joint committee is composed of the top men from the House Ways and Means Committee and the Senate Finance Committee). The Treasury, also, will provide the Committee with estimates of revenue effects and additional information, from broad policy statements to explanation of minute technical details.

As the Committee makes specific decisions by majority vote, its legal staff undertakes the unbelievably complex job of drafting the provisions in legislative terms. The staff also prepares a committee report which explains the purposes of the bill and defends the specific proposals. These explanations in nontechnical terms are important, not only to help Congressmen understand what is intended, but also to inform the public and later to guide the courts in cases involving the tax law.

When all decisions have been reached and all reports written and printed, often with dissents, the chairman of the Ways and Means Committee arranges to have the bill presented on the House floor. This is done under "closed" rule, whereby debate is narrowly limited and amendment is virtually impossible without specific endorsement by the Ways and Means Committee. The House must accept or reject the revenue bill as a whole. Individual members can discuss specific provisions for 2 to 5 minutes but rarely do Representatives have power to alter the bill as submitted by the Committee.

Senate action. When a revenue bill has passed the House it goes to the Senate and is taken under consideration by the thirteen-member Senate Finance Committee. Because much of the ground has been covered in the House hearings, discussion before the Senate Committee is usually briefer; it often benefits from more thorough analysis than was available to the House. The Senate Committee can and often does add amendments—sometimes of major importance. The legal staff of the Senate Finance Committee embodies its amendments in legislative form. A committee report is drafted, and the bill goes to the Senate floor. Debate here is unlimited and new amendments may be added.

Final action. If the Senate bill amends the House bill, it is returned to the House. Occasionally the House may accept the Senate changes as they stand. More likely the two measures are sent to a bipartisan conference committee composed of members of the revenue committees of the two houses. The primary job of the conference committee is to compose the differences. In doing so it commonly accepts many changes which the Senate, with the advantage of more extensive study, has made. In working out a compromise, the conference committee tries to avoid going beyond the position taken by either house or bringing in new provisions. Much bargaining and negotiating are often needed to reach agreement. The resulting measure is almost certain to be accepted by both House and Senate.

The bill then goes to the President. He must accept or reject it as a whole.

Evaluation. The federal procedure of tax legislation has many merits, some defects. On the whole it is more satisfactory than the appropriation procedure. There is less detail to be considered than in an appropriation measure, and the committees can do a more probing analysis. Expert assistance obtained from the staff of the Joint Committee on Internal Revenue Taxation gives valuable technical help. Thorough and competent economic analysis is sometimes presented. Slow turnover on the committees permits some members to gain mastery of one or more elements of the highly complex law.

A major defect in present procedure is the subjection of both Congressional revenue committees, and the membership of both houses, to group pressures. "Outside" witnesses that appear before the two committees are spokesmen seeking the special interests of their groups, regardless of whether these interests coincide or conflict with the general public interest. Groups sometimes organize tremendous campaigns to influence Congress. Treasury representatives speak, of course, on behalf of the Administration, and this may be the best approximation of the general public interest that good thinking by excellent brains can produce. But not always. On occasions the Administration has a political, social, or economic ax of one sort or another to grind. Then the true public interest may be hopelessly buried under masses of biased pleadings. Finally, tax laws have become so bewilderingly complex that anything even approaching informed public judgment is very often impossible. Only a handful of people may be qualified to appraise a proposal which, in fact, has considerable importance.

Enactment of state and local taxes. Procedures for enacting state and local taxes differ widely. In general, they have lagged behind the needs of changing times. At the state level, and even more at the local level, staffs to give informed advice to executive and legislative officials do not exist, or where they have been formed they are inadequate. Not so long ago state and local taxes were simple indeed compared with those today. Rudimentary research may have been tolerably satisfactory—but no longer. States and many cities need truly expert advice. Revenue estimating, among other things, requires greater, and more varied, skill than when tax systems rested heavily on the property tax. Only one out of three state legislatures has a staff for continuing study of fiscal problems; few staffs, if any, have yet been built to a size and quality permitting adequate analysis of today's problems. Special commissions have often served well, but they cannot give sustained effort.

The initiation of tax legislation sometimes comes from the executive, sometimes from within the legislature. Ordinarily, there is some form of public hearing, but nothing approximating Congressional hearings. It is rare that anything more than a short newspaper summary of arguments is made available to the public. Special interest pressures are influential. The effective decisions are ordinarily made in private by party leaders. Some of the normal reluctance to raise taxes is overcome by constitutional requirements that prospective spending *must* be covered by prospective revenues.

THE ADMINISTRATIVE PROBLEM

Taxes are not like market prices, essentially self-enforcing. When one seeks a product or service from a business, one cannot normally expect to get what one wants without paying the price. The supplier has a strong interest in collecting. Government services are different, however. We get them, with few exceptions, whether or not we as individuals pay the price to finance them. So we have incentives to try to avoid payment of tax, incentives which differ fundamentally from those we have to escape the payment of prices. In the latter case, we shall not get what we want unless we pay, whereas in the former we do, individually—though not, of course, collectively. Hence a problem of tax administration arises from the absence of any *quid pro quo* which the taxpayer can expect for his individual tax payment. He may seek to avoid tax, using legal or at least not illegal methods of escaping the burden. Or he may stoop to evasion, violating the letter of the law.[3]

[3] "Evasion" and "avoidance" are sometimes used as synonyms in connection with tax matters. A useful distinction may, however, be drawn between them. "Evasion" should be applied to the escape from taxation accomplished by breaking the letter of the tax law—deliberate omission to report a taxable item, for example. The term "avoidance" is then available to cover escape accomplished by legal procedures which may be contrary to the intent of the tax law's sponsors but nevertheless do not violate the letter of the law. A federal income-tax payer who deliberately omits an item of taxable income from his return *evades* the law. One who devises a trust arrangement overlooked by the framers of the tax law and thereby legally reduces his tax liability *avoids* the tax. Whereas the tax evader breaks the law, the tax avoider sidesteps it. The term "escape" is frequently used to cover both evasion and avoidance, and sometimes shifting as well.

Tax avoidance. Inadequate goals for tax legislation and improper drafting of tax laws, rather than administrative laxity, make tax avoidance possible. A few influential legislators may, for example, get into the law provisions which in fact open loopholes for some taxpayers. Avoidance also becomes possible when legislators list a series of taxable subjects intended to be all-inclusive but by oversight omit some items. Any taxpayer may then try to organize his properties, activities, or business as to come within the omitted classification. Even though the legislators never intended such exemption, the courts will hold the taxpayer beyond the reach of the taxing power by the express provision of the statute. The intent of the taxpayer is immaterial—transactions authorized within the provisions of a tax law do not lose their immunity because the taxpayer intends to avoid the tax.

Courts, too, have some responsibility for tax avoidance. It has been a long-established precept that: "In the interpretation of statutes levying taxes it is the established rule not to extend their provisions, by implication, beyond the clear import of the language used, or to enlarge their operations so as to embrace matters not specifically pointed out. In case of doubt they are to be construed most strongly against the Government, and in favor of the citizen."[4] At times in applying this principle, however, the courts have construed tax statutes with ferocious strictness and have applied the broadest of interpretations to constitutional limitations upon tax powers. In their anxiety to protect the individual's "liberty" from the "tyranny" of the taxing power, they have ignored clearly expressed legislative intent. However, the federal courts and a number of the state courts have in recent years experienced a change of heart. Current judicial construction is along the lines of sustaining legislative intent and administrative practice wherever a sound common-sense case can be made out in its favor. Federal tax legislation in particular has felt this judicial trend, admittedly at the expense of some uncertainty for taxpayers, much criticism, and some "hard cases."

In the last analysis, allowing for favorable court construction, the best preventatives for tax avoidance are simplicity, uniformity, and completeness in tax statutes, with exceptions and exemptions eliminated as much as possible and vigorous administration of the laws after they are passed. In some ways this is an impossible ideal. Our complex economy necessitates complexities in tax laws. The high rates of many major taxes require special exceptions and exemptions if laws are not to work impossible hardship in particular cases. The task of legislatures and courts is to strike a reasonable balance between simplicity and complexity, between uniformity and special provisions.

Tax evasion. Most tax evasion can be blamed on administrative weakness. Either the law has not provided adequate penalties for evasion, or

[4] *Gould* v. *Gould,* 245 U.S. (1917) 151.

the organization and technique of the administrative machine are at fault. Taxpayers evade the tax because they feel reasonably safe in so doing. But other factors also influence the tendency to pay a tax or to evade it—the general popular attitude toward the government and its expenditure program, popular feeling about the "fairness" of a particular tax, and whether a tax rate is low or high.

ADMINISTRATIVE PRINCIPLES

Over 175 years ago, Adam Smith set forth four canons or maxims of sound taxation.[5] The first, relating to the distribution of tax burdens, was quoted in Chapter 9. The remaining read as follows:

> II. The tax which each individual is bound to pay ought to be certain and not arbitrary. The time of payment, the manner of payment, the quantity to be paid, ought all to be clear and plain to the contributor and to every other person.
>
> III. Every tax ought to be levied at the time, or in the manner, in which it is most likely to be convenient for the contributor to pay it.
>
> IV. Every tax ought to be so contrived as both to take out and keep out of the pockets of the people as little as possible, over and above what it brings into the public treasury of the state.

These canons—certainty, convenience, and economy—are as applicable to the American tax system today as to the English revenue system of 1776.

No human being is expected to be enthusiastic about a tax he must pay. But passive acquiescence and a certain cooperation, albeit grudging, on the part of most taxpayers is necessary to the effective administration of any tax. No small corps of officials, however well intentioned and well trained, could successfully levy and collect a tax from a population stubbornly resisting them at every phase of their task. Having relieved their feelings by grumblings and complaints, taxpayers must be willing to subtract "the total of items P, D, and Q" from "the difference between items X and Y" in calculating net income, to report salaries and wages paid employees. The legislator and administrator cannot ignore public sentiment toward different taxes and different ways of collecting them. And to a great extent the degree of avoidance and evasion is determined by the certainty, convenience, and economy with which a tax is levied and collected and by the related factors of familiarity and tax consciousness.

Certainty. Confused provisions of law or regulations inspire taxpayer resentment and contribute to tax avoidance. If there are alternative interpretations of some detail, the taxpayer will naturally choose the one involving the lowest tax. Should the administration overlook the point, avoidance results. Or, if the administration spots the irregularity, the outcome is an imbroglio which leaves the taxpayer aggrieved if not embittered.

Simplicity in tax legislation is the first step toward certainty. Of course,

[5] Smith, *The Wealth of Nations,* Book V, Chapter 2.

a tax applying to a complex subject, such as net income or "corporate capital stock employed within the taxing state," cannot be covered by the phraseology of a children's primer. High tax rates have brought irresistible pressure for detailed and complex refinements—to provide justice or special favors. Nevertheless, the substance and language of many tax statutes could be simplified without materially impairing the situation of those whose complex personal and business interests cannot be taxed justly under an elementary law. Typographical tricks—the use of varied types in printing the law, catchwords, head-notes, indentations, and the like—can, without sacrificing legalistic exactitude, be used to guide the taxpayer. And no principle of lawmaking requires sections and clauses of a tax law to be jumbled in haphazard confusion, regardless of logic or common sense.

Legislators are not the sole contributors to the taxpayers' bewilderment. State tax commissions, which should share with their legislatures the responsibility for framing the revenue laws of their states, must bear part of the blame for the confusion of some state tax laws. After Congress enacts a tax statute, the Treasury supplements the law with regulations[6] (sometimes with booklets explaining the regulations) and interprets the regulations with frequent "decisions." Both published and unpublished rulings, interpretations, and mimeographs attempt to convey to officials the policy and attitude of the administration. Individual officials add personal and unwritten interpretations. In some states the discretion retained by administrators is excessive. A business, for example, cannot be sure of its tax liability until its case has been decided by an official.[7]

Judicial interpretation then enters. Every federal district court, the Tax Court, and the Court of Claims establish the law in those cases over which they have original jurisdiction. Circuit Courts of Appeals hand down binding interpretations. The Attorney-General's opinions on tax matters are controlling on the administrative authorities; the Chief Counsel governs the Service by determining the cases in which to apply for, or consent to, review and the cases in which to acquiesce in lower court decisions. And the Supreme Court has final word in the limited class of cases which, after years of litigation, finally reach it. A dozen or more sources, with diverse aims, backgrounds, and equipment, contribute to the stream of tax law vexing and confusing federal taxpayers. Somewhat similar complication of interpretative agencies confuses the meaning of state tax laws.

Lawyers, accountants, "taxperts," and the tax departments of large corporations are aided in their endeavors to thread the complexities of federal and state tax law by the looseleaf "tax services" published by

[6] Before a regulation becomes effective, it is published and comment is invited. Suggestions from interested members of the public often lead to modifications.

[7] This condition applies especially to taxes on the income of firms doing business across state lines. The possibility of favoritism exists, and the public has little way to check on what happens.

Prentice-Hall, Inc., and other commercial organizations, and by various "tax manuals." These services and aids coordinate statutory, administrative, and judicial tax law and report it in well-organized, clarified form.

With present tax rates, persons planning business decisions face a great obstacle if the tax consequences of the various alternatives cannot be foreseen clearly. Some progress has recently been made in devising arrangements under which a business, before making an important decision, can seek a ruling on the tax aspects, which will bind the Treasury. Unfortunately, the conditions that must be met to obtain such "closing agreements" are so strict that few businesses can benefit.

Upon administrative agencies rests the responsibility to prepare tax forms and regulations. In recent years, the federal Internal Revenue Service has made real progress, and the forms and regulations for various of its taxes have been markedly improved. Congressional simplification of some parts of the law has aided immensely. Some state tax administrations have also sought to reduce taxpayers' uncertainty by issuing clear, concise instructions. Professional associations of tax officials are helping to improve the quality and reduce the conflict of state laws and interpretations. Some tendency of states to follow federal practice simplifies the problem for the taxpayer.

Confusion resulting from arbitrary and hairsplitting judicial interpretations cannot be cured while tax issues remain subject to court review. And under a system of constitutional government, this means forever. Some uncertainty is part of the price paid to protect individual liberties and rights from arbitrary encroachment by government action.

Familiarity. In fiscal matters, familiarity breeds not contempt but resignation and understanding. Heated though the opposition to a tax may be upon the occasion of its first levy, opposition wanes as the tax survives. Taxpayers become accustomed to filling in the tax forms, and calculations which once seemed hopelessly intricate become simplified through repetition. Once a clear statement of the general principles has been provided, it should remain unchanged. Five years or more may be necessary for the great mass of taxpayers to become reasonably familiar with a new tax law or provision.

Administrative procedure crystallizes into efficient routine, and disputes between taxpayers and the administration decrease in number as regulations, rulings, and decisions clarify the tax law. More than once it has looked as though federal Internal Revenue Service might be swamped under the income tax disputes and unsettled tax cases piling up awaiting rulings. But as precedents have been established for the points in dispute, the staff has cleared away the backlog. Furthermore, long continuance of a tax permits the courts to pass upon the disputed points, and as these clear up, the task of administration is eased. Changes have been made in the federal income tax every year or two since it was enacted. The major body of the law, however, and most of the tremendous edifice of administrative and judicial interpretation, persist unmodified and familiar.

Administrators and legislators give much weight to acquiescence. Once a tax is well established, they are loath to change its base substantially or to substitute another. Unsatisfactory as the first tax may be in many respects, its general acceptance makes it a certain source of revenue. Popular prejudice may ruin a new tax, for all that it promises to be superior. Similarly, administrators faced by the need for additional tax revenue prefer an increase in the rates of existing taxes to the levy of a new tax. And taxpayers are often irked less by a heavier tax levied under a familiar system than by a lower, but new, tax requiring new calculations and procedure.

Special effort on the part of the tax administration can, however, avert much popular prejudice.[8] The alert administrator must turn missionary when some new tax is levied. He becomes a sales executive with a new "commodity" to sell, and he must advertise its virtues. The new tax can be publicized through press releases, through special articles and question-and-answer columns in trade newspapers, magazines, and the general press, and through speeches before civic organizations and taxpayers' associations. To gain taxpayers' good will, committees should be consulted upon practical details of accounting procedure when reporting forms are being prepared. Taxpaying groups may also be consulted in the formulation of the interpretative regulations. And no wise administrator is arbitrary or bureaucratic in the actual administration of a new tax. Where conciliation and compromise are warranted, he conciliates and compromises. Because of the great expense of taking a disputed point to court, the great mass of taxpayers are largely at the mercy of the tax official when a question arises. A tax administrator supervising the imposition of a new tax must be a referee, standing between the state on the one hand and the taxpayer on the other, with the sole idea and desire of seeing that both are treated fairly.

Convenience. Taxpayer convenience and administrative convenience or efficiency are not mutually contradictory. Rather, the two are in close harmony. To the extent that the details of a tax law and its regulations conform with taxpayer convenience, they contribute to popular acquiescence and ease the problems of administration. Payroll deduction of the federal personal income tax is a major step in providing more convenient means of tax payment, though imposing extra costs on 4,000,000 employers and some detail work for the Treasury.

Although most tax statutes are drafted with the convenience of the taxpayer in mind, this factor is occasionally overlooked. For example, the federal estate tax for a long time was unduly rigid in the time limitations

[8] A sad example of how *not* to act was New York City's failure year after year to issue official sales tax regulations. Business did not know what to do and had no firm basis for holding the administrators to any certain rules.

it set for payment of the tax. Usually, amendments correct these initial oversights. Sometimes, however, legislative indifference results in the persistence of a stupid provision. Instalment payment of property taxes would be a boon to most property owners, but until recently, provision for quarterly payment was exceptional. Inadequacy of tax administration, however, remains the most common cause of taxpayers' inconvenience. For a long time, overcentralization, compelling taxpayers to journey to state capitals or to Washington to settle minor disputed points, was a vicious source of irritation.

Although pressure from taxpayers plus rising competence of administrators have produced many devices to make taxpaying more convenient, shortage of staff and equipment have slowed progress. More funds for administration are needed to serve taxpayers as well as is reasonably possible—giving prompt answers to questions, good service in helping fill out tax returns, frequent audits so that the taxpayer knows definitely how he stands, service by mail to save waiting in line, evening tax office hours, frequent billing.

The growth in number of taxes has multiplied taxpayer inconveniences. Differences in federal and state concepts of taxable income, for example, are certainly a nuisance. State corporation taxes vary in all sorts of nonessentials. Fortunately, authorities are gradually reducing these conflicts, but there is still much that could be done.

Economy. Assessment and collection of any tax involve costs. Office space, equipment and materials, and salaries cost money. In fairness to the taxpaying public, these administrative costs should be held to a practicable minimum. But a low administrative cost is not *per se* an indication of a good tax or a good administrative agency. The problem of administrative economy is not that simple. What ratio administrative costs bear to tax collections depends upon a number of factors—the taxes imposed, the efficiency of the administration, and the intensity of administrative effort. And not to be overlooked are the costs of compliance imposed upon taxpayers.

The costs of administering the various taxes differ widely in absolute amount and per dollar of revenue. A specific tax on commodities or legal documents involves a minute administration cost if it can be collected by the sale of stamps which must be affixed to the articles or documents. Administrative and compliance costs of retail sales taxes amount to around 5 per cent of collections. A personal income tax, requiring detailed auditing and review of complicated returns, is expensive to administer well.[9] As a general rule, it will cost less to administer a commodity tax whose collection can be centered on a few large-scale producers or wholesalers

[9] The simplified return, however, permits very economical administration. On the other hand, the necessity of refunds of overpayments of tax collected from the employer adds to costs.

than one collected from a multitude of small dealers or consumers. For this reason, the states collect their gasoline taxes from the distributing companies rather than the service stations.

Within limits, the administrative cost of any tax varies inversely with its rate. A 1 per cent retail sales tax and a 2 per cent retail sales tax involve exactly the same number of returns, but the revenue of the latter, although not necessarily double, will be much larger. Administrative effort and costs will advance somewhat, since the higher rate will hold out more inducements for evasion, but—unless the rate of the tax is pushed beyond the optimum point—not pro rata to the increase in revenue. High minimum exemptions in personal and business taxes reduce the relative costs of administration. A personal income tax return submitted for a three or four dollar payment costs that much or more to audit, file, and possibly check—a cost which produces no net revenue.

The smaller the amount spent on tax administration, the poorer is the quality of the result. An efficient tax administration, of course, costs the public less than an inefficient one. *But a low ratio of costs does not necessarily indicate efficient administration.* A tax office that makes no attempt to discover avoidance or check evasion, that contents itself with accepting such revenue as is voluntarily paid in, can show a very low ratio of costs to revenue. An office that genuinely seeks to collect the full amount of taxes payable under the law, that seriously audits returns and makes sample checks, that provides the review machinery necessitated by its more intensive enforcement, will collect much more revenue, but it will also have a higher ratio of administrative costs.[10] Low costs resulting from administrative indifference are as much an injury to the taxpaying public as high costs resulting from waste. Ample evidence indicates that additional funds spent on administration would yield many times their amount in added collections, yet even governments starved for funds refuse to provide enough to collect taxes due under existing law. One commission in 1958, for example, tried to get an additional $1.4 million for enforcement, pointing out that careful studies of experience left no doubt that at least $10 million more would be collected in a single year. The legislature voted nothing. The revenue additions from audits made in one year will accrue indefinitely as taxpayers once caught refrain from repeating the same errors.[11]

Finally, most taxes impose "compliance" costs. A taxpayer who in the

[10] For description of rationally directed effort to learn how much should be spent on audit, see R. B. Welch, "Measuring the Optimum Size of a Field Audit Staff," *National Tax Journal*, Sept., 1954, pp. 210–221.

[11] Thus, when Iowa reported that it spent $1 to collect each $4 of sales tax deficiency in 1957, the cost, although obviously well worth while, may seem high. Yet the full benefits from the 1,500 audits will come only over the years as the businesses affected do a better job of compliance.

course of the year devotes hours to keeping special records and calculating income tax is spending valuable time without compensation. Well-to-do individuals pay substantial fees to lawyers or accountants to prepare their tax returns; even people with small incomes frequently seek the advice of "hole-in-the-wall" tax advisors—for charges which are often gross overpayments for the quality of the advice received. Large business concerns must employ a special staff to handle tax matters, must pay lawyers and accountants for tax services, must occasionally engage in expensive tax litigation.

Tax consciousness. When an individual is taxed in his private capacity on the income he earns or on the property he owns, he pays out funds which he could otherwise have used for a new suit of clothes, for an extension to his house, for a vacation trip, or for saving. To taxpayers, a personal tax seems a direct deprivation, and it is often resented accordingly. Government services received seem less closely tied to a personal tax payment than food and clothing are to the payments we must make for them.

Businessmen, on the contrary, are more likely to regard the taxes—other than net income taxes—paid by their enterprises as a cost of business operation. Such taxes are no more a special deprivation than factory or office rent, the prices paid for raw materials, and wages and salaries. Furthermore, many businessmen believe that all business taxes, even net income taxes, are shifted eventually to the consuming public. If the government wishes, let it impose business taxes; somehow, business will increase its prices and pass on the tax. So most business taxes are likely to appear less obnoxious to the concerns that pay them than personal taxes do to individual taxpayers.

The general shifting of commodity and business taxes to consumers results in a regressive burden. Economists, editors, labor leaders, and occasionally politicians tell the masses of their "exploitation" by such indirect taxes. But because consumers do not directly hand dollars and cents to a tax collector, they fail to recognize the tax burden imposed upon them. They are not *conscious* of any tax payment. And so commodity and business taxes, though generally shifted, invoke little popular opposition.

From the administrative viewpoint, a levy which arouses no "tax consciousness" is preferable to one which does—the problem of combating evasion is milder. Nevertheless, administrative considerations are not the only ones which enter this issue. The personal taxes which arouse "tax consciousness" are in closer conformity with current ideas of fiscal justice, and seem less likely to depress business, than shiftable taxes on commodities and business. And there is a school of thought which praises "tax consciousness" *per se.* Taxpayers who are made aware of a personal tax, it is argued, are more likely to become champions of economical government and enemies of public extravagance.

ADMINISTRATIVE ORGANIZATION

Federal government, state governments, and local governments have each developed distinctive tax administrative machinery.

Federal tax organization.[12] Two independent bureaus of the Treasury Department administer federal taxes. Customs duties are collected by the Bureau of Customs, whose existence began with the organization of the federal government. The Internal Revenue Service (formerly the "Bureau of Internal Revenue") collects all other taxes. It dates from 1861, but was a rather small unit until the flood of World War I taxes brought the staff to over 20,000. It shrank in the 1920's but began to expand in the 1930's. Serious efforts were then made to improve the organization. The most important were (1) improvement in the quality of the personnel, and (2) decentralization, which began in 1938.

World War II multiplied the workload many times just when personnel and equipment were scarcest. Despite tremendous obstacles, however, new and old taxes were administered at least moderately well. Improvement was quietly speeded when the war ended, although it was checked continually by shortage of appropriations. In the early 1950's, criticism of the Service became a major public issue. Evidence of corruption as well as inefficiency received headlines. The evil centered in the political branch of the Service. This branch involved the 64 collection districts, each headed by a politically-appointed Collector of Internal Revenue. The collection staffs contained many persons who originally obtained their jobs through politics. Suspicion also fell on a few high Service officials politically chosen.

Reform was demanded, and by mid-1953 the Internal Revenue Service had a new administrative organization. Only one position remained open to political appointment—that of the Commissioner of Internal Revenue. Washington headquarters has become more clearly a directing agency, setting policies and supervising. Responsibility for operations now rests with 9 district offices, each of which has final authority except in most unusual situations. Actual collection work is done by the staffs of 64 District Directors of Internal Revenue, at least one in each state. Collection work was reorganized primarily on a functional basis; auditing, for example, is done by the same staff for all taxes,[13] in contrast to the former system under which there was a separate staff for each function for each major tax or

[12] For current data, see the annual reports of the Commissioner of Internal Revenue. Much useful information can be obtained from the printed hearings on the annual requests of this agency for appropriations. A useful volume by a former official of the Internal Revenue Service is J. P. Crockett, *The Federal Tax System of the United States: A Survey of Law and Administration* (Columbia University Press, New York, 1955).

[13] The functional organization was abandoned for alcohol and tobacco taxes because of special problems, chiefly the large element of policing required in enforcing liquor taxes.

group of taxes. To help maintain uniformity and high standards of work and integrity, an Inspection Service directed from Washington was organized. Internal Revenue Service employees must now make regular disclosures of their personal financial affairs.

About 80 per cent of the Service's budget goes for salaries. At the opening of the 1959 fiscal year, the Service had 52,000 employees, less than 3,000 in Washington. Most employees are clerical, working primarily on the mass jobs of handling tax returns, payments, and records. Although the personnel has not increased in recent years, additions of mechanical equipment have improved operations significantly; the tax on a simple income tax return can now be computed in 1/70th of a second through use of punch cards. By 1958, most of the mass of clerical work—including the annual mailing of 150 freight cars of tax returns, and the processing of most forms—had been concentrated in 3 service centers.

Federal tax collection costs are about 40 cents for each $100 of revenue obtained. Indeed, total costs are under 20 per cent of *deficiency* collections —that is, supplementary tax payments to cover original underpayments— which are attributable almost entirely to the collection procedure. No one can say how much additional appropriations for auditing would yield in revenue, but probably the ratio would be 10 or even 15 to 1.

A few figures on work loads give some picture of the Service's job. In the 1960 budget it was estimated that the Service would process almost 97,000,000 tax returns, compute and verify tax in 61,000,000 cases, and handle 41,500,000 refunds. Its staff would investigate 200,000 plants, warehouses, and stores, issue 72,000 regulations and rulings, make 2,700,000 audits of tax returns in the Service offices and in the field, handle 6,600 cases in court, and issue 19,200,000 notices of taxes due. In 1957, it assisted 11,000,000 persons to fill out their tax returns.

The new Internal Revenue Service organization, like the old, provides successive levels of review of cases involving disputes. The taxpayer, if he wishes, can demand hearings and conferences with officials of increasingly greater experience and authority (although the costs of proceeding beyond the local level are prohibitive unless at least several hundred dollars are involved). Above the Service stands the Tax Court. This appointed, nonpolitical court of 16 judges has become a valuable link in the chain of federal tax procedure, deciding over 5,000 cases a year. Panels of its judges travel widely to hear cases near the taxpayer's home. Technically, it is an administrative body, not a part of the federal judicial system. Consequently its rules of procedure are simpler than those of other courts, although the early hopes for a cheap, simple, informal agency have been somewhat disappointed. Its findings on questions of fact are usually binding on the higher courts, and its interpretations of the law carry great weight with administrators and with taxpayers.

State tax organization. The characteristic organ of state administration is the state tax commission. More rudimentary bodies—state boards of review and equalization—are found in some states. A few states have achieved a further stage of development, and tax administration has been made a function of a state department of finance. But in two-thirds of the states, most tax administration is at present in the hands of state tax commissions.

Prior to the Civil War, the general property tax, administered locally, was the sole source of revenue in many states. State tax administration machinery first appeared in the 1850's, when Indiana, Iowa, Michigan, New York, and Wisconsin created state boards of equalization.[14] Within three decades, most states had established similar boards. Assessment of the operating property of railroads and other public service corporations was taken from the local assessors in many states and entrusted to these state boards. So, too, administration of special state taxes was increasingly delegated to these bodies.

State boards of equalization, with their characteristically large ex officio or elected membership, proved to be too cumbersome. Indiana in 1891, and many states thereafter, provided a state tax commission to replace the state board of equalization. A distinctive feature of these new bodies was their small membership, usually three, appointed by the governor for four- or six-year terms. To them were entrusted, as a rule, administration of special state taxes and more or less supervisory authority over local tax officials and property tax assessments.

Except for Florida, all the states now have some state official or body specifically charged with tax administration. A few states concentrate administrative powers entirely in the hands of a tax commission, a tax commissioner, or some board of finance or revenue. In most cases, however, responsibility for tax administration is split; the tax commissioner, tax commission, or board of equalization administers the property, income, corporation, and sales taxes, while gasoline and motor vehicle taxes may be placed under a state highway commission, liquor taxes under a state liquor commission, certain corporation taxes under the secretary of state, and still other taxes under other state departments or agencies. As states have added new kinds of taxes since 1930, the tendency has been to lodge their administration in the central tax body. By 1957, a single agency administered the six major taxes in 11 states, while in 18 other states such work was handled by only two bodies. Although the need for geographical decentralization within a state is less pressing than the needs which inspired federal decentralization, offices in two or three leading cities outside the capital are desirable.

Machinery for the *administrative review* of state tax assessments and levies is still unsatisfactory in many states. Only 11 states have special boards of tax appeals. The demarcation between the scope of adminis-

[14] For consideration of the function of state equalization, see Chapter 19.

trative review and that of judicial review is not always clear. Too often, issues which should be settled across an administrative official's desk are litigated. Rarely, too, is the reviewing authority of each grade of administrative official clearly defined, and subordinates, fearful of exceeding their hazy responsibility, prefer to "pass the buck" to their superiors. When, as often happens, a tax commission itself assesses some item for taxation, review is possible only if the commission subsequently sits as a board of review and passes on its own acts as an assessing agency. Independent state boards of tax appeal, with quasi-judicial status, similar to the federal Tax Court, would appear to be a necessary agency of state tax administration.[15]

A small but important role of many tax commissions is collecting and publishing tax data, making continuing and special studies of state and local fiscal problems, and advising the governor or legislature on proposed tax legislation.

Local tax organization. In rural districts, the local property tax assessor and the district or county tax collector comprise all the necessary tax machinery. Property assessment in cities is a more technical matter, and new types of local taxes often involve additional administrative problems of substantial variety and difficulty.

Tax administration in most cities was entrusted initially to an elected board of tax assessors, and many such boards still exist. Typically, they have suffered from lack of adequate technical competence, from shortage of assistance and equipment, and too often from the influence of dominant political machines. In recent years, however, progressive cities, large and small, have made many improvements in tax administration. Since these involve chiefly the property tax, discussion is postponed to Chapter 18.

Centralization of state and local tax administration. The movement for centralization of state-local tax administration has a double objective—to unify the tax administration of a particular government unit and to transfer tax functions from local to state officials.

A deplorable lack of administrative unity in tax assessment and collection is displayed in a number of states. The cause of such heterogeneity is to be found in the development of the tax system. Many state taxes were originally fees attached to particular state offices, and, although they evolved into taxes, no step has been taken to unite their administration with that of other taxes. When tax administration thus remains an incidental function of a series of departments whose main interests and duties lie in other directions, the development of consistent, effective tax administration is impossible.

Administration of all state taxes, except possibly those of a purely regu-

[15] A Model Tax Court Act has been prepared by the American Bar Association. It is designed to give the taxpayer speedy and economical remedy. The rules of procedure recommended are those of the U.S. Tax Court. For a discussion of present arrangements, see Federation of Tax Administrators, *State Administrative Tax Review: Organization and Practices* (The Federation, Chicago, 1958).

latory character, should be unified under a tax commission or department of finance. Such unification has among its advantages the following:

(1) Intensive and intelligent application to the work by executives;
(2) Wider experience and more practical knowledge of tax matters by administrators;
(3) Ability to assign adequate clerical forces for peak-load periods;
(4) Increasing elevation of standards of administration for each new tax;
(5) The development of specialists;
(6) Economy in administration by doing a wholesale rather than a retail business—in other words, quantity production;
(7) The convenience of the taxpayers;
(8) The adoption of a functional distribution of administrative powers;
(9) Ability to cooperate systematically with other states and with the federal government.

City governments which, in addition to property taxes, levy special license, sales, payroll, and other taxes should entrust their administration to the department charged with administering the property tax. Of course, no two taxes have identical administrative problems, but routines of assessment, inspection, audit, collection, appeals, and review are markedly similar. A larger, unified tax staff can develop specializations and effective, economical procedures impossible for small, scattered groups.

Administrative personnel. Traditional American mistrust of bureaucratic government has resulted in a penchant for elected state and local tax officials. The office of assessor is generally elective. Some of the higher tax administrative officials—members of the county boards of review, members of the state boards of equalization, even a few tax commissioners—are also elected.

Tax administrative functions are ministerial, not executive or legislative, and there is consequently no reason why tax officials should be elected. There are many reasons why they should *not* be elected. Election generally results in periodic changes of personnel, and the officeholder does not have the opportunity to master the complicated technique essential to administrative efficiency. Furthermore, elected officials, particularly assessors, are always tempted to subordinate their office to political considerations, to curry favor with their constituents by open or concealed underassessment.

The appointed tax official is the most effective administrator at the top directing level. Such officials should be appointed for a term long enough to insure thorough mastery by the incumbent of the details of administrative technique. Dangers inherent in long tenure can be guarded against, but not eliminated, by vesting power of removal in some higher official or body. The possibility of transforming elected into appointed officials is closely associated with the movement for centralized tax administration.

Membership on local and county boards of review is usually an ex officio function of such other local offices as mayor, town clerk, county clerk, county supervisor, and so forth. Ex officio functions, as a general rule, are not performed with a high degree of efficiency, since the individuals charged with their performance are likely to view them as incidental to the major functions of their proper offices. In the case of local and county review and equalization, however, except for the largest cities, the function is exercised for too short a period in each year to be attached to an independent office. Ex officio boards are probably the most practicable agencies.

Subordinate tax administrative personnel should be under the merit system, as in the federal Internal Revenue Service and many state fiscal agencies. Until recently there was a tendency to consider tax work a relatively low grade of civil service, and salaries for the most part were low. There has been significant upgrading of rankings and compensation of Internal Revenue Service examiners in the past few years. Except for beginners, few receive under $7,000, and a good many get $10,000 or more. This hardly constitutes over-pay. Actually, the work calls for much technical training, tact, and integrity.[16] Even in the subordinate grades, tax administration requires individuals of high caliber.

Federal and state tax offices succeed in obtaining a supply of able young men fresh from law and accounting schools but, in the absence of salary inducements and opportunities for advancement, many of the best do not stay long. After a few years of service, during which these men obtain valuable experience, benefit from the government's special training program, and establish useful contacts, they desert the tax offices for more lucrative private practice. Turnover among the federal and state tax personnel has in the past been unhealthily high, with consequent damage to the services in question. The federal Internal Revenue Service has taken steps to make its employment an attractive career service, and within recent years turnover has dropped substantially. States still rely more on pious hopes than on tangible rewards to hold their most competent personnel, but there *is* progress.

ADMINISTRATIVE TECHNIQUE

Through long experience, certain details of the administrative procedure of taxation have been marked as faulty and others as advantageous.

Assessment technique. A business enterprise numbering its clients or customers by the thousands must devote keenest thought and care to the development of filing and cataloguing systems through which it can reduce most of its relations with clients or customers to an orderly routine. A

[16] Few members of the public have any conception of the responsibility resting with relatively low-ranking tax officials. If an assessor of property values it too low, the owner will not protest, and there is almost no other check. If an income tax agent fails to detect, or refuses to report, an error on a tax return, it will not be caught. Much the same is true of sales taxes. Tens of thousands of dollars of tax liability often depend upon the judgment of an ordinary, rank-and-file agent whose salary is modest at best.

haphazardly run tax office can no more be successful than a carelessly conducted business enterprise.

The first requisite of a good assessment technique is a complete and constantly up-to-date record of persons and business concerns liable for each tax. In the case of property taxes, the tax assessor must keep files of all land transfers. For income taxes, information on salaries paid and on other sources of income must be obtained from the individuals and business concerns making disbursements. Corporation taxes require the administrator to obtain from the state official charged with recording the organization and entrance of corporations information about corporations active in the state. Obvious though this procedure may appear, it is neglected in a surprising number of cases. Until recent years, public opinion has been hypersensitive about the use of private and even public records in determining tax liability. Various state departments gather large amounts of information which would assist the tax office, just as the tax office receives information that would help other state departments to improve their operations. Government departments, however, are surprisingly reluctant to exchange information to aid the performance of each other's duties, and state tax officers are often denied the assistance of other state government units. This isolationist tendency among government departments is waning, however. Furthermore, interchange of tax information between federal and state tax units, and among the tax units of different states, is now fairly widespread.

Assessment technique differs according to whether the tax officials or the taxpayer makes the assessment. The one important tax assessed by tax officials is the property tax. Fortunately, as applied to real estate at least, official records provide a good basis for systematic administration. Some localities have made fairly good use of such records.

No such systematization is possible where the taxpayer makes the assessment or valuation. Nevertheless, the tax administration is not completely at the taxpayer's mercy in the case of income taxes, death taxes, sales taxes, and business taxes based on gross receipts, turnover, and so forth. It has two weapons against evasion in self-assessed taxes—information from outside sources and the sample check. In some cases, the obtaining of information from outside sources can be routinized. Newspaper clippings can supply an alert administrative staff with intimations of income tax evasion by prominent individuals. Cross-checks can be made between personal income, inheritance, and corporation tax returns. For the income tax, employers can be compelled to report salary and wage payments, corporations required to report dividend payments, and so forth. For a small fee, states can obtain photostatic copies of the federal income tax returns of their residents and in addition a transcript showing the nature and amount of all changes made during the federal audit. For all estates subject to federal death tax, the states can in effect obtain all the information gathered by the typically thorough federal authorities. Moreover, interstate co-operation has developed, especially in the exchange of information.

Sometimes a comparison of the taxpayer's way of life—his houses, autos, clothes, entertainment—with his reported income suggests the desirability of intensive investigation. Written complaints, frequently anonymous, disclose instances of evasion which might otherwise pass undiscovered. Some states have experimented with "tax ferrets"—informers paid a percentage of the evaded taxes recovered through their information. The system is used occasionally to uncover evasion of federal customs duties and the federal income tax.[17]

One weapon against both inaccuracy and evasion of self-assessed taxes is the sample check. A tax administration cannot, of course, minutely investigate every one of the tens of thousands of sales tax returns and the millions of income tax cases.[18] Only a small portion, about 4 per cent, of personal income tax returns submitted are carefully examined. But fear of possible detection is highly effective in preventing evasion. A small "flying squad" of auditors, settling for a few weeks in some town, then in some section of a large city, then in a farming community, then moving again to some unknown destination, can in the course of a year carefully examine into the reports of several thousand taxpayers. Evasions discovered in this check may be punished by heavy penalties—with full publicity, which is salutary warning to other prospective evaders. Each published case of tax evasion punishment usually results in a wave of voluntary "corrections" of prior tax "underpayments," most of which would probably not have been caught by routine audit procedure.

The sample check has been developed in another direction. Intensive study of selected cases—different types of retailers subject to sales tax, or various professions for income tax—reveals how to proceed most effectively in examining returns which cannot be investigated in detail.[19]

When a tax is self-assessed, an essential function of tax administration should be to protect the taxpayer against overassessment. The great mass of taxpayers cannot master the details of the income tax nor employ specialists. Nor should they. Accurate and impartial information should be provided by the tax office. If the taxpayer overpays, he should receive a refund as a matter of course. Such treatment is only fair. Moreover, it is essential for sustained success of a self-assessed tax. If the taxpayer feels that the administration is unfair and grasping, he will in self-defense decide doubtful questions against the government and possibly resort to deliberate evasion. If such a tendency were to develop on a large scale, tre-

[17] In 1957, the Internal Revenue Service received 3,900 informers' claims. During the year, it rejected 3,700 claims and allowed 624, totaling $518,000.

[18] Even the simplest income tax return can stand some investigation, if only a check on supplementary income and claims for dependents.

[19] The IRS announced in 1958 that plans were being developed to use the information gained from such studies for mechanical auditing of more complicated returns.

mendous increases in administrative staffs would not prevent large losses of revenue. Since the tax administrator must often press the government's case against avoidance and evasion, he may tend to forget his responsibility to protect the taxpayer. He may become arbitrary, overbearing, and unreasonable; the small taxpayer then has, in fact, no practical chance of getting justice. Or the tax administrator, feeling that his job is to turn up additional revenue, may focus attention solely on cases in which he suspects the tax was underpaid. American tax administration is far from perfect in its protection of the taxpayer. Improvement is needed, but for masses of taxpayers with small incomes the Internal Revenue Service now does very well in making prompt and accurate refunds.

Tax penalties. Honest, consistent, and expeditious administration will secure voluntary observance of tax laws from most taxpayers. Among this majority are many taxpayers who make mistakes through innocent ignorance or carelessness. They should be treated with lenience. Some occasionally succumb to venturesome impulses and seek "to put over" a little cheat on the tax bureau. And, finally, there are always some "tax outlaws" who will willfully evade if there is a chance of success. For these last two classes there must be penalties, mild for the venturesome, suitably severe for the "outlaws."

To make tax evasion a criminal act punishable by heavy fine or imprisonment is a punishment which can fail through overseverity. Juries may refuse to convict a person indicted for tax evasion, when such conviction would make him liable to a jail sentence.[20] Punishment for evasion should normally take the form of a monetary penalty specifically provided by statute, the amount proportioned to the size of the evasion. Imprisonment should be reserved for cases of very serious wrongdoing.

As a practical matter, it is sometimes advisable to waive penalties and even a tax liability itself. The taxpayer may not have the funds, or forced payment might do the Treasury more harm than good—it would not be good publicity for the government to bankrupt an honest but unfortunate businessman. Discretion in deciding such questions must generally be left to the administrative officials. Apparent abuses may result, but good administration requires that the authority exist and sometimes be used.

Tax liens. To aid in the collection of a tax which has been legally assessed, statutes frequently provide that the tax becomes a lien against the property or against the individual and his property.[21] The government can

[20] One state trying an income tax case found that 9 out of 12 jurors had failed to file returns. The federal government now gets about 1,000 convictions a year for criminal violation of tax laws. Six times as many taxpayers plead guilty.

[21] A government may in some cases require proof that tax has been paid before granting permission for some action the taxpayer desires. Aliens, for example, will not be given permits to leave the country until they have satisfied the Internal Revenue Service that any tax they owe has been paid.

seize the property and sell it for the taxes. The government can make it impossible for the taxpayer to effect a legal transfer of his property until the tax has been paid. The rules regarding tax liens vary widely depending upon the taxing jurisdiction and the tax—property, income, death, or excise. The use made of liens also varies greatly, but as a general rule, government officials make less effective use of tax liens than the law permits and than is desirable. Delay, lack of adequate staffs, and sometimes lack of determination seem to be the main obstacles to the full use of tax liens as an administrative aid.

Improvement. Federal tax administrative technique is generally effective and efficient, always granting possibilities of much continuing improvement by the wider use of methods that have proved successful and the development of still better ones. The same can be said for the tax procedures of some states and cities. For many states and most local governments, the operating efficiency of their tax units falls far short of what is reasonably possible.

Happily, much progress toward better tax administration at state and local levels in recent years can be reported. Four factors have contributed to this improvement: (1) the shift from elected to appointed tax officials, and the better caliber of tax staffs developed under civil service systems; (2) increasing use of machine techniques; (3) the influence of tax administrators' professional associations; and (4) collaboration of businessmen, lawyers, accountants, and professors.

State and local tax officials have organized a number of professional associations, chief among them being the Federation of Tax Administrators.[22] These groups hold annual conferences at which technical tax matters are discussed and ideas exchanged. They finance research and publish collated tax information which no single taxing unit could bring together. Some of the growing reciprocity among states in aiding each other's tax enforcement is undoubtedly due to the efforts of these groups and the personal contacts they develop.

Many business leaders—and increasingly the tax specialists of large corporations—have been of great assistance to state and local tax administrators. Both to simplify their own tax compliance problems and as a matter of public service, they have given generously of their time and effort in advisory capacities. They have opened the eyes of tax administrators to the possibility of applying effective business routine to tax work. They have helped tax administration conform to the complexities of business structure and operation, thereby reducing areas of fiscal friction.

[22] Many of these organizations have their headquarters in the same building, 1313 East 60th Street, Chicago, and cooperate closely. Their monthly *Tax Administrators' News* provides a wide variety of detailed information on state and local tax personnel, statistics, judicial decisions, and other relevant subjects.

PROBLEMS

1. Discuss the reasons for and against seeking stability, elasticity, and diversity of revenue sources at each level of government.

2. What conditions are likely to make for good decisions in enacting tax laws?

3. Study the hearings before the Committee on Ways and Means on a recent tax bill. Find out how your state legislature deals with the problems of enacting tax laws.

4. Discuss some of the major problems of administering tax laws well. What general methods of improvement would you suggest?

5. "An old tax is a good tax." Discuss from the point of view of administration.

6. What are the special problems of administering a self-assessed tax?

7. Discuss with businessmen their impressions of federal, state, and local tax administration.

8. What part does administration have in determining whether a tax is equitable?

9. How closely are the processes of voting taxes and of voting expenditures tied together at each level of government?

P A R T   T H R E E

Federal, State, and Local Revenues

THE next eleven chapters deal with the taxes levied by the 102,000 American federal, state, and local governments, and other revenue sources, except borrowings and grants received from other governments.

Chapter 11 (The American Tax System) is primarily statistical, and analyzes the trends and current dependence of the three different classes of governments on the various forms of taxation. In the next nine chapters, the wide variety of taxes actually levied is classified into six groups. Two chapters are devoted to the personal income tax, two to business taxes (including the corporation income tax), one to commodity taxes and related excises, one to highway taxes, two to property taxes, and one to death taxes. The final chapter deals with nontax revenues.

CHAPTER 11

The American Tax System

TAXES pay for most American government activity. They have become determining factors in our lives not only because of the importance of the services they finance but also because they are a major "cost of living." Perhaps in using the term "system" we give a somewhat misleading concept of orderliness and rationality. Without question, however, there is a whole which deserves our attention before we examine the parts.

COMBINED FEDERAL, STATE, AND LOCAL TAX COLLECTIONS

Government expenditures in the United States, as was shown earlier, have long been on the increase. Perforce, tax revenues have had to increase.

Over-all growth. From 1890 to 1913, American tax collections rose from $875 million to $2.2 billion, a 150 per cent increase. Federal war tax collections and some expansion of state and local tax systems lifted total tax receipts to over $9 billion in 1920. Three years later, federal taxes had been reduced by $2.7 billion, state and local taxes had increased $700 million, and the total figure stood at $7.2 billion. During the remainder of the 1920's, the country's total tax bill increased slightly, due to increases of state and local levies. Three years of economic recession, 1930–1933, caused tax receipts at all government levels to drop.

Since 1933 the country's tax bill has been multiplied over twelvefold. Between 1933 and 1940, combined tax collections doubled, primarily as a result of heavier federal taxation to finance defense. The war taxes of the 1940's, operating in a period of sharp inflation, lifted federal tax receipts from less than $6 billion in 1940 to over $42 billion in 1946. The end of World War II did not bring the reduction of tax load that had been expected. The international situation made it necessary to continue military and foreign aid outlays at a high level and these, combined with heavy postwar interest and veterans' aid costs, and rising welfare and farm aid, precluded any substantial reduction of federal taxes. State and local governments, meanwhile, with a backlog of unmet needs, and facing the results of considerable inflation, had to raise increasing sums by taxation. By 1959 combined federal, state, and local tax collections stood at about $113 billion.

TABLE 11–1

American Tax Revenues, Selected Years 1890–1959

	Amount (in billions)						
Fiscal Year	*Federal*[1]	*State*[1]	*Local*	*Total*	*In Dollars of 1958 Purchasing Power*[2]	*Per Capita Dollars of 1958 Purchasing Power*[2]	*Per Cent of National Income*
1890	$ .4	$ .1	$ .4	$ .9	$ 3	$ 48	7
1903	.5	.2	.7	1.4	5	61	7
1913	.7	.3	1.2	2.2	7	68	6
1917	1.0	.4	1.7	3.2	7	68	7
1920	5.7	.6	2.8	9.2	13	113	13
1923	3.1	.9	3.3	7.3	12	110	10
1927	3.3	1.3	4.4	9.1	15	127	11
1930	3.5	1.8	5.0	10.3	18	145	13
1932	1.8	1.6	4.7	8.1	17	138	16
1936	3.8	2.4	4.3	10.5	23	176	17
1940	5.8	5.1	4.7	15.6	31	236	20
1944	42.2	5.4	4.8	52.4	86	620	30
1948	42.2	7.9	6.6	56.7	69	470	26
1959[3]	79.0	16.5	17.5	113.0	113	650	31

[1] Includes Social Security tax receipts; at the state level, payroll taxes for unemployment benefits.

[2] Calculated by dividing the figure for each year's revenues by the corresponding index number of the U.S. Bureau of Labor Statistics index of consumer prices.

[3] Estimated for fiscal years ending in 1959.

SOURCES: The National Industrial Conference Board, *The Economic Almanac,* various years; U.S. Bureau of the Census, *Summary of Governmental Finances Series; The Budget . . . for 1959.*

One of the most significant facts of American taxation since 1940 has been the result of a fivefold increase in national income. Tax yields have grown automatically, reducing the need to raise tax rates. The public has been able to pay in taxes for a greatly increased volume of government services, including a huge military establishment, while also having more left for private consumption and investment. (Inflation, of course, has accounted for over a third of the postwar increase in national money income.) Persons subject to the progressive portions of the personal income tax rate structure, especially those whose incomes have risen in the range over $15,000, have very often suffered a real loss of after-tax purchasing power. But the country as a whole has paid more and more in taxes as the economy has prospered, while holding on to more and more private purchasing power.

The tax burden. The "burden"[1] of a tax or of a total of tax collections is determined partly by the actual amount of tax revenue collected and partly by three other factors—changing price levels, increasing population, and changing national income. Tax collections of a given dollar amount rest more lightly on taxpayers in a period of high prices, when

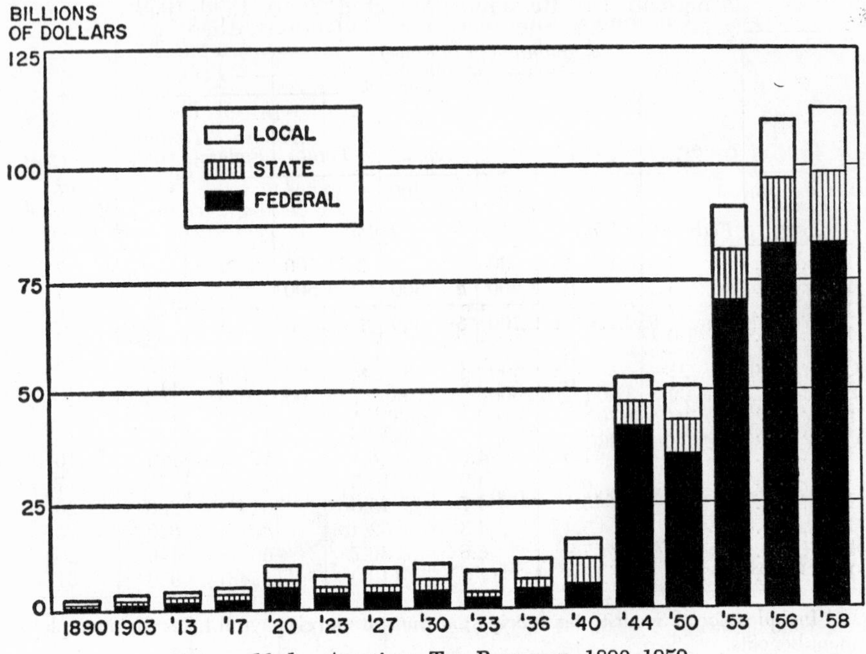

CHART 11–1. American Tax Revenues, 1890–1959.

money is worth less, than in a period of low prices. Relative burden of a given tax collection depends, too, upon the number of taxpayers among whom this amount is divided. And finally, if the same amount of tax is collected at two different times from the same number of taxpayers, and if each taxpayer's income is larger on the second than on the first occasion,

[1] The term "tax burden" can be misleading. It carries, and frequently is intended to give, the implication that tax collections are dissipated by the governments that receive them, with no corresponding return. Such implication, of course, is false. Part of the national income against which tax collections are measured is itself created by government expenditure. And the public benefits produced by government expenditure may exceed the personal deprivations occasioned by tax payments.

But taxes do constitute a forced diversion of purchasing power and productive effort from voluntary personal determination. Directly or indirectly they restrict the sphere of personal disposal of income. In this limited sense they may be considered a "burden" on the individual and business community, and it is in this limited sense that the term "burden" is used in the discussion above. Our interest is in comparative tax "burdens" in different periods of time or as between different countries, rather than in the moderation or severity of the "tax burden" in one particular time and place.

the burden of the second levy in relation to purchasing power is lighter.

The importance of taking "burden" into account in dealing with tax trends over periods of fluctuating dollar value and increasing population is indicated in Table 11–1. While tax collections in actual dollars increased sevenfold between 1940 and 1959, in dollars of a constant purchasing

TABLE 11–2

Combined American Tax Collections, 1958[1]

Type of Tax	*Amount (in millions)*[2]				*Per Cent of Total*		
	Federal	*State*	*Local*	*Total*	*Federal*	*State and Local*	*Total*
Personal income	$34,700	$ 1,600	$ 200	$ 36,500	46	6	34
Corporation income	$20,100	$ 1,000	...	$ 21,100	26	3	19
Other business[3] ..	...	1,200	$ 300	1,500	...	5	1
Total business	$20,100	$ 2,200	$ 300	$ 22,600	26	8	20
General sales ...	...	$ 3,500	$ 400	$ 3,900	...	12	4
Liquor[4]	$ 3,000	600	100	3,700	4	2	3
Tobacco	1,700	600	300	2,600	2	2	2
Other sales[5]	4,300	300	100	4,700	6	1	4
Total sales ..	$ 9,000	$ 5,000	$ 900	$ 14,900	12	17	13
Gasoline	$ 1,600	$ 2,900	...	$ 4,500	2	9	4
Auto license	...	1,400	100	1,500	...	5	1
Total highway	$ 1,600	$ 4,300	$ 100	$ 6,000	2	14	5
Customs	$ 700	...	...	$ 700	1	...	1
Property[6]	...	$ 500	$14,000	14,500	...	44	13
Payroll	8,700	1,700	...	10,400	11	5	10
Death and gift ..	1,400	400	...	1,800	2	1	2
Miscellaneous and unallocated[6] ..	100	900	600	1,600	...	5	1
Grand total	$76,300	$16,600	$16,100	$109,000	100	100	100

[1] For fiscal years ending in 1958; partly estimated. Because of rounding, details will not necessarily add to totals.

[2] Rounded to nearest $100 million.

[3] Includes franchise, utility, bank and insurance, and license (except auto and liquor) taxes; does not include gross receipts, payroll, federal sales, or other taxes collected from businesses but presumably shifted to consumers.

[4] Includes liquor license taxes; does not include profits from state liquor monopolies.

[5] Includes amusement and pari-mutuel taxes.

[6] Includes severance taxes.

SOURCES: U.S. Bureau of the Budget, *1959 Federal Budget, Midyear Review;* U.S. Bureau of the Census, *State Tax Collections in 1958* and *Summary of Governmental Finances in 1957.*

power the increase was less than fourfold. When population increase over these years is taken into account, the increase in tax burden was somewhat under threefold—heavy but not overwhelming. Per capita growth of state-local taxes in dollars of constant purchasing power is shown in Chart 11–2. Tax burden can also be measured by relating tax collections to national income. By this measure, the tax burden rose by one-half from 1940 to 1958.

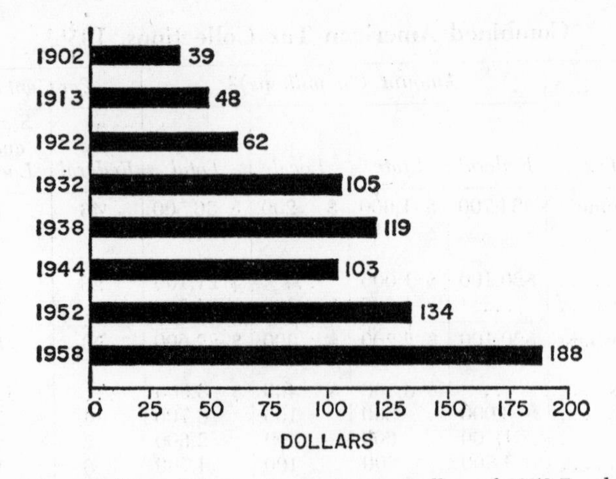

CHART 11–2. State and Local Taxes, per Capita, in Dollars of 1958 Purchasing Power, 1902–1958. SOURCE: U.S. Bureau of the Census, *Historical Statistics on State and Local Government Finances, 1902 to 1953,* and Table 11–2.

Political distribution of tax collections. Prior to 1940, federal tax collections were normally somewhat more than one-third of the country's total. Local taxes constituted a larger proportion. World War II financing raised the federal tax proportion to 80 per cent, but state-local collections had risen to about 30 per cent by 1959. There is every prospect that federal tax collections will henceforth dominate the combined total.

Relative importance of sources. The personal income tax is now the most important element in the American tax system, accounting for 34 per cent of total tax revenue. Its importance is as a federal source, even though a few states get significant personal income tax revenue.

"Business" taxes are next in importance, yielding 20 per cent of the total, not counting property and payroll taxes. If the employer's part of Social Security payroll taxes is added, business taxes make up almost one-fourth of the total.

Sales, commodity, and service excise taxes account for about 12 per cent of the 1959 total, with liquor and tobacco taxes making up half of the $15 billion total. If gasoline and motor vehicle licenses are included, the broad group of consumption taxes accounts for nearly one-fifth of the country's tax revenue.

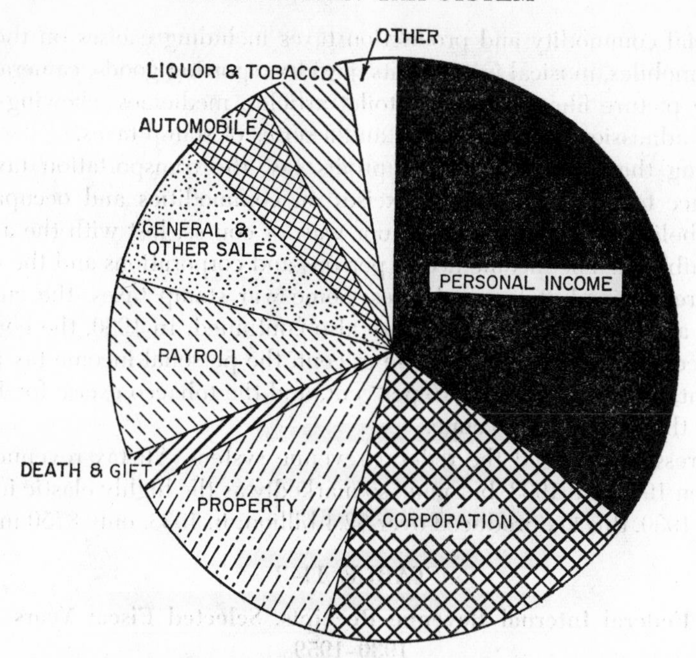

CHART 11–3. Sources of American Tax Revenues, 1958.

In fourth place today, although until the early 1940's it was the most important, is the property tax. It is still the dominating element of local finance. It produces 44 per cent of combined state and local tax revenue.

THE FEDERAL TAX SYSTEM[2]

Prior to World War I, customs duties and liquor and tobacco excises were the major sources of federal tax revenue. A property tax apportioned among the states was tried unsuccessfully in the 1790's and during the Civil War. Personal income taxes, death taxes, and various business taxes were imposed during the Civil War, and again briefly in the 1890's. The present federal tax system was foreshadowed when a one per cent corporation income tax was levied in 1909, a progressive personal income tax was enacted in 1913 (after ratification of the Sixteenth Amendment), and a progressive estate tax was imposed in 1916.

1917–1939. The rates of all existing taxes were increased, and many new taxes were levied, during World War I. Among the new taxes were an excess profits tax and a war profits tax to supplement the corporation income tax, a tax on transportation, a tax on insurance companies, a multitude

[2] An excellent description of the federal tax system, with considerable historical material, was prepared by N. B. Ture for the Joint Economic Committee in 1956 and revised in 1958. See *The Federal Revenue System: Facts and Problems* (Washington, 1959).

of special commodity and production taxes including excises on the sale of automobiles, musical instruments, jewelry, sporting goods, cameras and moving picture films, cosmetics, toilet articles, medicines, chewing gum, theater admissions and club dues, and a series of stamp taxes.

During the 1920's, the excess profits tax, the transportation tax, the insurance tax, and the special excises on commodities and occupations were abolished. The excise on liquor was, of course, lost with the advent of Prohibition. The income tax on persons and corporations and the estate tax were retained at lowered rates. Some war stamp taxes, the customs duties, and the tobacco excise were also continued. In 1930, the corporation income tax accounted for 35 per cent, the personal income tax for 32 per cent, customs duties for 16 per cent, and the tobacco excise for 13 per cent of the federal tax revenue.

Depression changed the federal revenue system. All tax revenues fell between 1930 and 1933, but none so markedly as the highly elastic income tax. In 1930, this tax produced over $2.4 billion; in 1933, only $750 million.

TABLE 11-3

Federal Internal Revenue Receipts, Selected Fiscal Years 1930–1959

Tax or Tax Group	1930	1932	1936	1940	1945	1948	1953	1959[1]
	Amount (in millions)							
Individual income	$1,147	$ 427	$ 675	$ 982	$19,034	$20,998	$33,394	$38,000
Corporation	1,263	630	849	1,272	16,027	10,184	24,000	18,000
Estate and gift ..	65	47	379	360	643	899	940	1,600
Liquor	13	9	505	624	2,310	2,255	2,700	3,000
Tobacco products	450	399	501	609	932	1,300	1,689	1,700
Gasoline and auto	2	...	299	377	646	1,212	2,307	2,900
Social Security ..	...	...	...	834	1,779	2,381	5,249	10,000
Other excise and miscellaneous	100	46	313	288	2,531	2,636	3,205	3,100
Total	$3,040	$1,557	$3,520	$5,346	$43,902	$41,865	$73,484	$78,300
	Percentage of Total Tax Revenue, Including Customs							
Individual income	32	23	17	17	43	50	45	48
Corporation	35	33	22	22	36	24	32	23
Estate and gift ..	2	3	10	6	2	2	1	2
Liquor	...	1	13	11	5	5	4	4
Tobacco products	12	21	13	11	2	3	2	2
Gasoline and auto	...	...	8	7	2	3	3	4
Social Security ..	...	...	...	15	4	6	7	13
Other excise and miscellaneous	3	2	8	5	6	6	4	4
Total	84	83	90	94	99	99	99	100

[1] Estimated. Because of rounding, details will not necessarily add to totals.

SOURCES: U.S. Secretary of the Treasury, *Annual Reports; The Budget . . . for 1959.*

Business recovery, higher rates for existing taxes, and several new taxes restored federal tax revenues by 1935 to the predepression level. Exemptions of the personal income tax were lowered in 1932, and the tax rate schedule was substantially increased in 1932, 1934, and 1935. Corporation tax loads were increased in one way or another in almost every year of the decade. Estate tax rates were increased. Most important of the new taxes, from a fiscal point of view, were the liquor excises reimposed in 1934 after the repeal of the Eighteenth Amendment, the gasoline tax, and the Social Security payroll taxes enacted in 1935. By 1940, the gasoline tax, liquor excises, and payroll tax accounted for over 30 per cent of the federal tax revenue.

1940 to the present. Except for the addition of the excess profits tax and some excises, the revenue acts of 1940 and 1941 did not change the general character of the federal tax system. The additional revenue was derived mainly from higher rates of existing taxes. Personal exemptions in the income tax were again lowered, and the rates were substantially increased. Besides the superimposition of the excess profits tax, all corporation tax rates were increased. Rates of the estate and gift taxes, the liquor taxes, the tobacco taxes, the gasoline taxes, and various other excises were increased.

During World War II, the Administration pressed vigorously for heavy tax increases to pay for the war and to minimize inflationary pressure. Congress refused to go as far as the President urged. It rejected completely Treasury proposals for a highly graduated tax on spending and for closing some costly loopholes. However, income and excess profits tax rates were raised greatly, exemptions were reduced, income tax collection at source and current payment were instituted, excise tax rates were raised and new excise taxes imposed, some postal rates were increased, and many refinements—some highly desirable, others of dubious value—were made.

With the cessation of hostilities, Congress repealed the excess profits tax, effective at the end of 1945; the corporation income tax rate and personal income tax rates were moderately reduced. With Presidential support, Congress voted to postpone reduction of some of the wartime excise tax rates which were due to expire. Most of these "temporary" levies have lasted to the present.

Congressional temper in 1947 favored tax reduction. Scheduled increases in Social Security tax rates were again postponed. Twice in 1947, Congress voted to reduce individual income tax rates, but Presidential vetoes prevented the bills from becoming law. The vetoes were prompted by the belief that inflationary pressures were still too great to risk tax reduction, that the public debt should be reduced during the prevailing prosperity, and that the form of the tax reduction proposed was far from the best possible. In 1948, however, Congress overrode a veto and made large reductions in the personal income tax and in the estate and gift taxes.

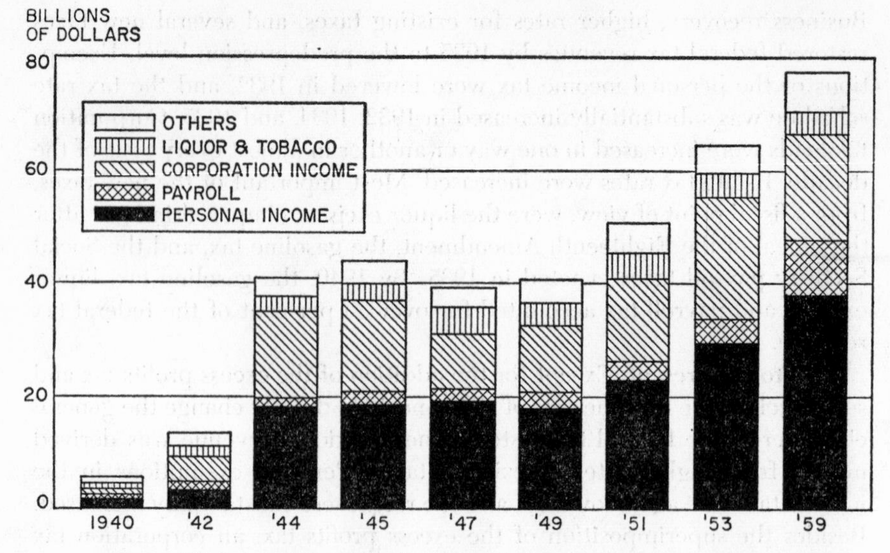

CHART 11–4. Sources of Federal Internal Tax Revenue, 1940–1959.

By early 1950, revision of the *structure* of many taxes was long overdue; there were crudities of many kinds, inequities, sources of administrative difficulty; various tax provisions tended to depress specific industries which needed to be spurred rather than haltered. Congress was in the midst of a detailed study of tax revision when fighting began in Korea. Then higher, not lower, taxes became the order of the day. Personal and corporation income tax rates were returned to wartime levels—higher in some cases. An excess profits tax was reimposed. Excise taxes were raised higher than they had been during the war, partly to reduce civilian consumption of products made of war-essential materials.

The "Korean" tax laws had provided for subsequent automatic reductions, but the Treasury, still needing revenue, opposed most of the scheduled reductions except for the abolition of the excess profits tax and small declines in the personal income tax. The Administration, however, strongly favored Congressional review of details of the tax structure. The resulting changes in 1954 constituted a sweeping revision of the income tax law. The net result was a total of modifications which reduced tax liabilities appreciably. Some of the changes were designed to help stimulate the economy, whereas some were intended to remove inequalities in the treatment of taxpayers.

During the 1950's, Social Security taxes were raised, along with benefits, on four occasions. A few modifications of the excise tax structure were made, the biggest being increases on motorists to help finance highways. In 1958 the "temporary" World War II levy on freight transportation was abolished, and several dozen other changes were made. Although some were technicalities of only narrow significance, a few, including measures intended to aid small business, involved both important modifications in tax structure and revenue loss of more than incidental amounts.

STATE TAX SYSTEMS

For the American colonies under English rule, land and poll taxes, liquor excises, and customs and tonnage duties were the primary sources of revenue. As states in the federal union, they were forbidden by the federal Constitution to levy customs or tonnage duties. The land tax, expanded into the general property tax, became their basic fiscal support. During the nineteenth century, some states tapped other sources of tax revenue—special bank taxes, insurance company taxes, railroad taxes, general corporation taxes, and inheritance taxes—but nowhere did these levies produce more than a small fraction of total state income.

More and more, however, toward the close of the century, the states came to rely on levies other than the general property tax. In the twentieth century this tendency accelerated. Corporation taxes became increasingly prominent during the first two decades, and motor vehicle license taxes and gasoline taxes moved to the fore after 1920. Two decades later, property taxes produced only one-sixteenth of state tax revenue. By 1959 the proportion was one dollar out of thirty.

The three principal state taxes currently are the general sales tax, the gasoline tax, and the payroll tax for unemployment insurance, as indicated in Table 11–4. Individual and corporation income taxes combined produce nearly $2.6 billion. Taxes on the retail sale of tobacco products and alcoholic

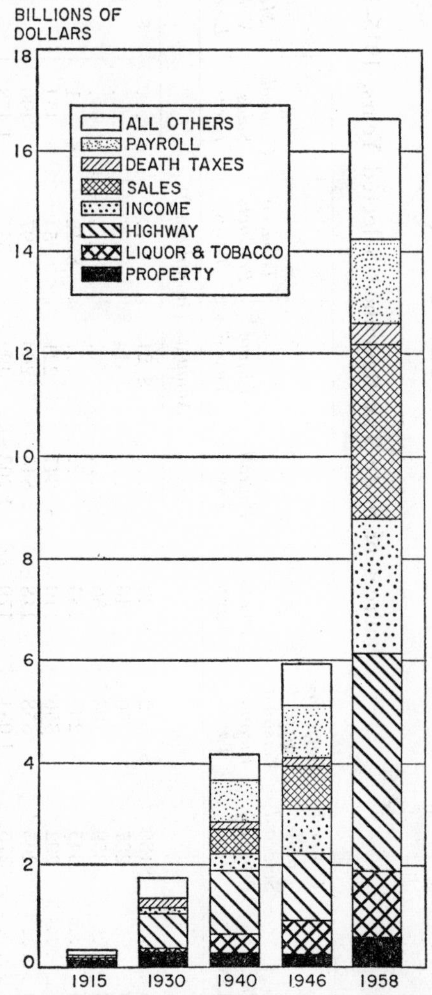

CHART 11–5. Sources of State Tax Revenue, Selected Years, 1915–1958.

TABLE 11–4

Sources of State Tax Revenue,[1] Selected Years, 1915–1958

Fiscal Year	General and Selected Property Taxes	Corporation and Personal Income Taxes	Death Taxes	Payroll Taxes	Liquor Taxes[2]	Tobacco Products Taxes	General Sales Taxes	Motor Vehicle Licenses	Gasoline Taxes	All Other Taxes	Total
Amounts (in millions)											
1915	$186	$ 2	$ 29	...	$ 21	...	...	$ 15	...	$ 115	$ 368
1919	237	50	46	...	14	...	...	65	$ 1	182	594
1925	359	103	86	...	...	...	...	261	148	349	1,305
1930	345	233	183	...	...	$ 12	$ 1	356	495	482	2,108
1937	292	356	116	$ 347	221	54	434	349	722	469	3,360
1940	265	358	118	843	260	97	490	388	845	507	4,171
1948	276	1,084	179	1,203	499	337	1,478	593	1,259	1,038	7,946
1958	533	2,560	351	1,700[3]	647	616	3,497	1,411	2,914	2,376	16,605
Percentage Distribution											
1915	51	...	8	...	6	...	...	...	...	35	100
1919	40	8	8	...	2	...	...	11	...	31	100
1925	28	8	7	...	...	...	...	20	8	27	100
1930	16	11	9	...	...	1	...	17	23	23	100
1937	9	11	3	10	7	2	13	10	22	14	100
1940	6	9	3	21	6	2	12	9	21	12	100
1948	4	14	2	14	6	4	19	8	16	13	100
1958	3	15	2	10	4	4	21	9	18	14	100

[1] Excludes local shares before 1937, includes them thereafter.
[2] Includes liquor license revenue; excludes profits from state monopolies.
[3] Estimated.

SOURCES: U.S. Department of Commerce, *Historical Statistics of the United States, 1789–1945, Revised Summary of Government Finances, 1942–1950;* U.S. Bureau of the Census, *State Tax Collections in 1958.*

beverages account for nearly $1.3 billion (not counting $400 million profit of state liquor monopolies).

State tax systems display elements of both uniformity and diversity. Payroll, gasoline, and motor vehicle taxes are imposed in every state. Tobacco products taxes are found in over 40 states. Three-quarters of the states have personal or corporation income taxes, or both, and 33 have general sales taxes. A variety of special levies are found. The relative importance of major and minor taxes differs considerably, as suggested by Table 11–5. Comparisons among states, however, are more difficult than

TABLE 11–5

Per Capita Tax Collections in Selected States, 1958

State	*Sales and Gross Receipts*[1]	*License*[2]	*Individual Income*	*Corporation Net Income*	*Property*	*Total*[3] *(Except Payroll)*	*Payroll for unemployment 1957*
California	$ 75	$11	$11	$12	$ 8	$120	$11
Georgia	65	6	7	5	...	84	7
Illinois	62	12	...	...	...	76	9
Massachusetts	31	21	22	6	...	85	13
Michigan	69	18	...	...	6	102	16
Nebraska	32	6	...	...	17	58	3
New Jersey	30	18	...	...	...	51	16
New York	28	12	32	16	...	95	16
Pennsylvania	46	16	...	12	...	80	13
Texas	34	14	...	...	4	73	4
Vermont	39	20	24	5	1	99	7
Virginia	28	11	16	7	3	68	3
Washington	113	11	...	...	9	137	15
United States	$ 51	$13	$10	$ 6	$ 3	$ 88	$ 9

[1] Includes general sales, gasoline, liquor, tobacco, insurance premium, public utility, pari-mutuel, and miscellaneous.

[2] Includes motor vehicle, business and other occupations, hunting and fishing, and miscellaneous.

[3] Includes sources not detailed.

SOURCES: U.S. Bureau of the Census, *State Tax Collections in 1958; Statistical Abstract . . . for 1958.*

appears offhand. For one thing, the relative importance of local taxes varies a great deal. In six states, for example, state taxes are over 70 per cent of combined state-local taxes, whereas in a few cases state levies are less than 40 per cent of the total. Then, too, it is difficult to judge how much of a tax collected in a state actually falls on its residents.[3]

Within a few years after World War II, several states had added new taxes and raised rates. Yet, in general, despite opinions to the contrary,

[3] For brief discussion of problems of comparison, see R. H. Johnson, "The Reliability of Comparative Tax Studies," *NTA . . . Proceedings . . . 1957,* pp. 66–76.

states were not subject to really serious financial pressure. By the mid-1950's, however, their problems were much more pressing.

LOCAL TAX REVENUES

Property taxes have always been the all-important source of local tax revenue. Of the $17.5 billion of local tax collections estimated for 1959, about $15 billion will come from property taxes.

In some states the yield of certain state-collected taxes is divided between the state and local governments.[4] Most cities and some counties derive some revenue from local licenses, permits, and various fees. To an increasing extent since World War II, local governments have been levying payroll, income, sales, gasoline, auto, and miscellaneous taxes.[5] For all cities, nonproperty taxes in 1957 averaged $17 per capita while property taxes were $44. The postwar period has also witnessed a surge of efforts to improve the property tax.

SOCIAL AND ECONOMIC DISTRIBUTION OF TAX BURDENS

Many are the generalizations made about the social and economic incidence of the combined federal-state-local tax system. Spokesmen for the rich say it confiscates their wealth and income. Champions of the masses frequently assert that the American tax system rests disproportionately upon the poor. Home-owners, farmers, business—each group complains of overtaxation in comparison with others.

Reliable statistics and careful analysis of the distribution of American taxes by income classes and by various groups—farmer and city-dweller, home-owner and renter, investor and employee and consumer, incorporated and unincorporated business, old and young, stockholder and bondholder, railroads and their competitors, smokers and nonsmokers—are almost nonexistent. It is astonishing, perhaps shocking, that so little acceptable material can be found. Taxes are so important in our economic and social life that we should know far more than we do for wisest selection of the available alternatives.

But the problems of determining such distribution are extremely difficult, and competent, objective observers sometimes reach substantially different conclusions. In recent years, one of the hardest problems has been the large and frequent changes in both the tax system and the country's economic and social condition. Data have often become obsolete before they have been published. More basic, however, is the dearth of

[4] See Chapter 22.

[5] Developments are covered in H. F. Alderfer and R. L. Funk, *Municipal Nonproperty Taxes* (Municipal Finance Officers Association, Chicago, 1956).

knowledge about our society. For example, there are gaps in our knowledge of how national income—money or real, gross or net, annual or decennial—is distributed among individuals or families. And what is meant by "income"? To what extent does it include changes in capital values? In comparing tax burdens, should the income be that which would have been received had it not been for taxes?

A major problem is selecting assumptions about the shifting of taxes. If it is assumed that much of the property tax was capitalized when present owners bought the property, the tax so capitalized might well be said to constitute no current burden. If the assumption is denied, a very different result is obtained. In measuring the tax on farmers or home-owners, as well as by income groups, this is highly important. Since the corporation income tax is now so great, the entire picture of national tax distribution will hinge on how much of the corporation tax is assumed to be shifted to consumers, passed back to employees or suppliers, or left on owners and creditors. Social Security taxes present somewhat similar problems.

To allocate the burdens of excise and sales taxes by income classes or by other groups, we need to know far more than we do about how much each group consumes of each taxed item—cigarettes, clothing, beer, taxed amusements, gasoline. Difficult as this is, more difficult still is accounting for excises that become business costs—taxes on electricity, trucks, telegraph messages.

Another hard-to-handle item is estate, inheritance, and gift taxes. Should they be allocated to the person transferring the property or to the recipient? Should they be spread over a period of years? What allowance for avoidance should be made in studying these and other taxes?

How far should one go in allowing for the fact that some taxes are deductible in computing others? How can one account for the wide variety of state and local taxes? In trying to allocate taxes according to characteristics such as occupation, residence, age, consumption, one must make many arbitrary assumptions, and any sort of multiple classification seems impossible.

Two other very fundamental problems defy simple solution. What, if any, validity is there in allocating tax burdens without also allocating the benefits of tax expenditures, especially expenditures that yield real, but not always immediate, money income, such as public education or national defense or highways or accruing Social Security rights? And is the significant problem really that of seeing how taxes are distributed, or is it the broader, more basic problem of learning how the effects of taxes (or taxes and expenditures) are distributed?

An estimate for 1954, summarized in Table 11–6, indicates that the burden of combined federal-state-local taxes is progressive. Families and individuals with incomes under $5,000 have about one-fourth of their in-

TABLE 11–6

Estimated Distribution of Taxes by Income Classes, 1954

Income Class	*Tax as a Per Cent of Income*									*Taxes Paid as a Per Cent of Total American Taxes*
	Federal Taxes					*State-Local*			*Total*	
	Personal Income	*Corporation Income*	*Excises and Customs*	*Estate and Gift*	*Payroll (Social Security)*	*Property*	*Sales and Excise*	*Other*		
Under $2,000	2.7	3.2	4.7		3.1	4.2	5.0	0.5	23.4	4.6
2,000 to 3,000	4.7	3.4	4.3		3.7	3.9	4.6	0.9	25.5	6.4
3,000 to 4,000	6.4	3.0	3.9		4.0	3.8	4.2	0.9	26.2	10.6
4,000 to 5,000	7.6	2.9	3.7		3.8	3.7	4.0	1.1	26.8	11.8
5,000 to 7,500	10.6	3.3	3.6		3.0	3.5	3.9	1.0	28.9	25.0
7,500 to 10,000	13.2	3.8	3.3		2.3	3.4	3.5	1.3	30.8	10.5
$10,000 and over	14.0	13.5	2.0	1.3	1.0	3.2	2.1	2.1	39.2	31.2

SOURCE: R. A. Musgrave, "Incidence of the Tax Structure and Its Effects on Consumption," *Federal Tax Policy for Economic Growth and Stability* (Joint Economic Committee, Washington, 1955), pp. 96–113. It is assumed that two-thirds of the tax on corporation income rests on stockholders and that one-third is shifted to consumers. The concept of income used includes the rental value of owner-occupied dwellings, and certain other items not included in taxable income; use of a narrower concept does not change the results significantly. Undistributed corporate profits are assumed to be income of stockholders.

comes absorbed, directly or indirectly, by taxes. This is true of even the lowest income group.

Taxes take one-tenth more of the income of families in the $5,000 to $7,500 group and still more from those going on up to $10,000. But it is above this latter point that the total tax burden becomes decidedly progressive, averaging almost 40 per cent of income.

Those with incomes over $10,000 not only pay a far bigger percentage of their income in taxes than persons with smaller incomes. The top group with about 8 per cent of the income units (families) and 25 per cent of total income pays almost one-third of *all* the country's taxes. The 8 per cent carried as much of the total tax as the entire lower half of the country's population in 1954. If the two extreme groups—under $2,000 and over $10,000—were divided into more subgroups, the results would reveal new contrasts. At the bottom of the income scale there are people with virtually no income as conceived here and for tax purposes—pensioners in some cases or persons with businesses that have suffered a loss—whose taxes are very high in relation to their net incomes. And at the income ranges above, say, $20,000 the total tax load is generally much above even the 39 per cent shown here—but, because of loopholes, sometimes a good deal less.

The tax system as a whole, or at least the part of the system where incomes are large, is more progressive than anyone would have dreamed a generation ago. What are the effects on American society? Clearly, the building of great fortunes is far more difficult than if we had the tax pattern of the 1920's or that when the princely estates of the pre-World War I era were accumulated. The extremes of personal consumption—ignoring eccentricities—have been much reduced by the growth of modern taxes. Our society, partly because of taxes, has less inequality in consumption and property accumulation than in the past. The social and economic results of this equalizing force are not by any means clear.

Another social effect of modern taxes is an outgrowth of efforts to minimize taxes. Business and personal actions are influenced increasingly by desires to escape taxes.[6] Again, however, it is impossible to measure the social significance of this trend to date, or the results in another generation.

Finally, we should note that prosperity and economic growth have not been killed by tax rates which thirty years ago would have been thought insupportable. We might have done better with a different kind of tax structure. The private economy would certainly have had a greater opportunity if we had not had the huge taxes made necessary by the burden of defense. Perhaps the inflationary forces at work in the past two decades have done more to conceal the deleterious effects of high taxes than we yet

[6] The same problem is found in many lands. For expert discussions of different national experiences, see Institut International de Finances Publiques, *Les Distorsions Économiques d'Origine Fiscale* (Établissements Émile Bruylant, Brussels, 1958).

realize. Perhaps man's ability to overcome the adverse pressures of heavy tax rates is greater than the serious observer has been inclined to predict.

PROBLEMS

1. Discuss the reasons for adjusting for price changes and national income in making historical studies of the growth of taxes.

2. Which taxes would you expect to increase in yield more than proportionately with national income? Why?

3. Account for the fact that federal personal income tax yields today are almost double those during World War II.

4. Explain the major changes in state taxation as indicated in Table 11–4.

5. Discuss difficulties of determining how the nation's tax bill is shared by different income groups.

6. "The striking fact about the distribution of American taxes is that the load is generally proportional throughout the range which includes the great bulk of the population, whereas most of the total is collected from income groups where the load is clearly progressive." Discuss.

7. Why do you suppose that the per capita totals of state taxes vary so greatly?

CHAPTER 12

Personal Income Taxes

PERSONAL income taxes are imposed by the federal government and by 31 states. A small but growing number of cities, towns, and even school districts also tax some forms of personal income. Nearly 60,000,000 Americans pay income tax; in the popular mind it is THE TAX. The $43 billion collected through federal, state, and local income taxes in 1960 will constitute one-third of the combined total of tax revenue.

THE FEDERAL TAX[1]

World War II gave the federal personal income tax the role economists had long felt it should have—the foundation of the federal tax system. The rates of the tax were raised to levels previously inconceivable, and exemptions were reduced. Methods of collection were revolutionized. The federal personal income tax became, for the first time, a mass tax, producing huge revenues and occupying a major place in most family budgets—a position it is likely to maintain for a long time. The form and use made of this tax are now recognized as an important element in the development of the national economy.

History. The first federal personal income tax was imposed during the Civil War, and repealed in 1870. Its rate schedule at first was progressive, rising eventually to 20 per cent; it was made proportional in 1867.

A proportional 2 per cent income tax was imposed in 1894. Before the tax could become fairly operative, the Supreme Court held it unconstitutional in two five-to-four decisions.[2] The Court's argument was that a tax

[1] There are a number of technical manuals and services on the tax, intended for lawyers and accountants to guide them in minimizing their clients' taxes; about three-fifths of the 7,000-page loose-leaf Prentice-Hall *Federal Tax Service* deals with the personal income tax, for example.

[2] *Pollock* v. *the Farmers' Loan & Trust Co.*, 157 U.S. (1895) 429, 158 U.S. (1895) 601.

on income derived from real or personal property is a tax on the property itself, hence a "direct" tax which must be apportioned among the states in proportion to population. With this decision, a federal personal income tax other than a tax on personal compensation was impossible until either the Supreme Court reversed itself or the Constitution was amended.

Within two decades, the Supreme Court did reverse itself on this very point. Meanwhile, however, the Sixteenth Amendment had been adopted in 1913. It provided that:

> Congress shall have power to lay and collect taxes on incomes, from whatever source derived, without apportionment among the several States, and without regard to any census or enumeration.

Thus authorized, Congress immediately enacted a personal income tax which was the progenitor of the present law.

The 1913 personal income tax was intended to complement a 1909 one per cent corporation income tax; dividend income would be taxed at source under the corporation tax, all other income would be taxed to the recipient under the personal tax. This linkage with the corporation income tax was responsible for the curious rate structure of the tax—the combination of "normal tax" and "surtax." The "normal tax," from which corporation dividends were exempt, was established at the same rate—a proportional one per cent—as the corporation tax. In this way, the corporation tax served as a partial collection-at-source arrangement for the personal tax. Minimum exemptions on the "normal tax" were $3,000 for single individuals and $4,000 for married couples; the progressive "surtax" applied to incomes in excess of $20,000, rising to a 6 per cent maximum on incomes over $500,000.

World War I brought large increases in rates and some declines in exemptions, but between 1919 and 1928, there were seven reductions in the tax. In 1932, exemptions were cut, and in 1932, 1934, and 1935, rates were raised. Defense and war financing resulted in a series of tremendous increases. A reversal of this trend started in 1945, when a modest reduction followed the end of hostilities. Rates were reduced, exemptions were raised, and other revenue-reducing changes were made in 1948. However, need for increased military expenditures led to new rate increases in 1950 and 1951, the latter resulting in heavier rates than in the war years.[3] A slight reduction was made in 1954.

STATE AND LOCAL PERSONAL INCOME TAXES

State income taxes were levied before the federal tax. Without exception, however, all nineteenth-century state income taxes were administra-

[3] The provision for "splitting" family incomes in determining the applicable bracket rates, introduced in 1948, made the higher 1951–1959 rates somewhat less onerous than the lower wartime rates on many families with a single or major income recipient.

tive failures. Of the 16 states that had enacted personal income taxes prior to 1911, only five still had them on their books by that year. The taxes in these five were all administered by local property tax officials, none could claim the slightest shadow of success, and students of taxation expressed great scepticism about the personal income tax as a possible source of state revenue.

Wisconsin opened a new chapter in American fiscal history in 1911 with an income tax administered by a state tax commission. The rate schedule of this tax was progressive, beginning at one per cent over a moderate exemption and rising to 6 per cent on the excess over $12,000. The success of the Wisconsin tax was immediate, and within four years five other states enacted centrally administered income taxes. There was a wave of adoptions from 1919 to 1923, and another after 1929, including an adoption by the District of Columbia. No more states were added to the list during the 1940's and early 1950's, and two states repealed their taxes.

Philadelphia in 1939 was the first city to impose a local income tax—more accurately an earnings tax. Similar taxes were levied later by Columbus (Ohio), Cincinnati, Pittsburgh, St. Louis, Scranton, Toledo, Dayton, Springfield (Ohio), and Louisville. In addition, several hundred smaller localities, chiefly in Pennsylvania, have a form of income tax.

Current status. Some similarity and considerable variance are found among the state income taxes.

The New Hampshire and Tennessee levies are not general income taxes but special levies on income derived from intangibles. Salaries, business profits, rents, capital gains—all major items under a general income tax—are not reached. These special taxes apply only to interest from bonds and mortgages and dividends from stock. Colorado imposes supplementary levies on income from intangibles. Massachusetts has fashioned its tax, not as a single levy upon all personal income, but as a series of three complementary taxes on income from intangibles, on income from trading in intangibles, and on income from professions, employment, trade, and business; different exemptions and rates apply to each class of income. The Maryland tax has a somewhat similar structure.

Other states generally follow the federal personal income tax in determining income subject to their taxes, with numerous variations. Alaska's tax is one-seventh of the federal tax. Like the federal tax, the general state income taxes allow personal exemptions, with additional exemptions for dependents.

The special income taxes of Maryland, Massachusetts, New Hampshire, and Tennessee have proportional rates. Otherwise, the state personal income taxes all have progressive rate schedules. Compared with the rate schedule of the federal tax, the progression of the state income taxes is mild and generally confined to the lower income brackets. A common arrangement is a one percentage point increase in rate for each $1,000 or

$2,000 of income, up to a maximum 5 or 6 per cent. Highest rates are found in Oregon where the tax reaches 11.6 per cent on income in excess of $8,000, and in North Dakota, where it reaches 11 per cent on income over $15,000.

The income taxes of local governments are relatively simple and moderate. The tax base is usually confined to wages, salaries, and earnings of unincorporated businesses. The rates are flat, ordinarily from one-half to one per cent. Personal exemptions are not granted, nor is the taxpayer allowed to deduct such items as interest or contributions. Withholding by employers is the rule.

CONSTITUTIONAL LAW OF PERSONAL INCOME TAXATION

The Sixteenth Amendment specifically empowers the federal government to tax "income"—with no restriction to "net income"—without apportioning the tax among the states according to population. This authorization covers only such receipts as the courts construe to be income; certain types of stock dividends, which the Supreme Court has held not to be income, may not be brought under the federal income tax.

Until the late 1930's, interest on state and local bonds and the salaries of state and local employees were generally believed to be beyond the reach of a federal levy; state income taxes had to extend a corresponding exemption to interest on federal bonds and to federal salaries. The Supreme Court shattered the federal and state instrumentalities limitations with respect to salaries.[4] Many authorities believe that the way has been cleared as well for nondiscriminatory federal taxation of the interest on state and local securities.

Where the "equality" and "uniformity" provisions of state constitutions are not construed to prevent state income taxation, a state income tax may be imposed directly upon income as such or may be levied as a tax on persons "measured by" the incomes they receive. But since a state has no jurisdiction over the persons of nonresidents, a state income tax whose subject is persons could not well be extended to the income derived by nonresidents from within the taxing state. Therefore, state income taxes specifically or impliedly have "net income" for their subject. The federal Constitution imposes no bar to the taxation of nonresidents' income originating within the taxing state, except for one limitation—state income tax rates and exemption provisions must not discriminate against nonresidents.

JURISDICTIONAL BASIS FOR PERSONAL INCOME TAXATION

Under constitutional law, the federal government and the states have full power to tax all income received by residents and all income originating

[4] See Chapter 7.

within their boundaries. Which of these two bases, or what combination, will be employed is determined by the discretion of Congress and the state legislatures. Congress has chosen to rest the federal personal income tax on both bases, allowing (1) a credit to citizens for foreign income taxes paid on the basis of origin, and (2) a reciprocal credit to alien residents for foreign income taxes paid on the basis of nationality. In effect, therefore, the federal tax primarily taxes income on the basis of where it originates rather than according to the residence of the recipient.[5] For the most part the states employ both bases, with some provision for reciprocal credits.

Critical opinion predominantly favors residence as the basis for personal income taxation. On "benefit" arguments, it is admitted, a case can be made out for taxation of personal income both by the state of the recipient's residence and by the state of the income's origin. The former protects and serves the recipient in his personal capacity. The latter protects the property from which the income originates and fosters the business which produces it. But as personal income tax rates are currently applied, residence-basis taxes conform to "ability" principles and origin-basis taxes do not. A progressive rate schedule has justification under "ability" doctrines only when it is applied to the entire income received by an individual or family group. Residence-basis taxes permit such application of progressive rates. When progression is applied to the accidental segments of individual incomes which chance to originate in one state or another, it lacks this justification. Given two identical incomes, such "segmentary" progression results in lower taxes on income originating in several taxing states than on income originating entirely within one state.

This defect of origin-basis income taxes might be cured by determining the tax rate on a segment of "origin" income by the taxpayer's total income. The rate so determined would then be applied to the "segment" of income derived within the taxing state. Let us assume that a state's income tax rate schedule is one per cent on the first $4,000, 2 per cent on the next $4,000, and 3 per cent on the excess. Of a total $10,000 income, $5,000 originates within the state. The rate determined by the total $10,000 income is 1.8 per cent. This would be applied to the $5,000 of "origin" income. The constitutionality of a similar arrangement in the case of state death taxes has been upheld. A combination of origin-basis income taxes levied by several states, with each state determining the rate on its segment of "origin" income by the individual's total income, would result in fair comparative tax burdens as among the individuals. As compared with residence-basis taxes, one disadvantage of origin-basis income taxes is the

[5] See Chapter 23. An American citizen who resides outside the United States for 17 out of 18 consecutive months is not subject to United States income tax on the first $20,000 of foreign earnings.

added compliance cost and administrative load resulting from the multiplicity of returns on segmented incomes.

A fair and sound nation-wide system of state income taxation can be developed either on an origin or a residence basis, but not on a combination of the two. If some states employ the one basis and some the other, or if states seek to augment their revenues by employing both bases at once, unjustifiable double taxation of some individuals is bound to occur. When but few American states levied personal income taxes, the occasional instances of double taxation could be ignored. Now that nearly two-thirds of the states have income taxes, scores of thousands are likely to be victims of double taxation. However, reciprocal credit clauses are included in the income tax laws of most states taxing on both residence and origin bases. Under these arrangements, some states allow credit to residents for income taxes paid in other states; several allow credit to nonresident taxpayers for taxes paid to the state of residence. But although reciprocity clauses dispel the injustice of double taxation, they leave the administrative authorities burdened with nonresident returns upon which little or no tax is paid. If the system of reciprocal credits becomes general, its necessity as a retaliatory weapon against states which maintain double tax bases will disappear. A single residence basis for state income taxes seems a reasonable goal.

City income taxes generally use both residence and origin bases; one major purpose of these taxes, in fact, is to reach commuters who work in the city but live outside.[6] This complicates tax compliance for traveling salesmen; one with customers in Pennsylvania, where nearly 300 communities have local income taxes, may well have difficulty keeping tax records of where he earned how much. Rates of these local taxes are low, however, and their crudities do not produce serious injustices.

THE INCOME CONCEPT

It is easy to assert that personal income taxes are measured by "income." Definition of the term "income" is not so easy. Economists express widely divergent views on what "income" is and is not. Accountants have their own concepts. Legislators and tax administrators have fashioned tax laws which involve arbitrary intermarriages of various economists' and accountants' concepts. Our problem is to analyze and understand the major issues involved in the various income concepts. The huge rises in income tax rates increase greatly the practical importance of perfecting a definition of "taxable income."

General concepts. Economic theorists have offered many inconsistent

[6] About 15 per cent of the yield of the Philadelphia tax, and 25 per cent of that of St. Louis, comes from nonresidents. R. A. Sigafoos, *The Municipal Income Tax* (Public Administration Service, Chicago, 1955), p. 78. See also J. C. Phillips, "Philadelphia's Income Tax After Twenty Years," *National Tax Journal*, Sept., 1958, pp. 254–264.

concepts of income. One concept identifies the term "income" with the monetary value of the *flow of services* enjoyed by an individual within a specified period of time.[7] Another definition[8] views income as the monetary value of the net *accretion* to an individual's economic power within a specified period of time, with no deduction for his personal expenditures. A third is much narrower; it holds that income consists of *recurrent*, consumable receipts.[9]

Under the "service-flow" concept, an individual's net income would be equivalent to his expenditures for current consumption, plus the estimated net monetary value of his nonmonetary or "psychic income"—the services enjoyed from such durable properties as an owned home, house furnishings, and an automobile, and the value of the uncompensated labor of the individual for his own comfort and welfare. Since funds devoted to savings and investment purchase no personal utilities or satisfactions, they constitute no part of "service-flow" income. The amount and character of receipts during the income period are irrelevant; a millionaire miser who spent $2,500 a year on living and hoarded the rest of his receipts would have exactly the same "income" under the "service-flow" theory as an unemployed man who lived for a year upon $2,500 drawn from his savings.

The "economic-accretion" concept considers as income the net receipt or accrual of economic power, measured in money value, during a given period. In addition to wages and other compensation for services, rents and royalties, interest, net business profits, and dividends, this concept includes capital gains and losses, bequests and gifts received, and "psychic income." What disposal the individual makes of his income after it is his—whether he spends it, saves it, or gives it away—has no bearing.

The "recurrent-receipt" concept also looks to the receipt rather than the disposal of income items. But it limits income to recurrent items—personal compensation, rents and royalties, interest, net business profits, and dividends. Nonrecurrent items—capital gains, gambling gains or other irregular receipts, bequests, and gifts—are excluded.

American personal income taxes rest primarily upon the "economic-accretion" concept combined with important elements of the "recurrent-receipts" concept. They deliberately ignore certain items which the econo-

[7] The most insistent American supporter of this concept was Irving Fisher; see I. Fisher and H. W. Fisher, *Constructive Income Taxation* (Harper & Bros., New York, 1942).

[8] See Robert Murray Haig, *The Federal Income Tax* (Columbia University Press, New York, 1921), p. 27; W. Vickrey, *Agenda for Progressive Taxation* (Ronald Press, New York, 1947); this treatise is an outstanding contribution to the study of all phases of the income concept. An excellent defense of the "economic-accretion" concept is found in H. C. Simons, *Personal Income Taxation* (University of Chicago Press, Chicago, 1938).

[9] The British law attaches considerable importance to recurrence as a test of whether or not a receipt should be treated as income. A thorough discussion of the British concept of income will be found in Royal Commission on the Taxation of Profits and Income, *Final Report* (H. M. Stationery Office, London, 1955).

mists regard as "income." In the interest of administrative expediency, the taxes generally do not apply to nonmoney income. Since a special form of taxation has been built up around bequests, inheritances, and gifts, these items are also eliminated from personal income taxation. The income of unincorporated businesses, including partnerships, is an element of the taxable personal income of the owners. So are gains and losses resulting from transactions in capital assets, but they generally receive special treatment.

Nonmoney ("psychic") income. "Psychic income," better termed "nonmoney income" or "imputed income," deserves special discussion. Assume that A owns a house, rents it for $2,000 a year, and himself lives in another house for which he pays $2,000 rent a year, while B owns a house which could be rented for $2,000 a year but which he chooses to use for his own dwelling. Accountants credit A with a $2,000 income, and B with none. Economists argue that B has obtained benefits from living in his house which exactly balance the $2,000 rent A received from his; B has received a "real" income exactly equivalent to A's monetary income. Exclusion of the net value of owner-occupancy removes about $5 billion from the tax base each year. Benefits from the use of other types of durable consumers' goods are also excluded. Similarly, a farmer who consumes his own produce and the person who receives payment in kind—such as lunches, medical care, or insurance coverage—receives an "imputed income" equivalent to the sales value of such items.

So also, a man who paints his own house and a housewife who does her own housekeeping receive benefits from their labors equivalent to the cost of having those operations performed for them by others. *Leisure* can also be considered a desirable nonmoney source of satisfaction and of relative difference between persons. If C and D, for example, each have net money incomes of $5,000 but C works 2,200 hours during the year and D works only 1,600 hours, there is likely to be a marked difference in the sums of their total psychic incomes.

Occasional attempts have been made to take account of "imputed income" in American income taxes. The federal Civil War income tax and the Wisconsin tax of 1911 provided that the rental value of premises inhabited by the owner should be listed as income, as in Britain. Such provisions proved administratively impracticable. Evasion was too easy relative to the small administrative staffs provided, and compulsion of payment in the individual cases that came to the administrators' attention provoked exceptional resentment.

So our current income taxes ignore—they rarely exempt specifically—"imputed income," with consequent discrimination between individuals and groups of taxpayers. High tax rates have led to growing deliberate use of payment in nonmoney forms ("fringe benefits") to enable the recipients to escape income tax, with labor unions and top executives both pressing for such tax advantages.

The man who lives in a rented home is discriminated against as compared with the man who owns his own residence; furthermore, the latter can deduct taxes on the property and mortgage interest in calculating taxable net income, whereas no part of home rental is deductible. The family raising some of its own food or doing its own housework and laundry, for example, is favored over the family which buys all of its food or which employs servants and patronizes commercial laundries. Injustice is often done to women who work outside the home.[10] Farmers are favored, because they generally own their own homes or can count rental as a deductible business expense and because they produce more than other groups for their own consumption. As a class, dwellers in the larger cities are subject to discrimination since they employ and pay others for domestic and personal services to a greater extent than do the inhabitants of small cities and towns, because they are more often renters, and because they can produce less of their own food. Persons with expense accounts may also receive real income that is not taxed. In recent years many businesses have become deliberately generous in their interpretation of officers' and employees' "expenses" chargeable to the employer, or close an eye to gross "padding" of expense accounts, as a tacit means of providing an additional element of nontaxable compensation. This method of getting around the tax, which often goes beyond avoidance into evasion, sometimes approaches scandalous proportions.[11]

Tax-exempt receipts. In the federal and most state income tax laws, taxable net income is defined as "gross income" less certain "deductions." Then, in a catch-all sentence or paragraph, "gross income" is defined in such a way as to cover practically all receipts an individual may get. However, two classes of receipts—certain nonincome items and certain types of income nontaxable because of contractual or constitutional reasons —are excluded. For social reasons, certain other classes of receipts are sometimes excluded. Only the more important *exclusions* can be noted here.

[10] So much criticism of this discrimination developed that Congress in 1954 granted an extra child-care expense deduction to working mothers and widowers. The child must be under 12 or mentally or physically incapable of self support. The deduction is limited to $600 a year, regardless of the number of such dependents.

[11] Probably a large part of some executives' really lavish living could not possibly be paid for out of personal income after taxes. No one knows what fraction of the night-club and country-club life is financed out of expense accounts, but it must be large. Tax administrators find it almost impossible to be certain what entertainment really serves a legitimate business purpose. Without doubt, a corporation president's limousine and chauffeur charged to the company help him to work more efficiently, and act more efficiently, for the company, but they certainly also make his personal life pleasanter. In 1957, the Treasury proposed that employees be required to report amounts received to cover travel and other expenses and then to substantiate the validity of claimed deductions. The outcry in opposition forced the Treasury to retreat.

Excluded nonincome receipts listed in the federal income tax law are: payments of life and casualty insurance claims; sickness and disability benefits; damages for personal injury; annuities above certain amounts; up to $5,000 death benefits received from a deceased's employer; scholarships and fellowships; military pay earned in a combat zone and mustering-out pay; all veterans' benefits; certain options to buy stock on favorable terms; and gifts, bequests, and inheritances.[12] The federal statute still specifically excludes interest from state and local bonds.[13]

A common "social" exclusion under income tax laws is the rental value of a residence furnished to a minister by his congregation. Social Security and Railroad Retirement benefit payments are excluded by the federal law. The portion of an annuity or pension to be included depends upon the portion of the total cost over the years paid by the recipient (or his spouse) and his life expectancy as computed actuarially.[14] The general exemption of benefit payments under life insurance policies frees the interest that has accumulated on paid-in premiums as well as the premiums themselves; the amounts so involved are substantial. Several states exempt pension receipts. A few states exclude interest on savings bank deposits.

States having general personal income taxes often exclude dividends paid by corporations already taxed by the state. Prior to 1936, the federal statute exempted dividends from the normal tax, though not from the surtax. This partial exclusion of dividends from personal income taxation rested on the theory that a personal income tax and a corporation income tax should operate as one single tax on corporation income with two complementary levies, rather than as two superimposed taxes. The corporation tax was viewed as a loose method of collecting at source the personal tax on dividend income. Today the personal tax is superimposed on the corporate, but the individual is allowed to exclude $50 of dividends and to take a tax credit of 4 per cent of any additional dividends. Thus, a person receiving $200 in dividends would exclude $50 and then deduct $6 (4 per cent of $150) from the tax otherwise due.

Business cost and expense deductions. Gain from unincorporated busi-

[12] The law is so complicated that numerous qualifications attach to the items listed here.

[13] This major defect of the federal income tax is discussed more fully in Chapter 26.

[14] Assume that a person paid the full cost, $12,000, of an annuity contract which will bring him $100 a month and that at retirement his life expectancy is 16 years. He stands to get $16,000. His cost has been 75 per cent of what he will presumably receive. Therefore, 75 per cent—$900 out of $1,200 a year—will be excluded from his income as computed for tax purposes. If an employer had paid some or all of the cost, and if such payments had not been included in the employee's taxable income—the typical situation—the employee's cost and hence the amount he may exclude each year is reduced correspondingly. The general objective of what are truly complicated rules is to exclude that part of an annuity which represents the return of funds on which the annuitant has presumably paid income tax before. In addition, the law seeks to spread the exclusion evenly over the period of the annuity, rather than bunching it in a few years. The taxation of pension funds is discussed in Chapter 14.

ness enterprises (including farms and independent professional practice such as law and medicine) is an element of the taxable personal incomes of the owners of such enterprises. Such profit is the total gross receipts of the business minus the expenses of obtaining them. Among these deductible business costs and expenses are the cost of material for manufacture or of merchandise bought for resale, employee compensation, supplies, other operating costs, interest on business indebtedness, business taxes, bad debts and other business losses, rent, repairs and other business property costs, and depreciation, obsolescence, and depletion allowances.

Every one of these business cost and expense deductions has been the subject of voluminous administrative and judicial interpretation. In many instances, these constructions relate to technical details. Some, however, involve fundamental elements of the concept of "business income." Chapter 14 deals with a few.

Expenses of an employee associated with his occupation and not reimbursed by the employer are deductible within only narrow and arbitrary limits—union dues, some educational expense of teachers, outlays for uniforms in certain cases, travel expense away from home. However, doctors, lawyers, and other persons engaged in independent practice are permitted to deduct operating expenses. Many unquestionably include some personal expenses in with the professional and boost after-tax income more than negligibly. Operating expenses of income-producing property, such as a building rented to another, may be deducted by an individual as a business expense.

Gross income minus these deductions and also minus capital and other losses is *adjusted gross income*. Chart 12–1 shows some figures for 1955.

Personal expense deductions.[15] A logical case could be made for the deduction, in determining taxable personal income, of the costs of keeping the taxpayer alive and healthy, so that he may earn the income. A logical case could also be made for allowing no deduction of such costs of living. In general, the federal and state personal income taxes permit no such deductions. *Interest* payments on personal debts are generally deductible. So are certain *tax payments* made by taxpayers in their individual capacity.

The *personal tax* deduction under the federal income tax is limited to state and local income taxes, property taxes, gasoline taxes, motor vehicle taxes, and sales taxes. The sales tax deduction is limited to retail sales levies paid by the purchaser and collected through the seller (not the manufacturer). The taxpayer is denied the deduction of many taxes which are shifted to him because technically they fall upon someone else. The deduction under state income tax laws is generally similar to that of the federal tax, except that (1) state income tax payments are not deductible

[15] See M. I. White, "Deductions for Nonbusiness Expenses and an Economic Concept of New Income," Joint Economic Committee, *Federal Tax Policy for Economic Growth and Stability* (Washington, 1955), pp. 353–366.

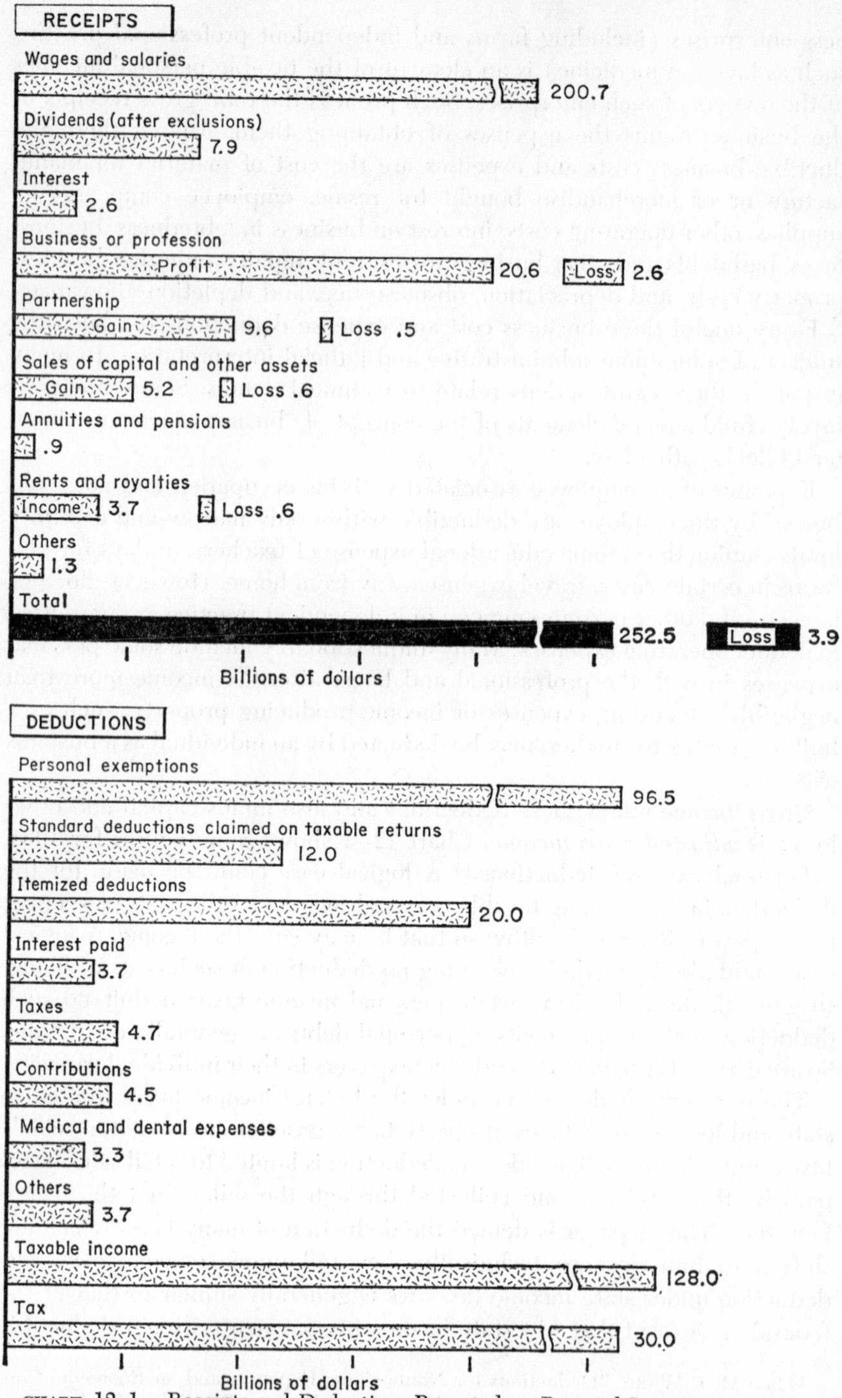

RECEIPTS

Wages and salaries 200.7

Dividends (after exclusions) 7.9

Interest 2.6

Business or profession

Profit 20.6 Loss 2.6

Partnership

Gain 9.6 Loss .5

Sales of capital and other assets

Gain 5.2 Loss .6

Annuities and pensions .9

Rents and royalties

Income 3.7 Loss .6

Others 1.3

Total 252.5 Loss 3.9

Billions of dollars

DEDUCTIONS

Personal exemptions 96.5

Standard deductions claimed on taxable returns 12.0

Itemized deductions 20.0

Interest paid 3.7

Taxes 4.7

Contributions 4.5

Medical and dental expenses 3.3

Others 3.7

Taxable income 128.0

Tax 30.0

Billions of dollars

CHART 12–1. Receipts and Deductions Reported on Personal Income Tax Returns, 1955. SOURCE: *Statistics of Income . . . 1955.*

and (2) 21 states allow federal income tax as a deduction. Federal excises charged directly to the taxpayer are also deductible in many states.

Partly to encourage certain socially desirable types of personal expenditure, partly to ease the burden of the heavy federal rates on taxpayers with certain types of expenditure obligations, the federal tax and some of the state taxes accord limited deductions for *extraordinary medical and dental* expenses not covered by insurance. The medical expense deduction under the federal tax provides for deduction of payments for medical and dental care and supplies in excess of 3 per cent of adjusted gross income to a maximum of $2,500 for a single person, $5,000 for most couples, and $10,000 for a family. Persons over 65 may deduct all such expenses except drugs and medicine under one per cent of income. Some state taxes provide for some deduction of life insurance and annuity premium payments and for expenses of schooling of members of the taxpayer's family.

Contributions to religious, charitable, scientific, and educational organizations are deductible under the federal and most state taxes. This deduction is intended to stimulate such contributions for the social advantages they produce. To prevent undue loss of revenue, this deduction is limited to a specified proportion of the taxpayer's income—to 10 per cent by a few states, to 20 per cent by the federal government plus another 10 per cent for gifts to churches, educational institutions, hospitals, and medical research organizations.[16] Some states allow the deduction only for contributions made to organizations operating within the state.

Alimony payments may be deducted by the payor; the payee must then include them in her gross income. A wide variety of *losses* from such casualties as fire, theft, automobile accident, and flood may be deducted to the extent that they are not covered by compensation from insurance or other source. *Uncollectible debts* are deductible in some cases.

Under the federal and most state personal income taxes, instead of listing his personal expense deductions item by item, an individual may elect to take a "standard" lump-sum or fixed-percentage deduction. For the federal tax, this "standard" deduction, which about 70 per cent of all persons filing tax returns use, is 10 per cent of the taxpayer's adjusted gross income, not to exceed $1,000.

Treatment of capital gains and losses.[17] An ever-open issue in income taxation is the treatment of gains and losses from the sale of capital items—stocks, bonds, real estate, etc. Are such gains and losses properly brought

[16] Under certain circumstances, a person would save more in income taxes by making a charitable contribution of property on which there has been a large capital gain than if he had sold the property and paid the tax on the capital gain.

[17] For an excellent discussion, see L. H. Seltzer, *The Nature and Tax Treatment of Capital Gains and Losses* (National Bureau of Economic Research, New York, 1951). It should be noted that persons who argue that changes in capital values should not be included in computing taxable income, will insist that depreciation, which is a change in capital value, should be deductible.

within the income concept, or should they be considered capital manifestations which never touch the income plane directly? If they are considered an element of income, should they be brought within the scope of a personal income tax? Or would the economy operate better if they were exempt from tax? If they are taxed, should they be accorded special treatment, and what should that treatment be?

Capital gains and losses would be completely separated from income under the "recurrent-receipt" theory of income; the English income tax, which rests largely on this theory, generally but not completely exempts capital gains and losses. Just as positively, however, the "economic-accretion" doctrine would include them in income. The federal income tax and most of the state income taxes treat capital gains as taxable income and allow capital losses under certain conditions as deductions. The Supreme Court has sustained such treatment, with the important proviso that the gain or loss must be "severed" or "realized" before it assumes the attributes of income.

The criterion of realization is reasonable. Capital values fluctuate so widely and so incessantly that it is not practical to try to take account each tax period of changes in value that are only "on paper." Funds for payment of tax may not be available until the asset is sold. Furthermore, the current value of many assets—stock in closely-owned businesses, for example—is often a matter of considerable doubt. There is, however, serious disadvantage in taxing capital gains or allowing capital losses as deductions only upon realization—the taxpayer has control over timing his sale. He is given inducement and power to realize losses while delaying realization of gains. Under present law, *by holding property with gains until death, he can escape income tax on the gain entirely.* It is the power of the taxpayer to determine realization that makes more generous deduction of losses seem dangerously costly to the Treasury. It is the ability to avoid tax *permanently* that adds a widely distorting factor in a property-owner's decisions about whether or not to realize gains.

Pros and cons of taxing capital gains. Inclusion of capital gains in the concept of taxable income, and the related allowances of capital losses as a deduction, has provoked a number of criticisms.

(1) It is argued that a man whose property or investment has increased markedly in value feels "locked in" and hesitates to sell because of the heavy tax which results.[18] This hesitancy, it is further argued, distorts business and investment decisions. As capital values rise, sales of securities and real estate are discouraged because the resulting capital gains would add an extra element of immediate tax liability. As values fall, many taxpayers are induced to sell so that they can deduct the capital losses. Two some-

[18] For analysis of the principles involved, see R. F. Gemmill, "The Effect of the Capital Gains Tax on Asset Prices," *National Tax Journal,* Dec., 1956, pp. 289–301.

what different results must then be charged to capital gains taxation. (a) Fluctuations in the *general level* of capital values are greater than otherwise. (b) *Relative prices* of assets reflect artificial tax factors as well as judgments about economic prospects.

(2) In periods of rising capital prices, many of the gains subjected to the tax are illusory—they represent only an enhancement in *prices* rather than any gain in basic *values*. Reinvestment of the funds must be at the new level of prices. Likewise, capital losses during periods of falling capital prices are not all true losses but partly monetary variations. In periods of sharp inflation or deflation, the taxation of capital gains and deduction of losses may work injustices by ignoring the illusory nature of the change.[19] When swings of capital prices are moderate, of course, the practical injury is not serious. Application of a "capital price index number" to taxable gains and losses might reduce this defect. But a satisfactory "capital price index number" has yet to be computed, and good administration of such a provision would be most difficult.

(3) Another charge against taxation of capital gains and deduction of capital losses is that it makes the yield of an income tax more variable. Toward the end of a period of rising capital values, realized capital gains—and therefore tax revenue—may be large. After a persistent decline of capital values, however, realized capital losses outweigh realized capital gains, and tax revenue is correspondingly reduced.

(4) If the accruals of a capital gain over several years are lumped in the particular year when the gain is realized, the application of a progressive rate schedule may result in overtaxation. Suppose a $30,000 capital gain accrued over 30 years at the rate of $1,000 a year. At 1959 rates (but without the provision for application of the tax to only half the gain on long-held property), such a gain realized in a lump sum at the end of the 30-year period by an unmarried taxpayer who had other income of only $1,600 would be taxed about 50 per cent. But had each year's $1,000 capital gain been taxed as it accrued, the tax on the total capital gain would have been only 20 per cent, since it would be subject only to the minimum bracket rate each year. Moreover, lumping capital losses in the year they are realized also works against the taxpayer's interest, since the saving reaches further into the lower income brackets subject to lower rates. Were the loss deductible as it accrued each year, the saving would appear as a yearly reduction in top income brackets, upon which the tax is heaviest.

(5) A large portion of capital gains results from plowing back of corporation profits which have already been taxed heavily. They have not, of course, been taxed as heavily as if they had been distributed as dividends and the remainder then put back into the business.

[19] Bonds, and to some extent real estate and stock prices, change in response to variations in interest rates which result from broad forces in the market which a seller may not be able to escape when reinvesting the proceeds of sale of an asset.

(6) Exemption of capital gains will help stimulate capital formation and business growth by encouraging businesses to retain earnings and prosperous individuals to finance ventures with uncertain chances of success but some of which will be highly productive.

(7) Taxation of capital gains and allowance of capital losses complicate the tax structure.

(8) Finally, exemption or highly favored treatment of capital gains offers one way to escape the bad effects of high bracket rates. If Congress will not face the political risks of cutting extreme rates, it can achieve some of the same ends—which many people believe to be desirable—by permitting some income to escape these rates. A crude device may seem better than none.

Proponents of including realized changes in capital values in computing taxable income argue that these criticisms are outweighed by other considerations.

(1) The rise and fall in property values simply cannot be ignored in measuring changes in economic power and ability to support government. An income tax exists to get revenue from people on a basis which discriminates rationally. What counts is the difference in personal economic circumstances, and changes in capital values are significant and relevant, certainly when realized. Assume, for example, that A and B have net salaries of $10,000 each but that A suffers a capital loss of $20,000 and B enjoys a capital gain of $20,000. The difference in their position must be considered, it is argued, in any equitable determination of the income tax they should pay.

(2) Capital gains often represent "unearned increment," such as a rise in site value of land, or a discovery of oil, or an increase in the value of corporate shares, or a rise in bond prices due to changes in market rates of interest, for which the owner is in no way responsible. By all principles of tax justice, unearned increments are appropriate objects of taxation.

(3) Although the yield of a personal income tax is made more variable by including capital gains and losses in the income concept, the fluctuations tend to fit well into a fiscal policy designed to reduce business cycle swings.

(4) If capital gains were not taxable, individuals with large incomes would try even harder than at present to convert other kinds of income into capital gains. Thereby they would avoid much personal income taxation and especially high progressive rates. Our economy provides a convenient and systematic way to convert business earnings into capital gains—retention and reinvestment of profit in the business.[20]

(5) Net capital gains are realized primarily by persons whose income is

[20] For analysis of this often neglected point, see C. S. Shoup, "Relation of Capital Gains Taxation to Tax Treatment of Undistributed Profit," *Federal Tax Policy for Economic Growth and Stability* (Washington, 1955), pp. 394–404.

well above average.[21] Capital gains are an important part of the total income of prosperous and rich families. Failure to tax such income would reduce the progressivity—and even the *proportionality*—of the income tax.

(6) Although the provisions necessary to tax capital gains (and take account of capital losses as deductions) are complex, the provisions that would be needed to exempt them would be even more complex—unless huge loopholes in the income tax structure were to be tolerated.

(7) Finally, for as long as the population and wealth of the country continue to expand, capital gains will tend to exceed capital losses, and capital gains taxation adds to the long-term yield of a personal income tax.

Special favorable treatment of capital gains. American legislators have been persuaded that the pros of capital gains taxation outweigh the cons. Capital gains are taxed under the federal income tax and under all general state income taxes except those of Iowa and Maryland. But general acceptance of the principle of capital gains taxation does not mean that such gains must be taxed at the same rates as other forms of personal income.

The arguments that support the taxation of capital gains at special low rates are:

(1) It reduces some of the injustices of capital gains taxation—application of high bracket rates to lump gains that have accrued over a period of years, and the "paper" character of gains in periods of rising prices.

(2) It reduces any tendency for the tax to distort the relative prices of capital assets.

(3) It produces a favorable economic effect. Low rates induce individuals in the upper income brackets—who constitute an important source of investment capital—to favor equities which combine probabilities of capital accretion with low current income yield and some degree of risk. This treatment thereby offsets some of the depressant effect which the heavily progressive federal income tax would otherwise have on the equity investment market, through reducing the capacity and willingness of wealthy individuals to take risks.

The arguments against special favoring treatment of capital gains are:

(1) It favors mainly taxpayers in the higher income brackets, thereby reducing the intended progressivity of the personal income tax.

(2) It offers loopholes for tax minimization, whereby capital gains are substituted for certain types of current income. Corporation executives, for example, arrange to take part of their compensation in the form of capital gains on stock of their companies purchased by them with funds loaned by the companies. Farmers treat their profit on sale of livestock owned for more than a year as capital gain instead of regular farming income.

[21] In 1955, individuals with incomes over $15,000 received 13 per cent of all adjusted gross income and roughly 60 per cent of realized capital gains.

(3) It makes compliance with, and administration of, a personal income tax more complex.

(4) It lowers the yield of any personal income tax.

To the Congressional mind, the pros outweigh the cons, and since 1921 capital gains have been taxed either at a special low rate, or on a fractional basis, or by a combination of the two systems. Although several states include capital gains with other income and apply the regular rates to it, the details of methods vary widely.

Treatment of capital losses. All "justice" arguments lead to the conclusion that if capital gains are taxed as personal income, capital losses should be deductible. From an economic viewpoint, to tax capital gains and not allow a deduction of capital losses would unduly discourage risk-taking investment, which is important to national progress. Two considerations, however, dictate some hedging of the privilege of capital loss deductibility.

(1) To some extent taxpayers can "time" sales of capital assets so as to realize capital gains and capital losses in years which will give them maximum tax advantage. When, as in this country, gains not realized before death are *never* subject to income tax, the opportunity to realize losses while avoiding the realization of gains would favor the taxpayer excessively. Limitations on the deductibility of capital losses restrict the possibility of tax avoidance.

(2) In recession years capital losses of some taxpayers could completely offset their income items. If full deductibility were allowed, the reduction of the yield of state income taxes would upset their budgets unduly.

Current status of capital gains and loss taxation. Present federal personal income tax treatment of capital gains and losses is unbelievably complex, and becoming more so. However, for the great mass of taxpayers the rules are not unduly intricate.

Highly technical provisions distinguish sales or exchanges which bring normal profit and loss from those getting capital gains treatment. Most of these provisions also apply to businesses, including, of course, unincorporated firms. The general rule is that sale of business property which is subject to depreciation—buildings and machinery, for example—brings capital gain or loss, whereas sale of stock in trade and goods held for resale to customers—inventory—is not a capital transaction.[22] Sale of livestock but not poultry can bring capital gains treatment. Sale of a patent but not a copyright, musical, or artistic composition created by the seller can qualify. Stock options and some pensions can be arranged to bring their recipient a capital gain rather than other form of income. The insistent and unremitting pressures on Congress are to get more types of sales and exchanges

[22] It requires a complicated body of rulings to distinguish from capital gains those profits which are the everyday earnings of business and commerce.

treated as capital transactions when they yield a gain—and as a regular business transaction when they result in a loss, for business losses are more fully deductible than capital losses.[23]

Federal law includes in taxable income most realized capital gains that exceed losses. One exception is the gain from the sale of a residence if the receipts are spent on another house within 18 months. The amount of the gain is the difference between the selling price and the "adjusted basis"; the latter is the purchase price minus depreciation, plus and minus a variety of other items whose computation is sometimes complicated. Capital transactions are classified according to the length of time the assets were owned. If ownership was 6 months or less, the transaction is *short-term*, if over 6 months *long-term*.[24] Short-term gains are included fully with other income for tax purposes, but only half of long-term gains are included. The allowance for losses is complex, but in general both short-term and long-term business and investment losses are deductible from corresponding gains. If the result is still a net loss, it may be deducted from other income up to $1,000 and any balance can be carried forward to subsequent years, but not more than five. The taxpayer has another alternative. If he has net long-term gains, he can elect to have the gain taxed at a rate of 25 per cent—a real bargain for a single person with income over $18,000 or a married person with income over $36,000, for whom the regular tax rates (applied to half the gain) would be higher.[25]

State treatment shows wide variation. Although the common practice is to tax business and investment capital gains at regular income tax rates, there are instances of special or fractional rates. Capital losses are generally allowed as a deduction, but frequently such deduction may be made only against gains reported for the year or during a two-year period.

Critique. Extensive dissatisfaction with the present treatment represents no agreement. True, the baffling complexity does provoke general disgust. Yet active pressures are not for simplification, but for enlarging the number of special provisions,[26] as one group seeks approximately what some other has. Objective observers will also agree that the present rules produce great inequality in tax burdens among people with essentially similar ac-

[23] Moreover, there is pressure to get more exchanges, and even outright sales, treated as "involuntary conversions" and thus not realizations for computing capital gain.

[24] The reason for distinguishing long from short gains is to meet the problem of lumping the income of more than one year into a single year's tax base. Consequently, the dividing line should be at least *more* than one year. It is hard to find any logic in the present treatment.

[25] Technically, half the net gain is taxed at a rate of 50 per cent. The rate on all the gain, then, is 25 per cent. The 22,000 taxpayers reporting incomes over $100,000 in 1955 were permitted to exclude from taxable income nearly $1.2 billion net capital gains—an amount large in relation to the $3.6 billion income on which they paid tax.

[26] For example, a 1958 change permits, in some cases, a person who sells property received as a gift to add the *donor's* gift tax to the purchase price in computing the basis for determining capital gain or loss.

cretions of economic power. But there is no agreement on the seriousness of the injustice that results nor on the significance of the economic consequences—good or bad "distortions."

Much of the difficulty comes, fundamentally, from the height of personal income tax rates. If the top rates could be lowered significantly to narrow the difference between the upper bracket personal income tax rates and the 25 per cent top rate on long-term capital gains (or if that rate could be raised), the practical dimensions of the problem would be much reduced. If transfers at death were treated as realization and permanent avoidance thus eliminated, one source of difficulty would disappear.

PROBLEMS

1. Discuss four problems of defining "income" for purposes of taxation, emphasizing the economic significance of your points.

2. "It would be simpler and no less fair to tax on the basis of adjusted gross income, minus exemptions, than to try to compute a net income which, being smaller, requires higher rates." Discuss.

3. Criticize the arguments for and against including capital gains and losses in taxable income.

4. What is the logic of the "realization" principle?

5. Explain the significance of the possibility of permanent escape of tax on capital gains.

6. Describe and criticize the present federal arrangements for taxing capital gains and for excluding capital losses.

7. Give reasons for and against allowing an individual to deduct interest, taxes, and contributions in computing taxable income.

8. What problems would arise in trying to include in taxable income the rental value of an owner-occupied dwelling?

CHAPTER 13

Personal Income Taxes (Concluded)

PERSONAL INCOME TAX RATE SCHEDULES

WHEN the federal personal income tax was under debate before World War I, the issue of a proportional versus a graduated rate was bitterly contested. In conservative quarters, the principle of progression was still denounced as "confiscatory" and "un-American." Today, popular and critical opinion not only accepts but approves progressive income taxation. But even though the principle of progression is generally endorsed, there is much honest and intelligent dispute over its application.

Personal exemptions. The federal income tax allows a $600 "personal exemption" to single persons, a $1,200 exemption to each married couple, and a further $600 exemption for each dependent. Moreover, each blind person and each person over 65 years of age receives an additional exemption of $600. Through the 1930's, the federal personal exemption was $1,000 for single individuals and $2,500 for married taxpayers. Personal exemptions under the state income taxes range from $2,500 and $5,000 in Louisiana to $500 per capita in Vermont and $600 per capita in six other states. In five states the personal exemptions take the form of deductions from the tax instead of deductions from the net income itself.

Four arguments are advanced in support of the personal exemption. (1) Provision of the necessities of human life is as much a "cost of production," it may be asserted, as any of the business costs allowed as deductions from gross business income; an individual's "clear" net income does not begin until the minimum costs of living have been covered. (2) Under "ability" arguments, a person or family has no "taxpaying ability" whatsoever if income just suffices to cover minimum living expenses. (3) From a social point of view, it is not desirable that an income tax force a person or family to adopt a "submarginal" living standard. (4) Personal exemptions reduce the number of returns and hence lessen the administrative costs of tax collection; in 1958 an increase in exemptions of $100 per capita would have freed about 4,200,000 taxpayers from all income tax.

Prior to 1942, federal income tax exemptions were considerably above the minimum-of-subsistence level. State income tax exemptions are generally still liberal. The earlier federal and numerous state exemptions represent a "minimum-of-comfort" exemption. Such minimum-of-comfort exemptions greatly reduce revenue and relieve millions from direct financial responsibility for the conduct of their governments.

"Broadening the income tax base"—lowering personal exemptions and thus increasing the number subject to the tax—was forced by World War II. The principal arguments for such action were: (1) the great revenue increase that would follow; (2) the awakening of "tax consciousness," which might lead to pressure for more economy in expenditure; (3) the absorption of purchasing power, which would help check the inflation threatened by other elements of the defense finance program; and (4) less desirable mass taxes, such as a sales tax, could be avoided. Rises in the cost of living have made the $600 per capita exemption less than a tolerable minimum for some taxpayers, especially single individuals living in high cost areas.[1]

There is some administrative advantage to a uniform per capita exemption instead of amounts that vary according to marital or dependency status. This advantage takes on increasing significance as the coverage of the law increases, especially when employers must withhold tax.

The main revenue effect of raising or lowering exemptions is not what the taxpayers just exempted or brought in by the change pay. Rather, it is the reduction or increase in the amount paid by all the taxpayers above the exemption level. Increasing the personal exemption by only $100 would cost the federal government $2.8 billion revenue, 60 per cent of the saving going to taxpayers with incomes over $5,000.

Taxation of nonresidents, under state personal income taxes, upon income originating within the taxing state raises a special problem with respect to personal exemptions. A substantial proportion of the states taxing nonresidents allow them full personal exemptions. A few states, with greater logic, prorate the personal exemptions in accordance with the proportion of total income derived within the taxing state. Two states have adopted the indefensible compromise of granting the single-person exemption to nonresidents, irrespective of their family status.

Application of progression. The federal and state income taxes accomplish progression by the "bracket" method, whereby each successive higher rate applies only to income in excess of the previous bracket maximum. Furthermore, "continuing" exemptions reduce somewhat the over-all bur-

[1] A person employed only 13 hours a week at the federal minimum wage of $1 an hour earns more than the $600 exemption plus the 10 per cent allowance for deductions.

den of the scheduled rates.[2] Actually, therefore, the over-all effective rates on total incomes are lower than the maximum "bracket" rates applying to these incomes. Under the federal tax from 1926 until 1931, for example, the top bracket rate on taxable incomes over $100,000 was 25 per cent, but the taxes actually paid on these incomes averaged only between 13 and 17 per cent.[3] In 1959, the bracket rate on taxable income between $10,000 and $12,000 was 38 per cent; the total tax, however, on a person with a net income of $11,000 was about 26 per cent of his net income if he was single and 16 per cent of his net income if he was married with two dependents and if his wife had no separate income. The top bracket rate in this year was 91 per cent on income in excess of $200,000 for a single person; the over-all rate on an income of $200,000 over exemptions was about 78 per cent for a single person. Moreover, a ceiling of 88 per cent on total income was provided.

The splitting of income between husband and wife that was introduced in 1948 reduces the steepness of the progression on married couples.[4] The tax on a single person with a net income of $10,000 is 25 per cent of his income, but for the married couple without dependents it is only 19 per cent. If the income is $100,000, the single person pays total tax of 67 per cent whereas the married couple pays 54 per cent.

For federal revenue purposes, the most important incomes have become those under $10,000 where most of the nation's income is concentrated. Before World War II made the federal personal income tax a mass tax by greatly reducing exemptions and raising rates, the broad income range from $10,000 to $100,000 was the most important. Table 13–1 shows an estimate of income and tax distribution for 1958. The 55 per cent of taxpayers with incomes under $5,000 paid 20 per cent of the total tax. The 38 per cent with incomes from $5,000 to $10,000 had almost 45 per cent of the total income and paid 38 per cent of the total tax. Only 7 per cent of taxpayers had incomes over $10,000, but they accounted for 24 per cent of all income and paid 41 per cent of total tax.

An increase or decrease in the rate schedule can be made either by changing the rates themselves or by imposing a flat percentage of the tax of a given schedule as an addition or a reduction. The first method has been traditional in this country. In 1945, 1948, and 1954, however, the second

[2] For long the federal personal income tax rate schedule consisted of *two* schedules—a proportional "normal tax" with a superimposed progressive "surtax." The distinction eventually lost its significance and no longer applies.

[3] This discussion of over-all rates does not take into account the substantial lowering of "effective" rates on large incomes by the special provisions for taxing long-term capital gains or by various procedures of tax minimization.

[4] A widow or widower can ordinarily get full benefit of income splitting for 2 years after death of the spouse. Any other "head of a household" is treated in effect as half single, half married. A special set of rates gives him or her about half of the married couple's gain from income splitting.

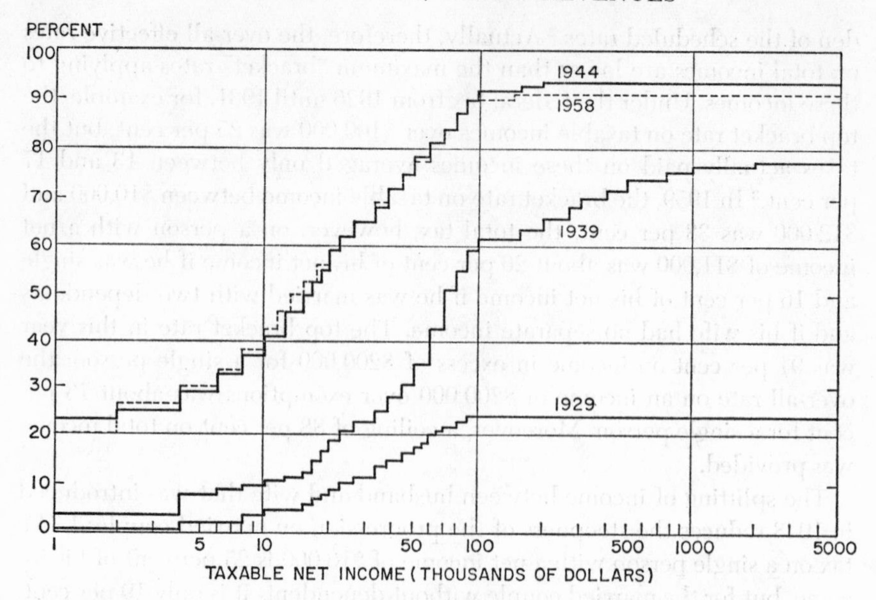

CHART 13–1. Federal Personal Income Tax Bracket Rates, Selected Years, 1929 to 1959.

method, described as an "across-the-board" cut, was employed. When the rate schedule is already progressive, an "across-the-board" change gives much different results at different ends of the income scale. The 1945 law, for example, permitted taxpayers to reduce their computed tax by 5 per cent of the *tax*. For a married man with two children and a net income of $3,000 this reduction cut the tax by $10, increasing his income after tax by one-third of one per cent; for those with net incomes of $102,000, however, the tax saving was $3,366, increasing the income after tax by 10 per cent. The merit of the "across-the-board" method is that Congress may feel politically safer in reducing or increasing the steepness of the scale of progression by making changes as a percentage of the tax than by modifying the stated rates.[5]

Limits to progression. Constitutionally, nothing prevents the federal government or any of the states from establishing 100 per cent rates on income over a prescribed amount.[6] Nor does economic theory dictate any maximum rate for income taxes. But the graduation of income tax rate schedules is not purely a matter of legislative discretion.

Graduation in state income taxes is limited by two considerations. (1) With the rates of the federal tax rising to over 90 per cent, were state

[5] New York State has maintained its basic income tax rate schedule unchanged for a number of years, with changing "across-the-board" reductions to accommodate budgetary revenue requirements.

[6] In effect, rates may exceed 100 per cent of *net* income, for example, when losses are not fully deductible.

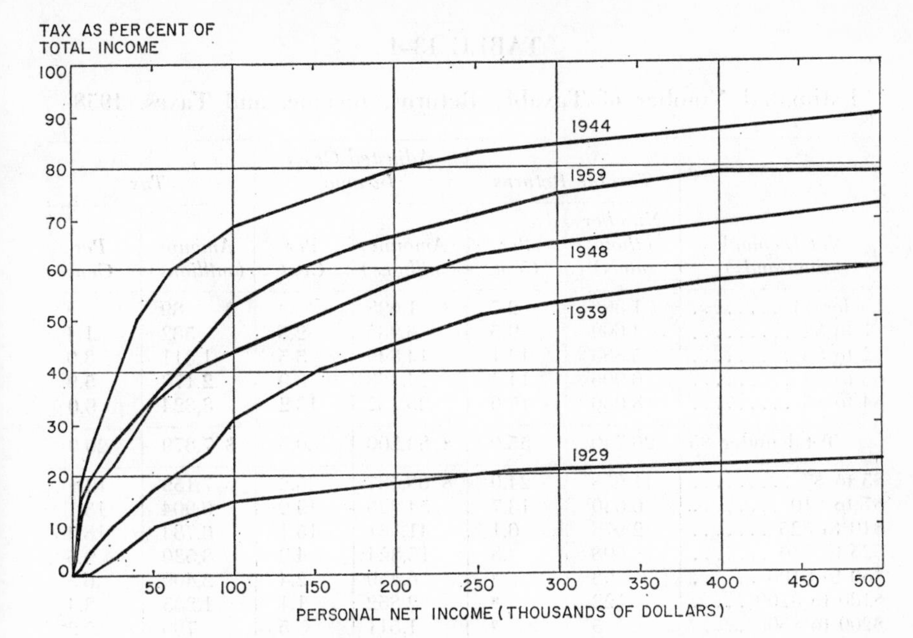

CHART 13–2. Proportion of Taxable Income of Married Couple, No Children, Absorbed by Federal Personal Income Tax, Selected Years, 1929 to 1959.

taxes allowing no deduction for federal tax payments to be higher than 10 per cent, they could occasionally result in complete confiscation of income in excess of some figure.[7] (2) If the top bracket rates of a state income tax are high, wealthy individuals may avoid the tax by moving to lower-taxing or nontaxing states. For a number of years, Florida and Nevada advertised themselves as income-taxless havens for millionaires. However, the deductibility of state income tax payments in computing federal tax liability reduces the effective differential in total personal income taxes resulting from differences in state tax rates, especially on large incomes. For example, a $5,000 state tax on a married man with $100,000 taxable income would deprive him net of $1,400—about 3 per cent of his income *after* tax. The $3,600 cut in his federal tax wipes out most of the difference between burdens in states with and without income taxes.

The federal government does not have to fear greatly the exodus of millionaires because of high income tax rates. National residence is not changed lightly or easily. Nonetheless, progression in the federal income tax is limited, although by a different set of factors. Let the top rates of the tax be set too high and recipients of larger incomes will find it advan-

[7] The federal law, of course, allows deduction of state income tax in computing federal taxable income. Therefore, a 100 per cent combined rate could apply only when the previous year's income was much less than that of the current year, so that the state income tax deductible in computing income for federal tax would be much less than the state tax currently due.

TABLE 13–1

Estimated Number of Taxable Returns, Income, and Taxes, 1958

	Taxable Returns		Adjusted Gross Income		Tax	
Net Income[1] *(thousands)*	*Number (thousands)*	*Per Cent*	*Amount (millions)*	*Per Cent*	*Amount (millions)*	*Per Cent*
Under $1	1,306	2.7	$ 1,098	a	$ 39	a
$1 to $2	4,609	9.5	6,933	2.5	532	1.4
$2 to $3	5,883	12.1	14,849	5.5	1,311	3.6
$3 to $4	6,906	14.2	24,188	8.9	2,173	5.9
$4 to $5	8,036	16.6	36,132	13.2	3,324	9.0
Total under $5	26,740	55.0	$ 83,200	30.5	$ 7,379	20.0
$5 to $7	11,658	24.0	$ 68,587	25.2	7,159	19.4
$7 to $10	6,640	13.7	54,328	19.9	6,904	18.7
$10 to $25	2,975	6.1	41,181	15.1	6,784	18.4
$25 to $50	398	.8	13,324	4.9	3,520	9.5
$50 to $100	98	a	6,459	2.4	2,409	6.5
$100 to $200	22	a	2,852	1.1	1,235	3.4
$200 to $500	5	a	1,511	.5	799	2.2
$500 to $1,000 ...	1	a	551	a	327	.9
$1,000 and over ...	a	a	624	a	369	1.0
Total over $5	21,797	44.9	$189,417	69.5	$29,506	80.0
Grand Total ..	48,536	100.0	$272,617	100.0	$36,885	100.0

Figures will not necessarily add to totals because of rounding.
[1] After deductions but before personal exemptions.
[a] Less than one thousand or one-half of one per cent.
SOURCE: Joint Committee on Internal Revenue Taxation, *Alternative Plans for Tax Relief for Individuals* (Washington, 1958), p. 1.

tageous to shift their investments from corporate securities and real property to tax-exempt government bonds or to take fuller advantage of avoidance devices—and to press Congress for more loopholes. The willingness to work harder and take risks may suffer—how much, no one knows—with probable loss of national economic effort. High personal income tax rates also reduce the amounts saved by the upper income groups and thus reduce one source of funds for new investment. High tax rates may prove costly in terms of economic progress by reducing both the ability and the willingness of the taxpayers affected to invest in new capital goods.

As top bracket rates approach confiscatory levels, the incentive to evasion and avoidance is heightened, for the gain to be derived is increased. Expert legal talent hopefully suggests all sorts of "dodges"—conversion of potential salaries, interest, and dividends into capital gains; treatment of "hobby farms" and racing stables as businesses so that the costs of operation can be deducted as current business losses; creation of trusts for relatives and dependents so that the income devoted to their support shall no longer be credited to the taxpayer; establishment of trusts to accumulate income for children until they reach age 21; gifts of capital to members of the family; formation of partnerships between father and sons and grandchildren to split up a single large income and remove it from the higher tax brackets; fringes and expense accounts as substitutes for part of what would be salaries; and other possibilities.

Some tax minimization procedures are disallowed by the courts, and changes in the law remove others, but many prove to be valid "loopholes" and provide an avenue of escape. Somewhere along the line, as rates are pushed higher and higher, a "law of diminishing productivity" comes into operation, and the long-run yield from the high income brackets falls off with further rate increases. Moreover, political pressures for the creation of new loopholes become so strong that Congress often cannot resist. Rather than cut the high rates, Congress chooses to provide means of escape from them.

What are the facts? A Tax Foundation study has traced changes in income as reported for tax purposes from 1916 to the mid-1950's.[8] It concludes that, for incomes from $10,000 to $50,000, the amounts reported for tax purposes have increased at approximately the same rate as personal income for the whole economy. However, incomes over that amount have risen much less. For example, in the $100,000 to $300,000 class, income in 1953 was less than half what would have been expected if income had grown in proportion with personal income under $50,000. Without any allowance for changes in the value of the dollar, income in brackets over $100,000 in 1953 was less than half that in 1916, and the average income on returns over $100,000 was considerably less than at any time between the two World Wars, though the number of returns had increased. These findings are certainly consistent with the prediction that upper income groups will seek to avoid tax.

The tax rate and family incomes. The weight of a tax with progressive rates depends in part upon whether a given income must be reported by one person or may be divided among several. For example, a net income of $20,000 reported by one person paid, at 1959 rates, about $6,942; two people reporting $10,000 incomes paid about $2,436 each, a total of $4,872; four people reporting $5,000 incomes paid roughly $944 each, a total of $3,756; ten people reporting $2,000 incomes paid about $280 each, a total of $2,800. Even if the person with the $20,000 income had had nine dependents, his total tax would have been $4,260, compared with a total of $2,800 for ten $2,000 incomes. Splitting or fractioning income shifts some of the income from higher to lower tax brackets, with a net tax saving

[8] Tax Foundation, *Are High Surtax Rates Worthwhile?* (The Foundation, New York, 1957).

which can be very great. In some cases, splitting may also bring additional personal exemptions.

Personal income tax laws generally provide that income must be taxed to its legal owner but that members of a family may pool their income and deductions. Where family net income above exemptions is more than the first bracket of the income tax—$2,000 under present law—tax can be saved by splitting the income, if splitting is possible. But in most cases, the taxable income belongs legally to one member of the family, so that it cannot be split. There are major exceptions, however.

One exception arises when the family has income from property. By dividing the property among family members, the future income can be distributed, perhaps widely, so that the tax is reduced. Transfer may require payment of gift tax and may deprive the former owner of effective control. But the income tax saving, especially for the wealthy, frequently warrants such sacrifices. *Trusts* are widely used to effect splitting without complete loss of control, but the law has been tightened so that little direct control can be retained by the donor if income tax is to be saved. In some cases, a large number of trusts can be created, each of which is treated as a separate "person" for tax purposes. Family partnerships, if they seem reasonably genuine, can sometimes be used to split income.[9]

Another possibility of income splitting results from the *community property* systems of several states. In eight states with property laws stemming from Spanish or French origins, generally half of the income of the husband is legally the income of the wife and vice versa. The federal income tax has recognized this principle. Consequently, families with taxable net incomes over $2,000 in community property states long paid less income tax than families with equal incomes in other states. At wartime tax rates, the benefits, even on modest incomes, were appreciable; in the upper ranges, they were tremendous.

The Treasury made several unsuccessful attempts to get Congress to solve the tax problem of community property and some other forms of split income by requiring husbands and wives to file joint tax returns, that is, pool their income for tax purposes. There would be a substantial increase in revenue, and the accident of residence would no longer bring great differences in tax to taxpayers in essentially similar economic circumstances. Congress rejected this proposal, however, and in 1948 met the problem by allowing all married couples to split their income for tax purposes. Such modification of the federal income tax removes a tax discrimination as between residents of different states. The taxes on single persons, however,

[9] To take an extreme example, if capital is an important element in a firm's earnings, a father may give an infant child some of the capital and make him a "silent" partner. The child's share of the partnership profit is reported and taxed separately. With the income from the business thus split, some of the higher bracket rates are avoided. If the father wishes, he may regain part or sometimes all of the income by charging the costs of the child's upbringing against the latter's partnership income.

may be unfairly high relative to those on married couples, and the reductions effected at the upper income levels have been criticized as disguised reduction of the effective progression of the income tax. For married couples with large incomes the tax is now less severe than a look at the rates in the law would suggest. Conversely, bachelorhood or spinsterhood for the rich has been made costly.

World War II tax laws broadened the definition of *dependency* to give more realistic and more generous treatment. Any person related by blood, marriage, or adoption, except where the relation is remote, can be claimed as a dependent by the person who provided more than half of the support during the year.[10] However, credit is not granted if the dependent has gross income of over $600 or is not a resident of the United States, Canada, or Mexico, unless the dependent is under 19 or attends an educational institution at least 5 months in the year. Some tax escape now results from overgenerous treatment of dependents because the income of a dependent is completely excluded from the tax base if it is less than $600; yet the person providing more than half of the support is allowed the full $600 deduction.[11]

Timing of income realization. Progressive income tax schedules make the timing of income realization an important element in determining tax liability. If a person realizes a loss greater than his income in one year and is not permitted to offset it for tax purposes against income of an earlier or subsequent year, he in effect pays taxes on more than the net total of his income over the period of years. Likewise, if a low-income individual has less taxable income than his exemption in some years, he cannot apply the unused part of these exemptions to years when his taxable income exceeds the exemption; hence over a period of years he may have to pay tax on more than the excess of his *average* taxable income over exemptions. If several substantial items of irregular income are realized in one year, part of the resulting aggregate income will be taxed at a higher bracket rate than if the income items had been scattered through a series of years. If realization of an income item is postponed, as capital gains are until the year when the asset is sold, tax liability is also postponed—possibly to a year of higher or lower tax rates. A person can completely escape income tax on capital gains by holding them until his death.

Some individuals, particularly investors, businessmen, farmers, and professional men, can control somewhat the timing of income receipts or the payment of deduction items. They can thus manipulate this detail of the tax law to their advantage.

[10] Scholarships received do not count in determining whether the parent provided half or more of support.

[11] All but a few states have recently modified their property law to simplify the transfer to, and ownership of, common stock and other property by minors. Therefore, it is more convenient than it was a few years ago to give minors a source of income that will fall under the $600 figure.

The inequities resulting from income fluctuation could be eliminated through an averaging of income for tax purposes over a reasonable period of years. Some steps have been taken toward such averaging—loss carry-over provisions and the treatment of capital gains and losses are examples. The possibilities of income-averaging over a period of several years deserve legislative exploration.[12]

ADMINISTRATION

Administration is the keystone of effective income taxation. If the administration fails, the tax must fail—as state income taxes did fail until Wisconsin showed that capable administration was possible. Federal administration is far from perfect, but it is generally effective. Many states can also boast now of sound accomplishment.

"Pay-as-you-go" collection of the federal tax. Prior to 1943, taxpayers computed and paid their federal tax on each year's income in the following year. The 1943 tax law placed the federal personal income tax on a "pay-as-you-go" basis. The greater part of the federal tax on wages and salaries is now "withheld" by employers from their employees' pay and is paid monthly by the employers into the Treasury's bank account. Over a dozen states now require withholding of personal income tax on wages and salaries.

Under the federal withholding tax system, each employee (except those in domestic service, agriculture, and casual workers) files with his employer a statement of the number of his dependents. The employer, using tax tables provided by the Treasury (or, if he wishes, somewhat more refined percentage rates which allow for the "standard" deduction), then computes the tax due on the employee's compensation for each payroll period, with allowance for the employee's personal exemption, and deducts such amount from the employee's paycheck. Such deduction approximates closely the tax due on any compensation income up to about $8,000 annually. Where earnings are higher, less than the full amount of the tax is withheld, unless the employee requests that more be held back. The employer must keep a record of the amount deducted for each employee and, at the end of the year or when the employee leaves his job, must give him a receipt for the tax so withheld. A copy of the receipt is sent to the Internal Revenue Service.

By April 15 of each year, a taxpayer whose income will exceed his personal exemption and dependent deductions by $5,000 if single or $10,000

[12] With modern electronic accounting and computing equipment, the mass of the administrative work could be handled without undue difficulty and cost. A description of possible methods and a measurement of results will be found in W. A. Steger, "Averaging Income for Tax Purposes: A Statistical Study," *National Tax Journal*, June, 1956, pp. 97–114.

if married, or who will receive income other than personal compensation over $100, must file an *estimate* of the income he expects to receive during the year.[13] He must calculate the tax on such estimated income, deduct the tax his employer will withhold, and pay the balance in four quarterly installments. Should subsequent developments during the taxable year indicate that this original estimate was faulty, an amended "estimated tax" return can be filed and the remaining quarterly payments adjusted accordingly.

An employer's "withholding," or the taxpayer's estimate of his ultimate year's tax liability, will generally be only an approximation of actual ultimate tax liability. On or before each April 15, every taxpayer must file his final tax return with a definitive determination of his previous year's income and tax. This tax calculation may either exceed or be less than the tax already paid under withholding tax and estimated tax. In the former case, the balance must be paid with the return. In the latter case, the taxpayer is entitled to a refund of the excess payment or credit on the next year's tax. Collection of the federal personal income tax is overwhelmingly on a "pay-as-you-go" basis.

Over $2 billion of interest, dividends, and similar income is not reported for tax purposes each year. The Treasury has tried to get Congress to require banks, corporations, and other institutions to withhold tax on interest and dividend payments. So far, however, objections to the amount of clerical work involved have persuaded Congress to forego this method of getting several hundred million dollars a year of tax due but unpaid.

Tax return simplification. An individual who derives a substantial income from a business, or from investment operations, or from properties, and who is entitled to various deductions of costs and expenses associated with obtaining such income must be provided with an intricate report form on which to calculate his taxable income. The federal Treasury long overlooked the point that most of the complexities entering into the calculation of such incomes do not exist for taxpayers who derive most of their income from salaries and wages.

A first long step toward "tax simplification" was taken by the federal Treasury in the 1930's, when a "short" two-page tax return form was developed for taxpayers with incomes under $5,000 who derived no part of their incomes from business, rents, royalties, or capital gain. A still longer step was taken in 1943, when provision was made for using the "withholding receipt"—the report of the employee's income tax withheld by the employer which every employer must give his employees—as a tax return. This supremely simple form of tax return met the needs of millions of tax-

[13] The detailed provisions are more complex than need to be described here. In the case of a fiscal year taxpayer, such return must be made by the fifteenth day of the fourth month of his fiscal year. Persons who receive two-thirds or more of their income from farming do not have to file this "estimated tax" return until the following February 15, at which time the full estimated tax must be paid.

payers, but its use was abolished in 1948 because it led to great confusion when used by persons who worked for more than one employer during the year. It was replaced by a form almost as simple. This "short form" is adapted to punch card and other systems of mechanical handling. Beginning in 1959, most taxpayers with income up to $10,000 may use the simple punch card form.

Simplified reporting procedures have also been incorporated in the regular tax return. Instead of making a detailed report of all his personal deductions, a taxpayer may take a "standard" deduction, up to $1,000. If his income is under $5,000, he may determine his tax liability from a simple table (which allows for the "standard" deduction). The format and language of the return have been planned with a view to simplicity and clarity within the limits possible when a tax has many complexities. Moreover, for millions of persons with low incomes, the Treasury now calculates the tax and bills the taxpayer for, or refunds, any difference from what has been withheld by the employer.

With some lag, the state tax administrations have followed the federal Treasury in simplifying their personal income tax forms. "Short forms," for taxpayers whose incomes are derived mainly from wages and salaries, have become common.

Information-at-source. With, or in addition to, statements of employees' tax withheld, employers must supply the federal Treasury with information statements showing the total wage and salary payments made to each employee receiving over $600 a year. The law also requires information returns covering partnership income, professional fees paid, insurance, pensions, annuities, rents, dividends, interest, expense accounts, large gifts, purchase and sale of securities, and other payments or possible sources of payments. Some small payments need not be reported—the limit varies—but most sizable items are covered.

These information-at-source reports provide the Treasury with means of uncovering attempted tax evasion through failure to report incidental items of income. Several hundred million dollars extra tax revenue is collected yearly by following up these information reports. Although there are vastly more of these reports than the Internal Revenue staff can examine carefully, improved mechanical devices are enabling the IRS to make more thorough use of this mass of data.

State and local income tax administrators likewise require information-at-source reports. In many cases, their requirements duplicate those of the federal Treasury, so that the state information report is literally a carbon copy of the federal report.

Audit, check, and review. The federal Internal Revenue Service receives about 60,000,000 personal income tax returns a year. In a year of good business nearly 50,000,000 report taxable income. Many cover the incomes of two or more members of a family. Only a small fraction can be examined thoroughly. The problem is to concentrate personnel and effort where they will be most productive.

Prior to the 1950's, federal personal income tax returns were segregated into two groups, with $7,000 income as the dividing line. All returns for $7,000 or less were verified as to their mathematics in the collectors' offices, and some were cross-checked with information returns. Refunds or additional assessments were made when necessary upon this verification. A small random sample—about one out of 200—would be selected for examination. The taxpayer would be called to the collector's office for an interview upon a questionable listing of a dependent, or a suspicious deduction, or for possible unreported income. The interview served the moral effect of indicating that the office was alert, often yielded a little revenue, and induced the taxpayer to report more accurately in subsequent years. A somewhat larger random sample of returns on incomes between $7,000 and $25,000, and almost all for incomes over $25,000, would be examined by an office auditor, and a few hundred thousand would receive field audits. This system turned up hundreds of millions in extra tax revenue each year, but it was too sketchy and unsystematic.

Early in the 1950's, the foundation was laid for a fundamentally new approach to federal income tax auditing. A scientifically selected sample of returns—around 500,000—was subjected to thorough analysis to ascertain the answers to such questions as: What kinds of errors are commonly found in the returns of different classes of taxpayers—employees, small businessmen, farmers, and so on? What claims for dependents are most commonly unjustified? How much of the cash fees of doctors is not reported? Who fails to report interest and dividends, and by how much? Do errors vary from region to region, or by age, or by racial group, or by occupation? The study found more serious weaknesses than had been suspected. One out of four returns had errors of over $2 in tax liability; in 90 per cent of these cases tax liability was understated, on the average by one-fifth. Erroneous returns on incomes over $100,000 understated tax liability by an average $3,600. Total net understatement of the 1948 tax, on the basis of the sample study, was about $1.4 billion.

These findings showed what everyone knew—that the Internal Revenue Service was much understaffed in view of the tasks assigned it. They were also used to reorganize the auditing work of the Service on a probability basis. Relatively inexpensive clerical workers sort out the 45,000,000 returns of those classes of taxpayers shown by the study to have low probability of errors involving significant sums; these returns are for the most part "filed and forgotten." The remaining 15,000,000 are then screened by a more experienced staff. On the probability basis established by the study, about 2,500,000 of these returns are reviewed by office and field audit. Reluctantly, the Internal Revenue Service must ignore 5 out of 6 returns whose audit would yield, upon the basis of past experience, more in tax deficiencies than the audit would cost. However, it now investigates 9 out of 10 returns in certain of the more important categories. Moreover, as time passes, taxpayers "caught" in one year will be wary of misreporting in subsequent years while the Service is devoting its attention to other cases.[14]

The federal Treasury has three years from the date an income tax return is filed to start collection proceedings based on the discovery of a deficiency through audit by the Internal Revenue Service. The taxpayer is notified of the deficiency and is allowed opportunity to confer with the Service agent who handled his return. If he does not agree with the agent's findings, he may have an informal conference with a group chief, then a somewhat more formal review with a chief reviewer. Cases still unsettled then go to an appellate hearing, still fundamentally informal, but outside the auditing staff entirely. At each conference level, the Service representative has wide authority to make final settlements. Appellate rulings are not often upset by the Tax Court, but the taxpayer has the right to take his case before that body. To help insure uniform policy throughout the country, the Washington staff of the Internal Revenue Service, and the new Inspection Service, conduct a post-audit of a sample of disputed returns after their final settlement.

State and local administration. Most states have made the basis of their taxes correspond generally with that of the federal tax, and their returns are modeled on the federal returns. Of course, exact correspondence is impossible, because the states do not tax income from federal instrumentalities and the federal tax does not extend to state instrumentality income, and because most state income taxes involve the taxation of nonresidents. These differences, however, are small and do not destroy the essential correspondence between the two sets of taxes.

State personal income tax administration varies greatly in thoroughness and ability. In some instances, almost complete dependence is placed upon the federal audit, and state taxpayers are simply required to report any federal tax adjustments to the state administration so that corresponding adjustments of state tax can be made. A few states make more searching inquiries and audits than does the federal Treasury, especially on small-income returns. One development which ought to be pressed much more vigorously is cooperative joint auditing by federal and state tax administrations. State and federal agents plan their auditing procedures so as to avoid duplication while obtaining data needed for both administrations. Copies of audit reports can then be used by both administrations. Massa-

[14] If a person has failed to keep records that seem accurate, the Treasury may use the "net worth" method of estimating his income. His assets minus debts in, say, 1956 are compared with those in 1948. If his net worth grew by $100,000 and his living expenses were at least $100,000, it is assumed that he had income of at least $200,000. This total can be compared with what he reported for tax purposes. If he cannot justify any discrepancy, he can be required to pay on the basis of the presumptive income.

chusetts quickly discovered 20,000 persons owing it income tax who had filed no state returns. Most states levying personal income taxes allow inspection of each other's returns on a reciprocal basis.

One-third of the states with personal income taxes now have general withholding. This recent development has unquestionably been a success —no panacea but a convenience to taxpayers and officials, at some cost to employers. In a few cases the increase in tax collections has been substantial, with six states estimating the improvement at 12 per cent or more.[15]

Local personal income tax administration varies widely in efficiency. One difficulty is the reluctance of small employers, especially those hiring domestic servants, to withhold the tax on employees' compensation or to give information. Inherently, of course, these taxes are simpler to administer than if a more refined concept of income were used.

Penalties. Substantial penalties are necessary to induce income taxpayers to file their reports when due and to report their income fairly.[16] The federal government exacts a penalty of 5 per cent per month, up to a maximum of 25 per cent, together with 6 per cent interest, for failure to file returns by the due date. Where intent to defraud can be proved, the courts may in addition assess fines up to $10,000 and impose prison terms. State penalties, in general milder than the federal, vary widely.

Innocent understatement of income on a tax return is rarely punished, the tax laws being content with an interest payment on the deficiency. Where "negligence" is established as a cause of the understatement, the interest charge is usually higher. Fraudulent understatement may be punished even more severely. Under the federal law, the taxpayer may have to pay an additional 50 per cent penalty tax and may be sentenced to fine and imprisonment. For many years, however, few income tax evasion cases were taken to court. Tougher policies were introduced in the 1950's. Many state laws provide a 100 per cent penalty tax for fraudulent understatement, but there is little criminal prosecution.

Evasion and avoidance. A self-assessed tax like the personal income tax might appear at first glance easy to evade by willful nonstatement or understatement of income items and willful overstatement of deduction items. And so it is, if administration is casual. But where administration is effective—where a serious audit is given at least to larger returns and to a broad sample of smaller returns, and where suitable penalties are enforced without favor or prejudice against all offenders—deliberate evasion of a personal income tax is reduced to moderate proportions. It is likely to be rare among recipients of large incomes because of the more careful scrutiny devoted to their returns and the heavier penalties that they would incur.

15 See W. W. Heller and C. Penniman, "A Survey and Evaluation of State Income Tax Withholding," *National Tax Journal*, Dec., 1957, 298–309.

16 As of 1958, despite penalties, the Treasury had outstanding nearly 1.5 million delinquent accounts covering $1.6 billion overdue tax. During 1957, it wrote off as uncollectible some $180 million.

As intensive audit has shown, some taxpayers in the lowest brackets may indulge in considerable concealment of minor items of income and may exaggerate their deductible expenses, but under the present system of withholding and allowance of flat deductions, the global total of the petty deceptions constitutes but a relatively small reduction of the total revenue. With respect to income to which withholding is not applied—earnings from farming, small businesses and professional activity, payments for domestic service, dividends, capital gains, rents, interest, tips—evasion probably produces a tax loss of $1.5 to $2 billion a year.

Avoidance has been a greater difficulty than evasion. Income tax avoidance—or "tax minimization" as it is more politely called—during the past quarter-century has assumed a multitude of ingenious forms. Purchase of tax-exempt securities still affords well-to-do individuals an opportunity for avoidance. Most other methods of income tax avoidance employed can be reduced to three basic types: (1) short-circuiting the flow of income, defined in broadest terms, into expenditure or investment so that it does not appear as realized income of the taxpayer or so that it can receive the favorable treatment accorded capital gains; (2) establishing fictitious deductions; and (3) fractioning a large income among a number of recipients so that high-bracket rates are avoided.

The most common types of *short-circuiting* income—conversion of other forms of income into capital gains and the use of expense accounts and payment in kind—were discussed in Chapter 12. Short-circuiting income used to be accomplished by inserting corporations and trusts between the taxpayer and some element of his income. One method was to incorporate an expensive hobby—an estate, a yacht, a "gentleman's farm," a racing stable.[17] A second method was to incorporate a "personal holding company" to which the taxpayer transferred his investments.[18] Some taxpayers formed corporations to receive salaries and other earnings. After World War II some taxpayers formed corporations to carry on specific ventures—making a movie or building an apartment house; the corporation would re-

[17] The taxpayer would transfer to such a corporation investment securities to provide it with a gross income sufficient to cover the expenses of the hobby. Thus he freed himself of an item of income that would otherwise have been taxable to him under the personal income tax. Since the expenses of the corporation–maintenance of the estate, or yacht, or racing stable–ate up all the return from its invested capital and since the owner paid the corporation only a dollar a year or so for services given him, there was no net income to be subjected to corporation income taxation. And, of course, such corporations could declare no dividends to add to the taxpayer's taxable income.

[18] Such part of the income of these corporations as consisted of dividends on the stock of other corporations was formerly nontaxable under the corporation income tax; interest on bonds was taxable as corporation income at a much lower rate than the higher bracket rates that would have applied to the taxpayer's personal income. The taxpayer could then borrow his living expenses from the personal holding company without incurring any personal income tax liability whatsoever, while the company reinvested all the excess over such borrowings as the taxpayer personally would have done. If the corporation was subsequently liquidated, any increase in value would be taxed at the favored rates given capital gains.

tain the income for a time and then be "collapsed"; its assets would be distributed to the stockholders who could then treat the enhancement of value as a capital gain subject to special low rates.

These "short-circuit" loopholes have been closed reasonably well. For example, the federal courts and the statute now look behind the fiction of the "expenditure" corporations and tax the income of these corporations directly to the taxpayers for whose benefit they operate. The "personal holding company" loophole has been plugged somewhat by a special penalty surtax on such corporations—75 per cent on the first $2,000 of a personal holding company's undistributed net income, and 85 per cent on the excess over $2,000.

Yet the personal holding company penalties do not generally apply if more than five families share ownership of a corporation or if its ownership income includes large fractions from rents, oil or mineral royalties, or business operations. A group of wealthy men who control a regular business corporation can utilize their control to restrict its dividends. Thus their taxable dividend income is reduced, and the corporation employs its undistributed income for further investment.[19]

Short-circuiting of income is also still possible by the use of trusts to accumulate income from investments, pension trusts to delay for long periods the receipt of salary and investment income, and annuities and life insurance with large savings elements that accumulate interest.

Establishing economically *fictitious deductions* once offered many tax avoidance possibilities.[20] For example, investments which had declined in value, but which the taxpayer still wished to retain, were extensively used to establish "capital losses," which could be deducted from other income or from realized capital gains. A "wash sale" would be effected—the securities would be simultaneously bought and sold at the current market price. Thus a loss was established for tax purposes, while the taxpayer retained the corporate interest involved. Statute amendments and court decisions have closed most of these "fictitious deductions" loopholes. Taxpayers, of course, still have control over the *time* when they realize capital losses; this power can often be utilized to advantage. A vacation may possibly be charged as medical expense, and every year sees more professional conventions in Europe. Enough can often be deducted as maintenance expense of buildings and equipment to pay for net improvement above the value remaining after deduction of depreciation. Finally, *fractioning* of a large income can be accomplished by splitting among the various members of a family the capital which produces the income, as discussed earlier.

There will never be an end to attempts at income tax avoidance, particu-

[19] The undistributed profits tax of 1936 was directed in part against this element of avoidance. With the abolition of that tax the only present check on the practice is a 27.5 to 38.5 per cent surtax on corporations "improperly accumulating surplus"; this penalty surtax is, however, difficult to apply.

[20] Depletion deductions in excess of cost are discussed in Chapter 14.

larly with the high rates of the federal tax now in effect. But these attempts can be exposed by an administration which makes the effort to go behind the face of tax returns and discover any such legal dodges. They can sometimes be frustrated by courts that construe the tax law according to its intent and by modifications of the statute to close loopholes that judicial construction cannot plug. Legislatures, however, sometimes tolerate loopholes year after year; much too often, instead of closing a loophole to remove the favoritism granted one group of taxpayers, they enlarge it to add more beneficiaries.

Persons who take advantage of these opportunities are free from the requirement to report some, or much, of what would be their income. Yet the income that *is* reported brings less tax in the upper ranges than one might suppose. If we look at *all* taxpayers reporting adjusted gross incomes over $100,000 in 1954, we find the tax was 48 per cent of the income.[21] But if we add the one-half of long-term capital gain not taxed and make a rough allowance for tax-exempt interest, the average tax falls to 38 per cent of the more complete income figure. Yet the effective rate on such an income is nominally 67 per cent, and 78 per cent at $200,000 (or 52 per cent and 67 per cent with income splitting). The taxes actually paid are decidedly less than a look at the rates would lead one to expect.

ECONOMIC AND DISTRIBUTIONAL CONSIDERATIONS

A general personal income tax cannot be shifted.[22] The argument behind this conclusion was given in Chapter 8.

Some nineteenth-century fiscal writers defended or advocated personal income taxes on "benefit" doctrines, arguing that individual benefit from government activities is in proportion to the income enjoyed under government protection. In modern times, the "benefit" doctrine is rarely mentioned in connection with income taxation, since "ability" theories give stronger justification. If, it is argued, "taxpaying ability" is best measured by the net income of each individual, what tax could be better than a personal income tax? Another defense stems from the principle that the nation's taxes must be paid out of its income and by persons, not things. It is better, the argument runs, to apportion the total tax according to the income of each person than according to other criteria. Any other bases must inevitably be distributed among individuals and families in ways quite dif-

[21] These figures are those of S. S. Surrey, in *Tax Policy,* Jan.–Feb., 1958, p. 9.

[22] Nor can a special income tax, such as those found in New Hampshire and Tennessee, be easily shifted. But a special income tax can be capitalized, since subsequent purchasers of investments whose yield is taxed can turn to untaxed investments, if the prices of the taxed items are not reduced to allow for the tax. To the extent that high-bracket rates may affect the work incentives of executives and professional men, a personal income tax may have economic repercussions (see Chapter 27), but not such as to produce "shifting" of the tax in the normal meaning of the term.

ferent from income. If these other bases—for example, real estate ownership or consumption buying—are used, the total tax load cannot, in general, be allocated among persons with the intelligent refinement that seems desirable in drawing on the total stream of income.

The federal personal income tax has become a "mass" tax rather than a markedly "class" tax. Progressive rate schedules, however, still give strong "class" characteristics to both federal and state income taxes. Since so many other American taxes, particularly state and local levies, impose proportional or even regressive burdens, the progressive personal income tax is frequently defended or advocated as a valuable fiscal counterweight. In any case, it would be difficult—most fiscal economists would say impossible—to find a major-yield tax better than the progressive personal income tax from an over-all point of view.

This general consensus has been strengthened by the placing of personal income tax payment on a "pay-as-you-go" basis; the tax has thereby been made to fit well into a fiscal structure designed to help reduce fluctuations in national income.

Yet there is considerable basis for serious misgiving. The present federal and state personal income taxes have many imperfections. There are many elements of inequitable treatment of taxpayers in special circumstances. When rate schedules were relatively low, these inequities were more irritating than serious. With the present high rates, these inequities may often be highly oppressive to the individuals caught by them. The structure of the tax should long since have been improved to eliminate or reduce these inequities.

The dominant pressures, however, are for further erosion of the tax base, to create and enlarge rather than to restrict and remove avenues for avoidance. As the base erodes, the rates needed to raise any given revenue must be higher.[23] We are in a vicious circle. Thorough reform is impossible while rates are at levels above 50 per cent, or some such figure. Congress just does not want to make these rates effective. (The situation in Britain in this respect is even worse.) The logical approach would be to broaden the base and lower rates. But no "bargain" between opposing interests is possible. Consequently, those who benefit from the loopholes will not support loophole-closing in return for lower rates. Who knows, rates might then go up again! Yet large, though perhaps gradual, reduction of high rates ought to relieve pressure for further emasculation of the tax base. Such a program could be a good bargain for the public as a whole.

Increases in the personal income tax since 1940 will profoundly affect the nation's social, economic, and political life. Accumulation of large fortunes has certainly been made more difficult. Unbiased minds and intensive

[23] For a masterly study of why the 1956 Personal Income of $325 billion produced a total taxable income of only $136 billion, see J. A. Pechman, "Erosion of the Individual Income Tax," *National Tax Journal,* March, 1957, pp. 1–25.

study will be necessary to determine what the true results are before they can be labeled good or bad. Are tax-motivated business and personal decisions significantly less beneficial to the economy than those that would be made if taxes were neutral? Have incentives to work been dulled, and if so, what are the consequences? Has saving, in the aggregate or of particular types, been reduced, and if so is this desirable (to establish a proper balance with investment) or undesirable (because capital formation and therefore national productivity will rise too slowly)? Has willingness and capacity for "venture" investment been reduced? Do the masses of voters, feeling that the costs of government can be imposed on others, support expenditure policies that are socially wasteful? Or do the masses, fearful of higher low-bracket income tax rates, force the government to forego expenditures of great social utility? What are the alternative methods of obtaining revenue?

POLL TAXES

Poll taxes are studied here because, as taxes on the person, they are related more closely to the personal income tax than to any other.

The poll, or head, tax is a fixed sum levied on persons as persons. No longer is it necessarily related to voting or the polls. In the United States, it dates back to colonial times. Large landowners particularly, who saw in the poll tax an opportunity to shift part of the tax burden to the small landowners and the landless, considered it especially just and appropriate. But as variations in wealth and income increased, the poll tax was held to involve serious discrimination, to be badly regressive, and to lack justification under both benefit and ability doctrines. Although criticism of the poll tax has never been hushed, the moderation of the levy has spared it serious legislative attack.

Nine states, mostly in New England and the South, still impose poll taxes for state purposes. Local poll taxes are found in most states. Sometimes the tax is exclusively a county levy, sometimes it is imposed by villages and towns. In some Pennsylvania localities—including the Pittsburgh School District—the yield is about 10 per cent of total tax revenue.[24]

The poll tax is everywhere limited to adults. To prevent the application of the tax to persons who may have no earning capacity, a maximum age limit is commonly set. Women are often exempt. So are soldiers and sailors, disabled individuals, paupers, the deaf, the blind, and the insane.

Poll taxes are flat charges, without graduation, and usually between two and five dollars. Some governments permit a man to commute his tax by

[24] For a revealing discussion, see G. H. Sause, Jr., "Municipal Poll Taxes in Pennsylvania," *National Tax Journal,* Dec., 1955, pp. 400–407. A married couple may be subject to more than one such tax and pay as much as $50 a year. Some communities hire outside collectors who are paid on a commission basis. Tax payment is not a requisite for voting.

working on the local roads. A few Southern states still make payment of the poll tax a prerequisite for voting. No attempt is made to collect the tax from Negroes, and their failure to pay is then utilized to bar them from the suffrage. The Southern poll tax has lost most of its fiscal significance and has become an instrument of politico-racial regulation. Condemnation of this use of the poll tax has aroused controversy in which the revenue issue has played no part.

The federal government cannot constitutionally levy a poll tax unless apportioned among the states according to population. Poll tax levies are made mandatory by a few state constitutions and are flatly forbidden by several.

Since the poll tax is levied on each individual as an individual, it relates to no class of business transactions which would permit its direct shifting. If a local poll tax were heavy, the floating population of the locality might conceivably move to other, lower-taxing districts and, by leaving a labor shortage in the taxing locality, cause a wage increase there sufficient to cover the amount of the tax. But with poll taxes rarely half a day's earnings, the probability of shifting is very slight.

The poll, or head, tax finds slight justification under the common doctrines of tax distribution except that it forces those who may pay little tax (directly) to the locality to share the expense of local government. It may also spur tax consciousness. A more sophisticated line of reasoning also lends support for a substantial flat-rate tax on adult males, with suitable exemptions for hardship cases. The government services we all receive are possible only because the public pays heavy fixed costs. Our existence depends upon the provision of these services. Then, one may argue, a fixed charge to help cover some of the basic cost is appropriate, one of the first claims on income. If government gets revenue in this way, it will have less need to use other taxes. It can avoid some of the high rates that would otherwise apply. Consequently, the adverse effects of consumption and property taxes on the pattern of consumption and investment—any deterrent effect of the income tax on incentives—would be reduced. Under some circumstances, the basic economic merit of this line of argument would be unquestioned, but today anything of the sort is likely to get no serious consideration.

The administration of the poll tax may seem simple, since only a list of names is necessary. Nevertheless, evasion is extensive, especially in nonrural areas with shifting population. In the South where poll tax payment is a prerequisite for voting, the fiscal element is subordinate to the political. Tax collection is pressed only where the dominant political party wants an individual to be registered as a voter. Even in other states, poll tax administration is very imperfect. Individuals who own no property escape the assessor's eye, and the poll tax has tended merely to supplement the general property tax. Wyoming makes employers liable for the tax.

PROBLEMS

1. What are the reasons for allowing personal exemptions?

2. Explain the significance of income splitting.

3. "The true limits to income tax progression are set by the willingness of government to close loopholes." Discuss.

4. Describe three methods of income tax avoidance.

5. What accounts for the conversion of the personal income tax into a mass levy?

6. Study the different federal income tax returns.

7. What are the major problems of administering an income tax?

8. What are the advantages and disadvantages of state withholding of personal income tax?

9. What scale of personal income tax rates would you consider fair? Why? How does your schedule compare with those shown in Chart 13–1?

10. To what extent is the personal income tax self-assessed?

11. State the economic arguments for and against flat-rate per capita taxes (not tied to voting) to yield revenue for local governments.

12. What would be the effects if income and price levels were to rise by, say, one third without any change in personal income tax rates?

CHAPTER 14

Taxes on Business

THE term "business taxes" is used here in a broad sense. It covers all levies, whatever their legal names, imposed on forms or classes of profit-seeking enterprise because of their existence in such forms. A gross income tax on railroads, a premiums tax on insurance companies, a severance tax on petroleum companies, as well as a general corporation tax are all "business taxes." Excluded from the "business tax" concept are commodity, property, and transaction taxes incidentally paid by business enterprises. Federal and state personal income taxes applying to the net profit of unincorporated businesses have already been considered.

Particular kinds of business activity and particular forms of business organization are favorite bases of taxation. Business taxes are generally impersonal, indirect, and largely shifted to consumers. Legislatures as a rule like such taxes because of their administrative simplicity, because some, at least, bring a relatively constant inflow of tax revenue, and because the masses of voters express little opposition.[1] Even when they cannot be shifted to the consumer, business taxes are sometimes defended on the ground that business enterprise as such benefits specially from government activities and its owners may properly be called upon to pay for such benefits. Justification is also found in the argument that some business taxes have been so capitalized as to impose no current burdens. State business taxes are frequently championed on the ground that out-of-state consumers and owners bear part of the burden.

Much criticism has been directed, however, at making business a special object of taxation. Since taxes must eventually be paid by persons, not things, is it not better to levy taxes on persons directly rather than indirectly and obscurely through businesses? May not business taxes depress economic activity and retard progress, thereby lowering living standards

[1] Legislatures have adopted a few special taxes on business to serve *in lieu* of property taxes.

and the growth of national income? Perhaps, by finding an alternative source of revenue, governments could free business of throttling burdens, with resulting social benefit. Perhaps the basis of some business taxes could be revised to give businesses greater incentives.

The pattern of business taxes is confused. Neither the federal government nor any of the states has found it practicable to develop a single all-embracing business tax—a tax applying to incorporated and unincorporated enterprises and covering all forms of gainful business activity. A universal business tax based upon gross income or net income might conceivably be levied, but to date, none such has developed. Instead, the American governments levy special taxes on particular classes of business enterprise—on incorporated concerns, on public service corporations, on banks and other financial enterprises, on mining and drilling companies, on specific occupations and professions.

HISTORY OF FEDERAL BUSINESS TAXES

Prior to 1909, the federal government had levied business taxes only during the Civil War. Business taxation as a source of federal peacetime revenue was inaugurated with the levy of a one per cent federal corporation income tax in 1909. It represented in part an outcropping of general distrust of incorporated "big business." To avoid possible constitutional complications, the tax was called a "corporation excise," but it was nonetheless a net income tax of the purest sort. In 1913, to form a general system of federal income taxation, the "corporation excise" was merged with the new personal income tax. Rate trends since are shown in Chart 14–1.

During World War I, the federal government relied heavily on business taxation. The corporation income tax rate was increased to 6 per cent and then to 12 per cent. A supplementary "excess profits tax" with rates from 20 to 60 per cent was levied in 1917 on the excess of a corporation's profits over a peacetime normal. In the following year, the rates of this tax were increased, and an additional "war profits tax" established for one year an 80 per cent minimum tax on corporation income designated as "war profits." Concurrent with the levy of the excess profits tax in 1917 was the enactment of a one-twentieth per cent tax on the capital stock of all corporations; the rate doubled in 1918.

From 1918 to 1932, the federal system of corporation taxation was steadily pared down. The excess profits and capital stock tax were abolished. In 1932, the corporation income tax rate was increased to 13.75 per cent, and then made progressive in 1935—from 12.5 per cent on the first $2,000 of a corporation's income to 15 per cent on the excess over $40,000. A year later, in connection with the levy of the undistributed profits tax, the rates on small corporate incomes were reduced somewhat. At the same time that these rate changes were being made, the character of the tax was stiffened by structural change which tended to increase burdens. A combined "excess profits" and "capital stock" tax was imposed in 1933, a payroll tax to finance the Social Security program was levied in 1935, and a provocative undistributed profits tax was added in 1936 but abolished in 1939. The corporation income tax rate crept upward.

World War II revenue acts involved additional heavy corporation taxation. Corporation income tax rates were increased to a peak ranging from 23 per cent on the first $5,000 of a corporation's income to 40 per cent on the entire income of corporations earning over $50,000. In 1940, a new excess profits tax was imposed.

The first tax results of the end of World War II were repeal of the excess profits tax, effective in 1946, repeal of the declared-value excess profits and capital stock taxes, and a small reduction of the corporation income tax rate. The Korean crisis, however, led to the rate of the corporation income tax being increased to 45 per cent in 1950 and to 52 per cent in 1952. In addition, a tax on excess profits was reimposed and lasted until 1954.

THE FEDERAL CORPORATION INCOME TAX[2]

The corporation income tax ranks next to the personal income tax as a major source of federal revenue. The average annual yield from 1954 to 1959 was $20 billion, roughly 30 per cent of total federal tax revenue. Table 14–1 shows highlights of receipt and deduction items for all corporations for 1955–56.

Taxable income. The *income concept* is much the same for the federal corporation income tax as for the personal income tax, as described in Chapter 12, due allowance being made for the fact that corporations do not receive certain elements of income received by persons.

Calculations of gross operating income and of business cost deductions for the two income taxes is almost identical. Capital gains and losses are treated in about the same way; the deduction for capital losses is somewhat restricted, however, while treatment of profits or losses from sale of business property tends to favor corporations. Four problems common to the definition of income for both incorporated and unincorporated businesses have been left for discussion here, for their chief significance is with corporations—treatment of depreciation, depletion, inventory valuation, and operating losses.

Allowances for *depreciation* of buildings and equipment—but not land—are treated as deductible costs in determining net business income. Although the principle of this deduction is uniformly recognized, its practical

[2] See R. E. Goode, *The Corporation Income Tax* (John Wiley & Sons, Inc., New York, 1951); J. K. Butters and J. Lintner, *Effects of Federal Taxes on Growing Enterprises* (Harvard University, Boston, 1945); D. T. Smith, *Effects of Taxation, Corporate Financial Policy* (Harvard University, Boston, 1952).

TABLE 14–1

Receipts and Deductions of Corporations Filing Federal Income Tax Returns for Period July, 1955–June, 1956[1]

(*Amounts in Millions*)

Receipts:		*Deductions:*	
Gross sales	$514,864	Cost of goods sold	$390,323
Gross receipts from operations	97,819	Cost of operations	58,242
Interest on Government obligations (less amortizable bond premium):		Compensation of officers	10,481
Wholly taxable	2,287	Rent paid on business property	5,682
Subject to surtax only	79	Repairs	5,624
Wholly tax-exempt	471	Bad debts	1,653
Other interest	10,370	Interest paid	7,058
Rents	5,176	Taxes paid	14,203
Royalties	698	Contributions or gifts	415
Net short-term capital gain reduced by net long-term capital loss	46	Amortization	2,590
Net long-term capital gain reduced by net short-term capital loss	2,205	Depreciation	13,419
Net gain, sales other than capital assets	1,017	Depletion	2,805
Dividends, domestic corporations	2,572	Advertising	6,602
Dividends, foreign corporations	772	Amounts contributed under pension plans	3,296
Other receipts	3,872	Amounts contributed under other employee benefit plans	1,147
		Net loss, sales other than capital assets	571
		Other deductions	70,187
Total compiled receipts	$642,248	Total compiled deductions	$594,299

Compiled net profit	47,949
Income tax	21,741
Compiled net profit less income tax	26,208
Dividends paid:	
Cash and assets other than own stock	13,592
Corporation's own stock	1,996

[1] Number of returns filed: 807,303

SOURCE: *Statistics of Income . . . 1955.*

application is subject to much dispute. What initial value should be allowed for the depreciating property? What records must be kept? What shall be the rate of depreciation allowed on each particular asset? It is inherently impossible to measure the useful life of an asset accurately until the end of that life. Any earlier estimate may turn out to be seriously in error. Obsolescence is even more difficult to forecast, but in the modern world of rapid technical change it can be very high. Inflation has created another serious problem. Replacement costs of equipment are sometimes very different from the original cost. Under such conditions, the use of original cost in computing depreciation means that the expense being charged and deducted is less than is needed to replace the productive capacity.[3] An element of fictitious profit is made the basis of a very real, and heavy, tax.

Congress has given the Treasury a wide area of independence in determining allowable depreciation deductions. In the 1920's, the federal tax administration was liberal in its concession of depreciation allowances; total depreciation of any asset was, of course, limited to 100 per cent of its cost, but such depreciation might be taken over a period much shorter than the actual operating life of the asset. During the 1930's, to increase the immediate yield of the tax, the Treasury stiffened its policy by insisting that depreciation allowances must be spread over a longer term of years; thus each year's deduction was decreased. Much injustice was done because firms suffering losses in some years were unable to get full tax deduction of depreciation of their capital. The deductions of loss years which brought no tax benefit could not be carried to profit years. The provision of loss carryovers in the 1940's, described below, met only part of the problem. Businesses claimed that the amounts they could charge as costs during the early life of equipment understated the loss of value.

The Treasury's rigid practices were condemned so strongly that in 1954 Congress specifically authorized use of new methods for new depreciable property.[4] The traditional straight-line method divides the cost of the item by the estimated years of useful life and allows the same fraction each year. A machine costing $50,000 and having a life of 5 years would be depreciated $10,000 each year. The two new methods allow much larger deductions in the early years, and less later. The double declining-balance applies double the straight-line rate but to the balance that has not yet been deducted, that is, one which gets constantly smaller. The sum-of-the-digits method applies a changing fraction to the cost of the property. The denominator is the sum of the years of useful life computed from the beginning of each year, that is, for a 5-year life, $5 + 4 + 3 + 2 + 1 = 15$. The numerator the first year is 5, the next year 4, the last year 1. The business can choose its method. The double declining-balance permits deduction of two-thirds of the cost in the first half of the useful life, whereas the sum-

[3] Prof. J. Backman of New York University estimates that for U. S. Steel the replacement cost of productive capacity used up during the period 1940–56 was $904 million more than the depreciation allowed for tax purposes, including special amortization and accelerated depreciation allowed on plant and equipment for military production. U. S. Steel, *Steel and Inflation: Fact vs. Fiction* (The Corporation, New York, 1957).

[4] The 1958 law grants limited deduction of 20 per cent in the first year on $10,000 of either new or used machinery. This provision is intended to help small business, including farmers, and to stimulate purchase of equipment—a doctor's X-ray machine, a retailer's truck or cash register, a manufacturer's lathe.

of-the-digits method permits deduction of almost three-fourths.[5] The following example illustrates the three methods as applied to a $50,000 machine with a 5-year life.

Year	*Straight-Line*		*Double Declining-Balance*		*Sum-of-the-Digits*	
	Annual Deduction	*Cumulative Cost Recovered*	*Annual Deduction*	*Cumulative Cost Recovered*	*Annual Deduction*	*Cumulative Cost Recovered*
1	$10,000	$10,000	$20,000	$20,000	$16,667[b]	$16,667
2	10,000	20,000	12,000[a]	32,000	13,333[c]	30,000
3	10,000	30,000	7,200	39,200	10,000	40,000
4	10,000	40,000	4,320	43,520	6,667	46,667
5	10,000	50,000	2,592	46,112	3,333	50,000

[a] This is double one-fifth of the $30,000 not yet recovered at the beginning of the second year.

[b] This is 5/15 of the cost.

[c] This is 4/15 of the cost.

Assuming that tax rates do not change and that other things remain the same, the business pays the same total tax over the years under all three methods of depreciation. The advantage of the new methods is that the business owes less tax in the early years and thus for a time has the use of more cash.

The new provisions have not satisfied business, however. The estimates of useful life are longer than critics believe accurate. Moreover, the use of original cost in computing depreciation fails to take account of the fact that current replacement cost would be higher. No satisfactory solution of this very real problem has been devised for this country.[6] If tax rates remain at present levels and if the prices of capital goods continue to rise, business can be hurt. It must treat as income—and pay tax accordingly—what, in terms of replacement, is not income.

Extraordinary *obsolescence*—amounts not covered in annual depreciation—can be deducted when their existence is clear. For example, a machine costing $5,000 was originally assumed to have a useful life of 10 years. However, at the end of 5 years, when $2,500 has been deducted in depreciation, the development of a new process had clearly reduced the machine's remaining economic life to 2 years. The remaining $2,500 undepreciated

[5] Under declining-balance depreciation, not all the cost is written off during the useful life of the property; if the property continues in use, the depreciation deductions will continue, or the unrecovered cost will be recouped when the property is sold or abandoned. However, this "defect" of the declining-balance method may be avoided by switching to straight-line depreciation, which the law normally permits the taxpayer to do at any time.

[6] In some countries where inflation has been much more serious, businesses have been permitted to compute depreciation on "written up" asset values. Special index numbers are provided for the purpose.

balance would be deductible in 2 years. It is generally difficult to prove extraordinary obsolescence.

Allowances for *depletion* of natural resources are also deductible in determining net business income, whether the business is a giant coal or oil company, a doctor or movie star taking a flyer in oil, an individual wildcatter, or the owner of the local gravel pit. Such allowances distinguish the *recovery of capital value* from *income*. Generous depletion deductions also stimulate exploration for new oil and mineral properties though most costs of exploration can be deducted as current expense when they are made, rather than being capitalized. There is no question of the general equity of the principle of allowing owners to deduct all costs at one time or another. However, under the federal tax the proportion of gross income from oil wells and many types of mining properties allowed as a "percentage depletion" deduction (27.5 per cent for oil and gas wells, but not to exceed 50 per cent of net income) has constituted special favoritism.[7] The deduction goes on even after the *entire* investment has been recovered taxfree.

The oil industry is a vigorous defender of the system. Industry leaders emphasize the great risks of exploration and hence the need for extraordinarily high profit prospects.[8] But is there national interest in allowing deduction of *more* than the costs expended? Most economists would probably answer in the negative. Such favoritism will attract investment from uses in which, without the tax inducement, their yield would be higher.

Yet assuming that we *do* decide to subsidize exploration, is this the most efficient way of doing so? One piece of evidence will suggest that from the public point of view this is an inefficient method: The Treasury has estimated that, by about 1946, owners of gas wells had on the average deducted in depletion allowances six times their total investments. The economy sacrifices alternatives worth nearly $2 for each $1 of benefit.[9] Depletion helps only the successful. The big companies which can spread their risks over many drillings somewhat as an insurance company spreads its risks can count on benefiting from high depletion deduction. The wildcatter who can try only a few holes may get nothing.

Is national defense aided? Well, the owner can benefit from the depletion allowance only if the oil or other mineral is *taken out* of the ground. While exploration is encouraged, so is exhaustion.

[7] Sulfur, uranium, bauxite, and lead are a few receiving a 23 per cent rate. Various metals get 15 per cent, whereas coal, brucite, and salt, among others, get 10 per cent; gravel, sand, and oyster shells are a few for which the rate is 5 per cent.

[8] The argument resting on risks of exploration has no validity in many cases—gravel or coal discovered long ago, for example.

[9] For an excellent economic analysis, see A. C. Harberger, "Taxation of Mineral Industries," *Federal Tax Policy for Economic Growth and Stability* (Washington, 1955), pp. 439–449. W. F. Hellmuth, Jr., "Erosion of the Federal Corporation Income Tax Base," *ibid.*, p. 898, estimates oil corporation depletion deductions at from 10 to 20 times the amount justified by cost.

Changing price levels give rise to a problem in valuing the raw material and other *inventory* that is to be deducted as a cost in any one period. One method is to value on a first-in-first-out ("fifo") basis. The items sold in any period are assumed to be made out of the earliest of the materials on hand or purchased in the period. Another method is last-in-first-out ("lifo"). The items sold are assumed to be made out of the most recently purchased materials. If the prices of materials are stable, the two methods give the same result. But if prices are rising, earlier purchased material will have cost less than its replacement. The amount allowed as a deduction in computing the cost of goods sold will be less than enough to replace the item. If the business must use "fifo"—and this was the rule before World War II—it will include the rise in price in its taxable income. It pays tax on what, in terms of replacement, is a "phantom profit." If prices fall, the opposite result will appear.

This kind of problem was not serious enough to warrant much concern when tax rates were low. But when they rose during a period of inflation which created great inventory profits, business pressed for recognition in the tax law. Congress gradually permitted the use of "lifo," subject to various restrictions.

Both federal and state laws allow *business losses* as a deduction against other income. With today's high tax rates, this problem is tremendously important. For long, there has been debate about whether the loss deductions should be limited to the current year or, other offsetting income being insufficient, should be allowed against income earned in earlier or later years. Agreement is now general that limiting the deduction of losses to income of the current year is both inequitable and dangerous for the economy. Without some provision for offsetting losses of one year and profits of another, the tax system would weigh with intolerable severity on businesses with high degrees of risk and wide swings in earnings. From 1921 until 1932, federal law permitted losses to be carried forward for 3 years; in 1932, the "prior year loss" period was reduced to 2 years and, in 1933, the carrying forward of losses was ended. In 1942, however, a loss carry-forward and a loss carry-back of 2 years each were provided. Losses may now be carried back 3 years and forward 5. Although there is criticism of details, the general principles seem satisfactory. If a business that has had net operating losses is acquired by a profitable firm under certain conditions, the losses of the first can be used to reduce the taxable income of the second.[10] One feature of the loss carry-back should be noted; it enables businesses suffering losses, because of general depression or other reason, to offset those losses against earlier profits and obtain tax

[10] Although this provision is desirable as a device for reducing the net risks of business, it has one feature that runs against national policy: It encourages mergers and the loss of independence of business organizations.

refunds when they are likely to be most needed for maintaining current operations.

Until 1935, dividends were completely exempt under the corporation tax because they had been fully taxed as income of the paying corporation; now, however, 15 per cent of the dividends received are taxable to the receiving corporation. Charitable contributions by corporations are limited to 5 per cent of net income.

One important deduction is available to corporations but not to unincorporated enterprises. *Salaries of officer-owners are a deductible expense for corporations;* the compensation paid to partners, or to a sole proprietor, is treated under the personal income tax as a nondeductible "withdrawal." The great majority of corporations are of modest size, each controlled by a few persons who are often officer-executives. In computing its taxable income, a corporation can deduct as an expense the compensation paid its employees, including those who are stockholders. By adjusting the salaries paid to owners who are employees, such corporations often endeavor to reduce taxable income and hence corporation tax to a nominal amount, or eliminate it entirely. If the salary payment can be defended as reasonable —and the range for honest doubt is obviously wide—the Treasury must allow the deduction. On the other hand, if the owners want to reinvest in the business, they can leave the profits in, pay only the corporation tax, and avoid personal income tax. Large corporations, whose ownership is generally separated from their management, cannot take advantage of these opportunities to adjust salaries to save tax.

Businesses—but not individuals in private professional practice[11]—may deduct payments into funds to provide pensions for employees if the plan has met the requirements of law, as discussed later. Business life insurance premiums on officers and employees are deductible if the business is not a beneficiary and if the cost is an ordinary and necessary business expense.

Research and experimental expenditures can generally be deducted as a current expense. However, the firm may elect to set up the outlay as a capital item and deduct it over the useful life of the property if that can be determined, otherwise over not less than five years.

Since 1942, affiliated companies have been allowed to file consolidated returns, offsetting the losses of some units against the profits of others, at the expense of an additional tax rate of 2 per cent. This penalty tax has induced some companies to simplify their corporate structures, eliminating separate corporate subsidiaries.

Special favoring treatment is accorded several important classes of corporations. Religious, educational, social, labor, and a number of other types of "nonprofit" corporations are entirely exempt. Businesses run by

[11] Lawyers, doctors, and others who cannot now get the substantial tax benefits of pension plans are pressing Congress for special legislation.

governments—federal, state, and local—are exempt. Regulated investment companies (investment trusts) are exempted from tax on income paid out in dividends if the latter equal 90 per cent of the total net income. Special provisions affect the determination of taxable income of cooperatives, insurance companies, mutual savings banks, savings and loan associations, companies operating outside the United States in the Western Hemisphere, and certain other classes of corporations. Public utilities may within limits deduct dividends paid on preferred stock. Some of these cases of special treatment are warranted under accepted interpretations of tax equity; the case for others is more questionable. Many special and highly technical provisions apply to limited extent. Those dealing with corporate reorganizations, for example, spell out in intricate detail six kinds of reorganization—merger, exchange of stock for property, acquisition of assets of a controlled corporation, etc.—which can be accomplished without being considered realization for tax purposes.

Rates. Corporations are taxed 30 per cent on their net profit under $25,000 and 52 per cent on the balance. The reason for this one-step pro-

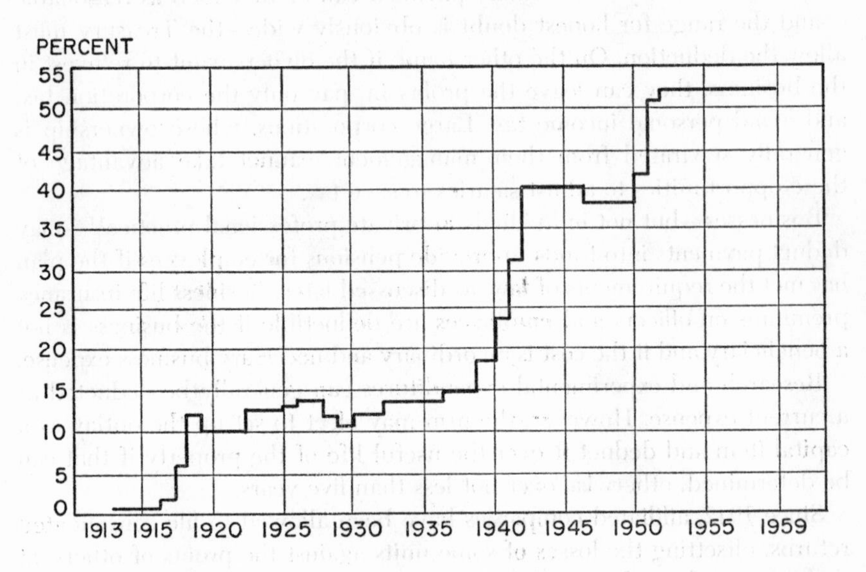

CHART 14–1. Federal Corporation Income Tax Rates, 1913 to 1959. (General rate of normal tax plus surtax. Excludes excess profits taxes and minor factors affecting corporations in certain special circumstances.)

gression is not any of the equity principles considered in Chapter 9, but a proclaimed intent to help small business. Unfortunately, it affords a tax avoidance loophole by enabling some corporations to split their business among a group of affiliates or subsidiaries, a number of which have net profits around $25,000, and so pay at the lower rate. Although the progressive rate element of the corporation income tax has elements of unwise fiscal demagoguery, there is some defense. Present corporation tax rates, without question, do impede the building up of equity capital by new and growing firms. Serious studies leave no doubt that many—but not all—businesses of modest size have difficulty getting equity capital. Taxes on income at the 52 per cent rate, by reducing the ability to reinvest earnings, would aggravate a problem for which the economy has yet found no satisfactory solution. Yet most small businesses are not incorporated and are therefore not affected by any favors in the corporation tax.

Supplementary rates on undistributed corporate profits. If a corporation fails to distribute any substantial part of current earnings as dividends, rich shareholders avoid personal income tax on the nondistributed earnings, although the value of their shares is enhanced through ploughback of profits. Here is an avoidance loophole which Congress has tried to plug in various ways.

Early laws provided that withholding "unreasonable" amounts of corporate profits would make corporations liable for a tax on the undistributed earnings in the same manner as if they had been distributed as dividends. This provision was eventually held to be arbitrary and unconstitutional. A different approach was tried in 1917—a special 10 per cent surtax on undistributed profits not reinvested in the business. Subsequent acts set various standards of "unreasonable" withholding of profits, and imposed varying penalty rates. The current rates, set by the 1942 law, are 27.5 per cent on "improperly" retained income (accumulation of surplus) under $100,000, and 38.5 per cent on the excess over $100,000. A workable definition of "unreasonable" withholding has been very difficult to frame. Every corporation is now permitted by law to accumulate $100,000, and the burden of proving improper retention above this sum has fallen on the Treasury.[12] In general, it will apparently consider imposing the penalty tax only when 70 per cent or more of income after tax is not paid out in dividends or invested in plant, inventory, debt, retirement, or other forms of warrantable "ploughing back." In fact, the penalties are rarely applied, and never to big publicly-owned corporations with large numbers of stockholders. Thus, substantial personal income tax avoidance is still possible, without fear of tax penalty, by retention of earnings within a corporation.

Recommendations for a general undistributed profits tax without punitive features have been made frequently since 1918. These proposals have generally been aimed at eliminating or reducing this possibility of personal income tax avoidance and at equalizing federal income tax burdens on in-

[12] For a careful study of experience under earlier provisions of the law and a discussion of the problems, see J. K. Hall, *The Taxation of Corporate Surplus Accumulations* (Joint Committee on the Economic Report, Washington, 1952).

corporated and unincorporated business. During the 1930's, the argument was advanced that such a tax would check corporate saving, which some economists considered economically undesirable.[13] For all of these reasons, though primarily to get higher tax revenues by forcing corporations to pay dividends which would go largely into relatively high personal income tax brackets, the Administration in 1936 pressed for an undistributed profits tax as a substitute for the corporation income tax. The tax that was passed, with progressive rates on undistributed profits ranging from 7 to 27 per cent, was imposed, not as a substitute for the corporation income tax, but as a supplement to it. Business and popular reaction was generally unfavorable. In 1938, the rate was reduced greatly, and the tax was repealed in the next year.

Excess profits taxes.[14] Two major reasons have motivated the levy of war and defense excess profits taxes on corporations: (1) yield—the World War II gross yield was about $34 billion—and (2) a popular belief that favorably situated businesses should not gain substantially from national distress. A possible supplemental motivation for the tax in the minds of some was the view that it penalized monopoly, "soaked the rich," and would make unions more willing to accept wage control.

The *basis* of a *war* excess profits tax is any difference between wartime and "normal" earnings. In general, wartime earnings can be determined readily, being simply copied, with some adjustments, from the ordinary income tax return. "Normal" earnings, however, are far more difficult to determine. Most countries imposing such taxes permitted a corporation to choose one of two methods. The first or "base period" method in our World War II levy was to take the average earnings for a prewar base period—1936 through 1939—as "normal"; in practice, many "relief" adjustments were permitted to ease the impact of the tax for growing firms or those with an abnormally low earnings record from 1936 through 1939. The second or "invested capital" method was to take as "normal" some ratio of earnings to operating capital. "Normal" earnings under the 1951–1953 tax were: (a) prior earnings basis—83 per cent of average 1946–1949 income, with many qualifications; (b) invested capital basis—12 per cent on first $5 million of investment, 10 per cent on next $5 million, and 8 per cent on the remainder, with qualifications.

Each method of calculating "normal" profit had certain disadvantages, which constituted the other method's advantages. The privilege of choosing one or the other method solved the problem of eliminating most discriminations against particular taxpayers, but retained all discriminations that favored any advantageously situated concerns. Inevitably, practical

[13] See G. E. Lent, *The Impact of the Undistributed Profits Tax* (Columbia University Press, New York, 1948).

[14] See Tax Institute, *Excess Profits Taxation* (Princeton, 1953).

administrative problems were immense, and the definition of taxable income under the excess profits tax became extremely complicated.

Logic would dictate that an excess profits tax should apply to partnerships, single proprietorships, and possibly to individuals as well as to corporations. The American tax sacrificed fiscal logic to administrative expediency. By limiting the tax to corporations, the Treasury was relieved of the task of handling returns from hundreds of thousands of small business units.

Wartime excess profits tax rates are usually high, particularly when superimposed on the ordinary corporation income tax. The rate schedule of the 1940–1945 tax was at first progressive, but the final rate was a flat 95 per cent minus a one-tenth postwar refund or credit for debt retirement. The total of the combined corporation income and excess profits taxes on a corporation in any year was limited to 80 per cent of its net income. The 1951–1953 rate was 30 per cent, with a 70 per cent ceiling for the combined taxes.

These high rates induced some corporations to engage in practices that may have been harmful to the economy. Avoidance and evasion were made tempting. Incentives to economize were weakened. Deductible expenses promising long-term benefits were concentrated, where possible, in the high-rate years. Advertising and other programs of little benefit to war effort flourished, since the government really "paid" most of the cost. Resistance to union demand for inflation-generating wage increases was weakened. Yet the effects that can be attributed to the tax effective during Korean hostilities—a period for which data for analysis are available—seem to have been smaller than generally assumed.[15]

"Rationalization" of corporation and personal income taxes. On the presumption that the federal corporation income tax is not shifted substantially forward to consumers or backward to suppliers, but rests essentially on common stockholders, the present federal system of corporation and personal income taxation, and those of most states, imposes a double tax on the dividend income of individuals. The corporation first pays a federal tax up to 52 per cent on its income, plus possibly a state rate. Then its stockholders must pay personal income tax, at rates determined by the sizes of their total incomes, on the dividends they receive. Income from other forms of personal investment is not so subjected to double taxation. Interest on savings accounts, mortgages, and bonds are subject only to the recipient's personal income tax. Property rentals are taxed only once—as income of the recipient.

To the extent that individuals have differing proportions of their total wealth in common stock, the double taxation of dividend income produces some inequality in the distribution of taxes. Of more concern, it discrimi-

[15] G. E. Lent "The Excess Profits Tax and Business Expenditures," *National Tax Journal*, Sept., 1958, pp. 254–264.

nates against investment in common stocks.[16] Thereby it penalizes some types of equity financing by corporations. Such treatment must handicap venture investment and encourage leasing and debt financing through bonds and mortgages. The first of these effects retards economic expansion. The second produces financial inflexibility, which makes economic adjustment more difficult and accentuates cyclical fluctuations.

Double taxation of dividend income also puts corporations at some tax disadvantage compared with unincorporated businesses.

Much thought has been given to "rationalizing" the federal income tax system so that it might operate equitably with respect to dividend and other investment income and with respect to comparable incorporated and unincorporated enterprises.[17] The following proposals have been advanced: (1) Either the corporation income tax should make dividends as well as bond interest and rentals deductible, or the deductibility of bond interest and rentals should be eliminated, so that the income tax system will not discriminate between equity and debt as instruments for obtaining business capital. (2) Corporations should be treated as partnerships and each stockholder should be taxed on his proportionate share of his corporation's total earnings, whether distributed or not.[18] (3) An undistributed profits tax should be reintroduced at a rate that will approximate the average burden of the personal income tax on dividend income. (4) Stockholders should be allowed a credit for the tax paid by the corporation on that part of its income distributed as dividends, as was done for many years under the personal income normal tax; a move in this direction was made in 1954 with the allowance of the exclusion of $50 of dividends and the granting of a 4 per cent tax credit. (5) Dividend income should be exempted from the low brackets of the personal income tax, or part of all dividend income should be exempted from all personal income taxation.

Each of the foregoing "rationalization" plans has certain merits. Each presents certain difficulties of administration and equity.

Some of the difficulties would be transitional. For example, persons who

[16] The lower rate on capital gains, however, enhances the desirability of common stocks that hold promise of accretion, at least for many individuals with large incomes. Apart from this consideration, under 1959 tax rates, an individual with a top-bracket income would have had to count on a *secure* pre-tax 115 per cent earning rate on share value by a corporation in which he held common stock to leave him as much after tax as he would have from a 5 per cent tax-exempt bond, assuming that the income of the corporation after taxes was fully distributed. The secure corporation earning rate would have to be 60 per cent to provide him as good a return as he would receive from a 3 per cent tax-exempt bond.

[17] H. M. Groves, *Postwar Taxation and Economic Progress* (McGraw-Hill Book Co., New York, 1946), pp. 20–73; U.S. Treasury Department, *The Postwar Corporation Tax Structure* (Washington, 1947); Goode, *op. cit.;* E. G. Keith, "The Future of the Corporation Income Tax," *Journal of Finance,* May, 1956, pp. 195–204.

[18] Partnerships and proprietorships are permitted in some cases to elect to be taxed as corporations. Congress in 1958 also allowed corporations with ten or fewer stockholders to be taxed as partnerships if all stockholders agree. The tax savings in some cases will be large in relation to income.

have bought corporate shares while the tax was in effect have presumably discounted or capitalized the prospective tax burden in the prices they paid for the shares; removal of the double tax would be capitalized into a windfall capital gain for them. The present prices and output of corporation goods and services have undoubtedly been adjusted to some degree to the present tax system. Several years might pass before outputs would increase and prices fall enough to undo all the accumulated adjustments to many years of double taxation. In the meantime, profits and dividends after taxes would rise, possibly above the levels justified by long-run economic necessity. Though difficult, of course, such transition problems should not excuse delay in starting long-run reconstruction.

Most plans for rationalization would involve large loss of revenue. To recoup the tax loss by either higher personal income tax rates or more consumption taxes would bring new strains and "irrationalities." Yet through refinement and combination of some elements of the plans noted above and possibly the development of others, such as long-run averaging of personal incomes for tax purposes, a practicable "rationalization" may be possible.

SOCIAL SECURITY PAYROLL TAXES

The federal government levies payroll taxes on both employees and employers to finance the Old Age and Survivors Insurance program. Both the federal and the state governments levy payroll taxes on employers to finance unemployment insurance.

A payroll tax on employees is a form of special personal income tax. A payroll tax on employers operates as a business tax. The two forms might accordingly be studied in separate chapters. It seems more advisable to combine their analysis here, however.

The OASI payroll taxes. Funds for Old Age and Survivors Insurance benefits are provided by two payroll taxes, one on "covered" employees and one on their employers.[19] The rate of each tax was originally set at one per cent of all wages and salaries up to an annual maximum of $3,000 per employee. The rate for the two taxes has been increased to 2½ per cent each on a maximum of $4,800 a year, and is scheduled to rise eventually—in 1969—to 9 per cent combined. At present one-tenth of receipts go to a special fund for providing disability benefits.

Receipts from these two payroll taxes substantially exceeded OASI benefit payments until 1958.

[19] The benefit aspects of Old Age and Survivors Insurance and of unemployment insurance were presented in Chapter 2. A special pension and payroll tax system with its own administration covers employees of railroads. Because benefits under this system are more generous than those for other employees, the payroll tax rates are higher—6 per cent on both employers and employees on annual earnings up to $3,600 per employee.

OASI benefits for self-employed individuals are financed by a supplementary income tax on their net earnings, with a rate 1.5 times that of the employee payroll tax.

Employers withhold their employees' payroll taxes and pay the total so withheld, together with their own equal payroll tax and the personal income tax withheld from the employees' pay, periodically in a single remittance. Employers of domestic servants, however, may absorb the employee's part of the tax. The typical worker has no compliance problem, and the employer's responsibility does not add greatly to what he must do for income tax withholding.

Problems of the OASI payroll taxes. Even with the future rate increases currently scheduled, actual benefit payments may soon outrun combined payroll tax receipts and earnings of the reserve fund. No one can be certain, however, if only because of the freedom of those insured to continue working beyond the stipulated retirement age. Having the power to tax when necessary, Congress is not compelled, as would be a private insurance company, to collect enough to pay for accruing benefits.

It is much easier for a politically-minded Congress to vote benefits than to vote the taxes needed to finance them—particularly when most of the payroll tax increase would go not for current benefits but only to add to a multibillion-dollar reserve fund. Furthermore, the idea of making OASI entirely self-financing through the payroll taxes has been criticized on certain lines of reasoning:

(1) As a *tax*, the employees' payroll tax is at least slightly regressive over the masses of the public, for it is measured only by personal compensation up to $4,800. Since it has no minimum exemption, it reduces income for living of even the poorest poor. This argument loses its force, of course, if the tax is considered not as a tax but as a life insurance and annuity *premium*.

(2) The employers' payroll tax can be viewed only as a *tax*, not an insurance premium. As a business tax not measured by net business income, it is largely shifted to the general public in higher prices (or backward as lower earnings). Hence its ultimate distributive effect is slightly regressive. By adding to labor costs, it may stimulate substitution of capital for labor and have some tendency to reduce employment.

(3) Excesses of payroll tax receipts over OASI benefit payments withdraw more funds from the stream of purchasing power than flow back through benefit payments. The net effect is to diminish inflationary forces or, under some conditions, accentuate an undesirable tendency toward recession. To attempt to adjust payroll tax rates to help offset business fluctuations is not out of the question. As a practical matter, however, it seems wiser to let benefit, rather than stabilization, needs determine OASI tax rates.

Unemployment insurance payroll taxes.[20] To compel creation of a nationwide state-administered system of unemployment insurance, the Social Security Act of 1935 imposed a 3 per cent payroll tax on employers of 8

[20] Railroad employees are covered by a special federally-administered system of unemployment insurance.

(now 4) or more persons other than employees engaged in agriculture, domestic service, government, and work for nonprofit organizations. The tax applies to the first $3,000 of annual wages and salaries. However, nine-tenths of this tax—2.7 per cent—may be covered by a credit for unemployment insurance taxes paid by the employer to any of the states. In other words, the federal government lets the states have nine-tenths of this 3 per cent payroll tax. The crediting device was used to compel the states to establish unemployment insurance conforming with the federal standards. All states have done so. Three have imposed supplementary payroll taxes on employees and most extend coverage to employees of firms with fewer than eight employees. If any state had failed to comply, its employers would have paid the same payroll tax as employers in other states but their employees would have received no unemployment benefits. Obviously, it was to the interest of every state and its employers to install a system of unemployment insurance financed by an employers' payroll tax with a rate of at least 2.7 per cent. The part of the payroll tax retained by the federal government is applied to the costs of administering the state unemployment insurance systems, in the form of grants to the states amounting to some $330 million a year.

All state unemployment insurance laws provide for "experience rating" or "merit rating" modifications of the employer's payroll tax liability. These provide that firms with relatively stable employment—the details vary widely—will be relieved of part or all of their state payroll tax. The national average tax rate is thereby reduced to about 1.5 per cent. The purpose of these provisions is partly to adjust costs among employers in some fair relation to the benefits their employees receive and partly to induce employers to stabilize employment. By cutting down fluctuations in numbers employed, a firm can hope to save in tax an amount which may be significant in relation to its total profit or loss. Many impressive criticisms of both the principle and the application of "merit rating" have been raised, but the plans are firmly established.

The states turn over to the U.S. Treasury the unemployment insurance payroll taxes they collect, which are invested (in federal bonds) to their separate accounts in a special federal reserve fund. The states draw on their accounts in this fund to pay unemployment benefits. The unemployment insurance reserve fund is not likely to grow much. At times it may decline substantially. During periods of high prosperity, experience rating cuts the tax of most employers, so that the intake of the reserve fund is held down. Meanwhile, the reserve is drawn upon for inevitable seasonal and frictional unemployment. When business turns down, bringing major unemployment, the fund faces heavy demands and tends to decline sharply.[21]

[21] In 1958, Congress revised the law to enable states to borrow from the fund to extend benefit payments, reimbursement to be made over a period of years.

PENSION FUND TAXATION

Private pension funds have grown rapidly since 1940. An important factor in this growth has been favorable tax treatment. There are three major features of this tax treatment. (1) An employer can deduct as a business expense his payments into a pension fund if it meets certain general requirements. (2) The income of the fund is itself exempt from taxation, that is, the interest, dividends, rents, or royalties earned by the assets of the fund are exempt from income tax. (3) The person to receive benefits does not pay tax until he gets the pension; thus, what would be his tax if he received the equivalent of the employer's contribution as salary can earn him income until his retirement. Moreover, when he is receiving the pension, his income will presumably be less than when he was employed, so that the benefit will fall into a lower tax bracket. The combined effect of these tax advantages is very great indeed, especially for executives who are subject to high bracket rates.

Perhaps the most significant of the requirements a pension plan must meet to qualify is that coverage when combined with that of Social Security must include the bulk of nontemporary employees. Plans may involve profit-sharing and stock-bonus arrangements. The details are complex, but the conditions are certainly not unduly restrictive. The total tax advantages are so great that Congress by the requirements it sets can indirectly determine the broad patterns of private pension plans. The only federal restrictions on investment of funds involve acquisition of the obligations of the employing firm. The bulk of the contributions—perhaps $5 billion a year—flows into insurance or trust companies who manage the plans. In general, this mass of wealth which yields largely tax exempt income will be channeled into relatively conservative assets. By 1960 $50 billion may have been accumulated.[22]

STATE CORPORATION ORGANIZATION AND ENTRANCE TAXES[23]

The act of incorporating any sort of business enterprise involves a small expense to the state agency performing this function. During the first half of the nineteenth century, newly organized corporations were customarily

[22] For a competent summary of the economic aspects, see C. H. Hall, Jr., "Retirement Contributions, the Spending Stream, and Growth," *Federal Tax Policy for Economic Growth and Stability* (Washington, 1955), pp. 786–797; D. M. Holland, "Pension Structure," *Federal Expenditure Policy for Economic Growth and Stability* (Washington, 1957), pp. 985–1009.

[23] An organization tax is levied on domestic corporations for the privilege of incorporating. An entrance tax is levied on foreign corporations for the privilege of entering the taxing state to do business. In some states, these taxes are called "charter taxes," "filing fees," "bonus taxes," "capitalization fees," and "initial fees."

charged a small flat fee to cover such costs. After the Civil War, the incorporation charge was recognized as a possible source of revenue. The transition from fee to tax was accomplished either by raising the amount of the flat charge above the costs of incorporation or by converting it into a capital stock tax. By 1902, 40 states levied either fixed or capital-stock corporation organization taxes. At present all states tax the organization of domestic corporations, usually on the basis of the amount of the capital stock.

Prior to the 1890's, "foreign" corporations (corporations organized in states other than the taxing state) registering their entry into a state for the purpose of doing business therein were not subject to any special tax. In 1894, Ohio taxed the "entrance" of foreign corporations on the basis of the amount of capital stock to be employed in the state. Other states followed suit. "Entrance" taxes are now almost universal.

In order to attract large corporations, some states graduate the rates of their capital stock organization and entrance taxes, applying lighter rates to large than to small corporations. With a similar end in view, many states set minimum and maximum charges for organization and entrance, the former to derive a sizable revenue from small corporations, the latter so as not to discourage large corporations.

Total revenue yield of these taxes is minor.

ANNUAL STATE CORPORATION TAXES

Until late in the nineteenth century, incorporated business other than financial institutions and public service enterprises—the incorporated manufacturers, merchants, butchers, bakers, and candlestick-makers—generally escaped special state taxation. The earliest form of general corporation tax, the corporate excess tax (noted in Chapter 18), was not a special tax but a modification of the general property tax to prevent corporations from evading intangible property taxes. At first, this "corporate excess" value was assessed and taxed to the shareholders; later, it was universally assessed to the corporations themselves. By 1912, corporate excess taxes were levied in 16 states. Thereafter, it found decreasing favor, and now only Massachusetts obtains significant revenue from its tax on corporate excess.

Capital stock taxes. Although the capital stock corporation tax developed later than the corporate excess tax, it spread more widely. Pennsylvania levied a capital stock franchise tax[24] on domestic corporations in 1840.

[24] The statutory designations of these taxes have been various and often quite meaningless. They are called "franchise taxes," "license fees," "privilege taxes," "corporation fees," and so forth. For the purpose of study, the statutory nomenclature has been ignored, and the various annual corporation taxes have been classified according to their inherent legal character. The term "franchise tax" has been confined to annual taxes on domestic corporations, and "privilege tax" is applied to annual taxes on foreign corporations. For a more complete discussion, see R. W. Lindholm, *The Corporate Franchise as a Basis of Taxation* (University of Texas Press, Austin, 1944).

Other states were slow to adopt this form of corporation tax—only 12 states had done so by 1902. Thereafter, the spread was rapid. Three-fourths of the states now impose capital stock franchise taxes. Annual capital stock privilege taxes on "foreign" corporations developed later than similar taxes on domestic corporations, but they were soon almost as universal. Capital stock taxes produce about $200 million a year. In Delaware, a "corporation haven" state, the annual corporation taxes account for one-sixth of the state's tax receipts.

Capital stock franchise and privilege taxes have three bases—authorized capital stock, issued capital stock, and capital employed in the taxing state. There is a marked tendency for taxes based on authorized capital stock to be replaced by taxes with one of the other two bases. Allocation is common in both franchise and privilege taxes based on authorized or issued capital stock, but it is obviously unnecessary for taxes based on "capital employed within the state."

Uniformity in the rate structure of capital stock taxes is conspicuous by its absence. Some rates are stated as a proportional permillage, others as a regressive series of specific charges for specified amounts of capital stock. Some, like Pennsylvania's five-mill tax, are substantial. Others are trifling, that of Maine being from one-tenth to one-fortieth of a mill. The quality of administration varies. In general, it has not been high.

Corporation income taxes. During the nineteenth century a few states experimented unsuccessfully with corporation income taxes. The modern movement, starting in Wisconsin in 1911, has extended to 37 states, whose taxes yielded about $980 million in 1958.

State corporation income taxes are based on earned net income. Unlike the federal corporation income tax, the state taxes frequently do not apply to public utilities, banks, insurance companies, and other groups of corporations reached by special taxes. In defining taxable income, the federal tax provides a general model for most states, but variation in details is wide. For example, most states for constitutional reasons exempt interest on federal securities, but several have framed their taxes as levies "on the franchise or privilege of doing business within the state as a corporation measured by net income thereby earned," thus taking advantage of Supreme Court decisions to include such interest in regular income taxes. On the basis of this subject-measure loophole, they tax "tax-exempt" interest. Capital gains are completely exempt in two states, taxed on a partial basis in a few others. Dividends received from other corporations are variously treated. All states allow bad debts as deductions, and almost all allow charitable contributions to be deducted within some limits. On practically every item entering gross income or calculated as a deduction, one or more states provide exceptions to the general rule.

Because of the U.S. Constitution, all states must provide for allocation of the incomes of foreign corporations. All states except Alabama also permit allocation of the incomes of domestic corporations.

Six states apply mildly progressive rate schedules. The others have proportional rates. The lowest proportional rate is 2 per cent, whereas 17 states have from 4 to 5 per cent. The highest rate is Minnesota's 7.3 per cent.

The yield of state corporation income taxes varies with changes in business conditions. This is a disadvantage because state borrowing or retrenchment to meet depression deficiencies is generally difficult. Massachusetts and New York stabilize the yield of their corporation income taxes somewhat by supplementing them with alternative capital stock taxes, the corporation paying whichever tax is higher. By the operation of the capital stock tax in this arrangement, an irreducible minimum revenue is assured even in depression years.

Allocation. State taxation of foreign (out-of-state) corporations is hedged about with constitutional limitations. A foreign corporation whose activities within the taxing state are indissolubly tied to interstate or foreign business may not be subjected to a capital stock or income privilege tax. If intrastate activity is present, however, a privilege tax may be imposed, but only upon so much of the capital stock or net income as may be attributed to the taxing state by separate accounting or by some system of allocation. A 1959 Supreme Court decision extended the authority of a state to tax the net income of a business engaged in interstate commerce but having no established place of business in the state. Although capital stock and net income franchise taxes on domestic corporations need not be allocated, nearly all states make such provision; otherwise domestic corporations would reincorporate in other states to avoid the extra tax burden.

For capital stock taxes, the most common standard of allocation is tangible property—a state capital stock tax is applied to such proportion of a corporation's capital stock as is determined by the ratio of its tangible property in the taxing state to its total tangible property. A few states employ a double basis of allocation—property and gross sales. More complicated and varied formulas have been developed for allocating net income under state corporation income taxes. Most common is the "Massachusetts formula," which employs the triple allocation basis of tangible property, gross sales, and payrolls. Various other combinations are found, while some states allocate solely on sales, or property, or cost of sales. In some states different formulas are used for manufacturing and nonmanufacturing businesses. The natural tendency is for a state to apply a formula which will tend to favor it by "importing," for tax purposes, income which more basically was generated outside. The chief opportunity for doing so arises in prescribing where sales will be presumed to have been made—the location of the buyer, the place where the contract was made, the point of shipment, or some other.

As a committee of the National Tax Association pointed out years ago:

All methods of apportionment . . . are arbitrary—the cutting of a Gordian knot. . . . There is no one right rule of apportionment, notwithstanding that there are probably a number of different rules, all of which may work substantial justice. . . . The only right rule of procedure is a rule on which the several states can and will get together as a matter of comity.[25]

However, economic analysis can provide some guidelines. A formula that recognizes underlying economic reality will have least tendency to distort business decisions and economic growth in general. Income in an area, the thing which the allocation formula seeks to determine, is created by human and material resources. The resources utilized can be measured reasonably well by dollar figures of payrolls and property, that is, other things the same, more of a corporation's income arises in the state in which it has large rather than small payrolls. Direct proportionality is an acceptable assumption. The same applies to property. However, the relative *weights* to be assigned in a formula to payrolls and to property is less clear. The proportions for the economy as a whole as revealed in national income accounts (around 4 to payrolls and 1 to property) would understate the relative importance of plant and equipment for much big business. However, an arbitrary weighting of perhaps 2 to payrolls and 1 to property ought to be satisfactory. The use of sales in allocation has, at most, slight economic justification—except, of course, for the effort involved in the selling which is included in payrolls. Selling is a part of the income-creating process whose contribution to the whole is represented *not* by the dollar volume of sales but by the remuneration of the human and material resources that perform the function. To assign sales an independent importance is to produce some inequity and to create an inducement to arbitrary, complex, and wasteful manipulation of sales arrangements.

Associations of businesses, legislators, and state tax officials have repeatedly recommended that the states agree upon a uniform standard of allocation for business taxes. The popularity of the "Massachusetts formula" indicates that some heed has been given to this advice. But there are still too many nonconforming states.[26] Because of variant allocation bases,

[25] "Report of the Committee on the Apportionment between States of Taxes on Mercantile and Manufacturing Business," National Tax Association, *Proceedings*, 1922, p. 201.

[26] In 1957 it appeared that a "break through" might come. The National Conference of Commissioners on Uniform State Laws agreed on a statute for income allocation, and the American Bar Association approved it. The proposed law deals with a great variety of major and minor issues. The allocation provided is the familiar equal weighting of property, payrolls, and sales, with the destination to determine the location of the sale. Considerable opposition has appeared, especially among the tax managers of businesses, and the prospects of general agreement and widespread adoption are apparently not high. *See* C. L. Harriss, "Economic Aspects of Interstate Apportionment of Business Income," *Taxes, The Tax Magazine*, April, 1959, pp. 327 ff.

corporations operating in two or more states still frequently find that combined state income taxes are based on more, or less, than their actual total income. Costs of compliance are increased by the need to keep accounts on different bases for taxes in two or more states.

States often fail to check carefully on figures used by businesses in computing their actual allocations. In many states the administrative agency has, in fact, a large range for the exercise of its discretion in specific cases.

STATE TAXES ON PUBLIC UTILITIES

To encourage construction during the early years of American railroading, many states exempted railroad companies from ordinary property taxation. Some states continued this policy of exemption well into the last quarter of the nineteenth century. Special railroad taxes also appeared, sometimes taking the form of individual taxes specified in the charters of the railroad companies. As a result, a single state might have several forms of railroad taxation.

Railroad tax systems have not shown the progressive development in which a more effective system replaces a less effective one. Instead, the various states have tried one or another system, sometimes changing, sometimes clinging to the one first established. Railroads have been subjected to the general property tax with or without centralized assessment, to gross receipts taxes, to capital stock and bonded debt taxes, to mileage taxes, and to other special levies. In some cases, railroads, even when losing money, have been taxed more heavily than profitable businesses.

Telegraph companies developed later than raliroads, and it was natural that taxes on such companies should be strongly influenced by railroad taxes. Some states have never withdrawn telegraph companies from the general property tax system. Others provided for the centralized assessment of telegraph property and sometimes for valuation by the "unit rule." With increasing frequency after 1875, the states resorted to gross receipts taxes. A few states turned to mileage taxes, generally proportional but occasionally graduated by some standard.

State taxes on telephone companies tended to parallel the earlier taxes on telegraph companies, though the rates were often differentiated where the two taxes were otherwise similar. Telephone companies were subjected to centrally assessed property taxes, to gross receipts taxes, and to mileage taxes. A few states developed a tax based on the number of instruments installed.

After the Civil War, express companies came to the attention of tax-hungry legislatures. More commonly than in the case of railroad, telegraph, or telephone companies, the tendency was to subject express companies to gross receipts taxes. Electric light and power companies came to be taxed generally on a gross receipts basis. Other classes of public service enterprises—pipe-line companies, water companies, steamboat companies—were subjected to special taxation in some states.

These special public utility taxes yield the states around $400 million a year.

Gross earnings taxes. The gross earnings tax is the distinctive form of public service corporation tax; it is employed in all but a dozen states. It may be applied to all public service enterprises, or merely to some, with the remainder taxed by other, special taxes.

Many public utilities gross earnings taxes are *in lieu* taxes—state levies substituted in the interest of administrative simplicity for general property taxes on the utilities' operating properties. *In lieu* gross earnings taxes may be based upon an allocated fraction of a corporation's total gross earnings, including earnings arising out of both interstate and intrastate services. But the general burden of an *in lieu* gross earnings tax must not be greater than the burden of the property levies for which it is substituted.

Revenues from *in lieu* gross earnings taxes must be distributed among the local governments which would otherwise have levied property taxes on the operating property of the taxed utilities. On this matter, the states were faced with a difficult problem—one which already troubled them if their gross earnings taxes were based on allocated total gross earnings—the problem of selecting a fair standard of distribution. As an example of the complexity of this problem, some of the standards of allocation and distribution considered for railroad gross earnings taxes have been single-track mileage, total-track mileage, total-track mileage with adjustment for value of terminal property, gross earnings, net earnings, car mileage, train mileage, car and locomotive mileage, "traffic units" calculated on tons of freight hauled and number of passengers carried, value of property. Each standard has minor merits and major disadvantages. And each class of public utility has different possibilities of allocation and distribution standards. Since a National Tax Association committee found it impossible to construct a fair, workable allocation and distribution standard for gross earnings taxes, the state legislatures cannot be severely criticized if they have not succeeded in solving this problem.

Public utilities gross earnings taxes are not always *in lieu* levies; several are independent taxes imposed in addition to property taxes or even in addition to *in lieu* gross earnings taxes. The entire revenue from such independent gross income taxes goes to the state governments, and hence no problem of distribution standards arises. Nor is there any problem of allocation, since these independent gross earnings taxes may be based only on intrastate receipts.

Rates of public utility gross earnings taxes vary widely, according to whether they are *in lieu* or independent taxes, according to the class of utility taxed, and according to the will of the various state legislatures. The most common range of rates is from 2 to 4 per cent; 6 per cent rates are found occasionally. In most cases, the rates are proportional; a few instances of progressive rates may be found.

Other taxes on public utilities. Public service corporations are frequently burdened with two or more special taxes, because the states commonly extend to them the general corporation capital stock, income, or corporate excess taxes. Furthermore, the states not infrequently levy special capital stock taxes, net income taxes, or special franchise taxes in the form of corporate excess taxes, on some or all of their public service corporations. Fixed taxes on certain public service enterprises are found in a few states. A few states tax railroads, streetcar companies, telegraph companies, and express companies according to the mileage of their tracks, wires, or routes. Kilowatt-hour taxes on electric power companies are found in a few cases. Some Southern states subject water, gas, and lighting companies, and sometimes other enterprises, to local license taxes based on the populations of the municipalities they serve. Telephone companies in Florida are taxed on the number of instruments installed.

Far from uncommon is the subjection of public utility enterprises to several independent taxes in the one state. Some classes of public service corporations in Virginia, for example, have been subjected to four special taxes in addition to their property tax. In recent years many local governments have added taxes on public utility earnings.

Critique. *Gross earnings* taxes on public service enterprises present one advantage—ease of administration. Complicated assessment problems of property taxation, as well as the deduction difficulties inherent in net income taxation, are avoided. But gross earnings taxes are hidden from the consumer and have regressive elements. Moreover, they sometimes discriminate among taxed enterprises, overburdening those which suffer losses or have a low ratio of net to gross earnings. In rebuttal to these charges, it is argued that gross earnings taxes on railroads and public service enterprises are shifted to users, so that the taxpaying ability of the enterprises themselves need not be taken into consideration. In fact, however, the ability of some enterprises to shift taxes may be slight; this has probably been true for most railroads for many years.

A flaw in the gross earnings tax arises from the federal constitutional limitation on state interference with interstate commerce. The Supreme Court has sanctioned a tax on an allocated portion of the receipts arising out of interstate commerce but only if the tax does not burden or interfere with interstate commerce. A gross receipts tax restricted to intrastate receipts is badly mutilated and does discriminate between enterprises otherwise identically circumstanced. By levying gross receipts taxes *in lieu* of property taxes, however, the state can avoid this constitutional difficulty. So generous is the attitude of the courts toward accepting the approximation of the burden of a gross receipts tax with that of a property tax for which it is substituted, that the states have a fairly free hand in developing this species of gross receipts tax.

Net income taxes on railroads and public service corporations may be shifted about as fully—or as inadequately—as property or gross earnings taxes, since rate-fixing bodies view all taxes as costs to be covered in the rates allowed. In this distributive aspect, then, net income taxes do not differ greatly from ad valorem or gross income taxes, except that the latter bear more heavily on firms with losses. Moreover, net income taxes are not subject to the constitutional disabilities which afflict a gross earnings tax. Compared with property taxes, they do not tend to discourage investment in new plant and equipment. Nor do they have quite the tendency of gross receipts taxes to reduce the purchase of services produced under conditions of decreasing cost. A net income business tax, however, is a variable source of revenue, productive in years of business boom and falling off in depression. Also—a practical fiscal point—the states appear disinclined to levy net income taxes with rates high enough to yield as much revenue as can be obtained from gross earnings taxes having apparently modest rates. Finally, net earnings taxes add another tax inducement to debt rather than to equity financing.

Ad valorem taxation of the operative property of public service enterprises is a needlessly costly method of taxation. The present ad valorem taxes should be replaced by gross earnings or net income taxes levied independently where possible or else *in lieu* of property taxes. No advantage is gained by subjecting public service corporations to combinations of taxes—gross earnings taxes, plus net income taxes, plus capital stock taxes, plus mileage taxes, plus whatnot else. The ideal of administrative simplicity is best satisfied by the levy of a single tax with rates high enough to produce all the revenue required from the group of public service enterprises. Such a single public service enterprise tax may be either a gross earnings or a net earnings tax.

Occasionally there has been some advocacy of a hybrid public service enterprise tax, combining the principles of both gross earnings and net income taxation. Maine has enacted such a tax for railroads based on gross earnings, but the rate is graduated by the ratio of net earnings to gross earnings. Behind this proposal is the argument that such a tax is more equitable than an outright earnings tax. But this argument fails to consider the circumstance that net income as a basis for public service enterprise taxation is little, if any, more equitable than the gross income basis, since either tax is largely shifted. The combination of the two principles adds complication without compensating advantages.

The exemption of government-owned utilities creates discriminations. The prices of the services do not contain a tax element which must appear in the prices of goods and services produced privately.

PROBLEMS

1. Show how the concepts of taxable income for the individual and for a corporation resemble each other and how they differ.

2. What, if any, advantages will a business receive from using rapid rather than slower depreciation in computing taxable income?

3. Describe the provisions for loss carry-overs and their significance.

4. Discuss with a businessman the taxes his firm pays.

5. What would you expect to be the results of a Social Security payroll tax of 5 per cent each on both the employee and the employer.

6. Explain why allocation formulae are needed in state business income taxation.

7. In what sense is the tax on business net income a tax on efficiency?

8. "Taxes on the gross receipts of telephone and electric utilities are easier to justify than taxes on the gross receipts of railroads." Discuss.

9. "The allowance of percentage depletion in excess of the owner's investment will invite new suppliers, lead to lower prices, and in the long run cost the Treasury heavily while benefiting the taxpayer relatively little." Discuss.

10. How would you define "excess" profits for purpose of taxation during a time of peace? Of war?

11. "Interest and dividends received by individuals are taxed. Those received by pension funds are not. The result is unfair. Moreover, a distortion of investment will result." Discuss.

CHAPTER 15

Taxes on Business (Concluded)

STATE BANK TAXES

THE pattern of state bank taxation is established by federal law. The Banking Act of 1864 as subsequently amended prescribes how *national* banks, as federal instrumentalities, may be taxed by the states. If states were to tax their state banks much more severely than national banks, the state banks would take out national charters. Therefore, state taxation of state banks as well as of national banks is conditioned by federal law.

States may tax bank shares to their owners as intangible personal property, but at a rate no higher than that imposed on "other moneyed capital." The Supreme Court has interpreted this provision to mean that states with classified property taxes which imposed special low mill rates on intangibles must impose no higher rates on bank shares.[1] The states may also (1) tax bank net income under general corporation income taxes, (2) if they have no general corporation income taxes, impose special bank excises "measured by net income," or (3) tax bank dividends at rates no higher than on personal income from other forms of investment.

Most states tax their banks by a bank share tax. The shares are generally assessed to the issuing banks instead of to the owners. Consequently, although other intangibles may escape listing for the general property tax, bank shares are listed and generally assessed at their full par value or at the full value of the capital, surplus, and undivided profit of the bank. Usually, but not always, the value of real estate owned by the bank and taxed under the general property tax is deducted from the assessed value of the shares. Some states also permit part or all of a bank's surplus to be deducted. Behind this deduction is the theory that taxes on surpluses and undivided

[1] *Merchants' National Bank* v. *Richmond*, 256 U.S. (1921) 635. Until this decision, states as a rule imposed higher effective property taxes on all banks than upon businesses in general. Bank earnings were good enough to make the total burden supportable without serious adverse effect.

profits discourage the desirable accumulation of bank surpluses. Assessment of bank shares is generally made by the county or local assessor, but often the state tax agency either assists or itself makes the assessment.

A quarter of the states tax the income of both national and state banks, generally taking advantage of the 1926 "excise" provision, which enables them to include the interest on tax-exempt securities in the income base.[2] Half of the states impose on state banks and trust companies supplementary levies such as capital stock taxes, gross or net income taxes, and flat fees, which are not imposed on national banks. Low, flat rate taxes on deposits in state banks are levied in a few states. Thus, in some cases the present system of state bank taxation discriminates against state banks.

The present restricted and complicated tax treatment of banks is largely the result of historic accident. There is agreement that changes are desirable, but no agreement on *what* changes.

STATE TAXATION OF INSURANCE COMPANIES

Insurance taxation presents some of the same problems as bank taxation. Insurance companies and banks both operate under special state authorization and are subject to regulation. Computation of net income is difficult because of doubt about how much to deduct for future losses—casualties or bad loans. The importance of intangible property as an element of insurance company and bank assets, moreover, makes for special property tax problems. Income from government bonds creates difficulties of income taxation in both cases. However, Congress has not set special rules for the state taxation of insurance companies, as it has for banks, and until recently, the courts did not consider the insurance business "commerce" under the interstate commerce clause. Consequently, states have had wide freedom in taxing insurance companies.

Present status. Gross premiums, less returned premiums and premiums paid on reinsurance, are the preferred basis for state insurance company taxation.[3] Capital stock as a basis for taxing mutual companies which have no capital stock value is out of the question, and as a basis for taxing stock companies it is far from satisfactory, since it fails to reflect the asset values of their reserves. Net income is almost impossible to determine for mutual companies and is a questionable concept for stock companies, especially for life insurance companies, whose contracts extend for very long periods.

All states tax foreign (out-of-state) life and fire insurance companies on a premiums basis. Somewhat more than two-thirds of the states also bring domestic insurance companies under special premium taxes; the remainder

[2] Under the "rule of subject and measure," such income excises have been upheld when they applied to interest on federal debt issues, and when applied to the interest on bonds issued by the taxing state itself as "exempt."

[3] The federal government, in contrast, imposes no premium taxes but has complicated formulae for taxing investment income of insurance companies.

subject them as best they may to general corporation capital stock or income taxes. In about half the states payments for annuities are also taxed. Premium tax rates vary considerably—from 0.4 per cent on domestic life insurance companies in Nebraska to 3.5 per cent on foreign companies in Wisconsin. Most common is the 2 per cent rate.

Insurance companies of different classes are frequently taxed at different rates and sometimes under different taxes. Such discriminations are established between life, fire, marine, and casualty insurance companies. Stock companies are frequently taxed more heavily than mutual companies. Fire insurance companies in many states are subject to a special tax—the "fire marshal or fire department tax," levied on the benefit principle for the support of state or local fire departments.

Discrimination against foreign insurance companies has been common. Sometimes, higher premium tax rates have been imposed on them; sometimes, they have been subjected to premium taxes while domestic companies paid lighter capital stock or income taxes. Fortunately, however, with the development of reciprocal and retaliatory provisions in insurance tax laws, this type of discrimination has been largely eliminated.

The states now receive over $450 million annually from special taxes on insurance companies. The yield in most states is around 3 per cent of total revenue. Virtually all of this tax would seem to be shifted to purchasers of insurance. It is in essence a "sales" tax on the purchase of a particular kind of service. Administration is relatively easy, and evasion is negligible.

SEVERANCE TAXES

A severance tax is a special gross receipts or gross product tax imposed on the extraction or "severance" of natural resources—mineral ores, coal, oil, and timber. In some cases these severance taxes have been levied in substitution for property taxes on the current value of the mine or well reserves or timber stands. The property tax tends to promote early and often wasteful extraction and use of mineral deposits and timber stands. Criticizing the effects of the traditional form of property taxation, the National Resources Board pointed out:

> Owners of mineral resources are driven to open mines in order to provide income enough to meet their taxes, and the ad valorem tax has been one of the causes of overdevelopment of mine capacity, especially of coal mines. It has a tendency to force selective mining, with attendant loss of low-grade material. It handicaps the development and extraction of the miscellaneous grades to be found in most mineral districts. It puts a premium on the use of methods of extraction which cost the least, regardless of the fact that these methods often involve the permanent destruction or locking up of important reserves costing more to extract.

Deforestation is also promoted by the application of property taxes to timber lands.

Substitution of severance taxes for property taxes on natural resource values promotes conservation at the cost of some temporary revenue loss. Furthermore, in many of the oil and mining states, there has risen the feeling that operators who tap the natural resources of the state are gradually, yet nonetheless steadily, impoverishing the state. Some of the net "rent" from gifts of nature, it is argued, should accrue to the people of the state. From this feeling have developed several systems of "compensatory" severance taxes levied in addition to the ordinary property and business taxes paid by the mining and oil companies.

Half of the states now impose severance taxes on mineral, coal, sulphur, oil and gas, and timber-cutting operations. The severance taxes on timber cutting are gross receipts taxes, based on the stumpage value of the cut timber, with rates varying between 2 and 12.5 per cent. Some of the severance taxes on mineral, coal, and oil companies are also gross receipts taxes with rates ranging from one-sixteenth per cent to 12 per cent. Most severance taxes have specific rates, as 3 cents per ton on iron ore in Alabama and seven-tenths cent per ton on coal in Colorado, or one-half cent per barrel of oil in Oregon and 4.6 cents per barrel in Texas.

Severance taxes now yield about $400 million in a year of good business. Texas' severance tax receipts, about 30 per cent of the state's entire revenue, constitute one-half of the national total.

Several local governments in Pennsylvania impose taxes on coal mined within the locality.

BUSINESS LICENSE TAXES[4]

Every state levies special license taxes on one or more particular businesses and occupations. In some Southern states the number of business license taxes is legion, and they come close to being a system of special business taxation with differentiated bases and rates. Special business license taxes elsewhere represent a rather casual tapping of incidental sources of revenue. Local governments in recent years have made increasing use of such taxes.

The manufacture and sale of alcoholic beverages require special licenses which are designed to raise revenue and sometimes to aid in regulation. A number of states and cities levy special license taxes on the sale of tobacco products. Peddlers, pawnbrokers, brokers, and a wide variety of service enterprises are subject to license taxes, particularly in the South. A con-

[4] Many state charges on special occupations prove, on close inspection, to be fees rather than taxes—their yield barely covers the costs of the regulatory activity to which they are attached. Such license fees are eliminated from present consideration, but are analyzed in Chapter 21. Also excluded from present consideration are license taxes on the manufacture or sale of particular commodities which are measured by the number of units or the values produced or sold. These are considered commodity taxes and are studied in Chapter 16.

siderable element of regulation and sometimes an element of protection for local business are to be found in many of these taxes. Theaters and other amusement businesses must bear special taxes in many states and localities.

Special business license taxes have little justification. Lightning-rod agents, dealers in musical instruments, cotton processors, or theaters are granted no special privileges by the state to justify special taxes according to any benefit theory. Because of finespun distinctions drawn between different business activities and occupations, some concerns can slip between classifications and avoid the tax in a manner not possible under a more general business tax. No legislative adjustment of fixed taxes, or taxes per county, or taxes per population of the city in which the business is operated, or taxes per machine employed can make a series of license taxes conform as closely with the principle of taxpaying ability as does a general income tax or some other general business tax. As regulatory devices, they are generally crude, ineffective, and inequitable. Some slight economic justification can be found, however, where the number of licenses to be issued is limited, perhaps for regulatory purposes; the tax may absorb some of the "monopoly" value given to the economic opportunities that are permitted.

TAXES ON RACING

Taxes on pari-mutuel betting and on racing licenses have become prominent in recent years. Half of the states and many local governments levy such taxes. The tax is ordinarily imposed as a percentage of the total bets placed through the pari-mutuel systems—5 to 7 per cent, as a rule, but 11 per cent in New York. In addition, states frequently take half of the "breakage"—the amount remaining after expenses have been paid and winnings computed to the nearest 10 cents or other convenient figure.

Some states impose heavy license fees on racing. Rates are sometimes fixed by the day—as high as $2,500 in Kentucky—or for each meet—$10,000 in New Jersey. Rate graduation is common, based upon the size of the community or the type of race or the attendance. Separate taxes are frequently imposed upon admissions.

Although betting at the tracks is for many people a form of amusement worth its cost, it is for others tragically expensive. Gambling can be the source of serious misfortune for the individual and his family—and the community. When governments develop the taxation of gambling as a source of revenue—and this rather than control and regulation is now the objective—the temptation to encourage gambling will not infrequently overrule rational evaluation of the net social results of extending the activity. Since 1950, the number of racing days has increased almost one-third.

Pari-mutuel taxes yielded about $240 million in 1958, all but a few millions going to the states.

CHAIN-STORE TAXES

In 1927, three states—Georgia, Maryland, and North Carolina—imposed special discriminatory taxes on chain stores. In support of these taxes, some argument was made that chain stores had special taxpaying ability because of their higher efficiency and the intangible value represented by their organization setup. Also, it was suggested, the personal property tax in these states discriminated in favor of chains and against independent merchants, so that the chain-store tax was a sort of compensatory levy. Actually, the motivation of these taxes was regulatory—to hamper the chains in their competition with the independent dealers.

Of the six chain-store taxes enacted in 1927 and 1928, five were declared unconstitutional. In these and later decisions, however, the Supreme Court established a permissible scope for this form of discriminatory taxation. With constitutional issues cleared, many states hastened to place chain-store taxes on their statute books. As of 1958, 15 states and several cities had chain-store taxes.

The chain-store tax is generally a lump-sum tax per store, graduated either by the number of stores in the state or in the country. Top rates range from Alabama's $112.50 for each outlet in excess of 20 to Texas' $825 for each outlet in excess of 50. Tennessee has a curious tax based on floor-space area; Michigan has a supplementary tax on the number of store counters and North Carolina one on motor fuel pumps.

Chain-store taxes yield little revenue—the total yield for all states with such taxes in 1957 was only $6 million. But that these taxes check the development of chain retailing is unquestionable—and this is their specific purpose. In some cases, national chains simply closed their outlets in heavily taxing states and left an unchallenged field to the independents. In other cases, especially oil companies, they sold their outlets to the former managers and reorganized their distributive system on a "voluntary group" basis in a manner to avoid tax liability. Some of the trend to supermarkets may have been due to taxes which penalized larger numbers of small chain units.

Impartial fiscal opinion generally disapproves of chain-store taxes except possibly at very modest levels to compensate for avoidance of certain other taxes by chain stores. Some authorities, hostile to regulatory use of taxes, condemn chain-store taxes on this ground alone. Others, who condone regulatory taxation, argue that the purpose in this case is economically undesirable because it discriminates against a form of business organization that may be, and often is, of more than average efficiency.

GENERAL UNINCORPORATED BUSINESS TAX

In nearly all states, incorporated businesses bear a heavier tax burden than unincorporated concerns. This discrimination has often been criticized and the suggestion made that a compensating tax be imposed on unincorporated business. In 1921, Connecticut imposed the first such tax. Because it was felt that the inadequate accounting records kept by many small concerns would make a net income tax difficult to report and administer, a gross income basis was chosen. Rates are now one-fifth per cent on manufacturing and retail business, and one-twentieth per cent on wholesale concerns.

New York made the bold plunge in 1935 of enacting a net income unincorporated business tax. Lawyers, doctors, and certain personal service firms which derive most of their income from services rendered by the owners are exempt. On other enterprises, the rate is 4 per cent on net income over a general $5,000 exemption plus as many additional $5,000 exemptions as there are co-proprietors or partners. The new income taxes of local governments generally apply to the net income of unincorporated businesses and professional persons.

Theoretical considerations give a strong balance of argument in favor of unincorporated business taxation—if business as such is to be subject to special taxation. The stumbling block is the difficulty of administering a tax applying to a myriad of small concerns. Connecticut sought to avoid this difficulty by use of the simple gross income base. New York took refuge in generous minimum exemptions that limited the number of firms liable for the tax. Neither solution is satisfactory, and whether a substantial but practicable unincorporated business tax can be developed remains an open question.

VALUE-ADDED TAXATION

A more general type of business taxation—one which in fact can also be considered a broad form of consumption tax—is the tax on value added. The tax base, in general, is the difference between a business's total receipts from sales and its payments for materials. The tax base, in other words, is the growth in value attributable to each firm's activities. In essence, it is a tax on wages, profit, and other payments for factors of production.[5]

The potential merits are impressive. The base would be very broad so that a low rate would yield substantial revenue. The universality of the tax would aid its general shifting and diffusion and minimize dangers of

[5] In terms of national economic accounting, the base may be either total product or total income.

excess burdens on part of the economy. The tax does not penalize efficiency as a net income tax may. The legal form of business organization, the degree of integration, and the proportions of equity to debt financing would not influence the tax due. Just as all economic activity requires the existence of government, all would pay—directly to the extent economic resources are used. Consequently, the tax would be more neutral than any other form of either business or consumption taxation. Nevertheless, this lack of discrimination may not be deemed an unmixed blessing; some people, for example, prefer a tax that hits profits especially.

In this country, only Michigan's Business Activities Tax of 0.55 per cent on "adjusted receipts" approximates the value-added form. The Michigan tax, however, has important features which depart from the basic nature of value-added taxation. For example, small firms are exempt. France makes heavy use of essentially this form of taxation, with rates that are high and with special provisions numerous.

Administration appears no more difficult than a net income (or general sales) tax. Of course, existence of special provisions to meet this or that need—deductibility of taxes, contributions, depreciation, and services, such as advertising, taxed to the supplier—would repeat familiar problems. At the state level, the difficult problem of allocation would remain, but it would not be worse than under income taxes. The French require a firm claiming a deduction—what it says it paid for materials or inventory—to provide a duplicate of the seller's report to the tax authorities of the gross amount of his sales. This system provides a check of considerable effectiveness. The problems of principle and practice—to be sure to count everything once but only once—will not all have easy solutions. Still, in casting around for a way to tax on a broad base, to substitute a more general for the more limited tax, states and the national government should seriously consider this form.

CONSTITUTIONAL LAW OF BUSINESS TAXATION

Express or tacit permission given by the states to individuals or associations to engage in various lines of business is viewed by the courts as a privilege which will sustain special state taxes on the resulting business activities. Furthermore, the conduct of business generally, and such specific aspects of business as purchasing, selling, earning business profits, and so forth, are considered activities which may be subjected to excises. The federal government, which accords no legal privileges upon which businesses may be organized or operated, bases its right to levy business taxes on this "excise" theory.

Neither the "due process" or "equal protection" limitations of the Fifth and Fourteenth Amendments, nor the majority of state "equality and uniformity" constitutional provisions, bar the classification of business enterprises according to form of organization or type of business activity. Nor do they prevent the levy of distinct taxes or different rates on the various classes of business enterprise. Corporations, for no other reason than that they are corporations, may generally be taxed differently from other private enterprises. Public service concerns, banks, mines, insurance companies may each be subjected to a separate system of taxation. Manufacturers may be taxed differently from merchants, butchers from bakers, railroads from truckers, steamfitters from plumbers, chain-store systems from single retail establishments. The courts ask only that there exist some reasonable economic or legal distinction between two business enterprises to uphold differences in their treatment under the tax laws.

Federal business taxes. The most important constitutional limitations on the federal government's power to levy business taxes were reviewed in Chapter 7. It will suffice here to repeat that the federal government cannot tax export trade or gross receipts derived from export trade, nor can it tax state property or the instrumentalities of state government.

State business taxes. Constitutional law distinguishes sharply between domestic and foreign corporations as to the care with which it guards them from questionable exercise of state and local taxing powers. Corporations are deemed to be the creatures of the states under whose laws they are organized, and the tax powers of states with respect to domestic corporations are plenary. The states are accorded no such absolute power over foreign corporations, and their taxation of such corporations is hedged about with restrictions. Organization taxes on domestic corporations may be based on total authorized capital stock; entrance taxes on foreign corporations, on the contrary, must be based on allocated issued stock or on capital employed in the state. Franchise taxes on domestic corporations may be based on total authorized capital stock and on nonallocated net income; privilege taxes on foreign corporations must be measured by allocated issued stock or by allocated net income.[6] Finally, a franchise tax may apply to a domestic corporation whose sole business is interstate commerce, but a privilege tax on foreign corporations could not be so extended, even if nondiscriminatory.

Constitutional limitations with respect to gross income or earnings taxes are strict. Receipts arising out of transactions in interstate commerce may not be taxed under a gross receipts tax levied as a state privilege tax, or not apportioned to the business done in the state. If a state levies a gross income tax on public service corporations in lieu of a property tax on their property, the tax may be measured by interstate as well as intrastate re-

[6] The Supreme Court will not nullify an apportionment formula unless it gives palpably disproportionate results that make it patent that the tax is levied upon interstate commerce rather than upon an intrastate privilege.

ceipts. The burden of such a gross receipts tax, however, must not greatly exceed the burden which would be imposed by the property tax it replaces.

ADMINISTRATIVE CONSIDERATIONS

In general, business taxes are somewhat easier and cheaper to administer than personal taxes. All but the smallest business concerns keep better records on their transactions and finances than do ordinary individuals. These records facilitate the computation of tax liability and reduce the likelihood of error, and they simplify the task of checking the tax returns when such checking is necessary. The complexity of the structure and operations of some concerns is so great, however, that inquiry into their returns is an administrative task of great difficulty and high cost.

Business concerns are, moreover, less likely to attempt tax evasion than are individuals. The adverse publicity that may follow disclosure of attempted tax evasion can seriously weaken a firm's position in the community. Since many businessmen are persuaded, rightly or wrongly, that they can pass their taxes on to the purchasers of their commodities or services, they are less inclined to impede levies whose burdens are thought to rest on others. As a rule, all but small businesses will find tax evasion difficult, even if they want to try it. But business concerns will not hesitate to seek means of tax avoidance. The businessman who is alert to find legal ways of outwitting his competitors can see no reason for overlooking any loophole in the tax laws. To aid him, he has the advice of legal counsel, expert at picking flaws in statutes and finding "jokers" in court decisions. If a tax law minutely classifies business enterprise and burdens some classes more lightly than others, the businessman will try to make his concern conform as closely as possible with the classes of business activity subjected to the low tax rates. If there is a possibility that some constitutional provision may protect his concern from a particular tax levy, the businessman will make the most of that possibility.

Hence, in the levy of a business tax, it is essential that the statute be worded in simple, inclusive, unequivocal language. Distributional considerations which dictate special treatment of particular classes of business activity must often be scrapped, lest such special treatment prove a breach in the uniform front of the tax statute and permit the escape of concerns intended to be subject to the full application of the tax. Legislative committees concerned with drafting business tax statutes, and administrative bodies charged with drafting regulations for the assessment and collection of the tax, might well seek the advice of business organizations interested in obtaining a tax law uniform and fair in its application.

Business tax laws and the regulations concerning them should be so composed that a minimum labor of reporting is imposed on the taxpaying concerns. Reduction of business tax "compliance costs" is as vital a goal for tax administrators as paring the direct costs of administration. Much unnecessary reporting and negotiating remain, however.[7] New tax laws and changes in the old frequently add further complication.

Intrastate uniformity. Complexity in a state's method of business taxation multiplies administrative problems, for the administrative agencies as well as for the taxpayers, and the possibilities of tax avoidance are increased. When various types of business enterprise are subjected to different taxes resulting in higher and lower tax burdens, many firms will employ legal subterfuges to place themselves in the lower-taxed category. Sometimes the subterfuge can be outlawed by litigation—to the expense and irritation of both parties. But often, when statutes are carelessly drawn, the courts uphold the subterfuge, and the avoidance is stamped with judicial approval. All too frequently, the subterfuge never comes to the attention of the tax administration and is successful in fact if not in law. Furthermore, scattering the attention of the administrative agencies over a dozen or a score of separate business taxes prevents the economies resulting from uniform regulations and large-scale handling of tax returns.

Because of these considerations, many students of taxation advocate the substitution of a general business tax for the series of special business taxes now found in many states. The National Tax Association has been an outstanding champion for the principle of uniform intrastate business taxation. This does not necessarily mean one single, general, state business tax, applying uniformly to manufacturing, mercantile, and service enterprises, to financial institutions, and to public service enterprises. Constitutional and economic considerations may dictate differing tax treatment for broad categories of enterprises. And special regulatory taxes, such as the levies on chain stores and on the liquor business, cannot be fitted into a uniform business tax system. But at the most, four or five basic forms of business taxation could be established within each state, with uniform application of each class of tax. Incidental business license taxes, unless imposed for specific regulatory purposes, or systems of arbitrary license levies like those found in the Southern states, are especially condemned.

ECONOMIC CONSIDERATIONS

Because of the diverse forms and characters of American business taxes, no single theory of incidence or economic effect, no single distributive argument, can be applied to them. Rather, the whole body of economic and distributive theory must be drawn upon to throw light on the various

[7] An illustration may be helpful. Some states, but not all, allow corporations in computing net income for state tax purposes to deduct federal income taxes. But the tax laws may be completely silent on how total federal tax is to be allocated among states. Corporation officials may then have to negotiate with state administrators—a shifting group—on actual application of the law.

and complex problems presented by this group of taxes. Various theoretical business tax issues have already been explored in earlier chapters.

Incidence of business net income taxes.[8] Because business taxes have become so very heavy, the economic aspects of these taxes is a vital current issue. Economic theory has long posited that a general net business income tax on *pure profit* in the sense of an economic surplus cannot be shifted, that its incidence is exclusively on the owners of the taxed concerns. American corporation income taxes, however, are not general taxes on pure profit, and any simple categorical conclusion that they are nonshiftable would be unwarranted. The same is true of personal income taxes to the extent that they apply to business income. It is now generally accepted that the burden of these taxes is divided. Part is borne by consumers, part by some of the suppliers and employees of the companies that pay these taxes. Part is borne, through capitalization, by former owners of corporate common stocks. And part remains on present corporate owners, notably common shareholders.

Unfortunately, this line of analysis does not take account of what would happen if the net income tax did not exist or were very much lower. What other revenue devices and what spending policies would differ, and how? We are dealing with magnitudes that might reach 6 per cent of national income. Some of the spending and tax could alter conditions in ways that would modify the results otherwise expected. Perhaps the most realistic conclusion is that the longer the tax is in existence, the more broadly and generally it is diffused through the economy.

In the short run, other things the same, a change in the tax on business net income would give the business no power to raise prices and no reason to lower them.[9] In the longer run, however, the tax will affect supply conditions. For one thing, a business net income tax tends to reduce saving and thereby the ability to invest. For another, together with the personal income tax, it reduces the attractiveness of risk-taking and consequently impedes capital formation somewhat. This result is most probable where risks are great. The higher the tax, the less the productive capacity that will be built and maintained. The supply of goods and services will tend to be less, and prices higher, than if the tax were lower or did not exist. To some extent the tax must be shifted in the long run to consumers in the form of higher prices.

Thereby it operates somewhat as a broad but uneven sales tax. It affects, however, a far wider spread of purchases than would the most general of

[8] A good summary of present opinion with references to other sources is B. U. Ratchford and P. B. Han, "The Burden of the Corporate Income Tax," *National Tax Journal*, Dec., 1957, pp. 310–324.

[9] There is the practical possibility that a business might seize upon a sizable reduction in a net income tax rate to lower its prices in the hope of getting a larger volume of business. This situation is not probable under the conditions ordinarily assumed in price theory, but it is by no means inconceivable.

sales taxes, since it influences the prices and charges of financial transactions, house rentals, transportation, medicines, and other items to which no sales tax would apply. Over short-run periods, moreover, part of the tax may be shifted backward to groups of suppliers who are in a weak bargaining position or to employees who cannot move to other jobs or who have special types of compensation contracts (for example, with profit-sharing arrangements).

This analysis of the shiftability of part of the federal corporation income tax does not complete the story of its incidence. Part of the nonshifted burden of the present tax has been capitalized. Investors who purchased corporate common stock subsequent to tax rate increases, upon the assumption that the higher tax rates would continue for some time, presumably took account of the tax in the price they paid for their shares. Former shareholders rather than new purchasers of corporate shares thus bear some of the tax. To the extent that present stockowners acquired their holdings prior to a tax rate increase, they currently bear part of the tax.

Incidence of other business taxes. Capital stock corporate franchise and privilege taxes constitute special discriminations against a particular form of business enterprise. Unincorporated enterprises are not subject to these taxes. Even where certain corporation taxes are intended to be substitutes for taxes to which unincorporated business concerns are subject, the burden of the special corporation tax is nearly always heavier than that of the tax for which it is substituted. Because of the inequality of the tax burden which they impose, much of the capital stock corporation franchise and privilege taxes may be nonshiftable. In those lines of business activity where the corporate form is so prevalent that unincorporated enterprises are a negligible competitive factor, capital stock taxes may be shifted to consumers. No general rules can be laid down on the business license taxes, although they are probably more often shifted to consumers than not. Many are fixed taxes which give a large concern an advantage over a smaller firm paying the same amount of tax.

The possibility of shifting state and local business taxes is affected by the circumstance that such taxes are levied by governments whose jurisdictions are geographically limited, whereas the markets in which many businesses compete are interstate. Variations in the business tax burdens imposed by different states result in inequalities which may not be offset by the quality of government services. Consequently, complete shifting of taxes levied by the heavier-taxing states may be impossible when the industries of both high-taxing and low-taxing states compete in a common market. Inequality in the general burdens of the business taxes of two states does not in itself cause the business taxes of the heavier-taxing state to be nonshiftable. The difficulty of shifting a business tax results from the inequality of tax burdens imposed upon *particular* enterprises located in different states but directly in competition with each other—the inequality in tax burdens between the steel corporation taxed under property taxes and a capital stock tax in State A and the steel corporation taxed under property taxes and an income tax in State B, the inequality in tax burdens between the shoe manufacturer taxed under a turnover tax in State C and the one taxed under a corporate excess tax in State D.

State and local taxes on insurance premiums and on public service enterprises, and even the federal income tax on utilities, are quite generally shifted. Regulatory commissions, federal and state, view these taxes as costs to be allowed in setting rates which will yield a reasonable return over and above all costs of operation. As noted in Chapter 8, however, several obstacles stand in the way of smooth and immediate shifting of public service enterprise taxes. In some cases, such as transit lines and railroads, demand may be inadequate, or so elastic that rate increases because of raised taxes will drive away so much business that, in effect, no recovery of the tax increase is possible. Political pressures on regulatory authorities sometimes prevent or delay authorization of tax-compensation rate increases. Consequently, there is commonly a lag between a change in tax burden on a public service enterprise and its shift to the consumer. Furthermore, the rate schedules of some public service enterprises are of such nature that a small change in tax burden cannot be compensated by a corresponding modification of rate schedules.

A consideration that confuses the incidence of all special business taxes is that they are deductible costs under federal income tax. Marginal businesses, operating at break-even or loss, cannot benefit from such deductions as do more successful enterprises. This condition tends to make these business taxes more shiftable than they otherwise would be. As an offsetting factor, to whatever extent federal income taxes on business income are shifted to the consumer, they are presumably rendered less shiftable by the deductions for the special business taxes. However, the amounts are so small as to be "lost in the shuffle."

Distributive considerations. The distributive aspects of business taxes are confused. When a business tax is shifted forward to consumers, its ultimate burden is likely to be generally proportional, but with a modest regressive element. When a business tax cannot be so shifted, its ultimate burden may embody elements of progression; the average income of owners of business enterprises is generally higher than that of the rest of the population, although there are many exceptions.[10] On a group with the

[10] For a scholarly analysis, see D. M. Holland, *The Income Tax Burden on Stockholders* (National Bureau of Economic Research, Princeton University Press, 1958). At the upper income levels, the corporation income tax rate of 52 per cent is less than the personal income tax rate. On undistributed profit, therefore, the corporation tax, compared with the personal income tax that would be due if the earnings were paid out in dividends, is relatively more burdensome on stockholders at lower income levels than on those at the top.

same income, say $15,000, the tax will impose burdens that vary widely depending upon the amount of stock owned.

Since the burden of business taxes can be traced to the general consuming public, to the owners of the taxed concerns, or to employees and suppliers, it may well be questioned whether such a roundabout method of imposing tax burdens on individuals is necessary or desirable. Were the economic factor the only one to be considered, it might indeed be difficult to make out a sound case for business taxes. However, those of states and localities get collateral support from a special "benefit" consideration.

Most individuals lead double economic lives—a private life of consumption, a business life of production. Government functions supplement both aspects of the individual's existence. Frequently, however, the individual's personal life is conducted in one taxing jurisdiction while his business activities are located in another jurisdiction. The government in whose jurisdiction the nonresident conducts his business activities may not tax the individual under a personal tax. Therefore, the argument runs, it is unjust to require governments to aid business enterprises within their territories if at the same time the firms do not compensate the state or local treasury because the owners of the enterprises or the consumers of the products have personal residence elsewhere. Consequently, state and local governments may properly draw part of their general tax revenue from business enterprises. Public service enterprises using streets and highways for their tracks, wires, and pipes are considered to enjoy "special" privileges or franchises which justify the special taxes imposed.

This "justification" of business taxation is, however, essentially an after-the-fact rationalization. The fundamental reason for business taxation is its convenience as a method of obtaining substantial revenue. Here, as in other fields of taxation, principles of "tax justice" are humble handmaidens to fiscal expediency.

Business taxation and the pattern of economic development. We have seen that different types and amounts of taxes are imposed upon different businesses. Consequently, burdens are higher on some businesses than on others. Unless the extra burdens are matched by extra benefits, businesses with the higher burdens are at a disadvantage relative to other businesses. The prices of their products or services may include relatively more payment for government services—taxes—than the prices of other products or services. If this is true, the more heavily taxed businesses will not develop as fully (unless demand is completely inelastic) as they would if they were taxed on a par with other businesses; fewer units of product can be sold because the unit price is higher. If the tax is not shifted to consumers, the returns to owners, employees, or suppliers must be less than the returns from other businesses. The survival of the more heavily taxed businesses will consequently be threatened, their development retarded. The adjustment to differential tax burdens may be very slow; it will be difficult to detect because adjustments to many other forces will be in process at the same time. Yet, adjustment is certain.

What businesses are most heavily taxed in this country? Unfortunately, we do not have enough data to answer this question clearly. There are variations from state to state. The stage of the business cycle has a bearing on the answer, as does the legal form of organization, the size of the business, the capital structure, and other considerations. It is hard to appraise the significance of these different causes of variations in tax burdens. Moreover, a discriminatory tax burden may be placed on a class of business by a special tax on the product or service of the business, though not on the business itself; the development of the alcoholic beverage and tobacco industries has certainly been affected by the heavy taxes on liquor and cigarettes.

Privately owned utilities, including railroads, are generally taxed more heavily than most other businesses. They have large amounts of property subject to property tax. They are burdened by many special state and local taxes. Railroads pay heavy taxes for employee pensions. As corporations, railroads and other utilities are subject to many general taxes imposed on general business corporations although, since many have large amounts of debt financing, their corporation income taxes are reduced by larger interest deductions than most other businesses.

The discussion of such variations in business tax burden could be continued at great length. An extensive list of businesses receiving some kind of favored tax treatment could be compiled—one might start with those allowed depletion deductions which exceed the owner's investment—as well as a list of businesses that are victims of fiscal discrimination. These differences in tax treatment help mold the pattern of our economic life and lead to a different allocation of resources than would develop if all businesses were taxed alike, or not taxed at all. Yet there are so many other factors of equal or greater importance than tax differentials, and the forces of economic adjustment may take such a long time to work their effects, that there are few specific developments that can be attributed with certainty to inequalities in business tax treatment.[11]

Taxation and business location. What is the effect of state-local taxation, including property taxes, on business location? This question has been of unusual interest in recent years, not only because taxes have been rising but also because the tremendous growth of the economy has heightened concern about *where* development is to take place. Unfortunately, however, it is difficult to learn just how much total taxes compare in different

[11] Depletion allowances stimulate more output than would otherwise appear. In the important case of oil, however, state restrictions offset some of the effect of the tax provision.

areas and what is the effect of the differences on business—in the short run and the long.

One of the most revealing of recent studies found that for 6,860 firms doing business in Minnesota, 1953 state-local taxes ranged from 10.09 per cent of gross receipts for one electric utility to 0.32 for petroleum and coal processing.[12] The average was 0.85. In general, the firms with high rates were in industries whose location was determined by their activity—utilities and real estate, for example. The great majority of firms with some freedom to shift activities paid state-local taxes considerably under 1 per cent of gross receipts—and undoubtedly shifted much to consumers.

Moreover, the significant consideration, perhaps, is not so much taxes in relation to gross receipts as in relation to net income. A rational business decision will rest on what can remain after all expenses in different locations. The range of tax in relation to net income was tremendous, but a substantial proportion of firms paid state-local taxes that were over 16 per cent of net income, with the average almost 19 per cent. Interstate differences in state-local taxes of a fourth or more can certainly be large in relation to net income.

The study then tried to compare taxes in eight states in the region in the case of a hypothetical corporation. It found four instances in which the total was less than half that in the top two states. Allowing for offsets due to deductibility of state-local taxes in computing federal taxes, and assuming the same shiftability, the four states imposed burdens at least one-quarter less than the two highest. Without doubt there will be cases in which differences in state-local taxes are large enough in relation to net income to have a significant bearing on a decision about where to locate or expand.

Other factors, especially labor and transport expenses, are usually much larger than taxes in costs. Yet to the extent that such expenses are otherwise equal, tax differences can be important. Another qualification, however, must be considered—the quality of public services. If higher taxes provide better services—better for the firms which must pay the larger amounts—the net effect may be to attract business.

The statements of businessmen regarding the importance of state-local taxes in location decisions cover a wide range of view. The following statement probably represents the view of most business leaders:

[12] Minnesota Tax Study Committee, *Staff Report* . . . (Minneapolis, 1956), Chapter 4. Other useful studies are C. C. Bloom, *State and Local Tax Differentials and the Location of Manufacturing* (State University of Iowa, Iowa City, 1956); J. S. Floyd, Jr., *The Effects of Taxation on Industrial Location* (University of North Carolina Press, Chapel Hill, 1952). A study of state-local taxes in the metropolitan New York area found wide variations, depending often upon the type of business. The absolute net differences, however, would rarely be as much as one per cent of sales. The prevailing tendency appears to be to reduce differentials in the region. A. K. Campbell, "Taxes and Industrial Location in the New York Metropolitan Region," *National Tax Journal,* Sept., 1958, pp. 195–218.

We have never sought tax-free status, special favors, special privileges or special advantages. On the contrary, we feel that, if we are associated with a community, we should bear our fair share of its operating expenses. We recognize the ever-increasing burdens placed on states and municipalities by the demands of education and other institutions. Industry by and large has not and will not dodge its responsibilities in this area.

Looking at the other side of the coin, we, in common with most other industrial enterprises, feel that we should not be exposed to special penalties or special harassments. We are well advised to avoid locations where there is a feeling that the corporate citizen, inanimate and voiceless, can be pushed around with comparative safety.[13]

Business taxation and economic progress. What about the economic consequences of our business tax system as a whole? Is it a drag on our economic progress? At first glance it would certainly seem so, since it burdens the very organizations we rely upon for most of our productive activity and our real income. Here, in a sense, is a tax on efficiency, and progress is less likely if efficiency is penalized than if it is encouraged.

But our business taxes could be eliminated or reduced only by substituting or increasing other taxes. We could replace half of the federal corporation income tax by adding about 10 percentage points to all the brackets of the personal income tax. Would not this hobble economic progress as much as the corporate tax burden thereby eliminated? Or we could replace some of the federal corporation income tax and some of the state business taxes by a system of general sales taxes. By absorbing consumer purchasing power, these would also constrain business. Most fiscal economists, after weighing the foregoing and similar questions, would probably agree that more of our present tax load should be placed *directly* on individuals and less on business. There is, however, no practical prospect of removing business taxes entirely.

It is sometimes proposed that the business system could be improved by incorporating tax *incentives* to encourage or discourage certain types of action. Still more liberal depreciation than provided in 1954 and 1958 is proposed to spur real investment. Favored business tax treatment to stimulate housing is widely discussed. These and more unusual incentive plans deserve careful study. As a general rule, the underlying premises of these incentive proposals are themselves the subject of sharp controversy, and the advocates of these plans tend to claim too much. Nevertheless, many incentive proposals undoubtedly warrant sympathetic attention, but attention which takes full account of costs and alternatives.[14]

[13] R. L. Hershey, Vice-President and Member of the Executive Committee of the du Pont Corporation, in an address, *A New Plant in Town,* July 11, 1958. Other business officials emphasize the importance of tax administration which does not abuse its power and discriminate against firms once they are operating in an area.

[14] Some of the highly impressive postwar recovery of the West German economy may be attributable to tax incentives granted industries of special importance. See R. G. Wertheimer, "Tax Incentives in Germany," *National Tax Journal,* Dec., 1957, pp. 325–338.

One of the more disturbing conditions, as we think of the needs for economic growth, is the difficulty present taxes create for new firms. Accumulation of equity capital by ploughing back earnings is harder than it would be if pre-World War II rates prevailed. And equity capital is important not only in itself but also because it makes borrowing easier. The established business has an advantage which does not result from any inherent element of productivity. In the case of large businesses, this relative advantage is not only the possession of capital. In addition, the firm has income from existing operations, perhaps a variety of types. As it spends on research or to get some new line under way, it can deduct the costs from the profits of other operations with consequent reduction of taxes. The Treasury, in effect, bears half of the development cost, just as it will reap half of the profit. The new firm must also expect to share profits with the government without, however, equal opportunity to share the costs of getting the new operation established.

PROBLEMS

1. Evaluate the reasons for and against taxing insurance premiums.

2. Find out the license taxes on business imposed in your state and in your locality.

3. "The insignificant revenue from chain-store taxes shows that these levies are no longer significant." Discuss.

4. "Although there is no prospect of a reduction in state taxes on business, there ought to be real opportunity for improvement. The 'value-added' base looks highly promising as a substitute for today's crude levies." Discuss.

5. "We should stop trying to answer the essentially unanswerable question of who pays the tax on corporation net income and concentrate our effort on trying to find its effects and to remove those that are undesirable." Discuss.

6. "There is no question that business taxes in themselves retard progress. But this is to be expected, because the function of taxes is to take resources from private use for governmental use." Discuss.

7. What would be arguments for and against doubling taxes on electric and telephone utility companies?

8. Try to find for a particular business the importance it attaches to state-local taxes in deciding where to expand its activities.

9. What taxes might be increased to make up for a substantial reduction in the rate on corporations? Give arguments for and against such a change.

CHAPTER 16

Commodity, Sales, and Related Excise Taxes[1]

TAXES on commodities and services—consumption taxes—are familiar, although because some are hidden these taxes are less familiar than their revenue importance would justify. Some of these levies fall upon specific things or services (cigarettes or airplane travel),[2] some upon sales generally. Although they exist primarily to produce revenue, and do so on a large scale, they exist for other reasons as well, and they do have nonrevenue effects.

Before the Civil War, tariff duties were the primary revenue source for the federal government. Since that time their revenue importance has declined, and today their significance lies in their nonrevenue effects. Other commodity and service taxes, however, have gained an important role, far different from the place once envisaged—as temporary sources of wartime revenue, plus the partially regulatory taxes on liquor and tobacco. A still more striking change has occurred at the state level, where general sales and specific excises, notably those on tobacco and liquor (and gasoline) have become major revenue sources. Hundreds of localities, too, are making significant use of consumption taxes.

CUSTOMS (TARIFF) DUTIES

A tariff or customs duty is a tax on imported commodities.[3] Local governments, especially in Europe, once levied import duties under the name

[1] Exclusive of gasoline taxes, which, because of their special relationship to highway financing, are considered in Chapter 17, and utility and insurance premium taxes discussed in Chapter 15. An excellent study is J. F. Due, *Sales Taxation* (University of Illinois Press, Urbana, 1957). The description and analysis draw upon long and intimate contact with the taxes here and abroad.

[2] Specific commodity taxes and general sales taxes are frequently levied as license taxes on manufacturing or mercantile enterprises, measured by the quantity or value of the commodities sold, rather than as excises on the commodities themselves. In this chapter, a business tax *measured by* the quantity or value of commodities produced or sold is considered a commodity tax.

[3] Export taxes imposed by some countries are also customs duties.

of transit tax or *octroi.* Today, however, in the United States (by constitutional provision) and in most other countries, import duties are reserved to the national government.

Tariffs may be levied for one or more of three reasons: (1) To raise revenue, rates may be imposed on commodities not produced in the taxing country but whose entry is easily watched. (2) A tariff may be imposed on the import of a commodity produced and subject to a domestic excise; the custom rate is identical with the excise, to equalize the tax burden on the domestic and foreign products. (3) A tariff may be set on imported commodities competing with articles produced domestically to reduce the competition of imports with the domestic products. The first is a "tariff for revenue only," the second a "compensatory tariff," and the third a "protective tariff." The "protective" aspect has always been of greater concern to Congress and to economists than revenue. Today's yield of $750 million in a year of prosperity is of less concern than are the effects of the tariff on the flow of trade.

The "protective" character of the American customs duties has been considerably modified during the past quarter-century. Since 1933, a number of treaties with individual countries, and then a much broader agreement—the 1947 General Agreement on Tariffs and Trade—now covering over 30 countries, have substantially reduced our tariff rates. Many important imports, chiefly raw materials, are not subject to any customs duty. However, burdens on many kinds of manufactured goods remain high enough to impede certain elements of foreign trade substantially, and considerable high tariff sentiment persists.

Economics of the protective tariff. The initial effect of a protective tariff is to increase the price of the imported article, thus persuading purchasers to turn to a competing domestic item. The increased demand for the domestic article tends to force up its price also.

Higher profits for a protected domestic industry encourage it to expand production. If a protected industry is in its "infant" stage, economies of larger-scale production and distribution may result from its growth. Conceivably, the price of the domestic commodity may fall to that paid for the imported article before the customs duty was imposed, or even below. However, if the protected industry is not well adapted to development within the taxing country, or if it is mature or must accomplish expansion on an increasing-cost basis, the tariff produces a new price higher than the old, though not necessarily by the full amount of the tax.

Proponents of protective tariffs advance four major arguments: (1) Assistance to an "infant" industry, as has been stated above. (2) In the case of maladapted or increasing-cost industries, the added cost to consumers is counterbalanced by expansion of domestic industry, with more employment, greater use of domestic materials, and higher profits—at the expense of the countries whose exports are reduced by the tariff. (3) Many foreign goods undersell domestic goods only because foreign wages are lower, so that high tariff protects American wage scales. (4) Some maladapted industries may need to be fostered for reasons of national defense.

Five major arguments are advanced against protective tariffs: (1) The principle of "comparative advantage" shows that each nation profits most by producing and exporting those goods and services for which it is relatively most suited and by importing items produced under relatively favorable conditions in other countries. A protective tariff offsets such "comparative advantages" so that, in the words of Adam Smith, "the industry of the country, therefore, is thus turned away from a more, to a less advantageous employment, and the exchangeable value of its annual produce, instead of being increased, according to the intention of the lawgiver, must necessarily be diminished. . . ." (2) Insulation from foreign competition leaves domestic firms with less pressure to become as efficient as possible. Monopolies are likely to develop in protected industries. (3) Reduction of imports from other countries reduces their receipts of dollars. This reduces their financial capacity to buy American exports. Export industries suffer, as do farmers. Moreover, the loss of real income by foreigners reduces their ability to finance defense—our loss if they are allies. (4) Protective tariffs breed retaliatory quotas, tariffs, and other restrictions abroad. These further reduce the export markets of American agriculture and exporting industries and curtail the advantages to be gained from specialization and the division of labor. High wage rates can rest soundly on high productivity; foreigners, no matter how low their wage rates, want to sell here to buy. What do they buy? Very largely products of factories where our wage rates are high—but also where productivity is high. (5) Most tariff revenue comes from the mass of consumers. Even more important, to the extent that rates are truly "protective," prices of domestic items are raised. Thus, the cost of living is increased, part of the increase going to the government (if the rate is not prohibitive), part going to the protected industries, and part being the economic loss resulting from production under conditions less favorable than in other parts of the world. Export industries and their workers bear a real but concealed burden.

Rate structure. Tariff rates, here and abroad, take two forms—specific and ad valorem. A specific duty is one levied according to the weight, bulk, length, or some other unit of measurement; sulphured cherries, for example, are taxed 5½ cents per pound if unpitted, 9½ cents per pound without pits. An ad valorem rate is levied as a percentage of value; roller bearings are taxed 17.5 per cent on their value plus 4 cents a pound. Both forms sometimes apply to the same product.

Specific customs rates tend to place a relatively heavier burden on the coarser and cheaper grades of goods than on the better grades, since the rates bear no relation to value. Such rates are markedly regressive. Interests seeking protection often like them because prohibitive levies on cheap goods can be concealed by rates which do not appear prohibitive when related to more expensive grades, and because higher rates can be imposed when expressed in flat, rather than percentage, terms. A great virtue is the relative ease of their assessment.

An *ad valorem* rate does not discriminate against coarser and cheaper grades of goods. Great administrative difficulties are entailed, however. Choice must be made between several prices—the foreign producer's price, the F.O.B. price, the C.I.F. price, or the American selling price. Arbitrary values must be established for consigned goods. Price changes on thousands of taxed items must constantly be taken into account.

American customs duties follow no consistent policy as to form of rates. For some items the rates are specific, for others ad valorem. Still others are subject to supplementary ad valorem rates superimposed upon basic specific rates. In some cases, alternative rates are established, the higher at any time being applied. Examples may be found of specific rates graduated according to the value of the import.

When a raw material or semimanufactured import is taxed, an extra cost element is added to the price of all articles produced from the imported item or similar domestic items. If American producers are to be placed on equal footing with their foreign competitors, imports of the final article must be subjected to a "compensatory" duty equal to the amount of the raw material duty entering into the cost of the finished article produced domestically.

Rate determination. The rates set by Tariff Acts are determined largely by pressure-group tactics applied to House and Senate committees, to individual members of Congress, and sometimes to the President himself. The interests of consumers and export industries are too diffuse to focus effectively. The schedules ultimately embodied in law tend to be a hodgepodge of logrolled "protections" for the industries whose lobbies are powerful enough or skillful enough to win their demands. The "dutiable list" contains about 1,500 paragraphs and hundreds of subparagraphs, bewildering in the complexity of their specifications and rate schedules, largely ignoring the new product developments of the past quarter-century, and with little interrelationship other than that of alphabetical sequence.

Since 1934, however, determination of many of the tariff rates actually applied has been by the State Department and other executive agencies rather than by Congress, under broad reciprocity powers granted by Congress. In this way, agreements for mutual tariff reduction have been negotiated with other countries without Congressional logrolling. However, Congress in renewing the authority for such agreements—for four years in 1958—has set conditions which make the permanence of these reductions uncertain. Foreign trade, therefore, cannot develop confidently on patterns of highest efficiency.

FEDERAL COMMODITY, SERVICE, AND TRANSFER EXCISES

Because of the constitutional requirement that direct taxes be apportioned, the federal government may not tax commodities as property unless the tax is apportioned among the states according to population. But the federal government has ample power to levy taxes on the manufacture or on the sale of commodities, such taxes being construed as excises on acts rather than as direct taxes on property. A federal commodity tax may not, however, be extended to goods intended for sale to foreigners, since export taxes are forbidden.

Besides taxes on the manufacture or sale of certain commodities, the

TABLE 16–1

Selected Federal Sales Tax and Excise Rates and Yields, 1959

Item	*Rate*	*Estimated Yield (millions)*
Alcoholic beverages:		
Distilled spirits	$10.50 gallon	$2,140
Beer	$9 barrel	760
Wine	17–67¢ gallon (some higher)	90
Cigarettes	8¢ package	1,700
Cigars	$2.50–$20.00 per 1000	46
Lubricating oil	6¢ gallon	76
Gasoline	3¢ gallon	1,710
Tires and tubes	5–8¢ pound	289
Automobiles	10 per cent	1,400
Trucks and buses	10 per cent	248
Automobile parts and accessories	8 per cent	170
Electric, gas, and oil appliances	5 per cent	75
Electric light bulbs	10 per cent	30
Radio sets, phonographs, television, and records	10 per cent	194
Mechanical refrigerators	5 per cent	46
Business machines	10 per cent	100
Furs	10 per cent[1]	32
Jewelry	10 per cent[1]	165
Luggage	10 per cent[1]	62
Photographic equipment	10 per cent	24
Toilet preparations, cosmetics	10 per cent[1]	108
Sugar	½¢ pound	95
Telephone, telegraph, etc.	10 per cent	698
Transportation of persons	10 per cent	230
Club dues	20 per cent	64
Admissions over $1.00	10 per cent	55
Stock transfer	varying	105

[1] On retail selling price.

SOURCE: *The Budget . . . for . . . 1959,* with allowances for August, 1958, revisions.

federal government imposes excises on the sale of certain services and on various transfers.

First from a revenue viewpoint are the liquor excises—$10.50 per gallon on distilled spirits, $9 per barrel on beer, and from 17 cents to $2.25 per gallon on wines. Tobacco taxes also embody varying rates, with the 8 cents per package tax on cigarettes being much the most important. The justifications for these taxes are their heavy yield, their ease of administration (except for the tax on spirits), and their imposition on items whose consumption many people feel should be, or at least can be, reduced. The tax on gasoline and to a smaller extent the taxes on oil, tires, and other auto products find special justification in benefit; the federal government spends large amounts to aid auto, truck, and airline transport and now earmarks most of the automotive tax revenue for highways. One set of excises has been justified as applying to "luxuries" and "semiluxuries." Club dues, amusement admissions over $1.00, radios, musical instruments, cameras, toilet preparations, furs, jewelry, perfume, luggage, film, sporting goods, playing cards, television sets, and firearms are taxed.

Related to these "luxury" excises are "control" excises imposed in 1941 to reduce consumption of articles whose production competed with the war effort. Among the articles subjected to such "control" taxation were automobiles and parts, mechanical refrigerators, electrical appliances, tires and tubes, and business machines.[4] These levies were retained after the war for revenue purposes; some were raised during Korean hostilities and remain at the higher level even though there is no desire to discourage consumption of these specific items any longer.

Telephone toll calls, telegraph and cable messages, electricity, and pipeline charges were all taxed in the 1930's for revenue purposes. During World War II, the rates of these taxes were raised and new taxes were imposed on freight (3 per cent) and on passenger transportation (15 per cent). The objective was twofold, added revenue and reduction of usage. The rate on passenger travel is now 10 per cent, whereas the tax on freight was removed in 1958. Electricity sales are no longer subject to federal tax. Transfer taxes on bond and stock sales, and on other conveyances, are imposed for revenue reasons only. A final group of federal excises is strictly regulatory, intended to discourage purchase of the taxed items, and produces little or no revenue. Sale of a machine gun is taxed $200. Gambling transactions are taxed 10 per cent, primarily to compel disclosures which will aid state and local law enforcement. Opium is taxed one cent a pound when sold for medicinal purposes, $300 a pound otherwise, marihuana $100 per ounce.

This "system" is hardly a model of a rationally balanced set of levies. Criticisms have led to some improvements, such as the removal of several

[4] The tax of nearly one-half cent a pound on sugar is part of the general system of agricultural controls. There is a compensating tariff.

minor crudities and the major reform of the abolition of the tax on freight.[5] The Treasury, however, has strongly opposed most proposals for change. It knows that these are predominantly aimed at reducing the revenue, that if one industry group succeeds, others will fight for comparable reductions, and that replacements for the revenue lost will also be bitterly opposed.

STATE AND LOCAL TAXES ON SPECIFIC COMMODITIES AND SERVICES

Prior to the 1920's, a few Southern states based special license taxes on value or amount of production or sales. Some of the pre-Prohibition state liquor taxes were based on sales. New York and a few other states taxed transfers of stock. In 1919, Alabama imposed a tax on carbonic acid used in soft drinks. Connecticut levied an admissions tax and Iowa a cigarette tax in 1921. These three laws marked out the main fields of state commodity and service taxation until state liquor taxation could be revived after 1933.

Constitutional considerations. States levy their commodity taxes as excises on the act of manufacture or sale. Unlike similar federal levies, such state taxes are subject to the interstate commerce limitation. A state commodity tax applying to merchants may not cover sales to customers outside the taxing state. A tax on the output of manufacturers or of mining companies, however, is not construed as a tax on sales but as an excise on the acts of manufacturing or of mining, measured by sales. The interstate commerce limitation does not apply to such taxes, on the theory that they do not involve any act of commerce, interstate or otherwise.

Liquor and beverage taxes. In addition to license taxes on manufacturers, wholesalers, retailers, and dispensers, every nonprohibition state imposes "gallonage" taxes on the volume of alcoholic drinks produced or sold within the state.[7] Rates vary. Beer tax rates are lowest; the top rate of almost 10 cents a gallon is the most common, but in one out of four states the rate is under 5 cents a gallon. Wines bear somewhat higher rates, varying with alcoholic content. The rate on distilled spirits is usually around $2 a gallon.

Several states tax soft drinks. In most cases the levy is imposed on the

[5] The excise on freight transportation, per dollar of revenue, was probably the worst of modern excises. It impeded the economic specialization that is imperative for best utilization of resources. It discriminated against cheap, bulky commodities such as grain. It discriminated against persons and areas remote from production or where freight rates are relatively high. It reduced the number of firms competing in any one area. It discriminated against firms that are too small or that for other reasons cannot or do not maintain their own transportation systems. It cut the scale of operation of a decreasing cost industry—the railroads; they lost business to trucks, which, if operated by a company to carry its own products, were exempt.

[7] In 16 states, however, all or most alcoholic beverages are sold by state-operated monopolies, and the state revenue on liquor sales is derived from profits instead of taxes.

extract, syrup, or carbonic-acid gas used to make the beverage. In a few cases, the levy is on the retail sale.

Tobacco products taxes. Forty-three states now tax the sale of cigarettes, eleven cigars, and nine smoking and chewing tobacco and snuff. The total yield is about $600 million a year. Rates for the cigarette taxes are commonly 3 or 4 cents per package of 20. Cigar tax rates are usually graduated according to weight or price of the cigars. Several dozen *cities* also impose cigarette taxes, most commonly at a 2 cents per package rate.

Other state commodity and service taxes. About half the states, and a good many cities, tax admissions to public amusements. The tax is generally collected on a gross receipts basis; Connecticut has a theater tax with a daily charge per theater graduated by seating capacity. Rates range from one-half per cent in Maryland to 10 per cent in Mississippi, South Carolina, and Texas. Several states impose special taxes on admissions to prize fights, athletic exhibitions, or horse races. Rates for these sumptuary taxes are generally higher than for the theater and motion picture taxes. New York State gets about $40 million a year from a tax on stock transfers. Three other states with such taxes receive insignificant revenue. A few cities tax the use of hotel rooms.

STATE GENERAL SALES TAXES

Modern state sales taxes are largely a legacy of the depression of the 1930's. By 1937, almost half the states had such taxes. Only 6 of these "emergency" levies were repealed. Another series of state sales taxes were enacted after World War II. By 1959, there were 33 such taxes in effect, plus 3 broadly based gross receipts taxes. The states using them get over a third of their tax revenue from this source—in a few cases over 40 per cent. New York City, New Orleans, the District of Columbia, many California counties and cities, and about 1,000 Illinois localities, and scores of other local governments in 10 states also levy local retail sales taxes. Most local sales taxes in California, Illinois, Mississippi, and New Mexico are administered as supplements of the state tax. Sales tax revenues naturally depend in part upon the general level of prices; one result of postwar inflation was a substantial increase in sales tax yields.

Scope. Economists distinguish five basic types of general sales tax: (1) retail sales tax; (2) single-stage excise on sales by manufacturers or wholesalers; (3) multiple-stage "gross sales" or "turnover" tax, applying to all sales by manufacturers, wholesalers, and retailers;[8] (4) "gross income" tax, applying not only to sales of tangible commodities but also to gross

[8] Germany imposes a general turnover or cascade tax, and several other countries have taxes which fall more than once on the same base during successive stages of a single series of transactions. Canada imposes a single-stage tax of 10 per cent on manufacturing; the yield is about 20 per cent of total Dominion revenue. Single-stage taxes at the wholesale level are found in Australia, New Zealand, and Switzerland.

income from services; finally (5) the tax on "value added" may be considered a general consumption, as well as a general business, tax. The manufacturers' or wholesalers' excise taxes are poorly adapted to state use, and no state uses either except incidentally. Michigan has a form of "value-added" tax. The other three forms are all employed by the states, with various intermediate forms common. Some retail sales taxes apply exclusively to commodity sales, some extend to certain services, some to public utility charges. "Gross sales" or "turnover" and "gross income" are taxed in a few states and in New York City. This variation in tax bases affects their productivity; for example, a gross income tax applying to all forms of business income will bring several times the yield of a retail sales tax with the same rate.

The most common goal is to tax sales of tangible personal property not intended for resale,[9] plus some utility services in about half the states. Constitutional considerations prevent the application of a state tax to sales made to customers outside the taxing state. Sales to federal agencies are also largely beyond the reach of the states' taxing powers. Real estate is exempt, but lumber and other materials that go into a building are taxed. Capital goods are rarely exempt, even though sales taxes are presumably intended to be impositions on consumption expenditure; to tax machinery and then the output of the machine is to tax the economic value of the machine twice. However, animal feed, seed fertilizer, containers, and industrial fuel are often exempt. To ease the burden on the poor, a few sales taxes exempt food. Rather frequently, sales to or by charitable institutions and local governments are exempt. Administrative and social considerations prompt the exemption of housing (except in some cases rentals to transients), domestic service, medical services, periodicals and newspapers, used property, isolated sales, and certain other categories. But one or more states specifically tax photography, pest control, dry cleaning, storage, rental of business machines, and repair services. Gasoline, liquor, and tobacco sales are sometimes exempted because they are subject to special taxes. And finally, the agricultural lobbies have obtained the exemption of sales of livestock and other farm produce in several states.

Retail sales taxes have an inherent weakness; business consumers of certain products, and even occasional individuals, will, if free to do so, make purchases in neighboring states or communities levying no sales tax. To check this form of avoidance, all sales-tax states but one have imposed "use" taxes, at the same rates as their sales taxes, on commodities bought outside of the taxing state but brought within it for use there.

Rates and minimum exemptions. Most state retail sales taxes have a uniform 3 per cent rate, but 2 per cent applies in 15 states and 3⅓ per cent in Washington. The Arizona, Mississippi, New Mexico, and North Carolina

[9] Sales by a manufacturer, miner, or wholesaler are taxed if not for resale. The tax is not limited to sales by retailers.

taxes, which apply to both wholesalers and retailers, have heavier rates for retailers than for manufacturers and wholesalers. California local rates are generally 1 per cent, those in Illinois and Mississippi 0.5 per cent. New York City, in addition to 3 per cent on retail sales, taxes gross income of certain financial institutions at 1 per cent and gross receipts of other businesses 0.25 per cent. Gross income taxes as found in Indiana and West Virginia may have anywhere from 2 to 9 rate categories.[10]

ADMINISTRATION OF COMMODITY AND SALES TAXES

Much experience in commodity and sales tax administration has now been accumulated by government officials. The businesses that must comply have also gained experience. Hence, administration is now much better than at first. Yet early hopes that these taxes would be easy to administer have proved vain.

A high tax invites evasion. The evasion of high liquor duties through "moonshining" is an old chapter in fiscal history. If, on the other hand, a tax is low, the risks and nuisance of evasion outweigh the benefits, and evasion is likely to be inconsiderable. A moderate tax on a commodity widely used in large quantities is preferable to a high tax upon a little-used item. Nevertheless, revenue necessities and a desire to subject "luxury" items to discriminatingly high rates frequently induce governments to ignore this principle.

The tax base in relation to administration. A universal tax that applied to all sales of all commodities and services by all business organizations, without any exemptions, would be the easiest to administer. There would be some problems on defining "sale," what to do about leases of equipment, when tax liability should accrue on installment sales, and on other points. But they would be trifling in comparison with the administrative problems created by the partial sales taxes and the special commodity taxes actually in effect.

A tax levied as a manufacturers' excise, for example, raises the issue of what constitutes manufacturing. Is a repairman a manufacturer? Is a contracting textile printing plant a manufacturer? And what is the value by which the tax is measured? Should it include manufacturers' charges for warehousing, finance, delivery, installation, servicing?

Who is a retailer, with the obligation of remitting the tax, under a retail sales tax? Must the tax administration try to trace down every wholesaler, manufacturer, or farmer who makes incidental sales at retail? Which sales are items not for resale? When a retail sale includes a substantial element

[10] Diversity of rates in a gross income tax, an admission that such a levy is not uniformly shifted, is a crude attempt to equalize the tax as among classes of enterprise. But unequal burdens as among firms within a class still persist.

of service, as with a restaurant or a prescription druggist, should the tax be based on just the material elements or on the service elements as well?

Exemptions in any sales tax multiply the difficulties of its administration. Every exemption involves dividing lines, and every dividing line adds points that must be watched by both the administration and the taxpayers. It is common, in order to avoid double taxation, to exempt materials which will become part of another item whose sale will be taxed. Yet determining which ingredients will be used up and which resold as physical things, presents difficulties.[11] If foods are exempted under a retail sales tax, what, for example, is the status of canned horse meat intended for dogs? Is a Good Humor food or a confection? If sales outside the state are exempt, how can shipments be checked? Businesses must keep separate records of taxable and exempt sales, and the government must provide some form of check if there is not to be costly evasion. The interstate nature of so much business forces many complicating, though perhaps minor, difficulties.

Point of collection. Commodity tax administration is facilitated if the tax can be levied at a stage in the manufacturing and distributive process where transactions are concentrated in relatively few hands. The earlier in the process of production and distribution that a tax is collected, however, the greater the likelihood that it will be "pyramided," as explained later. The greater also is the difficulty of granting exemptions, such as for items for government use or capital goods. Furthermore, since the manufacturer's price is below the retailer's, a tax expressed as a percentage of price will have to be higher at the factory level to produce any given amount of revenue. Moreover, making adequate allowance for differences in channels of distribution presents problems. If a manufacturer sells at retail, for example, what part of the selling price belongs in the tax base?

For some commodities the greatest concentration may be at the passage of the commodity through the hands of the wholesalers. A tax on such a commodity would be better charged to the wholesaler than to the manufacturer. Responsibility for the payment of state tobacco and liquor taxes is placed on local manufacturers for such part of their products as is sold within the taxing state; wholesale distributors are responsible for the tax on tobacco products or liquor brought in from other states.

The Treasury has estimated that there are nearly twice as many wholesalers as manufacturers and nearly 18 times as many retailers. Retail sales taxes thus impose tax liability at the point—retailing—where transactions are most widely diffused, where prices are highest, and variations

[11] The attempt to avoid taxing the same thing twice in successive stages is commendable. The "physical ingredient" rule, however, does not succeed in accomplishing the objective. It exempts the cloth that goes into a shirt but not the power or lubricants for the machines. Yet the final value includes both. In other words, to avoid taxing an element of value twice, the government must exempt, before the stage of final sale, more than merely the physical ingredients which can be identified in the ultimate product.

in methods of distribution have least significance.[12] But the states have little choice in the matter. A large fraction of the commodities consumed in each state comes from other states and could not be reached by a state manufacturers' excise. And for most lines of distribution, wholesaler-retailer interrelationships overlap state lines, so that a domestic wholesalers' sales tax would not impose a universal or uniform tax on commodity consumption within the taxing state. Most consumption purchases of commodities can be reached only through retailers, and even then—as the development of the "use" tax indicates—the coverage is not complete.

Manner of collection. When a commodity is regularly sold in packages, the tax can be levied in the form of a stamp tax. Manufacturers usually, but sometimes the wholesalers and retailers, are required to purchase revenue stamps and so attach them that the stamp is torn when the package is opened. Absence of a revenue stamp on a package advertises to all dealers and subsequent purchasers that the tax has been evaded. The offense is not easily concealed. Tax collection is accomplished by the sale of the revenue stamps to the taxpayers. The federal liquor, tobacco, and playing card taxes are administered as stamp taxes. State cigarette and liquor taxes are also usually levied as stamp taxes, the stamps being bought and affixed by the manufacturers and importing wholesalers; retailers are responsible for stamping any items that come to them unstamped through irregular channels of trade. Metering devices have been developed to the point where they can be used economically and effectively in place of tax stamps.

For taxes on bottled beer and soft drinks, the "crown tax," a derivation of the stamp tax, is possible. The manufacturers of the crowns, or caps, that are pressed onto the bottles pay the tax in accordance with their sales of bottle caps to the manufacturers of beer and soft drinks.

General sales and gross income taxes apply to many commodities and services for which stamping is not practicable. Such taxes are assessed on the basis of monthly or quarterly returns submitted by the selling concerns liable for the tax. The sellers must usually state and charge the tax to the purchaser as an item separate from the article or service itself. For small retail sales, listed tax schedules ordinarily provide that certain arbitrary amounts must be collected—for example, under a 2 per cent retail sales tax, one cent if the sale is between 15 and 64 cents, two cents if the sale is between 65 cents and $1.14, and so on. Several states allow retailers to retain one per cent or more of collections to compensate for costs.

Enforcement and evasion. Where the payers of a particular tax are few in number, the administration can exercise a careful supervision impossible where the number of taxpayers is large. A general sales or turnover tax suffers because it must be collected in small amounts from a large number

[12] G. E. Lent, "Manufacturers' v. Wholesalers' Sales Tax Base," *Taxes—The Tax Magazine*, Aug., 1958, pp. 573–601.

of taxpayers. The government cannot inquire carefully into the accounts of every little country cider mill and every corner candy store. Instead, it must trust largely to the skill and honesty of small taxpayers. The alternative—to allow an exemption which will eliminate the flood of returns from small firms—reduces the revenue potential. A small sample of all firms and most larger concerns are checked periodically by detailed audit.[13] For example, their figures for a particular day or week out of a two- or three-year period may be carefully scrutinized. If there is any tax deficiency for this sample period, the deficiency proportion is applied to the tax liability for the entire period. Much progress has been made in auditing techniques of state tobacco, liquor, and retail sales taxes. Where advanced methods are used, states can keep evasion and avoidance at perhaps 3 per cent or less. Courts have greatly expanded the authority of states to require out-of-state sellers to collect and remit the tax if the seller has a place of business or agent in the state, if title passes there, or if any of several other conditions exist. To utilize this legal power effectively is much more difficult.

Interstate evasion remains a problem, of course. Residents of a taxing state will buy from mail-order houses in other states or may drive into the nontaxing state and make bulk purchases of the taxed items. However, use taxes, applicable to commodities whose sale is taxable in the state but which have been purchased outside for consumption within the state, are increasingly effective except on small purchases brought in by the buyer. Most states with use taxes provide that, although they are *payable* by the purchaser, they are to be *collected* and *remitted* by the out-of-state seller. The large, responsible mail-order houses have long been required to cooperate with the state tax administrations on this matter. In recent years, states have found more ways to force out-of-state sellers to act as tax collectors. To help the states, Congress amended the postal law to require shippers of cigarettes by mail to charge and hold back any state cigarette use tax. Although there is still considerable evasion of use tax, one item on which "interstate" evasion of sales and use taxes has been well checked is automobiles. Because of the registration requirement, out-of-state purchase of an auto is immediately noted, and payment of the use tax can be enforced at once.

ECONOMIC AND DISTRIBUTIVE CONSIDERATIONS

Commodity and sales taxes can be good revenue producers. If the tax is general or if the specific commodity taxed is widely consumed, even a low rate will produce a relatively large revenue. It can do so with slight inconvenience to the taxpayer. Payment of many small amounts seems easier and more palatable than an annual remittance of the same total. Com-

[13] All returns as filed should also be checked for consistency and arithmetic accuracy. Businesses would generally like prompter final determination.

modity and sales tax yields, although not inelastic, vary less during business fluctuations than revenues from net income or business taxes. State and local governments find this an important merit. Furthermore, revenue from a commodity or sales tax begins to flow in immediately after enactment of the tax or a rate increase. Transients and persons escaping other taxes are caught within the sales tax net. Compared with income taxes, consumption levies may, per dollar of revenue, have less adverse effect on the accumulation of capital for business growth. They probably have a minimum of discouraging effect on incentives or on business location. Against these favorable considerations stand adverse economic and distributive effects which, until recently, economists have generally felt outweighed the favorable factors. Analysis of the incidence and social effects therefore assumes special importance.

Shifting and incidence. The incidence of taxes on particular commodities was studied in Chapter 8. Such taxes are largely shifted to consumers by an increase in price. The price increase will rarely be exactly the amount of the tax. Whether the price rises by more or less than the tax depends upon the elasticity of demand for the commodity and the circumstances of its supply. Prices of joint products or competing commodities are also likely to be affected. Taxes on commodities and services extensively used by businesses, such as the federal taxes on telephone and telegraph service and on business machines, are also eventually shifted in part to consumers.

A uniform retail sales tax should also shift to consumers, though not uniformly. Diminished consumer purchasing power resulting from the tax should unsettle the pre-existing distribution of consumption expenditures, reducing consumption of all items, but sales of luxuries more markedly than sales of necessities. Prices for all consumption items should be affected, according to the varied circumstances of their demand and supply.

Considerable friction, of course, may hinder the process. Merchants sometimes find themselves constrained to absorb at least part of the tax. Where large sales and substantial tax amounts are involved, customers may try to bargain themselves out of the tax. Location near a tax-free area puts a business at some disadvantage in shifting. To the extent that merchants fail to shift a retail sales tax, it operates as a gross income tax on retailing, unequal in its burden.

Still greater obstacles are encountered in shifting manufacturers' excises, and gross sales and gross income taxes applying to manufacturers as well as merchandisers. As a commodity passes from one handler to another in the chain of production and distribution, the tax element to be incorporated into its ultimate price is "pyramided."[14] Some commodities pass through

[14] The possibilities of commodity tax "pyramiding" have often been much exaggerated. There can be little doubt, however, that an excise imposed at an early stage in the manufacture or distribution of a commodity is likely to add more than its actual amount to financing, insurance, and other costs of distribution; there may at times be additions to the profit margins of producers and distributors.

more hands than do others before they reach their ultimate consumers. There is wide divergence in the total taxes attached to various commodities, with consequent repercussions on buying, cost of production, and ultimate price readjustments. Furthermore, a manufacturers' excise, a gross sales tax, or a gross income tax discriminates against a series of single-process concerns, each of which in succession is taxed upon sales; it favors any competing concern which engages in successive stages of production and distribution and whose output as eventually sold bears only a single tax. The single-process concerns must absorb the difference between the pyramided taxes on their product and the single tax paid by their multiprocess competitor. Attempts to alleviate this discrimination by "resale certificates" giving a reseller credit for earlier taxes paid on the commodity complicate administration and increase compliance costs. Moreover, a business may find itself unable to add a state gross sales or gross income tax to the prices of its output when it competes with firms located in states which do not levy such taxes.

The deductibility of some commodity taxes in computing federal and state income tax alters their net burden, and distorts their incidence as ordinarily conceived.

Distributive effects. To the extent that sales taxes are shifted forward, they constitute taxes on consumption. The poor spend a larger proportion of income on consumption items than do the rich. Consequently, a tax which imposes a proportional burden on consumption absorbs a larger proportion of the income of the poor than of the rich. A general sales tax, or an excise on tobacco or sugar, is relatively more burdensome on a family with a $2,000 income than on one with $10,000 or more. This regressivity is the main basis, and a most important one, for condemnation of general sales taxes and mass-consumption excises.[15] The large family with low income has valid reason to complain. Exemption of food items under a general sales tax, however, removes much of the regressive effect and also removes any discrimination in favor of families which produce their own food. Though a food exemption eliminates some of the curse of the sales tax, the higher rates that must be applied on other items to bring a given revenue also fall on the poor, though less onerously. When we look beyond the extremes of rich and poor to the great mass of families, the general sales tax is roughly proportional. Through the income range from $3,000 to $10,000, differences in burden on income groups (but not necessarily on individuals) depart only a little from proportionality. See Table 11–6. Much of the same applies to specific mass excises such as cigarettes, with one important exception—burdens vary not only with income but also with the pattern of consumption. People with different preferences are burdened differently for that reason alone.

[15] The worst effects of a general sales tax may not be felt by the poorest families. Their government welfare payments may be increased to absorb the tax. The "not quite destitute" are likely to be hurt most.

If, for any reason, sales tax cannot be shifted, it results in an inequitable burden on the taxed producers or sellers, bearing no relation to the relative abilities of taxpayers.

Sales taxes on "luxuries" are sometimes advocated as a method of accomplishing progressive taxation. A further argument advanced in favor of such "luxury" taxes is that consumers are under no compulsion to shoulder the burden; they can properly avoid payment by not buying the taxed "luxuries"; hence such taxes are largely "voluntary" payments. No one is really compelled to smoke, and anyone who does smoke is free to save the tax on cigarettes by "rolling" his own. No one is forced to drink beer or whiskey. Yet these taxes bring large revenue because the *masses do* prefer factory-made cigarettes enough to pay the tax and *do* drink alcoholic beverages. Moreover, one asks, where is the line between luxuries and necessities to be drawn?[16] A fur coat may be a necessity to a working girl in Duluth, Minnesota. A leather briefcase is an obligatory working tool for many lawyers and research workers. Are engagement and wedding rings "luxuries" when custom makes them mandatory? Is wine any more of a luxury than tenderloin steaks? There is hardly an item that may be brought under any definition of "luxury" which is not more or less of a necessity to some people. Although the over-all burden of a "luxury" excise or sales tax may rest somewhat more heavily on the more well-to-do than on the poor, this result is accomplished at the cost of many discriminatory violations of "ability" doctrine.[17]

Defenders of consumption taxes point out that not everyone with a high income—$15,000 or $150,000—pays the income tax which falls on most people with comparable incomes. Loopholes do exist in the income tax. However, there is no escaping many consumption taxes. In fact, therefore, consumption taxes offer a method of compensating a little for defects in the income tax that enable some prosperous families to escape the full impact of high bracket rates.

"Regulatory" excises. Taxes on selected goods or services, or even "general" sales taxes that do not reach all consumption items, lead to a different pattern of consumption, production, and the use of resources than would otherwise prevail. This result is sometimes termed "economic distortion" and is charged against commodity taxation. But no tax is altogether free of "distorting" effects; no tax is altogether "economically neutral." The income tax, for example, affects the distribution of income between consumption spending and saving, and may influence the incentive to work and the

[16] Probably the best economic definition is that "luxuries" are those items on which the individual or family spends the marginal or highest units of its income. If this definition is accepted, it seems to follow that the best way to tax luxuries is to tax income.

[17] The high flat-rate tax on hard liquor is a much bigger percentage of the purchase price of cheap than of higher quality liquor. Here is a source of discrimination against imbibers with low incomes. Moreover, it is they who are most likely to be induced to buy illegal liquor which is sometimes of very poor quality indeed.

relative attractiveness of leisure. The general "distortion" of the economic pattern produced by commodity taxes may be accepted as a natural incident of any form of taxation. But where specific excises are under consideration, a check should be made to assure that none of them will exercise particular harmful effects not warranted by their yield.

A different problem is presented when a commodity tax is imposed with a primary, or even secondary, intent of modifying some specific element of the established economic pattern. Then, as pointed out in Chapter 9, the problem divides into two parts. Is the objective desirable? Is the tax an effective—or the most effective—means of achieving the end?

Many defensible cases of "regulatory" commodity taxation exist. Since the federal government lacks police power to prohibit the sale of narcotics but can check the traffic by a "prohibitory" tax, such tax would appear to have unconditional warrant. A convincing case can be made for the imposition of regulatory excises on certain commodities whose market prices are not high enough to keep consumption down to socially desirable levels; possible examples, in addition to the familiar case of strong liquor, are items employing irreplaceable natural resources (e.g., petroleum and certain ores) or resources replaceable only at costs greater than are charged in the market price (e.g., timber). Moreover, during a war, free markets might bring prices above long-run competitive costs, thus providing needless windfalls for the lucky or unscrupulous operator, or they might divert resources from other uses of greater immediate national importance. In such cases, the argument for selected regulatory excises is convincing. Experience suggests, however, that "regulatory" taxes yielding any revenue live on even if the case for the regulation disappears. Hence, such taxes should hardly be adopted for temporary reasons unless they also seem desirable for the long run.[18]

FUTURE OF CONSUMPTION TAXES

Consumption taxes are here to stay. Considering the alternatives, they do not deserve the condemnation so generally placed on them. Is there not considerable appeal in the basic principle of taxing people on the basis of what they take out of the product of the economy (consumption) rather than on what they put in (income)? The refined way to achieve such an objective would be a tax on total spending during a year, with allowance for an exemption and possibly with graduated rates. Such a spendings tax

[18] A classic example is the federal tax on passenger transportation. When imposed during World War II, it could be justified to some extent as a measure to reduce demands on railroads, buses, and airlines, whose capacity was needed for war purposes. When wartime demand declined and trains, buses, and planes moved with much empty space, the chief reason for the tax vanished. Yet Congress continued it even when subsidies were being given to airlines and when railroads were losing money heavily on passenger service.

base would be, essentially, net income minus net saving. There is no near prospect of such a tax, however, whereas there is strong prospect that we shall make increasing use of general sales taxes and excises on selected commodities and services.

The old objections to consumption taxes have not disappeared. These taxes *do* fall more heavily on the low income groups than seems wise and fair. These taxes *do* discriminate among people according to their consumption patterns and with some results difficult to justify. For example, how would one justify the $30 a year federal tax on the person who smokes one package of cigarettes a day? These taxes *do* distort somewhat the allocation of resources, in production as well as in consumption, and often in ways that serve no useful purpose.

But what are the alternatives? If we did not have consumption taxes, we should still need revenue. Heavier use of income, business, and property taxes would create problems as serious as those produced by consumption taxes. Although these alternative taxes are not at their ultimate limits, more intensive use would accentuate their distorting effects and magnify existing inequities. Consumption taxes *do* reach those who for one reason or another get off lightly from the other taxes. As long as loopholes and discrepancies in the income tax remain, it is perhaps fairer to use another tax which reaches everyone than to concentrate still heavier burdens on those already paying income tax.

Payment of consumption taxes is generally convenient. Good administration is possible. Though compliance may impose special business costs, like other broad business costs these will generally become a part of price rather than a drain on the business. The improvement of public welfare systems and the development of social insurance offset some of the bad effects of these taxes as they fall on the low income groups.[19] There is an additional possibility of eliminating the worst effects of these taxes on the poor—refunds or perhaps some form of exemption. The general idea would be to enable a family with low income to get back some or all of the sales tax it paid, computed roughly. In essence this would be a sort of income tax the other way around, that is, the lower the income after personal exemptions, the bigger the refund. The tax could, in fact, be combined with the personal income tax.[20]

Widespread state use of general sales taxes at the retail level limits the federal government. If it were to seek substantially more revenue from commodity taxation, it would have the practical choices of using existing bases more heavily, of expanding the list of items or services subject to specific taxes, or of adopting a broadly-based tax at the manufacturing or

[19] The Labour (Socialist) Government of Great Britain relied heavily on tobacco and liquor taxes to help finance welfare programs.

[20] For a concrete proposal, see A. A. Rozental, "Integration of Sales and Income Taxes at the State Level," *National Tax Journal*, Dec., 1956, pp. 370–377. A special commission in Michigan has recommended just this type of refund.

wholesale level. The last is probably the best. To make substantially more intensive use of existing taxes would multiply the disparities between taxed and untaxed items, that is, their consumers and producers, with all the discriminations involved. Significant broadening of coverage—to food, clothing, and furniture, for example—would approximate a general tax. On balance, it would seem logical to make the tax general, with predominantly uniform rates and a minimum of exceptions. But these problems call for careful analysis before definite decisions are made.

Finally, most of the present taxes were established with little experience to draw upon and, in fact, often under emergency conditions. Defects have been discovered, and some have been remedied. Yet there remains an opportunity for considerable improvement in the structure of the system. The start should be a well-considered formulation of what we seek to accomplish in either a general sales tax or a specific excise. The next step would be to draw upon experience and the best of thought to judge how to make the taxes as efficient as possible for achieving these purposes. An essential element of a rational approach would be the effort to integrate broadly-based consumption and broadly-based business taxes.

PROBLEMS

1. Estimate the amount you spend in consumption taxes (excluding taxes on gasoline) a year.

2. Evaluate the possibilities of using the tariff as a major revenue-raising device in this country.

3. What would be the effects of removing taxes on tobacco products and alcoholic beverages?

4. If there is a sales tax where you live, examine a copy of the regulations. Discuss its administration with a businessman.

5. "Regressivity is, of course, bad. American consumption taxes, however, are not seriously regressive." Discuss, giving special attention to the evidence you would like to have for your answer.

6. Appraise the relative merits of a tax at the manufacturing level with those of a tax at retail.

7. "When a commodity tax is first imposed, or when a rate is raised, the producer as well as the consumer suffers. After a time, however, only the consumer really suffers." Discuss.

CHAPTER 17

Motor Vehicle and Fuel Taxes[1]

THE present system of highways—but not local streets and roads—has been financed for the most part with funds derived from special taxation of highway users. Motor vehicle license taxes will yield the states about $1.4 billion in 1959, motor vehicle fuel tax[2] about $3 billion. These two taxes—frequently termed "highway user taxes"—were once tacitly accepted as levies to which the states have prior and dominant claim. Since 1932, however, the federal government has imposed a gasoline tax. It now brings almost $2 billion a year. Since 1956, part of the receipts have been earmarked for highway aid. As noted in the preceding chapter, federal manufacturers' excise taxes are imposed on automobiles, trucks, auto parts, tires and tubes, and some auto accessories. These were originally levied to produce general revenue, but approximately half, along with revenue from a new tax on heavy trucks, now goes into a special trust fund for highways, to pay for 90 to 95 per cent of the 41,000 mile interstate system now being built. To evaluate these and other less important levies on motorists, one must also consider street-highway expenditure beyond points covered in Chapter 2.

MOTOR VEHICLE LICENSE TAXES

The motor vehicle license charge developed from the low fixed-sum auto registration fees established for control purposes by some states early in the century. When the revenue possibilities began to be exploited, the rates

[1] The following titles, in addition to those cited in later footnotes, will cover most of the points or suggest further sources: Tax Institute, *Financing Highways* (Princeton, 1957); W. Owen, *The Metropolitan Transportation Problem* (Brookings Institution, Washington, 1956); Papers in Part XIV, *Federal Expenditure Policy for Economic Growth and Stability*, especially those by J. F. Due, H. S. Houthakker, and R. M. Zettel; O. H. Brownlee and W. W. Heller, "Highway Development and Financing," *American Economic Review, Supplement*, May, 1956, pp. 232–250.

[2] This term is more accurate than "gasoline tax," since the tax is generally extended to other motor fuels, such as diesel oil; lubricating oil is sometimes taxed.

were graduated on such bases as horsepower, net weight, and value. License taxes on passenger vehicles and trucks were differentiated. Base modifications and rate increases continued into the 1930's. Since then, motor vehicle license tax rates have remained fairly stabilized, increasing less than the general needs for revenue might have led one to expect.

Auto licensing by the states for regulatory purposes is essential. Since this is the case, virtually no extra administrative expense is involved in making the license a source of net revenue. The ownership and use of motor vehicles is so widespread that such a tax is a broadly based revenue source. Drivers' licenses, required originally for regulatory purposes, increasingly yield net revenue as well—about $100 million a year.

A new federal tax of $1.50 per 1,000 pounds on commercial vehicles over 26,000 pounds is designed for revenue.

Local governments in several states are authorized to impose supplementary motor vehicle license charges. Total collections are not large.

Bases. What principles should guide legislators in framing the basis of a motor vehicle license tax? The possession of any vehicle could itself provide an appropriate basis for a uniform fixed tax on vehicles of all types if government is to make streets available at the option of the user. Such a tax could be a sort of payment for "readiness to serve." A large overhead or fixed cost is incurred to make the use of autos and trucks possible. It would be logical to cover some of the cost by a uniform fixed charge on all potential users. But there is no agreement on how much.

Most states have differing bases for passenger cars, trucks, and buses, with superimposed variations for private, commercial, and common carrier vehicles. No two states have an identical combination of bases.

For the taxation of private passenger cars, net weight is the most prevalent base, being used either as sole base or in combination with others. These net weight charges are generally progressive—the amount charged increases more rapidly than the net weight base. Other bases, however, are freely employed. Flat fees are common. Horsepower, value,[3] and age of car each appear as measure of the tax. Seating capacity and type of tire are occasionally taken into consideration.

Most states levy special additional taxes on trucks or else subject them to a different, heavier tax. Capacity is a common base for these truck taxes, but many states employ gross weight and net weight, the number of axles and wheels, or, more unusual, chassis weight and value. Some states discriminate between commercial and private trucks, and nearly all impose special taxes on buses and commercial passenger cars. Commercial passenger car taxes are levied on such diverse bases as value, gross weight, net weight, carrying capacity, seating capacity, mileage, passenger mileage, ton mileage, and the population of the city wherein operated. Most states

[3] When the license charge is in lieu of property tax, as it is in some states, the value of the vehicle is an appropriate element to consider in setting the amount.

also place heavier taxes on common carrier than on private or commercial vehicles.

A supplementary highway user tax, the *weight-distance,* axle-mile, or ton-mile levy—sometimes called a "third-structure" tax—has recently been adopted by several states. Although details vary, these taxes apply rates which are (a) graduated according to weight of the vehicle and (b) mileage in the state. In New York, for example, vehicles of less than 18,000 pounds capacity are exempt. Others pay at rates from 6 mills per mile to 35 mills per mile at 76,000 pounds, plus 2 mills per mile for each additional ton. New York's tax yields over a tenth as much as motor vehicle licenses. The purpose of such taxes is to get more revenue from operators of heavy trucks. Neither motor vehicle license charges nor motor fuel taxes, it is felt, impose a heavy enough burden on really big trucks, especially those from out of the state. However, good administration is difficult; there is honest difference of opinion about what rates are appropriate; reciprocity arrangements may be disturbed; compliance costs are high.

Many states have special license taxes for electric and steam vehicles, motorcycles, trailers, tractors, taxicabs, buses, and other special road-using vehicles. Diesel-powered trucks may be taxed more heavily to compensate for their advantage under the motor vehicle fuel tax. School buses are frequently charged a special low rate.

This complexity has developed from the laudable desire to apply the benefit principle to motor vehicle taxation. The chief objective has been to apportion tax burdens in accordance with the road *costs* caused by different classes of vehicles. Some differences, however, reflect a desire to apportion according to an estimate of *value* of service. Logically, however, each of the many bases cannot adjust taxes to benefit principles. With the development of the motor fuel tax, whose burden is closely related to road use, the need for some of these elements of presumptive benefit measure in license taxes has diminished.

Pioneering efforts have been made in applying the principle of incremental cost.[4] Some types of vehicles require more government spending than others. Road tests indicate that highway construction and maintenance costs depend upon such factors as truck weight, resiliency, and other physical characteristics. Therefore, it is argued, a logical basis for a motor vehicle license tax is weight, adjusted for other features of vehicle construction which affect wear and tear on highways. There is no ideal procedure for finding incremental cost; the basic principle, however, is to determine total costs, deduct whatever fraction seems appropriate for charging to the

[4] The actual computation is very much more complex than can be indicated here. For recent studies, see W. D. Ross, *Financing Highway Improvements in Louisiana* (Louisiana State University, Baton Rouge, 1955); and *Financing Kentucky's Roads and Streets* (University of Kentucky Bureau of Business Research, Lexington, 1956), summarized by J. W. Martin, C. R. Lockyer, and E. C. Holshouser, "Results of the Kentucky Highway Finance Study," *National Tax Journal,* June, 1957, pp. 126–137.

general public, and then divide the remainder among groups of motor vehicle users. Engineering estimates can indicate what part of a facility would not be needed if vehicles were less than a certain weight, allowance being made for other features. Then the vehicles over this weight must bear the full cost of the extra construction requirements plus a share of all other costs. Some part of their total share will come from what they pay in tax on fuels. The remainder will be their appropriate license charge.

Even if this more refined method is not used, a state should recognize that the cost of highway construction and maintenance is greater, and more than proportionately greater, for heavy commercial vehicles than for private cars. The former necessitate extra-width roadways, more solid and expensive roadbeds, and more substantial bridges. And road damage by vehicles increases progressively with vehicle weight. A motor vehicle license charge based on gross weight should, therefore, be progressive—the *rate* should increase as the gross weight of the taxed vehicle increases. However, allowance should be made for number of wheels or axles, with a *lower* rate for the extra axle or wheels and any other features that reduce road wear. Such a motor vehicle tax base would give incentives to types of vehicle construction and use that reduce highway wear and tear.[5]

Because urban congestion is a major problem, because the costs of meeting it by extra street construction are exceedingly (prohibitively) high, because bridge and tunnel costs depend partly upon vehicle width, and because length and width of vehicle affect the amount of street and parking space required, a new basis for license taxation of autos might encourage a better allocation of resources. The tax would be graduated according to length and width of vehicles. The graduation could be made sufficiently steep above some limits to give manufacturers an incentive to produce autos that would be more economical of a truly scarce resource—street space in urban areas. The charge could collect substantially more revenue from those who choose to demand more publicly provided resources—street space—by using large vehicles.

As public service enterprises, motor vehicle common carriers may logically be brought under a state's general system of public utility taxation. This is frequently done. Still, a number of states have developed special taxes, based on seating or carrying capacity of the buses or trucks, on mileage operated, and on gross receipts.[6]

[5] Passenger buses and trucks need not be differentiated under a progressive gross weight tax, since the greater gross weight makes them subject to the higher rates of the progressive schedule. Nor need there be discrimination between private and commercial vehicles. The latter use the public highways more extensively, and therefore pay more gasoline taxes.

[6] Unlike gross receipts taxes on railroads, gross receipts taxes on motor vehicle common carriers can be based, not only on gross receipts from intrastate service, but also upon allocated gross receipts from interstate service, provided that the tax is levied as an excise for the privilege of using the public highways. See *Aero Mayflower Transit Co.* v. *Montana,* 332 U.S. (1948) 495.

Rates. Each state is law unto itself in setting motor vehicle tax rates. Variation in these rates is tremendous. Charges for private cars run from a few dollars to over $200. For common carrier and noncommon carrier buses, rates range from $15 to over $1,000. Truck rates range from under $20 to almost $4,500 for giant diesel six-axle carriers. Increasing horsepower and weight of autos has made established rate schedules more and more productive.

Reciprocity. All states honor the registration of passenger cars bearing license plates of the state of the owner's domicile. Although a few states require special "entrance" registration of "foreign" cars, they charge no tax.

Such universal recognition of "home" registration does not apply to contract and common carrier buses and trucks. A complicated system of general reciprocity statutes and of bilateral reciprocity agreements between some states eliminates double taxation of all or certain classes of motor carriers in these states. But carriers with a "home" registration or operating in the other states must pay a registration tax to every state in which they operate. In some cases, the registration tax on "foreign" carriers is established at a fraction of the tax on "home" vehicles. This multiple taxation of motor carriers lends itself to abuse. In general, the extension of reciprocity is to be recommended. Yet "bridge" states complain that they provide facilities and get little revenue. The heavy demands on states for bigger outlays for highway facilities provide strong argument for taxing all commercial users regardless of their "home base." One proposed solution is a general mileage tax in lieu of other levies on trucks.[7] Another possibility is indicated by nine Western states which formed an interstate compact in 1957 to apportion truck weight and registration fees on a mileage basis.

Administration. The motor vehicle license tax has been described as a tax which can be neither evaded nor avoided. In one sense, this statement is true, since every car operating on the public highways must take out a license. But a certain routine is needed to prevent passenger car and truck owners from understating the weight, or capacity, or horsepower of their vehicles when applying for license. Initial license applications must be checked against dealers' certificates, and license renewal applications must be checked against the old registrations. If this routine is performed faithfully, a motor vehicle tax is almost impossible to evade. But if it is neglected, partial evasion is likely to become widespread.

Most of the states have not turned the administration of the motor vehicle license tax over to the state tax commission or state revenue department. County officials still administer the tax in a few states, the secretary of state or state auditor in some, and the state highway department in

[7] W. F. Scheffer, "Reciprocity in the Taxation of Interstate Trucks," *National Tax Journal,* March, 1956, pp. 75–83. Prof. Scheffer proposes a federally collected motor fuels tax specially tailored for distribution to the states according to truck mileage, on a formula reflecting each state's user tax system.

about twenty states. State highway departments can administer the motor vehicle license tax well. So can any state agency which is given adequate power and funds. Although local offices are essential for the convenience of motorists, county administration cannot be as efficient as that centralized in a state agency.

MOTOR VEHICLE FUEL TAXES

Originally imposed by Oregon in 1919 as a minor supplementary source of highway revenue, the motor fuel tax has become the major "highway" tax in most states.

Scope. A motor vehicle fuel tax is a special sales tax, collected usually on the sales by distributing companies to service outlets. Sometimes, however, it is collectible from service outlets selling to their customers. Like retail sales taxes generally, it encounters few constitutional restrictions. In clear-cut decisions, the Supreme Court held that once motor fuel has entered a state for disposal therein, it is subject to state taxation on its sale, storage, or use.[8] Gasoline sold to federal agencies is held to be a federal instrumentality and not subject to state taxation. Except for kerosene in some cases, all motor fuels, including diesel oil, are taxed. In all but a few states, motor vehicle fuel taxes are levied as highway excises, with exemption for fuel not used in highway transportation and with all revenue earmarked for road construction or maintenance. Most states have also extended their taxes to cover gasoline utilized by airplanes or have levied special supplementary taxes on aviation gasoline.

Rates. Motor vehicle fuel tax rates range up to 7 cents per gallon in ten states, with 6 cents the most common. To these varied state taxes must be added the federal tax of 3 cents and some local taxes. Most states allow a deduction on the tax to cover shrinkage in the handling of the fuel from the time the tax is paid until its sale to ultimate purchasers. A few states also allow the distributors a rebate to cover special accounting costs. Rates have not, in general, risen as much as the costs of street and highway construction.

Administration. The federal motor fuel tax is imposed at the point where the business is concentrated in the fewest hands—the producers and importers. Collection costs are extremely low, and evasion is insignificant.

States cannot impose their motor fuel taxes on the conveniently small number of producers and importers, since the gasoline produced in any state is not necessarily consumed there, nor is the gasoline consumed in

[8] Large-scale consumers of motor fuels—trucking companies, railroads, aviation companies, and others—formerly avoided some state motor fuel taxes by purchasing supplies from distributors in states with lower rates. Because of the interstate commerce limitation, such interstate purchases were not taxable by the seller's state. To check this avoidance, states have enacted gasoline "use" taxes. These apply to gasoline bought outside the taxing state for resale or use within its borders.

a state necessarily produced there. The best focal point for the state taxes is the wholesale distributor, and all states make him primarily responsible. If a retailer buys motor fuel from a distributor operating in another state, he is either reached under a "use" tax or he is made responsible for the payment of the regular gasoline tax when he makes his sales to customers. Motor fuel users who purchase from distributors or retailers in other states are individually liable under "use" taxes. Some states have "ports of entry" at the state boundary to collect "use" tax, especially from truckers. Kentucky reported in 1958 that shortly after setting up ports of entry it added 1,500 truckers to its tax rolls. Efficient interstate cooperation contributes materially to the effectiveness of gasoline "use" taxes.

Administration of the motor vehicle fuel tax has been given to the state tax commission or department of revenue in half the states, to the state highway department in a few. In the remaining states, the tax is collected by such diverse offices as the secretary of state, the state controller or auditor, treasurer, and the state department of agriculture. Years of experience have enabled states to overcome most administrative difficulties. The chief exception is the handling of rebates for gasoline not used on highways. The difficulties of administering a local gasoline tax effectively are obvious. Unless local distributors absorb a major part of the tax, local motorists, as well as truckers and passing motorists, will tend to buy their gasoline across the town or county line. Local "use" taxes are almost impossible to enforce.

ECONOMIC CONSIDERATIONS[9]

Since the motor vehicle fuel tax is a pure form of specific commodity tax, most of the theory of commodity taxation in the preceding chapter is directly applicable. Motor vehicle license taxes, though they raise slightly different theoretical principles, can be considered most conveniently in connection with the gasoline tax. Yet because of the tie to street-highway finance, these taxes do raise unique issues of theory—and practice.

Incidence. Motor fuel is a commodity for which demand, within the limits affected by present rates, is relatively inelastic. Hence, with minor exceptions, the tax is shifted to gasoline users.[10] When the taxed fuel is used in private cars, there is no possibility of further tax shifting. The tax on fuel used by commercial vehicles, however, is for the most part a business cost for which consumers must pay. Similarly, the license tax on private cars cannot be shifted, whereas in general that on commercial vehicles is passed on to consumers and more or less diffused through the economy. The same applies to other levies on business vehicles, with spe-

[9] Tolls are discussed in Chapter 21.

[10] Because these taxes are generally deductible in computing federal and state income taxes, minor complications not considered here arise in an exhaustive analysis.

cial frictions in tax shifting occasionally arising where utility commissions control rates charged by common carriers.

Distribution of the burden. "Highway" taxes are outstanding modern examples of "benefit" taxes. Motor vehicle users derive special individual benefit from the construction and maintenance of streets and highways. The taxes compel motorists to pay part of the cost of building and maintaining streets and highways.[11] Many legislatures, however, have not been able to decide whether they are taxing according to the "cost-of-service," or to the "value-of-service," doctrine. When vehicles having solid tires are taxed more heavily than those having pneumatic tires, the legislators clearly have in mind the greater destruction caused by solid tires. The "solid-tire discrimination" is an example of "cost-of-service" taxation. When commercial vehicles are charged more than privately-owned vehicles of the same size and capacity, it is probable that "value-of-service" is the principle behind the discrimination. The typical truck tax is generally a combination of the two principles.

Motor fuel taxes are also defended by both the "cost-of-service" and "value-of-service" doctrines. Gasoline consumption by autos is related to the mileage they travel and to their weight and power. Trucks and buses, though probably not private autos, strain and damage streets and highways somewhat in proportion to the distance covered and weight and power. Certainly, the quantity of street and highway facilities that must be provided depends upon the amount of driving. Therefore, a motor vehicle fuel tax prorates costs of constructing and maintaining facilities for motorists among those who make the expense necessary. On the other hand, the presence of such facilities benefits users more or less in proportion to the mileage they travel and the capacity of their vehicles. A motor vehicle fuel tax, then, distributes highway cost in rough proportion to the benefit derived.

The customers of business concerns using motor vehicles benefit from the existence of streets and highways through lower transport cost. Business concerns, in shifting the tax to their customers, pass street-highway costs to those individuals who derive the ultimate benefit from the use of the highways by commercial vehicles.

Highway user taxes in relation to street-highway costs and use. An economist sees many diverse considerations in analyzing the optimum role of highway user taxes. Most significant is the fact that there exist revenue devices which can obtain from users of streets and highways enough to pay the full costs of the facilities. These taxes can also be made heavy enough to yield revenues for other government services. Moreover, they can influence the amount of usage and hence the need for government to spend on streets. Yet streets and highways, besides specifically benefiting

[11] The same theory is applicable to the levy of airplane and airport license taxes and to the extension of motor fuel taxes to airplane fuel, to provide funds for airport construction and maintenance.

auto and truck users, confer a general social benefit by providing greater facilities for travel and communication. Cheap transportation is a powerful aid to economic progress. The creation of new streets or highways commonly enhances the value of neighboring property, but sometimes it also reduces values. And some of the most difficult problems of cities grow out of "overuse" of vehicles, creating costly congestion at peak periods.

Moreover, other transportation agencies which also serve the general public must be considered. Quite naturally, railroads, which have long been heavily taxed, partly to finance highways, would like to see their competitors—trucks and buses—pay equally high taxes.[12] Another complicating factor is the nature of street-highway costs. At any one time they are largely fixed, varying little with amount of use up to capacity.[13] Moreover, much of the motorist's cost in the short run changes little with auto use; an addition to variable cost that is great enough to affect usage greatly would be extreme.[14] A final reality must be noted—a preference of rural-dominated legislatures for using state-collected taxes on motorists to pay for highways and rural roads rather than city streets.

What principles of taxation would serve best over the long run? There is wide difference of opinion. Even though there is general public advantage in cheap transport, there are many other types of spending that also bring general benefit. To pay for schools, welfare, and other services, revenue sources which, judged by most standards, are inferior to "highway" taxes must be used. It would not be wise, then, to rely upon these other revenue sources to pay for streets and highways.[15] Yet there is at least one exception in principle; if localities raise the revenue themselves, they can retain the money for spending at home rather than help pay for spending in some other part of the state or nation.

It is reasonable that motor vehicle taxes should fall more heavily on

[12] The relative tax burdens on railroads and trucks is not easily determined. There is honest dispute about whether truckers pay approximately their reasonable share of highway and street costs in the form of taxes. The comparable expense of railroads—the cost of roadbed—is paid not in the form of taxes but as wages and materials. Then in addition, railroads pay taxes to support schools, welfare, streets, and other public services, a tax cost truckers generally do not bear on the roads they use. Land taken for streets and highways is no longer in the property tax base, but the railroad right of way remains subject to real estate tax.

[13] As usage goes beyond some point, of course, congestion creates heavy social costs. Yet it is not one that must be paid as a variable, or any other form of, cost by the government.

[14] Insurance, depreciation, and interest on the investment vary little per week or month, even with relatively large differences in use.

[15] Students of highway finance—and not only the powerful petroleum, auto, and truck industries—often dispute this point. Unfortunately, there is no clear basis for deciding the issue. However, advocates of the use of property, income, tobacco, or other taxes for streets and highways rarely consider explicitly the needs of education, health, police, and other nonhighway spending. The diversion since 1956 of federal auto tax revenue from the general fund to highways reduces the amounts available for other federal programs.

classes of vehicles that are responsible for extra costs of street and highway construction and maintenance. License charges on trucks and buses, graduated progressively on the basis of gross weight—and auto licenses graduated with length and width—can make such a desirable adjustment. Practical difficulties do arise, however, in adjusting the charges to take rational account of differences in costs of construction and maintenance. The gasoline tax helps relate the amount of tax paid both to over-all mileage and to the road-destructive character of the vehicle—the heavier trucks and buses use more gasoline per mile. The weight-distance tax also serves the same purpose. But measurement of proper amounts is still subject to great uncertainty. Perhaps the incremental cost principle, and more tests scientifically controlled and conducted, can provide helpful guidance. Moreover, as long as railroads are subject to heavy taxes for general purposes, their direct competitors, especially trucks, should probably be taxed not only to pay for their part of streets and highways but also for other costs of government. Otherwise the allocation of resources is biased in a way that serves no useful purpose. In fact, deliberate use of taxes to shift long-distance heavy trucking to railways would help make fuller and more efficient use of the unused capacity of railroads and relieve somewhat the pressures on governments to spend more on highways.

In one important respect, however, the combination of motor vehicle and fuel taxes cannot operate to meet a real need—the redistribution of street-highway use to cut peaks and to encourage fuller utilization when capacity would otherwise be idle. A gasoline tax high enough to discourage use at peak periods by casual motorists would far exceed a rate appropriate as a general levy. The costs of peak loads are tremendous. Much of the extra-lane capacity of our arterial highways is needed only during a few morning and evening hours and on weekends and holidays. Moreover, the loss of time due to urban congestion a few hours a day is a much greater economic cost than is generally recognized.[16] Unfortunately, we as yet have no practicable way of imposing charges to reduce peak use or to recoup some of the social cost of such use. Yet such a charge is badly needed. Where tolls will be collected in any case, or can be collected at certain times, higher charges at peaks may be feasible.

The typical city needs some form of charging "contact" population, specifically those nonresidents who drive to and from work. Heavy costs are usually required to provide facilities for such motorists. Charges would serve two purposes. The city could recoup some of the costs incurred for a generally identifiable group which otherwise pays little local tax. In addition, the charge might cause some commuters to use public transport which, per passenger, requires only a small fraction of the public facilities needed per person travelling by private auto.

[16] The person whose time is worth little adds to the congestion which burdens more wastefully the person whose time is highly valuable.

The issue of earmarking—or "dedication"—versus "diversion" of highway user revenues has been decided in favor of earmarking. Fiscal economists, however, have strongly favored the general policy of sending motor vehicle tax revenues, together with other receipts, into the general fund and then using the money available for purposes with highest priority. This principle might lead to spending either more or less on streets and highways than is received in taxes from motor vehicle licenses and fuels. Unfortunately, the pressure exerted by various interest groups tended to mislead the public by ignoring the expenditure on streets and focusing on highways. Thus, it was possible to paint a picture of the "short-changed motorist" which aroused support for earmarking. Today, in view of the need for street-highway spending, can there be any real harm in assuring that at least as much is spent as governments receive in highway user taxes? Perhaps not,[17] but there *is* a danger in earmarking systems as they operate —poor allocation of funds. Not enough of the revenue goes for city streets relative to nonurban facilities.

PROBLEMS

1. State arguments for and against a substantial increase in motor vehicle license taxes, assuming that the yield (a) will and (b) will not be earmarked for facilities for motor vehicles.

2. Would you consider it logical to adjust highway user taxes each year in accordance with costs of street-highway construction? Why?

3. What advantages might be gained from highway user taxes that discouraged use of highways? What disadvantages?

4. Discuss the relative merits of motor vehicle fuel and motor vehicle license taxes. In what, if any, respects may tolls be superior?

5. "Although everyone may agree that users should pay the costs of highways —streets are another matter—there is no economically sound method of apportioning the fixed costs." Discuss.

6. Find out how your state deals with the problem of out-of-state truckers.

7. "A fundamentally distorting feature of our present system of highway finance is that it frees truckers from the necessity of including the full costs of necessary fixed facilities in their charges, whereas railroads must include the full cost. Thus railroad rates must be higher, and their facilities used relatively less, than trucks." What evidence would be needed to judge this statement?

8. What features of our highway user tax system help show the willingness of the user to pay as much for new facilities as they will cost?

[17] The financial implications of the new federal highway program are not clear. Unquestionably, however, it will add pressure on states and localities to increase their own outlays for construction and maintenance of streets, roads, and highways outside the 41,000 mile interstate system. These pressures may be sufficiently strong to induce more spending on this one function than is justified in light of other public needs. Then a larger part of our taxpaying potential may be used for this purpose than is wise.

CHAPTER 18

Property Taxes

THE property tax, until the 1940's America's largest producer of tax revenue, is the major source of funds for local governments.[1] It is highly important to our economy, partly because vital public services which affect our lives every day depend upon the revenue it yields and partly because the condition of our housing, and the prosperity of the construction industry, depend to some extent upon real estate taxes. Often hidden, sometimes, as we shall see, burdensomeless, this tax pervades our lives more than we realize.

The American property tax started as a tax on land. During the early nineteenth century, one category after another of personal property was included with land and subjected to the same rate, and the tax evolved into a "general property tax." By the Civil War period, it was established as the basic local and state tax—in general, a locally-administered levy on the gross value of all property, at a uniform (proportional) rate in the jurisdiction, and, except for certain exempt groups, without regard for the total wealth or the identity of the owner. The next outstanding development was the centralization of certain aspects of administration, the state assessment of railroad and public utility property.

The twentieth century saw the property tax subjected to a ground swell of criticism. It was charged with imposing an undue burden on one subject of taxation—real estate—while other subjects escaped with lighter tax liability. Effective taxation of personal property was declared an administrative impossibility. Influenced by such criticism, legislatures whittled away at the weaker portions of the tax.

Most states have relinquished the property tax, completely or practically,

[1] At the beginning of this century, the property tax brought almost half of all government receipts and came to about 3.4 per cent of Gross National Product. In the 1920's, when it yielded a third of all government revenue, it was nearly 5 per cent of GNP; today, yielding about an eighth of all revenue, it is about 3 per cent of GNP. For an account of property tax developments, see M. Newcomer, "The Decline of the General Property Tax," *National Tax Journal*, March, 1953, pp. 38–51.

to local governments, though the state determines the kind of property localities may tax. In at least 22 states the property tax yields no state revenue or less than one per cent. It still provides almost 90 per cent of local tax revenue, however, and by 1958 yielded about $14 billion. The present *per capita* property tax of about $80 a year over the country as a whole, adjusting for price changes, is more than three times that of 1900.[2]

BASIS

The tax is not a tax on net worth, in no sense a levy upon net wealth. The legal *subject* of property taxes is either "all property within the jurisdiction of the state or district except for such exemptions as are allowed by statute," or "such classes of property within the jurisdiction of the state or district as are specified by statute." Legally, therefore, the property tax is imposed on *things* (*ad rem*) with little or no regard to the *persons* who must eventually bear the economic burden. "Value of the property as assessed for tax purposes" is the *measure.*

Classes of taxable property. Allowing for exemptions, all categories of *real property* are generally subject to taxation without any deduction for debts outstanding against the property.

Tangible personalty—furniture, livestock, machinery, autos, jewelry, inventory—is still taxed (or presumably taxed) in most states, but deep inroads have been made on this formerly universal levy: several states, including New York and Pennsylvania, have abolished tangible personalty taxation altogether. Many exempt motor vehicles and regard the annual license tax as a partial substitute. A few impose special license taxes on merchants *in lieu* of a property tax on their inventory. Tonnage taxes on vessels, severance taxes on cut trees *in lieu* of property tax on the growing trees, gross receipt taxes on railroads and public utilities, and the severance taxes on mines and oil wells, replace property taxes on these items in some places.

By law or practice, about half of the states already exclude all or practically all *intangibles* from their general property taxes. Most others have withdrawn specific classes of intangibles—bank deposits, cash value of life insurance policies, mortgages secured by taxed domestic property, shares and bonds of corporations otherwise taxed by the state. In a few states some intangibles are subjected to *in lieu* recording taxes; in others, the income tax is viewed as a substitute; elsewhere no specific replacement

[2] New York City property taxes are over $115 a person per year–$565 for a family of 5. Boston's per capita figure is even larger, about $140. Both cities bear the costs of schools. If all local property taxes in other areas were combined, many cases of levies exceeding $100 per capita would appear.

appears. There is good reason for this growing abandonment of property taxation of intangibles.

Application of a property tax to mortgages duplicates part of the tax on the gross value of the real estate. Taxing corporate stocks and bonds, as well as the real and tangible property owned by corporations, also duplicates tax burdens. Thus property taxation of most forms of "representative" *intangible personalty* involves double taxation. In general, these taxes on intangibles, when imposed, are evaded to such an extent that they are practically taxes on honesty. Perhaps they could be made effective by determined and costly administrative effort, but in view of the injustice involved, there is serious question whether such a goal should even be sought. For example, in a community in which property is assessed at full value and the tax rate is 3 per cent, the tax would take 100 per cent of the income from a savings account or a bond yielding 3 per cent. Fiscal authorities generally recommend that intangibles be withdrawn altogether from property taxation.

In 1956, property subject to tax was assessed at $272 billion, subdivided as follows:

	(*Billions*)
Residential (nonfarm)	$114
Farm and other acreage	29
Commercial	35
Industrial	23
Railroads and utilities assessed by states	20
Vacant lots	5
Other real estate	7
Total realty	$233
Personal property, tangible and intangible	47
Gross assessment	$280
Partial deductions	8
Net assessment	$272

The tax is overwhelmingly a tax on real estate, very largely in fact a tax on housing.

One-half of the 61 million separate parcels of real estate are residences. The tax is equivalent to a consumption tax of 20 per cent or so on expenditures for housing—the money being used to pay for schools, police, and other functions of local government. Perhaps one-third of the total falls on utility and other business property and is shifted to consumers in hidden form as a general element of price. Still, the amount falling on business is not large in relation to other business costs; all property tax on nonresidential business is less than one week's wage bill.

Exemptions. Probably 25 per cent of the real property values of the country are exempt. For constitutional reasons, no state or local government may tax property of the federal government or of its instrumentalities unless specifically authorized by Congress. In most localities the values involved are relatively unimportant, even though the federal government owns almost one-fourth of the total area of the country. But in some states, the presence of extensive federal forests, military installations, or Indian reservations seriously restricts the basis for local taxation, while the governments concerned must provide services, such as schools near air bases.[3] Federal bonds and other debt obligations are also exempt from property taxation; brief shifting of bank deposits and other personalty subject to personal property taxes into federal securities over property tax dates provides a convenient method of avoidance.

Were state or local governments to tax their own real estate, they would in effect be shifting funds from one pocket to another. Hence their own properties are generally exempt.[4] A clear conflict of interests arises, however, if a state park or forest reserve is established within some local taxing district, or if the water works or special institutions of one local unit are established within some other locality. The loss of taxable values to the unit within which the properties are located may be serious. In exceptional cases, permission is granted for the taxation of such public properties by the locality within which they are located. More commonly, a contractual payment by the government owning the property is substituted for taxes. Unfortunately for some localities, no provisions are being made as a part of the new highway program to compensate for removal of land and other property taken from the tax base for the new construction. (Some localities, however, will gain on balance as their property values rise.)

Statutes commonly exempt non-profit-producing properties used for educational, religious, or charitable purposes. The institutions owning these properties perform services which state or local governments might otherwise have to undertake or which, like religion, are socially desirable even though not a proper function of government. To limit the activities of these organizations by compelling them to use part of their resources for taxes would hardly further the public interest.[5] Several states grant farmers special exemptions on implements and growing crops.

A few states[6] authorize local governments to attract new industries by

[3] An attempt was made to avoid similar embarrassment over property purchased or developed during the New Deal and World War II, either by granting state and local governments permission to subject the property to nondiscriminatory tax rates, or, as had been done in the District of Columbia for many years, by providing for contractual payments as substitutes for property taxes.

The federal government now gives the states from 5 to 50 per cent of its revenues from certain public lands used for grazing and other private purposes; such payments come to $40 million a year. TVA pays the states roughly 3 per cent—about $6 million annually—of the gross proceeds of the sale of electric power. Federally-owned housing projects pay sums ("tax equivalent payments") presumed to be equal to the prevailing property tax rate. State and local governments are permitted by Congress to impose their regular property taxes on real property owned by federal lending agencies, including war plant and equipment of the Defense Plant Corporation.

[4] Such exemption, however, makes it harder to compare the full costs of private and government use of real estate—for example, the highway-railroad problem.

[5] A study in New York found that about 7 per cent of the privately-owned real estate in the state was exempt. There, as is often the case, real property owned by philanthropic and similar institutions for investment income is not generally exempt.

[6] Alabama, Louisiana, Mississippi, and South Carolina are leading examples.

the lure of 5- or 10-year property tax exemptions.[7] The exemption may apply to all new establishments or only to specified industries which the state desires to encourage, such as the exemption for beet-sugar factories in Wyoming. Sometimes the state law specifies the term and conditions of the exemption. Sometimes it merely permits local governments to make such exemptions at their own option. The general practice is to be condemned. From the point of view of the whole economy, any benefit to one area is likely to be obtained at the cost of another. To the locality, however, the cost *may* be zero. The possible benefit *can* be significant, for residents may get a chance at really better jobs than otherwise. Yet sometimes the local government must incur added expense to provide facilities for the business. More generally, businesses to which property tax seems important enough to influence location will not have a strong economic basis in the area. Relative property taxes ordinarily appear as minor considerations in studies of the factors determining the location of successful manufacturing and commercial enterprises. Still, the fiscal scholar who is inclined to condemn the practice of exempting new plants must recognize that, to the local officials desirous of spurring development, the temptation to grant tax exemption—or give a favorable assessment despite the requirements of law—is powerful. To a new business the difference may just be determining.[8]

Somewhat similar is the exemption of newly constructed housing to encourage home building. Some local governments exempt federally-financed housing projects; the exemption is treated as the contribution of the local government in matching the federal subsidy. New York State permits privately-owned limited-dividend slum-clearance housing projects to obtain commitments that for a period the property tax on the new property will not exceed the tax on the slum property it replaces. Even as thus limited, the exemption has the defect of throwing upon owners and users of other properties, including slums, any increase in the cost of government that must be met out of property taxes.

Special minimum exemptions for administrative or social reasons, such as a flat exemption of personal property under $500, have long been common. Sometimes, a minimum realty-personalty exemption is allowed to a

[7] In more than a few cases, property tax exemption can be supplemented by exemption of interest on borrowed funds. If the locality itself borrows to build a plant, its bonds are tax exempt. It can then lease the plant to a private user on terms that reflect both property tax and income tax exemptions.

[8] A careful study of one state in which data were available found a record of 609 exemptions granted for $355 million of plant and equipment. Yet only about $25 million could be definitely attributed to the exemption. Even though virtually all of the other $330 million would have been invested in any case, the owners took advantage of the law. The annual loss of property tax revenues was about $5 million–$51 million over the ten years. It seems highly doubtful that the people of the state benefited on balance. See W. D. Ross, "Tax Concessions and Their Effect," *NTA . . . Proceedings . . . 1957* (Harrisburg, 1958), pp. 216–224. See also Tax Institute, "State and Local Efforts to Attract Industry," *Tax Policy*, Feb.–March, 1957.

particular class of taxpayers—to veterans, to widows and orphans, or to the widows and orphans of veterans. During the 1930's, the idea of a general minimum exemption to all home-owners—the "homestead" exemption—gained headway. Texas initiated the movement in 1932 with a constitutional exemption of all "residence homesteads" under $3,000 in value. One-fourth of the states allow complete or partial "homestead" exemptions, ranging in value up to $5,000 in Florida and Mississippi and even more for farm properties in the Dakotas and Oklahoma.[9] Annual tax savings range from a few dollars to $300 or so. Veterans receive a variety of special homestead or similar exemptions in almost thirty states, but in some cases limited to disabled veterans. The homestead exemption limits sharply the tax base of some local governments; it shifts an undue tax burden upon the owners and occupiers of nonexempt properties—including rented properties occupied in substantial part by low income families. It may promote home ownership a little, but the revenue loss makes the cost of any resulting public benefit grossly excessive.

Property tax exemptions seek to make a tax on things conform to some desired standard for taxing persons. These attempts may reflect a welcome dissatisfaction with the crudeness of the property tax as a method of distributing taxes among persons. Yet, even if one is willing to tolerate great administrative complexity, there seems no reasonable prospect of setting up a system of property tax exemptions that will make the distribution of property tax burdens conform to any generally accepted criteria of the way taxes should be distributed among persons.

Jurisdiction to tax. The federal Constitution provides that a property tax levied by the federal government must be apportioned among the states according to population. Practically, this eliminates property taxation as a source of federal revenue. On three occasions only, the last time during the Civil War, has Congress tried to impose an apportioned property tax.

Real property is taxable only where it is located. *Tangible personalty*, once attributed to the state or district of the owner's domicile under the fiction of *mobilia sequuntur personam*, is now held taxable only by the state where it is physically located or where it is construed to be located. There is considerable divergence among the states, however, as to taxable situs of tangible personalty within state boundaries. Most states provide for the taxation of tangibles in the district where they are located. Other states assign tangible personalty to the district of the owner's domicile, but most of these permit such property to acquire taxable situs in the district where it is permanently employed for business purposes. The interstate commerce limitation prevents the application of property taxes to articles actually being transported in interstate commerce. But these articles may be taxed before they enter actual transportation and after they come to rest at the

[9] In most cases the exemption does not apply to all property taxes. In only five states, for example, does the exemption extend to all local property taxes. In four states it applies to state property tax only.

end of their interstate journey.[10] Property taxes may also be levied on property used in interstate commerce—such as vessels, tracks, wires, cars, and so forth—provided that no discrimination is exercised against such property and that apportionment of total value among the states is reasonable.

Intangible property is still generally taxed by the state and district of the owner's domicile. Some states, however, have made allowance for its acquiring a special situs in the district where it is permanently employed in business.[11] The state in which a trustee resides is authorized to tax the property in trust even though the trust and the beneficiaries are in another state. Neither federal nor state constitutions bar the double taxation involved when both real and tangible property and their representative intangibles are taxed. Thus, mortgaged real estate may be taxed on its full value to the owner while the mortgage is taxed to its owner. A corporation may be taxed upon the full value of its land and tangible assets and upon the intangibles it owns, while the shareholders and bondholders may be taxed upon their shares and bonds. The law views the mortgage and the mortgaged property, the corporation and its securities, as distinct and independent properties. Many states, however, prevent such double taxation by withdrawing specified classes of intangibles from general property taxation; others fail to enforce laws which would impose such double burdens.

"Taxable value." The *measure* of property taxes is the capital value of the taxable property as of assessment day, such as April 1.[12] But the legislatures have attached many qualifying terms to "value." Laws specify "true cash value," "fair cash value," "fair market value," "true value," "fair value," "actual value," etc. The courts have contributed to the confusion. In Louisiana, one court held that "cost" was "value." In one Connecticut case, a court accepted as the proper base the cost of replacement less depreciation, whereas in Alabama such a figure was held to have no bearing. A Wisconsin court said the thing to strive for was strict cash realization under prevailing conditions. A Washington court believed that the statute meant not "exchange value" but value to the owner using the property. A New Jersey decision, in admitting the probability of lack of an actual buyer for certain property, indicated that the assessors might properly estimate what a hypothetical buyer would pay. Underlying this conflict of phraseology and opinion is a general formula: "Taxable value is the price which a property would bring in an open market on a free, not forced, sale between a willing buyer and a willing seller." Yet this is inevitably vague and leaves assessors and courts with a range for judgment. (The possibility

[10] The location on tax day governs.

[11] Bank deposits can sometimes be shifted to escape tax.

[12] As of 1958 there were six states in which the law specifically authorized assessment at a fraction of current market prices.

of taxing land and buildings on "annual income" instead of capital value, essentially the British practice, has found little support.)

Assessment as of a particular date is awkward in its application to the inventory of merchants and manufacturers. Moderate ingenuity will enable a business to reduce its stocks to a minimum on the assessment date. Having obtained the tax advantage, it is then free to increase inventories to the requirements of business. To prevent such avoidance, over twenty states provide that merchants and manufacturers shall be assessed on the average of their stocks over the course of a year or some large fraction of a year. The single-day rule also makes for some inequities in taxing new construction and demolished buildings.

ASSESSMENT OF ORDINARY PROPERTY[13]

Assessment—the *listing* and *appraisal* of the properties subject to taxation (that is, the discovery of what exists and the judgment of what it is worth)—is crucial in property tax administration. Here are found the weaknesses and abuses which have opened property taxation to a barrage of criticism. Good assessment requires not only technical competence in valuation but also independence and integrity of a high order. The problems are inherently difficult. No two parcels of real estate are identical; location, at least, is always unique. Markets are thin, and knowledge of the full facts of transactions that are concluded is rarely possible. The owner of property has an interest in biased valuation; the downward pressure on valuation that he exerts will be a constant force eroding the tax base. There are no penalties on the assessor for failure to assess well.

Assessment organization. Assessment of personal and ordinary business properties is everywhere performed by local assessors—city, village, town, school district, or county officials. Duties of the county and subdistrict assessors frequently overlap, so that independent assessments of the same properties at different values may be made by two or more assessors.

Informed opinion is decidedly critical of village, town, and school district assessment. The assessment district should be large enough, in area and in taxable resources, to permit the employment of one full-time assessor and at least one assistant. Rarely, however, can a village, a town, or a school district afford a full-time salaried assessor. Too often, assessment is performed on a part-time basis at a compensation which compares unfavorably with a laborer's wage, and the function suffers accordingly.[14] The county, or a major city, is likely to be the more efficient unit. Even where

[13] Proceedings of the annual conferences of the National Association of Assessing Officers are published each year under the title *Assessment Administration* and are available from the headquarters at 1313 East 60th Street, Chicago, Ill.

[14] Over half the assessors in New York State spend 10 per cent or less of their time on assessment, and only about half get over $400 a year. Five out of six assessors in the state are elected.

a small poor county cannot support an adequate assessor's office, it can at least do better than any of its subdistricts. County assessment has the further advantage of removing the assessor to some extent from the influence—not necessarily willful and pernicious, but none the less dangerous—of his immediate neighbors and electors. In larger units, personnel can specialize on particular types of property—factories, stores, homes, personal property.

Most town, township, and county village assessors, and many city assessors are elected. Their terms of office vary from one to six years. Their pay is usually on a per diem basis, seldom over $10.

Experts favor appointment of assessors, preferably as part of a civil service merit system. The elected assessor is too often a vote-getter instead of a competent appraiser and administrator; worse yet, he may be a creature of the local political "machine" and misuse his office to further the "machine's" ends. When election puts an honest and able man into an assessor's office, he labors under a heavy handicap. He has a wide range of discretion, an ability to grant favors that is great indeed. If he hopes for re-election, he must continue to be politician as well as tax administrator; he must retain the backing of his party organization and curry favor with the voters. Such divided interests reduce his efficiency.

Dangers, however, also lurk in a system of appointment. If the office is at the disposal of a county board, it will often be made a political gift, a reward for political effort rather than fitness for the office. This hazard can be reduced by requiring appointment to be made from a list of candidates certified as to fitness by a competent and impartial agency—say, the state tax commission. As a further safeguard, the state agency may be empowered to remove appointed assessors upon proof of incompetence or malfeasance. Although the exercise of such removal power might be rare, its existence would help toward maintaining state-wide standards of assessment practice. Better yet, assessors should be made part of the permanent civil service, as in New York City. Tested competence should be the basis of selection and promotion, with examinations open to all.

State agencies for the supervision of local assessment procedure are found in almost all states. Too often this "supervision" is a mere "paper" power, seldom exercised. In some states, the commission performs the valuable service of preparing and prescribing assessment forms and compiling "manuals" of regulations and suggestions for the local assessors; and they frequently sponsor assessors' conferences. A few states go further and provide "supervisors" to train, advise, assist, and cooperate with local assessors; these "supervisors" help raise the quality of assessments.

Recently there has been a marked increase in state efforts to improve local assessment, with at least half the states doing decidedly more than before World War II. Oregon, for example, has a staff of about 50 field workers aiding local assessors and recently provided that only assessors approved by the state civil service commission could assess property. Maryland voted $500 a year extra pay to any assessor qualifying as a Certified Assessment Evaluator. In 1957, at least 25 state universities held special training courses for local assessors. Colorado completed a basic reappraisal in 1952, and at least a dozen states have thorough reappraisals in process. Nearly half have specialists for helping localities assess particular types of property. If the present rate of progress can be maintained for 10 or 15 years, most of the country can hope for good, if not distinguished, quality of real estate assessment.[15]

Use of private appraisal firms is growing. A community may hire an outside organization to make a thorough valuation of all taxable property. A staff which specializes in such work can quickly learn the general features of the local real estate market. It can then proceed systematically to value all property on a uniform basis and free from political pressures. The cost, considering the quality of the result, is usually modest. Thereafter, the local assessor has only the responsibility of making changes, to take account of new construction and other special developments. Another possibility is to use private appraisers on a temporary basis to value specialized properties—factories, hotels, and resort facilities, for example—for such properties often require detailed analysis and special competence beyond the capacity of even a good regular staff.

Despite sentiment for local autonomy, the actual assessment of certain classes of property has been widely transferred to state officials.[16] First to be subjected to central assessment was the operating property of railroads. Then central assessment was in many states extended to the property of other public service enterprises and more recently, to the property of motor bus and motor truck lines. Many industrial corporations also have properties which in their complexity and difficulty of assessment rival those of public service corporations. Their valuation is often beyond the capacities of the average assessor. When units of an industrial enterprise are scattered over a considerable area, no local assessor can value the enterprise as a whole. Central assessment of certain types of industrial property would seem desirable.

Annual assessment of all real estate is provided by the laws of half the states. From 2 to 10 years may elapse between realty assessments in the other states. In preparation for each assessment, the assessors are supposed to receive lists of taxable personal property from their owners, to "view and value" the taxable real estate and specified items of tangible personalty, and to enter the appraised values on a "tax roll."

Rural realty. Rural real estate "appraisals" are often farcical. Assessors frequently copy the tax rolls of their predecessors. Amazing values of prop-

[15] See J. A. Gronouski, *Equalization Programs and Other State Supervisory Activities in the Property Tax Field* (Federation of Tax Administrators, Chicago, 1957).

[16] See C. W. Macy, "The Theory and Practice of Central Assessment," *NTA . . . Proceedings . . . 1956*, pp. 501–510.

erty are omitted from the lists year after year. A marked general rise or fall of land values in the area is covered by a proportional raising or lowering of all values listed on the tax roll. Time and again, assessed values set against listed properties bear no recognizable relation to their true values. Assessors sometimes classify land into arbitrary categories, either establishing uniform unit values for each category or setting maximum and minimum unit values.

Happily, a growing number of assessors' offices are making a serious technical approach to their function. They check their property lists against tax maps based, in many cases, on aerial photographic surveys. They assess land and improvements separately. Shrewd rule-of-thumb methods based on experience and local knowledge enable them to make fair appraisals of farm and village buildings. They use sales data to check their listed valuations. And they apply various technical aids—filing systems and standardized entry cards for recording information about each parcel of property—to further and maintain the accuracy of their appraisals.

The best rural assessment is still far from perfect. Occasional parcels of land escape listing. Omission of buildings and other property is much more common, especially where farming has been undergoing dynamic change. Such omissions are easily remedied, however—given the desire and personnel. Inequalities of assessment occur—but they can be reduced by efficient review. The inevitable faults do not prevent a good assessment roll, so far as it relates to rural lands and buildings, from being the basis of a sound, fair tax levy.

Urban realty.[17] Urban realty assessment in many cities has become increasingly "scientific." It is a mass job which cannot give each property parcel more than a tiny fraction of the time a private appraiser would need for a professional appraisal. Yet techniques for reasonably good valuation on a wholesale basis have been developed. They require more skilled personnel and better records than the public will usually provide, but progress has been substantial. Separate valuation of land and improvements is usually employed to aid the equitable and speedy assessment of land.

City tax offices begin land assessment with a "block and lot map"—a detailed plan showing every block and lot, each with its own key number. Initial preparation and maintenance of such tax maps is expensive, but they earn their cost many times over.

The next step is to establish the value of a standard-depth lot in the center of each block. There will, of course, be wide variations between these standard-lot values from one section of the city to another and depending upon such specific features as traffic facilities. The current market value of occasional lots, here and there, alone or more probably with their buildings, can be discovered from sales records, by capitalization of the

[17] A comprehensive analysis of urban assessment techniques is National Association of Assessing Officers, *Urban Land Appraisal* (The Association, Chicago, 1940).

net rentals, by court decisions, or by private appraisal. When combined building-and-lot values are determined, lot values may be derived by the "residual" method of ascertaining building values and subtracting them from building-and-lot values. From a few lot values so calculated, the value of a standard-size center lot in each block can be estimated, by making allowance for value differences that exist between the center and end of each block. This center-lot value is then reduced to a "front foot" value by dividing the lot value by the number of feet of its width. These calculations have been standardized, and the assessors' manuals contain simplifying work-tables.

The "center foot value" calculated for each block is entered upon the "block and lot" map. For lots on either side of the central one, successively higher values per "front foot" are assigned by pre-established scale; maximum values are usually assigned to corner-lot frontages. To determine the value of a standard-depth lot, its particular "front foot value" is multiplied by its frontage. Lots of nonstandard depth, irregular shape, or influenced by special factors such as air rights or zoning, are valued by the use of tables constructed on principles that have been developed from experience. Assessed values are entered upon separate file cards for each lot. Essentially, the whole process is in large part a way to learn what is happening to land prices *generally* and to the pattern of *relative* prices from one area or use to another.

There are three methods used in assessing buildings and other improvements: (1) market price of the property or comparable property, (2) capitalization of the income earned by the property, or (3) reproduction cost minus depreciation. Each method, if it is to be used well, requires the careful assembly and review of facts on a massive scale—not facts for each building each year, but for all general types, and for each property altered since the last assessment. The more valuable properties are seldom sold. Consequently market price can rarely be used as a basis for their valuation, and one of the other methods, requiring much use of judgment, must be employed.

As a rule, city assessors' offices develop standard assessment record cards for various classes of structures—single- and two-family residences, apartment houses, office buildings, store buildings, factories, and miscellaneous buildings. Record notations include cubic space or floor area, type of construction, utility, age, obsolescence, state of repair, various classes of fixtures, and the facility with which the building could be remodeled to serve other uses. To some extent, tables and formulas can be used in evaluating these various factors, but the assessors' judgment must obviously be allowed considerable leeway. Once obtained, this information can be kept up to date by ordered reference to contractors' permit reports and records on sales, mortgages, foreclosures, leases, and court appraisals.

Where the assessor's office is politics-ridden or just understaffed as is especially true in many small cities, land and buildings assessments suffer from the abuses of the worst rural assessments. A survey in a New England manufacturing town with 16,000 population uncovered 1,896 buildings, lots, and improved parcels of land not entered on the tax map. Even more amazing, 49 of these omissions were on the town's main street—a mile or so long. New York State, in checking on local assessments in the 1950's, found cases in which real estate had been entirely omitted from the assessment roll. The vagaries of unequal assessments are likely to be even greater than those of nonlisting. In New York City, 1958 assessments averaged well over 90 per cent of selling prices in Manhattan but under 60 per cent in residential areas in Queens.

Personalty. The figure of $47 billion of all personal property assessed throughout the country in 1956 proves that only a small fraction of property other than real estate gets on tax rolls. The average was 17 per cent of total assessed values, with variations from 3 per cent in Maryland to 43 per cent in South Carolina.

Actual assessment of personalty commonly rests on sworn lists submitted by the taxpayers.[18] The taxpayer is likely to report only those items which he knows are already known to the assessor or are easily discoverable by him and to place upon them the lowest conceivable valuation. Where tax rates per dollar of assessment are, say, 5 per cent, the "penalty" for honesty is rather high. Upon information, inspiration, or guess, the assessor may add such values as he sees fit, knowing full well that his final figure is quite arbitrary and probably without relation to the actual value of the taxpayer's personal wealth. Should the assessment exceed the property's value, the taxpayer "swears off" the excess.

Some types of *tangible* personalty cannot well escape the assessor's list; others are notorious evaders. Farm flocks and herds and farm machinery—matters of public knowledge in rural regions and open to the eye of the assessor—can be listed rather fully. Merchants' and manufacturers' stocks of goods usually appear on assessment lists by compromise agreement between the assessor and the taxpayer, rather than on the basis of accurate appraisal. Machinery and store and office equipment are listed at purely

[18] The following effusion of the fiscal muse was submitted as a tax list for the Connecticut property and poll tax a century or so ago:

I have two poles tho' one is poor,
I have three cows and want five more,
I have no horse, But fifteen sheep,
No more than these this year I keep,
Stears, that's two years old, one pair,
Two calves I have, all over hair,
Three heffers two years old, I own
One heffer calf that's poorly grone,
My Land is acres Eighty two
Which sarch the Record youle find true,
And this is all I have in store,
I'll thank you if youle Tax no more.

nominal values, if at all. This slipshod practice can be avoided. Although machinery and equipment listings and book values as used for income tax purposes are not, as a rule, adequate for property taxation, they could give useful guidance. For some machinery there is a moderately satisfactory "used" market. Little short of scandalous is the nonlisting of household furniture and personal belongings.[19] Valuation of such tangibles, when reported, is commonly a compromise between taxpayers, who grudge what they consider an unfair, discriminatory imposition, and assessors, who have no intention of attempting an inventory of the taxpayers' possessions. City assessors sometimes approach the problem of assessing tangible personalty by fixing a presumptive value for each taxpayer's tangibles arbitrarily based upon such extrinsic indicia as the neighborhood of his residence, the character of his dwelling, and incidental information about his manner of living. Subsequently, the taxpayer is given an opportunity to prove that his tangible possessions are not worth the presumptive value set by the assessor. On the whole, listing and valuation of tangible personal property are seriously deficient.

Intangibles are rarely listed. If a taxpayer refuses to state what stocks, bonds, mortgages, or cash-surrender value of life insurance policies and annuities he owns, there is no way by which to extort a confession of ownership from him. Governments do not force individuals to open safe deposit boxes to permit the assessor to make an inventory. Nor can the assessor require banks to reveal the amounts on deposit. Intangible property in trust and intangible property before the probate courts are sometimes listed, because trustees, executors, and administrators are required to do so. Otherwise, taxpayers generally refuse to obey the law. Real property and tangible personalty may, after they are listed, be assessed at only a fraction of true value, but intangibles often bear their value on their face or are quoted regularly in the securities markets. Once they appear on the assessors' lists, they must be assessed at full value. At present property tax rates, the tax on some intangibles would absorb most of the income, sometimes more. Recognition both of this circumstance and of the injustices which result from taxing basic real or tangible property as well as its representative intangible property induces tax assessors to connive at the taxpayers' failure to list all, or even any part, of their intangibles.

Could the listing of intangibles be improved? It has been proposed that a record be kept of bequests received by beneficiaries, to indicate a probable minimum value of their future personal estates. Reports of dividend and interest receipts from income tax returns are in some cases successfully used as a guide to stock and bond holdings. Corporations doing business in

[19] "The burglar had discovered more diamonds in one of that city's many wealthy homes than appeared in the summary of diamonds reported for taxation by all the city's diamond merchants and their patrons in a body." P. H. Cornick, "The Tax on Tangible Personalty," in Tax Institute, *Should Taxes on Tangible Personalty Be Abolished?* (New York, 1950), p. 3.

the taxing state might be required, as are banks, to pay the tax on the shares owned by shareholders living within the state. Banks might be compelled to disclose the amounts on deposit and the collateral security for loans, and brokers might be forced to file lists of transactions.[20] But popular support has never been ranged behind such proposals because of the widespread feeling that the intangibles tax is fundamentally unfair and the more effective its enforcement, the more unfair its operation. The one partial solution to receive any approval is the classified property tax with special low rates on intangibles, described in the next chapter.

Underassessment and unequal assessment. State constitutions may specify full-value or equal and uniform assessment, but assessors, courts, and the public ignore the mandate. Underassessment and unequal assessments present a grave problem.

Once personal property is listed, a reasonable, if arbitrary, value can often be assigned to it without great difficulty. In practice, however, undervaluation is common. A 1956 study in Minnesota found inventories of auto dealers assessed for 14 per cent of book value, those of grocery stores for 45 per cent. In the valuation of real property, the assessor must exercise his judgment, and it often shoots wide of the mark. And when the assessor errs, it is likely to be on the side of underassessment, since the taxpayer would fight a valuation resulting in overassessment.

Several factors accentuate the assessors' natural tendency to undervalue. When a *county* tax rate is levied on the valuations of localities, every assessor is inclined to undervalue the property of *his* district in order to reduce the amount of county tax it must pay. Low local valuations, of course, necessitate a higher local tax rate, but the total amount of tax for the local district is not thereby increased. Similarly, the levy of a *state* tax rate encourages competitive underassessment by *both* counties and local districts. State aid distributed to local governments in inverse proportion to their original assessed valuations, presumably to equalize their respective resources,[21] may also encourage competitive underassessment. In a period of rising property values, assessments are rarely increased to keep pace with market prices.

Other factors, however, counteract somewhat the tendency toward underassessment. If part of a state-collected tax is distributed to local governments in direct proportion to their assessed valuations, local units find high assessments to their interest, since they thus obtain a larger share of the state-distributed funds. Also, where a constitutional provision or statute limits local tax rates and local debt by assessed valuations, a local government which is pressing close upon its tax rate and debt limitations may be

[20] Success of proposals such as these would depend upon the cooperation of all states. Otherwise, evasion could be effected by a taxpayer who is able and willing to shift his wealth to a state which is not willing to require disclosure. Interstate cooperation on the scale required seems most unlikely to develop.

[21] Discussed in Chapter 23.

forced to raise the level of its assessments in order to obtain more taxes or to float additional loans.

A nation-wide survey by the Bureau of the Census obtained data on the sale prices of a representative sample of real properties sold in 1956. The prices were then compared with assessments. In two states, South Carolina and Montana, assessments of nonfarm residential properties were less than 10 per cent of selling prices. The highest relationship was in Rhode Island, 60 per cent. In only two other states were assessments over 50 per cent of selling price. In most cases, the ratios were about equal for houses built before 1945 and those built after 1949. Farm properties and acreage were usually assessed at a lower rate in relation to sales than nonfarm properties —for less than half in several cases—but at higher rates in a few states such as Illinois, Iowa, and Kansas. Commercial property assessment-to-selling price ratios showed wide diversity. In New York the figure was 78 per cent compared with 47 per cent for residential property. The comparable California figures were 20 and 18, those of Georgia 25 and 22.

Assessment ratios of individual properties in particular districts in a state also show wide variation. County averages in Minnesota in 1955 ranged from 17 to 52 per cent, in New York from around 10 to 100 per cent. In one Kansas county, 39 per cent of properties varied 60 per cent or more from the median.[22]

City property assessment ratios are generally higher than rural, both because city assessors use more efficient methods and because many cities deliberately force up the assessment ratio to avoid pressure on debt or tax rate limits.

Underassessment as such does not involve injustice to individual properties or to classes of property. Were all properties assessed at exactly one-half or one-quarter their true value, tax rates would have to be double or quadruple the rates that could be levied if all property were assessed at full value. But underassessment would not change the tax paid on each individual property or each class of property. Improper discriminations result from *unequal* underassessment, which may go to extreme lengths. Within any district, individual properties may be assessed at anywhere from a minute fraction of their true value to considerably more than their true value. For example, study of one Pennsylvania county revealed that one property was assessed at 60 times its sale price while another was assessed at only one-fourteenth of its sale price.

Small properties are usually assessed at a higher proportion of market value than large properties. Owners of large properties find protesting high assessments worth their effort; moreover, assessors are less able to value complex properties well. In some places, however, such as New York

[22] J. D. Garwood, "The Kansas Citizens Examine Their Property Tax," *National Tax Journal,* Sept., 1956, pp. 258–267. The examples of inequality seem endless. J. K. Hall, "Sales-Assessment Ratio Survey in Washington," *National Tax Journal,* June, 1956, pp. 177–192, discusses another striking body of evidence of assessment inequality.

City, political considerations result in greater underassessment of small residences than of office buildings, factories, large apartment buildings, and other properties whose owners lack influential voting power. The further the general average of assessments falls from the standard of market values, the wider are assessment ratios of individual properties likely to vary. A difference of $10,000 in full assessment is more apt to be noticed than one of $1,000 when assessment is at 10 per cent of market price.[23]

The courts long offered no protection against inequalities of assessment ratio. If a taxpayer's property was assessed at more than true value, the courts would grant a reduction to true value. But they would not direct assessment to be lowered to the general level of the assessment of other property. The taxpayer's only remedy, they held, was to obtain an increase in the assessments of lower-assessed properties—a remedy legally unimpeachable but practically worthless. Recognizing the impracticality of this attitude, the federal courts have held that the equal protection of the laws guaranteed by the Fourteenth Amendment necessitates lowering the assessment of property overvalued in comparison with other properties of similar character. Taxpayers whose properties are relatively overassessed can seek relief in court. Actually, however, this remedy is for the most part available only to large businesses and wealthy individuals whose stake in tax discrimination is sufficiently high to warrant the expense of legal action; for the owner of an ordinary farm or residential property, litigation costs would exceed tax savings.

A few states have sought to prevent the injustice of unequal underassessment by providing that all properties be assessed at a specified fraction of their true value, in the hope that all properties would be equally underassessed. But this hope has not been fulfilled. In practice, the assessments fall below the statutory ratio and the variations in underassessment are apparently as wide as in the states where full value assessment is required. The strongest possibility of reducing unequal underassessment lies in the development of good assessment technique.

One untried possibility of improving assessment would be to base the tax on a moving average of value. Real estate prices *do* fluctuate, and one reason for underassessment is a reluctance to move values up and down with the general market. In effect, assessors do their own averaging and forecasting, often unconsciously and certainly crudely. But if the tax were based on this year's value averaged with that of the two or three prior years, the assessor might be more willing to seek and insert actual market values each year.[24]

[23] Assume that an individual property-owner wants to learn whether his real estate is overassessed relative to that of others. When underassessment is the rule, he must find the market values of the properties of others as well as the assessments. At full assessment he need worry little if his own tax valuation is the reasonable market price.

[24] See R. M. Haig, Carl Shoup, and L. C. Fitch, *The Financial Problem of the City of New York* (New York, 1952) pp. 170–173. Modern mechanical equipment would permit economical record keeping and computation.

ASSESSMENT OF SPECIAL CLASSES OF PROPERTY[25]

Certain types of property are so complicated that accurate appraisal is beyond the capacity of the ordinary assessor. Sometimes this difficulty is solved by withdrawing them from general property taxation and subjecting the enterprises owning them to other taxes—*in lieu* taxes, perhaps, imposed specifically as substitutes for the property tax, or general business taxes that have no legal or economic tie to property taxation. Often, however, the property tax is retained, but special assessment procedures are developed.

Mineral and timber lands. Mining and growing-timber properties present a peculiar appraisal problem—potential future profit must be translated into current valuations. And these ought to be good, for the economy can suffer from valuation and tax policy which encourage premature or otherwise wasteful cutting or extraction. The issues involved are too complicated and the values affected too considerable for the matter to be left to the rule-of-thumb procedure of the ordinary rural assessor. Tax commissions of states with extensive mining and forest properties generally provide their assessors with formulas for valuing these properties. Under one formula, the salable metal content of the reserve is first estimated *in toto*. Probable costs of recovery and sale are deducted and the resulting estimate of net proceeds is then discounted to present worth on the basis of the current rate of mining operations. Such assessment naturally discourages an owner from "proving" the existence of underground reserves much in advance of the time when he wants to extract them. Timber lands are sometimes valued by a formula which starts with an estimate of the value of the timber that will eventually be cut. From this figure is deducted an allowance for carrying charges from present date to the time of cutting. To this "present" timber value is added the stripped-land value—the value of land and growth below marketable sizes.[26]

Railroad and public utility properties. In most states a state body assesses the operating property[27] of railroads, airlines, and public service corporations. Rarely is the attempt made to value such property as a collection of individual items; it is generally assessed as a unit. The valuation of such properties, many of which are technically complex, is laborious

[25] Special procedures for assessing bank stock and taxing insurance companies are examined in Chapter 15. Massachusetts, Illinois, and Rhode Island still tax "corporate excess." This is the estimated difference between the full value as a going concern and the value of real and personal property as assessed.

[26] Many states, however, have adopted some form of postponement of tax on growing trees and then recoup with a tax on the yield when the trees are cut. Chapter 15 discusses severance taxes.

[27] "Operating property" is that property actually used in the performance of a public service enterprise's service. In the case of a railroad, it includes tracks and roadbed, engines and cars, terminals and stations, and possibly repair shops. In the case of an electric power company, it includes powerhouses, relay stations and transformers, wires, and poles.

and expensive. Appraisers must choose between original or replacement cost, although in periods of rising or falling prices neither basis fairly represents present value.

Assessing bodies more frequently seek to assess each enterprise as a "going" concern. When the "going" value of an enterprise is determined by a *capitalization of net income*, the assessing body is put to the laborious task of determining net income, only to have the income figure capitalized by an arbitrary rule-of-thumb ratio.[28] Furthermore, a valuation determined by capitalizing net earnings can fluctuate widely as net profit varies from year to year. When the *market value of a corporation's securities* is used to ascertain "going" value, the assessment is made subject to wide and erratic fluctuations on the stock exchange. Furthermore, if all or a large proportion of the shares are owned by a holding company, there may be no active trading to set a market value. In practice, the assessing commissions and boards rarely confine themselves to one of these two valuation methods. Instead, they seek by various arbitrary combinations to achieve some reasonable figure. Ultimately, ad valorem taxation of public service enterprises often resolves itself into a bargaining between the assessing body and the representatives of the taxed enterprises, with the latter defending themselves by the threat of litigation.

After the assessing body has determined a value for the entire enterprise, which may operate in half a dozen states, a fraction of this value must then be allocated to the taxing state. A number of standards of allocation or "unit rules" have been developed. A common "unit rule" is mileage—of railroad track, or telephone or telegraph wires, or piping. The fraction of the corporation's total assessed valuation allocated to the taxing state is determined by the ratio of its mileage in the taxing state to its total mileage. Gross collections, "traffic units," and location of tangible property are occasionally used as standards of allocation, frequently in combination with mileage. For express companies and car companies, "route mileage" is the common standard. The nonoperating property of public service corporations is ordinarily valued by the local assessors.

Utility property is usually taxed by each local district at the prevailing rate, although a few states apply special rates. Where such property is centrally assessed, the assessment must be equalized with other property assessments in the state, as discussed in the next chapter, and the general state valuation must be distributed among the local governments. Mileage is the most common standard for local distribution; it favors thinly-settled districts through which railroad tracks or electric wires run as against the heavily-populated areas which provide the traffic or consume the current. A few states use the location of the corporation's tangible property as the standard.

[28] Refined methods do exist, however. See J. W. Martin, "New Evidence on Tax Valuation of Public Service Property—Capitalization of Earnings," *National Tax Journal*, Dec., 1954, pp. 309–318.

The assertion is frequently made that the value of a public utility's property should be the same for tax as for rate-making purposes. Plausible as this may sound, the argument is nevertheless fallacious. In setting a value for rate-making purposes, a public utility commission tries to determine the investment on which the utility should be permitted to *try* to earn a fair return. If the utility is granted an appropriate rate schedule, if demand is adequate, and if costs are reasonable, then it should earn a fair return on its valuation; that valuation is then also reasonable for tax purposes (subject to equalization). However, the utility may not get an adequate rate schedule or demand may be too small. Then, even with efficient operation, it *cannot* earn a fair return on the investment which the utility commission uses in setting value for rate purposes. If its earnings are consequently depressed, the property would not sell for the valuation set by the utility commission. If the market value is thus lower than the valuation for rate-making purposes, the tax authorities may properly use the lower value in setting the tax value. In fact, if the lower value is not used, owners of the utility will be taxed more heavily than other property-owners.

PROBLEMS

1. Distinguish between tangible and intangible property and between real and personal property. What is the difference in tax treatment in your locality?

2. "If the state owns real estate in a locality, the state should pay local property tax." Discuss.

3. Discover the principles used in your community in determining the percentage of market price at which real estate is assessed. What are the reasons for failure to assess at full value?

4. What are the three methods of valuing real estate? What kinds of data are needed to apply each successfully?

5. Why is underassessment likely to lead to unequal assessment?

6. Find out how railroads and electric utilities are assessed in your state.

7. "The property tax must depend to a great degree upon the decision of the assessor. Hence, the public interest requires that he be both highly competent and of the highest integrity." Discuss each element of this quotation.

CHAPTER 19

Property Taxes (Concluded)

REVIEW[1]

BECAUSE a property tax is based upon a tax official's estimate of value rather than on a free market test (as is a sales tax) or on one's own report (as is an income tax), a chance to check the official's judgment is highly important. "Due process of law" clauses of the federal and state constitutions require that every taxpayer receive notice of his assessment and be given an opportunity for a hearing some time before the tax collection date.[2] During such period as prescribed by law or regulation, a taxpayer may protest his assessment and have it "reviewed."

Organization. No uniformity in organization for property tax review exists among the states or even within individual states. Where assessment is local, review proceedings may be conducted by an ex officio board of village, town, or school district officials, with privilege of appeal to the county board of review. In large cities, the assessing officials may sit as a board of review, or a separate bureau of review may be set up in the city's department of finance, or an independent board may be elected. When large values are involved, appeal from the findings of county boards of review can usually be had to a state agency. State bodies also act as reviewing agencies for their own assessments of special properties. Finally, appeal to the courts can be had from the decisions of review boards.

Procedure. Most local review procedure is farcical. The small property-owner, most likely to be relatively overassessed, is ignorant of review procedure or does not consider the trouble involved worth the small saving that may result. The large property-owner comes armed with political influence, legal talent, and mountains of evidence which the review board

[1] Review and equalization functions are discussed in National Association of Assessing Officers, *Assessment Organization and Personnel* (The Association, Chicago, 1941).

[2] The legal requirement is met if the preliminary assessment list is posted or made public in other ways.

cannot check and often cannot comprehend.[3] At worst, review is a matter of looking into the complainant's political antecedents and connections. At best, it is often a matter of wrinkling a brow, shutting one eye, and hazarding a guess. Both competence in appraisal and integrity are essential to good review.

Where an efficient assessment technique has been developed, the data entered upon the land value maps and the assessment cards for individual lots and buildings may provide the reviewing body with information that will enable it to pass intelligent judgment upon the owner's claims. The review procedure employed by some state tax commissions is very good.

The large element of unchecked discretion in both the original assessment and later in review opens opportunities for abuse. Lawyers taking cases on a percentage-of-savings basis, for example, may work in collaboration with an assessor or reviewing board, or both. A property-owner who hires the right attorney may have little difficulty getting a reduction, especially if the assessor was in on the racket and originally took care to set a high value. Part of the fee the owner pays the attorney may go to the political group or to the assessor. Next year the assessor may again place a high value, and the process is repeated. Methods of public check on the honesty and wisdom of reviewing boards hardly exist.

EQUALIZATION

If localities conduct independent assessments, their varying assessment ratios do not affect the relative burdens of their local levies, since each unit applies its own tax rate to its own assessment. But if these original assessments stand unmodified, a uniform county or state rate would impose a higher burden on property in the districts having high assessment ratios than in the districts having low assessment ratios. Unless inequality of assessment ratios among tax districts is neutralized, the more conscientious assessors who bring their valuations closest to market value merely penalize the taxpayers of their districts.

The procedure of modifying assessments to take account of differences in assessment ratios is called "equalization." Original assessments made by localities should be equalized before a county tax levy is imposed. Assessments of the high-ratio districts should be lowered; those of the low-ratio districts should be raised. Similarly, if a state tax rate is imposed, or if state grants in aid are based on assessed values, there should be state equalization as among the counties. A further refinement, found in many states, is state equalization as among classes of assessed property.

County boards of equalization are usually, though not always, identical

[3] Owners, in some states, may pay the tax under protest. After they have done so for several years, the amount of tax in dispute is large enough to justify the expense of litigation.

with the county boards of review. State equalization, now undertaken in four-fifths of the states, was originally performed by a distinctive agency—the "state board of equalization." Now it is ordinarily a function of the state tax commissions where these exist.

Procedure. Effective equalization can be developed for realty assessments. A state agency can consistently collect and analyze data on the sale prices of land and buildings throughout the state. It can also make some appraisals on its own. A comparison between these values and those listed by the assessors will give a basis for estimating the accuracy of assessment in each county or district.

Too often, however, equalization is either flatly neglected for lack of factual data or is performed in a casual, superficial manner. Customary equalization ratios are continued year after year, although the assessment inequalities they are supposed to correct may have shifted widely. Or perhaps, after the equalization board has submitted itself to an "ordeal by oratory" by representatives of the counties affected, heard a few witnesses, and noted a handful of sales values, the figure for one district is raised 5 per cent and that of another lowered by some equally arbitrary percentage. A county or state levy based upon such equalization cannot possibly result in a uniform or proportional burden. The general practice is to apply to personalty the equalization ratio for real property, but this only compounds stupidity by futility.

Nevertheless, experience of several states since World War II shows that good equalization is possible. Strong leadership by the state revenue officials together with support from the legislature can produce noteworthy results.[4]

Equalization can do nothing, of course, to correct *nonlisting* of personal property. No possible data are available to indicate the varying proportions of nonlisting as among districts or counties.

RATE STRUCTURE

Each school district, each village, each city, each town, each county, and with some exceptions each state determines its own property tax rate. Since every property is located within the territory of two or more superimposed taxing governments—a school district and a county at the very least—the taxpayer's bill embodies two or more superimposed independent rates. How high are actual rates in relation to full value of property? For the country as a whole, property taxes in 1956, the year of the comprehensive Census study, were around 1.8 per cent of estimated full value of taxable real estate. But this is a rough estimate. In some localities, clearly, effective

[4] W. G. Murray, "Overall Progress in the Field of Equalization," *N.T.A. . . . Proceedings . . . 1955,* pp. 449–455; other papers and discussion follow.

rates are much higher—perhaps exceeding 4 per cent over all, as well as on particular properties.[5]

Determination. Local property tax rates are of two kinds—mandatory "earmarked" rates and optional "general fund" rates. (Rates fixed by state law are discussed later.)

Mandatory special rates develop when counties or municipalities encounter strong demand for some particular function—schools, roads, poor relief, and the like—and either wish to avoid the odium that would arise should they increase their "general fund" rates to cover the expenditure or cannot raise their "general fund" rates because of legal limitations. The state legislature is persuaded to vote a mandatory "special" rate to finance the function in all counties or all municipalities. A dozen mandatory special rates may be found on the taxpayers' bills in some states. State universities and other state functions are occasionally financed by statewide mandatory rates.

Champions of special government functions support mandatory rates, since the functions are thereby freed of budgetary control by other local officials. And local officials generally approve, because with the costs of special functions removed they can make a better showing with their "general fund" budgets. Mandatory earmarked levies, however, breed a constant agitation for higher special rates, for splitting rates, and for new rates. They force the development of special functions in a pattern that is determined, not by need for the function, but by the productivity of an arbitrary tax rate in individual counties and municipalities. Ultimately, they entangle the local authorities who, with revenues earmarked, find themselves unable to develop effective accounting systems or to budget wisely.

When government functions were limited in scope and the property tax was almost the sole source of local revenue, tax rates were determined simply by dividing the figure for estimated expenditure by that for assessed valuations. This is less true today, when local tax rates are pressing against statutory or constitutional limitations or when an increase in tax rates may spell political suicide for the party in control. City and county officials are now less likely to make up a budget and then inquire what rate of taxation will balance it. First they note what funds will be available if the existing tax rate is maintained; then they try to judge whether added spending would be worth a higher tax rate.

Many state governments formerly used property tax levies as an elastic element in their tax systems; a few still do, Arizona and Nebraska for example. For the major part of their revenues, these states depend on such special taxes as income taxes, gasoline and sales taxes, and so forth. Should the revenue from these sources decline below current needs, the state prop-

[5] Estimates based on sample data in one study show averages more often under 1.5 per cent than over. E. S. Maynes and J. N. Morgan, "The Effective Rate of Real Estate Taxation: An Empirical Investigation," *Review of Economics and Statistics*, Feb., 1957, pp. 14–22.

erty tax rate is increased to cover the difference. Several state constitutions specifically empower the state government to make such elastic use of general property tax levies.

Ordinarily, property tax levies are voted as *per cents* or *per mills* on the assessed value of the taxable property.

Limitations. State legislatures, county boards, and local councils may not endlessly increase their property tax rates. Limitations are placed by both state constitutional and statutory provision.

Limitations on state property tax rates, found in one-third of the states, are stated as a maximum rate of so many mills on the dollar, commonly about 5 mills per dollar, or one-half of one per cent. Limitations on the levies of the counties and other local governments appear in all but the New England states and Maryland. The most common type of local tax rate restriction is the fixed limitation, varying usually between 10 and 20 mills for each class of government—counties, first-class cities, second-class cities, school districts, and so forth. Such a millage limitation is frequently graduated according to the assessed valuation or the population of the government units affected. Occasionally, this regular millage limitation may be exceeded upon referendum or upon review by the state tax commission or other central control body. A few states, instead of placing fixed millage limitations upon local levies, provide that any one year's levy must not exceed the levy of the preceding year by more than a fixed amount or stated proportion. Minnesota has used an exceptional limitation providing a maximum levy per capita for each class of local government. Finally, many states limit particular levies for specific government purposes, as well as the total levy for each class of government.

"Blanket" or "over-all" limitations, applying not merely to the tax levies of particular classes of government units but to the combined levies imposed upon property anywhere in the state, were adopted by several states during the 1930's. The stringent Ohio limitation establishes a maximum of one per cent for the combined tax levies on any Ohio property. The allocation of taxing power among localities using the same base—county, town, school district—creates difficulties.

Such limitations on local governments, which depend upon the property tax, may become a fiscal strait jacket. If the property tax rate imposed by local governments is restricted, but not their indebtedness, localities will resort to borrowing, even using money so obtained for current expenditures. If both tax rate and debt limitations are rigid, local governments may find it necessary at times to curtail highly desirable and even essential functions or improvements. After Ohio's one per cent "over-all" limitation went into effect, many Ohio municipalities had to curtail their educational functions, and a few were forced to close their schools completely for a time. Tax limitations are "an unintelligent and ineffective" device for trying to achieve a desirable objective. Sometimes they do not in fact limit, partly because the public resorts to other devices for raising revenue—the special district for example. They create confusion, lead to assessment manipulation, encourage borrowing, and generally complicate financial planning. Sometimes they prevent the development of desirable government services. They account for some of the growth of local government demands on state treasuries and the reduction of local autonomy. There is nothing in a rate limitation which helps discover or eliminate inefficiency in spending; if there are cuts in expenditure, very possibly it is the wrong thing that must be sacrificed.

A beneficial aspect of property tax limitations is that they sometimes force local units to break away from exclusive reliance on the property tax. This broadening of the local tax base is frequently desirable, for distributive as well as revenue reasons.

COLLECTION

All current property taxes—state, county, town, village, district, and any others—are usually listed on a single bill and collected by a single official, generally the county tax collector or county treasurer. In a few states, however, each taxing district has its own collecting office, so that the taxpayers must make from 2 to 6 separate payments.

Time and manner. Traditionally, property taxes are payable in a lump sum during the fall and winter. The arrangement is hardly conducive to efficient financial administration by the tax-receiving government, and is highly inconvenient for business concerns and urban taxpayers generally. But it fits farmers' financial arrangements neatly, for it is in the fall and winter that many get cash from the sale of crops. For other taxpayers, however, this arrangement is most inconvenient and helps account for some of the unpopularity of the property tax. Progress toward the generally rational goal—payment regularly in twelve or six installments, somewhat as utility bills are paid—has been slow. Half the states authorize two-installment, a few quarterly, payment. But thirteen still insist upon the single payment, a large and typically distressing amount. Fortunately, however, many property-owners pay one-twelfth of the tax each month as part of a mortgage installment. The lender then remits to the government. With modern mechanical equipment any government of even modest size could arrange to handle frequent payments to suit taxpayer convenience. The inertia to be overcome, however, is great because a complex body of legislation must be modernized.

Sending out bills would seem an indispensable element of property tax collection routine. Tax offices of large cities do so. But in several states rural collectors are not required to mail bills. In some others, bills must be sent on the taxpayer's request. Collectors, where they have the option, often content themselves with a general, published notice of the time and place for tax payment.

Delinquency and remedies. In one county, the firm application of effective tax collection laws by an efficient staff may in normal times produce almost complete collection of current levies as due. A neighboring county having the same collection laws but less efficient administration may make a very poor showing.

An unpaid realty tax is an obligation against the property, not upon the owner personally. But since the value of a property is normally many times larger than the amount of unpaid taxes that would be allowed to accumulate against it, and since real property cannot be readily removed from the area, the taxing unit would appear always to have ample security. Prior to the 1930's, no one considered property tax delinquency a serious fiscal problem. The penalties for late payment were high, half the delinquencies were paid up within a year, and rarely did more than a quarter of the delinquencies continue for over three years. Against continued and cumulated delinquency, the usual procedure was the "tax sale," at which liens for the amount of unpaid taxes, rather than the properties involved, were auctioned off. The purchaser paid the delinquent taxes and received in return a lien against the property covering the amount paid plus interest and certain other charges. If, within a specified period, the property-owner failed to pay off the full debt, the lien holder either acquired title to the property subject to certain qualifications or was given the right of foreclosure under the lien.

From 1932 through 1934, property tax delinquencies reached crisis proportions. In Michigan, the *average* for the state in 1933 was 40 per cent; for some cities the proportion mounted to 50 and 60 per cent. And a tremendous backlog was piling up. To have put all delinquent properties up for tax sale would further have wrecked the real estate market, might have led to vicious popular uprisings, and would have been useless anyway, since funds to buy all the tax liens were not available. Popular pressure forced the enactment of much "delinquency leniency" legislation—laws that extended the time of payment, reduced or waived penalties already accrued, or postponed the date of tax sale. By inducing many who might have paid their taxes to hold back, these laws only made matters worse. Years and economic recovery were needed to clear up the difficulty.

"Current" delinquency—payment delays of a year or less—correlates closely with the inefficiency of collection procedure. Reasonable penalties firmly applied by an efficient collection office are one cure; an even better one, possibly, is development of systems of installment payment so that tax payments can be easily fitted into the owner's budget. Continued cumulated deficiencies in "normal" times suggest that a farm or business enterprise is economically submarginal, that it is in the wrong hands, or that a home-owner has overextended himself. At times, reversion of land to state or local government and reincorporation of it into the public domain may be wise. More generally, the way must be smoothed through better "tax sale" laws so that the property may be transferred to holders more capable of managing or sustaining it. More expeditious methods have been developed in a few places. For delinquent rent-producing properties, a system of "tax receivership," under which the properties are administered by a public receiver, has been developed in a few states.

Some widely accepted theories of the use of fiscal action to reduce the cyclical swings of the economy might endorse property tax delinquency in depression and subsequent backpayment during a boom. The public would be left with more purchasing power when general demand was short; government spending would be maintained by deficits financed by inflationary borrowing. During the boom, opposite conditions would prevail. The crucial difficulty, of course, is that local governments need revenue badly during a depression and depend overwhelmingly upon the property tax. Barring fundamental changes in our entire economic and political organization, fluctuations in property tax collections cannot be encouraged as a stabilizer of the general economy.

PROPERTY TAX REFORM—THE CLASSIFIED PROPERTY TAX[6]

One basic approach to improving property taxation is the classified property tax, under which taxable properties are grouped for the application either of (1) varying assessment ratios, or (2) varying tax rates, or (3) special *in lieu* taxes. Proponents of this reform believe that these assessment or rate discriminations, properly adjusted, can eliminate many of the injustices of general property taxation. Even more important, it is argued, property which evades the current high rates of ordinary property taxation would be listed for the low assessment ratios or rates of the classified tax.

Most state constitutions permit property classification, and over a third of the states levy classified property taxes. In a few cases, the principle is applied rather comprehensively to all forms of property. More commonly, only specified classes of intangibles are subjected to low mill rates or to recording taxes.

Classified taxation of realty. Classified property taxes are extended to elements of real property in but few states. Louisiana assesses factories (not land) utilizing waste materials at 25 per cent of their true value. Since the purpose of the special assessment ratio is neither to make property taxation fairer nor to discourage evasion, this is hardly an example of true classified property taxation; rather, Louisiana's special assessment ratio is a sort

[6] For a thorough, though not a recent, analysis see S. E. Leland, *The Classified Property Tax in the United States* (Houghton Mifflin Co., Boston, 1928).

of bonus to encourage a particular class of industry. True applications of the principle are the special assessment ratios applied to various classes of land in Minnesota and Montana[7] and the varying limitations on the tax rates applied to three categories of real property in West Virginia. Occasionally, special low assessment ratios or low rates are applied to homestead properties, and special treatment of mining and forest property is provided in some states.

Classified taxation of tangible personalty. Some states apply their classified property taxes to tangible personalty. Their methods, however, differ. Kentucky places special tax rates on elements of tangible personalty. In Virginia, the rolling stock of railroads and motor carriers is taxed at 25 mills and other capital employed in trade and business at 7.5 mills. Minnesota, Montana,[8] and Ohio apply special assessment ratios to various categories of tangible personalty. West Virginia accomplishes classification by setting varying rates limitations for three classes of personalty.

Classified taxation of intangibles. In about thirty states there is at least a pretense of taxing intangible personalty. Of these, seventeen employ the classified property tax.

By far the favorite method of subjecting intangibles to a classified property tax is the *special mill tax* applied to specified classes of intangibles. In contrast, Montana assesses money and deposits at 7 per cent of actual value, bank shares and other moneyed capital at 30 per cent of their true value, and shares of corporations without taxable property in the state at 40 per cent of their true value.

A few states apply their special mill rates to all classes of intangibles, whereas the others so tax only certain classes of intangibles. Where only particular classes of intangibles are subjected to special mill rates, the other classes are generally altogether exempt from property taxation. Money and deposits are two classes of intangibles most commonly brought under the special mill rates. Business credits—accounts, bills, and notes receivable—are also a favorite subject of the classified property tax. Special mill rates are less commonly applied to corporation securities and mortgages; the former are often altogether exempt from property taxation, and the latter are more often subjected to recording taxes.

Special mill tax rates vary. For example, Ohio, which does succeed in getting personal property on the tax rolls, imposes a rate of 2 mills on deposit accounts, whereas Maryland taxes shares of financial corporations

[7] Minnesota assesses rural, nonhomestead land at one-third of its true value, urban real estate at two-fifths of its true value, and iron ore deposits at one-half of their true value. Montana assesses all land and improvements at 30 per cent of their true value.

[8] The proceeds of mines are taxed on their full value. Household goods, machines, motor vehicles, and boats are assessed at one-fifth of true value. Mining fixtures and supplies are assessed at three-tenths of true value. Live stock, farm implements, and stocks of merchandise pay on one-third of their true value. Other elements of tangible personalty are taxed on two-fifths of true value.

at 10 mills. Sometimes a uniform mill rate is levied on all taxed intangibles, sometimes two or more mill rates are levied on as many classes of intangibles.

Recording taxes. In several states, secured debts are freed of annual property taxes and subjected instead to recording taxes. Mortgages, bonds, and other instruments brought under such taxes usually have no legal validity unless they are recorded with a designated state officer and the tax paid on the occasion of such recording. Not only does such recording validate the instrument, but it also accords exemption from regular property tax levies. The exemption may be effective either for a specified period of years or for the life of the instrument while in the possession of the owner who recorded it. Recording tax rates may be fixed at so many mills on the dollar or per acre, or, as in Oklahoma, graduated according to the life of the recorded instruments.

Critique. In some respects, the accomplishments of the classified property tax would appear to sustain the claims of its proponents. Most states reported large increases in the assessments of intangibles following the introduction of low mill rates. Per capita assessments of intangibles are higher in classified tax states than in general property tax states. Without question, the application of low assessment ratios or low mill rates to intangibles increases the amount of such property on the tax list.

When attention is shifted from assessments to tax receipts, the picture is not so favorable. Increased assessments of intangibles were in many states more than matched by the consequent decrease in effective tax rates; tax revenues from intangible personalty fell off under the classified property tax. In some of the other states, where the change to a classified property tax apparently resulted in increased tax yields from intangibles, contemporaneous improvements in tax administration deserved as much credit for the increase as did the changes in the character of the tax.

Classification has served not to fill public treasuries but to make the property tax more equitable and more flexible. The general property tax posed a dilemma of equity—either intangible personalty escaped assessment and so its owners did not bear their "due" share of property tax burden, or it was assessed at full value and bore an excessive burden, while other property was fractionally assessed. Classification can relieve this injustice.

Just as the highest hopes of classified property tax advocates have failed of realization, so also it must be recognized that the worst fears of its opponents have proved groundless. Removal of the requirement of uniformity and proportionality, it was formerly argued, would throw wide open the door to favoritism in tax legislation. But the predicted logrolling has failed to materialize to any marked extent. The classified property tax has been treated as an instrument of fiscal reform, and there have been few attempts to turn it to ulterior ends.

PROPERTY TAX REFORM—ABOLITION OF THE PERSONALTY TAX

Because of the administrative difficulties of assessing tangible and intangible personal property, because of the destruction of respect for law that results from wide evasion, and because of the injustices arising from the taxation of such property, there is strong support for more basic reform —the complete abolition of personal property taxation and the transformation of the general property tax into a levy on real estate only.[9] One-third of the states so far have discarded the tax on intangibles. Several have dropped the taxation of tangible personalty.

If the personal property tax now imposes significant burdens, its abolition would favor, at least for a time, investment in securities, cash, machinery, inventory, and bank deposits over investment in new building. It would deprive local governments of badly needed revenue. Would it not work injustice among owners and users of property if, as seems certain, property taxation continues to be a major fiscal resource of local governments?

Personal property no less than real property embodies taxpaying ability. Exemption would throw a disproportionate tax burden on the owners and users of real property. Outright exemption of personal property would throw windfall gains to owners of such property who had capitalized the tax when they bought the property. Equity seems to require that the release of personal property from property taxation be offset by the imposition of other taxes indirectly reaching personal property values. Yet the theoretical and the practical difficulties of achieving equality of treatment are insuperable. When the taxes to be adjusted are imposed on things, as is the property tax, it is inherently impossible (1) to achieve equality of treatment of persons or (2) to distribute any inequality according to personal characteristics, such as income or wealth. Whatever the method used to replace the revenue loss resulting from the exemption of tax on personal property, there will arise another difficult problem.[10] How can *local* governments be adequately compensated? The devices discussed in Chapter 22 are available, but all raise problems of their own.

[9] A major exception might logically be made to keep business machinery and equipment in the tax base. There is about as much reason to tax such property as there is to tax business real estate. The tax would be shiftable to roughly the same extent. The property tax would then be neutral as among methods of production, not discriminating against methods that emphasize real estate. Inventory, however, is more movable, and variations from month to month are wide. The reasons for keeping it in the tax base are less persuasive than those for retaining machinery and equipment.

[10] An extensive study for a National Tax Association Committee by A. D. Lynn, Jr., and endorsed by the full committee discusses the defects of existing procedures and examines alternatives. Committee on Personal Property Taxation . . . of Tangible Personal Property Used in Business, "Report . . ." *NTA . . . Proceedings . . . 1953* (Sacramento, 1954), pp. 359–407.

Special business taxes and personal income taxes are most frequently suggested as substitutes for the personal property tax. Most business taxes are free of the practical shortcomings which mark a locally administered personal property tax. Transfer from a personal property tax paid by business concerns to a special business tax changes somewhat the distribution of the tax burden, by no means a clear disadvantage. Moreover, although the spirit of fiscal localism will not tolerate state administration of the personal property tax—which might give the tax some chance of success—it will permit a state-administered business tax to be substituted for the personal property tax.

Substituting a state personal income tax for a personal property tax paid by individuals also presents problems. Not all property yields money income—furniture and autos, for example. And if an income tax does not provide exemption for the income from taxed realty, the combined property and income tax system could be charged with imposing a double tax burden on real estate owners. Yet, if the income tax provides such exemption, property-owners whose property tax had been capitalized in effect escape taxation altogether.

What about the extreme case—removal of the tax on personal property with nothing added to offset the relative advantage of personal property over real property?[11] The forces of competition would tend to remove the differential, not in 2 years but perhaps in 8 or 10. An encouragement would be given to investment in personalty rather than real property. The resulting marginal shift in the flow of investment funds would lower the yield on personalty and raise the before-tax yield on realty. The yield on machinery, stocks, and bonds would be equated with the after-tax yield on realty.

PROPERTY TAX REFORM—THE LAND VALUE TAX

A final school of property tax reformers would eliminate, not only all personal property taxation, but also a part of the realty tax. They would confine property taxation to the site value and the natural fertility value of land and exempt all buildings and improvements. Land values, they argue, are only slightly the result of investment of labor and capital by man. It is predominantly "natural" value which owners can pre-empt because of the existence of government and the law it supports.[12] Moreover, a tax on such values would not diminish the quantity of pure natural resources poten-

[11] In fact, the revenues from taxes on personal property are rarely large. States which have made the full move, such as New York, have adjusted without producing either apparent economic distortions or injustices.

[12] An opposing argument is that settlement and development of new areas, to say nothing of fertilization and improvement of the land, require labor and capital whose return appears as "rent." Without the prospect of rising land values, such investment would often not be made.

tially available. Land values are therefore felt to be a peculiarly suitable subject for taxation in contrast to houses and factories, which result from effort and sacrifice of alternative uses of resources. Furthermore, it is argued that relieving buildings and improvements from taxation will stimulate new building; imposing additional burdens on land values will check the holding of unimproved land for speculative purposes. Taxes on land values generally rest on the owners, whereas taxes on buildings are shifted to tenants. Untaxing buildings and other improvements, by leading to more investment in housing, would ease the tax burden on the poor, who rent their homes.

"Single Taxers," notably Henry George, were the first active champions of the land value tax. One all-embracing tax on land values, they argued, would provide sufficient revenue for all government purposes. All other taxes could be dropped. Today, no such hope is realistic; all the pure rent from land would not pay costs of even local government. The impracticability of the *single* tax proposal, however, should not reflect upon the *land value* tax, which of itself deserves independent consideration.[13]

There is a strong case, in principle, for land value taxes directed primarily at *future* increases in land values. A heavy tax on *present* values, it is true, would not reduce the amount of land in existence. But present owners who bought the land in good faith before the tax would suffer indefensible loss. If the tax were confined to *future* increases, however, the inequity would be sharply reduced. And so would the revenue. Yet in view of the large growth of population that is inevitable in this country, big socially-created increases in land values, including many which will grow out of the new highway program, ought to provide an appreciable tax base.

A major stumbling block would be the assessment difficulties. In rural regions, an assessor cannot practicably separate the value of a farm into the value of its natural fertility and the value resulting from the labor of cultivation and from investment. Even in cities, where real estate improvement is embodied more generally in the structures than in the land and where relatively efficient assessment techniques are available, separate assessment of land value would present troublesome difficulties if different tax rates were to be applied. So few sales or leases of land without improvements are made that guides for separation of land and building values might often be inadequate. Inevitably, allocations of value would often be arbitrary. Hence, as a matter of justice, and to provide the owner with a positive incentive to make the best possible use of the land, a special tax

[13] Land value taxes have a history going back over 50 years in some of the Australian provinces and New Zealand. A number of Canadian cities have attempted to rely upon land value taxes as single taxes. In the United States, various California irrigation districts, Houston (Texas), and Pittsburgh and Scranton (Pennsylvania) have experimented with the possibility of "untaxing" improvements. In 1926 Mississippi provided for the exemption of all improvements on farm lands. Great Britain after World War II attempted, in effect, to confiscate future increases in land values in many important areas. The program was not a success and has been modified substantially.

rate on the increment in land value ought certainly to be well below the full amount of the increase.

ECONOMIC CONSIDERATIONS

The interest shown over the years in practical property tax problems has not been matched by exploration of the theoretical aspects. In part, the paucity of satisfactory theory results from the inherent complexity of the tax, in part from the wide variation of the tax as it operates.

Incidence. If the property tax were truly a general tax applying uniformly to all property values, it would be an unshiftable noncapitalizable tax. But the so-called "general property tax" is in practice a series of special taxes, sometimes at differing rates, on particular types of property. Moreover, unequal assessment and evasion make property taxation as it exists anything but "general." With these observations and the principles developed in Chapter 8 to guide us, we may lay down certain limited generalizations:

(1) Taxes paid on property held for personal use—owner-occupied dwellings, for example—cannot be shifted, but they may be capitalized when the property is purchased.

(2) Taxes paid on the natural fertility or site value of parcels of land cannot be shifted. They can be capitalized when the property is purchased.[14]

(3) Taxes on business structures, machinery, and other tangible personalty may be shifted by being incorporated in the prices of goods and services supplied through the use of the taxed property.

(4) Taxes on rented property may be shifted by being incorporated in rent charges, subject to the following qualifications:

(a) Long-term leases may block such shifting for considerable periods of time. Some leases, however, provide specifically that the tenant must pay all or part of any increases in tax.

(b) Rent controls may impede shifting.

(c) In communities and neighborhoods that are declining, demand for rented quarters is not likely to press upon the available supply in a manner to permit a shifting of the tax.

(d) The alternation of speculative building booms and collapse may prevent the tax factor from becoming a price determinant in the actual real estate market.

(5) Taxes paid on intangible personal property (a) can be shifted in varying degree to the issuer of the security and (b) can be capitalized when the security is purchased.

For some businesses, the property tax that has not been capitalized,

[14] The inclusion of taxes in the computation of parity for federal price supports and other aids to farmers adds a complexity.

whether paid directly or indirectly in rent, is proportionately heavier than for others. If the differences are not offset by variations in the quality of government services, the firms with heavier burdens may not be able to meet competition and shift the full tax to consumers. Conceivably, the net differences will sometimes be large enough in relation to other costs to have a significant effect on competitive position or net income. Beyond the railroad industry, however, examples of serious difficulties are probably rare.

The differences that have not been capitalized and that are not shifted back to the landowner in the form of lower economic rent tend to be shifted to price. To the extent that productive resources flow freely, they will move into some firms and out of others until the net return at the margin is equal. Prices must cover costs, except that economic rent on nonshiftable resources, such as good locations, tends to depend on the net return *after* other costs rather than to operate as a *price-determining* factor. Where taxes on improvements vary, the shiftable resources tend to move toward low-tax fields and away from high-tax fields until the final products sell at prices which yield the same net return on marginal investment. In practice, however, such shifting may be very slow; as among communities, the adjustment at best may be far from the most profitable.[15]

American property taxes fall far short of being universal. When they are not shifted, they tend to be capitalized—purchasers "buy themselves free" of special tax burden by paying lower prices. Since a majority of properties seem to change hands in the course of a decade or so, most present property-owners, we may conclude, are bearing as a true burden not more than the tax increases of the past 10 years or so. The burden of earlier tax increases was loaded, in capitalized form, on the previous owners.

Taxes on intangible personal property also tend to be shifted and capitalized. Some intangibles are exempt by law or by well-established practice. Federal government bonds are the outstanding example. Investors thus have an opportunity to buy securities which will be exempt from property tax. They will hardly buy securities subject to such tax unless the yield is correspondingly higher. Therefore, the issuer or the seller of the security must offer terms, or sell at a price, which will offset the extra burden of the property tax. There are so many other factors that affect the price of securities, however, that the process of shifting and capitalization doubtless works very imperfectly.

[15] A difficult case is that of a railroad which is legally obligated to maintain a service. A large minimum investment may be required in an area with very high tax rates—for example, New Jersey cities adjacent to New York City. The traffic which requires such facilities moves to and from dozens of states. Since the law requires that the facilities be maintained, the amount of railroad investment that can be shifted to escape the high tax rates will be small. The communities where the facilities must be available can effectively impose extremely high taxes on the railroad property. The pressure of competition and the slowness of regulatory bodies to adjust rates may make it impossible for the railroads to shift the tax for long periods.

Finally, the property tax is deductible in computing federal and state income taxes of individuals and businesses. Since the deduction typically comes out of the highest bracket if rates are progressive, a dollar of property tax will reduce the income tax by 90 cents in extreme cases and by over 20 cents for millions of persons. Despite complications and exceptions, it is correct to say that the net cost of the property tax is generally less, often much less, than the amount of the tax. The difference is, in effect, shifted to another government, predominantly the federal government and the general body of federal taxpayers.[16]

The property tax, we conclude, is widely diffused. The portion falling on industry, commerce, and most utilities and farms is probably distributed among consumers in about the same pattern as their spendings. This conclusion applies to the portion that has been capitalized, for it must, of course, be paid. Consumers in doing so make resources available to government. If the tax had not been capitalized, consumers now would be paying no less, but private owners rather than government would be the eventual recipients of the money. The part of the tax that falls on housing is distributed in approximately the same proportion as housing expenditure, with important differences arising from inequalities in assessment and variations in local government spending. In the lower income ranges, especially where consumption spending exceeds income as is the case for many retired persons, the property tax is regressive in relation to income (Table 11–6). Throughout the ranges where most families are found, the tax is essentially proportional. At the top it is again slightly regressive.

Distributional considerations. The justification first advanced for property taxation in the colonial and early federal periods was the *ability* theory. With income-producing wealth then mainly in the form of real property, the property tax probably worked well as an "ability" tax. Toward the middle of the nineteenth century, however, land-owning opponents of the expanding functions of government turned to the *benefit* theory as an argument against their being taxed for the support of these new functions. For a considerable time debate raged around the property tax primarily as a "benefit" tax.[17] Some argued that a tax on property distributes costs of government essentially in the same proportions as government benefits. Others believed that the benefits of educational and social expenditures are distributed far differently from property tax burdens, so

[16] Deductibility adds a regressive element to the property tax. An individual with a large income finds up to 90 cents, a corporation up to 52 cents, of each dollar of property tax saved in the form of lower federal income tax. Persons or businesses with no taxable income get no comparable benefit—they bear the full burden. This fact, incidentally, reduces the validity of whatever arguments there are for the property tax as an "ability" tax, as discussed in the next section.

[17] For a summary of (a) ways in which property (and its owners and users) benefits from government spending and (b) weaknesses of the "benefit" theory, see E. H. Spengler, "Property Tax as a Benefit Tax," Tax Policy League, *Property Taxes* (The League, New York, 1940), pp. 165–173.

that the property tax is unjust from a "benefit" viewpoint. In some cases, it was pointed out, there could even be an inverse "benefit" relation; for example, the owner of a "firetrap" building with a low value and low tax might get more benefit from fire protection than the owner of a fireproof building on which the tax is much greater.[18]

Later, "benefit" justification of property taxes again yielded to considerations of "ability." The "ability" argument for the property tax, however, is based on a false premise—namely, that gross property holdings are a good measure of ability. (1) Professional and salaried men with large incomes may pay less property tax, directly and indirectly, than persons with small incomes but large holdings of property. (2) Many forms of property escape the property tax. Such properties are sometimes subjected to special taxes which take the place of the property tax, but often enough the escape is absolute. (3) And notoriously, some properties are overvalued and others undervalued in the process of assessment. Rate uniformity avails not at all when rates are based on unequal assessments. A uniform rate levied on unequal assessments results in unequal burdens. (4) Furthermore, property-owners are not allowed to deduct their debts. Two persons with equal gross holdings will pay the same tax even though one owes no debts and the other owes debts in excess of his assets. (5) Some of the property tax has been fully capitalized and constitutes no true burden on present owners. And some is shifted to renters, to consumers of the products of a business, to users of a railroad or utility, and to investors. As a practical matter, it is impossible to determine how much of each year's property tax is a current burden or to demonstrate who finally shoulders it. Consequently, we cannot say how closely the tax conforms to any standard of ability—individual or family income, or wealth, or other measure.

In a community where there are no sharp inequalities in wealth and where the mass of property is of tangible, readily assessable character, the worst injustices of the general property tax do not develop. Given good administration, the general property tax may well prove satisfactory. But as a community becomes more industrialized, as the distribution of wealth and income diverge, and as the intangible forms of property values increase in importance, the property tax becomes an ever cruder device for distributing tax burdens among persons on the basis of commonly accepted measures of ability. It can certainly not be used to get progression, but it is probably about as successful as any tax in making burdens proportional on the great majority of families.

Effects on consumption, saving, and investment. Our knowledge of how

[18] Within any given community the distribution of the property tax among families is not likely to conform closely with any measure of benefit. As among communities, however, the burden does conform rather more closely to benefit when the property tax is a local tax. One exception is important, however. Some localities with concentrations of utility, industrial, or commercial property which serve a wider market may in fact impose burdens on outside property-owners or consumers, burdens which bear no discernible relation to benefits accorded them.

the property tax affects the balance between saving and consumption is certainly inadequate, but compared with alternative revenue sources, the practical significance of any differences is not likely to be great. The long-run effects on investment, however, are a bit clearer. Some types of investment are taxed more heavily than others. The differences do not seem to result from any careful social appraisal of the relative desirability of the different types of investment. Consequently, there is no presumption that the effects of property taxes on the flow of investment improve the allocation of resources and hence raise the community's real income. On the contrary, the chronic shortage of good housing at reasonable prices may be explained in part by the expense of the property tax. The cost of housing—20 to 25 per cent being tax, including, of course, any part capitalized—has come to include much of the cost of local government. The price is therefore raised relative to other prices; the pattern of consumption must be changed, with less being spent on housing than if all forms of consumption were taxed equally.

Unfortunately, the effects of the property tax on investment in housing are likely to be worse than has been generally recognized. The typical residence can be built under conditions of decreasing cost per unit of space within the range that is relevant.[19] Per square foot, a house of 1,200 square feet costs one-fourth less to build than a house half the size. To build a dwelling of 2,200 square feet costs one-third less per unit of space than the house of 600 square feet. The property tax, by raising the cost of housing, induces families to seek smaller units than otherwise. Consequently, the units built are smaller and thus more costly per square foot. The investment in housing, therefore, goes into forms that give poorer value than the housing that would presumably be built if the tax were substantially lower. The property tax, in other words, is to some extent a burden on production under conditions of decreasing cost. As such, it produces an unfortunate effect on the total allocation of resources.

Moreover, the total volume of investment in real wealth is doubtless lessened. Savings held in cash or bank deposits or invested in government bonds can escape property tax. Savings put into houses or factories or railroads bring the obligation to pay future taxes. Though the amount of these taxes is uncertain, the potential investor is assured that there will be an item of cost, taxes, which will have a claim prior to his on gross income, perhaps without any relation to his net income. Consequently, the tax, with its element of risk, must act as a deterrent to investment in new capital goods. The amount of the deterrent will depend, among other things, upon how effectively the competitive process alters the flow of investment to reduce differentials in net yields (and, of course, the benefits that come to property-owners and users from spending the tax revenue).

[19] The issues are discussed in W. A. Morton, *Housing Taxation* (University of Wisconsin Press, Madison, 1955).

Since there are genuine risks, however, some deterrent to investment in real property will persist.[20]

THE FUTURE OF THE PROPERTY TAX

Four considerations favor continued large-scale use of property taxation by local governments: (1) Capitalization has absorbed most of the tax's past inequalities, unless rates are raised considerably above their current levels; (2) the tax as it applies to real estate can be administered effectively, and even well, by local governments; (3) it is a major revenue producer for local governments, and equal or worse drawbacks attach to possible substitutes; (4) it will absorb some of the increment in real estate values resulting from general economic growth. Three major arguments against heavy use of the tax are: (1) administration by many local units is still distressingly bad; (2) the discouragement of building, especially housing, is unfortunate; and (3) the burden on the poor is heavier than seems good public policy.

The favoring considerations heavily outweigh the objections. Although property taxes will never regain their position as the largest single source of tax revenue in the combined federal-state-local system, they will long continue to be a major source, and for local governments the primary source. As new buildings are constructed, and if land values should continue to rise, the base of property taxes will be increased. They will automatically produce increasing revenues at the present levels of assessment and rates. Many local units can derive substantially greater revenues from property taxation without increasing their rates—by raising their current absurdly low ratios of assessment. Although there is much poor administration of the property tax, there is well-founded hope for improvement through extension of classification and through developing and applying better methods of administration.

PROBLEMS

1. Outline the requirements for an effective system of review of property tax assessments.

2. Why is assessment equalization desirable? What procedures are necessary to make it effective?

3. State the arguments for and against taxation of personal property on the same basis as real estate and also at a substantially lower rate.

[20] A discussion of many ways in which farmers are influenced by property taxes is F. D. Stocker, "How Taxes Affect the Land and Farmers," *Land, The Yearbook of Agriculture* (U.S. Dept. of Agriculture, Washington, 1958), pp. 240–253. In twelve agricultural states, property taxes range from 15 to 26 per cent of net rent on rented farms.

4. "A growing economy is foolish to permit private owners of land to reap the values that result from social development. A special increment tax should be adopted." Discuss, giving attention to the problems of administering such a tax.

5. In what sense is the property tax a benefit tax?

6. Assume that the property tax on residences in an area is increased substantially. Discuss the possible economic effects.

7. In what sense is the property tax a levy on a decreasing cost industry?

8. "Because he does not understand tax capitalization the typical owner of real estate seriously overestimates the net burden of the property tax." Explain and evaluate.

9. Can a community with its property tax impose burdens on nonresidents? Why?

CHAPTER 20

Inheritance, Estate, and Gift Taxes

"DEATH" taxes on the transfer of the property from a deceased person to his heirs are imposed by the federal government and all states but Nevada. Death taxes are of two types. An *estate* tax is levied on the entire net estate left by a decedent. An *inheritance* tax is levied on the share of a decedent's estate passing to each individual beneficiary or heir. Taxes on noncharitable *gifts* by living donors are imposed by the federal government and twelve states. Death and gift taxes yield nearly 2 per cent of total tax revenues—$1.4 billion to the federal government and $350 million to the states. Although the total revenue from gift and estate taxes may not seem large, it probably equals the yield from personal income tax rates over 43 per cent. As burdens on the wealthy, death taxes are impressive even when compared with the progressive ranges of the income tax. And death taxes have an influence on the way rich people invest and use their wealth that can have economic significance beyond anything the annual revenue would suggest.

FEDERAL ESTATE TAX

The present federal death tax dates from 1916. Prior to that, temporary use had been made of this tax form only in the Civil War and Spanish War tax systems.

The 1916 tax was an estate tax with an exemption of $50,000 and a rate schedule from 1 to 10 per cent. Later, the rates were increased and the progression sharpened. In 1924, after an attempt to abolish the tax had failed, a maximum rate of 40 per cent was applied. To help the states, this law also permitted state death tax payments to be credited against the federal tax up to 25 per cent of the federal tax. In 1926, the federal rate schedule was lowered, with the maximum reduced to 20 per cent, and the exemption was raised to $100,000. Credit for state death tax payments was increased to 80 per cent. In 1932, to obtain more revenue, an "additional" estate tax was superimposed. The state tax credit did not apply to this *additional* tax. Various changes in rates and exemptions were made during the next few years. The present rates, dating from 1941 but combined into a single schedule in 1954, are shown in Table 20–1.

TABLE 20–1

Federal Estate Tax Rates, Amount of Tax, and Credit for State Tax

Net Estate[1]	*Top Bracket Rate %*	*Total Tax*	*Maximum Credit for State Taxes*	*Net Estate*[1]	*Top Bracket Rate %*	*Total Tax*	*Maximum Credit for State Taxes*
$ 60,000	..	...	...	$ 1,310,000	39	$ 423,200	$ 51,880
65,000	3	$ 150	...	1,560,000	42	528,200	68,320
70,000	7	500	...	2,060,000	45	753,200	101,440
80,000	11	1,600	...	2,560,000	49	998,200	143,600
90,000	14	3,000	...	3,060,000	53	1,263,200	186,960
100,000	18	4,800	...	3,560,000	56	1,543,200	234,960
110,000	22	7,000	...	4,060,000	59	1,838,200	286,640
120,000	25	9,500	$ 160	5,060,000	63	2,468,200	398,320
160,000	28	20,700	560	6,060,000	67	3,138,200	518,000
310,000	30	65,700	3,920	7,060,000	70	3,838,200	645,680
560,000	32	145,700	12,400	8,060,000	73	4,568,200	781,040
810,000	35	233,200	23,280	10,060,000	76	6,088,200	1,076,720
1,060,000	37	325,700	36,560	over	77	+	+

[1] After expenses, contributions, debts, and other deductions *except* the $60,000 exemption and the "marital deduction." Amounts passing to the surviving husband or wife are exempt up to half of the estate.

STATE DEATH TAXES[1]

Several states enacted death taxes during the nineteenth century. A few were probate duties or fees—in effect, nonproportional estate taxes. Most were proportional collateral inheritance taxes which exempted the surviving spouse, the parents, and the descendants of the decedent. Toward the close of the century, some of these were extended to the direct heirs and some were made progressive. Administration was generally indifferent.

In 1903, Wisconsin imposed an inheritance tax with variation of the rates according to the relationship of the beneficiaries to the decedent, and with progressive rate schedules for each class of beneficiaries. This law became the model for most state death taxes enacted during the next 20 years. A divergent development during this period was the enactment of an estate tax in Utah and combined inheritance and estate taxes in two other states.

[1] For a discussion of the development of theory and practice see W. J. Shultz, *The Taxation of Inheritance* (Houghton Mifflin Co., Boston, 1926).

The 1924 federal estate tax credit for state death tax payments made it to the interest of the states to adjust their death taxes so that their rate schedules would measure up to the federal tax credit. At first this was done by imposing supplementary state estate taxes with such rate schedules, from which the older inheritance taxes were deductible. Some states subsequently abolished their inheritance taxes and relied exclusively on estate taxes adjusted to the federal credit.

Current status. Every state except Nevada levies an inheritance tax, an estate tax, or a combination. Although the rules for calculating the net taxable estate are broadly similar to those for the federal tax, treatment of gifts made in contemplation of death, charitable bequests, interests in trusts, insurance, and some other items varies, sometimes widely. Only a few states follow the federal precedent of exempting bequests of as much as half of the estate when made to a surviving spouse.

Nine states accomplish death taxation exclusively through estate taxes. Minimum exemptions under these estate taxes range from $10,000 to $100,000. Utah's estate tax has the lowest rate schedule—3 to 10 per cent; at the other extreme, North Dakota's rises to 23 per cent on estates over $1,500,000.

Rate schedules vary even more widely among the inheritance taxes. All these levies involve exemptions and rate graduation according to the relationship of the beneficiary or heir to the deceased. Minimum exemptions range from $75,000 for widows in Kansas to $100 or none at all in many states for distantly related beneficiaries. New Hampshire still clings to a collateral inheritance tax—no levy whatsoever on transfers to direct heirs and 8.5 per cent on transfers to other beneficiaries and heirs. A few states have only two rate schedules—one for direct inheritors and the other for collaterals. Inheritance taxes of other states differentiate three, four, and even five relationships.

Superimposed on this *relationship* discrimination in most of the state inheritance taxes is a rate progression based on the *size* of the beneficiary's share. The progression may be mild, as in Maine where the top rate on direct heirs is 6, and on collateral heirs 16, per cent. Or it may be sharp, as in Minnesota where direct heirs pay up to 18 per cent and distantly related beneficiaries up to 60 per cent.

Finally, most states impose a tax to cover the full federal credit. As a result there is considerable uniformity in the actual burden of state death taxes on estates over $250,000 despite the wide differences in inheritance tax rate schedules.

The diversity of state death tax laws is in itself a burden on property-owners and one that serves no useful purpose. Where people move as much as they do in this country, where property ownership extends so broadly and changes so easily as people buy and sell assets, and where heirs may be so scattered over different states, variations in the provisions of death tax laws—not rates and exemptions but in the definition of what is taxed—greatly complicate efficient investment planning and give rise to all sorts of arbitrary results. For more than a generation efforts by a few leaders to get substantial uniformity have accomplished little. Yet state governments have nothing of importance to lose by agreeing on uniform provisions, and they could serve the public by doing so.

State jurisdiction to tax. It has long been clear that a state does not have jurisdiction, under our constitution, to tax transfers of real property outside its boundaries, whether owned or received by residents. The state where real estate is located may tax its transfer even if the decedent and the heir are both nonresidents. In the 1920's, however, other property could be subjected to overlapping taxation by two, three, or even more states. Tangible personalty—for example, jewelry, furniture—would be claimed for taxation by the state of the deceased's domicile and by the state where the property was located. Corporation shares might be taxed by the state of domicile, the state where the certificates were physically located, and the state of the company's incorporation. Other intangible items could also give rise to multiple taxation.

A few states met the issue by limiting the base of their death taxes to property owned by resident decedents. A much larger number provided for reciprocal exemption of the intangible property of nonresident decedents. Under a reciprocal clause, a state levied no death tax on the intangible property of decedents domiciled in those states which did not tax the intangible property of decedents resident in the taxing state. By 1932, 39 of the 47 death tax states had reciprocal exemption provisions. It seemed possible that by this method of mutual accord, the states themselves would end the abuse of multiple death taxation.

Meanwhile the United States Supreme Court pruned away various possibilities of double death taxation by defining and limiting the taxable situs of different classes of property. First a single situs—the state of location—was assigned to tangible personalty. The same rule was subsequently established for money in a safe deposit box. Next to be outlawed was the Wisconsin system of taxing a nonresident decedent's holdings of the shares of foreign corporations which owned property located in the taxing state. Finally, government bonds were conceded a tax situs only in the state of the decedent's domicile, and a similar restriction was laid on the taxation of the most important class of intangible personalty—shares of corporate stock.

Thus, in the early 1930's it appeared that the states had their problem of double taxation settled. Property generally seemed to have but one situs for death taxation—realty and tangibles where they are physically located, intangibles at the domicile of the decedent. Nonresidents remained subject to state death taxation only when they died possessed of realty or tangibles physically within the taxing state. On such property they would not be taxed by the states of their residence.

Then, two disturbing trends appeared. One was double, or multiple, domicile. Domiciliary qualifications were so construed by the state administrators that a person might be held to be domiciled in two or more states at the time of his death; each could then claim the right to tax all his intangibles. The Supreme Court refused to assign single domicile in the specific cases and ruled that multiple domicile was not unconstitutional. Gross injustice can be done, but persons of means are now on notice and may be able to avoid subjecting their estates to such hardships. Revision of state laws would provide surer justice.

The second reversal of trend was the Supreme Court's overruling in 1942 of an earlier decision which had set the state of the decedent's domicile as the exclusive situs for taxing corporate shares. Once again, the Court permitted a state in which a corporation is chartered to tax the estates of nonresidents on the shares of stock of the corporation; Utah was allowed to tax the estate of a New York resident on stock in the Union Pacific Company. The justification was that Utah's charter was of benefit to the stockholder. This decision could have opened the door to an element of double taxation which would not only be inequitable but would also have discouraged interstate investment in corporate securities. Fortunately, most states either refrain from exercising this extension of their tax rights, or respect reciprocity provisions.

THE TAXABLE ESTATE

Determination of the gross estate or—in the case of inheritance taxes—the different shares and the determination of the allowable deductions both raise practical and theoretical problems. Table 20–2 shows the composition of estates for which federal returns were filed in 1955.

Elements of the gross estate or share. Most property of a deceased,[2] whether resident or nonresident, over which the taxing government has jurisdiction, is included in the calculation of "gross estate." By a fortunate quirk of judicial reasoning, the "federal instrumentalities" limitation has never been applied to state death taxation, nor the "state instrumentalities" limitation to federal death taxation. So-called "tax-exempt" bonds, therefore, must be fully listed. Federal law specifically excludes real estate abroad and certain pension rights.

Gifts of property before death were early utilized to avoid death taxes. To meet this threat, the federal tax and most state death taxes have been extended to apply to "deathbed" gifts and gifts made "in contemplation of death." Usually, the law provides that a gift made within a specified period

[2] For *state* death tax purposes, in the states where the system of community property obtains, only one-half of the joint property of husband and wife is deemed to belong to the estate of the first to die.

TABLE 20–2

Gross Estate, Deductions, and Tax: Estate Tax Returns Filed in 1955, Including Nontaxable Estates

Composition of Gross Estate:	*(Millions)*
Real estate	$1,560
U.S. bonds	457
State and local bonds	201
Other bonds	82
Corporate stock	3,074
Cash	748
Mortgages and notes	275
Taxable insurance	468
Other property	603
Total	$7,467

Deductions:	*(Millions)*
Funeral and administrative expenses	$ 308
Debts and mortgages	383
Marital deduction	1,372
Charitable bequests	398
Specific exemption	2,195
Property previously taxed	22
Total	$4,678

Unutilized exemption on nontaxable returns	$ 198
Net taxable estate	2,991
Gross tax	872
Tax credits	95
Net federal tax	$ 778

Because of rounding, details will not necessarily add to totals.
SOURCE: U.S. Treasury, *Statistics of Income*.

before death, ranging from 90 days in Kansas to 6 years in Arizona, is presumed to have been made in contemplation of death and therefore subject to tax. The law cannot go further than to establish a presumption of intent to avoid the tax, and such presumption may be rebutted by evidence to the contrary. In suits on this issue, the taxing government is usually at a great disadvantage. The federal statute now has a reverse provision—gifts made more than three years before death are *not* to be deemed made in contemplation of death.

The tax laws go far outside the boundaries of property law in determining the assets that must be included in the gross estate. The courts have upheld extreme provisions as reasonably necessary to prevent death tax avoidance. Many types of *trusts*, for example, may be included when the decedent had retained perhaps only a small part of the total "bundle" of property rights—control and income. It has become increasingly difficult for a person to remove property from his estate for tax purposes while retaining significant direct benefits.

The treatment of *life insurance* varies. The general principle of the federal law now is that all life insurance is included if the decedent possessed important "incidents of ownership" such as the right to change the beneficiary; however, if he had retained no such rights but had paid the premiums, the insurance proceeds are not included. State laws frequently exclude life insurance payable to a named beneficiary, a provision that costs heavily in revenue. *Jointly-owned property*, dower rights, property over which the decedent had a power of appointment, and other special types of interests are included to varying degree, the federal law tending to be more inclusive than state laws.

A major omission from the death tax base is property from which the decedent received the income but whose ownership did not pass at his death and over which he did not have full control. For example, A can put property into trust by his will, giving the income to B for B's life, then to C for C's life, and perhaps further control the disposition of the trust property even after C's death; there will be no tax at B's death or at C's death, even though each may have had, in addition to the income, considerable control over subsequent disposition of the trust property under a *power of appointment.* One, two, or more generations may escape tax. This is a serious loophole.

The definition of the gross estate for federal death tax purposes has become almost unbelievably complicated. The planning of estates, to save tax while achieving other objectives, is a growing, lucrative and important branch of law, accountancy, and financial supervision. It is also extremely complex.[3] Lawyers specializing in "estate planning" devise new methods of avoidance. Congress, the courts, and the administrative authorities may tolerate loopholes, or close them. Complexity increases year by year.

Deductions. Debts owed by the deceased and costs of administering the estate are deducted to determine the net estate subject to tax. The federal tax does not allow deduction of state death taxes in the calculation of net estate, but some states allow full deduction of the federal tax.

Bequests to government bodies or to private educational, charitable, or religious organizations are generally allowed as deductions. A wealthy person can therefore make a bequest to charity with relatively little net cost to his heirs. States, however, often limit the deduction to bequests made to institutions within their own borders.

To prevent rapid repetition of death taxes when an heir dies soon after receiving a bequest, a credit is allowed for death or gift tax that has been paid within a specified period on property in the estate. The federal law gives essentially full credit when a decedent dies within 2 years after the death of the former decedent. The credit then drops by one-fifth every 2 years so that none is allowed after the tenth year.

The marital deduction. Until 1942, residents of community property states enjoyed a substantial federal estate tax advantage. The federal law, recognizing state property law, in effect, exempted half of the estate of a husband or wife. This automatic division cut the total tax base and divided it so that the reductions permanently escaped the highest brackets. To put residents of all states on a more nearly equal basis, Congress in 1942 provided that for federal estate tax purposes, community property laws should be ignored.

[3] A nontechnical discussion of avoidance methods by a leading expert is found in A. J. Casner, "Property Disposition Under the Federal Estate and Gift Taxes," *Federal Tax Policy for Economic Growth and Stability* (Washington, 1955), pp. 847–855.

In 1948, Congress reversed itself. It provided that estates throughout the entire country should receive the community property treatment. The change was effected by granting each estate a *marital deduction*. This consists of the value of property passing to a surviving wife or husband up to one-half of the estate, providing that the surviving spouse is given substantially *complete control* of such property. Certain complex limitations apply, but the end result is a very large reduction in the tax on the estate of the first spouse to die and a somewhat smaller, but still very great, reduction in the total tax when the husband and wife die some years apart. For example, before the change, a net estate of $1,060,000 passing from a husband to his wife and the balance then passing more than 5 years later as her estate would pay roughly $550,000 under the 2 sets of death taxes; under present law, the total taxes would be about $415,000. The new provision permits a total net tax saving of almost $3 million on an estate of $10 million. The effective progression of the federal death tax was cut considerably. Where the marginal tax rate was formerly 22 per cent, it may now be zero. Where it was 59 per cent, it may now be cut to 45 per cent. Net estates of as much as $120,000 need pay no federal death tax at all if the husband or wife survives.

Time of valuation. Were property and investment values always stable, it would not matter when assets were appraised for death taxation. Value as of the date of the owner's death, value as received by the executor or administrator in the course of liquidating the estate, or value as transmitted to the heirs—all would be identical. But if property values rise or fall sharply, these three values may differ significantly. In a rapidly falling market, the value of an estate at date of death may be much greater than any subsequent liquidation price. Which value is chosen as the basis for taxation may be highly important to the government and to the heirs.

Legal theory assumes that an estate passes from the decedent to its new owners at the moment of the former's death. Under statutory provision or administrative practice, however, values as of other dates are often utilized. In 1935, the federal law was liberalized to permit the executor, at his own option, to have the estate valued for tax purposes either as of (1) the date of death, (2) the date of sale if the property has been sold, (3) the date of distribution if it has been distributed, or (4) one year after death in the case of property still undistributed by that date. Choice of the valuation date does not have to be made until 15 months after the date of death, so that the executor is able to choose the most favorable date.

PERSONAL EXEMPTIONS AND RATES

Major issues in death taxation are the amount of minimum exemptions and the degree of rate progression. In addition, fascinating theoretical questions are raised by relationship discrimination in inheritance taxes.

Minimum exemptions. Minimum *inheritance* tax exemptions are true personal exemptions—each beneficiary enjoys his particular exemption, its size usually determined by his relationship to the deceased. Generous allowances to the surviving spouse and to the direct heirs find ample justification. Frequently, such heirs were dependent upon the decedent and have now lost a provider. When their shares are small, to tax them would work real hardship upon the recipients because Social Security benefits and other income sources will not pay for reasonably adequate living.

But there is little justification for exemptions to other classes of beneficiaries. A brother, or a nephew, or a cousin rarely suffers diminution of financial capacity by the decedent's death. Their shares of the estate are pure windfalls. Even on administrative grounds, there is no reason for exemptions to collateral beneficiaries. If a total estate is large enough to be reported to the tax administration, the executor's tax report is audited as a unit, and "collateral" exemptions do not save any labor.

Under an *estate* tax, a minimum exemption does not operate as a true personal exemption—it does not benefit any clearly determined class of individuals. As most wills are drawn, death taxes reduce the amount of the residuary estate after all specific legacies are paid. Hence, an estate tax exemption benefits the residual legatee, whoever he may be. True, the residual estate often passes to the decedent's widow and children, in which case they benefit from the exemption. But this is not an invariable rule. Where direct heirs are covered by a specific bequest and a residuary estate is left to some special interest of the legator, the exemption favors this interest.[4]

With the personal effect of estate tax exemptions so uncertain, administrative and revenue considerations must be given predominant weight in setting the amount. One purpose is to save the tax administration the costs of checking and auditing thousands of returns on small estates, the tax receipts on which would hardly cover the costs involved. The $10,000 exemption allowed under the estate taxes of Oregon, Rhode Island, and Utah probably comes close to fulfilling this purpose.

The large exemption of the federal estate tax has a special background. Congress originally intended that the federal government would limit its death taxation to large estates and leave to the states the field of small estates. In effect, the federal tax was to be a sort of surtax superimposed on the relatively moderate state taxes. Incidentally, since only a relatively small number of estates would be liable for federal tax each year, administration would be easier and cheaper.

Relationship discrimination in inheritance tax rate schedules. A fairly convincing argument can be presented for lower taxes on the shares of an estate going to a widow, and to children, parents, and other direct de-

[4] An exception must be noted in the case of the New York estate tax. No exemption is allowed to the general estate but specific personal exemptions are allowed on the shares passing to direct heirs.

pendents of the deceased, than on the shares passing to other beneficiaries. Direct heirs gain wealth, but if they lose their provider at the same time, their inheritance is far from pure benefit. To justify lower rates on nephews than on cousins, on first cousins than on second cousins, on blood relatives than on relatives by marriage, is more difficult. French and Italian writers have argued that grief for the deceased varies in intensity with the closeness of the blood tie and that lower rates on nearer collateral relatives compensate for these varying degrees of grief. Also, they insist, inheritance tax rate discrimination according to the relationship of the beneficiaries to the deceased helps preserve a proper balance in the monetary side of the family edifice. Such reasoning is alien to American thought.

Progressive rate schedules. It is more difficult than often assumed to justify progressive rate schedules in death taxes under current doctrines of how tax burdens "ought" to be shared. The burden imposed by a progressive estate tax can bear no rational nor consistent relation to the "abilities" or "benefits" of various heirs and beneficiaries who receive different-sized bequests either by the testator's will or by the laws of descent. A poor heir to a small fraction of a large estate bears the same rate of tax as the rich heir to a large fraction. Just as obviously, "ability" and "benefit" can have no significance as applied to the deceased owner of the estate. "Ability" and "benefit" doctrines can properly be dragged into the controversy over progressive estate taxes only by interpreting an estate tax as a "back tax" on the owner of the estate.

Progression in inheritance taxes has little more logical basis. Relative taxpaying ability of the beneficiaries and heirs cannot be determined by exclusive reference to the shares they received from the estate of a decedent. In the first place, wealth alone is not a satisfactory measure of taxpaying ability. Moreover, the share of an estate received by a beneficiary or an heir rarely constitutes his entire wealth, so that rate progression based solely on the size of his share cannot by any theory approximate his taxpaying ability. Surely, a millionaire who receives a $1,000 bequest has a relatively greater taxpaying ability than a pauper who receives a $50,000 bequest. Yet under a progressive inheritance tax, the latter is taxed more heavily than the former. Moreover, since preplanning of an estate permits the owner to distribute the net amount that will remain after taxes as he wishes, the *actual* result of progressive rates may differ substantially from the *apparent* result.

In spite of the fallacies involved, glib "ability" and "benefit" justifications for progressive death tax rates are given and are popularly accepted. The real motivation for this progression, however, would appear to be much less any reasoned theories of tax justice than (1) the social intent to equalize distribution of wealth and check hereditary transmission of large aggregates of property, and (2) the pressure for revenue.

Possibilities of progression in state death taxes are limited. If any one state or group of states imposed rates much above the general level, wealthy individuals, to protect their estates, would transfer their residences and property to lower-taxing states. At the present time the federal estate tax credit more or less establishes the maximum for state death tax progression for estates over about $400,000. The federal government, however, is not bound by such considerations, since even confiscatory death tax rates are not likely to cause many people to move to another country. Its problems arise from the pressure that high rates create for tax evasion and especially for avoidance.

Avoidance possibilities are impressive. A big accumulation of life insurance can be built up outside the estate. Gifts may be made before death at "bargain" gift tax rates. Long-term trusts skipping generations may be established. The higher the level of death tax rates and the steeper their progression, the greater is the need for statutory "plugging" of avoidance loopholes. From time to time, the laws are tightened—and relaxed. The high level of federal tax rates inspires the employment of avoidance devices. The states, as a result, find their death tax bases depleted because of the efforts of wealthy persons to avoid the federal tax.

Where the rate progressions are identical, an estate tax imposes a heavier burden than an inheritance tax. If an estate is divided into many shares, each share is a reduced unit and comes only under the lower bracket rates of an inheritance tax. But if an estate tax applies, there can be no division of the estate to bring the shares under the lower bracket rates.

The federal estate tax credit for state death taxes. Bitter controversy has been provoked by the provision that state death tax payments may be credited, up to a prescribed fraction, in payment of federal estate tax. Does this not coerce the states to maintain uniformity and thus impair their freedom? Two arguments have been advanced in support of the credit. (1) The credit softens the burden of the federal estate tax and permits the states to levy correspondingly heavier death taxes. A similar result could be obtained more simply, however, by an outright reduction of the federal rates. (2) Prior to the enactment of this clause, some states had bid for the residence of wealthy individuals by competitive reduction of death tax rates. Florida adopted a constitutional amendment forbidding the enactment of a death tax and advertised this provision as a lure for rich residents. Without some check, such competition might have forced states desiring and needing death tax revenues to surrender this form of taxation. Within the limits of the credit, all death tax competition among the states has been ended. Whether a rich decedent was domiciled in Nevada or Massachusetts, his estate pays the same tax; if he was a resident in Nevada, the federal government collects all the tax; if he was a resident in Massachusetts, the state government takes part of the tax and the federal government part.

Coercion of the states is, of course, the very essence of the credit. A minority of the states is being restrained from "hijacking" the death tax revenues of the majority. Such coercion is not altogether to be condemned. The credit, instead of infringing upon the sovereignty of the individual states, may be said to increase it. Abolition of the federal tax, or of the federal credit, would only stimulate rivalry among the states and lead to reductions of the state rates on large estates. Such "cut-rate" competition among the states would magnify opportunities of death tax avoidance and substantially reduce net state revenue from this source. The credit might be modified to gain an original objective still to be achieved—greater uniformity in state definition of what is to be included in the taxable estate. Such coercion seems hardly a blow at essentials of state rights.

Tax rates on property of nonresident decedents. How to bring the death tax burden on the property of nonresident decedents into harmony with the burden on estates of resident decedents still bothers some states. Real and tangible property physically located within the taxing state is likely to be a small fraction of the total estate of a wealthy nonresident decedent. To subject it directly to a progressive death tax runs counter to the principle that such a tax should take into account the entire estate or the entire amount of a beneficiary's share. A special flat-rate tax on the taxable property of nonresident decedents is one solution. By sacrificing the progressive principle, it avoids improper discriminations between nonresident decedents.[5] An alternative is the application of the same progressive rates to nonresidents' and residents' property with the rates determined by the total estate or share rather than the amount of property actually within the taxing state. This so-called "New Jersey ratio plan" has Supreme Court approval.

Comparable discrimination is involved in the application of progressive death taxes to the property of resident decedents. The state of the decedent's domicile cannot tax real and tangible personal property located in other states. Therefore, the final rate actually applied to the property of a resident decedent may be determined by a fraction, instead of the entirety, of the whole. This shortcoming could be remedied by extending the "New Jersey ratio plan" to the taxation of the estates of resident decedents.

ADMINISTRATION

Administration of death taxes enjoys one great advantage. Assessment and payment are generally focused on executors who, as officers of the probate courts, act in quasi-official capacity. Their acts are under judicial surveillance. *Evasion,* therefore, is limited. Nevertheless, extremely high rates of tax undoubtedly lead to concealment of assets, deliberate undervaluation, and failure to disclose all the conditions surrounding gifts that may have been made in contemplation of death.

[5] In a small number of cases, the federal tax applies to property of nonresidents or property abroad belonging to residents of this country. Some progress has been made toward removing injustices by treaty.

Special problems. Death tax officials face special problems. They must sometimes pursue far-reaching inquiries into the background of large estates. Lifetime transactions of the deceased must be examined to determine whether any are subject to death tax. When this function is laxly handled, a death tax is doomed to partial failure. The legal problems are often intricate. Not all property subject to tax need be a part of the estate which comes under jurisdiction of the probate court; to an increasing degree, wealth passes in the form of interests in trusts, life insurance, property in mixed ownership, and gifts before death, which are outside the legal estate. Problems of valuation are often very difficult; since the tax is a one-time levy imposed at progressive and sometimes very high rates, a small difference in the principle of valuation may make a big difference in the total tax. Closely held businesses, large blocks of securities, and interests in trusts are apt to be hard to value. On the whole, the federal Estate Tax Division seems to operate well; it examines all estate tax returns, at least briefly. Additional assessments of estate (and gift) tax are about 11 per cent of total receipts, compared with under 2 per cent for the personal income tax.

Estate taxes are generally simpler to administer than inheritance taxes because the latter involve more separate interests, each of which may present special problems. Though actuarial tables can often be used with tolerable validity to value the right to income from a trust for life, or contingent interests, there are also interests which may not be determinable with reasonable accuracy until other heirs die or remarry. If tax rates are progressive, the tax may be far greater if one assumption rather than another is made in such cases. Equitable administration may then be very difficult.

In several states, the tax is still administered by the probate courts, although they are poorly equipped for the task. Elsewhere, state death tax collection is an incidental function attached to the office of the state treasurer, comptroller, or auditor—also an unfortunate arrangement. More than half the states, however, have wisely delegated death tax administration to state tax commissions or other central tax agencies. Rarely, however, is the staff adequate for administering what is an increasingly complex tax.

Existence of the federal estate tax with the credit facilitates the work of state tax administrations. On large estates they have available the careful investigations of the federal authorities as a check on their own audits. Most states have reciprocal legislation for cooperation in enforcing their death taxes—a provision that has substantially improved administration of the tax on nonresident decedents.

Time of payment. The federal estate tax is payable 15 months after death, but in most cases payment is made earlier to permit closing the estate and distributing the assets. Since liquidation of assets is at times difficult, the federal statute permits extensions up to 10 years from death in cases where prompt liquidation would bring undue hardship. The authorities require proof that forced liquidation would bring avoidable loss; where a reasonable case can be made, however, extensions are granted on a year-to-year basis. In 1958 Congress went further and *assured* an estate 10 years to pay if it consisted largely (35 per cent of the gross estate or 50 per cent of the net) of interests in a closely-held business. Interest on extensions is charged at 4 per cent. As a rule, the legal title to the property cannot be transferred until payment of the tax has been made or assured.

State *inheritance* taxes generally allow postponement of final tax payment in complex cases until any contingency is resolved, with current posting of a bond for the maximum tax possibility.

ECONOMIC CONSIDERATIONS

The economic theory of death taxation is in an unsatisfactory state. The highly complex nature of some of the conclusions about who bears the death tax burdens depends much less on economic reasoning than upon categorical assumptions about the nature of the tax and the way property-owners prepare for it. Four mutually contradictory views have been advanced: (1) Death taxes impose no burden upon anyone, since the deceased accumulator of an estate is inanimate by the time the tax is imposed and his successors have only a legal expectation without any economic basis. (2) A death tax is a "back" property or income tax, so that its incidence is the same as these other taxes—on the deceased. Somewhat related is the proposition that the deceased had to forego consumption to provide for the tax on his estate, so that it operates as a "back" consumption tax and has the incidence of such a tax. (3) The most common view is that the incidence of a death tax is on the beneficiaries, since they are deprived of wealth which they would otherwise have received. Today's death taxes as applied to large estates certainly reduce what the heirs receive. Yet, since the decedent can arrange the sharing of his estate *after tax,* no generalization can safely be made about how the tax burden is distributed among heirs—or the extent to which it may fall on people who get nothing but who would have received something had there been a lower tax. (4) The burden of the tax is divided between the deceased and his beneficiaries to the extent that the deceased may have been affected to some extent in accumulating his estate by anticipation of the taxes on it. There is no final basis for choice among these propositions, but the first and second seem less defensible than the third and fourth.

Effects on capital accumulation and business development. Death taxes are frequently denounced as taxes on capital. It is argued that, by absorbing a portion of the capital of decedents' estates, they deplete the productive resources of the country and thus check its economic progress. As will be explained in Chapter 27, however, no tax can destroy or absorb capital equipment. The true issue is the extent to which death taxes ultimately influence consumption spending, saving, and investment.

Unless there is sufficient insurance and cash to cover taxes and other expenses, part of an estate must be liquidated.[6] Eventually, assets sold by the taxed estate are purchased by individuals (or businesses or other institutions) who, except for such purchase, would have placed their current savings in other investment. Indirectly, the savings of these purchasers are thus diverted to government use. To the extent that heirs subsequently stint themselves because of the reduction of their inheritances by the tax and thereby restore some part of their wealth, such saving offsets the original diversion. But such offsets are probably slight; the reduction of inheritances by the tax reduces the incomes that heirs would otherwise enjoy, and hence their ability to save and to consume.

Individuals may prepare for death taxes by taking out extra life insurance—and the law now favors insurance. If the premium payments on these policies are covered by *extra* abstinence on the part of estate owners, one can argue that the death taxes are being covered in advance by a reduction of consumption spending. At today's income tax rates, however, a wealthy person is likely to find it absolutely impossible to pay for enough life insurance, by reducing his consumption, to preserve his estate entirely. The greater probability is that such insurance premiums are paid out of income which the estate owners would otherwise save; the money might otherwise be ploughed into the family business or used to buy securities rather than being turned over to the insurance company. Later, payment of the policy by the insurance company and utilization of the funds for tax payment are as much a dissaving attributable to the tax as if the tax funds were raised by sale of some of the estate's assets.

Death taxes thus tend to absorb, on the whole, funds that would otherwise have been saved and available for investment. They undoubtedly burden capital accumulation, relative to the revenue involved, more than any other tax levied in the United States. Whether this tendency operates for good or for ill is a matter of dispute. Many argue that, since investment is a foundation of economic progress, a tax which so predominantly operates upon saving slows economic growth. However, economists who believe that unemployment results from oversaving and underconsumption, consider the absorption of savings by death taxes an advantage.

A heavy death tax, to be imposed at some uncertain future date, probably has less deterrent effect on an individual's willingness to work hard and take risks than an addition to the income tax that will yield the same

[6] If insurance provides the cash, the liquidation problem is shifted from the estate to the insurance company.

revenue.[7] Postponement of tax until death rather than year-by-year collection has other advantages—the owner's security and his psychological confidence are enhanced, losses of bad years are fully offset against profits of good years, and—perhaps most important—more of current income is available for ploughing back into business. Although qualifications must be made—especially for the growing family business—the economic effects of death taxation are probably less depressing on business incentives than available alternative taxes.

Encouragement of trusts and estate liquidity. One popular method of reducing death taxes is to put property into certain forms of trust and other long-term ownership. Much property is tied up in such forms and more will be—not only property of persons now dying but vastly larger amounts of those who have died and of those who are setting up trusts now to reduce the burden on their heirs. A special study of one year's estates found that almost *half* of the property in estates over $500,000 had been put into trusts. This "trustification" tends to earmark property for relatively conservative, nondynamic investment, and so restricts the volume of capital available for economically desirable "venture" investment. We know too little about how much property is involved or the ways in which it is invested to judge whether this consequence of death taxation will seriously affect economic progress.[8]

Present death taxes have another influence on the way wealth is invested. They stimulate holding of cash, government bonds, life insurance, or other highly liquid assets as opposed to real estate and equity investment. Thus, the owner saves his heirs from danger of loss through forced liquidation. The economy, however, loses potential benefits of risky investment.

Philanthropic bequests. Religious, charitable, and similar bequests are certainly greater than if no death tax deduction for them were allowed. Philanthropic deductions now average about 5 per cent of all gross estates and 6 per cent on the largest. Here is one disposition of his wealth that the testator can make which is tax-free. Moreover, the bequest, or a transfer during life, may be made by the creation of a foundation or trust to which are transferred shares in a business which the estate owner desires to maintain intact; as trustees of the foundation or trust, members of the family or officers of the business can control the voting power.

Distributive theories. Older writers have tried to justify death taxes under the "ability" theory by two arguments: (1) If the tax be considered

[7] Until the early 1950's, the need for cash to pay death taxes, combined with features of the income tax, created powerful incentives for owners of closely-held enterprises to merge with larger corporations. Special provisions of the law now reduce the need for such mergers in some cases.

[8] The marital deduction leads to a growth in the amount of wealth under the control of widows, for the deduction is allowed only if the surviving spouse gets substantially complete control, not merely a life interest. Property control by old women, by trustees, and by life insurance companies, all encouraged by our death tax system, is not likely to make for a dynamic economy.

as upon the decedent, it strikes him at the moment of his supreme taxpaying ability—his death, when he has no further earthly use for his property. (2) If the tax be considered as falling upon the heirs, it applies to property on which at the moment they possess high taxpaying ability. Inherited wealth is in the nature of a windfall.[9] These arguments may convince a person who wishes to be convinced of the basic "justice" of death taxes. They collapse badly when the attempt is made to use them as justification for rate progression. Likewise, they offer but weak support for inheritance tax rate graduation according to the relationship of the beneficiary or heir to the decedent.

The more modern argument of those who emphasize "ability" is rather different. Death taxes rarely burden the very poor or even the low income families. Here is a tax which falls chiefly upon the more prosperous, with the bulk of the burden probably confined to the wealthy. A tax system which puts heavy sales, payroll, property, and business tax loads on the masses is strengthened by a revenue source which can draw heavily, even if unequally and crudely, from the rich. Compared with most other revenue sources, death taxes are better on grounds of ability because they fall on the prosperous, not the poor.

Another argument to justify death taxation—the "silent partner" doctrine—maintains that an individual can accumulate an estate only by reason of the business milieu provided by government. In effect, the State is a silent partner in the accumulation of all individual fortunes. Its share in the building of large fortunes is relatively greater than for small fortunes. A death tax is merely government's method of collecting its share in the partnership assets on the dissolution of that partnership. Although the "silent partner" doctrine may support estate taxes and rate progression—a dubious matter at best—it offers no justification for inheritance taxes and relationship discrimination.

Early in the nineteenth century, some economists argued that death taxes find their justification in the "benefit" theory of taxation. Sometimes, the "benefit" involved was stated as the government's protection of the estate between death and distribution among the heirs. Sometimes, the concept was extended to include the general protection afforded the property during the lifetimes of the owners. Proponents of the "benefit" theory were usually anxious to limit the death tax to a moderate transfer fee and advanced the argument as authority for so limiting the tax.

Some writers have argued that a death tax is a sort of lump-sum "back tax," taking the place of property and income taxes which might have been levied during the lifetime of the decedent or which were levied but were evaded or avoided by him. This argument would seem to be very weak support for a general death tax applicable to the estates of decedents who

[9] A third argument rests on legal theorizing of no appreciable economic merit. Until the beneficiaries and heirs receive their shares, it is argued, the taxed property does not belong to them, and they cannot be considered as burdened by any taxes upon it.

accomplished no tax evasion. A more convincing version runs as follows: Death taxes do not have the *same* loopholes as the income tax. If we wish to impose heavy tax burdens on the prosperous and the very rich, we can do so more fairly and more effectively by using the two taxes than by relying upon either one. Capital gains unrealized up to time of death, income taxed at capital gain rates only, tax exempt bonds, funds received as tax exempt depletion, and other sources or forms of wealth reached inadequately by the income tax may be subjected to death tax.

Finally, we may note the contention of some legalists that there is no "natural right" of bequest or inheritance. Transfer of property at the death of the owner is a privilege accorded by state law, and what the states give, they may take away or limit. Although this is true of transfer of property at death, it is no less true of any other civil status or transaction. Bequest and inheritance are no greater "privileges" than all the multitude of others we enjoy under civil government. Herein, therefore, there is no justification for a special tax on these transactions. Moreover, this argument provides no basis for federal death taxation, since the "privilege" of bequest and inheritance are accorded entirely by state law.

Death taxes fail badly on the score of neutrality.[10] The distribution of the burdens of few, if any, other taxes depends so much upon chance and upon considerations largely irrelevant to the underlying economic circumstances of those bearing the tax burden. The amount of the tax to be paid depends not only on the value of the estate or inheritance, and sometimes on the relationship of the beneficiary to the decedent, but varies also according to accidents of the value of the estate at and after death, the length of time between succeeding deaths, the kind of property involved, the skill in selection of an "estate plan," willingness and ability to employ avoidance devices, the quality of negotiation with tax officials, and other extraneous circumstances.

That death taxes find no consistent support in the theorists' canons of distributive justice does not condemn these taxes. As was indicated in Chapter 9, these "canons" are rationalizations rather than reasons and are primarily useful for propaganda purposes. Logically or illogically, popular opinion in the United States accepts death taxes as "just"—more "just" than sales, or business, or even high income taxes—and thus gives them pragmatic sanction.

Reduction of large fortunes. Death taxes are sometimes defended on the ground that they reduce the inequality of wealth and check the development of hereditary plutocracy. They do, but crudely. Avoidance loopholes afford substantial relief opportunities to possessors of large estates. There is little over-all adjustment of federal rates to the number of heirs or to their other wealth. The tax is not related to how the decedent

[10] C. L. Harriss, "Sources of Injustice in Death Taxation," *National Tax Journal*, Dec., 1954, pp. 289–308.

accumulated his wealth,[11] nor to how long his heirs will enjoy it, and rarely to how long he possessed it prior to his death. The present system is far indeed from an equitable, refined, or effective instrument for equalizing wealth. Yet, it does make substantial inroads on large fortunes. And certainly, this social consideration has been an important motivation of the high progressive rates of the federal estate tax.

GIFT TAXES[12]

A tax might be imposed on gifts as an incidental method of producing some additional revenue, just as taxes have been or are levied on other transactions—for example, the issuance of corporate securities, the payment of checks, the sale of theater tickets. Such a casual tax on gifts would be legally sound, but would have little else to recommend it. It would affront the popular sentiment that gift-giving is meritorious, and it would be difficult to administer.

Our current gift taxes, however, were not enacted as independent revenue measures. They were passed and they are popularly accepted as supplements to death and income taxes. Though they occasionally yield welcome revenue, their primary purpose is to check the avoidance of (1) death taxes by making *inter vivos* gifts, and (2) income taxes by the splitting of a large income-yielding capital among the members of a family or into many trusts.

The federal gift tax. The present federal gift tax dates from 1932. The rate schedule was set, and has been adjusted to remain, at exactly three-quarters that of the estate tax, on the theory that the earlier payment of the gift tax made the ultimate burden of the two taxes approximately even.

[11] A more refined use of death taxes to check the transfer of family fortunes from generation to generation has occasionally received favorable attention. Under this plan, the estate of every decedent would be divided into two parts—the first part would equal the amount of the property which the decedent inherited and received as gifts during his lifetime, the second would consist of the additional wealth he accumulated through his own efforts. Normal estate tax rates would apply only to this second part of the decedent's estate. An additional discriminatory tax would be levied on the first part. Certain features which recommend this project are lacking in other proposals to use death taxes as a means of equalizing wealth distribution. It is in harmony with the popular disapproval of the "idle rich." It cannot be charged with discouraging individual initiative. In this respect, its effect, if any, would be to stimulate increased efforts by rich men who had inherited their fortunes to accumulate fortunes of their own to transfer to their children at the lower schedule of rates. Its principle could be effected, without altering the death tax revenue, by simultaneously reducing the death tax rates on earned wealth while increasing the rates on unearned wealth. The practical difficulties, however, would be substantial.

For a more complicated proposal, see W. Vickrey, *Agenda for Progressive Taxation* (Ronald Press, New York, 1947). This plan would impose progressively higher rates, the greater the excess of the age of the decedent over that of the heir. The avoidance of death tax by skipping one or more generations would thus be reduced greatly.

[12] C. L. Harriss, *Gift Taxation in the United States* (American Council on Public Affairs, Washington, 1940).

The applicable rate is determined by the *cumulation* of gifts in various years. Gifts made in any year are taxed at a rate determined by the *total* of all gifts made by the donor since 1932. A donor, therefore, pays the same tax whether he makes a large gift in a single lump-sum or spreads it over a period of years, except for differences in the total exemptions. In general, the gift tax applies to the same kinds of property transfers as the estate tax[13] and administration is roughly parallel. Heavy reliance is placed upon the donor's voluntary disclosure of his gifts.

The tax advantages of gifts remain substantial. By use of gifts, the total tax on the transfer of capital from one generation to another can be reduced below what would be imposed by an estate tax on the full amount—in four ways: (1) Gift of *part* of a person's wealth avoids the high brackets of *both* the estate tax and the gift tax applied to the full amount. (2) The funds used to pay the gift tax are not part of the gift, and the tax does not apply to such funds; the estate tax base, however, includes the funds used to pay the tax. (3) By making gifts, a donor can get large total exemptions—at least $30,000 during his lifetime plus an "exclusion" of $3,000 *each* year for *each* donee. (4) Income tax savings from the splitting of investment yields on capital divided among a family group may be large.

The federal estate tax on a $10 million estate is roughly $6 million, ignoring the marital deduction. If gifts totalling $6 million were made, however, the gift tax would be about $2.3 million. The estate tax on the remainder would be roughly $570,000. Thus, the combined estate and gift tax would be well under half of what the estate tax would be if no gifts at all were made. The income tax saving resulting from the splitting of capital might well offset the loss of income from the funds used to pay the gift tax. The *marital deduction* also applies to the gift tax. In effect, for a married person the lifetime exemption becomes $60,000, and the annual exclusion per donee $6,000. As a result, the opportunities for tax avoidance are greatly increased.

There are some partially offsetting disadvantages to making gifts. The funds used to pay the gift tax are no longer available to earn income for the donor. His control over the donated property is reduced or lost. Estate and gift tax rates to which the wealth will be subject may be reduced after a gift has been made—if property values fall, for example. And finally, the donee may predecease the donor so that extra tax, instead of estate tax avoidance, results.

Figures on annual gift tax revenue—$134 million from 80,000 returns in 1958—do not represent the full productivity of the tax. Many gifts which would otherwise have been made to avoid income and subsequent estate taxation are discouraged. This indirect yield is unquestionably substantial.

State gift taxes. Wisconsin levied a gift tax in 1933; by 1958, eleven

[13] The gift tax applies to gifts of foreign real estate. If it did not, avoidance would be easy—foreign real estate could be purchased, a gift made, the property resold, and the proceeds returned to this country.

other states had followed suit. The Wisconsin tax is assessed to the donee, but most state gift taxes are assessed to the donor.

Two types of exemptions are allowed. The first is a specific exemption on the total of gifts made by the donor—a single lump-sum, such as $10,000 in Oregon. The second type of exemption is an annual exemption per donee, which may be uniform or may be graduated according to the relationship of the donee to the donor.

Rates of state gift taxes are generally graduated not only by amount but also by relationship of the donor to the beneficiary. The Minnesota tax, for example, has a rate schedule ranging from .75 per cent to 9 per cent on gifts to a wife or minor child, three scales of intermediate rates, and a fifth ranging from 3.75 per cent to 45 per cent on gifts to distant relatives and strangers. Generally, these gift tax rates are about the same as the states' inheritance tax rates. A few states employ the federal requirement that gifts made in successive years must be aggregated to determine tax liability.

These state gift taxes, like the federal levy, have been adopted not so much for their direct revenue yield—which is less than $10 million a year—as to check avoidance of the states' death taxes.[14] Little effort is spent on administration. It is improbable that large taxable gifts escape the tax, but many smaller ones undoubtedly do.

INTEGRATION OF THE DEATH AND GIFT TAXES

An outstanding defect of the present methods of taxing transfers of wealth is the use of two different taxes, one on gifts during life and another on transfers at death. The tax base is thereby split, largely at the option of the taxpayer. The total tax paid on any given amount of property transferred can vary tremendously, depending upon the proportion given away before death. By judicious use of the favorable features of both taxes, a person of wealth can cut the total tax to a small fraction of what it would be if he retained all the property until his death. Not all taxpayers, however, have equal opportunities to exploit these avoidance devices. Because of ignorance, capital requirements of a business, legal restraints on the disposition of trusteed property, uncertainty about future property values, early death, doubt about the capabilities of heirs, and other reasons, some persons find it much harder to make tax-saving gifts than do others.

To reduce opportunities of tax avoidance and to put all taxpayers on a more nearly equal basis, it has been suggested—and was proposed by the Treasury in 1950—that the present estate and gift taxes be integrated or consolidated into a single progressive tax on transfers. Gifts made during life would be taxed at progressive rates, the progression being based upon the cumulated total of gifts made during a lifetime, as at present. Instead

[14] States also receive an indirect yield from the federal gift tax since it operates to discourage gifts which would reduce state death and income tax revenue.

of allowing a new exemption and starting at the bottom of a new scale of progressive rates at death, the estate would be taxed as a final gift at a rate determined by the total of the decedent's transfers during life and at death. The logic of the proposal seems clear. The practical difficulties do not seem serious, and there would be important offsetting advantages because there would no longer be need to attach such weight to the question of whether or not a transfer should be treated as a gift for tax purposes. Unless some such integration is effected, the revenue from death and gift taxes will fall far below the potentialities, and the taxes will continue to impose vastly different burdens on transfers of fortunes of essentially the same size.

Part of any program seeking such reform should be reduction in rates, especially those over 50 per cent. Support for such rate reduction as part of a "package" including a more comprehensive base might enlist cooperation from more conservative elements, or at least dull their opposition.

Another, more fundamental, suggested reform would be the substitution of an "accessions" tax for the federal estate and gift taxes. Each person receiving bequests or gifts (above an exemption and annual exclusions) would be taxed on the total received, whether the individual "accessions" came from one or a dozen persons. The cumulative principle of the present gift tax would serve well. Each year's "accessions" would be added to those of earlier years to determine the bracket rate which would apply to receipts of the year. Whether the practical difficulties arising out of trusteeship of property and out of complex valuation problems could be overcome reasonably well is a matter of dispute. Otherwise, however, the proposal of basing an "accessions" tax on what is *received* seems generally more rational than the present death-and-gift tax system which is based on what is *given*.

PROBLEMS

1. Discuss the probable effects of abolition of the federal credit for state death taxes.

2. "Progression in an inheritance tax, and to some extent in an estate tax, can be justified on customary 'ability-to-pay' reasoning." Criticize.

3. Explain the cumulative feature of the federal gift tax, and its purpose.

4. Describe the purposes and operations of the marital deduction.

5. Discuss with an insurance agent how life insurance can be used to reduce death tax. What would you judge to be the general economic consequences of the widespread use of insurance for this purpose?

6. Describe a state's jursidiction to tax property passing at death. Find out what your state does in practice.

7. "The complexities of the federal estate tax have made it one of the most arbitrarily discriminatory taxes in our system." Discuss.

CHAPTER 21

Enterprise, Service, and Sovereign Revenues

THE 15 per cent or so of American government revenue not derived from taxation comes from many diverse sources—charges of government enterprises, sales of certain types of property, investment profits, dividends and interest, the federal government's coinage right, expropriation powers, fines and penalties, gifts, fees, tolls, and special assessments. The problems are not so crucial as those raised by taxation because the sums involved are not so important. But problems there are, many and varied, that deserve consideration.

GOVERNMENT ENTERPRISES

In communist states, government enterprises constitute the major part of the economy. But even in some noncommunist countries, the railroads, the telephone and telegraph system, electric power production, various classes of mines, and other fields of economic activity are government enterprises. The field of government enterprises is much narrower in the United States, but it is still significant.

General considerations. A basic theoretical justification for any public function is its inherent element of indivisible social benefit. Specific individual benefits are but incidental by-products. If these incidental individual benefits are measurable, the beneficiaries may be called upon to pay for them. Such payment, however, is not an essential element of ordinary public functions.

In the case of government enterprises the emphasis is inverted. Social benefit there must be, to warrant government operation of an enterprise, but specific individual benefits overshadow the general social benefits. A water system supplies water of measurable value to each user; over and above this private benefit is the maintenance of the community's living and sanitary standards. A city transit system likewise serves individuals; socially, it may be of great advantage to these same users—considered as a community—by providing better service than a private firm whose fares must cover costs.

Scope of government enterprises. The argument which is the mainstay of American proponents of "public ownership" is that only a government unit is in a position to purchase a social benefit through providing services and setting charges without primary regard to profit considerations. Even when private business is classed as a "public utility"—such as transportation, communication, or the distribution of water, gas, or electric power—it must be permitted to charge rates which will net a reasonable return upon its investment if the service is to continue. Often, however, some factor of general social benefit runs counter to the desire for profit. To encourage the plentiful use of water, it may be socially desirable to charge a special low water rate. It may be advisable as a form of education to transport newspapers and other publications through the mails at less than cost. City growth may be furthered by running a transit line into an unsettled suburb despite the heavy expense and the certainty of loss for several years. The military began to operate bakeries, laundries, typewriter repair shops, retail stores, and other such establishments because no private facilities were available near army posts and on ships. Enlightened private enterprise may sacrifice present profits for larger future profits, but it can never discard the profit standard outright. In the operation of an enterprise touched with a public interest, only a government may be able to put a broad concept of general social benefit before profit. People as taxpayers will meet deficits, or get along with a lower rate of return on capital, than when they invest privately.

A number of supplementary arguments apply to particular classes of government enterprises:

(1) Government ownership and operation of railroad, telegraph, and telephone systems permit lines to be so planned that they will contribute to military needs. This is a basic consideration of government ownership of these utilities in European countries. In this country, federal development of atomic projects is motivated largely by military considerations.

(2) The state liquor monopolies have been justified by the argument that control can thereby be exercised over the distribution of a socially pernicious commodity more closely than by any system of supervision over private retailers.

(3) Public electric power systems are sometimes justified on the ground that they provide a yardstick to determine what rates private utilities should charge.

(4) Government housing projects are defended as a means of directly aiding a small fraction of low-income families and of indirectly improving the position of those in the surrounding area.

(5) In war time, plants involving heavy capital investment may be needed to produce military supplies. Private enterprise may be unwilling to finance these plants, because with the cessation of hostilities the military demand for their output will end. In such case, the federal government may construct the plants. It need not operate them, but may turn them over to private operation on a contract basis; or it may assume all the costs of operation but arrange for their

management by private corporations that have the needed know-how. Such arrangements were common during World War II, and currently apply to the federal atomic enterprises.

(6) High federal corporation income tax rates, and some other taxes, create a special argument for state and municipal enterprises. A municipally-owned utility can earn a normal return on capital investment with lower charges than a private enterprise because the municipal plant is exempt from the federal corporation and state income taxes as a state instrumentality. Another related advantage of municipal enterprises is that the exemption of state and local bond interest from the federal income taxes reduces the interest cost of borrowing to finance such enterprises.

(7) If an industry requires a heavy fixed investment for practicable efficient development, and operates at decreasing cost per unit within the capacity established by such investment, it faces a pricing dilemma. A price schedule which equated marginal cost and marginal benefit to consumers of its products or services—the price schedule which would be most beneficial to the general economy—would involve a loss on total operations. Such industries if privately developed become monopolies or quasi-monopolies with "administered" prices. Such prices produce profit for the industry, but thereby sacrifice general economic welfare. If plants were operated as government enterprises, a wise management could establish lower prices that equated marginal costs and benefits—the resulting deficits to be covered out of tax revenue. Such deficits would be justified by the increased general economic welfare.[1]

(8) Finally, we occasionally meet the proposition that a government may reduce the tax burden by operating an enterprise to yield a net revenue. That is the primary basis for the European tobacco monopolies, and the argument has been advanced in this country as supplementary support for state monopolies of liquor distribution. Occasionally, a "taxless town" boasts that its electric power plant yields such a substantial net revenue that property tax rates have been abolished. This "revenue justification" of government enterprises, however, appears particularly weak. A net revenue is generally obtained only by sacrificing much of the general social benefit from low prices which is the primary justification for government operation.

Possible extension of the scope of government enterprises is not a lively issue in this country today. However, at least two wide movements are quietly under way. (1) Municipalities are undertaking the distribution of natural gas as new pipelines bring the fuel into more areas; the sad financial state of local transit has also led to some "municipalization" of facilities. (2) The Department of Defense is getting rid of dozens of activities and hundreds of individual establishments which perform services that can be provided privately without significant extra cost or impairment of security.

The "relative efficiency" issue. The principal charge against government enterprises is that they operate less efficiently than private enterprises.

[1] A possible alternative to government operation to safeguard the general economic welfare would be government subsidies of such industries which would enable them to set prices at marginal cost. Occasionally a government's normal operations may involve an activity which private individuals or businesses need and which they cannot provide without wasteful duplication of facilities owned by the government. For example, a city may pave its own streets. When a utility or builder must tear up pavement and then replace it, the city's own staff may be able to do the job at lower cost, charging appropriately, than the private firm to which such activity is incidental.

Two very different aspects of efficiency are involved. The more familiar is the relation between inputs and outputs, what the man-hours and materials paid for turn out with the capital equipment available. The second aspect of efficiency is one the economist also insists should be considered. It is the worth of the output in relation to what the public could get from the use of the productive resources in the best alternative. In ordinary markets, the price the public will pay indicates what the output is worth. However, if the price is held arbitrarily either above or below what people would freely pay for the output that would become available, inefficiency in resource utilization results, even though technically the plant operates with apparently the highest of efficiency.[2]

It is the former concept that the public ordinarily has in mind. Managers of government enterprises are not compelled to explore every avenue of efficiency, since they are under no compulsion to produce more profit for stockholders. Money and incentives for research, development, and modernization may be meager. The shadow of politics is ever present. The public, listening to short-sighted and perhaps demagogic pleas, insists upon prices which are too low to be economical.[3] Bureaucratic organization—inevitable under political management—means "red tape," inflexibility, and stagnation in the face of changing conditions.

Proponents of government enterprises insist that the charge of politics is overdrawn. Managers of government enterprise corporations stand on the same footing as managers of private utility corporations. Moreover, bureaucratic inflexibility in government can be matched by bureaucratic inflexibility of private utilities whose monopoly positions are buttressed by long-term franchises. Pressure to forestall rate increases which are needed for efficient use of productive capacity, and to induce expansion, can be exerted with force against regulatory commissions as well as against government operating agencies.

Fair comparison of the operating efficiency of public enterprises and government-regulated private utilities is difficult. Since a government enterprise may deliberately forego profit in the interest of a social benefit, ordinary earning and profit standards cannot be applied. Unit costs also fail as a yardstick. In the utilities field, the costs of production and distribution vary from locality to locality and from enterprise to enterprise. The high proportion of fixed and joint costs adds difficulties that often make fair comparisons utterly impossible. Then, too, for the sake of ultimate social benefit, a government enterprise may deliberately assume certain costs which a private enterprise would avoid, such as running pipes or transmission lines to isolated or sparsely-settled neighborhoods, or furnishing such services as street lighting without charge. Finally, cost items in-

[2] General social gains, of course, may be offsetting.

[3] Political pressures have made it difficult in many localities to raise the charges of municipal utilities to meet the higher costs of inflation.

cluded by a private enterprise, such as taxes and interest, may be excluded from the calculations of a government enterprise. For many years, federal agencies did not have to account for free postage; accounting for office rent and heat is not always required.

Probably the only sustainable conclusion that can be reached about the relative efficiency of government enterprise is that the best are above the standard for average private business, that the average is below the standard for the best private business. The best relative results of government enterprise operation can be expected in activities that involve large amounts of routine rather than pioneering, new processes, and imagination.

Prices versus rates. Government enterprises may charge either "prices" or "rates," though the terms are now often confused. A "price" is a charge per unit of material sold or service performed. A "rate" is based on some circumstance other than the unit of material or service. The postal service is operated on a "price" basis. Municipal gas and electricity is usually metered as it is delivered to individual consumers, and a "price" charged. Municipal water systems, however, may be financed by "rates." Instead of installing meters, a flat charge is made per house, or per family, or per faucet in each house. Such water rates are graduated, as a rule, according to whether the water is used for personal consumption or for industrial operations. A rate system has the advantage of saving the cost of metering. Since it fails, however, to apportion the charge directly to use, it does not serve to induce economy in use.

Profit or deficit policy of government enterprises. Government enterprises normally, except for liquor monopolies, earn little or no profit. However, in 1957, city enterprises other than liquor monopolies reported current *operating* expenses of $1.5 billion and receipts of $2.3 billion. Capital outlay was $1.2 billion.

Government enterprises commonly involve substantial "concealed" costs which do not appear in their financial statements. (1) These enterprises, with few exceptions, are established with funds supplied by the governments. In many cases, amortization of debt and depreciation of assets provided by government are not charged against the enterprises.[4] (2) Interest on debt is often paid by the borrowing government without being charged against the enterprise. (3) If these enterprises operated under private ownership, they would be subject to various taxes; as government enterprises they are usually exempt, so that the owning government and others lose an element of tax revenue. (4) Employee pensions are often paid for out of general, rather than enterprise, revenues. These cost "concealments," although still common, are declining; to an increasing extent, debt amortization, interest, pensions, and a "calculated" tax are charged against re-

[4] Much of the plant and equipment of water systems and other government enterprise-type agencies was acquired at price levels much below those of today. Depreciation computed on a replacement cost basis would be higher than is ordinarily used in current accounting and in rate fixing.

ceipts in determining net revenue or loss. Moreover, some enterprises "conceal" what should be an element of income. They provide city buildings with water, gas, or electric power without charge. Such "concealed" income, however, probably falls far short of balancing the costs that are still "concealed."

Should a government enterprise be run at a loss? Or just cover costs? Or earn a profit?

No uniform principle applies to this issue. Where a state operates a liquor sales monopoly to restrict consumption through limited sales and high prices, the enterprise should earn large profits. Where a government seeks to encourage the circulation of magazines by low mailing costs, the mail service will probably incur a deficit. Since government enterprises are primarily justified by some element of general social benefit, fiscal considerations are secondary. Sometimes the charges that can be made for the services of a government enterprise without sacrificing social benefit will cover all its costs, overhead as well as operating, and yield a net profit besides. The *social* benefit produced by the enterprise is then obtained at less than no cost to taxpayers. Under these circumstances, however, the case for government operation is likely to be slight. In other cases the best charges for the enterprise's services from a social viewpoint fall short of covering some part of its costs; the public must pay for the social benefit out of general tax revenues.

Deficit operation of a government enterprise is not *per se* a cause for criticism. It may well be, however, that the charges for the services of an enterprise are set substantially below what would be their socially desirable level. The deficit which must then be met from general tax revenues constitutes a shifting of cost burden from consumers of its services to taxpayers. Since these two groups are not likely to be identical, definite inequity can result. Moreover, the low charges are also likely to mean that the system of charging will not adequately induce economizing in use.

Setting government enterprise charges.[5] The principle that government enterprise rates or prices should be set at "socially desirable" levels, and that if a deficit results it is justified by the social benefit produced by the enterprise and may properly be covered from general tax levels, does not provide any yardstick for determining what "socially desirable" levels would be. In practice, government enterprise charges are all too often set "by guess and by gosh." If privately-operated utilities around the country provide similar services, their prices may be used as a guide for pricing by the government enterprises. Political pressures play a big part, sometimes in the direction of high charges, sometimes low. If profits result, they are happily viewed as fiscal windfalls. When deficits result, if they are moderate in relation to the government's general budget, they are casually

[5] For a pioneering study, see Jules Backman and Ernest Kurnow, "Pricing of Government Services," *National Tax Journal,* June, 1954, pp. 121–140.

absorbed. If they are large, the enterprise charges are increased so that the deficit is reduced to some acceptable figure or eliminated altogether, with no calculation and little thought given to "social desirability."

Some economists suggest that pricing the services of government enterprises on the basis of marginal cost would maximize public benefit. If an enterprise's fixed costs are heavy, which is quite common, service charges high enough to cover these fixed costs, as well as operating costs, might be so high as to discourage full use of the enterprise's capacity. The resulting idleness would be a waste of potential production. At lower "marginal" charges that covered only operating costs, the community would use more of the enterprise's services. The fixed plant would be operated more fully. The community's real income would be increased by the added contribution of the enterprise's capacity that would otherwise have remained idle. This net addition to real income would be an unqualified economic gain. In addition, users of the service would gain from the lower rates. Somehow, of course, the costs of the fixed plant have to be covered. Taxes provide the answer. The public is better able to pay the added taxes since its real income is greater than if higher rates had been charged and part of the capacity of the enterprise had remained unused. Private industry, not having the taxing power, cannot be expected to set prices at marginal cost and thus achieve optimum use of fixed plant. Government can.

The proposal has merit on grounds of economic principle. There are, however, serious practical and economic difficulties. It would be hard, to begin with, to determine the marginal costs of many government enterprises, especially so since in many cases a single set of facilities is used to produce different classes of service. And what marginal cost ought to be used—short-run or long-run, the two being significantly different? Still more difficult would be the determination of the quantity that would be used at different prices. Although the general contribution of a government enterprise would be maximized by marginal-cost pricing, this is not necessarily the same as maximum social benefit—for health reasons, a municipal water system might wisely encourage more liberal use of water than would result from strict economic pricing. Finally, experience does not inspire much confidence that the political process will deal with such a complicated economic problem as marginal costs and marginal benefits. These difficulties do not preclude all possibility of applying the principle, but they do indicate that cautious experimentation would be initially preferable to any broad adoption.

Not only does determination of the *level* of enterprise charges raise problems for which there can be no clear solution; so also does their *structure* for any given level. Should the price be the same for all users of the enterprise's services, or should the users be classified with a different charge for each classification—different water charges to industrial and home users, for example, or special lower bus fares to school children? If there are to be classified prices, how should the differentials be determined? Should users of large amounts of the service, or of service at "off peak" periods when equipment would otherwise be partially idle, be given a reduced rate? What should be the "measure" of use for which the charge is made—should bus fares be a flat amount regardless of distance or on a mileage basis, should water-use charges be calculated per faucet or metered?

Equity and economic considerations generally point to rather complex schedules for enterprise charges—a multiplicity of classifications, and refined adjustments to quantity and circumstances of use. Complexity of enterprise prices, however, usually increases operating costs. Popular comprehension frequently cannot grasp the intent behind the complexity, and resentments may be aggravated instead of being reduced. The door is opened to special interest groups to seek modifications that specially favor them, and the task of rate-setting is bedeviled by political pressures. Each group can, and likely will, argue that others ought to bear the common fixed costs.

Incorporation of government enterprises. Traditionally, government enterprises have been operated under departmental authority. Their activities are subject to legislative control like those of any other administrative function. Their staff is part of the general personnel of the government unit, and ordinarily subject to the same civil service and salary regulations. Finances are part of the general finances of the unit.

A number of early federal enterprises could not follow this tradition. The First and Second United States Banks obtained their capital from private investment as well as from the federal government and were established as federal corporations. The same arrangement, for the same reasons, was worked out for institutions of the federal Farm Credit System. In acquiring properties and rights necessary for the building of the Panama Canal, the War Department obtained, and retained, a complete operating corporation, the Panama Railroad Company. The Wilson Administration found it advisable to incorporate a number of its special war agencies in order to obtain the important advantage of flexibility of policy and freedom from administrative red tape.

When the Roosevelt Administration inaugurated its program of federal credit insurance and power enterprises, it found the corporate form well suited to its plans. Incorporated enterprises would be relatively free of Congressional interference after their initial establishment. With their independent capital structures, such corporations, although accountable to Congress for their operations, would not be beholden for annual appropriations. They would possess somewhat the same freedom of operation, personnel, and financial policy as private incorporated enterprises, including exemption from the legalistic auditing procedure of the General Accounting Office. Subsequent drives for economy, however, and concern over growth of executive power prompted criticism of the remoteness of these corporations from public control and led Congress to limit their authority and funds. By 1946, the accounts of all government-owned corporations, with minor exceptions, were included in the Budget and subject to regular Congressional control over funds.

State and municipal governments have not generally endowed their enterprises with the quasi-independence of incorporation. There is, however, a tendency to give considerable autonomy to newly established entities, in setting them up as authorities.[6] The lack of legislative control, or even systematic review, of operations warrants attention. In some cases the finances and policies of authorities might wisely be tied in more closely with those of the regular government.

Federal enterprises. Prior to the 1930's, the federal government evinced little interest in establishing and operating enterprises. The postal system, which dates from the first years of the republic, was long viewed as a sovereign, rather than a commercial, function. The various federal enterprises established between 1900 and 1933—the Panama Canal, the reclamation projects, the Shipping Board, the Inland Waterways Corporation, and wartime operation of the railroads—were generally by-products of other interests. Under the Roosevelt Administration, the federal government deliberately "went into business"—power development and distribution, housing, credit, insurance, the merchandising of electrical equipment. Wartime exigencies caused further expansion of federal enterprises. The war also elevated Post Exchanges and Ships Stores into substantial merchandising organizations.[7]

Today one could prepare a long list of federal government agencies with enterprise-type activities. Table 21–1 presents balance-sheet data of what are officially termed business-type activities, but it is not complete. The two dozen or so corporations covered by the budget would comprise only a modest part of the whole. Some entities, such as the Alaska Railroad, have predominantly enterprise characteristics. Many others, such as the Government Printing Office, have a significant, but by no means overwhelming, enterprise nature. Clear lines cannot be drawn. There is literally no way to analyze all such activities without dealing with a large fraction of our federal government.

Some of the agencies extend credit, directly or indirectly, by insuring loans for a premium. Others provide transportation facilities or insurance or irrigation or housing. The armed forces operate a tremendous merchandising business and run thousands of laundries, theaters, and similar opera-

[6] One of the country's largest enterprise-type government agencies is the New York City Transit Authority. Its status was shifted from that of a city department to that of an independent authority—largely to reduce the political difficulies of setting fares that would cover costs.

[7] Sales of Army and Air Force Exchanges were $830 million in 1957, chiefly outside the United States. Most of the net income goes for welfare services, a small amount for expansion.

TABLE 21–1

Federal Business-Type Activities, Selected Assets and Liabilities, 1958[1]

Assets:	*(Millions)*
Loans	
To aid agriculture	$ 7,605
To aid home-owners	4,917
To industry	645
To financing institutions ..	710
To aid states, territories, etc.	275
Foreign	8,965
All other	393
Less reserves ... $354	
Investments	
U.S. Government securities	$ 4,523
In international institutions.	3,385
Other	368
Inventories[2]	21,206
Land, structures, equipment[3]	10,020
Other	9,594
Total	$72,242

Liabilities:	*(Millions)*
Bonds, notes, and debentures	$ 4,798
Other	3,472
Private proprietary interest ..	1,183
U.S. Government proprietary interest	62,789
Total	$72,242

[1] Excludes Atomic Energy Commission and other agencies in which the U.S. Government interest totaled about $20 billion at the end of the 1957 fiscal year. Does not include Federal Reserve Banks.

[2] Includes $10,866 million of Department of Defense.

[3] Includes electric power facilities, Panama Canal, Post Office Department, General Services Administration, and other.

Because of rounding, details will not necessarily add to totals.

SOURCES: *Treasury Bulletin, Federal Reserve Bulletin,* and *Survey of Current Business.*

tions for which a charge is made—and which private businesses say offer unfair competition. Space limits force us to restrict the discussion here to two activities—the postal service and sale of electricity.

The postal system. The Constitution gives Congress specific power "to establish post offices and post roads."

During its first fifty years, the Post Office Department earned moderate surpluses. From 1841 to 1959, it avoided deficits in only twelve years. A deficit of over $500 million was anticipated for 1959 on the basis of a total postal expenditure of around $3.6 billion. In some respects the quality of service has deteriorated even while expenditures have grown. Possibilities of postal profit have consistently been foregone in order to handle expanded volume in an economy of rising prices without commensurate increases in charges. First-class mail has normally earned a profit. After the 1958 increase to 4 cents an ounce, it will certainly continue to do so. The biggest loss arises from the handling of magazines, but there is no agreement on the amount. Honest differences of opinion—to say nothing of biased differences—about how overhead costs ought to be shared and how to allow for variations in quality of service make it impossible to get a consensus on the amount of loss from each type of service. The same problem makes it difficult to determine what charges would be most appropriate in relation to costs.

Postal operation has not been a model of efficiency. Most post offices are rented, and it is virtually impossible to check on the terms to see if the government is getting the best bargain possible. There has been no systematic effort to try out a variety of methods in different offices and to apply throughout the system practices which prove most successful. Lax accounting methods have permitted petty losses to occur. The failure of Congress to vote funds for more efficient equipment has slowed modernization. But to attribute all postal deficits to mismanagement is misleading. At any time from 1841 on, with even more inefficiency than could fairly be attributed to it, the postal department could have earned profits by maintaining high rates or by limiting operations to profit-yielding lines. Instead, Congress chose to sacrifice profit for other ends—popular education, or at least help for newspaper and magazine publishers and subscribers, and aid to transportation, farmers, and advertisers.

The postal system needs large funds to finance modernization and expansion of facilities. The growth of capacity has not kept pace with the huge expansion in the volume of mail. Mechanization offers possibilities of economy. Yet the processing and delivery of mail is inherently a personal service type of activity. As such it cannot be inexpensive in a country with wage rates as high as ours.

The best way to cover costs is by charges for the services rather than from general taxes. One gain from higher charges would be more compelling inducement for the public to economize in the use of mails, to refrain from imposing on the system costs for mail handling which are greater than what the sender is willing to pay.[8]

Power enterprises. Federal activity in the provision of electric power has grown rapidly. Three great river systems—the Tennessee, the Colorado, and the Columbia—have been harnessed for the production of hydroelectric power, and there are smaller projects in other areas. These embrace flood control, transportation, irrigation, and land reclamation, as well as hydroelectric power development, so that appraisal of the power features alone depends largely upon assumptions about the division of costs common to two or more activities.

From the outset, controversy raged around the power features of these projects. Proponents argued that their relatively low but profit-yielding

[8] Any sudden move to put the services now responsible for large losses on a self-sustaining basis would disrupt some businesses. A change over a five-year period would be preferable.

rates provided "yardsticks" for measuring the efficiency and rate charges of private power companies. Representatives of private utilities retort that fair comparison is impossible, because the fraction of total capital costs being allocated to the power elements of the project is inadequate, because the federal enterprises are free of many taxes borne by private companies, and because, in some cases, little or no allowance is made for interest on the government's investment. Where, under the torrent of charges and countercharges, the truth lies submerged cannot be ascertained beyond dispute.[9] The projects as a whole *do* impose costs, some not obvious, on taxpayers. This is not the dispute. The argument is the adequacy of the charges for electricity. Looking at the projects as a whole, it seems probable that government's only real advantage over a regulated private utility is an ability to develop nonpower aspects more effectively. Regional interests, of course, are eager to have the national taxpayer finance the development of power and other facilities in their areas.

State enterprises. In comparison with the scope of their general functions, state governments enter less into the field of enterprise activities than either the federal or municipal governments. Partial explanation is the unfortunate state experience with banking, canal, and railroad enterprises during the 1830's and the 1850's. Another reason is the anomalous economic character of state areas—they have, as a rule, no relation to broad regional service needs, yet they are too extensive to provide local services effectively.

Sixteen states monopolize the sale of hard liquor. Seven provide harbor facilities; the Port of New Orleans facilities are the largest present state enterprise, excluding toll highway authorities. Two states operate canals. Irrigation projects, printing plants, toll bridges, ferries, electric railroads, coal mines, cement plants, warehouses, and grain elevators are among the other state enterprises.[10] The liquor monopolies earned a net profit of

[9] On TVA's accounting—for example, with only minor allowances for taxes—in 1959 it will show a return from the sale of electricity of about 3 per cent on the investment in power facilities—hardly an impressive result for the taxpayer who put up the money. The TVA's status as a government enterprise has hindered it recently in getting capital for expansion. Congress will not vote money nor allow TVA to borrow in public markets as it wishes to do. A discussion of cost allocation is found in M. G. Glaeser, "Water Resources," *Federal Expenditure Policy for Economic Growth and Stability* (Washington, 1957), pp. 668–682.

[10] Outstanding among state enterprise ventures have been those of North Dakota and South Dakota. At the behest of agrarian interests, North Dakota, during the 1920's established a creamery, a grain elevator, a flour mill, a system for insurance against fire, hail, and tornadoes, a state bank with agricultural credit as its main field of activity, and —a sop to urban interests—a home-building program. Subsequently, the state undertook to extend farm mortgage credit. In the same period, South Dakota embarked upon a rural loan system, state hail insurance, state bank deposit guaranty, the manufacture and sale of cement, coal mining, and gasoline distribution. In addition, it undertook the management of farm properties acquired by the state through foreclosure on rural credit loans and operated by tenant farmers under lease. Most of the Dakota enterprises were failures. The capital cost of South Dakota's cement plant exceeded estimates, and construction was so long delayed that the plant could not fulfill its purpose—the provision of cement to be used in constructing state roads. The state

$229 million in 1957. These state liquor monopolies, without much capital investment, bring in relatively more revenue than do the comparable alcoholic-beverage taxes in the nonmonopoly states.

State universities rent dormitories and engage in other activities for which charges are made. Some prison and recreational operations have elements of enterprise functions. Many states operate workmen's compensation systems not unlike private insurance covering the same risks.

Municipal enterprises. Enterprises are rarely operated by counties, towns, and other units of rural government, but they are a common item of city government. All cities with populations over 25,000 operate enterprise-type agencies.

Water supply systems account for nearly two-thirds the total investment and half of the operating finances of municipal utilities. In this field, municipal ownership and operation overshadows private enterprise. On the whole, operations seem to be efficient; although data are incomplete, all costs, even an estimated allowance for depreciation (on the basis of historical cost) and interest on capital, appear to be covered.

Over half of the country's electric power systems are municipally owned —mostly by small cities. Half of these are both producing and distributing systems; the other half confine themselves to distribution only. Compared with the average private plant built to service a large area, the average municipal plant is small. Municipal plants have nearly 7 per cent of the nation's electric generating capacity. The earnings appear to cover all costs; in some cases, profits are substantial. In arranging for the local distribution of power from its huge hydroelectric projects, the federal government has given some preference to municipally-owned systems.

Among other instances of municipal enterprises may be noted the hundreds of airports established in recent years, ferries, tunnels, radio stations, abattoirs, gas systems, street railway systems, a large number of bus systems, and occasional municipal toll bridges. The largest single municipal enterprise is the New York City subway system, representing an investment of nearly $2 billion. State law directs it to charge fares which will cover operating costs, except interest; the taxpayer foots the bill for borrowed money.

One may debate whether the school lunch program is an enterprise-type activity, but there is no doubt that its annual gross sales of $900 million constitute a big undertaking, though one made up of thousands of small units.

Toll roads. Toll charges have long been employed to finance bridges, ferries, and tunnels. In the 1930's, a practice which had fallen into disfavor

---

hail insurance and bank deposit guaranty were not managed on proper actuarial principles, and involved loss, as did the coal mine and gasoline distribution system. In North Dakota, the state bank, the flour mill, and the grain elevator all incurred losses. The outstanding reason for the failure of these enterprises seems to have been the surrender of critical economic judgment to political pressure.

almost a century earlier—the use of tolls to finance highways—was revived with the opening of the Pennsylvania Turnpike. Many such projects were initiated just before World War II but discontinued during hostilities. The first decade of the postwar period then brought enthusiastic revival and expansion of the development of toll highways, usually constructed and operated by special "authorities."[11] By 1958, however, with over 3,000 miles of such facilities, the growth seemed at an end.

The toll roads were newly constructed, and their limited-access facilities offered services superior to those of free highways. The public proved willing to pay charges substantially greater than those involved in gasoline taxes. Much of the use has been by trucks and out-of-state motorists, and a considerable part of the traffic has been newly generated rather than diverted from other highways. Accident rates have been low in relation to the amount of use. With a few exceptions, the systems have proved financially successful.

Yet the toll system has disadvantages. The cost of toll collection is much higher than that of gasoline tax collection, and to the economy the difference is almost complete loss. Tolls bring social loss by discouraging some usage of facilities at other than peak periods. Limited access also reduces usage. The existence of these facilities makes more difficult the planning of a rationally integrated highway system. Only a small part of the whole highway network has traffic of sufficient density to support tolls; the toll system is entirely unsuited to urban areas, just where density is highest. The new federal Interstate and Defense Highway system, for a variety of reasons, seems to have killed any prospect of extension of toll highways. However, for bridges and tunnels there is still both opportunity and reason to use tolls.

PUBLIC DOMAIN AND OTHER PROPERTIES

The *public domain* is the land which governments own. Local governments generally use their land for building sites, parks, and streets. Much of the land owned by the federal and state governments, on the contrary, is waste or unoccupied land, free of government buildings and not used for government activities, though often of value for agriculture, lumbering, or mining.

During its early history the federal government received significant revenue from the sale of its public domain. Then nonfiscal considerations came more and more to dominate its disposal policies. Rapid settlement and national development were encouraged even at the risk of profligate

[11] J. F. Due, "The Rise and Decline of the Toll Principle in Highway Finance—1940–1957," *National Tax Journal*, June, 1957, pp. 97–113. Special highway authorities financed construction by borrowing, at interest rates which were above those paid by the state governments themselves. One attraction of this method was the escape from legal limits on state borrowing.

use and sheer waste. Gratuitous distribution encouraged not only the expansion of agriculture but also mining and lumbering and helped to lower the prices of many raw materials. Land was also given to aid in the development of public schools; over 200,000 square miles were granted to railroads in return for large reductions granted on freight shipments by the federal government and the travel of its military and civilian personnel.

There was never any compelling reason why the government should have freely disposed of its timber and mineral lands. On the contrary, logic pointed to the desirability of maintaining some control over timber and mineral exploitation by retaining title to, or subsurface rights in, such lands. Nevertheless, millions of acres of valuable mineral and timber land passed from national to private ownership freely or at nominal prices. Although the "conservation movement" of the 1900's closed the stable door after most of the best horses had been stolen, the mineral resources saved to the public as a whole are not inconsiderable. The mineral areas of the remaining domain are estimated to contain large reserves of coal, phosphate, potash, oil and gas, and deposits of oil shale. Potential waterpower on federal lands is substantial. These natural resources represent a possible source of revenue. Royalties on lumbering and mining patents and sales of timber and other products currently yield about $250 million a year.

The annual rental income from the public domain and from space in federal buildings and the use of federal equipment now approaches $200 million a year. Nearly one-third comes from over 30,000 ranchers for grazing.

The thirty states organized out of federal territory did not have title to the unoccupied land within their boundaries, but the federal government made generous grants to the states. The most recent was the transfer of title of offshore oil deposits to the coastal states in 1953, after the Supreme Court had ruled that such title was vested in the federal government. Most states squandered their original domains. School lands, with a few exceptions such as in Minnesota, Montana, and Texas, which still have valuable school funds, were sold for a song.

Large areas reverted to state and local governments during the 1930's because of tax delinquencies. In some states, the government units acquiring such reverted lands are empowered to convert them into forest preserves and public parks. But in many states, legal provision is lacking to give the government units clear title. Whether these states and localities wish it or not, the reverted land must be restored to private ownership irrespective of the possibilities of sound economic use. Unfortunately, cities have seldom taken advantage of opportunities to assemble land for such purposes as parks or housing projects by careful use of space obtained through tax delinquency.

Governments often find on their hands worn-out or obsolete equipment which has a sale value, even if only as junk. Sale of such material brings states and localities a small stream of current government revenue. Disposal of World War II surpluses produced about $7 billion. Congress provided a scale of preferences to be granted to other government bodies, veterans, schools, some relief agencies, and small business. Consequently, prices and sales proceeds were less than could have been obtained through unrestricted sale. Sales of surplus and other federal property—other than agricultural surpluses—bring about $350 million a year. The federal government has also liquidated its interest in various agencies—the Home Owners Loan Corporation, for example. In such cases do the terms of sale bring the taxpayer the best results possible? The public has little basis for determining.

Today, by far the largest sales of government property are disposals abroad of agricultural surpluses accumulated under the farm-aid programs. Payment is received in foreign currencies and is generally restricted for spending there. Some is used for technical assistance and other types of foreign aid, some for military support, the expenses of our diplomatic staffs, various types of educational and informational activities, loans to private businesses, and purchases of strategic materials. The equivalent of well over $3 billion will have been received by the end of 1959.

States and localities got $100 million from sale of property in 1957.

INVESTMENT INCOME

Incidental to their carrying out various functions, some government units derive income from interest, rents, and royalties. Such income is not the reason for the functions that produce it, but a secondary effect.

The federal government has accumulated a reserve in connection with Old Age and Survivors Insurance financing, and the states have built up unemployment reserves. In addition, the federal government, and most state and local governments, are building up funds to help pay for employee pensions.[12] Some government units also have trust funds, usually accumulated from bequests and contributions, that aid the financing of colleges, museums, hospitals, and similar institutions.

The OASI reserve is invested in a special issue of federal bonds. Other government reserves and trust funds are invested as a rule in the debt issues of the government maintaining the fund, or in bonds of the state, or in federal bonds. Because of shifting interest rates and investment opportunities, managers of government trust funds have a continuing job in getting the best income consistent with other objectives. The amounts involved are large enough to warrant more skilled attention than is commonly devoted to this task. Fortunately, some states provide guidance for localities whose officials cannot be skilled in investment.

[12] Many governments also maintain sinking funds to assist the retirement of debt, as discussed in Chapter 26.

Interest on federal, state, and local insurance trusts, including those for OASI and unemployment insurance, was about $1.8 billion in 1958. Other state-local interest receipts were about $500 million. Federal interest income, largely of lending agencies, was also about $500 million, but this is not so much investment income as operating revenue.

State governments ordinarily have little rentable property. With the exception of the offshore oil deposits, they have slight opportunity to derive royalty income from timber and mineral leases. Cities, however, have an important rental opportunity—their streets. Banks, stores, and business houses often build extensive vaults under city streets, under permit of course; a rental can be attached to such privilege. Building contractors can be charged for storing materials on sidewalks and streets during construction. Auto owners can be subjected to metered daytime parking charges and to monthly or annual charges for overnight street parking, payment being evidenced by a windshield sticker. After long ignoring these street rentals as a source of revenue, many cities are now developing them. Parking meters are now used widely, and with other charges for parking, yield perhaps $150 million annually. In addition, docks and wharves are city property in a few cities, and New York, Philadelphia, and Los Angeles receive several million dollars annually in rents from this source.

Deplorable housing conditions combined with the desire to help stimulate business in the 1930's led several localities, with aid from Washington, to finance some residential construction projects. After a lapse during the war the general program of "public housing" was resumed in the late 1940's and under newly created local authorities has advanced, though slowly. Federal law sets general terms, offers some subsidy, and provides for some national control. The details of the arrangements for financing, ownership, and rental vary, but in essence cities—or especially created agencies—own and operate the projects. Rental income is received and operating costs are paid by the local agency. The net results, as well as those of housing projects having only state or local assistance, are hard to judge. Subsidy is intended, but some elements, notably tax exemption, are difficult to measure. Rents are deliberately held below the free market price. Total state-local receipts in 1957 were $268 million.

FEES AND LICENSE CHARGES

The primary benefit from government activities is general and cannot be apportioned among individuals. But supplementary individual benefits attach to many functions. Thus judges are part of the general judicial system—but each decision settles a dispute between particular sets of litigants. Or a government unit may undertake a regulatory function to protect the community against the shortcomings of some types of businesses; for example, a municipality must inspect barber shops because, in the absence of such inspection, some barbers would not maintain desirable public health standards.

What could be more reasonable than the assessment of part of the cost of a government function to individuals or businesses who derive special benefits or who occasion the functions? For many functions, of course, the individuals who derive supplementary individual benefits or who occasion the activity cannot be isolated from the general public. There is no means by which the federal Department of Commerce can determine the particular firms which profit by its reports on the business outlook. Furthermore, for many "social" functions of government, the individuals who derive a particularized benefit are manifestly unable to pay for it—their very poverty gives rise to the function. But often the special beneficiaries or the people who necessitate a function can be identified—or made to identify themselves by the requirement of a license—and a special charge can be imposed. A litigant can be required to pay a service fee for filing each legal document essential to his case. A fisherman who benefits from a state's fish-protective and fish-stocking expenditures can be made to pay a license fee. So can a barber whose occupation necessitates a municipal inspection service.

Service fees. A service fee is a charge by a government to defray the cost of an administrative service or function which confers a supplementary special benefit upon individuals.[13] A definite *quid pro quo* relationship is present—individuals receive a particularized benefit from a government activity and they pay for it. Examples of federal service fees are those attached to federal court procedure, to consular services, and to the issuance of patents. State and local governments charge fees in connection with court procedure, for the recording of legal titles and transfers, for examinations in connection with regulated professions and trades, for some hospital services, and for a multitude of other varied services.

Service fees bear a close resemblance to the charges of government enterprises. Both involve a *quid pro quo* relationship between a government agency and individuals, and in both cases, the payment is made when a specific service is performed by some government agency. The distinguishing feature is the nature of the service rendered. An enterprise price is the charge for commodities or services of an *economic* character—for units of water, or electric power, or a government publication, or mailing a letter, or transportation, or credit. Service fees are charged for services of a *government* or *administrative* character—for elements of court procedure, for the filing or recording of legal documents. But the distinction between the two types of charges is not hard and fast. If a city maintains a college and charges "fees" for registration or instruction, these payments could be in-

[13] Definitions of "fees" are numerous. Some ignore the supplementary character of the individual benefits involved. Others include the qualification that the revenue from the charge must not exceed the cost of the service. Still others include the stipulation that the revenue must be earmarked to the service or function to which it is attached.

terpreted either as enterprise charges or as service fees. And often the line between service fees and taxes is also hard to draw.[14]

Should the fee be measured against the cost of the particular service to which it is attached or against the cost of the general government function of which the particular service is but one detail? The narrower view is that a service fee must not produce a revenue greater than the cost of the particular service involved; otherwise, it is a tax. A sounder view, perhaps, is that frequently taken by legislatures. Service fees are established in excess of unit cost to contribute to the cost of the general function.

License charges. If the special supplementary benefits of a government function accrue indirectly to a definable class of people instead of directly to individuals through the rendering of some specific service, the service fee cannot be employed. Nor can it be used where a government is seeking reimbursement for a special regulatory expense caused by some definable class of people or some type of business. In such cases, however, the activities which cause or benefit from the government function may be made illegal except upon government grant of license or permit, and a charge—a *license fee*—can then be levied on the license or permit.

Examples of the "class benefit" license fee are fishing license fees, the revenue from which goes to support state fish hatcheries, and hunting license fees, the revenue from which supports state game preservation activities. Examples of the "group cost" license fee are restaurant license fees whose revenue is applied to the cost of inspection to insure maintenance of proper sanitary standards, poolroom license fees, and license fees covering expenses of inspecting elevators in apartment houses and business buildings.

The line between license fees and taxes is even harder to draw than that between service fees and taxes. The *quid pro quo* relationship does not stand out so clearly in license fees as in service fees. Furthermore, the license requirement is a common instrument of tax administration. Our best point of differentiation is the relation between revenue derived and cost of the function involved. If the revenue does not exceed the cost, we may call the charge a license *fee*. If a revenue surplus results, the charge is a license *tax*.

License fees sometimes evolve into license taxes. When a class of individuals, compelled for regulatory purposes to take out licenses, becomes more or less coextensive with a group specially benefited by some general activity of government, a tax may justifiably be attached to the licensing. This procedure accords with the "benefit" principle of taxation. Thus, it

[14] A legal act which might provide a basis for a service fee—the recording of land transfers, for example, or the legal authorization of the transfer of the estates of decedents—can also be made the legal "subject" for a tax. Since taxes are sometimes justified on the "benefit" principle, the *quid pro quo* relationship between government agency and individual is not an absolute touchstone to determine whether the charge is a tax or a service fee.

was early realized that motorists, who were compelled to license their autos as a matter of public safety, were specially benefited by road building. The motor vehicle license charge, at first merely a fee to cover the cost of recording the license and issuing license plates, evolved into the license tax of today. In many cases, the driver's license has become, in effect, largely a tax. Or again, a class subject to a license tax may be a business group making sales to so broad a market that a charge levied on them can be passed on to the general public as an indirect tax. Thus, liquor license charges, originally levied as fees to cover the inspection of saloons, developed into license taxes and became a fruitful source of revenue.

Revenue considerations. Service and license fee revenue is relatively insignificant for the federal government—less than $100 million a year—but it is an important item in state and local budgets. Although statistics are not complete, we may fairly assume that service fee revenue accounted for most of the $1 billion reported by the states in 1957 as "charges for current services" (exclusive of highway charges) and for a significant fraction of the larger amounts so reported by local governments. State-local hospital charges yield about $700 million a year, almost one-fourth of the costs; federal hospital receipts are $30 million. Practice and policy in demanding reimbursement and in setting charges vary widely. Sanitation charges yield almost $300 million a year. Other important sources are charges—whether enterprise-type, fees, or license, we cannot clearly distinguish—for garbage collection, refuse disposal, services to neighboring localities, use of parks and recreation facilities, and a big "miscellaneous," the last totalling over $1 billion for the federal government and almost $900 million for states and localities.

Nevertheless, fees and charges are relatively neglected as a state and municipal revenue source. Many occupations and types of business cause the city extra expense in waste removal, street cleaning, police protection, or supervision in the interest of public health or morals, but only a minority are subjected to license fees. Careful study of municipal activities to determine the special costs caused by particular occupations and enterprises, followed by the enactment of license fees, would aid city finances.[15] Many states, too, have opportunities. They already provide that banks, insurance companies, and certain public utilities shall be subjected to fee charges to cover the costs of regulation. Increasing use of fees has been made to help finance public higher education, notably state universities. The federal government is trying to make greater use of fees and related charges. Yet there are doubtless many unutilized possibilities.

[15] A detailed study of Los Angeles finances concluded that charges for services could be increased substantially without imposing costs on individuals and businesses that would impair the general public interest. Charges related to identifiable costs, plus proportionate overhead, for a long list of activities could bring in about $70 million a year. This amount is significant indeed in relation to the city's total revenue of $190 million. J. S. Stockfish and L. B. Strifling, Jr., *Revenue Problems of the City of Los Angeles* (Planning Research Corp., Los Angeles, 1958).

In many cases, attaching fees and charges to particular government services would not only produce revenue but would limit the use of the service without thereby doing social harm. This would contribute to government economy. Sometimes, however, reduced use of a government service because of a fee or charge requirement would be socially undesirable.

Service fees are frequently attached to particular government offices instead of being payable into the general treasury. The practice is to be utterly condemned. As population grows, the fees attached to an office are likely to increase out of all proportion to proper compensation for its incumbent. The fees attached to the offices of sheriff and county clerk sometimes run into tens of thousands of dollars; upon occasion, they have exceeded the hundred-thousand-dollar mark. Such an office necessarily becomes an object of political "sale," and any candidate aspiring to it must promise a large share of the proceeds to his political party. The fees attached to the office become a source of *party revenue* instead of *government revenue.*

SPECIAL ASSESSMENTS[16]

The Census defines special assessments as:

> Compulsory contributions collected from owners of property benefited by specific public improvements (street paving, sidewalks, sewer lines, etc.) to defray the cost of such improvements (either directly or through payment of debt service on indebtedness incurred to finance the improvements) and apportioned according to the assumed benefits to the property affected by the improvements.[17]

Either constitutionally or by statute, all states permit local governments to levy special assessments, though many states place restrictions on such assessments.

Special assessments were a major item of city revenue before 1930. During the next two decades they were relatively neglected. Following World War II, cities turned to them once again as a means of financing many of the substantial capital improvements then undertaken. Total municipal receipts from this source in 1958 were about $300 million, more than four times the 1950 total.

The special assessment as such has no established place in state and county revenue systems.

Nature. A special assessment is a charge against property regardless of ownership. Furthermore, special assessments are levied for one purpose only—to compensate a government body for its expenditures in creating or maintaining a material improvement. Unlike a tax, a special assessment

[16] See Municipal Finance Officers Association, "Special Assessment Financing," *Municipal Finance,* May, 1957, entire issue.

[17] In some cases, charges are made under the *police power;* an example is public removal of snow where the property-owner has failed to meet city requirements. Benefit or an increment in the value of property does not have to be shown to establish a police-power special assessment.

is imposed to cover special supplementary benefits accruing to the property of individuals and must be strictly proportional to the benefits accruing to the parcels of property, regardless of any taxpaying ability of the persons who must pay.[18]

Although the levy of a special assessment is undoubtedly an exercise of the sovereign taxing power, it is a limited exercise of this power, and subject to certain restrictions which do not apply to taxes. (1) In many states, government expenditures financed by special assessments must be approved by a referendum of the owners of the property to be assessed. (2) A government activity financed by a special assessment must be of direct monetary advantage to the property to be assessed. That it adds intangible values to the lives of those residing in the district is insufficient. It must add dollars and cents to the value of their property. (3) Special assessments are as a rule based solely on land values. The value of improvements on the assessed property and of the owners' personal property is not taken into consideration. (4) A special assessment on any particular parcel of land must not exceed the value added to the land by improvement. (5) The total amount of a special assessment must in principle be distributed among the various parcels of land in proportion to the monetary benefit each derives.[19] (6) Finally, in most states, a special assessment cannot become a personal liability on the owner of the land; it exists solely as a charge on the land. A landowner who sells his land subsequent to a special assessment cannot be reached by the levying government.

Special assessments are most commonly levied in a lump sum to finance a capital improvement. Where the project is extensive and costly, special assessment bonds may be issued, to be repaid out of special assessment receipts over a period of years.[20] Current government activities benefiting a limited district—such as caring for the lawns of a boulevard—are sometimes financed by an annual special assessment.

Assessment. An issue arising at the very outset of a special assessment project is the extent to which the cost should be borne by adjacent property-owners and the extent to which it should be financed out of general tax funds—in other words, how the general social benefit and special individual benefit of a project should be apportioned. By what fraction does the

[18] One argument made in favor of a special assessment is that it can be applied where the property is exempt from the regular property tax, such as church property or houses with homestead exemptions.

[19] The courts have relaxed rules (4) and (5) somewhat and will uphold a special assessment levied according to one of the well-recognized rules of apportionment, even where, because of special circumstances, the charge on some particular parcel of land exceeds the resulting increase of selling value or is more burdensome than on other parcels. The fact that other properties may fall in value is universally ignored.

[20] Such bonds are frequently exempted from constitutional and statutory limitations on local borrowing powers. One reason for special assessment financing is to escape debt and tax rate limits.

paving of a street, or the creation of a park, benefit the property fronting on it and by what fraction the city as a whole?

No hard and fast rule exists for specifically determining the beneficiaries of such improvements. Since most public improvements carry both a *general* and a *special* benefit, legislative authorization of special assessment levies sometimes provides for a specific apportionment of the costs of particular improvements between special assessments and general tax funds. In other cases, the division of costs is within the discretion of some city board. Either way, the division of costs is highly arbitrary. Engineers have no yardstick by which to apportion accurately the general and special benefits of public improvements, the full effects of which may not be known for many years.

The next problem is to determine the radius of special benefit for the particular improvement. The nature of the improvement makes a difference. All property within a half-mile may be benefited by the creation of a park or playground. Building an arterial sewer or a boulevard may benefit property for a few blocks on either side. Paving an isolated side street may be of special benefit only to the fronting property. Where the area benefited by an improvement is extensive, the special assessment district must be divided into zones, a relatively greater part of the cost being apportioned to the nearest zones and a smaller share to those more distant.

Once the area and zones of the special assessment district have been determined, the costs must be allocated to individual properties. The ideal, of course, but one difficult of attainment, is the allocation of costs in proportion to the special benefit derived by each parcel of land. Three methods of allocating special assessments among individual properties have been developed: (1) the frontage rule, (2) the area rule, and (3) the depth-curve rule. Most common is allocation by street frontage, a method which discriminates in favor of deep properties and cannot take lot irregularities into account. Allocation by area fails in the opposite direction. Although a deep lot benefits more than a shallow one from a street or other improvement, such special benefit is not strictly in proportion to depth. Several cities have sought a middle road out of these difficulties by the use of "depth-curves" similar to those employed in property tax assessment. A specified value is determined for frontage with a given lot depth, a higher value (but not a proportionately higher value) for frontage with a greater lot depth, and similar higher values for stated greater depths.

Conclusion. Special assessments should be an item of major importance in the finances of a growing community. They must decline in importance when a community has completed a reasonable program of public facilities. Since many American localities probably have decades of growth and improvement ahead, the problems of special assessments will long remain.

In addition to the administrative issues already mentioned, there is the problem of devising some machinery of control over the initiation of special assessment improvements. A "shoestring" real estate operator interested in developing some semi-suburban section may prevail upon a city council to install an expensive set of improvements—graded and paved streets, sewerage, and water systems—before settlement in the area is sufficient to warrant such undertakings. Installation of the improvements helps sell the operator's lots, of course. But if the operator's dream development never shows more than a scattered handful of homes, the special assessments to finance the improvements are bound to encounter difficulties. The operator takes refuge in bankruptcy, the city acquires some worthless bare lots by tax delinquency foreclosure, and the costs of the improvements must be met out of general revenues. Or the unpaid balance of an assessment may pile up against the few properties that have been sold, imposing crushing burdens.

An alternative worthy of serious consideration is an "increment tax." Instead of trying to guess the value of a new project to a particular property before or during the building of the project, the community might impose an additional property tax on increases in the value of the property after the assessment is completed and as the community is adjusted to it. Such a tax would operate more equitably than special assessments, because only realized benefits as reflected in market prices of property would be taxed. It would not necessarily assure enough revenue to pay for the improvement.

EXCESS CONDEMNATION

Excess condemnation is the policy, on the part of the state or city, of taking by right of eminent domain more property than is actually necessary for the creation of a public improvement, and of subsequently selling or leasing this surplus. Theoretically, the city or state should acquire the land bordering on a proposed improvement at a price that does not include the benefit of the improvement and should sell the property at a price including the benefit of improvement. The land so acquired may instead be employed to protect parks, open spaces, schools, and public buildings against undesirable neighbors by incorporating restrictive covenants in the subsequent sale or lease of the land. Excess condemnation is thus allied to the special assessment. In contrast to the special assessment procedure, the government obtains the entire special value of the improvement to the surrounding property. This value may be greater than the cost of constructing the improvement, whereas the special assessment never reimburses the government for more than the cost of the improvement.

Excess condemnation is constitutionally permitted or authorized in about one-fourth of the states, but has been utilized only slightly. Government bodies are rarely so alert as to condemn all the property they intend to acquire before some part of the anticipated increase of value is worked into the condemnation price of the condemned parcels of property. Equitable pricing is difficult. Once the land has been acquired, the government body finds that it has assumed the occupation of land speculator, an occupation it is not well fitted to pursue. Yet, as communities develop in the coming decades, there will be many cases—slum clearance projects for example—in which excess condemnation could be used justly and with good results if public officials are both honest and able.

A vast immediate problem looms—the great highway program. In and around cities decisions which will determine land use (and human lives) for innumerable decades must be made during the next few years. Here is an opportunity for imaginative, constructive, and equitable use of the powers of excess condemnation such as has never before existed. Yet hardly a handful of localities are prepared to seize the opportunity.[21]

SOVEREIGN REVENUES

Sovereign revenues are those which government receives as incidents of its status as the sovereign political power. In the case of the federal government, these sovereign revenues are tribute,[22] the net profit of the currency privilege, expropriation under the power of eminent domain, fines and forfeitures, and gratuities.[23] The sovereign revenues received by the state governments, or by localities under grants of power from the states, are subsidy, expropriation under power of eminent domain,[24] escheat, gratuities, fines, forfeitures, and penalties.

[21] Another related opportunity—of an expenditure rather than a revenue nature—is the purchase of *development rights*. The golf course, private estate, or other low-density form of land use often benefits the *general* public. As population grows, however, the private owner of such property can expect a price which reflects the value of more intensive use of the land. The loss to neighbors is not relevant to his calculations. Yet it is to the community. Therefore, the local government, or perhaps the state, may be wise to buy the legal right to the *change* in the land use and thus keep the change from taking place while compensating the owner for the gain he would get if it did.

[22] *Tribute* is the payment exacted by a conquering government from a conquered government. Under the terms "war costs" and "reparations," it played a disturbing role in the finances of the Allied and American governments during the 1920's. The United States demanded no payments from its World War II enemies, except some of the costs of occupation, patents, some technical knowledge, and property to help meet the claims of American subjects. We shall collect hardly a trifle of the costs of occupation and of the economic aid given our former enemies.

[23] Recoveries from the renegotiation of contracts are contractual rather than an exercise of sovereignty.

[24] Government necessity prevails over private right. Therefore, when a government needs a particular piece of private property for public purposes, the government can appropriate it under the sovereign power of eminent domain. The federal, state, and local governments all possess this power. Yet it cannot be a source of profit to a government in the United States, because constitutional provisions compel the expropriating government to reimburse the private owner. Further limiting the power of eminent domain is the requirement that the *expropriation* be for a public purpose. The compensation of the individual may be determined either by contract with the expropriating government or by the courts in cases where no agreement can be reached.

Minting metallic money in the United States is the exclusive prerogative of the federal government. Since the bullion value of all silver, nickel, and copper coins is less than their face value, the Treasury makes a profit, called *seigniorage,* on every coin issued from the mints. Coinage profits average about $55 million a year.

The right to print paper money can be made a major source of national government revenue, at least for a short period. Chapters 27 and 28 discuss the principles and problems involved.

In 1933 and 1934, the American government used still a third method whereby a national government's monetary power may contribute to its Treasury. The dollar was devalued by slightly more than 40 per cent, and a Presidential order "nationalized" all gold in the United States. The Treasury thus netted a capital gain of $2.8 billion on its gold holdings as the dollar value was "written up."

Creation of the Federal Reserve System was an exercise of the federal government's monetary power. Federal reserve profits in excess of the amounts needed to pay member banks the established dividend, are paid to the federal Treasury. In 1958 this refund amounted to $650 million.

The ultimate title to all property, real and personal, is in the State as sovereign. Only because the State waives that right can individuals claim to have any title. Only by provision of law can an individual transfer his title in property to another. When the title of individuals fails for any reason, title reverts to the State.

Individual title to a property fails where an individual, not having any heirs within the relationship provided by law for intestate inheritance, dies without making a will. Intangible personal property then reverts to the government of the state of his domicile, and real property and tangible personalty to the government of the state wherein they are located.

Few individuals die or disappear without having made wills or without heirs capable of inheriting under the liberal inheritance laws of this country. Thus states derive an annual revenue of only a few million dollars from *escheats,* including bank deposits, life insurance, and corporation dividends unclaimed for long periods.

Crimes and infractions of the public laws are punished by imprisonment or fine and sometimes by forfeiture of property involved in the crime. Breaking bail forfeits any bail bond. Such punishment visits retribution on the offending individual, and in addition, *fines, penalties,* and *forfeitures* contribute to government revenues. These items yield the federal government about $12 million a year. The state governments receive about the same amount, but local governments get substantially more.

The fiscal aspect of fines and forfeitures, of course, should never be other than secondary, since the endeavor to derive a sizable government revenue from fines leads to miscarriage of justice. Nevertheless, it is not unknown for villages located along main-traveled highways to establish "speed traps," mulcting the unwary motorist on the excuse of his having exceeded a local speed limit. Some "speed trap" governments may find that the revenue they derive from such fines enables them to keep local taxes very low indeed. Even more reprehensible is the practice of letting local police and judicial officials pocket such fine revenue for private use.

During World War II, *gifts* were made to the federal government at the rate of $2 million a year. This was unprecedented. Governments rarely receive gifts or bequests solely for the purpose of aiding them in carrying on their ordinary government activities. Instead, such bequests and gifts are made to them as trustees for some public and charitable purpose. Gifts to governments for schools, libraries, and museums are common. Yet by far the most important "gift" is the time and effort of innumerable citizens who devote untold hours of effort to school board or other local activities, or to services of major and minor importance at every level of government. Such services, freely given, are worth hundreds of millions a year. If, as taxpayers, we were compelled to pay at commercial rates for the time and skill donated to our governments, tax bills would be uncomfortably higher.

PROBLEMS

1. "There is nothing in the nature of the postal service which makes it inherently a government function." Discuss in the light of the reasons why governments may conduct essentially business-type operations.

2. Examine the arguments for and against pricing the services of government enterprises to bring a substantial rate of profit.

3. Determine how some specific locality sets the charges for water, and appraise the method and the probable results.

4. What are the arguments for and against using fees and licenses as a source of revenue?

5. Show how special assessments differ from property taxes.

6. What methods might governments use to get more revenue from the exercise of the powers of sovereignty?

7. What are the advantages and disadvantages of systems of charging for government services in ways that influence the amount of service used?

8. What are the merits and weaknesses of tolls as a method of financing highways?

9. "Marginal cost pricing may permit more extensive use [of utility facilities] than full cost pricing, but it also adds to the need for taxes." Discuss.

PART FOUR

Intergovernmental Fiscal Relations

THE multiplicity of governments in the United States creates two special sets of fiscal problems: (1) a *vertical* one of how functions and revenues shall be shared between different government layers—between the states and their local units, between the federal government and the states; and (2) a *horizontal* one of relations between governments within the same layer—between metropolitan cities and their surrounding suburbs, between states, between the American federal government and other national governments. These are studied in the next two chapters.

CHAPTER 22

State-Local and Intercommunity Fiscal Relationships[1]

DURING the nineteenth century, state and local *functions* were sharply differentiated. States engaged in few "service" functions, limiting themselves to the provision of judicial systems and the machinery of political government. Local governments performed such service functions as the times demanded. Municipalities supplied police and fire protection, streets, garbage and rubbish disposal, education, and a few welfare services. Counties and towns were responsible for protection, road building and maintenance, and the care of the aged poor. School districts provided education.

State and local spheres of *taxation,* on the contrary, were not so clearly separated. Most state revenue was derived from property tax rates superimposed upon local rates. Local officials collected both the local and state levies, and the states received their shares from the local units. Each unit of government exempted from its property tax the property of other units. State agencies often assessed the operative property of public service enterprises and reported these assessments to the local units. But the nineteenth-century trend was toward the elimination of even this interrelationship. New taxes—corporation taxes, inheritance taxes, and others—were levied, collected, and retained exclusively by the states. Some early American writers on Public Finance anticipated that eventually there might be as complete separation of sources of revenue between state and local governments as there was of functions.

The twentieth century has seen the collapse of this state-local fiscal compartmentalization. Many long-established local functions are now

[1] The literature on intergovernmental financial relations is huge. A volume with a variety of useful papers and an excellent bibliography of materials published up to 1954 is Tax Institute, *Federal-State-Local Tax Correlation* (The Institute, Princeton, 1954).

recognized as having extra-local aspects. Children educated in one community, for example, may at maturity scatter all over the state and carry the good or ill effects of this education far beyond the bounds of the locality that schooled them. Furthermore, local "service" functions have expanded to overreach local administrative capacity and local revenue resources. Serious state-local fiscal problems have been created. Should state governments take over all or any part of various local functions which have developed extra-local character or have expanded beyond local revenue capacities? Should the states do anything about the inability of local property tax revenues to cover the expansion of local "service" expenditures? To what extent are the merits of political democracy and alert civic responsibility achieved more fully at the local than at the state level?

BASIC PRINCIPLES

Searching study has been devoted to the issues of state-local fiscal relationships. The following three conclusions or canons have been evolved:

1. *Some government functions are better performed by one level of government than by another.* A function affecting primarily the residents or property of a locality, with no important secondary effects on other persons or property, is best administered locally. State administration could not have the flexibility to do what people really want, to meet widely diverse local peculiarities and problems. Local handling of police and fire protection is generally more effective than state administration. Where there is no localization of the causes or benefits of a function, state administration is indicated. A state university to which residents of the entire state are admitted must be the responsibility of the state, not of the municipality in which it chances to be located. However, some functions primarily caused by, or of benefit to, the locality have important secondary effects on other persons and property—for example, road construction and various public health procedures. If the local and extra-local elements of the function can be separated, local authorities may retain the local features while state authorities take over the extra-local. To some extent, this has been the procedure in highways. Where the two elements cannot be separated, the entire function may be left to the local authorities, subject to some degree of state control.

2. *Some taxes can be better administered and collected by some levels of government than by others.* Except for the property tax and some minor business license taxes, this rule generally means state, rather than local, tax administration. But is not a state only the sum of its parts? Do not all localities combined have the same tax potential as the state? They do not because the total of what all localities acting individually can do is distinctly less than what the same public can accomplish by using the state.

Localities cannot levy personal net income, death, sales and excise, and most business taxes with real success for two reasons: (1) intercommunity competition and migration of large taxpayers and (2) the magnitude of the administrative problems.[2]

3. Unfortunately, the most advantageous distribution of government service functions according to the canon of functional fitness does not coincide with the optimum distribution of tax administration. Local governments are best fitted to perform the larger proportion of the functions. State governments are better fitted to levy, administer, and collect most taxes. Unless there is some help, local governments are compelled either to restrict their functions below a socially desirable point or to press to an unbearable extent upon the property tax and other revenues available to them. And so we come to the third canon of state-local fiscal interrelationship: *The states must put part of the revenues they collect at the disposal of their local units.*

The sections that follow discuss a variety of problems, but virtually all have one thing in common: Their solution is complicated by the rural and semirural domination of state legislatures. Urban populations suffer because they are under-represented. Moreover, our system of government provides no formal mechanism by which local governments as such can deal with problems of common concern.[3]

STATE-LOCAL DISTRIBUTION OF FUNCTIONS

Nearly all government "service" functions were begun by local units. When they started, most of these local "service" functions conformed to the canon of the functional fitness—they referred exclusively to local needs, or to what were believed to be exclusively local needs. They were best handled by local governments. Today, too, this is truer than we may realize. Preferences in public services, as in food, clothing, and recreation, vary. It is at the local level that differences in what people want—and want seriously enough to pay for—can be expressed and satisfied. Yet there are strong forces reducing the relative importance of local autonomy in performing functions.

Shift of extra-local functions. General economic and social development has imposed extra-local significance upon functions that were once purely local in character. Roadways, for example, were essentially a medium of local transport during the nineteenth century. When the auto made inter-

[2] Large cities may possibly be able to administer these taxes tolerably well. Even the biggest city, however, cannot solve the other problem–the movement of taxpayers and the shifting of taxable transactions.

[3] Municipal leagues have been formed in almost all states to serve local governments which choose to join. The leagues provide a variety of services, including representation in dealing with state governments.

urban traffic common, arterial highways had to be built. These served needs far wider than those of the local districts through which they passed. Through no act or choice of the road-building units themselves, highway construction had expanded beyond the legitimate scope of the individual localities.

Some functions—education especially—had extra-local significance from their inception. Even in the nineteenth century, shifts of population and economic, social, and political interdependence carried the products of education out of the communities originally providing it. Yet recognition of this fact dawned slowly.

State governments have generally been reluctant to take over, and local governments have been equally reluctant to surrender, functions which originated locally but became of broader concern. Even where the local and extra-local elements are separable, the entire function is likely to be left to the local authorities, with some form of state financial assistance and possibly control. Not until broader interests far outweigh purely local elements, and local administration obviously fails, will states take over a function.

Despite inertia, however, the states are gradually assuming functions of more than local concern which they are better fitted than the local governments to administer. Most state governments now build and maintain all arterial motor highways. Some have gone farther and taken over responsibility for county "feeder" roads, not primarily because of the extra-local significance of these roads, but because it was felt that the state highway departments could do a better and cheaper job than the local authorities. States, with federal aid, have taken over an increasing portion of the welfare function. Where state assumption is not complete, various elements of state control may be introduced in connection with financial support so that local control over the function is reduced substantially.

Rarely does a state take over an entire local function because some extra-local element has developed or become recognized. Usually, the state takes over the element with broader interest, leaving other elements with the local governments—the function becomes "shared" between the state and the local governments. In the field of public health, for example, care of the insane and of the victims of special diseases is made a state function, the number of patients per local unit being too small to permit of efficient care and treatment; other important public health responsibilities are left largely to the local units. Similarly, certain specialized elements of public education are handled through state agencies, while public education generally remains a local responsibility. Still another example of this sharing of functions is the development of state police.

In shared functions, lines of demarcation between state and local elements are sometimes difficult to draw or are drawn at the wrong points. Conflicts of authority and lack of comity between state and local police are not uncommon. Every motorist has learned to dread the changes in highway construction which occur where village authorities remain responsible for the stretches of state highways passing through village limits. But these imperfections of function-sharing are minor flaws and do not invalidate the fundamental soundness of the arrangement.

Local revenue deficiency and functional shifting. Inability of local units, particularly poor units, to finance various purely local functions adequately has sometimes given rise to demands that state governments take over the functions, even where state administration would probably be inferior to local. Compliance with such demands would, of course, contravene the principle of functional fitness. Attempts at such functional shifting have met with little success, except for instances of care of the aged and some other welfare functions. The more general solution is to aid local governments in financing of these functions, by one of the methods discussed below.

SEPARATION OF REVENUE SOURCES

Tax scholars writing in the early 1900's thought the disparity between local revenue sources and needs could be met by so-called "separation of revenue sources." States should forego their property tax levies, and possibly also their liquor license taxes, and derive their revenue exclusively from special corporation, income, death, and other taxes which local governments could not administer. Localities would then increase their property tax levies without making burdens intolerable.

It was also pointed out that the value of real estate depends substantially upon the activities of local governments. Reserving the property tax to localities would contribute to tax justice by limiting the taxation of property values to the government agencies which help create them. Furthermore, such separation would force the state governments to develop other sources of revenue, which would give a more rounded character to the combined state and local tax systems.

At present only half a dozen states make appreciable use of property tax levies. This application of the separation principle has not worked as well as hoped. State tax systems have lost a valuable element of flexibility. Minute adjustment of their property tax rates to state-wide assessments previously permitted states to equate expenditure needs and tax revenues with some degree of exactitude. Corporation, income, sales, and death tax rates do not lend themselves to such adjustment and fractioning, and in addition, the yield of those taxes is highly variable. Freeing the property tax for local use did not solve local revenue problems. State property tax levies never were very heavy. Their elimination did not generally give local governments much additional fiscal leeway.

The major advantages once thought inherent in giving local governments primary claim to property taxation have proved largely illusory. But although no panacea, it has been of some help. Meanwhile, there is growing pressure for some further applications of the principle. The states (and the federal government) are being urged to forego admissions taxes so that such levies, which can be administered well by local governments, may be more fully exploited by them. Taxes on electric power consumption and local telephone services, and various business license taxes, might also be reserved for local use. Such further applications of the separation principle will not aid local government much, but they will help somewhat; and such aid should not be despised.

SHARED TAXES

A second solution to the problem of unbalance between local revenue needs and local revenue sources is for state governments to redistribute to their local units part of the revenue from state-administered and state-collected taxes. Such tax-sharing began even before 1900.[4] After 1910, it spread rapidly. The impetus came from abolition of various elements of intangible property taxation, with the substitution of state-collected *in lieu* taxes. These reforms of the general property tax tended to deprive the localities of part of their property tax base, and elementary justice dictated that they be allowed to share in the special taxes substituted by states. Local governments thus were granted a share in the proceeds of state-administered mortgage taxes, motor vehicle license charges, bank share taxes, severance taxes, and personal and corporation income taxes.

TABLE 22–1

State Financial Aid to Local Governments, Selected Years, 1902–1958

Year	*(Millions)*
1902	$ 52
1913	91
1922	598
1932	801
1938	1,516
1948	3,283
1950	4,217
1958	7,985

SOURCES: U.S. Bureau of the Census, *Historical Statistics on State and Local Government Finances, 1902 to 1953;* and *Governmental Finances in the United States: 1957.*

During the 1920's, tax-sharing was increasingly motivated by the recognition that local property tax revenues were insufficient. In many in-

[4] Early state corporation franchise or privilege tax levies were usually accompanied by the release of corporate securities from general property taxation. To compensate local units for whatever loss of revenue was thus incurred, a dozen or more states before 1900 gave counties or other local units some share of the corporation tax collections. One state shared its inheritance tax receipts. New York and a few other states redistributed part of their state liquor tax collections back to their local governments.

stances, probably, the circumstance that local functions involved extra-local elements was an influencing factor. This functional tie-up is indicated by the fact that the tax shares were often earmarked to particular functions. Shares in motor vehicle revenues were earmarked to roadway construction and maintenance, shares in income and corporation tax revenues were earmarked to educational expenditure.

Later tax-sharing legislation turned away from the earmarking principle. The drop in local property tax collections, as a consequence both of the Depression and new tax-limitation laws, made property tax revenues in many localities inadequate to cover even purely local functional expenditures. Their need was not for more street funds or school funds, but for sufficient revenue to enable them to survive.

At present, almost all states share one or more taxes with their local units, providing in all probability over $2 billion a year.[5] The most important, shared tax, from a revenue standpoint, is the motor vehicle fuel tax.

Bases of distribution. With what local units—counties, townships, cities, villages, school districts, special districts—should a state share its revenue? All are likely to be afflicted with a fundamental insufficiency of tax base in relation to the functions they are called upon to exercise. It might be possible to work out a system of distributing shared taxes that would do justice to the claims of all classes of a state's local governments. What actually happens is that one tax is shared with the counties because relief of the farm tax burden was forcibly urged at one time upon a legislature or because champions of highway construction or charitable work—functions exercised primarily by the county governments—pleaded successfully for more county revenue for these functions. Another tax with a different unrelated yield is shared with the cities because their mayors once made an effective lobby. Still another tax is shared with the school districts as an alternative to state school aid. Such haphazard sharing is inefficient and certain to produce inequity.

The simplest method of distribution is to return to each locality a prescribed fraction of the tax *actually collected there*. Motor vehicle license tax, sales tax, and liquor tax collections are usually shared on a "source" basis. "Source" distribution of shared income, death, and corporation taxes is open to obvious criticism, however. Conflicting bases for deciding "source" can be developed, as the long history of conflicts in tax jurisdiction proves. A community "colonized" by wealthy individuals might receive more shared income and death tax revenue than it could fairly claim, whereas poor communities, where the need for shared revenue is much greater, would receive but trifling assistance. "Source" distribution of corporation taxes is still less justifiable. Large corporations having widely-

[5] The Bureau of the Census no longer reports shared taxes and grants-in-aid separately.

scattered operating properties pay state taxes through their head offices, and these are likely to be grouped together in one or two leading cities. "Source" distribution of the taxes would give these cities or their counties a royal revenue, whereas all other communities would receive mere driblets. Sharing gasoline, motor vehicle, and sales taxes on a "source" basis results in a more even distribution of the revenue, but still one with many crudities. Moreover, relative needs of the sharing communities are still ignored.

Shared revenues may also be apportioned on some *presumptive* basis of collection, such as population or property tax assessments, preferably equalized valuations.[6]

Still another basis for distribution, frequently employed where the shared revenue is earmarked to some particular function, is some measure of the *relative obligations* of the localities in connection with that function. Several states, for example, distribute part of their shared gasoline tax revenues on the basis of highway mileage. Tax revenues for schools may be apportioned according to school census or school attendance. Such sharing systems are a step toward the goal of equalization—but only a step, since they do not take into account the varying capacities of the localities to support the functions to which the revenues are earmarked. If equalized support of some local function, particularly one with extra-local elements, is desired, a grant-in-aid which entails an element of state control may be more effective than an equalized sharing of some tax revenue. This criticism would not apply to an equalized tax-sharing if the shared revenue went into the general funds of the benefited local governments—but until now, equalizing bases of distribution have not been applied to general-fund revenue-sharing.

Critique. Shared taxes are a useful means of relieving local revenue stringencies. They eliminate duplicate costs of administration and compliance. State legislatures have given the technique of distribution inadequate attention, however, with the result that in many states serious but correctible defects mar the sharing system. One disadvantage, however, is inherent in the system itself. Local governments are compelled to depend for part of their revenues upon an outside source unrelated to their individual peculiar necessities, and arbitrary elements enter the distribution. What is more, the local shares of certain taxes—personal and corporation income taxes, for example—vary through successive phases of the business cycle, with unpredictable and unfortunate consequences for local budgets.

[6] However, some tax administrators champion the use of original assessments as a distribution basis, on the theory that it will induce local assessors to increase the ratio of property assessment and make extra efforts to discover unlisted property in order to secure as large a share of the distributed revenue as possible for their own districts. It is argued that the advantages of a vigorous incentive to good assessment—and full use of property tax potential—outweigh the injustices involved in possible disproportionate distribution of the shared revenues.

SUPPLEMENTARY LOCAL RATES

Localities could be aided by being authorized to superimpose supplementary rates upon various state taxes collected within their jurisdictions. Cities and counties would be authorized to add an extra per cent or two to the state income taxes imposed on their inhabitants, or perhaps an extra cent on gasoline sold within their territory, or perhaps an extra half per cent on local sales. State agencies would remain fully responsible for administering the tax, would collect both the state tax and the supplementary local levy, and would remit the supplement to the locality.

This system opens to localities the possibility of revenue from taxes which they themselves could not successfully administer but without subjecting them to an arbitrary financial arrangement imposed by an outside authority—the state legislature. Within limits, each locality can set its supplementary rates at the levels dictated by *its particular needs* and can vary them as circumstances change. Individual communities need not fear being burdened by taxes imposed by others. No duplication of administrative machinery is involved, but there may be some additional compliance costs.

Still, supplementary local rates have limitations. In essence, such taxes are voluntary instead of universal sharing on a "source" basis and are subject to the weaknesses of "source" sharing. A supplementary rate can hardly yield the amount that in effect can be credited to localities under sharing arrangements. A state can give half of a rich man's 6 per cent income tax to a locality, but were that localitv to levy a special supplementary 3 per cent rate, the rich taxpayer might well move to some other community which imposed no supplementary rate. Therefore, the threat of intercommunity competition may lead to pressure for state or county compulsion on all localities to adopt a uniform policy.

Since World War II there has been extensive use of local supplements to state sales taxes in Illinois and California. Some Southern counties and villages levy supplementary gasoline taxes. Localities turning to income taxation would do well, if their state would permit, to impose their taxes as supplements to the state tax.

STATE-LOCAL GRANTS-IN-AID

The most important method by which the states give financial assistance to their local units is the grant-in-aid. Unlike the shared tax, it usually is an appropriation of a definite sum to a specified local function, rather than an appropriation of an uncertain and varying tax revenue. Grants-in-aid are generally earmarked to particular functions, in contrast to shared taxes. And finally, a grant-in-aid generally carries with it some degree of state control, whereas such control is exceptional in the case of shared taxes.

State grants-in-aid to assist communities in financing their *schools* were the earliest American application of this fiscal device—and still the largest. The first school grants were made from the income of funds—sometimes directly from the funds themselves—derived from the sale of public lands granted for this purpose by the federal government to the states. In time, these were supplemented by grants from earmarked state taxes. Later came appropriation of regular and growing amounts from the states' general revenues, at first to encourage the educational activities of the local school districts, subsequently to equalize relative educational opportunities between rich and poor districts.

TABLE 22–2

State Financial Aid to Local Governments, by Function, 1957

Function	*(Millions)*
Education	$4,094
Highways	1,071
Public welfare	1,025
Health and hospitals	253
Other	867
Total	$7,310

SOURCE: U.S. Bureau of the Census, *Summary of Governmental Finances in 1957.*

State *highway* aid to local units started in the 1890's. By the turn of the century, nearly all states had highway aid systems. Dominant from the very beginning was the intent to "buy" some state control over local highway functions in order to impose unform standards of construction and maintenance. State *welfare* aid on a small scale has a long history, but did not become important financially until the 1930's. The Social Security Act laid a foundation for major enlargement of a few types of local welfare functions accomplished with increased state assistance.

State control. When states distribute school, road, welfare, or other aid to a locality, they usually provide that the local activity for which the aid is granted must measure up to certain state-prescribed standards. If a school or a piece of local highway construction fails to conform to the state standard, the local government cannot share in the state distribution. Partisans of local self-government have been bitter against this feature, claiming that the state governments are in effect buying out the independence of local communities. The charge cannot be denied. But buying out the "anarchy of local autonomy" in functions such as public education and highway construction which involve extra-local elements may be amply justified. Were local governments left to themselves, the indifference, ignorance, and inertia of some might result in reprehensibly low levels of educational, roadway, or welfare accomplishment. State control, accepted because of the opportunity to share in state funds, guarantees at least a *minimum* level of achievement. Individual communities fortunately situated as to resources and willing to employ those resources are not prevented from expending more than the required minimum. Moreover, state coordination of operations over a large area—especially in highway construction—may enhance the value of the accomplishment beyond what would be achieved by separate localities acting independently.

There is, however, a latent danger in achieving state control of local functions through state aid if no element of equalization enters into the distribution aid. The minimum standard of accomplishment required for participation in state funds may be set so high as to be beyond the fair capacity of some local districts. A state-standard school program putting no burden upon a prosperous community might strain to the breaking point the resources of a city on the decline. Poor districts which do not meet this standard are excluded from any share in the state fund to which their taxpayers have contributed and which they need much more than their more prosperous neighbors. Yet, if the standard of accomplishment is set low enough to be within reach of the poorest communities, it is likely to be so low as to be practically meaningless. Equalization aid, of course, does not create this problem.

Bases for distribution: supplementation, stimulation, equalization. The bases for the distribution of state aid to local governments will differ according to the major purpose sought.

If the purpose of the grant is to *supplement* local revenue, if it is to meet the fundamental inadequacy of local revenues—if, in other words, the purpose is to substitute the superior taxing power of the state for the inferior taxing power of localities—a per capita grant will serve well. The locality gets a block of money which it is free to use as it wishes. New York, for example, grants each city $6.75 a year per inhabitant, with varying amounts to other localities. No restrictions at all are attached to use. In no other state, however, have voters provided themselves with such freedom in the use of grant funds at the local level.[7]

The typical form of supplementation ties the grant to expenditures for particular functions. The state will distribute fixed or proportionate amounts to local districts irrespective of their relative needs or accomplishments. School or road aid distributed on the basis of population or area would ease the local burden of financing these functions, but it would not necessarily improve the character of the education or roads. Localities might accomplish no more with the state aid than without it, merely substituting state aid for funds they would otherwise raise themselves. The distribution of school aid on the basis of school enrollment, and of funds for highway maintenance on the basis of existing highway mileage, might be fairer methods, but they would be equally bare of assuring extraneous

[7] Part of the explanation is that state legislators who must bear the responsibility for imposing the tax feel that they will get more credit for use of the money if it is directed toward some specific, and popular, function.

accomplishment. Supplementary state aid distribution had historical precedence over other bases. It can serve to relieve local tax burdens, and accord each community varying opportunity to use the money as it wishes. These wishes, however, may not take adequate account of broader public interests.

Grant distribution can be arranged to *stimulate*. A relatively small state grant can be devised to exert considerable leverage. A matching grant will do so. If the state, for example, agrees to give $1 for each $1 spent by a locality on a function, the locality will be stimulated to spend more on that function than it would otherwise. The same result can be obtained if funds are distributed on condition that the locality carry out some program. For example, a small, state school-fund might be distributed pro rata to school enrollment with the proviso that the school curriculum or construction in each district receiving state money must first be approved by the state school authorities. State school-aid might also be distributed to encourage local school activity by relating it to average teachers' salaries in each district or to school costs per pupil in each district, thereby encouraging the employment of higher-salaried teachers or an increase in school expenditures. A small, state road-fund might be distributed pro rata to local highway expenditure or mileage of motor highways maintained by the local units. Distributed on such bases, small amounts of state aid may inspire local activities much greater than could be financed by the direct expenditure of the state fund. One danger of such methods of distribution is that the more prosperous districts, which can make large expenditures on the aided functions without straining their resources, will obtain a disproportionate share of the state fund. Moreover, poorer localities, straining to get grants, may sacrifice alternative functions of greater value.

Relatively more may be given poor districts. A deliberate policy of using grants to *equalize* is now common. The widespread endorsement of equalization grants gets much of its support from a belief that differences in living standards among *people* ought to be reduced. Grants, however, are based on *area* differences. Consequently, they are an inefficient means for transferring real income from upper to lower income families. For example, the prosperous families in poor areas may in fact benefit at the expense of poorer families in prosperous districts. *Areas* neither pay taxes nor receive benefits of government spending—the *people* in the areas do. To frame policy in terms of areas rather than people is to resort to a crude means of achieving the goal of rational discrimination among people. Admittedly, however, where the amounts for distribution are as big as they are in most states, the grants to poorer districts can be large enough to reduce significantly the differences that would otherwise exist between the quality of their public services and those of more prosperous areas.

State money enables poor districts to provide vitally necessary school, road, welfare, and other government functions which, because of their poverty, they might not otherwise be able to finance.[8] State control over the subsidized local functions can still be maintained by requiring the subsidized local activity to conform with state standards before any state money is paid over.

A thoroughgoing equalization grant would have to combine several separate elements in its distribution basis. First, the relative *needs* of the localities in connection with the function would have to be taken into consideration. In the case of school aid, this would involve the number of children of school age in each district, with some modifier to cover school attendance customs. For highway aid, the factors would be area, population, character of traffic to be served, and also costs of construction as determined by topographical features and roadway character. For each class of welfare aid, a suitable set of need determinants would have to be formulated, a difficult task in a changing world.

A second factor which must enter into an equalization basis of state aid distribution is the relative *ability* of the various localities to support the function out of their own fiscal resources. Since the property tax is practically the sole source of most local tax revenue, the basis of distribution must be related—inversely—either to property assessments or to the revenue which can be raised by some prescribed property tax levy. Assessed valuations give, of course, a notoriously poor indication of the relative ability of local districts to support particular government activities. But since no state possesses accurate statistics on the income or wealth of the residents of its local subdivisions, property tax data have been the best measure available. Fortunately, good state tax equalization can eliminate the worst crudities. Moreover, data on local retail sales, taxable income, use of electricity and telephones, auto registration, and other objective and obtainable indices of economic strength can be used. Even if localities have only one tax base—real estate—their *relative abilities* to use it may be indicated reasonably well by these measures of economic strength. Yet not for certain, and as formulae get complex, new injustices may be created.

The trend for many years in state aid distribution has been toward equalization. Yet states, without a clear understanding of the difference between using a state fund to encourage local effort and using it to equalize local capacity—and restrained by constitutional restrictions and inertia—have grafted elements of equalization piecemeal into a grant and shared-tax system built originally around a small state fund for encourag-

[8] This welcome result is not certain. If the taxes which the state uses to finance the grant take more out of the district than the aid provides, the locality suffers. Ordinarily, however, the poorest districts will gain. Yet for any large number of "poor" localities, the net benefit may be slight. It will consist largely of the advantages of using state rather than local revenue sources, not in the fact that the people in the area get back many more dollars than they pay.

ing local effort. Though legislatures are gradually removing old incongruities, new complexities and rigidities appear.[9]

State aid and government efficiency. In general, by holding some local governments to standards of performance higher than they would achieve on their own account and by establishing elements of uniformity in extra-local functions having more than purely local concern, state aid combined with state control has helped improve the quality of particular local government activities. Under certain circumstances, however, aid may perpetuate or create inefficiency. Localities may be induced to spend in ways that do not accord with their highest preferences and that do not, in fact, benefit the rest of the state significantly. Political pressures or failure to adapt to changing conditions can lead to poor distribution of state funds. One example has been the failure of the grants in some states to take account of the improvement in the relative economic condition of rural areas since the late 1930's.

Scattered over the country are many "submarginal" school districts, road districts, villages, and counties too small in area or population, or too poor, to be able to undertake functions which are necessary for their existence. Were no equalizing state aid available, their provision of schools, or roads, or poor relief, or other functions would be so inadequate that, once called to legislative attention, a fundamental solution of the problem would be sought. In many cases, the difficulty might be met by consolidating or reorganizing the submarginal districts into better-balanced units. In extreme cases, it might be advisable to finance resettlement of population from areas which cannot provide normal livings and junk the government organizations of the submarginal areas. But a liberal state aid policy may enable governments in such areas to drag along a parasitic existence and defer the reorganization or scrapping process.

Nor can it be assumed that the state standards of accomplishment that must be accepted as a consideration for receipt of state aid are always the best. If they are inappropriate, their imposition throughout the state multiplies the harm they do. And *any* set of absolute standards is certain to fail to suit some situations.

Friction between state and local officials, especially in states with one or more very large cities, is a common result of grant systems. Another occasional, unfortunate consequence is perpetuation through state aid of local administration of functions whose extra-local significance dwarfs their purely local elements and which should be transferred to state ad-

[9] When equalization distribution was still in an experimental stage, some states made the mistake of distributing funds inversely to original property tax assessments, before these had been equalized by a state agency. It was soon evident that it was to the interest of each local district to assess its property as low as possible in order to obtain a larger share of state aid. Part of the reason for the postwar efforts of numerous states to improve property tax administration and equalization has been a desire to help make grant distribution more satisfactory.

ministration. Local officials are more likely to cling to the power which the administration of a function—highway construction, for example—gives them when, because of state aid, it involves little direct cost to their constituents. Finally, a matching type of grant may lead to laxity in spending if local officials know that the state will pay an appreciable fraction of the bill. Or the system may lead to wasteful red tape and rigidity as state officials enforce rules controlling local administration.

Treatment of cities. Officials of big cities may be justified in complaining that legislatures under rural domination shortchange urban areas in distributing grants. Each state-city case has its own special elements. Measurement is difficult, especially if there is an honest attempt to relate taxes collected in an area with state aid. Some mayors, without proposing how the state should raise the money, argue that grants for cities should be increased. Yet the cities might suffer. The taxes which the state legislature would increase might very well take more out of the cities than any increase in grants would put back. The issue hinges upon the distribution of the increase in taxes compared with the distribution of the increase in grants. This issue is decidedly different from that of a grant increase alone.

EXTENSION OF LOCAL TAXING AUTHORITY

Several states have recently turned to another method of solving the financial problems of local governments. This method violates the third principle of state-local fiscal relationship. Sometimes, as in New York, Ohio, and Pennsylvania, local governments are granted permission to employ taxes not already used by the state. More commonly, states authorize all local governments, or all of a certain size, or a single large city, to impose a particular tax or a group of taxes. A host of new local taxes has resulted.

Such extension of local taxing authority removes some of the *legal* restrictions which have prohibited local governments from trying to raise adequate revenues. Within the scope of the state-granted authorization, local units gain a measure of fiscal autonomy, and responsibility. There remains, however, the problem of *economic* restriction on local governments. Can they effectively impose taxes on income, sales, business, or special services? Can they use the best tax for drawing on the stream of income—the net income tax—or must they resort to indirect and regressive taxes or taxes that may discourage business in the community?

Experience indicates that local governments can obtain large amounts of revenue from low-rate taxes on income or sales or business receipts. Smaller but highly welcome amounts can be obtained from taxes on amusements, hotel rooms, liquor, and other such bases. In the short run, there may be little migration of business or population to neighboring communities which for the time being forego imposition of a similar tax. Even in the long run, the same may be true if the rate of tax is low and, more important, if better public services are provided in the community with the tax. However, if one community imposes substantially heavier rates than neighboring ones, or if the rates are made progressive, or if the tax structure is refined to try to discriminate more equitably, the local economy will suffer in competition with others. It seems inevitable that a part of the revenue obtained by local governments from these taxes must come from persons with small incomes. Costs of administration and compliance, too, are likely to be greater than if the state were to raise the same revenue.

One can easily understand why state officials welcome a solution to the state-local fiscal problem that places on local governments the unpopular responsibility for raising additional taxes. Nor can one deny the desirability in principle of tying spending and taxing decisions together as closely as possible. Yet, despite the difficulties involved in the other solutions discussed earlier, the best general answer will still seem to be for states to raise more of the total tax bill and improve the methods of distributing funds to local governments. The economic power of local governments to tax effectively and uniformly and equitably is too limited. Extension of their taxing power cannot remove the underlying economic limitations where population and capital are as mobile, and competition as extensive, as they are in the United States.

CITY-SUBURB FISCAL RELATIONSHIPS[10]

Serious fiscal issues sometimes arise between local government units. City-county problems are of long standing. Today, however, the most pressing current problem of intercommunity fiscal relationships is probably that posed by the rapid growth of metropolitan suburbs and the changing character of the older city areas.

Families prefer the suburbs to more crowding into centers of cities. Many businesses find it advantageous and practicable to build new plants and stores outside city areas. The growing communities must provide new streets, sewers, schools, water systems, parks, hospitals, and fire, police, garbage collection, lighting, and library facilities. Highways and bridges must be expanded or built to connect the offspring communities with the parent city. The necessary costs and taxes greatly exceed the amounts expected when most of the new families bought their houses.

The parent city must provide transit and traffic facilities to accommodate the great numbers of persons who enter and leave each day at about the same peak times. The parent city's school, welfare, and other costs do not, of course, increase as much as if the suburban population growth occurred within the city. City officials may exaggerate considerably the

[10] Tax Institute, *Financing Metropolitan Government* (The Institute, Princeton, 1955) contains useful discussion and an excellent bibliography.

adverse fiscal effects of suburban growth, or put the emphasis in the wrong place. Rarely do the people who earn their incomes in the central city and live outside put the city to expense, except for transportation facilities. The buildings in which they work will bear property tax ample to cover fire and police protection. Many high-density land uses, the types that support high assessments, would not be feasible without suburban populations. The chief dangers to the city's net fiscal problem, in addition to the costs of facilities to transport workers at peak periods, seem to be the degeneration of older areas into slums. The property tax base falls while needs may rise. The areas become the homes of the poor and under-privileged.

Low-income immigrants are attracted from outside areas; the large numbers of Negroes and Puerto Ricans that have moved into New York, Chicago, Detroit, and Los Angeles in recent years illustrate this tendency. Demands upon the city for medical care, relief, education, and protection grow, even though population is stable or actually shrinking.

In the growing suburban areas, land values rise and new buildings provide a base for higher property tax revenue, although owners may protest the taxes needed to pay for the vast increase in outlays. Conditions are favorable for special assessments. In the parent cities, the rise of property values is slow, not keeping pace with the costs of city government. The cities are driven to supplement the property tax with special business, utility, license, sales, income, and other levies, plus charges and fees.[11]

The metropolitan fiscal problem created by this situation is serious, its solution difficult. To an increasing extent, central cities are collecting fees from surrounding towns for use of city facilities such as police, fire, water, sewage, and garbage disposal systems. At best, such methods meet only part of the problem. And even such mutually advantageous arrangements are sometimes difficult to establish because of lack of good methods of accomplishing effective cooperation between cities and their suburbs, and among neighboring suburban communities.

Ultimate solution of this fiscal problem involves state, and sometimes interstate, action. State legislation is needed to authorize, and at times to compel, city-suburban cooperation. Problems of transportation, water and sewer systems, policing, welfare, air and water polution, public health, and park and recreation facilities cannot be solved efficiently, or perhaps solved at all, except with the participation of every community in a metropolitan complex. Fundamental decisions must be made within a few years as part of the new highway program. Sharing of costs and benefits—to say nothing of deciding on what specific programs to adopt and press—will inevitably create conflicts. Some of these will defy solution on a voluntary basis if unanimity is required.

[11] The imposition of such taxes and charges may hasten the exodus of business and more prosperous families, but evidence on this score is inconclusive. For equal quality of government services, suburban areas probably offer little net tax advantage, if any.

State grant and tax-sharing arrangements should be deliberately adapted to recognize the special problems of metropolitan areas. Each such urban complex presents unique problems, and no single fiscal pattern will meet all needs. Moreover, not *all* local governmental problems of an area must be solved on a common basis. An efficient system will result in differences. Suburbs will settle on different levels and patterns of spending that reflect the choices of their taxpayer-inhabitants. Clearly, the job ahead is one of the most difficult and the most challenging of modern life. It involves more than money, but it cannot be solved without great efforts in the area of city-suburb fiscal relationships.

PROBLEMS

1. In what sense are localities better able to spend money to perform functions than they are to raise taxes?

2. Make a study of shared taxes and grants-in-aid in your state.

3. "The problems of deciding how to share taxes and of how to make grants are essentially the same." Comment.

4. Describe the difference between stimulating and equalizing grants.

5. "The advantages of state grants of new revenue-raising power to localities outweigh the disadvantages." Discuss.

6. Show how the problems of public finance of separate local governments in a metropolitan area are inevitably related.

7. "A city should not spend money unless the services obtained are worth their cost. Why, then, should local taxpayers seek state aid?" Discuss.

CHAPTER 23

Interstate, Federal-State, and International Fiscal Relationships

RARELY, during the nineteenth century, did the fiscal activities of one state impinge upon those of another. Their functions could not possibly overlap. And with most states depending for their revenues primarily on property tax levies, there was little chance of tax competition among them or of double taxation problems. The federal government and the states were also dissociated functionally and fiscally.

Interstate and federal-state fiscal compartmentalization are now things of the past. Tax bases overlap as between states. States enter into tax competition, bidding for personal and business residents by the lure of low taxes. The federal government interests itself in functions once exclusively state or local prerogatives, while state and local officials look to Washington for money to finance their own programs. And the states and the federal government encroach upon each other's tax realms.

On the international level there are two familiar problems—excessive taxation of some individuals and businesses subject to the tax laws of two or more countries, and inadequate taxation of others who can use various loopholes resulting from differences in the tax laws from land to land. A third problem, related slightly to the second, arises from the desire of some countries to use tax concessions to attract outside business.

INTERSTATE FISCAL RELATIONSHIPS

Each state is a distinct territorial unit. Their service activities have been predominantly separated. Of course, interstate cooperation occurs in highway and bridge construction, water supply, forest fire protection, unemployment insurance, conservation, police work, tax administration, and in some other fields, but such cooperation does not ordinarily extend to fiscal provision for these activities.[1]

The insularity of state functional activities is not duplicated in the revenue field. A single economic element may be subject to taxation on different bases by more than one state. Compliance costs of businesses having interests in more than one state are increased by the lack of uniformity in state tax systems. And personal and business mobility is sufficient to establish the states as competitors, on the basis of relative tax burdens and public service benefits, for certain classes of persons and businesses.

Double taxation. Three major forms of so-called multiple or double taxation appear in the United States:

(1) *Multiple-aspect taxation* by a single taxing jurisdiction. This occurs when the federal government taxes corporation income and then the stockholder when he receives dividends, or when a state subjects corporations to a capital stock organization charge, a net income annual franchise tax, a property tax on their property holdings, a sales tax on their sales or purchases, and perhaps still other special license taxes.

(2) *Superimposed taxation* by taxing jurisdictions of different grades. This occurs when the federal and state governments both tax personal or corporation income, or when a state and various grades of local governments superimpose property tax rates on the same property.

(3) *Overlapping taxation*. This occurs when two states or two coequal local districts impose similar taxes on occasional taxable objects because judicial construction of their tax powers allows of overlapping jurisdiction. Such overlapping taxation arises in state inheritance, business, and personal income taxation.

No direct discrimination among taxpayers is involved in multiple-aspect taxation—or at least, no more than may be involved in each individual tax in the multiple series. In the light of its effect on the distribution of tax burdens among individuals, therefore, it is not inherently "unjust," though actual applications may appear unfair.

Superimposed taxation, likewise, works no discrimination among individuals otherwise similarly situated. It may, however, profoundly affect the economic character of a tax. A federal income tax by itself may be heavy without being confiscatory. So too, a state income tax may impose

[1] Where fiscal as well as functional unity is necessary to some interstate activity, the state governments may step out of the picture, transferring the function and its fiscal provision to an independent service agency created by interstate compact. New York and New Jersey established such an agency—the Port of New York Authority—to develop the traffic facilities of the New York and Jersey City port area. A few other "authorities" have been established to deal with other interstate service problems. Financing is accomplished through tolls and other charges.

The federal Constitution permits states to make compacts subject to Congressional approval. Compacts have been made successfully to deal with numerous problems. But the only important tax compact is that noted in Chapter 17, apportioning truck fees in the West. Compacts are generally slow to complete, relatively inflexible, and not easily enforced. Yet some students now believe that greater use of compacts to deal with fiscal problems is to be recommended.

Several states now have permanent commissions to deal with problems involving other states.

a fairly moderate burden. But superimpose the two without allowing credit or deductibility, and the result may be confiscation.

Overlapping taxation by two states does discriminate, among individuals and among businesses. A, who lives in Mississippi and earns his $25,-000 income there pays an income tax of $750. B, who also lives in Mississippi but receives $25,000 for services performed in New Orleans, would pay $750 to Mississippi and $750 to Louisiana (assuming no reciprocity between these two states). This double tax on B is unjust, since his government benefits are no more numerous than A's, nor is his taxpaying ability greater, nor does he sacrifice less in paying taxes.[2]

Overlapping double taxation can exist only when both of two conditions are present. (1) *Judicial construction must impute two or more tax locations to a taxable subject.* Income receipt, for example, is construed by our courts to occur in both the state where it is earned and the state of the recipient's domicile. Transfer of intangible personalty—such as corporation stock—on the owner's death is sometimes construed to occur in more than one state. (2) *The taxing states must levy their taxes on two or more allowable bases.* Overlapping double taxation cannot occur if two states tax income solely on the basis of the recipient's domicile. But if two states tax income on the bases both of source and of domicile or if one uses a source basis and the other a domicile basis, some individuals will be caught by the overlapping.

One possibility of eliminating overlapping double taxation would be a reversal of judicial construction to allow only one situs for any taxable item. As was noted in Chapter 7, the Supreme Court has twice reversed itself on situs in state inheritance taxation, eliminating and then reimposing double taxation in this field. The broad trend of court decisions in recent years has been to enlarge the state's taxing power. The prospects of judicial solution of this phase of the problem are thus slight.

Limitation of state taxes to some single base is a second possibility for eliminating overlapping double taxation. But individual state self-denying ordinances are difficult to obtain. Officials may express willingness to take such action—after neighboring states have done likewise. By *reciprocity* clauses in their tax laws, however, the states have been able to eliminate some overlapping double taxation without sacrificing their interests to those of their laggard neighbors. Under a "reciprocal" income tax statute, the levy is made on the two bases of source and domicile. The law provides, however, that should the income tax law of any other state exempt income earned within its borders by residents of the first state, then the first state will extend a corresponding exemption to income earned within

[2] As noted in Chapter 14, state laws taxing business income contain provisions for allocating total income. Presumably such provisions should eliminate the possibility of more than one state taxing the same portion of income. In fact, however, allocation provisions can produce double taxation on business income because the details of the provisions differ.

its borders by residents of the other state. As more and more states make provision for reciprocal exemption of "derived" income, overlapping double taxation of income is progressively reduced. Almost all state death taxes and most of the state income taxes have reciprocity clauses.

Interstate tax uniformity. No advantage would be sustained if two or more states made their poll or private auto tax laws identical as to language and administration. No disadvantage is suffered if such taxes vary widely from state to state. A poll-taxpayer or auto owner is concerned with one tax and one only—that of the state of his residence or the state of the car's registration—and it does not matter to him if other states employ different forms of the tax or if different judicial constructions are placed on the taxes of other states. But most taxes have to be paid in more than one state by a larger or smaller number of taxpayers. An individual may pay income tax not only to the state of his residence, but to several others from which he derives elements of income. The executor of an estate must prepare forms and pay taxes in the state of the deceased's residence and in every state where any of the real or tangible property is located. Incorporated enterprises must pay special taxes in every state in which they do business, and almost every business pays unemployment insurance tax wherever it has employees.

Nonuniformity of state tax laws is responsible for some of the overlapping double taxation noted in the preceding pages. Moreover, each different basis on which a taxpayer must calculate tax liability means additional accounting and tax compliance costs. Perhaps different accounting systems may be required to comply with different state laws even though the net effects of differences on actual tax bills are insignificant. And dissimilar tax statutes lead to variant judicial constructions, further adding to the taxpayers' worries, troubles, and costs. Although interstate uniformity in tax laws is not as absolutely necessary as uniformity in negotiable instrument laws or sales laws, it would at the very least be a trouble-saving and money-saving convenience to many taxpayers.

To achieve interstate tax uniformity, it is not necessary that every state impose exactly the same taxes at exactly the same rates. Uniformity could not extend to identity of tax rates and exemptions or even to identity in the taxes imposed. But, to serve taxpayers best, the basis of any one kind of tax should be uniform from state to state; the included and excluded elements, the language of the laws, the regulations, and the tax return forms should be reasonably uniform in all points except the calculation of the tax on the basis of the statutory rate.

Interstate tax uniformity has long been held a desideratum, but positive action has been needlessly slow. Two dozen or more different state formulae are used for allocating corporation income. What is needed is a series of model uniform tax laws—a model uniform sales tax law, a model uniform personal income tax law, a model uniform gasoline tax law, and so forth—each complete, except for rate and exemption provisions, and ready for enactment. Some progress in formulating model uniform tax laws has been made, but it is only a beginning in the movement toward uniformity.[3] Interested organizations must make concerted drives to persuade the state legislatures to enact the model laws. And finally, when and if uniform tax laws are on the statute books, the various associations of state tax officials will have to formulate a procedure for maintaining uniformity of regulations and report forms.

Uniformity in income, estate, and gift taxes could be achieved to very large degree by using federal law and regulations as the model for state taxes—as several states have done. Taxpayer compliance would be eased, and state administrators would get maximum benefit from the use of federal administrative aids that are now available.

Interstate tax competition. Real property cannot be moved from one state to another to avoid tax burdens. The location of new housing or industrial construction, however, may depend somewhat on relative property tax loads and the government services provided. Moreover, some elements of tangible personalty are shiftable. When choosing states of incorporation and when locating factories and offices, corporations can take relative tax burdens into account. Some sales can be legally consummated in one state or another, according to the relative tax liabilities involved. And men of wealth can choose their states of domicile (or for locating trusts) to minimize income, intangible property, and death taxes.

For most state taxes, the margin of taxpayers who can shift from one jurisdiction to another is so small that high-taxing and low-taxing states cannot be said to compete with each other. When one state imposes a sales tax, or a gasoline tax, or a tobacco products tax and its neighbor does not, some residents living close to the boundary line will go to the trouble of making purchases in the nontaxing state, but these few lost purchases do not seriously threaten either the revenue of the taxing state or its economic structure. Moreover, business enterprise migration to minimize taxes has probably been exaggerated by pressure-group propaganda.

Progressive personal income and death taxes, however, are more vulnerable to competitive interstate rate-cutting. Personal domicile can be so superficial a legal fiction that numerous wealthy Americans may, with little trouble, establish residence in almost any state of their choosing. Yet, this casual fiction determines whether a million-dollar income is taxed $100,000 a year in New York or nothing in Florida.

Rich residents, for all that their domicile may be largely a nominal matter, bring a degree of prosperity to a state. They buy property, build

[3] Some progress has also been made in joint auditing. Yet in view of the fact that many states impose essentially the same kind of tax on large businesses, the extension of joint auditing has been meager. Differences in statutes are only part of the explanation. Legal obstacles and administrative inertia are others. Needless costs to complying taxpayers and to the governments involved remain.

homes, and make purchases in the state; they give personal service employment to local labor. These advantages have been sufficient to induce Florida, Nevada, and some other states to advertise themselves as "tax havens" for millionaires who wish to avoid state income taxes. Before the federal estate tax credit was enacted, these two states also advertised themselves as havens for death tax avoidance. Wealthy individuals to whom these lures are addressed are a relatively mobile group, and if these "tax haven" states offered any substantial tax saving to the rich, they might "hijack" the tax systems of other states. Certain details of the federal tax system prevent this. The federal estate tax credit provides a protection for progressive state death taxes on large estates. The federal personal income tax provision for deductibility of state personal income taxes reduces the effect of rate differences in state taxes on large incomes. As of 1959, a million-dollar income, which would be taxed $100,000 in New York and nothing in Florida, would actually be reduced only $13,000 by the New York tax, because the recipient would save roughly $87,000 on his federal tax by reason of the deduction. For so long as federal personal income tax rates remain at anything like their present high level and the federal estate tax credit remains in effect, the advantages offered by the "tax haven" states will be much less than appears at first glance.[4]

Tax barriers to interstate commerce. Prior to 1930, the federal Constitution seemed to be an effective barrrier to state taxation that might interfere with interstate commerce. Indeed, the complaint was that the Supreme Court had extended its construction of the interstate commerce limitation so widely that it interfered with legitimate and nondiscriminatory business taxation. But the Twenty-first Amendment, adopted in 1934 to repeal the Eighteenth (Prohibition) Amendment, provides that once alcoholic beverages enter the state of destination, state regulation supersedes federal; this allows the states to impose liquor "import" duties. During the 1930's, a combination of Supreme Court relaxation of interpretations of the interstate commerce clause and state provincialism and protectionism, led to use of state taxing power to burden out-of-state business. Since World War II, however, the problem has been much less evident.

FEDERAL-STATE FISCAL RELATIONSHIPS

Overlapping of federal functions and revenues with those of the state and local governments is a relatively recent phenomenon. Some of the growing concern is really over the total load of taxes, not the fact of overlapping. A different type of concern results from distrust—though by

[4] Discussions ordinarily omit reference to differences in the quality of governmental services in the states with different tax systems. It is possible that for the rich person the difference in quality of service may be less important than differences in the *gross* tax but still greater than the difference in his tax, *net* after allowing for deductibility.

well-meaning people—of the ways others choose to use their income, that is, their failure to pay for education or welfare or highways to the extent the critics would prefer. Deeply significant issues exist, and they are accentuated by the weight of the total tax burden.

Through the first quarter of the twentieth century, the *functional* activities of the federal government and of the states were distinctly separate. Then some overlapping of services began through state activity in agricultural aid and conservation, fields previously occupied by the federal government, and through federal activity in arterial motor highways and criminal investigation, services previously provided by state and local governments. A climax in the mingling of federal, state, and local functional interests was reached in the handling of relief efforts after 1933. Today, as state and local governments find themselves pressed to enlarge existing functions and undertake new ones, and as taxpayers rebel at the growing burden of state and local taxes, there is mounting pressure for the federal government to assume phases of activity heretofore exclusively state or local responsibilities, or at least to share in their financing. The Constitution places no significant limits on the functions which the federal government can undertake through use of the spending power.

Federal and state-local sharing of a function may take either of two forms: (1) The federal government may directly perform some part of the function. The federal effort may be limited to phases beyond state jurisdiction and so avoid duplicating state-local efforts. Duplication has occurred in many instances, however, involving waste of public funds, failure to provide unified control, and conflicts of authority. This has been true to varying degree in the fields of agricultural aid, criminal investigation, and relief. (2) The federal government may leave the administration of a function partly or entirely to state or local agencies and content itself with distributing grants-in-aid to the state and local units to compensate them for the extra-state elements of their activity and to establish some federal control.

In their sharing of functions, the federal government and the states have in general worked cooperatively, with federal effort supplementing state or local activity.[5] In the *revenue* field, by contrast, there has been conflict and discord. Local acquisition of utilities reduces federal corporation income taxes. High federal liquor taxes stimulate bootlegging, which cuts state liquor tax revenue. Widespread state sales taxes make Congress reluctant to impose a broad federal sales tax. Federal purchase of real property reduces state and local property tax bases. State community property laws were largely responsible for the split income provisions of the federal personal income tax. The federal death tax base is vitally affected by state

[5] More friction may arise in highway construction as federal influence grows while fundamentally difficult problems of building in urban areas create serious new conflicts.

laws of property. All income taxes are reduced by the exemption in varying degree of interest on government bonds. When the federal government levied personal income, death, corporation, and gasoline taxes, it encroached upon fields originally developed by the states. When the states imposed liquor and tobacco products taxes, they trespassed upon fields previously considered part of the federal fiscal domain. In thus establishing duplicate revenue systems, the federal government and the states limit each other's revenue resources, impose double tax and reporting burdens upon taxpayers, and maintain duplicate administrative systems.[6]

The major reforms proposed—separation of revenue sources, shared taxes, tax credits, deductibility, supplementary rates, and grants-in-aid—parallel in some respects the solutions proposed for the state-local revenue problem. But there are several important differences between the state-local and the federal-state tax issues: (1) The states have inherent tax powers, limited only by the federal constitutional provision against imposing import or export taxes. Local governments have only such taxing powers as are delegated to them by state law. Therefore, in relation to the federal government the states have wider taxing powers than local governments have in relation to states. (2) Mobility of persons and businesses among states is less than their mobility among localities. Hence, in relation to the federal government states are not so *economically* handicapped in the levy of income, death, and business taxes as local units are in relation to the states. (3) States can administer effectively most of the taxes in dispute between them and the federal government, whereas efficient tax administration at the local level is limited. As a consequence of these three differences, whereas the state-local fiscal problem is one of *providing* the local governments with revenue, the federal-state problem is one of *allowing* them a sufficient revenue. Two other supplementary points are relevant. Federal intervention can help eliminate interstate double taxation, interstate tax competition, and duplicate costs of compliance and administration. Cooperation of forty-nine states is well-nigh unobtainable on a voluntary basis.

Separation of revenue sources. Separation of revenue sources is sometimes suggested as a solution of the federal-state revenue problem.[7] Un-

[6] See J. A. Maxwell, *The Fiscal Impact of Federalism in the United States* (Harvard University Press, Cambridge, 1946); and the U.S. Treasury, Tax Advisory Staff studies, such as *Federal-State Tax Coordination* (Washington, 1952). The best-known recent study is by The Commission on Intergovernmental Relations, *Report* . . . (Washington, 1955) and the sixteen studies prepared for the Commission and published by it. The Commission was established by Congress and included members of Congress and federal officials, state governors, and leading citizens appointed by President Eisenhower.

[7] The federal Constitution, in effect, requires some separation. Customs duties can be levied by the federal government only, and the apportionment requirement on federal direct taxes, other than on income, effectively bars a federal property tax.

fortunately, proposals for separation nearly always provide for the federal government's surrender of various taxes to the states, without any compensating surrender by the states to the federal government.[8] When and if separation is accomplished, a primary consideration must be the respective merits of federal and state administration of certain types of taxes and the suitability of such taxes to the federal or state tax systems.

On the basis of administrative considerations, the federal government might surrender to the states the taxation of admissions and gasoline (as it has given up taxation of electrical energy); in compensation, the states might surrender tobacco or liquor taxation. On administrative grounds, sales taxes should be left to the federal government, which can impose a manufacturers' excise; state retail sales tax administration is more costly and weaker—but too well-established for change to warrant serious consideration. The federal government is also the logical agency to administer corporation taxes.

Revenue needs have removed any possibility of federal withdrawal from the taxation of small incomes, but states now have to themselves the field for taxing the great masses of estates.

Partial federal-state separation of revenue sources on a *quid pro quo* basis, with due consideration of administrative capacities and tax characteristics, has some advantages. In certain respects it would give the states greater freedom in modeling their tax systems, it would reduce the widespread dissatisfaction with superimposed tax burdens, and it would end some of the uneconomic duplication of administrative machinery and tax reporting. But it now appears to offer little hope of practical accomplishment. Administrative considerations would dictate turning most of the large-yield taxes over to the federal government, leaving the states even harder pressed for revenue than they are today. Separation would not create the interstate uniformity of taxation which would result from a system of supplementary state rates or which could be enforced by a system of federal tax credits. Nor would it give the federal government the elements of control over state revenue systems and the elements of state functions with nation-wide significance which can be obtained through a system of federal tax credits or federal grants-in-aid. And it is not possible to equalize state resources through the separation of federal and state revenues, as it is through grants-in-aid.

Shared taxes. The states might surrender certain taxes to the federal government—or give up grants or take over responsibility for certain func-

[8] The Joint Federal-State Action Committee of governors and federal officials appointed by President Eisenhower in 1957 has recommended that the federal government give up 40 per cent of the tax on local telephone service. In return, the states would take over financial responsibility for two functions by giving up grants now received for vocational education and construction of waste treatment (garbage) facilities.

tions—on condition that the states receive a share in the revenues from one or more taxes.[9]

A shared-tax system could eliminate some double administration and reporting and might improve the net financial position of most or all state governments. This would be a logical step to follow a separation of revenue sources which for administrative reasons gave the federal government most of the large-yield taxes. But under a shared-tax system, each state's share would necessarily be determined by the arbitrary basis of distribution, not by the state's revenue needs. Some states would fare relatively better than others. All would be relieved of some direct responsibility to the taxpayers.

In some ways it would be easier, in others more difficult, to choose the bases of distribution in federal-state tax-sharing than in state-local sharing. Much better data are available on state than on local income. For practical purposes, there is less extreme unevenness in the spread of population, property, tax collections, and other standards of distribution among states than there is among localities; hence, there would not be the disturbing unevenness in the distribution of the shared revenue so frequent in systems of state-local sharing. But if income tax revenue were to be distributed on a source basis, which "source" should be the basis—the state of the taxpayer's residence or the state of the income's origin? Whichever the "source" chosen, some states would lose, and they could not be expected to view the system with marked approval. The distribution of power in the Senate, where a few million voters in sparsely-settled states have far more influence than many times their number in populous states, would tempt distortion in sharing.

Finally, unlike the states in connection with their local governments, the federal government could not force a general system of tax-sharing on all the states. It could on its own initiative institute sharing and reduce grants or give up a function. But if sharing were to involve state surrender of their own taxes of the type covered by the sharing arrangement—the usual and certainly logical proposal—state action on a voluntary basis would be required. The federal government could not collect a higher-rate tax in the cooperating states and a lower-rate tax in others, since this would be contrary to the "uniformity" clause of the Constitution. However, tremendous pressure could be brought to bear on all states to participate in the arrangement. Taxpayers in nonsharing states would have to pay the higher-rate federal tax, but these states would receive no part of the revenues contributed by their taxpayers. Therefore, despite the superficial appearance of a voluntary arrangement, the federal government could in fact virtually coerce the states.

[9] The federal government gives Puerto Rico the United States internal revenue tax collected on articles produced in Puerto Rico and consumed in the continental United States. The tax on rum is by far the most important. The federal government shares certain nontax revenues with states; the totals are around $60 million a year.

Supplementary state rates. A system of supplementary state rates superimposed on taxes administered and collected by the federal government would avoid the elements of state coercion and arbitrary revenue assignment involved in federal-state tax-sharing. Administration and collection would be left entirely to the federal government. Each state would add such supplementary rates as it chose to impose on the basic federal rates, which, of course, would be uniform throughout the country. Collections would be remitted to the states.

Like the shared-tax arrangement, the supplementary rate plan would eliminate duplicate administrative machinery and interstate diversity of tax bases. There would be no coercion on the states to forego their own taxes and accept an arbitrary revenue sum unrelated to their revenue needs. Each state's supplementary rate would represent the choice of its own legislature. A state which desired no part in this cooperative arrangement could stay out—impose its own tax, or impose no corresponding tax of its own, at its choice—without its taxpayers being subjected to any extra tax burden. The only constraint involved is that all states concurring in the arrangement would have to accept the basis of the federal tax as the basis for their own supplementary levies, and this would be a voluntary matter.

But the plan has its weak points. It could not apply to certain important taxes. State supplements could hardly be added to federal excises on tobacco or liquor manufacturers or to federal manufacturers' excise, since the uneven distribution of manufacturing facilities among states makes federal taxes unsuitable as sources of state revenue. Taxpayers' residences would have to be the basis for state supplementary levies on personal income taxes. Any attempt to levy state income tax supplements on the basis of the source of the income would either open a door to evasion or unduly complicate administration. For corporation income tax supplements, a uniform allocation arrangement would be needed. Finally, state supplementary rates in personal income and death taxes would have to be moderate; otherwise, the menace of interstate tax competition would again be raised.[10]

State credits against federal taxes. Since 1924 the federal government has allowed payments made on state death taxes as a credit, within prescribed limits, against its own estate tax. A similar credit applies to the state unemployment insurance payroll taxes.

A credit arrangement unquestionably divides the revenues from a tax between the federal government and the states, but as a revenue-sharing device it is inefficient. Duplications of tax administration and diversity of state tax bases continue. There would be little to recommend the credit arrangement were revenue-sharing its only accomplishment. But the credit

[10] Supplementary state rates could not well be made deductible in determining taxable income for the federal tax. This deduction is currently a major factor in suppressing "tax haven" competition among the states.

arrangement has an ulterior motivation not present in the other devices so far considered—it is an instrument of coercion whereby the federal government can more or less compel the states to levy particular types or forms of taxes. A state which fails to levy the kind of tax allowed as a credit saves its taxpayers nothing. They pay the same amount of tax, only the federal instead of the state treasury receives the revenues.

The coercion involved in the federal estate tax credit was the elimination of interstate rate-cutting competition in the death tax field. The payroll tax credit compelled the states to levy their own payroll taxes to provide revenue for unemployment insurance systems. Credit arrangements have been proposed in the corporation and personal income tax fields with a view to forcing interstate uniformity. Opinion on the propriety of such fiscal coercion is divided, on political as well as economic grounds.

Deductibility of state taxes from federal tax base. One major device for coordinating federal and state-local taxes often passes unnoticed. It is the deductibility of one or several taxes allowed when figuring other taxes. In computing taxable income for federal taxation, a taxpayer may deduct income, property, and many excise taxes paid to state and local governments. If a corporation is subject to a federal tax rate of 52 per cent, each dollar of state business or property tax on a profit-earning corporation reduces its federal tax by 52 cents. If an individual is subject to a marginal federal tax rate of 60 per cent, each dollar of deductible state and local income, property, and excise tax reduces his federal tax by 60 cents; the net burden of each dollar of state and local tax is only 40 cents. Some state income taxes permit similar deduction of federal tax.

This system is simple. It presents a minimum of administrative and compliance problems. Although it resembles the tax credit, it operates less forcefully. The net burden of state and local tax systems yielding the same revenue can be varied by adjusting (1) the relative use made of taxes allowed as deductible by federal laws, and (2) the relative amounts deductible from high brackets of the federal income tax. A progressive state personal income tax might actually impose an ultimately proportional burden, since the larger incomes paying the higher state rates would be saving relatively more through the federal deduction. Deductibility reduces the differences between total income tax burdens in income tax states and in states without income taxes. It removes almost entirely the possibility of combined federal and state rates exceeding 100 per cent.

Grants-in-aid. Federal grants-in-aid to the states and localities now appear as the most important aspect of federal-state-local fiscal relations. Whereas there seems to be little more than talk about modifying revenue relationships, there is impressive action on grants. Although they may be viewed as an arrangement for easing the fiscal burden on the states, their existence has been primarily the result of Congressional desire to secure state cooperation in introducing and developing specific services. Another force of increasing importance has been the tendency of urban areas to look to the national government for the solution of problems which state governments cannot, or will not, handle. Perhaps an outmoded state constitution, perhaps a legislature dominated by rural minorities, perhaps fear of interstate competition if taxes are raised, holds up the action which some groups desire. Sometimes there seems to be a feeling that the federal government can finance the program without imposing the same tax burdens on the beneficiaries as if states or localities were to undertake the job. Whatever the reason, the tendency to look to Washington is clear.

Grants to states are not new. Under the Hatch Act of 1887, each state and territory was offered a $15,000 federal allowance annually to establish and maintain agricultural experiment stations. Beginning in 1890, annual grants were made to the states to aid their agricultural colleges. Federal money was voted for agricultural education in 1914 and for vocational education in 1917. In 1911, Congress made a first appropriation to aid in forest-fire protection. Federal contributions for the National Guard were placed on a grant-in-aid basis in 1916. In the same year, appropriations for highway aid began. Until 1920, however, the amounts were trifling.

TABLE 23–1

Federal Grants to States and Local Units, Selected Years 1915–1959

(Amounts in millions)

Fiscal Year	*Highways*	*Education*	*Agri-culture*	*Health, Relief, Welfare*	*Other*	*Total*
1915	...	$ 3	...	...	$ 2	$ 5
1919	...	5	...	...	7	12
1925	$ 92	12	$ 8	...	2	114
1930	83	12	13	...	2	110
1932	188	13	13	...	3	217
1938	235	33	23	$ 215	121	627
1940	120	27	33	411	4	595
1945	78	89	36	525	11	739
1950	438	345	106	1,355	31	2,275
1957[1]	946	604	382	1,913	266	4,111
1959	2,400	680[2]	400[3]	2,870	250	6,600

[1] Includes amounts paid directly to local governments. In 1957, this was $350 million.
[2] Includes loans of $140 million for college housing and $220 million for school lunches.
[3] Includes $246 million of surplus commodities for the school lunch program and for other public agencies.
SOURCES: *Budget of the United States . . . for 1960; Governmental Finances in the United States: 1957*. Shared revenues—$106 million in 1959—are not included.

Beginning in 1933, the grant system was tremendously enlarged. Much of the "recovery and relief" program of the 1930's was accomplished through grants. The Social Security program established by the act of 1935 makes large use of grants-in-aid for old-age assistance, aid to dependent children, aid to the blind, maternal and child welfare services, and the administration of state unemployment compensation. Highway aids have soared as the programs themselves have become bigger and more costly and as the percentage of cost borne by the federal government has increased to 95 per cent, in some cases, and to 90 per cent for the most expensive. Federal grants-in-aid for 1959 are shown in Table 23–1. Today the bulk of these funds is covered by permanent appropriations with little or no periodic reconsideration by Congress. Federal grants for airports, hospitals, and school lunches go directly to localities, not states. About 90 different grant programs are now in operation.

No conditions other than the general purpose in view were attached to the early federal grants. No obligations were imposed on the recipient states, and no federal machinery was established to supervise expenditures. Commencing with forest preservation grants in 1911, Congress imposed definite conditions, including (1) state appropriation of sums equal to those contributed by the federal government and (2) federal approval of the activities supported by a joint fund. Agricultural extension grants after 1914 were conditioned upon state acceptance by legislative assent and upon approval of the work program by the federal government. Federal control was carried a step further under the highway aid act of 1921, which authorized the Secretary of Agriculture to cooperate with the state highway departments in designating a system of main interstate and intercounty highways, eventually to total about 200,000 miles, to whose construction and maintenance the federal aid should be applied; state work on these roads had to conform with federal standards. A 1958 "control" provision is federal assumption of 0.5 per cent more of the cost of interstate highways where roadside advertising limits meet federal standards. Ultimate responsibility for the functions involved has been largely transferred from state to federal agencies by the terms of some grants.

Though the principle of equalization occupies an important place in state-local grants-in-aid, it was originally given little consideration in federal-state aid. Prior to 1933, stimulation of state activity in particular fields, or purchase of control over particular state functions, were the primary motivations for federal grants. Such grants were made on a "matching" basis—the federal government contributing toward some function the same amount as the state appropriated—or the federal government contributed some fraction of the total cost of a function. The tremendous emergency relief grants of the 1930's, however, took into consideration local variations in relief needs, costs, and financial ability. Some of the cost and need factors determining the distribution of these funds were the relief load, geographical variations in living standards and relief costs, and relative amounts spent by local units for welfare purposes other than direct relief. On the "ability" side, ten indices—including number of gainfully employed, reported income, volume of retail sales, volume of wholesale sales, and motor car registrations—were utilized. Case studies were made of economic conditions in each locality, and consideration was given to existing state-local debt burdens and to the yield which would result from the application of a uniform tax system to all of the states.

The permanent federal aid programs now employ allocation factors other than matching, chiefly population and various measures of fiscal capacity, such as per capita state income. For aid to the needy aged the federal government pays 80 per cent of the first $30 a month and 50 to 65 per cent of the next $35, depending upon the state's per capita income.

There is little criticism of the general principle of federal grants-in-aid.[11] They have induced state and local governments to develop certain constructive lines of activity more fully than would otherwise have occurred. The federal staff brings to many states expert knowledge which they could not otherwise afford. At least informal state cooperation is encouraged. Grants have spread part of the cost of functions which generally have significance extending beyond state boundaries more equally over the national body of taxpayers. In periods of economic recession, grants can be financed by federal borrowing from the banking system and thus help stimulate the economy, while meeting real needs. Despite such gains, much of the growth of federal aid has been of a hit-or-miss variety, and there are criticisms of varying significance:

(1) Some programs are excessively rigid, and lack cohesion and consistency. Rigidity prevents funds from being distributed where they would be most useful in the light of changing conditions. Riders to appropriation bills can, and have, disturbed operations of even established programs.[12]

(2) Formulas for allocating funds are too complicated and arbitrary.[13] Other grants give too much discretion to federal officials, who are not so closely in touch with particular needs as state and local officials.

[11] See *Replies from State and Local Governments to Questionnaire on Intergovernmental Relations,* House . . . Committee on Government Operations (Washington, 1957). Many replies expressed the view that the federal government should bear more of the total cost.

[12] In the early 1950's, universities with R.O.T.C. units were embarrassed by a rider to an appropriation bill setting requirements on proof of loyalty of employees of institutions receiving grants. The law was not clear, but there was good reason to believe that it might profoundly affect academic freedom. And what if more restrictive provisions were added?

[13] The Hospital Survey and Construction Act sets the following rule for grants. "Each state . . . shall be entitled . . . to an allotment of a sum bearing the same ratio to the sums authorized to be appropriated . . . [each] year as the product of (a) the population of such state and (b) the square of its allotment percentage . . . bears to the sum of the corresponding products for all states . . . the allotment percentage for any state shall be 100 per centum less that percentage which bears the same ratio to 50 per centum as the per capita income of such state bears to the per capita income of the continental United States (excluding Alaska), except that (1) the allotment percentage shall in no case be more than 75 per centum or less than 33⅓ per centum. . . ."

(3) The desire to protect federal aid funds leads federal agents to participate in review of detailed state-local decisions. Federal control also induces state centralization of some activities; at the same time, however, the authority of the state executive is reduced because federal officials with real power deal directly with subordinate agencies of state governments.

(4) Grants are largely beyond state-local budgetary controls. The amounts of federal grants and thus the amounts the states and localities must provide in matching to take full advantage may not be known until after the state legislature has adjourned.[14]

(5) The matching provisions of some grants strain the fiscal resources of the less prosperous states. To obtain matched federal aid they tend to concentrate their efforts on activities associated with such aid, to the detriment of other activities for which need may be greater. For example, states slight general relief, for which there is no federal grant, to favor categorical relief for which grants are relatively large. Another example has been the concentration of state highway spending outside urban areas.

(6) The control exercised by federal authorities is not necessarily the best for particular states and localities. This country is so huge and diverse, and its economic and political development so varied, that uniform policies in many fields of government activity cannot be equally effective in all parts of the nation and at all times. Sometimes the centralized control associated with federal grants-in-aid is constructive in the best sense of the term, but not always. On occasion, "service becomes subordinated to administrative requirements." Delays in the issuance of federal regulations sometimes hamper states. Laws themselves tend to be too detailed and too specific for a world of change.

(7) The very large number of individual grant programs and the lack of coordination among them leads to waste in both administration and in the use of money and effort where they can do the *most* good.

(8) Shift of state-local responsibilities for some functions to the federal government may have gone too far, or may tend in that direction. This is not purely a case of federal "usurpation." Political considerations frequently induce state and city officials to press the federal government to assume responsibility for a function not really of great *national* significance, along with part of its financing. The states and cities hope to get more without a proportionate increase in the taxes *they* impose. Regardless of whether functional responsibilities have been unwarrantably assumed by, or forced upon, the federal government, some aspects of this shift threaten basic concepts of both *federal* and *democratic* government. The federal system will be threatened by the preponderance of one level of government, both in spending and in taxing to raise the funds spent. Democracy may be weakened if public initiative and participation in these functions are reduced. There will be no agreement about when the country will cross either line. Still, the apparent impossibility of reducing a grant program once it is established argues for caution.

Federal grants now exert something of an equalizing force as among states. One careful study indicated that in 1952 the sixteen lowest-income states received, per capita, $17.56 in federal grants. The sixteen highest-income states received $13.01 per capita. Yet four of the states with *highest* per capita incomes received *over* $20 per capita and four of the *lowest*

[14] Delays in reimbursing states, awaiting federal audit, sometimes create temporary strains on a state's cash position.

received *less* than the $15 which was the national average.[15] As an equalizing device, therefore, the present grant system is certainly inefficient. This conclusion is reinforced by the fact that comparisons of states are not comparisons of people. There is no way of comparing the *net* effect (1) on the relative economic position of prosperous and poor people of (2) the present (a) grants and (b) the taxes that would not exist if the grants were not being made. Who knows what part of the federal tax system would not now be operating if the grants had not developed?

Many students of grants favor more emphasis on equalization in distribution. Yet as a practical matter, and certainly as a matter of principle, the spending and the raising of funds must be considered together in a rational effort to achieve the aims of equalization. Such broad consideration would probably lead to the conclusion that it is the revenue system which can be the most efficient and effective device for equalizing—the personal income tax and the estate tax. These levies can put the costs of government on a graduated basis on people wherever they live—relatively modest burdens on most people in poor states, relatively heavy burdens on the prosperous families in high or low income states. The grant system which seems practically possible is not likely to be as efficient for equalizing, partly because the money goes to *states* and partly because it may be financed out of proportional or even regressive taxes. However, there are strongly-held views that grants themselves should be tailored more to emphasize equalization.

A possible improvement, a method which lends itself better to equalization than the present arrangements, would be the substitution of *block grants* to be used at the discretion of the individual states to finance broad groups of functions. Such grants would be particularly desirable in the social welfare field, to replace specific grants for aid to the aged, the poor, dependent children, and other specific groups. Each state ought to be able to divide such block grants among various functions more wisely—from the standpoint of its particular needs—than the money could be divided using any uniform formula applying to all states.

Finally, there is need for more coordination of programs at the federal level. A highly-placed staff agency would more than pay its cost by helping the scores of federal offices administering grants to work together more efficiently. A still greater contribution would result if this agency developed an over-all view, one which would help Congress to judge individual programs more wisely.

Conclusion. Although there is much criticism of the present fiscal relations between the federal and the state governments, the situation seems fundamentally less serious than in the case of state-local fiscal relations.

[15] Selma Mushkin, *Statistical Materials on the Distribution of Federal Expenditures Among the States* (U.S. Dept. of Health, Education, and Welfare, Washington, 1956). See also H. G. Schaller, "Federal Grants-in-Aid and Differences in State Per Capita Incomes, 1929, 1939, and 1949," *National Tax Journal,* Sept., 1955, pp. 287–299.

Federal tax policy is not materially hindering the states from obtaining enough revenue in reasonably good ways to finance essential state functions. As a rule, states are in better financial condition than they have permitted their own major subdivisions to achieve. Of course, virtually every unit of government "needs" more money, and beyond doubt present federal-state fiscal relationships are far from perfect. Important state functions are not being performed as well as our national interest warrants and as our national income would permit. Yet, the fiscal situation of the states can hardly be called critical.

Our constitutional organization and our political practices make improvement of federal-state fiscal relations inherently difficult. Institutions for achieving agreement between the federal government and the states are lacking. The Supreme Court has gone far in abdicating its potential role as dictator. The federal government can settle a great many questions unilaterally for state and local governments. But one Congress cannot bind another, nor can one state legislature agree that its successors will or will not levy certain taxes or provide funds for certain functions as required by any federal-state fiscal arrangement that may be agreed upon at one time. No effective bargaining is possible. Economic, social, and political conditions are so diverse that a plan which is attractive to one state may be bitterly opposed by another. As a result, it is difficult for all states to agree on a broad fiscal program that will have any chance of Congressional support. Issues arise and are settled on an *ad hoc* basis. A comprehensive, integrated solution seems highly improbable.

INTERNATIONAL FISCAL RELATIONSHIPS[16]

When businesses or individuals conduct economic operations or make investments in more than one country, they may become subject to more than one set of tax laws. It is common, for example, for at least two countries to claim taxing jurisdiction—the land in which the economic affairs are carried on, and that in which the business is legally organized (incorporated) or of which the individual is a citizen. The country of an individual's residence, or of the location of assets, may also claim jurisdiction. Obviously, if two or more taxes at today's rates are piled on each other, burdens can become terribly oppressive.[17] International business and investment could become throttled. Governments, therefore, have generally made some provision to meet the problem, but they have not always acted consistently. Arrangements over the world by no means harmonize.

The basic, long-standing U.S. practice has been to tax U.S. citizens, residents, and corporations on all income, whatever the country of origin, but to allow as a credit against the U.S. tax the income tax paid to the

[16] Foreign-aid spending is discussed in Chapter 1.

[17] Compliance problems are also difficult and their solution sometimes very costly.

government where the income originated. In general, then, the total tax is the higher of the U.S. or the foreign tax. Corporations, subject to various limitations, may take credit for foreign taxes paid by their subsidiaries even though no dividends have been received.

Although the broad rules seem fundamentally satisfactory, there are many criticisms and proposals for change. Unfortunately, the issues are often extremely intricate and technical, and what is appropriate for one type of business or area or type of legal organization may be oppressive to another and open a loophole in still other situations. The following points are made: (1) There are questions about the kinds of taxes abroad which qualify for credit, the country where income actually originates, and many problems of the concepts of income and expense. (2) If profits appear in one country and losses in another, tax offsets are not complete. (3) The legal form used by a business to conduct operations abroad can make a big difference in its taxes; for example, the use of branches rather than separate corporations is a difference in form which sometimes has a tax outcome completely disproportionate to any difference in substance. (4) If a foreign country wants to give a tax concession to attract U.S. business, the benefit will be offset by correspondingly higher U.S. tax. (5) Even with full credit, U.S. firms point out, they suffer because they must compete in foreign markets with businesses whose governments impose rates well below our 52 per cent. (6) Special avoidance opportunities have been created. In some countries—Canada, Liechtenstein, Liberia, and Panama, for example—it is possible to set up corporations which will be subject to almost no tax. A U.S. firm, therefore, can incorporate subsidiaries in such tax havens, conduct profitable operations abroad, retain earnings rather than distribute them as dividends, pay neither U.S. nor foreign tax, and accumulate wealth far more rapidly than if taxes at rates effective in most of the world applied. If accumulations are eventually returned to the United States, they may be subject to rates no higher than those on capital gains. Substantial avoidance possibilities exist, but they are hedged by many technicalities.

Since the mid-1930's, the United States has concluded about 35 special tax treaties to deal with problems not satisfactorily covered by statute, and they are legion. No two tax treaties are identical, because of the differences in the tax and business laws of the various countries with which they are negotiated. In general, however, they set up arrangements for (1) avoiding double taxation in situations not covered by statute, including those that apply to estates in some cases,[18] (2) exchange of tax administrative infor-

[18] A tax treaty with Pakistan, not ratified by the Senate up to 1959, would make a fundamental break with U.S. policy. It provides for "tax sparing," the allowance for credit against U.S. tax of amounts "spared" or forgiven by the foreign government. Thus Pakistan would determine the *amount* of tax paid by U.S. firms on their income earned in Pakistan and not, as under our established practice, the *division* of a total amount fixed by U.S. law between the two countries.

mation between the two countries, and (3) cooperation in tax collection.

From various sources come proposals that the United States reform its law to reduce tax inequalities for companies operating abroad and, as a means of stimulating foreign investment, to allow more generous tax treatment of income earned abroad.[19] If economic growth of the free world is to our national interest, there is much to be said for encouraging U.S. firms to expand abroad. Perhaps tax concessions to these businesses would bring higher returns, per dollar, to us as taxpayers than outright aid to the foreign governments. Unfortunately, it is impossible to judge whether tax concessions would be an efficient means to pursue the objective. Most proposals would grant U.S. tax concessions to investments abroad that would be made in any case, perhaps even to those that have already been made. The *additional* stimulus to development abroad, then, might cost our Treasury heavily in terms of general tax loss. Moreover, one wonders about the equity of taxing Americans with income from abroad at lower rates than apply to those deriving their entire income from within the country.

Because of the unparalleled complexity of the issues, and the diverse situations in this world of differences, no one set of rules can meet all desirable goals well. It is the world's high tax rates, and differentials in rates, that make the problems really serious. Under these conditions, the advisability of major changes in the basically generous U.S. practice is doubtful.

PROBLEMS

1. In what sense do people in one state have an interest in the spending policies of governments in other states? In the taxing policies?

2. "The major reason for interstate tax competition is not the differences in taxes to provide government services, but the effort to use taxes to transfer real income, that is, to tax one group to help another." Discuss.

3. Discuss the relative merits of tax-sharing and supplementary rates as methods of improving federal-state revenue relations.

4. Describe the tax credit.

5. Make a study of the grants received in your state from the federal government.

6. What are the criticisms of present federal grants? How might the arrangements be improved without fundamental change in the system?

7. Describe the general principles now applied by this country in taxing income from abroad.

[19] Although foreign *personal* holding companies have been subject to special penalties on undistributed income, the law now deliberately permits larger investment trusts to accumulate income abroad, paying virtually no U.S. tax. Several such companies have been organized in Canada, their stock being sold in this country. The general hope of those purchasing the stock is to accumulate wealth that will be free of tax during the years it is building up and never subject to more than the rates on capital gains.

PART FIVE

Government Borrowing and Indebtedness

IN 1959, the combined total of federal, state, and local debt passed the $340 billion mark. This is almost as much as one year's net national income. It is certainly an economic fact of broad significance. In the next three chapters we shall study, first the history and status of American government debt, next the principles of government borrowing, finally the principles of debt management.

CHAPTER 24

History and Status of American Government Debt

WITH the exception of the federal government's Civil War loans, borrowing and debt were relatively unimportant features of American public finance until the twentieth century. The $2.8 billion outstanding in 1902—nearly two-thirds of it local debt—amounted to only $36 per capita. No other world power could boast of so moderate a government debt.

After 1900, however, borrowing and debt assumed a prominent place in the American fiscal picture. From 1900 through 1916, local governments stepped up their borrowing to pay for construction of highways, schools, and public buildings. Between April, 1917, and November, 1919, the federal government incurred a $24 billion war debt. It paid off nearly $10 billion during the next 11 years, but state and local debt increased by a larger sum; in 1930, the net[1] total of American government debt stood close to $29 billion.

Local borrowing after 1931 fell off to a trifling amount. In fact, local debt declined almost 15 per cent from 1932 to 1938. But state borrowing expanded somewhat, and federal debt grew by almost $27 billion from 1930 to 1940. As of 1940, the total net debt of American governments was almost $68 billion. Deficits during World War II raised the federal debt to $279 billion in February 1946 ($25 billion being offset by cash in the bank); net state and local debt decreased by over $3 billion. The federal debt was reduced by $25 billion in the next 2 years, but, largely as a result of Korean hostilities and rearmament, it was back to around $275 billion by the mid-1950's. The recession beginning in 1957 accounted for new growth to over $280 billion in early 1959. The more striking postwar change was a quadrupling of state-local debt, as the total rose to nearly $60 billion in 1959.

[1] "Net" debt is used here to mean the total of all outstanding bonds, notes, certificates, bills, and similar evidences of debt minus amounts of such obligations held in government sinking funds.

State and local debt policy, as well as federal debt management, have progressed from the irresponsibility of hit-or-miss procedures to policies which, if they are not all that the scientific analyst might desire, are generally reasonable and sometimes excellent.

THE FEDERAL DEBT[2]

Since its creation, the federal government has been free of debt for only one year—the fiscal year 1835–1836. At all other times, it has been engaged either in borrowing to meet emergencies of one sort or another, or in carrying or retiring debt.

1790–1917. The federal government started its career by borrowing $170,000 from two banks to cover its initial operating expenses. By 1803 it had floated loans totalling $84 million for various purposes, among them assumption of the Revolutionary debt and the purchase of Louisiana territory. It started to retire this debt, and had redeemed nearly half when the War of 1812 compelled further borrowing. Retirement was resumed after the war, and by 1835 the federal government was absolutely debt-clear. Depression caused the Treasury to borrow in 1837, and the Mexican War led to further borrowing in the 1840's.

The Union government financed nearly three-fourths of its Civil War costs by borrowing and currency issues. By the close of the war the federal debt exceeded $2.5 billion. From 1870 on, retirement was steady; during the 1880's, the Treasury, at a substantial premium, bought in bonds before they were due. Borrowings during the 1890's and 1900's, among other purposes to finance the Spanish War and construction of the Panama Canal, with some intermittent retirement, brought the federal debt to $1 billion on the eve of World War I.

1917–1930. Between 1917 and 1922, the federal Treasury borrowed over $26 billion. To bridge the gaps between continuing war expenditures and intermittent "Liberty Loan" bond drives and tax receipts, the Treasury issued short-term certificates of indebtedness.

[2] "Federal debt," as the term is used in this volume and in most discussions, is not the total of the federal government's acknowledged obligations for future payments of funds. Promises have been made to provide Social Security, veterans', and farm benefits, for example, which will require payments not unlike those for redemption of formal debt. These promises are not contracts; no Congress can bind another by law, nor can a private citizen use court processes to enforce a government promise without the government's consent, whether to collect bond interest, gold for a "gold" bond, or a Social Security pension. Nevertheless, the promises are politically and morally almost as binding as the more formal bond debt. The amounts involved are uncertain but huge. The government has also guaranteed private lenders against loss on billions of dollars of loans to veterans and smaller amounts to businesses; the present debt figures contain no allowance for possible losses on such loans. Moreover, it has leased 24,000 post offices and garages under agreements running for several years which are as binding as formal debt. Yet they escape the debt totals. Finally, we do not ordinarily think of *currency* as debt of government, but in an important sense it is.

TABLE 24–1

American Government Debt, Selected Years 1790–1958[2]

Year	*Debt (Millions)*				*Per Capita Debt*
	Federal	*State*	*Local*	*Total*	
1790	$ 75	(1)	(1)	(1)	(1)
1800	83	(1)	(1)	(1)	(1)
1810	48	(1)	(1)	(1)	(1)
1820	90	(1)	(1)	(1)	(1)
1830	39	$ 26	(1)	(1)	(1)
1840	5	175	$ 20	$ 195	$ 11
1850	68	190	27	285	12
1860	90	257	200	547	17
1870	2,353	353	516	3,222	83
1880	2,055	275	849	3,179	63
1890	852	211	926	1,989	32
1902	969	235	1,630	2,834	36
1912	1,028	346	3,477	4,851	51
	(Billions)				
1919	$ 25.5	$ .7	$ 5.3	$ 31.5	$ 308
1922	23.0	1.0	7.8	31.8	289
1926	19.6	1.6	11.5	32.8	282
1930	16.2	2.2	14.7	33.1	269
1932	19.5	2.6	15.2	37.3	300
1937	41.1	2.8	14.7	58.6	454
1940	48.5	2.9	15.2	66.6	505
1946	269.9	1.8	12.5	284.2	2,014
1948	252.3	3.7	15.0	271.0	1,856
1950	257.4	5.4	18.8	281.6	1,862
1956	272.8	12.9	36.3	322.0	1,900
1958[3]	278.0	55.0		333.0	1,900

[1] Not available.

[2] Data as of end of fiscal year. Data for 1902 and later years are gross debt minus sinking fund holdings. The data for different years are not fully comparable, but any inconsistencies are unimportant. Federal data include guaranteed obligations.

[3] Partly estimated.

Sources: National Industrial Conference Board, *Economic Almanac for 1946–47;* P. Studenski, *Public Borrowing;* U.S. Secretary of the Treasury, *Annual Report,* for various years and *Treasury Bulletin; Statistical Abstract . . . for 1958.*

Between 1919 and 1930 the Treasury pursued a twofold debt policy—retirement and conversion. Part of the retirement of the war debt during the 1920's was automatic. The acts authorizing the Liberty Loans had provided for a federal "sinking fund," to be built up by mandatory annual appropriations, certain minor earmarked revenues, and all repayments on the loans that the United States had made to its allies. Most of the debt retirement during the 1920's, however, was accomplished through the surpluses that occurred in every year of this decade. By 1930, the debt had been reduced to $16 billion.

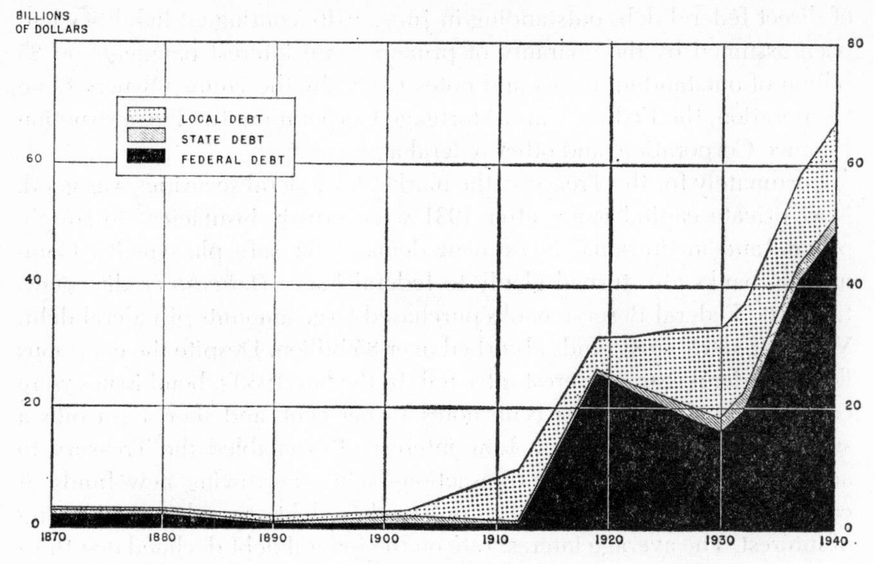

CHART 24–1. American Government Debt, 1870–1940.

The fall in interest rates during the business collapse of 1920–1921 cleared the way for conversion of the debt to achieve two objectives: (1) to relieve the maturity pressure of several outstanding issues, and (2) to save interest. As the various war bond issues became payable, the Treasury offered new issues bearing lower interest and with conveniently spaced maturities. The funds from their sale were applied to retiring the maturing issues; in many cases, investors made direct exchange of old "called" issues for the new ones. The average interest rate fell from 4¼ to 3¾ per cent.

Occasionally, the objective of saving interest clashed with the objective of rearranging the debt to have maturities fall at convenient dates. The particular category of debt—long-term, intermediate-term, or short-term—offering the greatest interest economy at the moment might be ill-adapted to maturity convenience. Compromise was required. Sometimes, too, the Treasury had to consider the extraneous effects of its offerings on the money market. Savings securities, for example, were withdrawn after 1923 because bankers and other groups insisted that these issues were diverting deposit money from savings accounts and that their relatively high interest rate was forcing an artificially high market rate. Furthermore, the Treasury was inclined to maintain a large floating debt as a safeguard against Congressional proposals for extravagant expenditure; the "pressing problem" of short-term debt could always be cited in opposition.

1931–1940. From debt retirement, the Treasury switched abruptly in 1931 to large-scale borrowing. Between June, 1930, and March, 1933, $4.7 billion was borrowed. The "recovery and relief" programs that began in 1933 required continued large borrowings. In addition to nearly $43 billion of direct federal debt outstanding in June, 1940, contingent liabilities had been assumed by the guaranty of principal and interest payments on $5 billion of outstanding bonds and notes issued by the Home Owners Loan Corporation, the Federal Farm Mortgage Corporation, the Reconstruction Finance Corporation, and other federal agencies.[3]

Fortunately for the Treasury, the market for federal securities was good. New private capital issues after 1931 were grossly insufficient to supply private and institutional investment demand for safe placements. Commercial banks also turned gladly to federal issues. To ease credit conditions, the Federal Reserve banks purchased large amounts of federal debt. Various federal trust funds absorbed over $5 billion. Despite the enormous flow of federal issues, interest rates fell. In the late 1930's, bond issues were costing only about 2.5 per cent, notes 1¼ per cent, and short-term bills a small fraction of a per cent. Low interest rates enabled the Treasury to accomplish a most unusual transaction—while borrowing new funds, it converted over $12.5 billion of its outstanding debt at a substantial saving of interest. The average interest rate on the federal debt declined one-third —from 3.8 per cent in 1930 to 2.6 per cent in 1936.

In its borrowing operations from 1931 to 1936, the Treasury was always anticipating that it would soon recommence retirement. Consequently, it consistently kept the federal debt in a form suitable for subsequent retirement, that is, issues with short maturities. Another reason for using short-term debt was the low interest rate at which it could be sold. A new policy on maturities was inaugurated in 1936. The Treasury saw that large debt retirement was unlikely in the near future and, as interest rates were favorable, it began to clear itself of intermediate- and short-term debt, so that it would not be harassed by constantly recurring maturities. Between 1936 and 1940, over $4 billion of notes were replaced by bonds with maturities arranged to take account of their probably eventual acquisition by the Social Security trust funds. Although the long-term bonds had to offer a higher yield, the Treasury tried to take advantage of market opportunities to replace high-interest with lower-interest issues.

1940–1945.[4] The debt problems of World War II dwarfed those of all prior periods. The Treasury's major war borrowing objectives were: (1) to obtain funds because, though tax collections were high, they fell short of war expenses by over $200 billion; (2) to borrow in ways that would be noninflationary; (3) to keep interest charges low; and (4) to maintain a debt pattern that would permit a reasonable degree of debt control, during

[3] These figures for gross liabilities take no account of offsetting assets. Over $3 billion of the funds borrowed by the federal government was invested in various government corporations created during the 1930's. Many received valuable collateral for the loans made with funds obtained from the Treasury. Valuable public works had also been built.

[4] See H. C. Murphy, *The National Debt in War and Transition* (McGraw-Hill Book Co., New York, 1950).

hostilities and later in peacetime. Unfortunately, these objectives—especially the second and third—were often conflicting.

The most important methods employed were: (1) a series of intensive war bond drives, offering a wide variety of debt issues (including "savings bonds") and designed to absorb periodically the cumulated savings of individuals and institutions; (2) continuous sale of "savings" bonds, accomplished in part by voluntary payroll deduction arrangements, to absorb current individual savings; (3) continuous sale of short-term low-yield bills and certificates to commercial banks, which were induced to buy them more readily by a "pegging" of interest rates at low levels and by adjustment of Federal Reserve rediscount rates and member bank reserve requirements.

Soon after the United States began rearmament on a serious scale, the Treasury increased its pressure for the sale of savings bonds to the public. During the 1941 fiscal year, however, most of the increase in the debt was bought by commercial banks. Since there was still much unutilized productive capacity, this inflationary source of funds probably helped stimulate and speed the expansion of output. During 1942, however, the drive for noninflationary sale of bonds to the saving public began to be pressed more vigorously. It was supplemented by payroll savings plans, on which the Treasury was to place great reliance. The Treasury was desirous of keeping bond purchases voluntary, but felt that the great masses of the public needed prodding. It induced employers, who as a group cooperated very well, to provide a convenient method whereby the ordinary wage-earner could buy bonds automatically without trouble and before he got his hands on the funds to spend. Considerable social pressure was exerted, and many employees felt that the plans were not truly voluntary, but large amounts of savings were thus obtained.

Eight big drives raised $157 billion. Limits were placed on the amounts and issues which commercial banks were permitted to buy. The World War I mistake of encouraging the public to borrow from banks to buy bonds was not repeated, but some such borrowing did occur.[5]

Although the details of the issues offered in the drives varied, savings bonds were always offered; the other issues ranged from short-term $\frac{7}{8}$ per cent certificates to 2.5 per cent long-term bonds. In addition, the Treasury borrowed regularly from the commercial banks on 90-day bills at a cost of $\frac{3}{8}$ per cent. Federal government agencies and trust funds bought over $15 billion net during the period.

[5] One reason was that some of the more desirable and limited issues typically rose in price after issue so that buyers could borrow, buy, sell quickly, and make a small easy capital gain. Another reason was that commercial banks would lend large amounts on the bonds at lower interest charges than the bond yielded; since the banks required only small margins of security from borrowers, and since the government was pegging the prices of the bonds, generous net yields—sometimes up to 15 per cent—on the borrower's equity could be obtained with little risk.

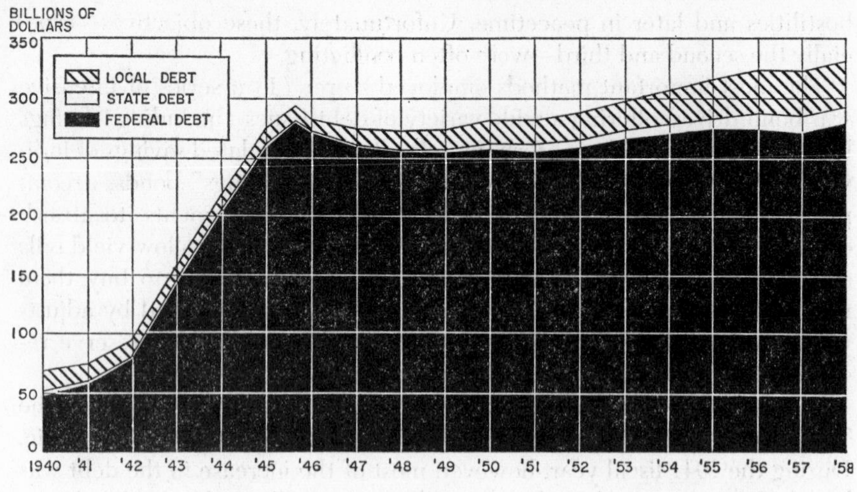

CHART 24–2. American Government Debt, 1940–1958.

The Treasury prided itself that, while it borrowed $210 billion net, the average interest rate on the entire federal debt fell from 2.52 per cent to 1.94 per cent. The disappointing feature was that so much of the borrowing—about $80 billion—came from commercial and Federal Reserve banks; the bulk of this borrowing was paid for by newly created bank credit, which played a major role in the war and postwar price inflation.

Postwar debt policy. On February 28, 1946, federal debt issues outstanding stood at a peak of $279 billion. Bonds accounted for two-thirds, shorter-term issues for the balance. Ownership is shown in Table 24–3.

Reduction and growth.—Prompt reduction was accomplished by applying $21 billion of the Treasury's cash balance to retire short-term debt. A series of cash budgetary surpluses permitted an additional $7 billion reduction by 1949. Then Korean hostilities and a restoration of the country's military potential during the early 1950's raised expenditures over revenues, and a series of cash deficits resulted. The program of debt reduction had to be replaced by one of borrowing, until 1954. Then after 3 years with small cash surpluses, business recession reduced tax revenue and required more borrowing. By 1959 the debt was about $25 billion above the 1950 level. In terms of purchasing power, however, per capita federal debt in 1958—about $1,600—was $170 less than in 1950.

Reorganization of maturities.—In arranging debt maturities, the Treasury was limited in what it could do. In 1946 it faced the following facts: (1) Over $120 billion was in the form of callable-term bonds, with maturity dates running to 1972. These long-term issues were held largely by banks and institutions. Some would fall due in the near future. The maturity of others could be anticipated by a few years through exercise of the "call" privilege, but the Treasury could hardly use this privilege to advantage, since replacement issues would have to be marketed at higher interest rates. (2) Nearly $50 billion consisted of "savings" bonds held by individuals. These would mature in periods up to 10 years, or might be redeemed by the holders any time before maturity. Mass redemption might create difficulties for the Treasury. For reasons unconnected with maturities, however, the Treasury wished to maintain or, better yet, increase this element of the federal debt. It had to continue to accept the risk of mass redemptions. (3) Short-term debt, in the form of low-rate Treasury bills and certificates, exceeded $58 billion. This heavy floating debt reflected wartime policies of holding down interest costs. Although some short-term debt would have to be maintained as an aid to flexible debt management, a much lower volume would suffice. Through use of the large 1946 cash balance and subsequent funds from surpluses, the short-term debt was brought down to a level of $35 billions, around which figure it was subsequently maintained. The Eisenhower administration felt more strongly than did President Truman's that so much short-term debt—plus the great amounts maturing or redeemable—was undesirable as a source of inflation threat and as a potentially disturbing factor in financial markets. The Treasury made a start in 1953 toward shifting to longer-term debt, but a decline in business made continuation of the policy appear unwise. Over the mid-1950's, then, the average maturity of publicly-held debt actually declined. However, small issues of bonds with maturities running to 40 years were sold. In 1958, almost half of the marketable debt was due

TABLE 24–2

Federal Debt Outstanding June 30, 1958

	Interest Rate Per Cent[1]	*Maturity Date*[1]	*Amount (Billions)*
Bonds:			
Marketable	2.25–4.0	1959–95	$ 90.9
Nonmarketable			
Savings bonds, all issues	3.25[2]	1958–68	52.0
Investment series	2.75	1975–80	9.6
Special issues for government trust funds	2.6[3]	. . .	40.5
Notes	1.5 –4.0	1958–63	20.4
Certificates	1.25–3.75	1958–59	32.9
Bills	1.0[4]	1958	22.4
Miscellaneous			7.7
Total			$276.4

[1] Minor exceptions ignored.

[2] Average rate on new issues if held to maturity. During the life of the bond, the rate at which interest accrues on some issues varies considerably.

[3] Average on all issues.

[4] Sold on a discount basis. In June the yield was about 1 per cent, but by December new issues were yielding around 3 per cent.

SOURCE: *Treasury Bulletin.*

TABLE 24-3

Estimated Ownership of Federal Debt, February, 1946, and October, 1958

	February, 1946		October, 1958	
	Amount (billions)	*Per Cent*	*Amount (billions)*	*Per Cent*
Commercial banks	$ 94	34	$ 67	24
Federal reserve banks	23	8	25	9
Individuals, partnerships, personal trusts	64	23	65	23
Insurance companies	24	8	12	4
Mutual savings banks	11	4	7	3
Other corporations	20	7	16	6
State and local governments	7	3	17	6
Federal agencies and trust funds	28	10	55	20
Miscellaneous	9	3	16	6
Total	$280	100	$280	100

Because of rounding, details will not necessarily add to totals.
SOURCE: *Treasury Bulletin.*

within 15 months and two-thirds within 4 years. The average maturity of the marketable debt *excluding bills* was less than 6 years in 1958, compared with 10 years in 1947.

Policy on interest rates.—The interest rates at which the short-term debt, and also the long-term bonds, had been sold during the war were abnormally low. This was the result of "easy money" policies reflected in the "pegging" of rates by the Federal Reserve.[6] There were three arguments for maintaining interest rates at these artificially low levels: (1) The federal government would continue to save interest as it refunded debt. (2) Banks and other institutions had bought tremendous totals of long-term bonds with low interest rates, on the implied pledge of the Treasury that interest rates would be maintained at a low level and that the capital values of the bonds would be thus supported; if market interest rates were to rise, the prices of outstanding marketable debt issues bearing the old, lower interest rate would fall. (3) A low interest rate would help stimulate private borrowing to finance housing, plant expansion, and other types of capital improvement.

The low interest rates, however, were an indirect but powerful inflationary factor, and mounting inflation now threatened the country's economy. The "pegging" of short-term yield rates was gradually ended during 1946 and 1947, and they rose, compelling the Treasury to offer higher rates on its

[6] The government was compromising between (a) the issue of interest-free currency and (b) borrowing from banks, which could create the money at very tiny cost in terms of sacrificed alternatives. Banks did not really need to be paid much for lending to the Treasury under such circumstances.

bills and certificates. Naturally, long-term rates were also affected, and as they rose, it appeared that the outstanding 2.5 per cent federal bonds would fall to a discount. The Treasury persuaded the Federal Reserve, against its wishes, to "peg" these bonds at par—that is, to be prepared to purchase offerings at that figure. The Federal Reserve realized that this policy made impossible an adequate anti-inflationary monetary program.

With debt retirement progressing during the late 1940's, the Treasury did not have to make any new bond offerings at the 2.5 per cent rate. But after hostilities started in Korea, creating the need for new federal borrowing, and as private borrowing continued to force up market interest rates, the inappropriateness of the "pegged" 2.5 per cent rate for federal bonds became increasingly obvious. In March, 1951, an "accord" between the Treasury and the Federal Reserve removed the "peg." A new issue of federal bonds yielding 2.75 per cent was offered, and in 1953 another, with a 3.25 per cent rate. Naturally, the prices of the outstanding older bond issues fell—to less than 90 per cent of par in some cases—but this proved less disturbing to the financial world than had been feared.

The Treasury, since 1951, has not used its power to try to determine market rates of interest except on a temporary basis when refunding operations are in process.[7] It has taken advantage of rates that appeared relatively favorable, but other considerations have been equally or more important than temporary interest changes. The average rate paid in 1958 was 2.6 per cent.

Policy on debt placement.—During the years of war borrowing, the Treasury had, within a framework of interest rates deliberately kept low, endeavored to place its debt issues in ways that would restrain inflation. It tried to sell bonds as much as possible to individuals, savings banks, life insurance companies, and other institutional investors rather than to commercial and Federal Reserve banks. Still, to raise the funds it needed, at the low interest rates it had decided to offer, it had had to resort heavily to the two latter markets. In February, 1946, commercial banks held $94 billion and Federal Reserve banks $23 billion.

Postwar developments helped the Treasury to shift the ownership of federal debt in ways that exercised a slight anti-inflationary influence in a period when other debt management policies were inflationary. Modest budget surpluses made possible a reduction of commercial bank holdings. An increase of $30 billion in amounts owned by federal trust funds between 1946 and 1959 was a major change.[8] Promotion of "savings" and "invest-

[7] This statement does not mean that the Treasury and its problems have no influence on Federal Reserve monetary policy, which does make short-run adjustments to accommodate the Treasury. It does mean that the Treasury has not sought to dominate the market as it did before 1951.

[8] States and localities have become major customers of the Treasury. See C. D. Campbell, "Investments in United States Government Securities by State and Local Governments," *National Tax Journal*, March, 1957, pp. 78–87.

ment" bonds increased private holdings of these issues by a small amount. Federal Reserve holdings fluctuated only slightly after 1950. More could have been done to shift federal debt ownership to offset inflationary forces during the postwar period if higher yields had been offered. Yet instead of anti-inflationary absorption of bank-held debt by insurance companies and other private corporations, for example, these institutions reduced their holdings $16 billion from 1950 to 1958.

Critique.—The treasury must be adjudged to have "muddled through" in its debt policy during the first postwar decade, with a combination of good and bad results. The volume of savings bonds outstanding, thanks to vigorous Treasury effort, dropped only one-tenth in the 1950's even though yields elsewhere became much more favorable. Larger net redemptions would have added inflationary pressures. The Treasury can rightly claim credit for this achievement. It must be debited, however, with poor judgment in maintaining so large a part of the debt in short-term form; this made the government vulnerable to any sudden desire of the public to reduce its holdings of public debt, perhaps to buy assets offering better protection against inflation, as well as to short-run disturbances in the money market. A more serious error was the insistence that the Federal Reserve hold the yield rate at an artificially low level until 1951. This policy was partly responsible for the inflation that plagued the economy during the early postwar years. Moreover, we have not prepared ourselves to finance another war or international crisis producing a large deficit.

STATE AND LOCAL DEBT[9]

The first public borrowing in America was done by the English colonial governments, the direct sovereign predecessors of the later state governments. These colonial loans were in the form of "bills of credit" which circulated as money. They had inadequate redemption arrangements, fell to discounts, and were eventually prohibited by England in the 1750's and 1760's. An orgy of irresponsible state borrowing occurred during the Revolution; these state debts were assumed by the federal government in its initial years.

Nineteenth century—state. Large-scale state borrowing began again in the 1820's, when several of the Eastern states undertook to build canals. By 1837, $193 million of state bonds had been sold, a large proportion to foreign investors. The depression period which stretched from 1837 to 1843 cut heavily into state revenues. Debt service charges became even heavier. By 1840, the pressure had become too heavy for seven states, and they defaulted temporarily on their interest payments; two Southern states

[9] For history and analysis up to World War II, see B. U. Ratchford, *American State Debts* (Duke University Press, Durham, 1941). The U.S. Bureau of the Census compiles and publishes statistical data on state and local debt annually.

repudiated bond issues floated to provide capital for banks which had failed. State borrowing practically ceased between 1840 and 1845, both because a halt was called to improvement projects and because the previous defaults had weakened state credit. Later, to assist railroad building, a number of Western states borrowed considerable sums.

During the Civil War, both the Union and the Confederate state governments offered enlistment bonuses and raised and equipped regiments which they placed at the command of the central governments. With civil expenditures already rising because of inflation, these added military costs could be covered only by borrowing. Investment capital was scarce in the South, wary in the North, but both groups of state governments succeeded in their borrowing efforts.

For the next 35 years, the Northern states were more active in retiring outstanding debt than in new borrowing. The war indebtedness of the Confederate states was flatly canceled by the Fourteenth Amendment. But during the period of "carpetbag rule" which followed the Civil War, the Southern states were saddled with an outrageous debt load. The funds obtained were not wisely used to add to the productive capital of the area, and service on this debt burden could not be carried by the economically exhausted region. In spite of bitter protests by Northern and English investors, the Democratic administrations which replaced the carpetbaggers in the 1870's either repudiated or scaled down many of these bond issues. In all, $115 million of the "carpetbag" state debt was sloughed off. No new Southern state borrowings were made during the rest of the century.

Nineteenth century—local. We have only scattered items of information on the borrowing activities of local governments prior to the Civil War. By 1843, the seventeen leading cities had some $26 million of debt outstanding. During the late 1840's and early 1850's, cities and counties borrowed heavily to erect public buildings and to aid railroad construction. Default was common. Warned by these failures of some of the dangers of unrestricted public borrowing, a number of states imposed constitutional restrictions on the borrowing powers of their local units.

Until 1850, each local loan generally required a special enabling act passed by the state legislature. From 1850 on, constitutional amendments or general municipal laws delegated broad independent borrowing powers to local units. Generally, these were hedged with limitations, as noted above, but all too often there were either no limitations or overgenerous ones. Consequently, in the 15 years following the Civil War, local governments were able to indulge in extravagant and irresponsible borrowing. Local debt increased from approximately $200 million in 1865 to nearly $850 million in 1880. Railroad aid, funding, and refunding issues accounted for nearly half the total. Defaults, many of them willful, were widespread during the depression of the 1870's. This financial irresponsibility inspired another wave of restrictive legislation. Prohibitions against lending public credit to railroads and other private business enterprises were enacted in a number of states; by 1880, local governments in half the states were bound by this limitation. The debt-to-property ratio limitation on local government, first applied by New York and Iowa in the 1850's, was widely adopted during the 1870's.

As a consequence of the defaults of the 1870's, local units found it difficult to borrow during the 1880's. By the next decade, however, a new generation of investors had apparently forgotten earlier unhappy experiences; they again lent freely to cities for schools, street construction, and public buildings, and to rural units for road construction.

1900–1932. Local borrowing, mainly for the construction of schools, highways, and city streets, continued at accelerating pace from 1900 until 1917. New local loans far exceeded retirements of old debt. Local debt outstanding had been $1.9 billion in 1902; by 1912, it had more than doubled to $4.1 billion; by the time of America's entry into World War I, another $3 billion had been added. State debt, much smaller in total, doubled during this period as an increasing number of state governments undertook the responsibility of constructing arterial motor highways.

After the war, state and local governments engaged in construction spending on a greater scale, and consequently borrowed more heavily, than ever before. Despite an increasing volume of retirement, net state and local debt increased after 1923 at the rate of $1.4 billion a year. State issues accounted for a relatively small fraction of the state-local total of new borrowings during this period. Even counties borrowed more than state governments. The most insistent borrowers were the cities, a result, partly, of growing urbanization. By 1930, nearly $18 billion of state and local debt was outstanding; interest exceeded $800 million annually.

At first, the onset of depression in 1929 had little effect on state and local borrowing. If anything, the market for municipals improved as savings sought the safety of bonds. By 1931, however, local governments were hesitant about undertaking new construction projects, and a general fall in bond values increased the difficulty of placing municipal issues. Although state governments increased the tempo of their borrowing, local borrowing between 1931 and 1933 exceeded retirements by only $100 million. As shown in Chart 24–3, the debt per capita in 1932 expressed in today's dollars was larger than that in 1958. In relation to income it was four times as great.

1933–1940. Beginning in 1932, relief provision for the victims of depression imposed upon state and local governments new expenditure obligations; in many cases these could be met only by borrowing. States, cities, and counties whose credit was still sound borrowed nearly $500 million from 1932 to 1938.

Meanwhile, however, three states and over 3,000 local units defaulted on their debt services. Practically every city whose debt exceeded 15 per

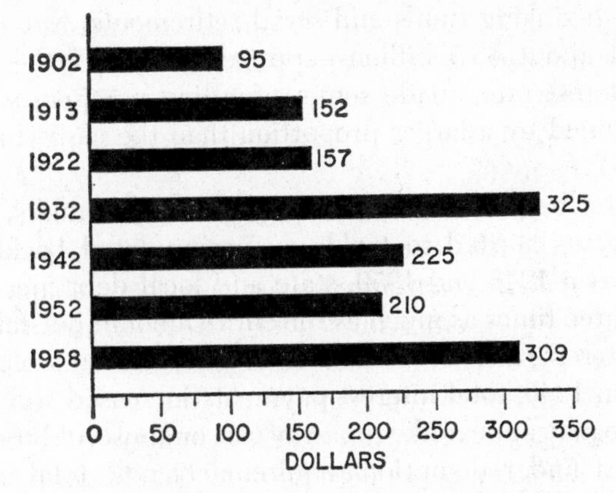

CHART 24–3. State and Local Debt per Capita in Dollars of 1958 Purchasing Power, 1902–1958.

cent of its taxable wealth became involved in "debt trouble." Investment capital shied away from the issues of all but the soundest governments. Most states could and did borrow for relief purposes, though on a diminishing scale after 1933. Gross state debt outstanding increased slightly in the 1940's. Local borrowing was so reduced, however, that for several years after 1933, the few new issues floated were more than offset by the obligatory retirements taking place. Annual interest charges fell substantially during the 1930's—almost one-fifth.

TABLE 24–4

Local Debt (Net), Selected Years 1912–1957

(Millions)

Borrowing Units	*Gross Debt Less Sinking Fund Assets*					
	1912	1922	1932	1942	1952	1957
Counties	$ 371	$1,273	$ 2,391	$ 1,846	$ 1,957	$ 3,501
Municipalities	2,872	4,679	8,842	6,442	10,831	17,110
School districts	119	1,053	2,040	1,701	3,596	9,009
Townships	78	123	344	273	414	1,078
Other	36	626	1,599	2,853	3,689	5,845
Total	$3,476	$7,754	$15,216	$13,115	$20,487	$36,543

SOURCES: U.S. Bureau of the Census, *Financial Statistics of State and Local Governments, 1932; Governmental Debt in 1952; Summary of Governmental Finances in 1957.*

Since 1940. State and local capital construction programs were largely "frozen" during the war years. Little new borrowing was needed. With tax receipts running high, surpluses occurred which in many cases could be used for debt reduction over and above what was being regularly accomplished through sinking funds and serial retirements. Net state and local debt declined about $3.5 billion—approximately a fifth—from 1941 to 1946. Low interest rates made some refunding possible, so that interest payments declined by a larger proportion than the capital amount of the debt.

In 1946, states began to borrow to pay veterans' bonuses, and state and local governments started to tackle an accumulated backlog of capital projects. Between 1946 and 1959, state and local debt increased by over $40 billion—three times as much as the entire amount outstanding in 1946. With rising interest rates, in some cases double those at which funds could be borrowed in 1946, total interest payments increased still more rapidly.

The increase may appear like runaway use, or abuse, of borrowing power. Annual interest and redemption requirements now total about one per cent of national income. When increase of population, rise in national income, and decline in the purchasing power of the dollar are all taken into account, however, the weight of the current debt is lower than that of many previous years. Practically all the postwar increase of state and local debt, except that incurred for veterans' bonuses, has been balanced by the creation of tangible assets—schools, roads, public buildings, public housing projects, subways. There are no measures for evaluating these assets, but inflation has undoubtedly made the replacement value (less depreciation) of most of them far greater than the currently outstanding state and local debts for which they were responsible.

There is every reason to anticipate still further increase of state and local debt. Many major projects whose finance requires borrowing—schools, streets, hospitals, sewers, and water supply systems—are far from complete. A considerable fraction of new debt will be self-servicing and self-liquidating; the projects financed bring revenue which will pay interest and amortize the principal. This is true of debt of state and local government authorities, a type that has been growing. One reason for the growth is the issue of debt by local housing authorities.

PROBLEMS

1. "Our federal debt is now, and always has been, the product of war." Discuss.

2. Compare the Treasury's debt management records after the two World Wars.

3. Who owns the federal debt?

4. Show why federal debt has grown relatively less since World War II than state-local debt.

5. How would you account for the fact that the average interest rate on new borrowings by the federal government in World War II was substantially below the rate paid in World War I? Note that the amount borrowed in World War II was about eight times that of the earlier period.

CHAPTER 25

Principles of Government Borrowing[1]

BORROWING, as a rule, is a supplementary method of government financing. By far the greatest part of government expenditure must be financed out of taxes and other current revenues. Yet, despite its supplementary character, government borrowing raises problems as far-reaching as any connected with expenditure and taxation. Every aspect of public credit—the purposes, the manner, the methods, and the control of borrowing, the management of outstanding public debt, the economic consequences of borrowing and debt retirement—is a subject of controversy. The increase of American government debt from $5 billion just prior to World War I to $340 billion in 1959 has had—and will have—profound effects on our economy. Management of existing debt—to say nothing of new borrowing—has become a major problem of government. The use of government power to borrow may go far toward helping to maintain prosperity and insure economic progress; abuse will foster grave economic troubles.

LAW OF AMERICAN GOVERNMENT BORROWING

Like the power to tax, the power to borrow is inherent in all sovereign governments. All American state governments consequently have full inherent power to borrow, subject only to such limitations as they have imposed upon themselves in the federal Constitution and their own constitutions. Although the federal government has only such borrowing powers as are designated in the federal Constitution, by the terms of that document (Art. I, Sec. 8, § 2) and the construction of the courts, these powers are full and untrammeled. Although Congress sets legal limits on the total federal debt at any particular time, Congress is always free to change the

[1] Exclusive of important effects of government borrowing on national income, which are covered in Part Six.

limit. Local governments have only such powers of incurring debt as are delegated to them by state constitutions and statutes.

Constitutional limitations on state borrowing.[2] By ratifying the federal Constitution, the states sacrificed only one detail of their inherent borrowing powers—they prohibited themselves from issuing debt instruments in the form of "bills of credit" intended to circulate as money (Art. I, Sec. 8, § 10). Borrowing powers of the state governments are, however, sharply restricted in many state constitutions.

Before 1850, several states underwrote the bonds of railroad companies which subsequently failed, leaving the governments saddled with onerous debts. To prevent any recurrence of such misfortune, provisions forbidding the legislatures to lend state credit to individuals or corporations were written into most state constitutions.

Today all but five states have constitutional debt restrictions. In twenty states, bond issues over some specified limit can be authorized only by constitutional amendment. Occasionally, the limit within which the legislature can act upon its own initiative is a double one—a low figure for general borrowing and a higher one for some special purpose. In over one-third of the states, bond proposals must be submitted to the electorate by referendum. Sometimes, this requirement applies to all proposals, in other cases such submission must be made only for issues which exceed a constitutional limitation.

Where limitations are established on the freedom of legislative approval of debt issues, the limitation is generally in the form of a fixed sum. A few states, however, limit state debt to a specified per cent of the assessed valuation of property within their borders. Borrowings to cover casual deficits or to suppress insurrection or to repel invasion are generally exempt from constitutional limitations.

Some state constitutions also cover various terms of state borrowing. In most cases the debt must be for a specific purpose. In many states, maximum maturities for state bonds are constitutionally established, ranging from 5 years in Wisconsin to 75 in California. State constitutions commonly require the legislature to levy a special tax sufficient to cover debt service at the same time that it authorizes a bond issue.

Constitutional limitations on state indebtedness have often proved irksome. Particularly was this true in 1934 and 1935, when a number of states found themselves temporarily unable to obtain federal relief funds because they could not borrow funds to match the federal grants. Debt limits are in a sense crude and superficial methods of controlling expenditure. They represent the imposition of one generation's judgment—or emotions—on another generation which will inevitably face different conditions. To some extent they are ineffective because they lead to circumvention. Borrowing responsibility is put upon localities or upon authorities, boards, commis-

[2] The Tax Foundation, *Constitutional Debt Control in the States* (New York, 1954).

sions, state universities, and governmental corporations, agencies whose debts the courts generally hold are not debts against the state. Yet, hampering and delaying as they appear, restrictions are a protection against the squandering of state credit. Whenever a real necessity for incurring a heavy state loan arises, it is possible in most states to obtain authorization by special referendum or constitutional amendment. The delay and publicity involved in such procedure help to insure serious consideration of the proposed bond issue and to check one year's legislature from yielding to pressures that bind taxpayers for a full generation. The tendency is for state electorates to approve most "loan" amendments. However, in states requiring constitutional amendment or popular referendum, per capita state debts were appreciably lower in the mid-1950's than in states with essentially no limits on legislative borrowing. The restrictions are not in fact meaningless.

Constitutional and statutory limitations on local borrowing. Constitutional clauses and legislative enactments usually delegate limited borrowing powers to local governments. But this rule is not universal. New England county governments ordinarily cannot borrow. And many of the special districts created in the 1920's were given taxing, but no borrowing, powers.

Local borrowing powers are generally regulated in greater detail than those of state governments. Many communities in a state may find borrowing more difficult if a few have bad debt records. Moreover, some localities do not have the competence, and some lack the will, to borrow wisely. The purposes for which local governments may borrow, the methods of incurring debt, the amount of local debt, its interest rate, its term, provisions for retirement, and the form of local debt issues are all regulated, in one state or another, by constitutional or statutory provision.

Local governments in a majority of the states are forbidden to lend their credit to corporations and individuals. Otherwise, restrictions as to the *purposes* of local borrowing are few and generally unimportant.

The most common limitation on the *amount* of local borrowing is a provision that the outstanding total of indebtedness must not exceed a specified proportion of the assessed value of property within the borrowing district. Usually, different assessment-ratio debt limits are established for the various classes of local governments. The sharpest limits are ordinarily set for cities, the highest for school districts. This assessment-ratio limitation frequently excludes self-supporting debt (discussed later), city indebtedness for water, gas, or electric systems, and special assessment debt. A majority of states provide that all or certain of their local governments can issue bonds only after approval by a local referendum. A few states permit local governments to exceed the assessment-ratio limits by specified amounts for certain purposes on local referenda.

Relating debt limits to assessed valuations may seem logical, since assessments partly determine property tax levies, and the property tax is the major source of local tax revenue to pay interest and retire indebtedness. Assessment ratios vary notoriously among communities, however, so that a uniform debt limit based on unequalized assessments operates with differing degrees of restriction among local units. Furthermore, to an increasing extent local governments obtain revenue from sources other than the property tax; local debt limits based on assessments only are economically obsolete. Moreover, such limitations on the total amount of local indebtedness often fail. Local governments circumvent them by raising the ratio of their property assessments, thus raising their debt limits, or by camouflaging their borrowings under a form exempt from the general limitation. Some state legislatures have connived with localities to exceed constitutional debt limits by creating special government units to take over particular functions of the original debt-laden governments, giving each new unit a new debt-incurring capacity. Superimposition of government districts in New Jersey made possible in some cases a total debt of 30 per cent of assessed valuation despite a 7 per cent debt limit. Some Detroit suburban communities built up superimposed debts amounting to 50 per cent of assessed valuations. Local governments which have borrowed up to their debt limits can be caught in a disastrous fiscal strait jacket, particularly if property values decline as they did during the 1930's.

A number of states fix the maximum interest rate, usually 6 per cent, which the bonds of their local governments can carry. Another fairly common provision is that local bonds must not be sold below par or under a certain discount.

Some states set maximum durations for local bond issues, such as the life of the improvement to be financed, or specific periods for various types of local improvements. The provision that the loan-term shall not exceed the life of the improvement is directed against irresponsible governments which seek to dodge their proper obligations by creating debts of such distant maturity that the present generation will not need to repay the debt. Yet limitations on maturities have proved of doubtful value. Local governments too often interpret the limitation as an authorization. The period intended to be a maximum is taken as a standard. Several states now require the issue of local bonds in serial form (discussed in the following chapter). Most states which permit sinking-fund bonds require localities to levy a tax sufficient to cover all debt charges on the issue. No matter how wise such rules prove in general, they cannot fit all needs efficiently.[3]

[3] A leading authority, criticizing "local bond and tax laws . . . so outmoded and unduly restrictive as to handicap a reasonable and judicious use of borrowing and taxing power," concluded: "Too many states and municipalities have exercised their ingenuity in recent years in devising borrowing instruments that have enabled them to pay investors from ½ of 1 per cent to 1½ per cent more than if they had issued bonds with a pledge of their faith and credit. Much of this, but by no means all of it, has been forced evasion of . . . constitutional prohibitions. . . ." F. L. Bird, *Tax Policy*, Nov. 1956, p. 6.

Central control of local borrowing. Central control of local finances by either a state or county agency, described in Chapter 5, may cover review of new and refunding bond issues. The board of review should have the authority, within limits of objective rules, to condemn a proposed bond issue and to direct that the intended expenditure be financed from tax funds if such procedure should appear desirable. It should also have power to modify the maturity and other terms of any proposed bond issue. The board should also have the responsibility, and the facilities, for giving positive help to localities—expert advice on policy and competent technical assistance in the mechanics of borrowing and repayment.

North Carolina pioneered in state control of local borrowing, and no other state has yet gone so far. Proposals for local bond issues must be submitted to the Local Government Commission for approval before either the bonds are issued or the question of issuance is presented at election. Upon receiving the application, the Commission considers the necessity, expediency, and adequacy of the bonds, the financial condition of the applicant, and its ability to pay the proposed bonds. The advice of its staff of specialists may be of real help. Rejection by the Commission does not deny the locality the opportunity to proceed. If the borrowing proposal is approved by the voters, the bonds may be issued regardless of the Commission's decision.

All bonds are advertised and offered for sale by the Commission at its office at Raleigh. Sealed bids are invited at public sale, and unless a representative of the unit present at the sale objects, the award is made to the highest bidder. All bonds are delivered to the purchaser through the State Treasurer, who collects the purchase price and turns over the proceeds to proper local authorities.

PURPOSES OF GOVERNMENT BORROWING

Borrowing, as a rule, merely postpones need for payment of a government expenditure. The borrowed funds must eventually be paid for out of current revenues.[4] Meanwhile, a continuing item of interest is added to the cost. A government must have special reasons to justify the financing of expenditure by borrowing instead of taxation or other current revenues. Four such reasons often are: (1) to finance large emergency or irregular expenditures—including wars, (2) to finance capital construction projects, (3) to harmonize the divergent rhythms of current expenditures and current revenues, and (4) to refinance existing debt. A fifth reason has tended to eclipse the others in much recent academic discussion—government borrowing can stimulate the economy when business is sluggish. We shall now explore the first four purposes, leaving the fifth to Part Six.

[4] Exceptions to this general conclusion will be noted in the next chapter.

War loans.[5] Outbreak of a war, or an "all-out" defense program, may justify a national government in immediate borrowing. The need for heavy military expenditures is pressing. No system of war taxes could be levied and collected quickly enough to provide the funds required.

The "emergency" argument applies less forcefully to later war loans. Within a year, a tax system geared to produce any desired revenue could probably be established. If borrowing policy is continued thereafter, its justification must rest on other grounds. These might be:

(1) The real costs of waging war must be borne while the fighting is going on. The labor, the materials, and the plant capacity of the future cannot be used to fight an enemy today. Even though the real costs cannot be shifted to future generations, some of the money costs can be so shifted by giving to those who bear real costs during the war money claims against the future—that is, bonds to be redeemed at a later date.

(2) Personal income and business taxes, and even excise taxes, would often hit individuals with disastrous harshness and inequity at the extremely high rates necessary to cover the full money cost of a major war by taxes. Borrowing relieves some of the pressure on the tax system, so that tax rates do not have to be pushed to extreme levels. Part of the borrowed funds may come from individual and business savings that can be surrendered more conveniently than equivalent sums taken by taxation.

(3) Very high tax rates might impair incentives to effort and efficiency.

(4) Payment with borrowed funds might stimulate productive effort. If the economy (as in 1941 but not in 1950) had a substantial amount of unemployed plant and labor resources, increased output for war purposes could be obtained without net sacrifice in total production for civilian use, or with only minor reduction. If the government tried to pay for all of its war purchases out of higher taxes, civilian consumption would be cut about as much as war production was increased, and full utilization of the idle capacity would be difficult. Within limits that are hard to define, but that are set by the amount and type of unutilized resources, including people's ability and willingness to work longer hours, borrowing to pay for a part of the war purchases might be economically sounder than an all-tax program.

(5) Even when resources are fully used, some continuing inflation produced by borrowing might maintain individual and business effort at a higher level than otherwise.

The chief argument against financing a substantial part of the war cost by borrowing is that inflation is likely to appear—and on a scale which works hardship of many kinds, which will impede the war effort, and which can cause great postwar distress. A second objection to borrowing

[5] This discussion applies to the kinds of wars known in the past. The financing of a nuclear war is hard to imagine.

is that the debt will add a heavy item of interest to other war costs, an item that can continue indefinitely long after hostilities end.

The connection between borrowing and inflation is more complex than sometimes assumed. If war bonds are paid for entirely with funds that individuals and businesses would otherwise have spent currently or utilized for tangible investment, war borrowing would not have an inflationary effect. More simply, and almost as accurately, we say: If bonds are paid for out of net new saving, the borrowing and the spending are not inflationary. To some extent, however, individuals and businesses buying war bonds pay with money that would otherwise remain partially idle, having a slow average turnover. When used by the government for war expenditure, the money circulates with higher velocity. Any such increase in velocity acts to raise the level of prices in essentially the same way as the injection of new money.

The chief inflationary force of borrowing, however, results from the sale of debt to commercial and Federal Reserve banks. They pay with newly created deposits. These added deposits are new means of payment, new money. If there can be no significant expansion of production (because resources are used fully) to balance this added purchasing power, prices in general tend to rise. Rationing and price controls may restrain the price rise, but rarely with complete success.

But why borrow from the banks if they merely create deposits—money to turn over to the government? A national government can itself create the money and save the interest on debt. One justification for borrowing from banks rather than issuing currency is that the interest paid to banks compensates them for operating the country's payment mechanism. The bank-using public gains in lower service charges what it loses by rewarding the banks for creating deposits.

Is inflation really more bad than good? Yes—the undesirable consequences are likely to outweigh benefits—by far. (1) To the extent that price increases cannot be prevented by controls, such increases affect the prices of what the government must buy, and thus add to war costs. (2) The general increase of prices affects some groups cruelly while others may benefit, without regard for relative contributions to the war effort or for social justice. (3) The controls used to limit (or perhaps circumvent) the inflation add to the costs and difficulties of production and reduce individual freedom. (4) Inflation leads to waste in consumption and business methods, and less obviously to inefficient use of resources.

No economist of consequence has ever suggested that a government finance major war activities by borrowing alone. Few have advocated an all-tax program of *war* finance. Informed opinion favors a combination tax-and-borrowing approach, with no agreement whatsoever as to the best proportion between the two. In 1917, the Treasury proposed the division of World War I costs half and half between taxes and loans. Later the proportion was set at one-third and two-thirds. Actually, if the Allied Loans are eliminated from the picture, taxes covered 45 per cent of the federal government's 1917–1918 expenditures, and 28 per cent of those of the following year. These proportions placed too much dependence on borrowing, especially since there was not a large amount of unutilized productive capacity upon which to draw in 1917. For 1940 and 1941, the Treasury aimed at a ratio of two-thirds taxation to one-third borrowing. After Pearl Harbor, it set the tax fraction somewhat lower. For the fiscal years 1941 through 1946, tax collections covered nearly half of the federal expenditures. Larger use of taxes would have been advantageous during the war years, especially after full employment was reached. Borrowing during the years of fighting in Korea was roughly one-tenth of total defense spending.

Other emergency borrowing. When a river overflows its banks and submerges the neighboring countryside, when a tornado cuts a swath of destruction across a populated territory, when an earthquake demolishes a city, the local and state governments affected, and sometimes even the federal government, must make heavy expenditures to repair at least part of the damage and, in the case of floods, to guard against a repetition of the disaster. The outlays demanded may exceed the cash resources available at the moment. Even were special taxes hastily levied to provide the desired funds, there would still be a considerable lapse of time before the receipts were actually available. Moreover, such widespread disaster weakens the financial structure of the communities affected, and heavy taxes would delay recovery. Expediency may dictate the reduction of existing taxes for a year or two, rather than an increase. Emergency expenditures necessitated by natural disasters are properly financed by borrowing.

Governments sometimes neglect their institutional facilities, such as prisons and hospitals. Buildings become seriously overcrowded; obsolete or improvised structures not adapted to present needs must be used. Suddenly a prison riot, or a hospital fire which proves a holocaust because the structure turns out to be a firetrap, awakens legislators and the public to the pressing need for new buildings. The cost is too great to be embodied in any "pay-as-you-go" program or in any long-term budgeting of capital construction. Though the responsible officials may be open to censure for having permitted such a condition to develop, the situation itself is an emergency warranting resort to borrowing.

"Emergency" justification may be extended to certain other public borrowings where the expenditures causing them, although not of a strictly "emergency" character, are large-scale and irregular. Cities may experience some winters when snow removal costs only a few thousand dollars and others when they run into millions of dollars. Under such circumstances, these cities cannot cover snow removal costs in their current budgets. Quite properly, they finance heavy snow removals by special intermediate-term debt. A sudden, large influx of population can create a very real emergency.

Facilities that might ordinarily be paid for gradually out of current revenues must be acquired at once. There is no practical alternative to borrowing.

Borrowing to finance government enterprises. To raise funds for acquiring or creating property, a private corporation which operates a bus line or an electric power plant will often borrow. Although technically the debt may be a mortgage on the property, the real security for the debt is the fact that the company's income from charges is expected to be more than sufficient to maintain the property in first-class condition and to pay interest on the bonds. If the property has a limited life, company revenues must in addition be sufficient to accumulate a fund which will either renew the property when it is worn out or redeem the bond issue. A municipality which operates an enterprise in a manner to cover both current costs and capital charges by the rates charged for services will be following standard business practice if it finances capital costs by a bond issue. It would be wasteful to forego construction or expansion rather than borrow, if the full costs of the borrowed funds were less than the full value of the additional services the community would obtain. About $6 billion of municipal "enterprise" debt of this character is outstanding. State "enterprise" debt, other than for toll highways, is relatively unimportant.

The federal government has substantial commitments of a partial enterprise nature. Some, like the postal system, the Alaska Railroad, the Bonneville and Boulder Dam projects, the reclamation and resettlement projects, and the revolving funds of the military, are handled through current departmental accounts, with no special earmarking of the capital costs involved. But to the extent to which these projects have added to deficits or reduced current surpluses at any period, they have indirectly added to the total of federal debt. Panama Canal construction resulted in a specific debt item of $135 million.

Debt incurred for government enterprises whose charges cover interest and principal payments is commonly called "self-supporting debt." Unlike ordinary government debt, it represents no drain on tax receipts. State constitutions and statutes generally recognize the distinction and exempt "self-supporting debt" from many limitations which bind other debt. Sometimes, however, for social reasons, municipalities prefer to set the service charges of an enterprise so low that the revenue received does not cover interest charges and debt retirement. Or mismanagement may so reduce government enterprise revenues that they do not cover its debt service. In either case, since part of the cost of the debt must be met by funds from the general government treasury, such "enterprise debt" is no longer "self-supporting."

Borrowing to finance ordinary capital construction. On the grounds of pure economic principle, resources should be put into capital construction, or even into an intangible long-term investment such as education or health, up to the point where the present value of the services of additional investment (determined by discounting the value of the future services at an appropriate rate of interest) will just equal the value of the current consumption sacrificed.[6] Governments, like businesses and individuals, will often see opportunities of using resources in capital construction that will bring increases in real income much above the costs; yet there may be no way of getting the resources except by borrowing. If the full costs of borrowing are less than the expected benefits, then borrowing for construction is economically wise. The capital equipment added will create more real income than it costs. This is good investment.

In practice, however, the calculation is very difficult. Precise—perhaps even rough—measurement of the full social benefit of a public investment is impossible, just as is the measurement of the value of the sacrifices the taxpayers must make to service the debt. American experience illustrates the sad inadequacy of the economic principle of borrowing as a guide for political action. We must look for more practical approaches.

When a small school district decides that its existing schoolhouse is unsuited to present needs and votes to construct a new and larger one, the expenditure can hardly be viewed as emergency. The old school building could be continued a while. Sooner or later, however, and the sooner the better, a new schoolhouse will be needed. Were the entire cost thrown into the tax levy of a single year, that levy would be crushing for the taxpayers of the small school district. Moreover, residents who moved out of the district shortly after paying the heavy construction tax would have been compelled to share in the cost of a school from which they would not derive a due share of continuing benefit.[7] If a bond issue to cover the cost is floated instead, the taxes necessary to retire the debt can be spread over a term of years. In each year's levy, the construction cost element will be small. Furthermore, taxpayers ten or fifteen years hence who help pay the debt will be sending their children to the school and so deriving a benefit from it. The same arguments can be advanced for financing a county hospital, a town hall, or a state capitol by borrowing. In general, a government may prudently finance by borrowing to build a project (1) of lasting benefit, (2) which will not soon be duplicated by the same government, and (3) whose cost is heavy relative to the financial resources of the community.

A large city or state with a growing population and a developing economic life faces a different problem—and has a different opportunity. Many capital expenditures of such a city or state are as continuing and ordinary a phase of government activity as its current expenditures. Year

[6] For an excellent brief discussion of the central issue, see A. C. Harberger, "The Interest Rate in Cost-Benefit Analysis," *Federal Expenditure Policy for Economic Growth and Stability* (Washington, 1957), pp. 239–241.

[7] Perhaps they could recoup, however, from persons moving in who will pay more to get property in a community whose new school is paid for.

after year, New York City, Chicago, Los Angeles, and other large and growing cities must expect to build a certain number of new school buildings. Each year, too, they must extend their water supply systems, open and pave new streets, and purchase additional fire-fighting apparatus. Capital replacement needs are also steadier in such metropolises than in small communities. Large states also require additional hospital and other institutional facilities each year. Some cities and states do, and more could, through moderate foresight, engage upon a basic program of capital construction which would progress in yearly installments paid for out of taxes with only occasional peaks to be financed by borrowing.

The effects of borrowing to finance continuing capital expenditure of the type just indicated should be distinguished from the effects of borrowing to finance occasional, rarely repeated capital projects. In the latter case, the item of indebtedness having been incurred, there follows a long period during which no additions are made to the debt. Meanwhile, the debt is paid off, or a sinking fund is accumulated against the time of its maturity. When, years hence, the community borrows for some other item of capital construction, it does so without pyramiding costs of debt service. But, if government loans are floated to finance continuing capital expenditure, borrowing must continue year after year. Total outstanding indebtedness mounts and with it the interest and debt retirement charges to be met out of each year's current budget. Eventually, annual payments for interest and debt redemption may equal or even exceed expenditures on present capital projects. Such a borrowing policy, moreover, pushes the debt close to the legal limit—or perhaps to the practical limit of the area's taxpaying ability—a condition which in the event of an emergency would hamstring a government.

If cities and states would plan their capital construction programs on a long-term basis, they could preplan their capital expenditures in reasonably even installments. Then they could properly adopt a "pay-as-you-go" program and finance each year's quota of capital construction by a tax levy. The "capital construction" levy would continue unchanged for a considerable time because of the uniform budgeting of the construction projects. Borrowing powers would be reserved for emergencies, for occasional unavoidable "peaks" of capital outlay, and for occasional special projects not comprehended in the budgeted program.

Where the yearly expenditure on capital projects varies considerably, a complete "pay-as-you-go" program cannot be applied. Substantial yearly variations in tax rates, necessary to cover varying capital expenditure, would irritate the taxpayer; they would not treat fairly those who enter and leave the community from year to year. Widespread adoption of a strict "pay-as-you-go" program to finance continuing capital expenditures is dependent upon the application of budgetary principles to capital expenditure. It may also depend upon major forces outside the control of any single government. For example, the public construction backlog built up during World War II, combined with the great growth of population and demand for additional improvements, created a situation in the late 1940's and early 1950's which few governments could meet on a "pay-as-you-go" basis; heavy borrowings were the only practicable means of financing massive construction programs.

Even the states and cities which do not budget their capital expenditures can partially apply the "pay-as-you-go" principle. In the past, the capital expenditures of large cities and states, undertaken without foreplanning and budgeting, have exhibited a cyclical rhythm, swelling in periods of business optimism, contracting in depression. Economists widely recommend a contrary rhythm, borrowing to build in depression, contracting in prosperity. Either rhythm offers a city and state the opportunity to provide a "capital construction" tax levy covering all capital expenditures during the low ebb of its construction cycle and covering a large part of costs even in the peak years. To determine the amount of such a levy for a 5- or 10-year period, a government might review its capital expenditures during the past decade, note the rough outline of their cycle, and establish the "capital construction" levy on the basis of the lowest capital expenditure made. Should the capital expenditures of some year be less than the amount of the "capital construction" levy, the surplus could be paid into a sinking fund or used to buy bonds on the open market for direct retirement. A program combining a "capital construction" tax levy to finance the minimum of continuing capital expenditures with borrowing to cover the excess of capital expenditures over this minimum is recommended to cities and states which do not preplan and budget their capital expenditures.

Constitutional limitations on incurring state indebtedness would not bar states from adopting the program suggested above. Some cities, however, might find legal obstacles. Constitutional or statutory limitations on local tax levies might prevent a city from shifting from a program of borrowing for public improvements to even a partial "pay-as-you-go" program. If the current expenditures absorb all or the greater part of the tax rate the city is permitted to levy, it cannot impose an additional "capital construction" tax which would bring its total tax levy over the prescribed maximum. Improvements can be financed only by borrowing. In several states, constitutional or statutory limitations on local taxing and borrowing powers must be modified if localities are to adopt more rational debt programs.

Finally, there must be noted the supreme political obstacle to "pay-as-you-go" financing. If a state or city administration increases tax rates, it is likely to antagonize taxpayers whose votes will decide whether it continues in office after the next election. Announcement of a bond issue to finance a government improvement arouses less hostility, since a bond issue does not immediately take money from the pockets of the taxpayers. Even though over the years a strict tax policy may be better for the community than a borrowing policy, holders of political office cannot be expected to injure their careers by forcing a tax levy on a public which would rather mortgage its future than pay cash today. Enlightened public opinion is prerequisite to any form of "pay-as-you-go" program for financing government improvements.

Two special factors have recently reduced the appeal of conservative "pay-as-you-go" finance. For almost a quarter of a century a level of interest rates which, by historical standards, was low has reduced considerably the appeal of saving interest. Moreover, inflation of costs has made delay in construction depressingly expensive. Waiting to build has been more costly than borrowing.

Whether or not the federal government should borrow to finance capital improvements depends upon broader considerations of over-all economic policy, discussed in Part Six.

Borrowing to smooth budgetary irregularities. Government expenditures are generally spread fairly evenly through the fiscal year. Some current revenues flow in with considerable regularity. Important taxes, however, are generally paid on a quarterly, or even annual, basis. Some governments harmonize these divergent rhythms of expenditures and receipts by operating on a cash balance periodically lowered by expenditure payments and replenished at intervals by lumped receipts. Other governments, however, adjust by short-term borrowing—by bank loans in the case of local and state governments, by open-market sale of short-term debt in the case of the federal government. Many governments undoubtedly have room for reducing interest payments a little; improved financial planning could reduce irregularities that now require short-term borrowing.

Borrowing for refinancing. Federal government bonds are commonly issued on a "callable-term" basis—the Treasury may, at its option, "call" them for redemption after a certain date, must redeem them at a later maturity date. If, when the optional "call" period arrives, current interest rates are lower than the face rates of the original bonds, the Treasury can borrow at the current lower rate and retire the higher-rate old issue, saving interest without reducing the face amount of the debt.

"Refinancing" borrowing is also useful in readjusting the maturities of outstanding debt to simplify the problem of retirement. A long- or intermediate-term bond issue may be floated to clear a heavy accumulation of short-term indebtedness which the government is unable to retire immediately. Sometimes, a large "callable" long-term issue is "converted" into short-term debt so that it can be retired in convenient installments over several years. In contrast, intermediate notes and short-term bills may be replaced by long-term bonds whose maturities will not soon inconvenience the Treasury. The mere existence of short-term debt over any significant period requires repeated borrowing. During and after World War II, Treasury refinancing amounted to tens of billions of dollars each year, largely because some short-term debt matured every few weeks and was not funded into long-term debt.

Few state or local governments have debt of sufficient magnitude or with sufficient market standing to permit them to engage in sound "refinancing" borrowing, except under special conditions. Declining interest rates after 1930 provided well-justified exceptions; refundings permitted large savings of interest. No repetition of this possibility seems probable, however; interest rates will hardly drop below the level at which most existing debt was incurred.

When a state or local government "funds" short-term debt with a long-term bond issue, the transaction may be a sign of bad fiscal management—the unit has failed to balance its budget for a series of years and is taking a spendthrift's way out of its difficulties. "Refunding" a *maturing* state or local bond by a new issue often means that the government has failed to accumulate funds sufficient to retire the loan and is irresponsibly continuing the debt.

Borrowing to pay bonuses. After World War II, a major reason for state borrowing was to obtain funds for veterans' bonuses. Over $3 billion of state debt was incurred for this purpose. In some cases special increases in taxes were voted to retire the bonds. The discharge of the nation's obligations to its veterans is primarily a national, not a state, responsibility. Use of state borrowing power should be reserved for purposes that are more urgent for the states than bonuses for veterans. Public support for bonus debt, however, was overwhelming.

Supplementary nonfiscal reasons for borrowing. Never, apparently, has an American government borrowed funds it did not need, merely to serve some ulterior nonfiscal end. But a nonfiscal consideration is frequently offered as supplementary justification for borrowing which has a primary fiscal purpose. When Alexander Hamilton recommended the assumption of the Revolutionary Debt by the newly created federal government, he suggested that the federal bonds might serve as a large-denomination currency. Civil War "greenbacks"—a form of forced loan—were defended on the ground that they filled the currency vacuum created by the disappearance of gold from circulation. During the 1840's and 1850's, state bonds fulfilled a secondary function as the basis for banknote issues under various "free" banking systems. Certain federal bond issues served an identical purpose under the national banking system until the 1930's.

Finally, government borrowing has sometimes been justified on the ground that it provides a form of supersafe asset for investors who must seek security and ready marketability.[8] Some trust funds are invested largely in government issues. Funds to finance pensions for government

[8] Government bonds, even federal issues, are not really so safe as often assumed. The price of other than short-term issues fluctuates considerably. In a few months in 1958, some issues dropped in price by as much as three years' yield. Moreover, continuing inflation reduces the purchasing power of government debt of specific money amounts.

employees must generally be invested in government bonds rather than in the debt of private businesses. Our banking system would have to be radically changed if there were no government bonds for bank ownership. The Social Security system is based on the expectation that a reserve fund will be accumulated, all of which must be invested in federal debt. Opponents of "pay-as-you-go" government financing have sometimes argued that governments should provide an ample supply of government securities for investors who must have this type. The huge volume of debt now outstanding, however, removes whatever merit the argument ever had.

THE GOVERNMENT BOND MARKET

The government bond market covers the entire economy—rich and poor individuals; financial institutions such as federal reserve banks, commercial banks, savings banks, and insurance companies; public and private trust funds; businesses; and other government bodies. Holdings of federal debt by categories of owners were shown in Table 24–3. These owners have responded to varied buying motivations; the channels through which government bonds are distributed to them differ widely. These considerations are important to officials responsible for government debt management.[9]

In analyzing marketing appeals and marketing procedures for government debt, we must distinguish between the normal sale of these bonds to their regular buyers upon a strictly investment basis, and the extraordinary techniques employed in wartime.

Normal buying motivations. In ordinary peace times, a government bond issue must be sold on its merits as an investment. A commercial bank is not influenced in its purchase of federal bonds by the consideration that the proceeds will refund a war loan or build a new atomic power plant. Nor does an insurance company or a pension fund buy the bonds of some city or county because the former intends to build a school or the latter a stretch of highway. Normally, decisions on buying a government bond rest upon the same considerations that influence investment purchase of other securities. These considerations, to be discussed in the next chapter, are: (1) The income yield, (2) special incidents that may affect the yield, (3) redemption provisions and other security elements, (4) the period to maturity, (5) the credit standing of the issuing government, and (6) special features and conditions, such as tax exemptions.

Normal marketing procedure. The federal government normally sells some of its debt issues directly to its own trust funds and the rest directly to banks and institutional and private investors. A few states and large

[9] Congressional practice has been to set broad limits within which the Secretary of the Treasury may use his judgment about interest rates, terms of debt, timing, and conditions of sale. Because of the relation of the federal debt to the country's financial system, the range now granted the Treasury for the relatively free use of its discretion gives it tremendous economic power.

cities have also had some success in selling bonds directly to investors. Most state and local governments, however, utilize the services of investment bankers.

Since 1935, federal "savings" bonds for individual investors have been sold through post offices, banks and other financial institutions, and employers. Subject to annual limits for each purchaser, the Treasury has been willing to sell whatever quantities of these bonds investors want, whenever they want to buy. Since these sales are only a small fraction of the federal government's total debt transactions, other elements of federal debt policy can be adjusted readily to accommodate variations in "savings" bond sales and redemptions.

Federal technique for other borrowing starts with an estimate by Treasury officials of the interest rate and other terms which must be attached to an issue to sell it in view of current market conditions.[10] Tradition and prestige demand—illogically, perhaps—that every federal offering be oversubscribed. Consequently, a slight generosity in yield rate is required—but not much, because the Treasury does not want to obligate itself to pay unnecessary interest. Market yields on outstanding debt and discussions with the financial community provide Treasury officials with a good basis for forecasting what yields the market will absorb. Often, however, new issues rise slightly in price immediately after issuance, suggesting that the Treasury might have obtained more favorable terms.

When the offering yield rate has been determined to a minute fraction of a per cent, the Treasury, through the Federal Reserve banks which act as fiscal agents in the transactions, sends a description of the issue and subscription blanks to a long list of potential institutional and individual purchasers. Then, with the usual oversubscription before it, the Treasury allots the issue, each subscriber ordinarily receiving an allotment pro rata to his original subscription. Small subscribers, however, may be allotted the full amounts of their subscriptions, which they can sometimes sell at once for a "free-ride" profit. Once marketable federal debt has been sold to the public, owners seeking to sell, or anyone wishing to buy, can deal through a bank or broker. A very highly specialized market for federal debt centers in New York.

A state or local government marketing a debt issue through investment banking firms follows a different procedure. (1) An interest rate is established at approximately the current market rate for comparable issues. In many cases, the government must choose the nearest fractional interest rate *above* the probable yield rate, since state constitutions and statutory limitations frequently forbid the sale of a debt issue below par. If the issue is a serial one, each maturity group may have a different interest rate; more commonly a single interest rate will apply to several maturity groups, which will then be sold at different premiums. (2) Next, the fiscal officer

[10] An exception is the weekly sale of short-term bills on an auction basis.

charged with selling the issue advertises to the investment houses which handle such issues and asks for competitive sealed bids on all or part of the amount. (3) Bids are ordinarily made in the form of offers of premiums over par value. (4) The issue is sold to the investment house or syndicate of underwriters making the best bid. (5) Resale by the underwriters to ultimate customers at a higher premium to cover costs, including risk, and to return a profit is the problem of the underwriters, not of the borrowing government. Resale spread on government bonds is generally narrow. Municipal bond distribution is a highly skilled, low-cost operation; a coordinated series of jobbers, wholesalers, and retail distributors all squeeze a profit from this narrow margin. Small issues of minor government units are sometimes handled by local banks which negotiate a local sale. Occasionally, issues are sold directly to insurance companies or other institutional investors.

"Patriotic" loans. In time of war or other national emergency, a government can ordinarily harness the intense feeling of popular patriotism to help the sale of bonds. Although one purpose of using a patriotic appeal is to help the government get money, a more important purpose is to improve the terms or conditions on which the bonds are sold. The major objective, for example, may be to induce the great masses of the public to cut their consumption to get money to buy the bonds; to the extent that people do so reduce their consumption, bond financing is not inflationary. If patriotism is a major factor in a bond drive, the securities offered need not carry as high an interest rate or be as attractive in other respects as if sales depended upon investment considerations alone. A feeling of popular participation in the war effort may also be obtained.

"Drives" highly charged with emotional appeal whip up enthusiasm. Subtle social coercion is exerted. Large sums may be obtained. There are dangers, however. To make a good showing, some persons may borrow from banks to get funds to buy bonds; such borrowing is apt to be just as inflationary as if the government borrowed from the banks—and more costly. When the emotional appeal weakens, the "patriotic" loans may seem less attractive than other investments or consumption; bond prices may fall, disorganizing the regular bond market, or the Treasury may lose some control over its financial policies as bondholders turn in bonds for redemption. Moreover, individual sacrifices may be very unequal, since some persons are more responsive to patriotic emotional appeals than others and since social coercion will operate unevenly. Finally, an intensive bond program may seem to be a substitute for higher taxes.

In the calendar years 1942 through 1945, roughly the war period, sales of "savings" bonds slightly exceeded $48 billion, and redemptions came to almost $8 billion. The most popular issue, Series E bonds, accounted for about $35 billion of the sales and $6 billion of the redemptions. About half of the Series E sales were in bonds with face value of $50 or less, indicating wide popular participation. After the end of the war, sales pressure continued, but sales fell off greatly and redemptions rose. Patriotic appeals were also made after Korean hostilities began, but with less apparent effect.

Forced loans. Compulsory or forced loans were employed in Europe during and after World War I; they were more widely employed in World War II.[11] They were long viewed as the last desperate resort of governments whose credit had collapsed and which had exhausted the appeal of patriotism. In World War II, however, new arguments were advanced. The huge demands of modern war, it was claimed, called for far greater withdrawals of consumer purchasing power than could be effected by taxes and voluntary loans. Moreover, taxes and patriotic bond drives would not in fact operate with the degree of equity appropriate to such great demands. A compulsory loan would absorb purchasing power to check inflation, but with a minimum of inequity because the funds would be returned eventually.

It was also argued that individual and business incentives would be dulled less by a high marginal levy that would eventually be returned than by a tax that was lost to the payer forever. Some adjustment to individual conditions could be made equitably—allowance could be given for heavy voluntary saving commitments. Finally, repayment of the bonds in the postwar period could be used to stimulate purchasing power. Occasionally the suggestion has been made that some form of forced saving be instituted to help curb inflation during peacetime.

YIELD ON GOVERNMENT BONDS

The "price" which bondbuyers receive for lending to a government, the "price" which the borrowing government must pay for a loan, is generally expressed in terms of the "yield" of the bonds. "Yield" takes account of three factors: (1) the "face" rate of interest, (2) calculated against the bond's selling price, which may involve either a discount or a premium on par value, (3) with an allowance for annual amortization of the discount or premium.[12] A nine-year 3.5 per cent bond sold at 94.58, for example, would have a yield of 4.23 per cent to maturity.

[11] Except to a limited extent in connection with the excess profits tax applying to some corporations, forced loans were not used in the United States. The short-lived Victory Tax had a small forced-saving feature. The Social Security system also forces the community to loan to the government, but the considerations are much different from those discussed in this section.

[12] The offering terms of new issues often have such apparently queer features as a 1958 Detroit issue with 2-year maturities bearing a 5 per cent coupon, and priced to yield 1.90 per cent, and also a 22-year maturity with a 3.75 per cent coupon priced to yield 3.90 per cent. The explanation is that in some cases interest can be converted into capital gain—or other income tax advantages secured from special situations. Moreover, at any moment the yield of specific outstanding issues may be influenced by the desire of owners to hold a little longer, or sell a little sooner, than they would otherwise choose in order to benefit from the difference in tax treatment of short-term and long-term capital gains and losses.

Yields on government debt issues marketed within the past 30 years have ranged from a minute fraction of one per cent to over 8 per cent. Chief among the many factors which affect "yields" of government securities are the credit standing of the borrowing government, maturity and redemption terms, tax exemption and other special incidents, the trading market which will exist for the issue after its flotation, and the current market rates of interest.

Credit standing of a government is the investment market's estimate of the probability that it will pay in full the interest specified and ultimately redeem the debt in cash exactly according to the terms specified. The higher a government's credit standing, the lower is the yield its bonds need carry. An outstanding consideration is the economic resources of the territory embraced by the borrowing government relative to its outstanding debt. Many investors prefer bonds of a government whose economy is diversified rather than dependent upon a single industry. With all the resources of the nation to draw upon, the federal government enjoys an unparalleled advantage in this respect; hence its issues bear low yields, though not the lowest, because the interest on federal debt issues is not exempted from federal income tax as is the interest on state and local bonds. State governments generally are better off than their local units. Obviously, a wealthy community has greater leeway in imposing debt-service taxes, and thus avoiding default, than one whose inhabitants have low average incomes. And other things being equal, a community with a small debt is better able to service it than one with a large debt. A local government's credit standing is improved by state control provisions, such as those which compel New York City to impose real estate taxes adequate to cover its debt obligations. Investment manuals covering government issues inform their readers in minute detail as to population, assessed valuations, tax rates, tax and debt limitations, and outstanding issues of all state governments and most local units.[13] The investment market studies this information and insists on yield variations to cover these differences in bond safety.

Another consideration which affects government credit standing is the prior debt record of the community. If it has once defaulted, with or without justification, it is thereafter branded with the stigma of irresponsibility. Rightly or wrongly, its issues are stricken from the "approved" lists for savings banks, trusts, and other regulated investments. To overcome the prejudice, subsequent issues must bear high yield rates. State and local governments in the South suffered for decades because during the 1870's they repudiated the "Reconstruction" debts incurred by the previous "carpetbag" administrations.

[13] These manuals rate government bonds by their "quality." Such quality ratings are based on marketability, yield, the community's credit reputation and the nature of its economy, and eligibility for bank, insurance company, and trust purchase. It is difficult to estimate to what extent subjective judgment and objective data determine these ratings.

The *maturity term* of a debt issue also affects its yield. The longer the term, the greater is the probability that intervening events may interfere with eventual redemption; hence, the risk is greater and the yield tends to be higher. Also, there is greater chance that better investment opportunities may subsequently appear. But these considerations may be offset by others. Important institutional investors such as life insurance companies and pension funds dislike the trouble and risk involved in frequent turnovers of their portfolios; they may be willing to take a slightly smaller yield for a longer term of a safe issue. Furthermore, suppose that a locality wants to borrow at a time when market interest rates are abnormally high. Then, the longer the term of the issue—and hence the longer the continuation of its high yield through later years when current interest rates may fall—the more willing are investors to take a yield rate somewhat below the current market level. And contrariwise, if the issue is floated with a low yield in a period of abnormally low current interest rates, investors will demand somewhat more than the current yield rate to assure them a reasonable average return over the entire life of the issue. For several years, until the early 1950's, yields on short-term issues were considerably below yields on long-term issues, in line with general market conditions; by 1958 the gap, though remaining, was less than in the 1940's.

Tax exemption or any other special benefit feature of a government debt issue lowers the yield of a government bond, of course, in accordance with the measurable value of the feature. Yield on federal issues is influenced by the fact that bank examiners favor them in bank portfolios and that they are par collateral for member-bank borrowing from Federal Reserve banks. Until 1951, the yield on federal issues was reduced by the fact that the Treasury had convinced the market that the government could and would keep prices of its bonds from falling significantly, reducing the buyer's risk. Government bond prices and yields have been influenced by state-imposed restrictions on the investments of banks, life insurance companies, and trust funds. In the 1940's especially, these institutions had difficulty finding other qualified investments and thus bid vigorously for government issues.

Presence of a *continuous trading market* in a government's securities after they are issued gives them an element of "liquidity" highly valued by many investors. This is reflected in the lower yield accepted. Although the holder is not *compelled* to release his bonds until their maturity or call dates, he knows that he can sell them at any time. Listing a public bond issue on a stock exchange insures a high degree of liquidity, but only federal issues enjoy this privilege. Constant over-the-counter dealings in many state and local bonds outstanding in large blocks give them relative liquidity. No organized trading market exists for the small issues of many thousands of minor communities, and they often become relatively "frozen" investments immediately after initial placement; buyers can usually be found at any time through brokers who specialize in "municipals," but some sacrifice in price may be necessary.

Underlying all individual variations in "yield prices" of government securities is the common factor of *current interest rates.* Like any other borrower, governments must pay more for their borrowings when investment funds are "dear"—when alternative investments are attractive—than when funds are "cheap." Five-year Treasury notes issued in the summer of 1957 bore 4 per cent interest, for example, as against 2.63 per cent on notes with essentially the same features issued in April, 1958. When the market rate fell in the 1930's, short-term federal issues could be sold with a yield of a fraction of one per cent.

The federal government and some state and local governments have tried to reduce borrowing costs by selling different issues with varying characteristics. By thus "tailoring" offerings to the special "needs" of different parts of the over-all investment market and by attaching conditions that prevent free transfer of issues, the "best" price—in terms of lowest yield—can be obtained from each category of investor.[14]

Zero yield. Can a government market its debt without interest or discount, that is, at "zero yield"?

Obviously, a dictatorship, relying upon force rather than economic persuasion, can "borrow" from its subjects without offering them any return for their "loan." The most absolute dictatorships, however, while having recourse to forced loans, generally sugar-coat the pill by promising interest.

Banks could be compelled to purchase zero-yield federal debt without serious inequity to these institutions, particularly if they were paid a service charge to cover costs of handling larger accounts. Banks would pay for such debt by creating deposits, a process which can be costless. Such federal borrowing might be inflationary, but perhaps no more so than if interest-bearing bonds were sold to the banks. The charge has been made, as noted earlier, that if federal debt is sold to banks, the payment of interest is in effect an unwarranted subsidy because the deposit creation in fact costs the banks very little. There are conditions in which this charge will be true; but if the banks, being pressed for reserves, sacrifice other opportunities to lend to earn income, the charge is false. So far in this country, "zero-yield" debt has not been used, except that the Federal Reserve returns to the Treasury most of the interest on its holdings of federal debt.

The federal government can also "borrow" from the community by issuing currency, which has no interest cost. The situations in which this practice is economically appropriate—periods of depression—are, we hope, rare. But they can exist.

The basic issue is whether the government wants (1) to borrow the voluntary savings of the community or (2) to get funds by the issuance

[14] In so doing, the Treasury in effect is acting as the discriminating monopolist of the economic textbooks.

of currency or the creation of bank credit. To get voluntary savings, interest must be paid. If "zero-yield" new currency or credit is issued, the inflationary results may force the community to "save" in the form of reducing consumption because prices rise. Much depends upon whether resources are, for practical purposes, fully utilized.

Actually, with no element of compulsion involved, the Treasury has at times marketed short-term issues at discounts so minute that the yield was practically zero; at least during World War II, however, the economy paid in the form of inflationary price rises. In rare instances, the Treasury has sold small short-term issues at a premium, that is, at "minus yield." The reason for this paradox was that certain investors were willing to forego any return on their funds, or even to pay a little, for the absolutely secure placement of idle funds in debt issues exempt from property taxes.

BURDEN OF GOVERNMENT DEBT[15]

Our combined federal-state-local debt amounts to $1,900 per capita and comes to over 90 per cent of one year's net national income. Is this a heavy "burden"—or any at all—on the American people?

First, we look at local debt. The obligations it creates are clearly burdensome to those who must pay the interest and retire the principal. But the schools, streets, and other facilities built with the borrowed money yield benefits. The relevant issue, then, is the size of (1) the advantages from the things serving the community that would not exist except for the borrowing in relation to (2) the costs of the debt. The advantages may greatly exceed the costs, and they may also fall short. The results depend upon the wisdom of the project-planning and the efficiency of spending. From the lender's point of view, the relevant consideration is whether he gets as good a net return, allowing for risk, as he could have from other employment of the money which he used to buy the locality's bonds.

The same considerations apply to state debts. However, because states are larger, there is greater possibility than in the case of localities that those who get the benefits are not those who pay the cost—or, more accurately, the benefits can be distributed among individuals in very different proportion from the costs of servicing the debt. Thus, even though the public of the whole state benefits, on balance, from a debt-financed project, there are some people who may clearly be worse off.[16] Compared with conditions that would exist if the debt had not been incurred, some taxpayers are truly burdened. So far as the holders of the debt are concerned, the issue again is whether they get as satisfactory compensation for lending to

[15] See J. M. Buchanan, *Public Principles of Public Debt* (R. D. Irwin, Homewood, 1958).

[16] The same kind of result is possible locally, of course. The difference between states and localities is one of degree.

a state as they could have obtained from other use of their savings. In free markets they must believe that they do.

National government debts raise somewhat more complex issues. The holders of the debt, we can generally assume, have acquired it freely. Since they continue to hold it, they are presumably getting at least as good a return as they would expect from alternative use of their wealth. Of course, their net benefit from holding *government* bonds compared with some other property is *not* the income from the debt; if the public debt did not exist, bondholders would have used their savings to acquire other assets and would receive at least almost as much benefit. The national government in paying interest to bondholders, therefore, confers no appreciable benefit above what the owners of the debt would have enjoyed in any case.

Unfortunately, conditions are not symmetrical. Taxpayers *are* worse off because of the debt. To them it is a burden. However, if the debt made possible the acquisition of benefit-yielding assets, taxpayers—or at least the general public—may gain as much as the debt costs, or more. There is then no net burden on the public as a whole, though there can certainly be net burdens on groups of taxpayers. Since most of our national debt was incurred to fight wars, any current benefit is intangible and impossibly difficult to appraise. Consequently, national debts seem more burdensome than a state or local debt; for they are matched by little or no apparent benefit accruing to taxpayers.

Further complications exist. For one thing, some of the debt was acquired by commercial and Federal Reserve banks through what was essentially money creation. The banks may not have sacrificed desirable alternatives. To this extent the interest they get is a gain which to them is rather different from the interest an ordinary person receives on a government bond acquired by sacrificing the purchase of a corporate bond. A second complication is that—assuming that the debt is owned within the country —the same broad public which owes the debt also owns it. In a sense, the two sides of the accounts balance and cancel out.

This "we-owe-it-to-ourselves" point has been greatly emphasized since the 1930's. Economists have pointed out that the interest paid on the debt is income to the bondholders who receive it. If the debt is retired, the funds received are assets of the former bondholder. For the country as a whole, the amount that is received equals the amount collected to pay it. This emphasis has grown out of a desire to reduce fears about the size of the debt. The argument, however, is easily overdone. The neglected aspect is the fact that most holders of the debt sacrificed alternative investment opportunities to invest their funds. Whereas the taxpayer is worse off by the full amount of the interest he must pay—assuming that the spending of the money in the past is bringing no public benefits today—the bondholder, to a large degree, is getting little if any more than if he had used his funds in other ways.

Continuing controversy about the nature of any burden of national government debt is certain. On some points, however, there is agreement. (1) Even if the interest is a transfer and the benefit to the recipient is as great as the cost to the taxpayer, the taxes do influence the economy beyond the dollars they raise. The taxes required to raise the $8 billion to cover interest on federal debt produce effects on business and on personal welfare that are not precisely offset by the receipt of the funds. Depending upon the conditions prevailing, the ultimate effects may be beneficial or harmful. (2) Government debt operations are not neutral for the economy as a whole. For specific individuals and parts of the economy, the effects of incurring, retiring, and servicing large government debt may be substantial. (3) The debt in the hands of the owners is a specific asset, a clear property right. The obligation to pay taxes to service the debt, on the other hand, is general. It does not fall on the individual in the same way that he can own a bond. Therefore, the public feels wealthier, its sense of being financially liquid is greater, than if the debt did not exist.

It is sometimes said that the debt creates a distributional burden, because the tax-interest payment process shifts funds from lower to higher income groups. Although prosperous families are certainly more apt to own government bonds than are poor families, the prosperous also pay higher income taxes. The redistributive effects of payment of interest cannot be determined because there is no way of saying *which* taxes pay the interest. If the debt did not exist, the interest saving might result in reduction of taxes on the poor only. Or it might mean a cut in high bracket rates. One cannot say *who* pays now. Moreover, Social Security, state and local government, insurance company, and saving-bank ownership of so much debt is largely for the great mass of middle-income families.

PROBLEMS

1. Give arguments for and against constitutional restrictions on state and local government borrowing. Assuming that there are to be restrictions, what types seem most likely to produce the results to be desired?

2. "A local government ought to borrow to pay for major capital projects. A national government should not." Discuss, taking account of possible differences in sizes and stages of development of localities.

3. Show how wartime borrowing can shift money costs of fighting to the postwar public.

4. Make a study of the planning and sale of an issue of state or local bonds.

5. "The national debt is not really a burden because we owe it to ourselves." Discuss.

6. What factors affect the cost of new borrowing to a locality? To the federal government?

CHAPTER 26

Government Debt Management[1]

To a government, the management of its debt is always important. Its credit standing, servicing expenses, the costs of new borrowing, its very ability to borrow to meet crises or normal needs—all depend in part upon how well it handles its outstanding debt. Yet the consequences of government debt management go far beyond the costs of borrowing to the borrowing governments. *Government debt management now affects vitally and directly the nation's entire financial system, the degree of its prosperity, the level of its prices, and the relative welfare of its citizens.*

The possible variations in the detailed provisions of a government debt issue are almost infinite. All of these variations affect the investment character of debt issues and influence their yields. They also produce various costs or savings, various conveniences or inconveniences, for the issuing government. If the officials who are responsible for the borrowing policy of a government unit exercise an intelligent choice among the many possibilities, the outstanding debt will be maintained in convenient manageable form, the government's credit standing will be supported, and the cost of its borrowing will be held down. The penalty for poor public debt management may occasionally be fiscal stringency to the point of bankruptcy and will always involve higher borrowing costs.

MATURITIES OF GOVERNMENT LOANS

Government loans are marketed with maturities ranging from a few days to several decades. For the purposes of this section, government loans are divided according to their maturities as of date of issue into: "long-term" loans, with maturities over five years; "intermediate" loans, with maturities over one year but not more than five years; and "short-term" loans, with

[1] The relation of debt management to changes in the level of economic activity is discussed in Part Six. The February, 1957, issue of *Municipal Finance* contains nine articles by specialists on municipal debt management.

maturities of a year or less. A brief preliminary survey is made of "perpetual" loans, a variant of long-term debt that has had little place in American borrowing policy.

Perpetual loans. Several European governments have issued bonds without definite maturities but with provision permitting the government to "call" them in after a stated period. Such issues need not be redeemed unless and until the government wishes. The individual owner of a bond, of course, is able to sell it in the security market, at a price determined by prevailing interest rates and other conditions. A government with "perpetual" debt of this kind need never make an appropriation for debt retirement; yet it can never technically be in default as to the principal. Since the government is under no pressure to redeem such loans, it is not likely to do so. Consequently, the debt does, in fact, tend to become permanent, perhaps thereby weakening the future credit of the government.

American governments have rarely avowedly incurred permanent debts.[2] Some local debt, however, is somewhat like permanent debt, because of the practice of issuing bonds with maturities adjusted to the life of specific improvements. If 30-year bonds are issued to cover the construction of a highway expected to last 30 years, a new bond issue to finance replacement of the highway must be floated as soon as the old issue is paid off. Thus, as long as any particular improvement is maintained, an item of local debt must be continued. Successive refundings of state and local obligations for which no adequate retirement provision has been made have also had the effect of burdening the governments involved with a quasi-permanent debt. The tendency today, however, is to provide for more systematic retirement of debt.

Since it now seems certain that we shall have a large federal debt for a long time—indefinitely—issue of some perpetual bonds has been strongly urged.[3] Debt management would be simplified as refundings would become unnecessary.

Long-term loans—"callable-term" provision. Maturity dates of federal bonds have ranged from 5 to 50 years. In addition to a maturity date, fed-

[2] The single American example of the European type of nonmaturing government loan was the federal $600 million Consolidated Debt ("Consols") of 1930, floated in 1900, and redeemable after 30 years, but without any specified maturity date. This issue was retired in 1935 as an incident of eliminating national banknotes from the currency system. When the National Banking Acts of 1863 and 1864 required the deposit of federal bonds for the issue of national banknotes, continued maintenance of a substantial federal debt was made an element of the country's currency system—at least while national banknotes remained a part of the currency system. With the elimination of the national banknote circulation in 1935 and 1936, this "freezing" of the "currency-privilege" federal debt was ended.

[3] H. C. Simons, "On Debt Policy," in *Economic Policy for a Free Society* (University of Chicago Press, Chicago, 1948), pp. 220–230. Retirement of such bonds could be made when desired by open-market purchase or by exercise of call provisions. If a stimulating effect on business is desired, issue of currency (or borrowing from banks) to buy in such bonds would be possible.

eral bond issues ordinarily carry an earlier "call" date. Thus, the first Liberty Loan bonds had to be redeemed in 1947 but could be "called" any time after 1932. Callable Treasury bonds now outstanding have a spread of 5 years between the "call" and maturity dates. Certain federal issues, such as savings bonds, are not callable but are *redeemable* before maturity at the *owner's* demand. Many states and a few cities also have "call" provisions in their bonds.

A "call" provision makes it easier for a government to convert old debt into new to smooth out retirement operations or to save interest. Even where no conversion intervenes, callable-term issues make debt retirement easier than fixed-term issues, since the government has an optional period during which to redeem or not, according to its financial circumstances. The investment market, however, dislikes the element of uncertainty thus introduced. This dislike translates itself into insistence upon slightly higher yields for callable-term than for fixed-term bonds. This cost consideration has discouraged state and local governments from issuing callable-term bonds as often as they might. Legal limitations sometimes prevent local governments from issuing such bonds.

Long-term loans—maturity period. Recent issues of federal bonds sold publicly have had maturities as high as 40 years. Most long-term issues are for around 20 years. Since there is no prospect of retiring the total debt within that time, the chief purpose of limiting maturities is probably to save interest costs, which have been lower on shorter-term debt.

Most state and local bonds are issued to finance capital projects. The principle is widely accepted that the life of the improvement is the proper maturity for the debt. Since future generations as well as the present will benefit from the improvement, it is argued that the payment should be spread among all who benefit. Accordingly, during the 1920's and 1930's, bonds were issued with maturities up to and over 50 years, with a median period of 15 to 20 years.

As indicated earlier, the adjustment of government loan maturities to the life of the improvements tends to result in a perpetual debt. Under this system, debt piles up until it reaches the legal limit. Then, no matter how vital the need for further improvements, they cannot be constructed. If every dollar of public improvement is matched by a dollar of debt, legal limitations on state or local borrowing become limitations on the value of the public improvements which can exist at any time. Nor does the principle take account of conditions in financial markets. When interest rates are low, a government may be justified in borrowing for a long term, but when interest rates are high, the shorter the maturity or call date of its borrowings the less it is likely to be saddled with heavy interest charges over a long period. Although the life of an improvement may properly be viewed as setting a *maximum* maturity for a loan, a shorter maturity is often preferable.

A program of borrowing to finance only the excess of a year's capital expenditures over a minimum covered by a tax levy, recommended in Chapter 25, runs flatly counter to the theory that the maturity of a government loan should be measured by the life of the improvement it finances. Excess-capital-expenditure loans would apply to no particular improvement. The costs of paving streets, building schools, and constructing parks would be lumped together, although the schools might outlast the streets, and the parks would outlast both. Such indebtedness would cover part of the cost of capital construction undertaken during the course of the year, rather than the entire cost of paving some street, building some school, or constructing some park. There would be no particular improvement to whose life the maturity of such loans could be related. Instead, their maturities would be determined by such factors as the maturities of the borrowing government's outstanding loans, expected development of the local economy, and the possibility of future changes in interest rates.

Intermediate loans. Intermediate government borrowing, with maturities from 1 to 5 years, has limited but definite uses. When an emergency or war loan is certain to be the last of a series and it is probable that efforts will be made within a few years to refund the debt resulting from the emergency or the war, a loan of intermediate duration simplifies the subsequent refunding procedure. Intermediate debt maturities also permit early payment of a portion of an outstanding government debt after it has been refunded. At times, intermediate-term securities may be issued to take advantage of yield rates lower than for long-term issues.

Intermediate loans are also used occasionally by some state or city governments. A city whose outstanding debt is in the form of callable-term bonds may discover a favorable opportunity to convert a portion of such debt by floating a new loan at a lower rate of interest. To insure continued retirement during the years immediately following the conversion, part of the new loan may be of intermediate duration. A city operating on a "pay-as-you-go" program may also resort to loans of intermediate maturities when exceptional expenditures cannot be met from current revenues.

Short-term loans. Short-term government borrowing takes various forms —bills, certificates, or notes sold to banks or other investors, bank loans, warrants paid out in place of cash, and unpaid bills and claims. Short-term borrowing is properly employed to smooth out irregularities between expenditure and income flows and to finance a government temporarily during a period when tax receipts unexpectedly fall off. Some cities have also found it more convenient to finance the construction of a series of improvements by short-term borrowings, subsequently funding them into consolidated long-term debt, than to float a separate long-term issue to finance each individual improvement.

During World War I, the Treasury used temporary *certificates* to obtain funds in anticipation of the Liberty Loans, retiring outstanding certificates from the proceeds of each loan. Certificates were again employed during the 1920's to obtain current funds between quarterly income tax payments. Since 1929, a new form of short-term debt instrument, the Treasury *bill* sold on a discount basis, has been utilized as the flexible element in the federal debt structure. Some issues may be used in payment of certain federal taxes. They provide a convenient short-term investment for funds accumulated to pay taxes.

In the 1930's and more strikingly during World War II, the Treasury made great use of bills and certificates with maturities of less than a year. Their attraction was their cheapness—a cost below one per cent a year. They were bought largely by banks and formed the basis for much of the wartime expansion of bank credit. There were $51 billion of these outstanding in 1945. The figure was reduced to $20 billion by 1951 but had risen to $55 billion by 1958.

Some state and city governments also issue short-term debt. As of 1958, state governments had about $200 million, and local governments about $2 billion, of such short-term debt outstanding.

A *warrant* is a departmental order to a government disbursing officer to pay the holder. It is an established part of the financial administrative machinery and, if properly used, is not subject to criticism. Local governments, however, finding themselves pressed for cash, make their warrants payable in 3 or 6 months instead of on demand. In some cases, the warrants are made payable out of some subsequent tax receipt. Holders of such warrants are, in effect, compelled to extend credit to the government for the term of the warrant. They may discount the warrants at local banks—at a cost. All parties having business dealings with such governments, except their salaried employees, can usually take this circumstance into account and make a corresponding addition to their charges. The practice of allowing bills to go long unpaid leads to similar excess charges.

"Moneyness" as related to debt maturity. Modern analysis of public debt, especially that of the national government, places considerable emphasis on the extent to which different debt forms have characteristics of money. Currency is a demand obligation of government in monetary form. Some other obligations of government are almost payable on demand—a Treasury bill or a long-term debt maturing tomorrow. The holder of such debt knows exactly what it will be worth in dollars in a few hours. Such debt, and others with a somewhat longer time to run to maturity, perhaps a few weeks, will serve most of the functions of currency or demand deposits and can vary in dollar price only minutely. This debt has a very high degree of "moneyness."

Some debt, however, will not mature for many years, and the marketability and transferability of some is restricted. Debt of this type differs from money in vital respects—its dollar equivalent tomorrow or next month is uncertain; it cannot be used or converted easily on specific dollar terms into something that can be used to make payments.

Some of the outstanding public debt is hardly distinguishable from money, some is a close substitute for money, and some is essentially different. The time to maturity is the main factor distinguishing the degrees of moneyness of government debt. By arranging the maturity composition of any given total amount of debt, the Treasury can increase or decrease the proportions that come very close to constituting part of the money stock of the country. When it puts debt in very short-term form, we say that it "monetizes" debt. Chapter 27 will show how such changing of proportions can tie in closely with control of the general monetary system and thus with changes in the level of business activity.

To anticipate, however, let us note that the short-term and redeemable nature of so very much of federal debt is a source of justified worry. This debt can accentuate forces making for inflation. If the Treasury, the public, and Congress were to recognize the "near money" nature of so much of the debt and the potential threat to monetary stability its existence creates, they might be willing to pay the price of funding really large amounts into long-term issues, as Canada did with marked success in 1958.

REDEMPTION PROVISIONS AND OTHER SECURITY ELEMENTS

Bonds of two government units, alike in all features, may sell at widely variant yields. As we have seen, the explanation is the "credit standing" of the two governments—the respective probabilities that each will redeem its bond issue in full on the date of maturity. Part of a government's credit standing rests upon its past record. Part is the investment market's estimate of the relationship between the debt burden of the government and its capacity and willingness to carry that burden. But part of the market estimate of a government bond issue turns on the issue itself—provisions made by the government for accumulating funds to retire the issue at maturity, "earmarked" revenues, and other safeguards that reduce the likelihood of default before or at maturity.

Default. Default is an unthinkable and tragic contingency in public credit—but it happens. The federal government has never been put to the shame of default. But seven states fell temporarily behind in interest payments on their debts in 1839 and 1840; during that depression period, Mississippi and the territory of Florida repudiated outright the principal of two bond issues. During the 1870's, ten Southern states repudiated $115 million debt incurred by their "carpetbag" governments. Three states fell behind on debt service payments in 1933. Local governments beyond count have willfully or unwillingly defaulted, particularly in depression periods. Because of prior overborrowing and revenue deficiencies resultant from depression, over 3,000 municipalities in 1935 were in arrears as to interest payments or were unable to pay principal due. In 1941, 1,261 were still in default, but prosperity eventually solved the problem.

Outright repudiation of debt is an irreparable blow to a government's credit, and usually every attempt is made to avoid it. Where cash is not available for interest payments, a government tries to persuade its bondholders to accept scrip, redeemable after some stated period. Where constitutional difficulties prevent use of scrip and default is inevitable, the debtor government tries to repair the injury as soon as possible by the payment of back interest. Defaults on principal have often been avoided by refunding issues. When default does occur, repayment is generally made at the earliest date permitted by the debtor government's finances. The three states reported in default in 1933 had cleared themselves by 1935.

As the 1929–1933 recession proceeded, it seemed that many of the communities slipping into default might never be able to redeem in full the tremendous debts with which they had loaded themselves during the earlier years of optimism. Two types of remedial legislation were passed. (1) Four states provided for court receiverships of defaulting municipalities. Maine, New Jersey, and North Carolina provided for "administrative" receivership under a state agency, and Massachusetts passed special receivership statutes for particular defaulting communities. All these laws provide for the appointment of a temporary "receiver" or "financial administrator" to manage the finances of a defaulting community until the debt default has been cleared. (2) A federal Municipal Bankruptcy Law of 1934 provided that, upon state authorization, adjustment and reduction plans for defaulted local debts could be worked out under court supervision and enforced if creditors holding two-thirds of each class of a community's debt and three-quarters of the total debt agreed. The measure was held unconstitutional in 1936. A second Municipal Bankruptcy Act passed in 1937, similar in its general provisions to the 1934 law but limited to a three-year period, was sustained by the courts.

Against federal or state repudiation of debt, the bondholders have no remedy, since suit against such governments is a revocable privilege accorded by the governments themselves. The Eleventh Amendment to the federal Constitution makes it impossible for the citizen of one state to sue another state in federal courts. However, some possibilities of action are available in case of local defaults. In the New England states, bondholders can proceed against officials' and taxpayers' property. Elsewhere they may bring suit for mandamus orders to compel the levy of such taxes as are possible within constitutional or statutory limitations, to raise funds for debt service. This remedy is generally more effective on paper than in practice. The mandamus order may compel the levy of a tax rate, but it cannot insure collection, and the local tax officials may not be able—or may not choose—to collect the levied rate.

"Credit" bonds. A "credit" loan may be defined as one for whose redemption no specific statutory provision is made. Bonds of such a loan may have a stated maturity, or they may be callable, but nowhere on their face or in the act authorizing their issue is there provision for accumulating any fund for their redemption. Such bonds rest flatly on the credit of the issuing government.

If a credit loan is small relative to the current budget of the borrowing government, a treasury balance sufficient to redeem the entire debt may be built up in preparation. Most bond issues are too large relative to current government resources to permit such practice. At best, credit loans are often partly redeemed, partly refunded at maturity. At worst, when the due date occurs in a period of financial stringency, the debtor government must acknowledge itself in default and negotiate some compromise.

When an open market has been established for government debt issues, the debtor government may not have to wait until the maturity date to retire an issue. Current surpluses can be utilized to buy in parts of the issue.[4] Such purchases, either at a discount or at a premium, may so reduce the outstanding total of an issue that only a small amount remains for retirement at the maturity date.

Federal bond issues have always been, for all practical purposes, credit loans.[5] In the past, all federal borrowings have in fact been retired out of current surpluses. The only real security behind federal bond issues is the Treasury's past debt record, which is perfect (ignoring inflation and the repudiation of the gold clause).

During the nineteenth century, state and local governments made frequent credit loans with sad results. Rarely was preparation made for redemption, and at maturity there could be no choice but to refund for another period. State and local governments, it is now felt, cannot generally be trusted to issue credit bonds, and constitutions and statutes tend to restrict new debt to the sinking-fund and serial forms.

Sinking-fund bonds. The principle of the sinking-fund loan is simple. When a bond issue is sold, provision is made for paying a specified annual amount of tax or other revenue into a "sinking fund," which will be in-

[4] If the trends of interest rates and market values favor it, the debtor government may be able to purchase blocks of its bonds below par, retiring its indebtedness at a cost below the face amount of the debt. Lack of foresight in planning the terms of a bond issue or unfavorable market and interest rate developments, however, may give the government no choice but to buy in its bonds at a premium. The federal government was in this position during the 1880's, when it was faced with a series of large treasury surpluses and no part of its Civil War debt was due for redemption or was callable.

[5] It is true that from Hamilton's time down to the present there has been a federal "sinking fund." But appropriations to the fund have generally been without discernible relation to the amount or maturity of the loans covered by the fund. In the past the federal sinking fund caused part of the expense of federal debt retirement to be listed as current expenditure, to be covered by current revenues. It thereby helped maintain federal tax rates against campaigns for tax reduction during the 1920's, so that the debt was reduced more rapidly than would otherwise have been politically expedient.

vested in various approved securities. Annual contributions to the sinking fund are so calculated that, at the maturity of the bond issue, the sum of the annual contributions plus interest on the investment of the sinking fund will exactly equal the amount of the bond issue to be retired. The principle of the sinking-fund is commended by investors, and a sinking-fund bond will generally sell higher than a corresponding credit bond.

Sinking-fund loans suffer, nevertheless, from serious practical defects. According to one authority, these are:

> First, legislatures must be persuaded to make the annual appropriations regularly. If there is difficulty in balancing the budget and if the maturity date of the bonds is fifteen or twenty years in the future, legislators are likely to be indifferent on this point. Second, after the fund has been accumulated, the legislature, in difficult years, may be tempted to "raid" it; that is, borrow from it and fail to repay the loan. Third, the administration of a sinking fund requires much routine clerical work and a considerable degree of financial judgment to insure a fair return, to protect the principal, and to maintain a sufficient degree of liquidity so that cash will be available when needed. Finally, since these funds are outside the stream of current funds and are accumulated in large sums, they present a greater temptation to public officials who might be dishonest.[6]

Some governments have made an important modification in the basic principle of the sinking fund. Instead of investing sinking funds in extraneous securities, they use funds to "call" one of their own issues or to buy in portions of their own noncallable debt when such bonds come into the general market. Bonds so purchased are canceled. (Good sinking-fund practice demands that the government thereafter pay into the sinking fund the value of the interest it would have had to pay during the life of the canceled bonds, in order to accumulate the total funds eventually required of the fund.) This procedure has the advantage of preventing the formation of fluid resources which may be raided subsequently by the borrowing government. Where debt limitations are based on gross rather than net debt, the immediate cancellation of bonds purchased by such sinking funds reduces the outstanding indebtedness and enlarges future borrowing capacity. The accumulation of a sinking fund of the ordinary type would not have this effect.

This "self-obliterating" sinking-fund procedure, unfortunately, has a limited application. It can be used only by government units with callable issues outstanding or having bonds that are readily purchasable in the general market.

Serial bonds. Provision for the retirement of a bond issue in a series of annual installments makes a sinking fund unnecessary. Installments of the principal can be adjusted to payments of interest, so that the annual payments for total debt service are nearly uniform.

Serial bonds are free from the disadvantages of sinking-fund bonds. The

[6] B. U. Ratchford, *American State Debts* (Duke University Press, Durham, 1941), p. 268.

prices or yields of different maturities adjust to variations in market conditions. Since the 1920's, most state and local borrowing has been in the form of serial bonds. Many debt limitation laws now require local bonds to be issued in serial form.

Other elements of security. If a government's credit is weak, it may have to earmark various revenues for debt service in order to reassure purchasers of the bonds. Foreign loans floated in this country during the 1920's were frequently backed by such earmarkings. The federal government has never resorted to such extraneous buttressing of its issues. Constitutional provisions frequently require state and local governments to impose tax levies sufficient for debt service.

The Liberty Loans and Treasury bonds sold during the 1920's all carried a "gold clause"—an obligation to pay principal and interest on the loan in gold coin "of the current weight and fineness." So did many state and local bonds. When these bonds were issued, there was not the slightest indication that any suspension of gold payments would occur. But when the dollar was devalued in terms of gold in 1933, this "gold clause" became abruptly important—if enforceable, it would give every bondholder a 69 per cent premium in current dollars. Congress specifically voided all "gold clauses" by a joint resolution; the Supreme Court held that though the "gold clause" in federal bonds was a binding contract and could not be voided by Congressional action, it was in practice unenforceable, since to sustain their suits bondholders would have to show monetary loss—and from the nature of dollar devaluation, no loss in monetary terms could be established. Congress also closed the courts to suits over the gold clause. The original Congressional resolution was fully valid as to gold clauses in state and local bonds, since the currency powers of Congress override all other arrangements for monetary payments.

Although the record of the federal government in honoring the dollar claims of its bondholders is flawless, inflation during the past two decades has wiped out a large part of the real purchasing power of earlier-issued bonds. If this trend continues, the investing public may become unwilling to lend to the Treasury except at very high rates of interest. To forestall this development, it has been proposed that a new security element be offered investors—the promise of repayment in terms of a price index. If the price level were to rise, the bondholder would receive enough more dollars to permit him to purchase goods and services equivalent to what he turned over to the government plus interest. If prices were to fall, he would get correspondingly fewer dollars. This proposal has fundamental merit, and if the process of inflation is not checked, it should receive sympathetic and exhaustive analysis.[7] It would permit the government to

[7] Some foreign countries have issued debt with interest and maturity tied to a price index. Among the more developed nations, France is the outstanding example. The immediate results have been good, that is, the public bought the new debt issues at moderate interest rates when it would not freely buy conventional debt.

accord bondholders fairer treatment. One objection is that the existence of such a bond provision might suggest that the government was unable or unwilling to prevent the dollar from falling in value. Even worse, relaxation of efforts to check inflation might seem to be invited.

The record of local defaults affects the estimate of safety that investors attribute to local issues, even to those of governments with clear records. Furthermore, the relatively limited taxable capacity behind local, as contrasted with state, issues lowers the "safety" factor of local issues. Consequently, local issues in general must be sold at a higher yield than comparable state issues. A saving in local interest payments could generally be effected if the states would underwrite the issues of their local units and thus substitute their own superior credit standing for that of the localities. A more extreme proposal is that the states themselves purchase the issues of their localities and sell their own bonds to raise the needed funds.

State underwriting of local debt issues would have to be tied up with some degree of state control of local borrowing. It would not be fair—or wise—to saddle state governments with every debt local units might choose to issue. The directors of the state "local debt fund" would have to be given discretion as to acceptance or rejection of local issues, taking into consideration both the purposes of the issue and the resources of the community. Such discretion would inevitably involve control over local functions. Even were the borrowing unit free, after the rejection by the state fund, to offer its issue through regular market channels, knowledge of the prior rejection would probably make it unmarketable except at high costs. Local fiscal independence might suffer.

"Revenue" (government-enterprise) bonds. Many state and local governments, and special government "authorities," borrow to finance their enterprises by a special type of debt issue called a "revenue" bond. The issuing government does not pledge its "full faith and credit" to these issues; it has no obligation to pay interest or redeem the bonds out of its own revenues. Instead, the bonds are secured by the earnings of the enterprise whose construction they finance.

Since government credit does not support these revenue bonds, investors must judge them as they would those of any private utility, taking into account engineering calculations of the value of the plant, present and anticipated market for the services of the enterprise, costs of operation, and rates charged. These enterprise bonds tend to sell to yield—and to cost the borrower—more than ordinary state and local bonds.

State and local governments often favor such debt because it is not subject to legal debt limits. By issuing enterprise bonds, they do not reduce their borrowing capacity for other purposes.

Although government enterprise bonds date back to the turn of the century, their widespread use is a recent development. They are now issued to finance such enterprises as municipal utility and sewerage plants, toll bridges and toll highways, airports, housing projects, and state university dormitories. Such bonds accounted for about one-third of state and local debt in 1958.

TAX EXEMPTION AND OTHER "BONUS" INCIDENTS

Special privileges or advantages attached to government debt enable such issues to be sold at lower cost and to reach markets which would otherwise be closed. An extreme example is the lottery prize drawing with which a few foreign governments have sought to "sweeten" some issues. In this country, the major special privileges have been tax exemption and bondowner's option of redemption prior to maturity at fixed prices.[8]

Basis and extent of tax-exempt bonds. Although there is a strong probability that the Supreme Court would uphold nondiscriminatory taxation of the interest on state and local bonds under the federal income taxes, and nondiscriminatory taxation of interest on federal bonds under state income taxes and of the capital value of such bonds under property taxes, the interest on state and local bonds is specifically exempt under the federal tax. Congress has not given states and localities permission to tax the principal and interest of federal bonds. Furthermore, prior to 1941 the federal government partly or wholly exempted from federal income taxation the interest on some of its own issues and on the issues it guaranteed. It now exempts interest on local government housing bonds which also have federal guarantee. Most state and local debt issues carry exemption from the property and income taxes of the states where they were issued. This privilege, of course, does not extend beyond the boundaries of the issuing state, and if such bonds are held by residents of another state, they are fully subject to the tax laws of that state.

As of 1959, interest on over $50 billion of publicly-held debt was exempt from the federal income tax. All federal, and much state-local, debt is exempt as to principal from state and local property taxes and as to interest from state income taxes.

Fiscal and social effects of tax-exempt bonds.[9] Exemption of the interest on a bond from income taxation, and exemption of its capital value from property taxation, unquestionably make the bond more valuable to certain owners. Such an owner will pay more for a tax-exempt bond, through accepting a lower yield, than for a taxable one. If every purchaser paid, in lower yield, exactly what the tax exemption privilege was worth to him, then whatever loss was sustained by taxing governments would be balanced by gain to the bond-issuing governments. If some can buy the tax-exemp-

[8] Some states prior to 1863, and the federal government from 1863 to 1935, had outstanding "currency privilege" bond issues. These bonds could be pledged by banks as security for their bank note issues.

[9] For a scholarly discussion, see L. C. Fitch, *Taxing Municipal Bond Income* (University of California Press, Berkeley, 1950).

tion privilege for less than it is worth to them—that is, if their tax saving exceeds their sacrifice in yield—then the taxing governments lose more than the issuing governments gain. Should any buyers pay more (through lower yield) for tax-exemption than it is worth to them, then the issuing governments gain more than the taxing governments lose. Which of these situations applies?

The value of tax exemption varies widely. To the millionaire paying a 91 per cent tax on the excess of his income over $200,000, tax exemption is worth ten-elevenths of the yield, a tremendous proportion. If only a few hundred million dollars of tax-exempt securities were in existence, they would all be bought by millionaires who would be willing to purchase them at a yield rate up to only one-eleventh that of comparable taxable securities. With more tax-exempt securities in existence than are needed to meet the demand of the millionaires, however, new issues must be sold to people and institutions for whom tax-exemption is less valuable. For example, the bonds may have to find a market among married individuals with incomes around $40,000 for whom tax-exemption is worth less than a three-fifths reduction of yield—still a big fraction. Bonds must today be sold to corporations for which tax-exemption is worth only a 52 per cent reduction in yield. They must be sold to small trust accounts and perhaps even to people with modest incomes for whom tax exemption may be valued at 20 per cent of the yield. As a service with such diminishing utility, tax-exemption (in terms of yield reduction) has a "price" which must be determined by the marginal buyers—the group farthest down the scale to whom tax-exempt bonds must be sold in order to market the entire supply. With over $50 billion of fully tax-exempt securities publicly held by 1959, and with the total steadily growing, new issues must be sold to people and institutions to whom exemption is worth little and who therefore offer little extra to obtain such securities. This conclusion is borne out by Table 26–1, which shows the distribution of tax-exempt securities, by classes of holders, as of 1957.

TABLE 26–1

Ownership of Tax-Exempt Securities, 1950 and 1957[1]

Owner	*1950*	*1957*
Commercial banks	$ 7.4	$13.4
Insurance companies	2.2	7.4
Other corporations	.5	1.5
Individuals	9.2	22.0
States and localities[2]	3.5	5.8
Other	.6	1.7
Total	$23.4	$51.8

[1] Amounts in billions.
[2] Includes sinking funds.
Source: U.S. Secretary of the Treasury, *Annual Report, 1957.*

Measurement of the market significance of tax exemption is difficult, because the influence of other factors cannot be isolated with certainty. In 1958, a composite index of yields of state-local general obligation bonds was almost identical with that on long-term federal debt but almost 0.85 per cent less than on good quality corporate bonds. A great number of state-local issues, however, were yielding substantially more than federal debt and even more than top quality corporate bonds. States and localities were evidently being forced to sell to marginal buyers to whom the exemption feature was not worth a great deal—perhaps around 0.6 per cent (the 20 per cent income tax rate applied to a 3 per cent yield). A very rough estimate suggests that issuing governments are saving $300 million a year.

This gain to bond-issuing governments is far outweighed by loss to the federal government. In addition to the federal income tax saving of marginal bond buyers—the saving passed on to the state and local borrower—a great number of purchasers in higher income tax brackets save much more than they sacrifice in yield. Assume a man subject to a 90 per cent marginal rate. He buys a top quality long-term state bond yielding 0.4 per cent less than a federal bond, $4 less a year per $1,000. At 1958 figures his state bond would bring him about $27 tax free, the federal bond $31 taxable. He can *keep* the entire $27, compared with only $3.10 from the federal bond. He buys the state bond, and the state government saves $4; the federal government loses the $27.90 tax he would pay if he owned the federal bond. The net loss of the two governments together is $23.90. Of course, there are not many people subject to a 90 per cent marginal rate. But if we assume a 50 per cent rate—and there are many individuals and corporations subject to this rate or more—the federal government loses $15.50 if the taxpayer buys a tax-exempt instead of a federal bond. This is nearly four times what the state saves. Although data are not complete, it seems probable that the federal government loses at least three times as much as states and localities save.

This *fiscal* loss from tax exemption varies according to a number of circumstances. (1) The more the volume of tax-exempt securities outstanding increases, the greater is the relative as well as absolute loss. To the new marginal buyers, the tax-exemption privilege is worth less than it was to the former marginal buyers; hence, the issuing governments obtain a smaller "yield reduction" benefit to offset the losses sustained by the taxing governments. (2) If market interest rates decline, the "yield reduction" gain of the issuing governments will shrink; consequently, there is less gain on their part to offset the loss of the taxing governments. (3) If tax rates rise, the net fiscal loss is increased, since the "yield reduction" benefit originally obtained by issuing governments was based on the earlier lower tax saving, and there is nothing to offset the subsequent greater tax loss of the taxing governments. Contrariwise, if tax rates are reduced, the net fiscal loss is decreased.

Besides this fiscal objection to tax-exempt bonds, two other highly important disadvantages exist. (1) The exemption reduces the effective progression of the federal and state income tax schedules by providing a legal means of avoiding the higher rates of the upper brackets. (2) Tax exemption induces rich men to invest capital not employed in operation or control of established businesses in the security of government issues. Yet much of this is the very capital that should, from the viewpoint of the economic advantage of the nation, be active in venturesome operations.

Abolition of tax-exempt bonds. Elimination of the tax-exemption privilege of government bonds would involve two separate procedures. (1) States, presumably upon their own initiative, would have to follow the federal government in ceasing to issue securities whose interest is exempt from their own taxes. (2) Federal tax laws would be applied to the interest on state and local issues, and state and local tax laws would be made applicable to federal issues.

Neither the federal nor the state governments should consider applying their taxes to any of *their own* securities previously issued as tax-exempt. Provision for exemption was a solemn covenant binding upon the issuing governments. To repudiate it would be unfair and would injure their credit. Furthermore, the state and local governments are prohibited by the federal Constitution from impairing the obligation of contracts, including their own. Only the *future* issue of exempt bonds can be stopped.

Subjecting the interest on state and local bonds to federal income taxation, and the capital and interest of federal securities to state and local taxes, involves different issues. Until 1939, the "state instrumentalities" and "federal instrumentalities" constitutional limitations seemed to establish categorical bars against mere legislative action in these directions. Now, however, the bar of the "state and federal instrumentalities" limitations has apparently been brushed aside by the Supreme Court, although no decisions are absolutely clear.

Though Congress can probably now apply the income tax to the interest on state and local bonds—outstanding issues as well as future ones—and state legislatures can reach interest on federal bonds, there is great hesitancy to take this step. Local governments feel that they would have to market their bond issues at higher cost. Undoubtedly they would, though they may exaggerate the difference. Their present slight advantage is gained at the cost of a much greater revenue loss to the federal government and serious weakness in the income tax structure. Nonetheless, it is *their* advantage, and they fight—effectively—to retain it.

The Treasury, perhaps somewhat surprisingly, has pressed no compromise proposals. The public benefit would be served by an arrangement for new issues that would give states and localities no less benefit than they now receive, while eliminating the excess to upper-bracket income groups.

Bondholder redemption option. In 1935, the Treasury once again started to sell "savings" bonds, an earlier venture in this type of debt management having been made during World War I. These bonds, termed Series E Bonds,[10] are issued in a graded series of denominations from $25 to $10,000. They were sold from 1935 to 1952 on a discount basis to yield 2.9 per cent at their redemption in 10 years; in 1958 the yield rate on newly issued bonds was 3.25 per cent. They are nontransferable, except at death, and cannot be used as collateral for bank loans. After maturity, interest continues if the bonds are not redeemed. Income tax on the interest can be paid each year or postponed until maturity.

The original purpose of these "savings" bonds was to "democratize public finance"; the major purpose today is to absorb individual savings that their owners will probably not draw upon for a period of years. Such borrowing has minimum inflationary effects.

The mass of the American population, who constitute the market for such bonds, tend to be fearful of "tieing up" their savings for as long as 10 years. Accordingly, the "savings" bonds were "sweetened" by two major provisions. One was the relatively high yield rate—at the time higher than the federal government paid on its "commercial" issues of comparable duration and higher than individuals then received on deposits in savings banks accounts.[11] The second was the optional redemption provision, a new feature in government debt management. Sixty days after purchase, the owner of a federal "savings" bond can redeem it at any time prior to its maturity in accordance with a schedule of prices stated on each bond certificate. This schedule of redemption prices is so determined that the net yield rate of a "savings" bond increases the longer the bond is held. Redemption 2 years after purchase, for example, results in an annual yield rate of 2.10 per cent; the annual yield with redemption at 5 years is 2.52 per cent; with redemption at 8 years it is 2.79 per cent. Redeemability confers a high degree of "moneyness" on this debt. The Treasury is always subject to threats of a wave of redemptions.

Other bonus features. In pursuit of its policy of tapping special investment markets for federal debt issues, either to gain yield advantages or to effect special noninflationary placement of federal debt, the Treasury has made extensive use of special bonus features in its debt issues. Besides the savings bonds, certain other bond issues may be directed at the individual savings market and made attractive by offer of a higher yield than the current market rate. Certain bond issues, as an appeal for individuals who wish their estates to be sufficiently liquid at the time of their deaths to cover death tax liabilities, may be redeemed at par at the owner's death or may be used at par to pay the federal estate tax. Some short-term notes may

[10] Series H savings bonds are issued in larger amounts, bring about the same yield, and are redeemable.

[11] It was partly because of this, then generous, yield that the bonds were not made salable in the open market. Another reason for prohibiting such sale was to prevent their use as indirect backing for inflationary bank lending.

be used to pay federal income, estate, or gift taxes. Some issues have been given "rights" which afford the bondowner a preferred position in the buying of other debt issues. Some issues intended for purchase by commercial banks permit the banks to use the issues as security for government deposits; others have entitled the buying banks to obtain preferential borrowing rates and terms when these bonds are used as collateral for loans from the Federal Reserve banks.

To accomplish its objective of placing and holding special bond issues in the special markets for which they are intended, the Treasury has accompanied the bonus features of these issues with various restrictions. Certain issues, like the savings bonds, are nontransferable. Others are transferable only within a specified class of individuals or institutions. Some may not be used as collateral for bank loans. In some instances, these restrictions apply throughout the life of the issue; in other cases, they operate only for a period of years, after which the bonds assume the unrestricted characteristics of the Treasury's general "commercial" issues.

CONTROL OF INTEREST RATES AND BOND PRICES

State and local governments can exercise little control—other than to establish and maintain themselves as good credit risks—over the yields that must be offered on their new debt issues and the market quotations on their outstanding obligations. Their debt management problem is largely one of passive accommodation to the circumstances and demands of the investment market.

Federal debt operations are of such magnitude, however, and their influence on the financial institutions of the country is so great that the Treasury can, within limits, influence the yield it must offer on its obligations and their prices. With over $280 billion of federal debt outstanding, a change of as little as one-half of a percentage point in the average yield rate on federal securities adds, or subtracts, more than $1 billion a year to the federal government's interest costs. Therefore, the Treasury has reason to prefer low interest rates. It also has grounds for preferring stability—or at least orderliness—in the market for federal debt. Some investors will be repelled a little by fluctuations in bond prices; as a result, instability in quotations makes borrowing more costly—and refunding needs make the Treasury always a heavy borrower. Most important, however, is the fact that monetary control and the country's economic life are intimately tied to management of the outstanding debt.

Short-term stabilization. Shifting conditions of demand and supply for federal debt issues may at times raise or lower prices appreciably above the longer-run average. Many financial developments here and abroad can produce such short-run price fluctuations. It is the considered opinion of financial authorities that many of the fluctuations that would develop in a completely free government debt market would be more upsetting to the economy than adjusting. Consequently, the Federal Reserve, acting to some extent for the Treasury, tries to limit the hourly, daily, weekly, and even monthly price changes of certain kinds of federal debt. The Federal Reserve buys and sells the various issues—generally only bills—to offset much of what it believes are abnormal market forces. It seeks to produce a more orderly market and not, in these operations, to determine the level of the market. Yet these short-term stabilizing moves cannot be divorced from open-market operations and general monetary control. Consequently, actions to keep markets orderly may intentionally or by accident influence the direction in which the market moves. If judgment proves wrong, correction later is possible.

A very different type of short-term stabilization was conducted for many years during and after World War II. The Federal Reserve, at the desire of the Treasury, "pegged" the prices of federal issues that were freely traded in the market. A stabilization point or range was established. When there was general pressure to sell at this point, the Federal Reserve bought enough to maintain the price. Contrariwise, the authorities met buying pressure by selling. If the stabilization price was close to its normal market level—the level that other forces of demand and supply tended to determine—Federal Reserve purchases and sales would more or less balance over an extended period, say a year. If not, longer-run problems had to be faced. These involved the *general level* of debt prices—interest rates—and the *structure* or *relative prices* of debt. Whatever the possibilities of stabilizing either in the short run, the problem over longer periods is much more complex.

Long-run control of interest rates. Can a government over any sustained period borrow at interest rates below those which would be determined by the underlying forces of demand and supply? One possibility is the use of compulsion to require the public, or some part such as the banking system, to hold debt for less interest compensation than would result from free-market forces. The Social Security system now contains elements of this compulsion. No one can say how much the average level of interest rates could be depressed over time by use of one or another kind of force. The public, or part of it, pays in the form of sacrificed alternatives rather than directly in taxes. The concealed costs must be at least as great as those that would result from open bargains in financial markets. Moreover, force and concealment are themselves to be condemned.

Another general possibility is to use the monetary system. In effect, the Treasury and the Federal Reserve can create money—or enable the banks to do so—for purchase of government debt. The demand for debt increases, and the Treasury can sell at a lower interest rate. Such debt monetization occurred during and after World War II, and it could be utilized again. If the nation's productive capacity is fully employed, the process is inflationary. It involves the creation of new money and the use of this money to pay the government for newly issued bonds or the public for existing bonds. As the price level rises, the public suffers from inflation—instead of paying interest it pays higher prices.

If the government is insistent, it can unquestionably succeed for a time in holding the level of interest rates below a free-market level. Yet for how long? No one can be sure. If the Treasury at the same time feels that it must sell debt to the public on a voluntary basis, the depression of the level of interest rates will be checked by public reluctance to buy debt whose yield is not high enough to offset the price rise. Assume that the pure interest rate is 3 per cent and the price level is rising 4 per cent a year. Nominal interest rates on publicly-sold debt would then have to rise to 7 per cent after the public realized what was happening. However, if the Treasury is not marketing new debt to the public, no real testing may occur. The process of debt monetization to depress the level of interest rates may continue about as long as the public will tolerate inflation.

Long-run control of the structure of interest rates, the relation of long- to short-term rates, for example, appears impossible even with considerable compulsion. Money and credit are fluid. They cannot for long be kept in compartments which do not respect the lines set by basic forces of demand and supply. The efforts during and after World War II began to fail when the public realized what was happening. When rates in one part of the market become abnormally different from those in another, the public will borrow where rates are low and lend where they are high. Under such conditions discrepancies cannot be maintained for long.

REDUCTION OF THE NATIONAL DEBT[12]

Being in debt can certainly cause trouble, for individuals or nations. It need not, but it can. And being in debt is costly, especially if the person who pays the interest does not have some creative property acquired in spending the borrowed funds, property which makes his income higher than if he had not gone into debt. Although the amount of the burden of the present federal debt can be disputed, taxpayers would be better off if the debt did not exist. Bondholders would be in at least almost as good a position as they are now. They could use the money obtained in payment for the debt to buy other assets. But both the economic and the practical problems of reducing an existing national debt are complex.

First, however—we are under no compulsion to reduce the debt. The government must meet every contractual obligation, repaying each issue as it falls due. But the Treasury can continue indefinitely its long-standing policy of borrowing anew to refund. Every bondholder would be satisfied. Every individual as a member of the nation gets rid of his part of the debt by dying. Governments, indeed, are in a very different position from a pri-

[12] The relation of debt reduction to employment and price levels is covered in Part Six.

vate debtor in being able to pass the obligations made at one time on to those who come later.

National debt could be reduced legitimately—we rule out repudiation—by using funds from (1) an excess of tax and other operating revenues over spending or (2) sale of federal assets. Moreover, (3) there may be times when some interest-bearing debt can be replaced by currency without indirectly involving repudiation, that is, without bringing inflation.

The sale of property would presumably do little more than permit the reduction of assets along with liabilities, bringing no net gain. Of course, there may be federal assets not really producing as much public benefit as the 3 per cent or so that debt costs. Generally, however, if the public were to sell, say, military bases and lease them back, operating costs would rise at least as much as the saving of interest on the debt that could be reduced.

Budgetary surpluses to retire debt involve burdens on taxpayers today to permit lower burdens on taxpayers in the future. Such surpluses can be achieved, currently and in the foreseeable future, only by holding or cutting back federal operating expenditures without reducing taxes. There is no practical likelihood of deliberately increasing taxes for the express purpose of producing surpluses. Such spending restraint would represent lowered evaluation of benefits from present government expenditure in relation to future tax savings. Yet today large portions of the American people by their private borrowing clearly indicate relatively high evaluation of the present over the future. Maintaining taxes higher than federal spending would compel families that are paying perhaps 12 per cent on installment debt, or 6 per cent on a mortgage, to pay out taxes to reduce government debt costing under 4 per cent. A program of consistently maintained federal surpluses to accomplish debt reduction would seem to run flatly counter to present popular preferences. Yet there is no denying the fact that a reduction of debt and annual interest costs would be welcome.

Fortunately, however, population and economic growth in themselves reduce the per capita burden of a national debt of any given size. Assuming no depreciation in the value of the dollar, future taxpayers will find a debt of the present size—or one even larger—less of a weight to carry, in real terms, than we bear today. At least there is reason for this hope, our conviction that national income will grow.[13]

[13] Long-run growth of the economy requires an increase in the quantity of money. This necessary growth could come from Treasury issue of currency to retire some bonds, rather than from bank creation of demand deposits. Such substitution of currency for interest-bearing public debt could, over half a century, reduce the total bonded debt appreciably, while remaining on a scale which is appropriate to the economy. The obstacles, however, are formidable. Public misunderstanding is probable. One result might be irrational fear of inflation and psychological repercussions tending to upset the economy. A greater danger, perhaps, is that the method would be carried to excess. If a little of this easy way to reduce the annual interest cost of debt works, why not more? The answer, "When the 'more' becomes inappropriate, inflation results," may not convince the public in time. Finally, banks would hardly welcome measures which would reduce their sources of income.

PROBLEMS

1. "Since much of the national debt is certain to remain for as long as we can foresee, the logical procedure would be to convert some into perpetual debt." Discuss.

2. Show how very short-term federal debt is more like money than is long-term debt.

3. Explain the difference between a serial and a sinking-fund bond.

4. "Exemption of municipal bond income from federal income tax does aid local and state governments; but the aid is an inefficient form of federal subsidy, because the Treasury loses more than the borrowing governments gain." Discuss.

5. What difficulties would the Treasury have in keeping the level of interest rates artificially low over a period of five years?

6. Give arguments for and against retirement of the federal debt out of tax revenues. Under what conditions might currency issue to retire debt be worth serious consideration?

7. What measures can a government take to keep the cost of any given amount of borrowing at a minimum?

8. Calculate the advantages to individuals at different income levels of the tax exemption of municipal bond interest at current yields.

PART SIX

Fiscal Policy*

TIME and again in the foregoing analysis, it must have been sharply evident that fiscal actions are not economically "neutral." Intentionally or unintentionally, they influence the level of economic activity—they have inflationary or deflationary effects upon employment, prices, and business activity in general. Prior to the 1930's, orthodox economic doctrine endeavored to ignore, and to deprecate where it was impossible to ignore, these economic effects. Achievement of the objectives of government finance should be sought by expenditure, tax, and debt procedures that would exercise a minimum of by-product economic reactions. It was anathema to orthodox economic theory to use fiscal procedures as deliberate means of economic control.

Depression and war brought a revolution in economic thinking. Economists now agree that the broad economic repercussions of government finance must receive explicit and high-priority consideration in decisions on problems of government expenditure, taxation, and debt management.

* The literature on this subject is now extensive. A few of the many useful books are: M. F. Millikan (ed.), *Income Stabilization for a Developing Democracy* (Yale University Press, New Haven, 1953); Joint Economic Committee, *Federal Tax Policy for Economic Growth and Stability* and *Federal Expenditure Policy for Economic Growth and Stability;* testimony before the Joint Economic Committee each year on the current outlook; A. Smithies and J. K. Butters, *Readings in Fiscal Policy . . .* (American Economic Association, R. D. Irwin, Homewood, 1955); J. S. Duesenberry, *Business Cycles and Economic Growth* (Harvard University Press, Cambridge, 1958); J. A. Maxwell, *Fiscal Policy, Its Techniques and Institutional Setting* (H. Holt & Co., New York, 1955); Committee for Economic Development, *Defense Against Inflation* (The Committee, New York, 1958); *Policies to Combat Depression* (National Bureau of Economic Research, New York, 1956); A. F. Burns, *Prosperity Without Inflation* (Doubleday & Co., Garden City, 1958); J. P. McKenna, *Aggregate Economic Analysis* (Dryden Press, Inc., New York, 1955); A. H. Hansen, *A Guide to Keynes* (McGraw-Hill Book Co., New York, 1953).

The term "fiscal policy" is now applied to the body of economics which deals with the effects of government spending, revenue raising, and borrowing upon price trends, employment, and, less generally, economic development.

We begin with a discussion of theory and then examine problems of implementation.

CHAPTER 27

Fiscal Economics

FISCAL ECONOMICS is the study of how government finances influence national income—the volume of employment and the level of prices. The basic principles are part of the Theory of National Income.

NATIONAL INCOME THEORY

This body of theory has grown to huge size, and economists still differ about many feaures. Our discussion will rest on the major, and widely accepted, elements of the theory, while drawing upon the increasing knowledge gained from developing analysis and accumulating experience.[1] It begins with the assumption of a closed domestic economy without foreign trade and without government spending, taxing, or borrowing.

National income. National income is one measure of the total economic accomplishment of an economy in a given period. It is a money figure. Its size reflects two quite different things—the quantity or volume in a physical or real sense of what the economy accomplishes, and the general level of prices. Certain basic elements of the processes involved are:

(1) In the course of production and distribution during any period, business enterprises make *payments to individuals* in the forms of personal compensation, interest, rent, dividends, and distributed profits. Many enterprises also *withhold* some of their earned *profit*. Business payments to individuals and profit withholdings, plus compensation payments by nonprofit institutions and service payments by individuals to individuals, constitute the country's national income, ignoring for the moment foreign trade and government.

[1] A different approach utilizes some form of the equation of exchange with emphasis on the velocity of money. Space limits prevent us from drawing fully here on the insights which one may gain somewhat better from this approach than from the presentation in the text. Throughout our discussion there will be points which cannot be developed adequately without a depth of monetary theory which is not assumed here.

(2) That part of the national income which individuals receive is utilized, apart from tax payments, in two ways: (a) the major part is spent on consumer goods and services; (b) the balance is saved. What is saved is potentially available: (i) for future consumption, debt repayment, or "consumer investment" (that is, *purchase of consumer durable goods* such as autos, houses, and household furnishings), (ii) for transfer to business units for "business investment" (that is, *creation or purchase of new capital properties*[2]) or for retirement of previously incurred debt. Withheld business profit is also a form of saving. It, too, can be used to buy new plant, equipment, and other types of business investment goods or to retire debt.

(3) Assume that all of the saved income is utilized promptly to buy investment goods, for either consumers or businesses.[3] Then dollar demand for goods and services exactly equals the quantity of such goods and services supplied at current prices. In other words, the income created by production purchases, at prevailing prices, the goods and services produced. The economy is in equilibrium. This equilibrium could involve considerable unemployment; "equilibrium" means only that economic forces are in balance and do not work toward further change.

(4) However, the amount spent on investment goods in any period may fall short of the amount saved. Some of the saved income may be held idle —"hoarded," not necessarily as currency but perhaps as a larger but unused bank deposit. In such cases the purchasing power flowing back to business is insufficient to buy all output at current prices. Either the physical volume of production must be cut, or prices must be lowered, if all output is to be sold. But either action reduces business payments to individuals or undistributed profit—that is, the dollar volume of national income must contract.

(5) Contrariwise, if savings accumulated in earlier periods are "released" or "dishoarded" to buy investment or consumption goods, more purchasing power comes upon the market than the current dollar value of output. Then output must increase or the prices of current output rise. But either of these actions increases business payments to individuals or withheld profit—that is, expands the dollar volume of national income.

(6) The balance of income produced and income spent may be upset in other ways than by hoarding or dishoarding of funds that have been saved out of income. New money can be created, existing money destroyed. Most money consists of demand deposits in commercial banks. These deposits rise as banks extend credit to borrowers and fall when the latter repay. As banks create credit in the form of deposits for borrowers, the latter obtain new purchasing power. As they spend it, national income expands. When

[2] Accumulation of business inventories is considered "investment," and decline of such inventories is "disinvestment."

[3] We also assume that the purchases are voluntary, that is, that the final owners wanted to acquire at these prices.

savings out of income are used to retire bank debt, the flow of national income contracts.

The "Multiplier." When national income begins to change, new conditions develop. The total ultimate effect of the initial change is likely to be greater in dollar amount than the original impulse. Keynes developed a simple concept, the "multiplier," for helping understand the process of income growth after a change such as an increase in investment.

(1) When a business increases its investment spending, national income rises initially by the amount of the added spending. Someone, of course, receives this addition to national income and in the next period will spend some, but, in the typical case, not all of it. A fraction is *saved*. The share spent on consumption flows back to business, to be paid out again as wages, dividends, and other income. Again the recipients save a fraction. Again and again the cycle is repeated, but each time the amount flowing back as consumption is smaller. By how much? This depends upon the recipients' marginal propensities to consume, that is, the proportion of an addition to income that will be spent on consumption goods and services.[4] If the marginal propensity to consume were two-thirds, the total eventual increase of national income produced by an added element of purchasing power would be three times the initial addition—the original investment plus twice its amount. The Multiplier would be three.

(2) The Multiplier can also work in reverse. If the flow of purchasing power contracts, spending drops not only in the period of the initial contraction but in later periods as well.

(3) Consumption and savings patterns in actual operation vary from time to time. Consequently, the size of the Multiplier for the economy as a whole cannot be predicted reliably. Moreover, forces other than those we commonly think of as aspects of consumption also influence the change in national income—and the tendency of change to cumulate—in an industrial economy.

The savings-investment relationship. Investment has a crucial role in national income change. We mean by the term "investment" newly created productive equipment, including houses and business inventory. The term does *not* include the purchase of financial assets such as stocks and bonds.

(1) Part of the country's saving is done by business units. Some is true net saving in the form of retained profit. Some is a retention of part of gross income to cover depreciation. The motives for such business saving are varied—accumulation of "safety" reserves, anticipation of possibilities of

[4] Something depends, of course, upon what happens to the portion of income saved. If the savings finance investment that would not otherwise have been made, the expansive effects are obviously larger than if the savings were held as idle funds. For the full effect of the Multiplier to be realized, an infinite period would be needed. Within a period of 18 months, however, most of the increase would have appeared. For an exhaustive analysis see Hugo Hegeland, *The Multiplier Theory* (Lund [Sweden] University, 1954).

future profitable investment, repayment of debt, avoiding personal income tax, and in the case of depreciation, replacement of productive capacity.

(2) Other saving is done by individuals. Their motives are many—anticipated purchase of securities or consumer durable goods, general safeguarding against "a rainy day," preparation for retirement, repayment of debt.

(3) Some investment, in the sense of spending on newly created capital properties, is done directly by the savers. Much business investment and consumer purchase of durables are of this type. In both cases, however, there is often a time lag between the saving and the investment, so that the total volume of investment spending by savers in any particular time period is unlikely to be identical with the total of the saving they have planned for that period.

(4) A large proportion of individual savings is channeled through such institutions as savings banks, insurance companies, and savings and loan associations, and through financial markets. In a sense these act as "savings reservoirs." From them business units and families that wish to buy new equipment, houses, and other capital goods seek funds by borrowing or by sale of new stock. Thus, large proportions of investors and of savers belong to totally different groups. There is no reason whatsoever why there should be any coincidence between the saving intentions of one group and the investment desires of the other. The interest rate, which is the "price" of loans and savings, is not fully effective in balancing the two sets of forces.[5]

(5) The normal situation is for amounts saved and the amounts that businesses and individuals plan to invest in any specific period to be unequal, one way or the other. (a) When investment intentions exceed what people want to save, the difference may be made up by drawing on "hoarded" savings of earlier periods or by an expansion of bank loans—bank credit extended to consumers or businesses. This credit is injected as added purchasing power entering the income flow as it is used to pay for investment goods. As the Multiplier operates, national income in subsequent periods is higher than it would otherwise be, but by dwindling amounts. As national income rises, the volume of savings increases until it equals the higher rate of intended investment. Thus, if intended investment exceeds intended saving, self-correcting forces appear. An important part of this self-adjustment process includes expansion of the national income.[6] (b) If consumers and businesses try to save more than they want

[5] The discussion in the text is in terms of intended, planned, *ex ante* saving and investment, that is, what people *try* to do. What is actually realized, saving and investment *ex post,* are always equal. Both realized saving and realized investment equal the income that is produced minus consumption (ignoring government and foreign trade).

[6] The expansion may be in the form of higher prices, higher output, or some combination. Changes in interest rates may play a part in the adjustment process. Moreover, as explained later, other forces operate to accentuate rather than offset a move once it has started.

to spend to buy new investment goods, national income contracts. The excess of saving is used to reduce outstanding bank loans or is held idle in bank accounts, which has the same effect. Part of the income produced by business thus does not flow back to business as either consumer or investment purchasing. The reduction of purchasing power continues to be felt in later periods as the Multiplier operates.

(6) Any factor that increases the desire to invest—improvement of profit prospects, for example—tends to affect national income expansively. Any factor that discourages investment reduces national income.

(7) When *amounts saved decline* because individuals spend more on consumption, the immediate effect is to stimulate business. The reduced availability of savings, it is true, may force interest rates and the cost of equity capital up somewhat, discouraging investment. It is not likely, however, that for this reason alone business plans for investment spending will decline by the full amount of the increase of consumption spending. When people try to *increase their savings* from a given level of income, there is less consumption spending, and business declines unless investment increases by as much as saving. Although interest rates may fall, any resulting stimulus to investment will not be likely to balance the decrease of consumption spending; the net over-all effect is to contract national income.

Cumulative change: cyclical ups and downs. Once national income begins to rise or fall, the change itself creates forces making for more change in the same direction. For a considerable time—well over a year on the average—the new forces generated push and pull the economy in the direction it has started. These involve more than the Multiplier. For one thing, the "acceleration principle" operates. A modest percentage change in the demand for consumer goods may, for a time, lead to a very much larger percentage change in the demand for inventory and for producers' plant and equipment. As the outlook improves, businesses borrow more from banks, thus increasing the quantity of money, which in turn helps finance rising consumption and investment. Psychological factors enter. Changes in costs and prices, and their relations to each other, have various effects, especially on profit and the profit outlook. Developments in international trade sometimes accentuate movement in a given direction, sometimes act to check a tendency toward cumulation.

Business cycle theory is much more complex than the theory of national income sketched above. The latter deals with broad aggregates of the economy—consumption, saving, investment. It does not go far enough behind them to determine the "why's" of relationships and without helping much to understand change in the specific parts—a simultaneous sag in auto sales and boom in motor-boating—which are of decisive importance in short-term fluctuations. No two cycles are identical, but there are elements of similarity. Consequently, we can draw upon an organized, though incomplete, body of knowledge of cycles to guide action. Fortunately so, for today it is clearer than in the 1930's that national income theory as developed by Keynes and his followers to study the forces determining the *general level* of income does not meet the needs for a theory of cycles, of short-run ups and downs. And fiscal action must deal not only with problems of the general level of employment and prices but also with short-run cyclical change and the tendency of change to cumulate and then eventually to reverse itself.

Employment and prices in national income expansion and contraction. (1) Any factor that increases or decreases the flow of purchasing power—total buying of consumption and investment goods and services—and thereby expands or contracts national income, does so by influencing volume of production (and thereby employment), or prices, or both.

(2) In the expansion of national income, *if there is considerable unemployment,* the major effect of the expansion is to raise employment, with minor effect on prices. As the level of "full" employment is approached, the effect on prices becomes more marked. After "full" employment is reached, further expansion of national income is almost completely inflationary—that is, price-raising.

(3) Contraction of national income reduces employment and lowers prices, though the result is not the exact inverse of that for expansion. Some prices, especially wage rates, now seem to move in one direction only—upward.

(4) Expansion of national income is not *per se* good, nor is contraction of national income *per se* bad. The desirability or undesirability of either depends on the state of business activity, employment, and price trends at the time the change occurs. If the country has unemployed labor and other productive resources, expansion of national income can involve added employment with relatively less increase in prices and will be beneficial. Contraction that would bring still more unemployment would, of course, be detrimental. If production facilities are being operated at capacity, labor employment is close to "full," and the price level is rising, further expansion of national income could only aggravate the inflation—a definitely undesirable development.

Fiscal operations and national income. Now government finances can be considered. Actually, part of the national income consists of what individuals and business units receive from government spending. And taxes absorb part of the national income that would otherwise be available for private spending on consumption and investment. Let us see how government expenditures inject purchasing power into the income flow, and taxes withdraw it.

(1) We start with a generalization which, though not subject to definite proof, seems valid: The private economy, for the most part, adapts itself to a *continuing* pattern of public finance—spending, taxing, and borrowing or debt retirement—that remains more or less unchanged for some

time.[7] Whatever special effects any particular pattern of public finance had on national income when it was first instituted are eventually compensated, within reasonable limits, by modifications of the prior patterns of consumption, saving, and investment.

(2) *Changes* in government financing, however, can profoundly affect national income, and thereby employment and prices. (a) An increase of government spending adds to the total demand for goods and services and hence to the flow of national income; (b) a decrease of taxes releases purchasing power and thus enables private individuals and businesses to increase their consumption, investment, debt retirement, or "hoarding."

(3) By coincidence, the magnitude of a government expenditure increase and a tax increase—or of a government expenditure reduction and a tax reduction—may exactly balance. Even so, the combined effect probably would not be neutral as regards the level of national income. Changes in government expenditure affect the total of received income, which is then divided between private spending and saving as the recipients wish. Any tax change, though of the same amount, will fall on somewhat different persons and businesses. Their spending on consumption and investment and their saving will change. Only by accident will such changes exactly offset those made as a result of the change in government spending.

(4) Usually, related changes in government spending and taxing do not balance exactly. Differences too large to be offset by changes in government bank balances lead to borrowing or debt retirement. If loans by commercial banks are involved in these public debt changes, the expansion or contraction of bank credit alters the country's stock of money. Government borrowing can truly increase—and debt retirement can truly reduce—rather than merely redistribute purchasing power. Currency issue or reduction, perhaps more obviously, alters the money stock.

(5) Changes in tax rates and tax structure, in types and methods of government spending, and in forms of government debt management, can influence the incentives, as well as the abilities, of individuals and businesses to spend and save, to consume, invest, and hoard. Such changes in the pattern of private economic activity can affect national income, often significantly.

National income models, "gaps," and fiscal action. Study of the past enables us to build "models" of the national economy. We can see the size of the parts, their relationships to each other, and how changes in different elements of the economy seem to have been related to each other. From what we know of the national income in the last few months, and of things largely certain in the months ahead, and what we can judge of the present, we can prepare a National Economic Budget for, say, the next year. This budget may indicate a total demand for output that will require the use of

[7] This conclusion assumes general stability in other aspects of economic life, especially monetary policy.

all productive capacity at current prices. If so, no change in fiscal plans is required to balance the accounts. But there may be "gaps." The total prospective demand may fall short of what is needed for full employment at current prices. Or demand may be excessive, creating an "inflationary gap," that is, the difference between prospective total dollar demand and the value of output at current prices will tend to *pull up* the level of prices. In either case, fiscal action can eliminate the gap.

Creeping inflation. One weakness of the foregoing theory is that it does not throw as much light as we need on a problem of great current importance in most of the world—creeping inflation. If the people of a nation try to spend more on consumption, investment, and government than the value of full employment output at current prices, then in a period of substantially full employment the level of prices will rise. Such a rise need not be the great percentage increases per year which we often associate with "inflation." Yet many installments can add to a large total. For example, if prices were to continue to rise at the 1956–57 rate, the dollar would lose half its purchasing power in less than 25 years. This is a far more dreadful prospect than most Americans, especially young people, can imagine. What can cause such a "creep"?

It is not enough to answer, "People want to invest more than they are willing to save." What creates this condition, or set of conditions? Good profit prospects, distrust of the value of money, inadequate self-discipline, lack of confidence that personal saving is desirable, perhaps high taxes and great social pressure to consume rather than save—all these are part of the answer. Some explanation, too, is found in the availability of funds to finance investment from the commercial banking system. A huge volume of short-term government debt that hinders restrictive monetary policy plays a part.

Yet quite another approach gets increasing attention—the "cost push." Labor unions insist upon wage rate increases, including fringes, which are appreciably above increases in productivity. Businesses then must raise prices. Some, whether local groups or nation-wide industries, have enough insulation from competition to boost prices even more than the increase in their costs. Farm groups with federal price supports can count on receiving higher prices when the price level rises. Escalator clauses in union contracts and in business pricing arrangements automatically raise many prices when other prices rise. There is a sort of vicious spiral, not necessarily rapid but certainly dangerous.

The "cost push" is less powerful than commonly assumed. Over-all price levels will not rise unless there is the money to support the rise.[8] Yet if wage

[8] In the past, periodic depressions wiped out part of the money stock and forced price levels down. Thus, the rises of prosperity were partly offset by declines during recession. But if in the future periods of prosperity predominate, and periods of recession are mercifully short, the upward drift of prices will be greater than in the past, other things the same.

rates go up, threatening unemployment by pricing out of jobs workers no longer worth the wage rate, government may create money to finance full employment at the higher level. Government thus "validates" the elements pushing costs upward. Without doubt, upward pressures on costs—chiefly wage rate increases above any growth in productivity—aggravate a condition which would be troublesome in any case. The analytical tools of Keynesian theory give inadequate help for dealing with this problem.

But whether it is the push of costs or the pull of aggregate demand financed by increases in the money stock or in the velocity of circulation, an upward trend of prices does seem to threaten us.

GOVERNMENT EXPENDITURE

To begin more detailed study, it is desirable to separate the effects of government spending from the effects of the measures taken to get the money to pay the bills.

Domestic expenditure. Most federal, state, and local government expenditure is for services and materials. These provide direct employment for millions. Over 10 million people, including those in the armed services, work directly for American governments. Large numbers are also employed by private industry to produce the myriad material items governments buy. Government expenditure for services and materials obviously leads to employment.

"Transfer" expenditures, however—subsidies to farmers, veterans' aid, welfare and Social Security benefits, perhaps interest on the public debt—are not payments for current services. However, they are part of the disposable income of the recipients, just like compensation payments to government employees. Changes in transfer payments affect the flow of purchasing power approximately as do changes in government spending for direct employment or purchase of materials.

Anyone receiving an increase in income from government—perhaps a person who had been getting none—will tend to use some for consumption, some for saving. If he gets less, he must reduce his consumption and/or saving. Of course, not all marginal propensities to consume are the same. A person receiving an unemployment check will probably spend more of it on consumption than would a government attorney receiving a salary increase of the same amount. Yet both will raise their buying from business.

A stabilized volume of government spending becomes, in time, an integral element of the flow of received income to which the economic system adapts itself. Any *increase* or *decrease* of government expenditure, however, like any other addition to, or subtraction from, the income flow, will tend for a time to lead to somewhat larger change in national income as the Multiplier and the other forces of cyclical change operate.

Some types of government spending are more "high powered" in creating jobs or affecting prices than others. Government purchase of goods or payment for a service, as contrasted with transfers, is itself employment-creating. Some spending may also induce relatively greater private spending; for example, a small amount to insure mortgages on new construction and thereby reduce private risks may induce many times the same total of private outlays on housing. Or spending to develop a region may activate a great expansion of other spending in the area. Some government expenditure, perhaps as a result of deliberate intent, may raise specific prices—of wheat, cotton, or a type of labor working on government contracts. Some expenditures may discourage private activity by displacing it, by competing, or by raising costs. Something, and perhaps a great deal, thus depends upon the *type* or *pattern* of government spending as well as upon the aggregate amount.

Expenditure abroad. The post-World War II spending of the federal goverment for aid and defense in other lands gives importance to the question of how the economic effects of such foreign expenditure may differ from those of domestic spending. Most "foreign" expenditures, in fact, have involved employment of Americans in this country to produce food and equipment to be sent abroad, and to transport it. The effects upon our national income are like those of domestic outlay, that is, people in this country get the income paid out in production. Americans, however, do not have the goods and services to add to their consumption and productive capacity.

When expenditure is used to employ foreign nationals abroad—to build air bases, for example—or to buy foreign-produced goods, it adds nothing directly to the American income flow. Indirectly, however, it will have some effect, since it provides foreigners with dollars which may be used to purchase goods and services in this country, creating more demand for labor here.[9] This is not a necessary consequence, however, since the dollars may be used to reduce foreign indebtedness to the United States or to buy securities or gold.

The persons in this country receiving more dollars from domestic government spending will use some of those dollars to buy imported items—newsprint, bananas, oil. This is a form of "leakage" which can be large for small lands but for the United States is rarely important because the dollars are usually respent here without great delay.

TAXATION[10]

Taxes influence the general level of economic activity in four ways: (1) by absorbing purchasing power that would otherwise be spent or saved,

[9] A German wholesaler supplying food to the U.S. Army may in effect use the dollars received to buy fruit from Italy, not meat from Chicago. The Italian, however, has dollars to spend in the United States. These dollars can be spent, finally, only here.

[10] For some purposes the discussion should specifically include nontax revenues, such as postal charges. These, too, absorb purchasing power. However, to indicate the significance of nontax items would unduly complicate the analysis.

(2) by affecting the related propensities to spend and to save, (3) by affecting investment, and (4) by affecting incentives to work and to operate businesses economically.

Absorption of purchasing power. Every tax absorbs purchasing power. Income taxes, and sales and other shifted taxes that raise prices of purchased items, absorb realized income. A nonshiftable business or property tax also absorbs purchasing power, but before it has been recorded as income.

Individuals and businesses burdened by a tax, having less disposable income, must save less or spend less. We cannot conclude, however, that any increase or decrease in taxes of a given amount has the same effect on national income. Taxes differ in their effects upon consumption, investment, and saving. The differences depend less upon the particular type of tax than upon the characteristics of the taxpayers. For example, per dollar of revenue, a tax on expensive jewelry, although a commodity tax, would probably reduce saving relatively more than would a retail sales tax on food. Let us examine the reasoning.

Our first premise is a set of conclusions concerning the way people at different income levels alter their consumption expenditure and saving as disposable income changes. The mass of the population lives largely from hand to mouth, and sometimes permits the mouth to anticipate the hand through installment buying. Some do not save. The greater number who save do so generally in the form of life insurance premium, home mortgage, and annuity or pension payments, or repayments of installment debt, or other procedures which in the short run offer little flexibility. Consequently, a tax borne to any large extent by the mass of individuals with small and moderate incomes absorbs, per dollar collected, considerable purchasing power that would otherwise have been applied to consumption buying. Commodity taxes like tobacco and liquor taxes, and retail sales taxes, have this effect. So also do property taxes on ordinary dwellings, payroll taxes, and personal income taxes to the extent that they apply to small incomes. Business taxes that are substantially diffused into the general price level have much the same result. As a rule, a change in any of these taxes will be reflected largely in consumption spending.

In contrast, taxes borne primarily by persons with very large incomes absorb purchasing power that, for the most part, would otherwise have been saved. Personal income taxes on upper-bracket incomes do this. So also, to some extent, do corporation income taxes, both because they cut corporate saving and because they reduce corporate dividends, which generally go to individuals with above-average incomes. Finally, per dollar of revenue, death taxes have perhaps more power than any other levy to absorb or offset savings; such taxes will reduce consumption somewhat, but the major influence will be on capital accumulation.[11]

[11] See Chapter 20.

The tendencies just described seem reasonably clear. However, increasing knowledge of family budgets has revealed much more variation in spending patterns than one might assume. As disposable income changes—perhaps because of a tax change—the consumption-saving response may be appreciably different from what had been expected. For example, even fairly high in the income scale, families may be so weighted down by fixed commitments that "discretionary income"—the amount not in fact earmarked for the settled standard of living and commitments—is small. Then tax changes may influence consumption spending much more—and saving much less—than one would expect. In short, prediction of the effects of any tax change on consumption and on saving has a larger margin of error than Keynes and his followers originally believed.

As taxes absorb income that would be spent on consumption, they reduce total demand. National income will be less than otherwise, and to some magnified extent as the forces of cumulation in the economy operate, powerfully or mildly.

Tracing the effects of a change in savings that results from a tax is more difficult.[12] We assume that saving and investment have been in balance, and that investment plans remain the same. Then taxes are raised and savings drop. A "shortage" appears. Bidding for funds tends to raise interest rates and the cost of equity capital. These higher rates discourage some marginal investments which would otherwise have been made. The resulting decline of investment spending reduces national income. Businesses, however, especially in the short run, need not rely entirely upon new savings to finance investment. They may borrow from banks, or try to do so. If banks have capacity to enlarge their lending, and do so, there is a net expansion of purchasing power. The contractive effect of the tax is offset.

If savings had been exceeding what people had wished to spend on new investment, the reduction in saving, if relatively modest, would probably have only minor effect on investment and on national income. Suppose, however, that investment had been running ahead of what the public had wished to save, with banks financing the difference. Any tax-induced reduction in saving would aggravate the tendency of business to seek funds from banks. Other possible situations can exist, of course. The net results will depend to considerable degree upon monetary policy. They will also depend upon the factors affecting the desire to invest; these, in turn, will almost inevitably be tied in (a) directly with any changes in taxes and (b) indirectly through the repercussions of taxes on consumer demand.

Effect on propensities to spend and to save. Taxes can also influence incentives to spend or to save the income which is left after paying other taxes. We illustrate with two possibilities.

Imposition of a heavy general sales tax, or a heavy tax on personal spend-

[12] Remember that our present analysis is limited to effects of the tax considered by itself, without regard to the effects produced by spending of the funds raised by the tax.

ing such as was proposed during World War II, would cause consumers to receive less in commodities and services per dollar of spending. The return that they could obtain on money saved and used to buy securities or other property might not fall. For some families, then, the relative attractiveness of saving would rise, and so would their saving. This result would be most probable if the tax increases seemed temporary. Current consumption would fall to permit more saving now to finance more consumption later. National income would drop as a result.

In contrast, a tax on any aspect of saving itself, such as the tax on saved personal income or the undistributed corporate profits tax enacted in 1936, would tend to stimulate consumption spending. A tax on saved income, by penalizing personal saving, would directly stimulate personal spending. The undistributed profits tax induced some corporations to distribute more of their net profits as dividends than they otherwise would have; some of the stockholders who received larger dividends undoubtedly spent the extra income for consumption purchases, instead of saving it as the corporations would have done.

Effects on investment. Taxes may affect investment (that is, creation of new capital) in two significantly different ways: (1) by reducing saved funds available to pay for new plant, equipment, housing, and other productive capacity, and (2) by affecting incentives to invest.

If taxes reduce the savings available for investment, the total volume of investment will tend to be less than otherwise. But there are exceptions. For one thing, bank lending may fill part of the gap. Or if the reduction of savings occurs because the tax has somehow stimulated spending, the rise in consumption buying might exercise a greater expansive effect on national income than the contractive effect of any increased cost of investment funds. Another exception arises during depression. The demand for investment goods may be so low that a reduction in savings has no perceptible tendency to cut investment further.

Quite different is the case of a tax that specifically discourages investment by reducing its prospective rewards. Income taxes on profit, dividends, interest, and capital gains may become high enough to deter investment, especially if risks are more than nominal. However, the tax law may favor investment, by design or accident creating special incentives. If tax burdens on the fruits of new investment are lower than the taxes on other income, investment will be greater than otherwise. Such favors may be permanent and general. Or they may be granted only to capital projects undertaken in a given period of time, a specific area, or a single industry. Again, the tendency is clear—taxes can hurt investment incentives and thereby depress national income, or tax provisions can add to incentives and stimulate business. Unfortunately, the measurement of the effects requires better techniques than are now available.

Effect on incentives to work and to operate businesses economically. An increase in the tax burden may affect individuals' incentive *to work,* in diametrically opposed ways. Some individuals, finding their disposable income so reduced by rising taxes that their standard of living is lowered, may take on additional work to make up the difference. Indirectly the tax increase produces an expansion of economic activity and of purchasing power produced by that activity.[13]

In contrast, there are individuals, particularly those with large incomes and "working wives" whose earnings supplement those of their husbands, who face the prospect of paying a substantial fraction of their top bracket income in taxes. They may conclude that the effort to earn the final increments of income is not worth the take-home return. Professional men —doctors, lawyers, consulting engineers—may restrict the amount of work they take on. Whether professional men or business executives, they may retire earlier than otherwise. "Working wives" decide to become housewives. The economy loses productive services and income, and is the poorer thereby. Moreover, raising income taxes at a time when inflation threatens, some people argue, may actually make things worse. The impairment of incentives may do more harm by reducing production than the tax increase does good by absorbing purchasing power. Unfortunately, we do not have the evidence needed to answer this extremely important question.

Heavy business income and excess profits taxes remove an *incentive* to economical and cautious business practice. Why should management risk a strike when faced by a labor demand for increased wages, since half or more of the extra wage is offset by income tax saving? Faced with a proposal for an extravagant advertising program which may or may not return its cost, why should management not take the gamble, since the government bears much of the cost? The tax-induced extravagance is wasteful, and thereby reduces real national income. Moreover, in a period when other inflationary forces are already rampant, it may add fuel to the fire, boosting national income in monetary, but not real, terms.

Conclusion. The preceding analysis is far from complete. Many potentially important relationships have not been mentioned. The forces making for an upward drift in price levels, as different from the forces making for cyclical fluctuations of business, require more attention. And what is the comparative influence of tax and spending changes? A dollar of tax and a dollar of government spending may have equal and opposite effects on national income. Yet one may have significantly more influence than the

[13] A carefully conducted study in Britain, where the higher taxes might lead one to expect the problem to be acute, found that accountants in private practice in general worked about as industriously as they thought they would if tax rates were appreciably lower. G. F. Break, "Income Taxes and Incentives to Work," *American Economic Review,* September, 1957, pp. 529–549. When taxes exceed one-fourth or somewhat more of the national output, it has been argued, they do more to encourage than discourage inflation. For critique of this line of argument and for a bibliography, see Tax Institute, *The Limits of Taxable Capacity* (The Institute, Princeton, 1953).

other—depending not only upon the nature of the tax and the spending but also upon the condition of the economy. The effects at one stage of the business cycle, or when monetary policies of one sort are in force, will differ from the effects when other conditions prevail. Fortunately, however, the broad outlines are clear enough to serve helpfully.

BORROWING AND DEBT RETIREMENT

It is commonly assumed that any form of government borrowing to finance spending has an expansive effect on national income, and any debt retirement a contractive influence. This is an oversimplified view, and in at least one case is categorically wrong. The economic effects of government borrowing differ according to whether such borrowing: (1) absorbs funds that would otherwise be spent for consumption; (2) absorbs savings that would otherwise finance investment (that is, creation of new capital properties); or (3) results in the creation of money, that is, new deposits in commercial banks. Moreover, the effects are intimately related to what happens in the monetary and financial system.[14]

Absorption of funds that would otherwise be spent. When the federal Treasury persuades the employed masses to buy "savings" bonds through payroll-deduction plans, or other arrangements which involve commitments to buy regularly, the economic effect of the borrowing may be much the same as that of a payroll tax. The purchasers have small or moderate incomes. Much of the purchasing power they divert into bond purchases would otherwise have gone into consumption spending. The over-all effect is to contract national income, probably by about as much as spending the loan proceeds expands it.

The economy in time readjusts to any maintained *rate* of such borrowing. Hence, as in the case of taxes with similar effects, it is primarily the *start* of such borrowing, or an *increase* or *decrease* in its *rate*, that changes the level of economic activity.

Absorption of funds being saved or already saved. When individuals or institutions other than commercial and Federal Reserve banks buy newly issued government bonds with funds they have saved or received from savers, the immediate effect is much the same as if the accumulated savings had been absorbed by a tax.[15] Businesses and individuals seeking

[14] The analysis of debt policy could run in terms of operations in debt with different degrees of "moneyness."

[15] The effect may be the same whether the bond purchaser uses funds on hand and awaiting investment, or sells some other form of investment to buy the government bond. In the latter case, the securities or properties sold may eventually find their way to some holder of accumulated savings who uses them in this way instead of financing new investment. However, if the eventual purchaser of the assets which are sold borrows from a commercial bank to pay for them, the situation falls into the third category of government borrowing, in which bank loans and demand deposits are created.

funds to pay for new investment goods find conditions tighter. Greater reliance on commercial banks may be possible, but borrowing costs will certainly rise. Some planned investment will be foregone because of higher interest rates and costs of equity capital. Government absorption of private savings tends to contract national income, more or less offsetting the expansion effects produced by spending the proceeds of the loan. In this case also, it is chiefly the *beginning* or *change* of such borrowing that changes the level of national income. A maintained rate of such borrowing tends to produce a new income equilibrium.

Borrowing that results in creation of money (deposits created by bank lending). Government borrowing can result in the creation of money—new demand deposits at commercial banks—in two ways: (1) the purchaser borrows from a bank to buy the government bond; (2) the government sells the debt directly to commercial or Federal Reserve banks. In the first case, the loan to the individual or institutional bond-buyer is accomplished by crediting the borrower with an additional deposit on which the borrower writes a check to the government to pay for the bond. In the second case, the bank pays for its purchase by establishing the purchase price as a deposit in the account of the government. Either way, the borrowing government gets newly created purchasing power, upon which it draws to pay its expenses.

Expenditure of the borrowed funds has an expansive effect upon national income, as does any government expenditure. The newly created deposits move into the country's stream of monetary payments. The public has more money to spend than it would otherwise. Total spending, and therefore national income (at least in a monetary sense), are above what they would be if the money had not been created.

However—and this point is often overlooked—the net effect of government borrowing depends upon what happens to private borrowing. If bank lending capacity is so limited that lending to government leads to less lending to business, the net expansive effect is correspondingly smaller than one might expect from looking at government actions alone.

When a government borrows from the central bank, in this country the Federal Reserve, a substantial monetary expansion is likely. Government employees and businesses selling to the government get payments from the proceeds of the loan. Their deposits in commercial banks rise. In turn, the commercial banks receive what was in the Treasury's account at the Federal Reserve. Such deposits at the Federal Reserve are the legal reserves of member banks. Any increase adds to the capacity of banks to make loans to businesses and consumers. The enlargement of the commercial banks' lending capacity facilitates expansion of demand deposits, which are the major element of the country's stock of money.

Debt reduction. When a government uses an excess of current revenue to retire a debt issue held by banks, the economic effect is the reverse of floating such an issue. The government repays the debt with bank deposits which it has accumulated, and these deposits go out of existence. Although, in a strict sense, the actual transaction of the debt retirement does not affect national income, the process of obtaining the money withdraws purchasing power from the public. The destruction of deposits in a significant sense passes the contractive effect on into the future—unless private borrowing from banks rises to offset the drop in government borrowing. The raising of the funds to retire the loan would, of course, involve more or less contraction of national income. If these funds were held for some time as idle deposits before they were applied to debt retirement, the contraction would precede the debt retirement. This emphasizes the point that it is the obtaining of funds for debt retirement, and not the debt transaction itself, that contracts national income.

Yet one possibility of an offsetting expansion may be present. Assume that the debt had been held by commercial banks. If their reserve position had previously limited the extension of commercial loans, the reduction of their loan to government would enlarge their capacity to lend to business. However, if the debt repaid had been held by Federal Reserve banks, the utilization of deposits in commercial banks to pay off Federal Reserve banks would reduce the member banks' legal reserves, which are deposits at the Federal Reserve. Bank lending capacity would drop by a multiple of the debt retirement.

When a government retires a debt issue previously bought by individuals or institutions with saved funds, the effect of the retirement is the reverse of that of the borrowing. The funds received by the bondholders are now available for new investment or consumption spending. The added availability of funds, plus any increase in consumer spending, would stimulate investment, but some time would be required to offset the bulk of the contractive effects of the taxation that raised the funds.

Retirement of government debt originally purchased with funds that would otherwise have been spent tends to reverse the original effect, but not exactly. To the extent that the former owners of savings bonds use the funds they receive to buy new houses, TV sets, automobiles, medical services, etc.—or squander the money in extravagances—the economy gets a stimulus which offsets the contractive effect of any taxes that raised the funds. But some individuals may use these funds to pay off mortgage or other debt, or acquire stocks, bonds, or other assets. In such cases the national income gets correspondingly less stimulus.

Debt and currency. As noted in Chapter 25, currency is, to some extent, a substitute for federal debt. The most pronounced effects of debt policy would be those interchanging debt and currency. If government were to issue currency to retire some debt, the stimulating effect would be great indeed, especially if the debt were that held by private savers. Or if the government were to borrow from savers to retire currency, the contractive effects would be substantial.

In general, the higher the moneyness of the debt form, the closer it is to currency and the less the effectiveness of interchanging it with currency—and vice versa. Today, most of our huge federal debt has a high degree of moneyness. In a world where upward pressures on the price level are as insistent as they now appear, this mass of essentially short-term debt is a greater danger than the public realizes. Large, though not necessarily sudden, funding into long-term issues seems increasingly desirable to reduce the average moneyness of the debt.

CONCLUSION

So far, with a few exceptions, we have discussed the economic effects of government expenditure, of various taxes, and of borrowing and debt retirement as though these were independent. Actually, all are closely interrelated. Fiscal Economics, therefore, cannot stop with the results of expenditure, borrowing, or debt operations studied in isolation. It must consider the combined effects.

Tax-financed expenditures—balanced budget financing. First, we ask, what is the effect of an *increase* of expenditure financed by a corresponding tax increase, or a *decline* of tax revenues which leads to a corresponding reduction of expenditure?

An increase in government expenditure tends to raise national income whereas a tax increase tends to lower it. Both the immediate and the longer-run effects depend upon (a) a variety of possible reactions of those who pay the taxes and those who are influenced directly by the outlay, as well as upon (b) the nature of the taxes and of the spending, and (c) the state of the economy. In view of the many cross-effects, we cannot conclude that an increase in government spending financed by taxes will leave total national income unchanged. Most probably, the net contractive effect of a tax increase will be a little less than the expansive effect of the expenditure increase it financed. Over all, then, an increase in a government budget which remains balanced will be, under modern conditions, expansive, but not greatly. Yet no one can be certain of the size of the net effect. (The so-called "balanced budget multiplier" now seems to be a less promising analytical device than once assumed.) And in time the economy will probably adjust so that the influence on the level of national income of any expenditure-and-tax increase or decrease fades away. This result, however, is not certain. What *is* certain is that no really large changes in national income are likely to result from equal but opposite changes in taxes and government spending.

Deficit financing. Deficit financing may come about in three ways: (1) Expenditures may be increased while the level of taxes remains unchanged;

(2) the level of expenditure may be maintained while taxes are reduced or while tax collections decline; (3) both expenditures and taxes may increase with the greater expansion in the former, or both may decline with the greater fall in taxes. In the first case, we start with a clear expansive effect produced by the expenditure increase. In the second, the effect of the tax reduction may range from marked to mild expansion in private spending on consumption and investment. In the third situation, there will be a combination of effects from both the expenditure and tax changes. The results will depend not only upon the amounts involved but also upon the *kinds* of tax and spending changes.

More important is the way the money to cover the deficit is raised. If the borrowing is accomplished by selling "savings" bonds in a way to absorb purchasing power that otherwise would be spent on consumption or investment, the ultimate net effect of the whole process may be little change in national income. But if the debt is sold to commercial banks, the economy can get a true stimulus as net new purchasing power is injected. The expansive force can be much larger still if the debt is sold to the Federal Reserve or if currency is issued instead of debt.

Surplus financing. A shift from deficit or balanced or budget financing to surplus financing operates, in essence, as the reverse of a shift to deficit financing. In general, a move to surplus financing has a contractive effect on the economy as more money is taken from the taxpaying public than is paid back in expenditure. The crux of the matter is the use of the funds received by the former holders of the debt. If banks are repaid and the money stock thereby reduced, the downward pressure on national income can be substantial. If currency is retired, the contractive effect is still greater. But if the surplus funds go into financing an increase in private investment, or consumption, the contractive result will not be significant.

Budget balance over the long run. Surpluses and deficits that are ideal from the point of view of national income needs will not necessarily offset each other over a period of years. Either deficits or surpluses may predominate. Whatever the merits of the annually balanced budget rule for other purposes, such as preventing wasteful spending, this rule is not the best guide for economic stabilization. Nor is there convincing reason to expect budgets to balance over a business cycle. The surplus that is best during a boom may be either larger or smaller than the deficit that is appropriate for a recession.

Interrelation of Fiscal and Monetary Economics: debt management. We have emphasized that changes in national income resulting from fiscal operations depend partly upon increases or decreases in bank loans and thus in the country's stock of money. We have dealt with these changes in bank lending simply as the agency through which fiscal operations introduce purchasing power, or withdraw it, from the income flow. Yet changes in the volume of deposits in commercial banks are, in themselves, monetary developments with widespread significance to the economy. Government, of course, exercises monetary controls which, quite independently of fiscal action, influence national income. The two may work in harmony. They may also conflict.

When selling debt issues, the Treasury is interested in placing them at low interest cost. The yield rates at which a federal debt issue can be sold depend in large part on the current market monetary rates. These can be controlled to some extent by the Federal Reserve. The Treasury, therefore, may seek the cooperation of the Federal Reserve in holding down interest rates. If such cooperation is given, budgetary considerations become a factor influencing monetary policy—inducing greater ease than otherwise. Assume that the borrowing is for refunding with the budget completely in balance. Then the desire to save interest on the debt refunded can induce a monetary policy which is expansive because it eases borrowing for the private economy. There is no reason, of course, for concluding that the Treasury and Federal Reserve officials will adopt policies which in total are inappropriate. Yet there is that possibility.

Although monetary and fiscal action are inevitably related, they are by no means identical. Government spending and taxation operate *directly* on the income stream. In contrast, monetary control, including debt management, operates *indirectly*. This distinction has many ramifications which cannot be explored here, where we emphasize the major fact: Fiscal action can change the level of national income directly, whereas monetary action works indirectly by making money more or less plentiful.

Compatibility of growth and stability. A final point in conclusion looms ever more important: Healthy long-run growth and short-run assurance of full employment often appear to require different policies. To an increasing number of economists, full employment seems to be incompatible with avoidance of creeping inflation. Some of the issues are discussed in the next chapter, but this whole problem-area is still a "frontier" of economic theory.

PROBLEMS

1. What happens to national income if the public tries to save more than it wants to spend buying investment goods?

2. Under what conditions may an increase in government spending tend to raise the level of employment? The level of prices? Neither?

3. When will a rise in taxes tend to help curb a tendency toward inflation? How can a tax reduction stimulate employment?

4. How are borrowing and debt policy related to general policies to change the level of national income?

5. "No country can spend itself into prosperity." Comment.

6. "What is truly important is not so much the change in taxes or the change in spending, as the change in the surplus or the deficit." Discuss.

CHAPTER 28

Fiscal Policy

THIS concluding chapter examines the practical problems of applying Fiscal Theory, with our institutions of government, in our complex economy.

DEVELOPMENT OF THE FISCAL POLICY CONCEPT

A short but sharp depression of 1921 stimulated interest in the possibility that fiscal operations might be shaped to head off recessions and mitigate the suffering they entailed. President Harding's Conference on Unemployment in 1923 suggested that government capital expenditures might be timed to act as a business stabilizer. Congress gave the proposal some consideration in 1925, 1926, and 1928. The 1929 Conference of State Governors debated the problem, and the members resolved to bend their efforts toward bringing about a programming of state capital expenditures with economic considerations in mind. In 1931 Congress authorized a six-year preplanning of federal public works, and a Federal Employment Stabilization Board was created to program the undertaking of such projects.

The severity of the 1929–1933 recession, with mass unemployment on a scale previously inconceivable, focused attention more sharply than ever on the control possibilities. At the same time it pushed cyclical "counterweight" programs for government expenditure into the background as inadequate for the current emergency. A new theory of government expenditure came to the fore—"pump-priming."[1] The federal government, and to a lesser extent the states and localities, ought to "prime" the economy by special rapid large-scale expenditures financed by borrowing.

[1] When a water pump has become dry, the air in the cylinder slips around the head of the piston, and there is no suction. The pump must be "primed" by pouring a small amount of water into the cylinder chamber to seal the space between the piston and the cylinder wall. The pump then has suction, which is thereafter maintained by the pump's own action.

The spending could take two forms: (1) "work relief"—public projects of any sort that could be immediately devised to create jobs; such "made" employment would maintain morale and provide the unemployed with purchasing power which their spending would put into circulation; (2) "home relief"—allowances to the needy who could not be employed; this would relieve suffering and also push purchasing power into circulation. The added buying power poured into the economy would, it was hoped, be a "primer" for the dried-out business system, which would thereupon regain "suction" and return to "pumping" in normal fashion. Between July, 1933, and June, 1937, the federal government spent over $10 billion on "pump-priming," and states and local units spent several billion more.

Now that partisan controversies of the 1930's have subsided, the program can be appraised objectively. It was a stab in the dark, undertaken without any sound measures of the magnitude of the economic needs involved or of what was being accomplished from period to period. Unquestionably the "priming" expenditures helped stimulate business. But there were offsetting influences: (1) Tax rates were substantially increased, depressing the economy; (2) the business community mistrusted the New Deal, and the resulting lack of confidence reduced the contribution of private enterprise to recovery; (3) to the extent that the program raised price and wage levels, some of the new purchasing power created was "lost," and rising costs hindered business revival; (4) international economic disruption was too profound to be cured by American action alone, and the international economic situation continued as a drag on the American economy. Beyond question, the "pump-priming" program exercised a *net* expansive influence. From 1933 to 1937 there was substantial recovery. We see now, however, that the deficits were much too small to give the economy a stimulus of the size it needed.

Meanwhile, Keynes' *The General Theory of Employment, Interest, and Money* appeared in 1936. This landmark in economic literature fashioned tools of theoretical economic analysis which came to be widely used, even by economists who disagreed strongly with many of Keynes' policy proposals. A wide literature appeared during the second half of the 1930's. Most dealt with the expansive possibilities of Fiscal Policy. Exploration continued during the 1940's, with attention directed on the one hand to problems of inflation control, and on the other hand to the preparation of fiscal counteractives to an anticipated postwar slump. Both Republicans and Democrats came to endorse the principle of using national government finances to help stabilize the economy at high employment. Congress, in the Employment Act of 1946, formally committed government to the deliberate use of Fiscal Policy to help determine the level of national income. However, three recessions and considerable inflation since 1946 have revealed that our problems cannot be solved by the relatively simple prescriptions that once seemed so promising.

OBJECTIVES OF FISCAL POLICY

Economists are far from unanimous as to what should be the economic objectives of Fiscal Policy—or, more accurately, the priority among desirable objectives which may, or do, conflict. Although we speak of "stability" as a goal, we do not want rigidity and absence of change. Opportunity and the chance of bettering ourselves call for change—but in an orderly framework. A host of major and minor objectives of public policy—from national defense to beautiful parks—are in some way related to Fiscal Policy action. However, the dominant concern, for good reason, is with *jobs* and *prices.*

Full employment and avoidance of inflation. There is little need to explain here why each of the goals—full employment and the avoidance of inflation—is desirable. We must note, however, that the concept of full employment is not so clear as one might think. Problems arise in deciding how many people are of necessity out of jobs at any one time because of the inevitable, and constructive, changes that characterize a dynamic economy. How much weight ought to be given to the amount of part-time and over-time work? What if employers list many jobs unfilled but offer pay that is below what people seeking jobs demand? Many such questions must be answered in any decisions about action in specific situations—and clear principles for answers are still in dispute. A reasonably satisfactory working goal is probably a seasonably adjusted rate of employment, as now measured, of at least 96 per cent of the labor force.

The Employment Act does not include the avoidance of inflation among the goals it sets. Nor does the public seem forcefully attached to price stability as something worth serious sacrifice. Rampant inflation, of course, would have no supporters. Milder rises in the level of prices, however, appear to arouse little more than grudging complaint from the housewife and fiercer determination of the breadwinner to get his pay raised. Yet even small inflation in each of several years can bring not only great injustice but also lead to economic waste. Increasingly, for example, debt contracts would be unacceptable except at interest rates which would be high enough to compensate for the possibilities of further price rises. Such rates would certainly impede many otherwise desirable economic developments. Stability of the price level ought to be an objective of Fiscal Policy.[2]

These two goals—full employment and avoidance of inflation—are closely related. And in the modern world they conflict. The higher the level of employment, the greater the danger of upward pressure on prices. The stricter the action to keep prices from rising, the greater the probability of some unemployment—avoidable unemployment. Either goal could be obtained easily, by sacrificing the other. Unfortunately, we have no basis for

[2] The Consumer Price Index can serve satisfactorily as the measure of the price level.

evaluating the worth of one in relation to the worth of the other. Is X per cent of inflation worse than Y per cent of unemployment?

Any policy for action must consider not only the short-run but also more persistent needs. What is decided for the next few months ought to depend in part upon needs for the years ahead. Thus we now look at possible longer-run objectives which, if accepted, must be considered in any decision-making.

Combating chronic economic stagnation. During the 1930's, some leading economists concluded that sustained full employment in this country was highly improbable under "normal" conditions. They argued that the era of great economic expansion through rapid population growth and territorial development was past, and that further technological development offered an inadequate basis for continued expansion; that when incomes are at prosperity levels, business and personal saving programs constitute such powerful "built-in" mechanisms for large-scale saving that, with a national income high enough to provide full employment, saving would tend to exceed the investment demand for savings, and thus automatically set in operation contractive influences which would pull national income below the full employment level. The economy was doomed to "stagnate," not in the sense of ceasing to grow, but in the sense of being unable to provide full employment through its normal operation.

What type of Fiscal Policy would be suited to such an economy? The "stagnationists" tended to favor fairly continuous deficit financing—spending for expanded programs of welfare, public works, and other government services, financed by borrowing from banks. This would pump more and more purchasing power into the economy. Saving, they thought, should be repressed by heavy taxes on the upper income classes to absorb income that they would otherwise save, by undistributed profits taxes to discourage corporate saving, and even by special taxes on individual saving. Investment should be stimulated by debt management policies that would keep interest rates low, as well as by the stimulus from the boost in consumer demand brought by higher government spending.

Combating chronic inflation. Today another worry grows—that our economy contains elements of "built-in" inflation. This fear results from the combination of several factors: (1) The prevalence of "administered" prices—from haircuts to spare parts to steel girders to farm products having government price support—favors rising prices, hinders price declines. The economy is plagued with all sorts of monopolistic factors which reduce somewhat the full force of price competition. (2) The power of organized labor has grown until it exerts a decisive influence. Unions force costs up by holding out for wage increases that are greater than productivity growth. (3) Private saving tends to lag behind the needs for investment. (4) Monetary authorities may not restrain adequately the growth in money stock, because to do so risks creating unemployment and also adds to the costs of managing the huge public debt. (5) Congress tends to increase spending and reduce taxes, with the result that deficits occur more often, and are larger, than is consistent with price-level stability. (6) To the extent that we succeed in sustaining prosperity, we reduce the old-time forces of depression which used to wipe out some of the wage and price increases, as well as inefficiencies, maladjustments, and excesses, of the boom.

The experience of the 1950's has tended to confirm the fear that creeping, chronic inflation is a continuing threat. If so, how can Fiscal Policy help prevent what is probably more dangerous than the public seems to realize? We cannot answer for sure, except to say that government should seek for bigger surpluses, and smaller deficits, than would develop if the long-run threat did not exist. Such a mandate, obviously, is not a very precise guide for Congress, but it is nevertheless better than none.

Pragmatic stabilization. Fiscal Policy is a tool of economic control, to be used sometimes to expand employment, sometimes to check inflation. Unlike many other factors that tend to force our economy into inflation or depression, fiscal procedures can be controlled by responsible national leaders acting deliberately for the public interest. They can be used to counter the noncontrollable factors. If some development triggers a recession, a counteracting expansive fiscal policy can be set in operation. If an inflationary swing begins, a contractive fiscal policy can check or mitigate it.

Wise action requires attention not only to the big aggregates but also to the many elements that combine into each. "Disaggregation"—the analysis of, for example, the major elements of the total aggregate of investment or consumption—will reveal both uniformities and differences in trends. It is only a pragmatic approach that will permit reasonable adaptation of policy to the realities of a varied economy.

Fiscal Policy so employed cannot be embodied in any formula for long-term application. It is a matter of constant adjustment and readjustment to changing circumstances.

Economic growth. Our long-range economic growth can certainly be influenced by the ways our governments spend and raise the stupendous amounts now involved in American public finance. Chapter 3 indicated several classes of government spending that have strategic effects on economic growth. In general, the more spent for such purposes as education, research, transportation facilities, a high quality legal system, and development of natural resources, the broader is the foundation laid for long-range economic growth—provided such expenditure is not financed by taxes that undermine the future. "Developmental" expenditures have had a large place in past government budgets, and there is every reason to believe that they will continue to do so.

The relation of taxes to economic growth is harder to identify clearly than the role of spending. A tax that checks creative private investment, either by reducing savings that would otherwise be available, or by reducing the incentive to invest through reducing the prospect of "take-home" returns from investment, damps economic growth. We must always be trying to discover and then to minimize the use of forms of taxation having such adverse effects.

Government borrowing that absorbs funds which would otherwise be used for private investment tends to hold back economic expansion—unless the government use of funds is more productive.

Still another possible Fiscal Policy goal is stimulation of efficiency in the use of our economic resources. The amount an economy produces depends not only upon the resources available and the completeness with which they are used, but also upon the relative efficiency with which they are used. A small relative difference in efficiency in use of resources may be more important in terms of national real income than an extra million or so of employment. Government spending and taxation should be planned to avoid distortions of desirable balance in the utilization of productive resources. Possibly, though this is more difficult, Fiscal Policy may upon occasion be directed at correcting maladjustments by the private economy, or at stimulating more efficient resource allocation. Competition is one instrument for stimulating efficiency. The Employment Act specifies that employment policy shall "foster and promote free competitive enterprise."

Finally, American Fiscal Policy may sometime have to be directed at a goal that heretofore has not been important to this country, though it has been vital for others—keeping the domestic economy in balance with those of other countries to prevent unfavorable developments in the international financial situation.

Conflicts in objectives. These objectives may sometimes conflict with each other. Tax policies that tend to reduce saving may stimulate immediate consumption and employment, but check long-run growth. Increased taxes to provide funds for construction of capital improvements may contribute to long-range growth at the expense of current consumption.

Since World War II, three other possible conflicts of Fiscal Policy objectives have become obvious: (1) The most serious has already been mentioned. As an economy approaches full employment, it must choose between the alternatives of some avoidable unemployment and of inflationary pressure on prices, wages, and costs. Should Fiscal Policy be directed toward full employment with inflation, or should it be directed toward checking inflation and thereby maintain some unemployment? (2) Full employment tends to reduce the efficiency of labor. The spur of economic necessity is blunted. Any Fiscal Policy directed at maintaining true full employment over an extended period would, besides stimulating inflation, cause some lowering of general economic efficiency.

(3) Some Fiscal Policy programs might lead to an expansion of governmental controls, with a threat to economic and social freedoms.

Furthermore, Fiscal Policy goals often clash with other governmental objectives. Reducing public debt relieves the taxpayers of an interest burden; but Fiscal Policy directed toward economic expansion may require government spending financed by borrowing. In a period of inflation, a contractive Fiscal Policy might be achieved by the imposition of a heavy general sales tax to provide a surplus for debt retirement; the added burden on the lower income groups, however, might be condemned as unfair. Freeing capital gains from income taxation, applying a special low rate to dividend and bond interest income, or allowing a five-year exemption to business profits attributable to new capital properties, would stimulate investment, but might seem to favor some taxpayers unduly.

Such conflicts of objectives are not, of themselves, categorical bars to deliberate use of Fiscal Policy. They indicate merely that goals are to be achieved at a price—not a price in dollars and cents only, but one measured by the sacrifice of various other objectives. The goal must be weighed against its cost. Sometimes a particular goal will be well worth the price; in other cases the sacrifice in alternatives may be too great to be warranted.

CONDITIONS FOR EFFECTIVE USE

The practical problems in wise use of Fiscal Policy are substantial. Assuming that goals have been agreed upon, let us look at four prerequisites of success: (1) accurate economic forecasting, (2) legislative, administrative, and popular understanding, (3) administrative discretion on timing, and (4) coordination with other economic control policies.

Economic forecasting. In the depression-ridden 1930's, no acute economic forecasting was needed to guide Fiscal Policy. Large unemployment for at least several years seemed inevitable. Expansionary Fiscal Policy was called for and would continue to be needed indefinitely. Likewise, during the war no complex forecasting techniques were needed to establish the fact that inflationary forces were exceedingly powerful, and that Fiscal Policy should be contractive, more contractive than seemed politically possible.

Since the war, however, we have seen that responsible Fiscal Policy cannot be predicated on such all-out economic anticipation. The economy rises and falls, but we never know for certain what lies ahead. Changes, at least in their initial stages, are not likely to be of great magnitude or to be readily anticipated by simple forecasting procedures. Yet Fiscal Policy, to be most effective, should be applied at the early stages of any shift away from good economic balance, and in magnitudes commensurate with those involved in the shift. Too little correction of an adverse tendency means loss of an opportunity. Overcorrection may do more harm than good. Moreover, most elements of corrective Fiscal Policy cannot be put into operation, or discontinued, at short notice. Sometimes months of preparation are required. The success we can expect depends upon the accuracy with which we can forecast the direction of change, its momentum, and its size; and more—we must be able to predict the effects of any actions taken.

Since most practical problems arise over changes that are not large in relation to the entire economy, forecasting that is not far off in relation to a national total may be off 100 per cent or more in relation to the change involved. As of 1959 our economic forecasting techniques still leave much to be desired. Tremendous effort is going into improvement, however. More data needed for forecasting are becoming available. Improved methods of analysis are being developed. Still, no one can be certain that a formula useful in the past will be as accurate in the future. Men's actions are always somewhat unpredictable, and so the Fiscal Policy appropriate to the months ahead cannot be predicted with certainty.

Legislative, administrative, and popular understanding. Among the federal government's economists are some of the best in the country. They appreciate as fully as anyone can the possibilities and limitations of Fiscal Policy, and can advise top officials competently. Some members of the Congressional finance committees are keenly aware of the Fiscal Policy implications of measures under their consideration. To other members, however, the subject remains one of bewildering confusion. Many officials, in and out of Congress, are not so much confused as firm believers in obsolete notions; they tend to brush aside advice, especially if it is for unconventional or unpalatable policies. Fortunately, understanding of the more modern theory has grown. Yet the recession of 1957–1958 prompted a distressing amount of confused talk even in high circles. Views of men with access to the best advice and facts seemed to differ sharply, not only about the dimensions of the problem that called for solution but also upon the results to be expected from different kinds of policies, such as income tax reduction.

It is too much to hope for widespread popular comprehension of the complexities of Fiscal Policy. But leadership outside government can play a vital part. Nongovernmental economists, financial and business leaders, editors and commentators advise and press for action. The greater their competence, the better the chances that policy will be wise. Moreover, popular confidence in government policies *does* make a difference in the results. Some of the potential accomplishment of the federal "pump-priming" expenditures in the 1930's was canceled out by the mistrust with which the business world viewed this policy. In contrast, some of the success of the "savings" bond element of federal debt management during the 1940s, even in the postwar period when patriotic motivation subsided, rested on the confidence of the country's millions in their federal government. Popular confidence is not only a matter of economic knowledge—but also of general trust in the President, his advisors, and Congress. Part of their job is to explain their policies frankly but without creating alarm or complacency—difficult at best when public finance is involved and more so when issues of politics can be introduced so easily to confuse the layman.

Administrative discretion on timing. Successful Fiscal Policy requires good timing. To have maximum effect, fiscal action to check a business fluctuation that would develop cumulatively must be instituted promptly at the initial stages of the movement. Delay not only reduces the potential effectiveness but may result in more harm than good as the action exerts its full force late, aggravating a new "distortion" instead of offsetting the older one. Unfortunately for this purpose, Congressional procedures to authorize a particular action may involve months. In states with biennial legislatures, authorization may be delayed a year or longer from the time the need is first realized, unless the governor calls a special session.

Present law allows the executive some discretion on expenditure policy. As a countermove against inflation, the President could call for "economy," with slashes in departmental spending. The unspent appropriations would either lapse or go into some sort of reserve, presumably to be used later. Unfortunately, the possibilities of such flexible policy are very limited. A somewhat more promising policy would seem to be for Congress and state legislatures to vote maximum appropriations for certain items, with discretion given to the executive to use none, part, or all of such appropriations, and at such time as his judgment dictated. At best, however, the amounts involved would hardly be large enough to exert much force. Potentially greater opportunity lies in changing taxes. For example, some taxes could be voted with rate *ranges*, discretion being left to the President to set and change rates within such ranges.

There is little popular or legislative support for giving the executive branch of government broad discretion over spending and taxes. (British, Canadian, and some other Parliamentary systems permit far prompter action than is ordinarily possible in the United States.) Congress and the state legislatures prize their fiscal powers too highly to favor any broad relinquishment. But there is some precedent for giving limited fiscal discretion to the executive branch. The Treasury has long had almost untrammeled authority to borrow up to some over-all limit, and to exercise its judgment freely as to the forms and provisions of debt issues. Billion-dollar military expenditure authorizations are voted with the understanding that a substantial part may carry over to later years as part of a longer-range program. The President has discretionary power to raise or lower many tariff rates within a wide margin. Perhaps, then, Congress and state legislatures, educated to the possibilities of economic control through Fiscal Policy, may in time authorize tax changes and "contingent" expenditures to be made when, as, and if the executive so decides.

Coordination with other policies. Fiscal Policy is not the only instrument of government for influencing the level of employment and prices. Monetary Policy, in fact, may be equally or even more important. Economists for many years have debated the relative efficacy of the two and the reliance which ought to be placed on each. One very clear advantage of monetary action is that it can be taken more promptly and much more easily by Federal Reserve officials than can action that requires Congressional decision. However, monetary controls operate indirectly; as a rule, their effects appear only after a considerable lag. The Federal Reserve's powers are by no means close substitutes for fiscal action.

The success of fiscal and monetary stabilization policies will depend upon the general economic framework within which they must operate. Government has a good deal to do with this framework; but in a predominantly free economy, government does not actively participate in the great mass of decision-making. Government, therefore, is not in full control of all factors that bear significantly on what it seeks to accomplish. Since World War II we have seen that labor-union pressure for wage increases has, year in and year out, worked to raise prices. So have the pricing methods of some businesses in reacting to higher wage rates and to other cost increases. Economists are by no means certain about the true strength of such forces. But there can be no doubt that the kind of upward pressure on wage rates that we have seen for many years creates problems which our fiscal and monetary controls cannot meet—problems which involve the levels of both employment and prices. Public policy has for many years supported collective bargaining. Public policy has certainly not opposed the use of union power to boost employment costs more rapidly than productivity. Unless there is some change, however, we must recognize that full employment with stable prices is probably unattainable.

Of course, various kinds of direct government controls on prices and wages are conceivable. Yet there is overwhelming agreement that, except in most unusual circumstances, the potential advantages of such controls are slight compared with the disadvantages. On the contrary, stabilization as well as general economic efficiency are furthered by freedom, flexibility, and easy adjustability in the economy. Competition will help. The more effective antimonopoly policy, the more successful our society is in stimulating competition, the greater are the chances for success in getting full employment without an upward creep in prices. Competition restricts the opportunities for individual businesses, whole industries, and unions to raise their own prices and thereby contribute to a higher price level while tending to reduce the number of jobs. In any one year or two, a vigorous antimonopoly policy cannot make much difference in the achievement of stabilization goals. In a decade it will, and in a generation it may possibly have a decisive effect.

International trade policy can also strengthen or weaken Fiscal Policy.

The effects will depend largely upon the relative importance of imports and exports in the economy. In this country tariffs, quotas, exchange restrictions, and other government controls on international trade and finance have relatively less bearing upon internal stabilization than is the case in most lands.

ECONOMIC CONTROL THROUGH EXPENDITURE POLICY

We saw in Chapter 27 that an *increase* in government expenditure raises national income and exercises an expansive influence on the economy, provided, of course, that the means used to finance this extra spending do not have an offsetting, contractive effect. If normal government spending plus consumer and business spending is insufficient to buy the full-employment output of the economy, expanded government spending may fill the gap. A *decrease* in government spending has the opposite effect. The problem is how to accomplish increases when they are needed, in the magnitudes needed—and how to accomplish expenditure reductions when the time for them comes. A simple way to enlarge federal expenditure quickly would be to fly airplanes over the country dropping currency or federal "bearer" checks. In most cases the finders would spend these windfalls, and the effect would be similar to that accomplished by any expenditure program. But the public would gain nothing else, no schools, no defense, no post offices. Would it not be wiser, then, to seek additional benefits from the increases in government expenditures that are made primarily to stimulate business? As we now seek to answer this question, we must be mindful of the fact that for very good reasons most, but not all, spending provided in government budgets is highly inflexible from year to year.

Timing of regular expenditure. Gross federal spending is more than a fifth of the Gross National Product. Even a small change in this regular expenditure could be significant in relation to *changes* in national income. There is always a possibility of speeding up or slowing down spending that will be made in any case. In fact, some success has been achieved in attempting such short-run variations to offset postwar cyclical movements. The results, however, have not been impressive. The great mass of regular spending is determined by considerations that override the gains to be expected from changes in such spending to meet short-run stabilization needs.

Programmed public works. The first approach to stabilizing the economy through Fiscal Policy was the idea of long-range programming of public works, state as well as federal, in such a way that they would act as a "counterweight" to cyclical ups and downs. Public works construction would be held to a minimum in periods of boom. This in itself would reduce the upward pressure on prices and costs. Meanwhile, a backlog of projects, unbuilt but fully planned, would be established. It would consist not only of plans for new structures but also, within some limits, for maintenance of existing facilities. When recession came, this backlog would be drawn upon. Resources that would otherwise be idle would be employed in construction—a clear economic gain, since any offsetting sacrifice of desirable alternatives would be slight. Payments for these "counterweight" government construction projects would enter the economy with a multiplier effect.

We should distinguish sharply between a "counterweight" public works program and the "pump-priming" effort of the 1930's. In the latter, projects had to be devised on an emergency basis. Immediate direct labor employment in areas of major unemployment was the primary objective of many of these projects. As a consequence, many were of ephemeral character—leaf-raking and "boondoggling"—with only trifling longer-run value. "Counterweight" projects, in contrast, would be regular public works which the governments concerned would undertake *in any case* without regard to the effect on jobs and price levels. Projects would be definitely needed and wanted, but not immediately urgent, things which could be delayed a few years without major loss to the communities involved. The Fiscal Policy aspect of these "counterweight" projects would lie, not in the schools, prisons, hospitals, or military bases themselves, but in the *timing* of their construction.

The first requirement of a sound "counterweight" public works program would be that the projects should be authorized and fully planned in advance.[3] If the period were one of inflation, these plans would be laid "on the shelf." This does not mean they could be ignored for years, then abruptly hauled out and used as originally formulated. Conditions that entered the initial planning would often change over even relatively short periods. Periodically—semiannually or annually—all plans held in reserve would have to be brought up to date. Planning for six years ahead is now a part of normal federal operations. States and cities, too, do more advance planning than before World War II.

A second requirement is the integration of federal with state-local planning. Much of the more important government construction is normally done by states and localities. Their cooperation can help greatly. One way to get such cooperation is to arrange some federal financial help for construction projects that are timed to fit national economic needs.

A third requirement would be the creation of some agency to study economic trends and to give the go-ahead signal for "counterweight" projects to be undertaken at the right time and in appropriate areas of the country.

[3] An indication of the importance of advance authorization and planning is the fact that it took five years for the President to approve all housing units authorized by Congress in 1937. For more extensive discussion see *Policies to Combat Depressions* (Princeton University Press for the National Bureau of Economic Research, Princeton, 1956).

The present Council of Economic Advisors might be given this responsibility.

Unfortunately, there are serious limitations to "counterweight" timing of public construction. They apply, in general, with more force to big projects than to modernization, repair, and maintenance of existing facilities.

(1) Public works differ significantly from the general average of private construction as to types of labor and materials employed. Building of superhighways would take up practically none of the slack created by a slump in consumer-goods industries; it would provide little direct compensation for a decline in house construction. Starting "counterweight" projects would introduce a general expansive force offsetting a general contraction, but the particular impact of these projects might be upon sectors quite different from those with the most serious recession. A "counterweight" public works program cannot directly offset slumps in particular lines—in textiles and apparel, home appliances, or autos. It can help them only indirectly by stimulating construction and the industries that are related to it as suppliers.

(2) The territorial areas where "counterweight" construction projects would be undertaken might not be those where unemployment was developing. Starting work on irrigation projects in the Mountain states would not directly relieve industrial unemployment in the Eastern states resulting from a contraction of dealers' inventories of consumer goods. Again, although there would be a favorable general expansive effect, there would be no solution of specific local unemployment problems.

(3) Even with advance authorization and planning, there might be long delays before public construction contracts could be awarded, condemnation of private property concluded, and construction expenditure started.[4] This reality reduces the value of "counterweight" project programming for dealing with minor fluctuations, since a project started in a short recession might get into full operation only as later expansion develops into a boom.

(4) A major project once started can rarely be stopped before completion without great waste, even though the economy may have started to boom. Spending on such a project might have to continue into a time when it would add to inflationary pressures and use resources better employed elsewhere. Political considerations, too, might make it difficult to end "counterweight" spending after the true economic need had passed.

(5) A final difficulty is that increasing public works construction during a recession tends to hold up wage rates and materials costs when they might otherwise decline. As a result, some private construction that might otherwise have been undertaken may be discouraged by the continued high levels of wages and costs. This, of course, would be an offset to the stimulating effect of the public works construction.

The limitations restrict the potentialities of "counterweight" planning. It could not be used for delicate, timely adjustments of the economy, except

[4] One study found that on the average only one-third of the federal public works spending was accomplished within a year of being started, and for some programs, notably reclamation, a significant part of the spending was not done until the third year. Some economists have made this lag in public works spending the basis for arguing that "counterweight" programming of such works would be more likely to exaggerate than to reduce business fluctuations.

for construction projects that could be completed in a year or less. Quite another matter is the possibility of holding construction plans in reserve against serious recessions that give marked indications of being protracted. Increases of government spending through "programmed" public works of some $4 billion a year or $8 billion over 18 months are practicable, and under some conditions could be definitely beneficial. Such amounts may not seem large in relation to national income, but they and their multiplier effects would be significant in relation to likely short-term *changes* in national income. They could exercise *strategic* expansive effects on the national economy. Postponements waiting for a boom to pass, although difficult, are always possible within some limits.

The speeding up, or slowing down, of work in process offers a little room for flexibility. The new highway program could be modified to provide greater anticyclical effect than is now scheduled.

In a serious depression, relief needs may outrun substantially the provision of the regular unemployment insurance and home-relief programs. Humane considerations dictate that the unemployed should not suffer severe destitution. States and localities are now responsible, wholly or partially, for such relief, but if the need outruns the financial capacities of state and local governments, as in the 1930's, the federal government could assist. It might enlarge the fraction of the grants regularly made for four categories of aid, and it might make special grants for general assistance. Conceivably, but not probably, the federal government might find it wise to institute some specific work-relief programs of its own.

Emergency relief expenditures in times of depression should be financed, not out of current tax revenues but by funds borrowed from banks.[5] Then the expenditure can do more than meet a humane need. It can really stimulate business. New purchasing power is injected into the economy. The federal government, far more than states and localities, has access to the money-creating system.

Three aspects of special relief expenditure add to its potential Fiscal Policy merit: (1) Some basic machinery for administering relief exists already in that established for the handling of regular local and state relief. (2) There is now little time lag in putting a special relief program into effect, once the appropriations are made. (3) As the economy recovers and the need for stimulation subsides, the social need for the special relief declines. Tapering off is decidedly easier than it is for construction.

Automatically stabilizing expenditure. The difficulties of timing specific expenditure changes properly, plus the difficulties of locating them to offset efficiently the differing degrees of recession in particular industries and territories, do not apply to all government expenditures. Some types automatically expand when and where employment and business activity de-

[5] Currency issue would involve no interest cost and be even more stimulating to the economy than borrowing from banks. Retirement of currency during a later period when the price level was moving upward would afford an anti-inflationary weapon.

cline, and automatically contract when the economy expands. No special legislative or executive action is required to make such automatically stabilizing expenditures sensitive and effective instruments.

In postwar recessions, unemployment benefit payments have been extremely important in preventing not only family want but also the cumulative economic spiralling downward that used to work such havoc. In September, 1957, such benefits totalled $113 million; 7 months later they were $404 million. The larger the scale of payment, and the longer the duration of benefits, the greater the anticyclical effect—and the cost. State and local relief grants, and in some cases farm benefit payments, also have some automatic countercyclical variation. Moreover, an increasing number of people at work have rights to OASI benefits. If they lose their jobs, they can quickly get a welcome source of income which involves no increased taxes on others.

The very stability of most government spending helps put a high floor under national income. The mass of federal, state, and local spending remains relatively fixed. It is a significant fraction of all spending for goods and services. Here, then, is a big part of the economy which is largely immune to the forces that cause other parts to rise and fall; this is also a section of the economy which is relatively immune to the effects of monetary policy. Yet at times *changes* in defense spending have been large enough to make an appreciable difference in national income.[6]

ECONOMIC CONTROL THROUGH TAXATION

Tax changes influence the level of national income in three ways. Let us review the major points of the analysis.

(1) Consumption spending can be stimulated by (a) repealing or reducing taxes that absorb disposable income, the change thus leaving families and individuals with more money to spend; (b) cutting taxes that discourage personal spending more than they discourage saving; (c) imposing or increasing taxes that discourage saving more than they discourage spending. The reverse of these three types of tax action would repress consumption spending. For practical purposes, the taxes that affect consumption most are the mass levies—the first bracket income tax, the payroll tax, broadly-based excises. Raise these to cut consumption, reduce them to raise it.

[6] Are huge military outlays necessary for continued prosperity? Most emphatically not! A drastic reduction in defense spending would, of course, greatly disturb some areas and industries. However, tax reduction could be large enough to permit maintenance of a level of aggregate demand which would help speed the conversion of industry and the shifting of employment so that necessary readjustments could be made with a minimum of serious disturbance. Then we could also keep taxes low enough so that the public could buy the full output of the economy working at full employment at a level of prices involving neither inflation nor deflation.

(2) A tax change that stimulates investment to a greater extent than it does the saving to finance such investment tends to raise national income.[7] One which discourages investment more than it does saving is likely to be contractive. Tax action to stimulate investment, relative to saving, would take the form of cutting taxes that reduce the prospects of net or "take-home" yield from projected investments. Imposing or increasing such taxes would discourage investment relative to saving.

(3) Looking to the longer run, tax changes that lead to increased investment promote long-range economic growth. Tax changes that tend to reduce investment check such economic growth. The tax effect on investment may be direct; it may also be indirect, working through the quantity of saving.

Other things the same, any sizable tax cut of whatever kind will increase consumption, investment, and saving. There will be some stimulus to business—perhaps a great deal, relative to the size of the tax reduction, perhaps rather little. Tax increases, on the other hand, will cut consumption, investment, and income—but in amounts and proportions no one can know for certain.

There is a major difficulty in the way of using specific tax changes, or general changes in the tax level, as instruments for controlling the economy in the short run. Considerable time must generally elapse between the recognition of an economic trend that might be countered by tax measures and the actual effectiveness of a tax change. Congressional deliberations take time. Months must usually pass between the time a tax measure is proposed and its final passage—if it is passed. Many groups press their own special interests, and the inevitable logrolling can delay action week after week, and distort the final outcome. If a new tax is involved, more months may be necessary to set up the administrative machinery. By the time the added tax collections start coming in, or the effect of a reduction is felt by the taxpayers, the economic trend may have changed. Yet prompt action *is* possible. In 1940 and 1950, for example, Congress did act quickly to raise taxes. Personal income tax withholding rates could be changed on short notice, influencing the stream of disposable income within a few weeks of Congressional action. However, temporary tax changes have a way of becoming permanent, and responsible officials may oppose what they believe good for the near future because it would be bad in the long run. One possible temporary measure would be to accelerate or postpone tax payment, chiefly by altering withholding rates.

Still, if a protracted depression or inflationary period is foreseen, tax action with Fiscal Policy objectives ought to be undertaken in spite of possible delays. Fortunately, there are other possibilities that will avoid stultifying delay—(1) "building into" the system taxes whose effect is auto-

[7] One stimulant of investment is an increase in consumer demand. Some economists argue that the tax changes most likely to lead to changes in investment are those that stimulate or depress consumption.

matically stabilizing, levies we now discuss, plus three other possibilities: (2) administrative tax rate discretion, (3) formula tax rate flexibility, and (4) special economic control taxes.

Automatically stabilizing taxes. The collections of certain taxes rise and fall automatically in response to economic fluctuations in such a way as to exercise an exceptionally valuable stabilizing influence on the economy. As business booms, tax collections are high. As business droops, tax collections sag. Yet more is involved. Tax collections change *more than proportionately* with income. A 5 per cent change in national income leads to considerably more than a 5 per cent change in tax receipts, that is, in the amount government withdraws from the income stream. This tax response helps to correct unfavorable developments before they generate much momentum.[8] (1) The yield of the personal income tax rises and falls with economic fluctuations, and in amounts proportionately greater than the fluctuations themselves. Roughly, a 1 per cent change in personal income produces nearly 2 per cent change in personal income tax liability. Collection-at-source plus quarterly declarations assure a close connection between any change in national income and personal income tax collections. (2) Corporation income tax yields are also highly "flexible." More than half of a change in profit is offset by a change in tax. Moreover, corporation income tax payments have been put on a more nearly current basis; consequently, the timing of tax payments conforms moderately well with what is effective for general economic stabilization. (3) The operation of the loss carry-back provisions under both the personal and corporation income taxes actually makes the burden of federal income taxation on unprofitable businesses *negative* as business recedes—that is, some firms obtain refunds of prior-year tax payments. (4) Excise and payroll tax collections also rise and fall, though not with swings as wide in relation to business change as income taxes.

State and local taxes score poorly as built-in stabilizers. Collections of sales taxes of various kinds do fluctuate, though generally less than income. Property taxes respond little, and unemployment payroll taxes tend to be slightly destabilizing because of experience rating. The relatively small state use of income taxes means that their maximum contribution to stabilization is tiny.

Administrative tax rate discretion. Is there not some way to overcome the delay and the uncertainty of Congressional action on taxes? One possibility is the surrender to the President of a limited power over certain tax rates, subject perhaps to the approval of an appropriate Congressional group. He could be delegated the authority, for example, to raise or lower all statutory bracket rates of the personal income tax by as much as five points, or the total tax payable by perhaps one-tenth, whenever he deemed

[8] There is, however, a seasonally destabilizing element—the bunching of income tax collections during the first half of the calendar year. Monetary policy is only partly successful in counteracting the economic disturbance that results.

that the economic situation warranted such action. The dollar effects of such rate changes could be very large in relation to ordinary fluctuations in national income, big enough to have a powerful corrective effect if the right action were taken at the right time. Any uniform change of all bracket rates would have the greatest proportional effect upon individuals with low-bracket incomes who account for the mass of the country's disposable income. Such administrative rate changes would affect personal income tax collections immediately through payroll deductions and estimated tax amendments.[9]

Should a federal retail sales tax or general manufacturers excise ever be enacted, a similar executive discretion over rates might be incorporated. However, power to change specific excise taxes would raise special problems. An expectation of administrative change would of itself lead to postponement of buying if a reduction were likely, thus further depressing the economy. Expectation of a rise would prompt anticipatory buying and accentuate a boom.

Formula tax rate flexibility. Another approach to countercyclical tax rate flexibility would be for Congress to establish specific rate increases and decreases for income and other taxes, to become effective when particular price, employment, or output indexes rose or fell to certain levels. The rate levels of major federal taxes could thus be utilized as instruments of economic stabilization, without Congress sacrificing any of its legislative control over tax determination.

The crucial weakness of such a plan would be its mechanical character. We do not know enough yet about the causes and cures of economic fluctuations to construct hard and fast formulae for their treatment. Probably in most cases such arbitrary formula modifications of tax rates would do more good than harm, but there would always be the danger that in any particular instance the harm might outweigh the good. Moreover, any tax rate control formula, no matter how sound at the time of its adoption, would tend to become less appropriate with the passage of time, and so increase the possibility that harm would outweigh good. Yet, once adopted, such a formula would acquire a statutory inertia which would militate against frequent desirable modification.

Possibly in the range of compromise between administrative tax rate discretion and formula tax rate flexibility, there may be some procedures that would meet the tests of both political expediency and current economic practicability.

"Control" taxes and tax features. Many unusual tax proposals have been advanced for dealing with depression and inflation—a money-and-deposits tax, a tax on savings, or an undistributed profits tax to stimulate business.

[9] The difficulty of calculating final tax liability for a year in which different rates applied for different periods could be met by a provision for averaging the rates on the final return, regardless of when the income was received through the year.

To check inflation, a tax on expenditures is suggested—a sort of income tax allowing deduction of amounts saved but including spending paid for out of past savings, inheritances, or capital gains. Except possibly for the undistributed profits tax, each poses difficult administrative problems. Yet if such taxes could be administered well, they might at times help produce a better level of economic activity. Under modern conditions, however, there are superior means of accomplishing whatever national income benefits these would achieve. Still, if serious inflation were to threaten, an expenditure tax would deserve serious consideration. The great merit is that it could have strong contractive effects, since it would not only absorb income otherwise spent but also stimulate saving.

Particular features of existing taxes may be useful instruments for controlling the economy primarily on a long-run basis. For example, merit rating in the state unemployment insurance payroll taxes on employers—rate reductions based on low rates of unemployment—induces employers to stabilize employment, but may force higher tax payments in the worst of a recession. Low-rate treatment of capital gains under income taxation stimulates investment in "venture" enterprises. Increased depreciation allowances for plant and equipment under income taxes would stimulate faster replacement of old equipment by new. Temporary changes in the rates of depreciation deductible may hasten or delay purchase of new capital goods.[10] As economists come to learn more about economic growth, other tax measures designed specifically to stimulate such expansion may be devised.

ECONOMIC CONTROL THROUGH DEBT POLICY

It is an oversimplification, but not fundamentally wrong, to assert that it is the *deficit* or *surplus* that "does the trick." It is the deficit that injects money into the economy to stimulate consumption and investment. And what will withdraw purchasing power to restrain an inflation? A surplus! Yet the effectiveness of either the deficit or the surplus depends in part upon the way it is financed. Moreover, the Treasury can influence the economy by the way it manages an outstanding debt of any given amount.

The opportunity, in essence, is to shift between debt with a low degree of "moneyness"—long-term obligations of the kind purchased with real savings by individuals and financial institutions—and debt which is nearly money—the issues sold to commercial banks or the Federal Reserve.[11] To

[10] Numerous proposals undoubtedly deserve serious attention. One, for example, would offer corporations inducements to save and purchase a special government debt issue during periods of high employment and then redeem the security and use the proceeds to finance new investment in real goods during recession. See J. P. Shelton, "A Tax Incentive for Stabilizing Business Investment," *National Tax Journal*, Sept., 1956, 232–246.

[11] Substitution of currency for debt and its opposite would be even more powerful, as noted in Chapter 27.

help check inflation, the Treasury would sell more long-term debt and use the proceeds to pay off debt held by commercial and Federal Reserve banks. To stimulate the economy, the Treasury would increase its borrowings from the banking system and repay life insurance companies and private savers. Such a debt management policy might be considered as an element of monetary policy—the terminology is not important. What *is* important is the fact that the debt *must* be managed and that the methods used will affect the availability of money throughout the economy and the public's general liquidity position—and thereby spending and the price level.

Valuable results can reasonably be expected from debt management geared to stabilization needs. Here again, however, we have no certain way to measure what any given action will do. The policy would not be costless. It would require the Treasury to do more refunding into long-term issues than it might otherwise do during the boom when interest rates would be high—and forego the opportunity to refund into long-term issues when interest rates are low during a slump.

STATE AND LOCAL GOVERNMENT POLICY

Neither states nor localities are responsible for the national economy. Yet they account for enough government activity so that changes in what they do can influence the level of national income. The national public, therefore, has an interest in encouraging state-local actions that will help stabilize, and certainly not destabilize, the economy. Moreover, the states and localities themselves have an interest in managing their own finances to meet the needs of economic fluctuations. If the states do what is in their own longer-run interest, they will thereby contribute to over-all economic stabilization.[12]

State-local revenues fall off during recession, while spending needs rise. During a boom, when revenues are relatively high, projects are undertaken which are less desirable than the spending programs, or tax relief, which must be foregone during bad times. A better average result would be obtained by some form of accumulation during high prosperity to help finance spending or tax reduction when business is poor.

One possibility is to accumulate tax reserves. Tax rates would be set high enough to meet expected requirements when business is "normal." If business is better, a revenue surplus will appear. It can go into the bank to be used to cover the deficit when a recession appears. The accumulation is a form of saving which will help restrain the economy; the dissaving later will help stimulate business. The advantages to the state or locality

[12] For a concise discussion with nine concrete proposals, see E. A. Myers and R. S. Stout, "The Role of the States and Local Governments in National Fiscal Policy," *National Tax Journal*, June, 1957, pp. 171–175.

of more stabilized spending would be great enough to justify the sacrifices involved in a modest plan.

A practical modification would be to use the accumulations to retire debt more rapidly than scheduled and then cut down, or stop temporarily, debt retirement during recession. With few exceptions, states and localities could not undertake such flexible debt programs without many changes in their laws—even in their constitutions—and certainly in attitudes. The experience during the 1957–1958 recession should prove to many governments that recessions *can* occur, despite the determination of the federal government to prevent serious depression, and that reserves can fill a great need. The practical difficulties of accumulating surplus tax revenues, however, are formidable. Insistent, short-run pressures on states and localities to spend and to keep taxes low will remain so great that building reserves is almost politically impossible. Conceivably, federal leadership for a new kind of state-local program would be possible.

EFFECTIVENESS OF BUILT-IN STABILIZERS

By accident much more than by design, this country, along with other more developed lands, has built into its system of public finances powerful stabilizers which operate automatically. When the stabilizing effects of expenditures and revenues, discussed above, are added, they now offset around 40 per cent of a change in national income. The consequence is that the normal forces of cumulation are greatly reduced. The tendency of a business expansion or contraction to feed on itself is significantly smaller than it would otherwise be. The mildness of fluctuations since World War II has been due, to considerable extent, to the offsetting forces of automatic stabilizers.

Can these built-in stabilizers, when reinforced by monetary controls, now meet our needs? For over a decade this has been debated among economists. The debate is not about whether we are now immune to undesirable fluctuations, for no one believes that we are. Moreover, most economists will agree that the long-run price and employment outlook is by no means ideal. But there is a real issue on which opinions differ—the extent to which we should look beyond automatic stabilizers. Putting the problem differently, can we expect deliberate, discretionary—often called compensatory—Fiscal Policy actions to be beneficial on balance? Clearly, surpluses or deficits produced to compensate for expected unbalance in the economy, *can*, when superimposed on automatic offsets buttressed by Monetary Policy, be excessive at the time they actually exert their force. If so, they may do more harm than good. The risks of just this outcome are too real to be ignored. Just as clearly, however, there is a potential for good in fiscal actions beyond those from automatic stabilizers. When built-in stabilizers have done their job, and when the monetary authorities have done their best, there will be opportunities more than once every decade to adjust public finances deliberately to help stimulate or restrain business.

CRITIQUE

The art of using Fiscal Policy to help control the level of national income is still in its childhood. Only within the present generation have economists formulated the basic principles. There are still areas of dispute in the theoretical foundation, and a tremendous task of verification, refinement, and keeping up to date lies ahead. We lack much of the statistical data needed for continuous economic diagnosis and prognosis, and for determining the magnitudes of the effects of the Fiscal Policy instruments at our command. We are much like a nineteenth-century physician without thermometer, stethoscope, or X-rays of his patient and with a kit of drugs whose characteristics are partly known but whose potencies are uncertain.

We do, however, have enough knowledge to avoid major errors of expenditure, tax, and debt policy. This is no small advantage. Should the occasion ever again arise, we will know better than to finance "recovery" expenditure by increasing taxes, as was done in the 1930's. It was a real achievement of Fiscal Policy in the 1940's that "savings" bonds were not made usable as collateral for bank loans, and that no "borrow and buy" slogan was used in the war bond drives, as during World War I—even though the favorable consequences of this achievement were largely tossed away during the postwar years by a debt management policy that needlessly promoted inflation.

In addition, we know enough to apply Fiscal Policy positively against serious recessions. We will not—or ought not to—hesitate either (a) to spend billions for recovery or (b) reduce taxes by billions, and to finance the deficits by selling debt to banks, should we ever find ourselves in another deep depression like that of the 1930's. On the matter of combating inflation through Fiscal Policy, we are more hesitant. Throughout the inflation since the 1940's we have been reluctant to raise taxes and reduce spending to produce budgetary surpluses that would be adequate to restrain the forces which have caused prices to rise. We still do not know whether such a policy could succeed without creating more unemployment than is desirable and tolerable.

It cannot be too strongly emphasized that Fiscal Policy should not be implemented exclusively through spending, or taxing, or debt management. All three should be coordinated. This is not to say that every particular objective should involve simultaneous use of particular spending, tax, and debt measures, although there are many situations that would warrant combined utilization of all three instruments of Fiscal Policy. Differing secondary effects may at times dictate the choice of one, rather than another fiscal device, to accomplish general economic objectives. For example, increased government spending, and tax reduction, both have general expansive effects. Spending has the advantage of producing hospitals, schools, highways, and other capital construction of a public nature that may be sharply needed. Tax reduction has the advantage of leaving individuals free to choose for themselves how the released purchasing power shall be applied. This freedom may channel such purchasing power into better patterns than could the government spending. More important today than before Korea, tax reduction may ease unfavorable distortions of the economy produced by high-level taxes and stimulate individual and business incentives. Nor can we ignore the varying time lags before various fiscal measures can begin to exercise control effects on the economy.

The federal fiscal picture at any time is also a factor in determining which instruments should be used to achieve a particular economic effect. If federal spending and taxes were both relatively low in relation to national income—as in the 1930's—economic expansion could be more readily stimulated by expenditure increases, and economic contraction by tax increases. With spending and taxes both as high as they are today, the more attractive Fiscal Policy approach to expansion would be tax reduction. To check inflation, on the other hand, expenditure cuts would be preferred to tax increases, except for the tremendous difficulty of making sizable reductions in the absence of betterment in international relations. Debt management, however, can help materially in preventing inflation by reinforcing monetary controls—if we will pay the price.

Major responsibility will rest upon the federal government, partly because its operations so dominate the fiscal picture, partly because it is one entity, not dozens or hundreds, and partly because it has access to, and responsibility for, the monetary mechanism. Still, there could be more collaboration by state and local governments, particularly in the matter of timing "counterweight" public works and perhaps incorporating more automatically stabilizing elements in their expenditure and tax systems.

More accurate diagnoses and prognoses of economic activity than we now have will be available. There will also be more accurate determinations of the quantitative effects of various fiscal policies. Then, if an analysis indicates that national income during a coming year threatens to run, let us say, some $25 billion short of the figure needed for full employment at a desired level of prices, immediate action can be taken to start spending on several billion dollars of public works, already planned, state and local as well as federal. At the same time, if the President has received discretionary authorization on certain tax rates, the income tax rate may be lowered by several points. The Treasury will discontinue for a time current sales of "savings" bonds. It might even start a campaign for "savings" bondholders to redeem their bonds and spend the proceeds. Debt issues will be sold to the commercial and Federal Reserve banks—or currency issued—as needed to cover these "savings" bond redemptions and any deficit. The magnitudes of these various operations will take into account Multiplier and savings-investment effects making for cumulative or self-correcting change, in the light of the fuller knowledge that should then be available on these subjects. As events develop, other expansive fiscal steps may have to be taken. Or extraneous factors may cause the economic tide to change, and Fiscal Policy will be shifted to one of contraction to head off inflation.

Such a picture may seem to fall in the range of fantasy. Still, it is not outside the possibilities foreshadowed by our current understanding of the subject. But more than an advanced *understanding* of economic factors and control techniques will be needed to insure that the powers will always be used to advance the *national* interest. Fiscal policy is a political instrument, and as such can be perverted to group interests. Labor, farm blocs, and business groups all tend to be short-sighted where issues of economic expansion and contraction are concerned. At a given period a contraction involving some shrinkage of "over-full" employment and "boom" prices may be desirable. Are the political representatives of labor, farmers, and business, however, likely to countenance government action that will produce such a shrinkage? Will not willful pursuit by group interests of superficial group benefits cause Fiscal Policy to be used as a one-way instrument of never-ending inflation? That is a real danger, unless those in control can combine a broad disinterested statesmanship with technical understanding of the complicated economic factors involved.

PROBLEMS

1. Why is it difficult to maintain full employment without a rising price level?

2. Find examples of predictions of national income. Evaluate them and judge what would have happened if government had used them in tax, spending, and debt management policies.

3. What would be the advantages and disadvantages of giving a few leaders of government power to change taxes to influence the level of national income?

4. What are the merits and weaknesses of automatic stabilizers?

5. There is now less optimism about timing public works to stabilize business than in the past. Why?

6. What are the relative merits of reducing expenditures or raising taxes to curb inflation? Be specific.

7. Outline a program for using Fiscal Policy to offset a moderate recession and a serious inflation. What part may debt management play?

8. Why is it said that Fiscal Policy can work *directly* on the income stream, whereas Monetary Policy works indirectly? What is the tie between the two?

APPENDIX

History of Public Finance

Public Finance in antiquity. Archeological studies indicate that, besides the Egyptian, several of the early east Mediterranean, Mesopotamian, and Indian civilizations achieved a high degree of political integration. In marked contrast with the revenue policy of modern states, the fiscal systems of these early civilizations depended heavily upon tribute from conquered peoples and slave labor employed by the State. Nonetheless, the ancient governments developed broad systems of indirect taxation, whose major elements were charges on land transfers and on commercial transactions. Imperial Rome levied an inheritance tax and a general sales tax.

Writings and treatises from the Roman and Greek civilizations have survived to modern times, but the written word of older civilizations has, with a few fragmentary exceptions, perished. From the Greek era there is left a short treatise, the *Athenian Revenues*, by Xenophon; incidental comments on fiscal matters are found in the writings of Plato and Aristotle. Analysis and criticism of Roman fiscal systems are encountered frequently in the writings of the Roman historians and commentators.

Public Finance prior to Adam Smith. When Imperial Rome collapsed, western Europe entered upon a period of political anarchy which eventually crystallized into the semigovernmental order known as the feudal system. Exchange of services and payments in kind to the nobility and the Church in effect paid for what government there was; custom fixed the terms. From the eleventh century onward, a group of commercial cities grew and flourished in Italy and northern Europe. In time, they gained political independence from the feudal lords under whose protection they were first established, and became true city-states. Their government activities and their revenue requirements were extensive. Treatises on Public Finance were written in several of these Italian and north European city-states; the most notable were written at the close of the fifteenth century by the Florentine historian Guicciardini and the Neapolitan councilor Diomede Carafa.

Fiscal problems of increasing magnitude were placed before the thinkers of Europe with the establishment of national states in western Europe and the growth of principalities and kingdoms in central Europe. Jean Bodin, the French writer, examined the sources of public revenue in his study on political science, *Six livres sur la république*, published in 1576. Mercantilist disputation in seventeenth-century England stimulated a flood of controversial literature upon the effects of excise taxes. The outstanding work was *A Treatise of Taxes and Con-*

tributions (1662) by Sir William Petty. To this period also belong the fiscal writings of John Locke, William Temple, and Charles Davenant.

During the eighteenth century significant contributions to the study of Public Finance were made in France, in Germany, in Austria, and in England. Vauban's *Projet de dîme royale,* a criticism of the French system of indirect taxes, which appeared in 1707, was an important French contribution. Boisguillebert, writing in the same year, and Montesquieu in his *L'Esprit des lois* (1748) also gave close attention to the tax system of the French monarchy. The Physiocrats Quesnay, Mirabeau, and Turgot, prominent in the second half of the century, proposed a single tax on land to replace all existing indirect taxes, which, they believed, were in all cases shifted to the landowners.

Eighteenth-century German writers on Public Finance were chamberlains and ministers of the reigning petty kings and princelings of central Europe. Their major interest was the practical technique of raising revenue for their royal masters; they dealt with the problems of Public Finance essentially from the position of the official and administrator. Their viewpoint having been that of the royal chamber, they have been given the group name "Cameralists." Von Justi, author of *Staatswirtschaft* (1775) and *System des Finanzwesens* (1776), is representative of the group.

To the English writers of the eighteenth century, Public Finance was incidental to the broader subject of Mercantilism. Sir James Steuart's *Principles of Political Economy* (1767) is the outstanding example.

Adam Smith and the English school. Adam Smith's *The Wealth of Nations,* published in 1776, was a broadside attack on the accepted doctrine of Mercantilism rather than a general textbook exposition of the principles of Economics. Book V of *The Wealth of Nations* was devoted to questions of taxation, but it was not to be expected that Adam Smith should present a full and well-rounded study of all phases of Public Finance. Nonetheless, such was its broad scholarship and keenness of argument that both in England and on the Continent it became the foundation for subsequent study on Public Finance. *The Wealth of Nations* put emphasis upon the role of principles of equity in the distribution of tax burdens. Smith also stressed the relationship between Public Finance and Economics, and made frequent reference to the economic effects of particular taxes, but he developed no broad theories of incidence.

English economists after Adam Smith devoted occasional attention to the problems and principles of Public Finance. First of a series of studies in this field was David Ricardo's *The Principles of Political Economy* (1817). To the extent that it dealt with problems of taxation, Ricardo's work complemented *The Wealth of Nations,* since it developed the field of tax shifting and incidence. Subsequent English writers in this field were not numerous, but a distinguished line may be traced through McCulloch and J. S. Mill to C. F. Bastable and A. C. Pigou. They continued essentially within the tradition established by Smith and Ricardo, occupied themselves with the theories of proper distribution and incidence of taxes, condemned the use of the taxing power (through tariffs) or subsidies to favor special groups, and gave little attention to the history of taxation or to its social or administrative aspects. During the last thirty years of the nineteenth century, several writers turned their attention to the special problems of local finance, and enriched fiscal literature with valuable studies on this subject. The more recent developments of British fiscal thinking and practice are covered in *Public Finance* (1947) by U. K. Hicks.

Public Finance on the Continent. Nineteenth-century French writers were interested in the theoretical aspects of Public Finance. P. Leroy Beaulieu's great treatise, *Traité de la science des finances* (1877), was an encyclopedic presentation of contemporaneous scholarship rather than a further probing into fiscal problems. Two other general studies of public finances by French economists—G. Jeze's *Science des finances* (1896) and E. Allix's *Traité élémentaire* (1907)—achieved an international reputation. R. Stourm's trail-blazing book *Le Budget* (1889) became a classic. After World War I French students of Public Finance became acutely concerned with problems of fiscal administration.

Germany was the seat of the greater part of nineteenth-century research and scholarship in Public Finance. A number of treatises on Public Finance, all strongly influenced by Adam Smith and Ricardo, appeared in rapid order early in the century; the most important of these was the *Grundsätze der Finanzwissenschaft* (1832) by K. H. Rau. These early studies not only covered the subject of taxation, but extended to problems of government expenditure, borrowing, and credit.

Toward the middle of the century, German fiscal scholarship made several new departures of great importance to the future study of Public Finance. Together with other economic subjects, Public Finance was taken up by the "historical school" of German economists. Although the work of Schmoller and Schäffle bore only incidentally on Public Finance, many of their pupils spent a lifetime of research upon the history of taxation, ancient and modern; under the editorship of Georg Schanz, the pages of Germany's great fiscal periodical, the *Finanz Archiv*, were ever open to studies of tax history. A second divergence of German scholars from the Adam Smith tradition was the propensity of several writers—noteworthily, Von Stein—to treat Public Finance as a branch of government or political science. For ultimate authority, they looked to the Cameralists rather than to Adam Smith. Through the far-reaching influence of Adolf Wagner, the social aspects of Public Finance—the possibility of utilizing the fiscal elements of government as agencies of social reform—came to be recognized. A monumental compendium which brings both theory and practice up to date is now available—*Handbuch der Finanzwissenschaft* edited by W. Gerloff and F. Neumark.

During the latter part of the nineteenth century and the first quarter of the twentieth century, Italian scholars also were active in Public Finance. To some extent the Italian fiscal economists derived their inspiration from German writers and devoted considerable attention to historical studies and to the social aspects of taxation. Another source of inspiration for the Italian writers was the Austrian development of the doctrine of marginal analysis; unfortunately, in pursuing this line of analysis the Italian economists tended to forsake practical realities for tenuous speculation. The most significant Italian fiscal study was A. Graziani's *Manuale della scienza delle finanze* (1893). A later Italian treatise of considerable merit is A. de Vitti de Marco's *First Principles of Public Finance*.

American writers on Public Finance. When a national government finds difficulty in disposing of a revenue surplus, as the American federal government did during the 1880's, scholarship in Public Finance is likely to go begging. Not until the close of the century did American writers make significant contributions to the study of Public Finance. Then, within fourteen years, from 1887 to 1900, there appeared six important American studies. Three of these, *Public Debts* (1887) and *The Science of Finance* (1898) by Henry C. Adams, and *The Theory and Practice of Taxation* (1900) by David A. Wells, showed a derivation from the English school of fiscal thought. The other three studies, *Taxation in American States and Cities* (1888) by Richard T. Ely, and *The Shifting and Incidence of Taxation* (1892) and *Progressive Taxation* (1894) by Edwin R. A. Seligman, were clearly influenced by the German doctrines of scholarship, emphasis being laid upon a historical approach, and consideration being given to the social aspects of taxation.

But neither the English nor the German school of fiscal thought gained predominance in the United States. Here, the federal government, the growing number of independent states, and the thousands of local governments having fiscal semi-independence, present a factual problem so stupendous that American students of Public Finance long found little opportunity for extensive studies in the general history and principles of taxation. Pressing problems of state and local finance drew American fiscal scholarship into localized fields, into studies of the fiscal systems of individual states, or into critical analysis of fiscal problems particularly affecting the states and the local governments. Many of our fiscal administrators are keen scholars of a "Cameralist" type. Many of our ablest academic fiscal scholars are drafted into administrative harness or serve on "advisory commissions." In consequence, until very recently American fiscal scholarship was held too closely to the immediate and the practical. Theoretical first principles were accepted from classical sources with a minimum of careful re-examination or were sometimes improvised casually in the course of rationalizing arbitrary conclusions.

Beginning in the 1930's, Public Finance in all its branches came to be tied in more closely with other fields of Economics as well as Law, Political Science, and other disciplines. Inspired and influenced by the writings of J. M. Keynes, an expanding group of American fiscal scholars proceeded to apply highly abstract national income theory to show how government finance might be used to influence the national economy and change the allocation of resources to increase welfare. For a time the most impressive developments in Public Finance were those which relate it to the determination of national income—the analysis of the forces affecting the levels of employment and prices. Public Finance has come to be so closely integrated with monetary theory that it sometimes seems that budgeting, government spending, taxation, and monetary policy are a single unit.

Since World War II, however, problems of state and local finance have required wide attention. Although much excellent work has been done, much is not generally available in libraries over the country. Inevitably, such study must often center upon specific problems, usually of a single locality or state. Yet this is where some of our most pressing problems lie. Fortunately, there are some facilities for finding what is being done elsewhere and profiting from such work—but not yet enough.

The tremendous growth of taxation has created a new and highly specific literature concerned with technical and often narrow problems in this field. Tax issues are blended with those of law and accounting, and the legal and accounting journals now include many articles of direct importance to students of Public Finance. Similarly, many of the best writings on government borrowing and debt management appear in financial publications of various types. Thus the student of Public Finance now finds much of the essential literature of his subject crossing traditional boundary lines between disciplines. The following bibliography indicates this fact, while listing some of the major titles and sources of information.

Bibliography

References to sources of information, and analyses of various types, on the subject matter of Public Finance appear throughout the text. The student seeking additional material can generally count upon the sources cited in footnotes to start him on the road to more complete coverage. The presentation here is designed to list in one place some major sources including several not in the text, and to comment briefly on the problem of Public Finance literature.

One major bibliographical caution should be observed. Materials on Public Finance often become out of date very quickly. A set of data or an analysis which is accurate this year may be misleading next year and quite wrong in five years. The rapid change of economic affairs, and especially the finances of government, creates a high degree of obsolescence in much of the writing on Public Finance. Great care is needed therefore in using materials only a few years old, except for historical purposes.

A second bibliographical pitfall is that much literature on Public Finance contains an element of special pleading—sometimes obvious, sometimes not. The purpose of the pleading may be honorable, the method forthright —but not always. The student must be especially on guard in dealing with writings on controversial issues. In his own interest he should seek materials representing more than one point of view.

BIBLIOGRAPHICAL AIDS

The American student has excellent aids for locating articles and books on general or specific fiscal topics. Perhaps the best starting advice is to ask one of those unusually helpful and specially trained persons, a librarian. General sources of bibliographical aid are the *United States Catalogue of Books,* the *Readers' Guide to Periodical Literature,* the *Industrial Arts Index,* the *Public Affairs Information Service,* and the *New York Times Index.* The student of Public Finance has a uniquely valuable specialized aid in the *Tax Institute Bookshelf,* published quarterly by the Tax Institute and presenting a comprehensive listing by topic of writings on government finance, including many foreign publications. The bibliographical sections of the *Book of the States* and the *Municipal Yearbook* are also excellent. Legal materials are listed in the *Index of Legal Periodicals,* and because of the importance of legal writings in Public Finance today this source should not be overlooked. None of these sources, however, provide critical guides on the contents of materials or suggest what is best.

SOURCES OF FISCAL STATISTICS

Sources of statistical data on American Public Finance have improved tremendously in the last generation. The work of the Governments Division of the Bureau of the Census of the U.S. Department of Commerce has been outstanding in the field of state and local government tax, expenditure, and debt statistics. Data for states and large cities are assembled promptly, organized uniformly, and released within a few weeks of the end of the fiscal years to which they apply. Detailed data on federal tax receipts and the public debt are published monthly in the *Treasury Bulletin,* along with major items of spending and the various trust fund accounts. For details on federal spending the best source is the *Budget,* published in January; the hearings before Congressional appropriations subcommittees are often very revealing. The *Annual Report of the Secretary of the Treasury* provides a textual summary of tax, spending, and debt developments each year and in addition very extensive statistics, with some series going back many years or decades. The annual reports of other federal agencies provide fiscal data of varying importance and are generally the best source of detail on spending.

Statistics presented by states and localities vary so widely that generalization cannot be very helpful. It has been the authors' experience that state and local officials are generally anxious to help anyone making a serious inquiry and that, in addition to materials published regularly, these officials will often provide supplementary data on specific problems. The *Book of the States* and the *Municipal Yearbook* contain much state and local fiscal statistical information, chiefly secondary but often supplemented by valuable analyses by experts on the various topics.

The *Federal Reserve Bulletin,* the *Social Security Bulletin,* and the *Survey of Current Business* are monthly publications with statistics on various aspects of Public Finance. The annual *Statistical Abstract of the United States* contains extensive information on Public Finance assembled from various sources and presented in historical series. The annual volumes of *Statistics of Income* prepared by the Internal Revenue Service provide a vast amount of detail taken from tax returns. A very convenient compilation of data on Public Finance is the annual *Facts and Figures on Government Finance* published by the Tax Foundation; the *World Almanac* and the National Industrial Conference Board's *Economic Almanac* are also useful and readily accessible sources of secondary information. They also indicate original sources.

PERIODICALS

Most original research on Public Finance appears in the form of articles in journals of many types. Professional journals for accountants, economists, lawyers, political scientists, and other groups, and the business and trade journals in innumerable fields, contain articles from time to time on topics in Public Finance. The *National Tax Journal,* published quarterly by the National Tax Association, is designed chiefly for economists and public officials; each year *The Journal of Finance* includes several scholarly articles on taxation, debt management, and government spending; the *Tax Law Review* (New York University School of Law) concentrates on legal aspects of taxation; *Taxes—The Tax Magazine* (Commerce Clearing House), *The Tax Executive,* and *The Journal of Taxation* are monthly publications appealing chiefly to accountants and lawyers practicing on tax problems; the *Monthly Digest of Tax Articles* (Newkirk Associates, Albany, N.Y.) presents condensed versions of articles appearing chiefly in legal and accounting journals. The monthly *National Municipal Review* is valuable for local developments and contains an extensive listing of other publications. *Municipal Finance* is a quarterly designed especially for local government officials; the monthly *Tax Administrators News* is of value to anyone interested in Public Finance. *Tax Policy,* published several times a year by the Tax Institute, presents the results of specific studies of tax, or occasionally spending, problems. The annual proceedings of the National Tax Association are published in a volume running to several hundred pages. The annual conferences of tax administrators, government purchasing agents, and other groups are also published to varying extent. New York University sponsors an annual Institute on Federal Taxation designed for practitioners; the printed papers provide discussions of several score specific tax topics. Finally, no listing of periodical literature should ignore the varied materials published regularly and to meet special situations by Prentice-Hall, Inc., Matthew Bender & Co., Inc., Commerce Clearing House, Inc., Research Institute of America, and other organizations providing business service publications.

The *Bulletin for International Fiscal Documentation* contains, in addition to articles, valuable brief digests and reviews of writings on Public Finance with excellent coverage of materials appearing outside the United States. Other foreign publications devoted to Public Finance are *Public Finance, Canadian Tax Journal, Finanz Archiv,* and *Revue de science et de législation financière.*

Each issue of the *American Economic Review* lists the titles of new books of interest to economists and the articles appearing in major journals.

SPECIAL STUDIES

Much original work on Public Finance appears in the form of special studies. Generally they are published as monographs with limited circulation. Some remain unpublished but perhaps accessible through library interchange services. The student or librarian will find the *Tax Institute Bookshelf* most valuable in locating such materials, but anyone interested in the problems of a particular locality, state, or federal agency should ask directly if any special studies have been made. Some of the work done by special study groups for states and localities has been very valuable, not only in analyzing the problems of the government involved but also in comparing them with corresponding problems and situations of other governments. The most valuable studies are those directed by, or having the active assistance of, professional economists.

At irregular intervals the U.S. Treasury prepares studies of special aspects of taxation. The Joint Committee on Internal Revenue Taxation and the Internal Revenue Service also make special tax studies, and the Joint Economic Committee has dealt with both tax and expenditure problems. Although not well indexed, the volumes of *Hearings on Revenue Revision* before the Committee on Ways and Means and the Senate Finance Committee contain a great deal of useful material as well as special pleading which has little basic merit. The Appropriations Committees' hearings as well as those dealing with money and banking, the reduction of nonessential government expenditures, and other special topics are valuable for different aspects of spending and debt management.

Many private groups include special studies of problems of government finance in their broader programs of research. Among these are the AFL-CIO, the American Enterprise Association, the Committee for Economic Development, the National Industrial Conference Board, the National Association of Manufacturers, the National Planning Association, the Twentieth Century Fund, the National Bureau of Economic Research, the United States Chamber of Commerce, and various trade associations and labor organizations.

TEXTBOOKS

Other American textbooks in Public Finance are:

Allen, E. D., and O. H. Brownlee, *Economics of Public Finance*, 2nd ed. (Prentice-Hall, New York, 1954)

Due, J. F., *Government Finance: Economic Analysis*, rev. ed. (R. D. Irwin, Homewood, 1959)

Groves, H. M., *Financing Government*, 5th ed. (Henry Holt, New York, 1958)

Kendrick, M. S., *Public Finance* (Houghton-Mifflin, Boston, 1951)

Plank, E. H., *Public Finance* (R. D. Irwin, Homewood, 1953)

Poole, K. E., *Public Finance and Economic Welfare* (Rinehart & Co., Inc., New York, 1956)

Valuable volumes of readings are:

Bullock, C. J., *Selected Readings in Public Finance,* 3rd ed. (Ginn, Boston, 1924); still useful for understanding the development of Public Finance
Colm, G., *Essays in Public Finance and Fiscal Policy* (Oxford University Press, New York, 1955); a variety of essays by an expert in budgeting and the use of fiscal policy for economic stabilization
Groves, H. M., *Viewpoints on Public Finance* (Holt, New York, 1947)
Musgrave, R. A., and A. T. Peacock, *Classics in the Theory of Public Finance* (Macmillan, New York, 1958); translations from European classics
Shoup, C. S., and R. A. Musgrave, *Readings in the Economics of Taxation* (R. D. Irwin, Homewood, 1959); an extensive selection of major writings not readily accessible
Smithies, A., and J. K. Butters, *Readings in Fiscal Policy* (R. D. Irwin, Homewood, 1955); leading articles of varying difficulty

SPECIAL STUDIES

Three books valuable for historical fiscal materials in addition to statistics are:

Ratner, Sidney, *American Taxation, Its History as a Social Force in Democracy* (Norton, New York, 1942)
Shultz, W. J., and M. R. Caine, *Financial Development of the United States* (Prentice-Hall, New York, 1937)
Studenski, P., and H. E. Kroos, *Financial History of the United States* (McGraw-Hill, New York, 1952)

The following volumes dealing with the subjects indicated will be useful. In some cases it has seemed wise to include titles already included in the text, but the general policy has been to avoid duplication.

Abbott, C. C., *The Federal Debt* (Twentieth Century Fund, New York, 1952); a discussion of general principles and of practices in the post-war period
American Commonwealths Series (Crowell, New York, various dates); one volume for each state describes government organization and operation
Birch, A. H., *Federalism, Finance and Social Legislation* (Oxford University Press, Oxford, 1955)
Blakey, R. G., and V. Johnson, *State Income Taxes* (Commerce Clearing House, Chicago, 1942); excellent for background
Blough, R., *The Federal Taxing Process* (Prentice-Hall, Englewood Cliffs, 1951); a professional economist draws upon years of experience as the chief of tax analysis in the Treasury
Brown, E. C., *Effects of Taxation on Depreciation Adjustments for Price Changes* (Harvard Business School, Boston, 1952); careful analysis of a problem made serious by inflation
Burkhead, J., *Government Budgeting* (Wiley, New York, 1956); a leading analysis of the economic and administrative aspects of budgeting with special reference to the federal government; contains excellent bibliographical materials
Burns, E. M., *Social Security and Public Policy* (McGraw-Hill, New York,

1956); a thorough analysis of broad issues and specific practices of social insurance and welfare

Butters, J. K., *Effects of Taxation on Inventory Accounting and Policies* (Harvard Business School, Boston, 1949)

———, J. Lintner, and W. L. Cary, *Effects of Taxation on Corporate Mergers* (Harvard Business School, Boston, 1951); though now somewhat out of date, this volume is an excellent analysis of issues and of business response

De Podwin, H. J., *Discharging Business Tax Liabilities* (Rutgers University Press, 1957); a study of tax compliance by an economist associated with a leading corporation

Due, J. F., *Sales Taxation* (University of Illinois Press, Urbana, 1957); a comprehensive study drawing heavily upon experience here and abroad

Goode, R. F., *The Corporation Income Tax* (Wiley, New York, 1950); in spite of changes in tax laws which have made parts of this volume out of date, it remains a leading economic discussion of business taxation

Groves, H. M., *Postwar Taxation and Economic Progress* (McGraw-Hill, New York, 1946); a careful examination of broad issues written for the serious layman and still valuable for the general analyses

Hall, C. A., Jr., *Effects of Taxation on Executive Compensation and Retirement Plans* (Harvard Business School, Boston, 1951)

Hansen, A. H., *Monetary Theory and Fiscal Policy* (McGraw-Hill, New York, 1949); one of several volumes by a leading student of the problems of fiscal policy

Hansen, B., *The Economic Theory of Fiscal Policy* (Allen and Unwin, London, 1958)

Hart, A. G., *Money, Debt, and Economic Activity* (Prentice-Hall, New York, 2d ed., 1953); especially useful for analysis of ways by which Public Finance and monetary policy are related in influencing employment and the level of prices; includes stimulating critiques of unusual ("crank") plans to stimulate the economy

———, and E. C. Brown, *Financing Defense* (Twentieth Century Fund, New York, 1951); though directed chiefly toward the problems raised by the Korean conflict, this study contains much of value on general problems of Public Finance

Harvard Law School, International Program in Taxation, volumes dealing with the tax laws of different countries (Little, Brown, Boston); of special interest to businesses operating abroad

Isard, W., and R. Coughlin, *Municipal Costs and Revenues Resulting from Community Growth* (Federal Reserve Bank of Boston, 1957); a pioneering study

Kaldor, N., *An Expenditure Tax* (Macmillan, New York, 1955); a British economist's analysis of an alternative method of progressive taxation

Kimmel, L. H., *Taxation and Incentives* (Brookings Institution, Washington, 1950); a tabulation and discussion of the findings of a questionnaire investigation

Lutz, H. L., *Public Spending and the Private Economy* (National Association of Manufacturers, 1949); an economist's arguments against the use of fiscal policy to try to offset business fluctuations

Mikesell, R. M., *Governmental Accounting*, rev. ed. (R. D. Irwin, Homewood, 1956); a comprehensive discussion

Montgomery, R. E., and others, authoritative volumes on federal taxation, of interest chiefly to attorneys and accountants (Ronald, New York, currently)

Organization for European Economic Cooperation, *The Influence of Sales Taxes on Productivity* (OEEC, Paris, 1958)

Oster, C. V., *State Retail Sales Taxation* (Ohio State University, Columbus, 1957); a statistical and economic analysis with realistic attention given to administration

Paul, R. E., *Taxation for Prosperity* (Bobbs-Merrill, Indianapolis, 1947); especially interesting for its discussion of federal tax history during World War II by the man who headed much of the Treasury's work

———, *Taxation in the United States* (Little, Brown, Boston, 1954); essays on a variety of topics by a leading tax attorney with a wide and informed interest in economic issues

Perry, J. H., *Taxation in Canada,* 2nd ed. (University of Toronto Press, Toronto, 1954)

Pigou, A. C., *A Study in Public Finance,* 3rd ed. (Macmillan, London, 1951); outstanding for theoretical analysis of taxes

Reck, D., *Government Purchasing and Competition* (University of California Press, Berkeley, 1954); contains a discussion of purchasing which is somewhat broader than the title suggests

Roberts, W. A., *State Taxation of Metallic Deposits* (Harvard University Press, Cambridge, 1944); a comprehensive analysis of a complex problem

Rolph, E. R., *The Theory of Fiscal Economics* (University of California Press, Berkeley, 1954); an advanced theoretical analysis of major issues

Sanders, T. H., *Effects of Taxation on Executives* (Harvard Business School, Boston, 1951); contains the findings from the study of the experience of a group of executives

Simons, H. C., *Economic Policy for a Free Society* (University of Chicago Press, Chicago, 1948); a group of stimulating essays of special value for their treatment of fiscal policy

———, *Federal Tax Reform* (University of Chicago Press, Chicago, 1950); a rare combination of excellent economic analysis and thorough grasp of the intricacies of tax law

Smith, B. B., *Liberty and Taxes* (Foundation for Economic Education, Irvington-on-Hudson, no date); a strong statement of arguments against redistribution of income by taxation

Smith, D. T., *Effects of Taxation; Corporate Financial Policy* (Harvard Business School, Boston, 1952); the findings from an intensive study of a selected group of corporations together with a general analysis of the problems

Stocker, F. D., *Nonproperty Taxes as a Source of Local Revenues* (Cornell University Press, Ithaca, 1953); a discussion of theoretical and practical problems

Strayer, P. J., *Fiscal Policy and Politics* (Harper, New York, 1958); a clear statement of the economic theory of the use of public finance to stabilize the economy with emphasis on the political problems

Tax Institute, *Tax Institute Bookshelf Supplement, Twenty-Five Years of Tax Institute Publications* (The Institute, Princeton, 1957); a complete bibliography of the Institute's many publications, arranged by topic

Vickrey, W. S., *Agenda for Progressive Taxation* (Ronald, New York, 1947); a thorough and imaginative analysis of the taxation of income, spending, and inheritances and gifts; the descriptive materials are no longer up to date

———, *The Revision of the Rapid Transfer Fare Structure of the City of New York* (Mayor's Committee on Management Survey, New York, 1952); a specialized study which has general value because of the discussion of fundamental principles

Weidenbaum, M. L., *Government Spending—Process and Measurement* (Boeing Airplane Co., Seattle, 1958); a scholarly analysis of spending as it influences income flows in the short run

Welch, R. B., *State and Local Taxation of Banks in the United States* (N.Y. State Tax Commission, Albany, 1934); while somewhat out of date, this study is still useful

Willis, J., *The Mitigation of the Tax Penalty on Fluctuating or Irregular Incomes* (Canadian Tax Foundation, Toronto, 1951); an extensive study of the problem of averaging income for tax purposes

Index of Subjects

(Pages whereon a topic is given major treatment are printed in **bold face** type.)

A

Ability-to-pay doctrine (see *Distributive theories*)
Accounting, government, 3, 91, **93, 125–128**
Administration, tax, 188, **210–228, 278–286,** 289, 303, 325, **327–328, 346–349,** 354, **361–362, 374–394, 418–420,** 459–460, 484, 606, 607
  organization, **219–224**
  principles, **212–218**
  techniques, **224–228**
  (see also *Compliance costs, Tax consciousness,* and under particular taxes)
Admissions taxes, 205, 238, 322, 343, **344,** 472, 484
Agricultural aid, **25,** 39, 54, 59, 181, 370, 488, 569
Airports, **44,** 489
Alabama:
  budget, 105, 121
  taxes, 323, 343, 370*n*, 373
Alaska, taxes, 251
Alaska Railroad, 437, 521
Alcoholic beverages taxes (see *Liquor taxes*)
Allocation, tax, 150, **310–313,** 314, 326, 385
American Bankers Association, 103
American Society of Municipal Engineers, 102
American Public Health Association, 102
Amusements taxes, 205, 238, 322, 343, **344,** 472, 484
Appointed fiscal officials, **92, 96, 223–224,** 228, 375
Appropriation procedure, federal, **108–121**
Appropriations Committee, House, 116, 119
Arizona:
  expenditure, 39
  taxes, 345–346, 390, 412
Arkansas, finances, 39, 150
Assessment:
  property tax, 95, 144, 146, 221, 223, 225, **374–386**
  special, 181, **449–452**
Atomic development, 15, 22, 25, 54
Audit of local accounts, state, **93**
Auditor, government, 91, 92, 93, **121–123,** 419
"Authorities," 88*n*, 140, 477*n*
Automobile taxation (see *Motor vehicle fuel tax* and *Motor vehicle license tax*)
Avoidance, tax, 141, 198, 205, 210*n*, **211,** 274–276, **283–286,** 301, 303, 327, 345, 374, 411–413, 426, 427

B

Bank taxes, 91, 147, 241, **318–319,** 326, 463
Banknote tax, 134, 148, 201
"Benefit" doctrines:
  expenditure, **59–62, 70–73,** 286, 363–364, 429–430, 445–448
  taxation, 72, **180–182,** 194, 253, 332, 358, 363, 402–403, 416, 423
Beverage taxes (see *Liquor tax* and *Soft drinks tax*)
Boards of equalization and review, state, 221
Bonds, government:
  callable-term, 504, 525, **538–539**
  "credit," **544**
  currency-privilege, 453–454, 526, 538*n*
  gold-clause, **546**
  interest rates, 26, 501–507, 516, **530–534,** 547, **553–555,** 580
  intermediate-term, 501, 502, 525, **540**

Bonds, government (*cont.*)
marketing, **527–530**
maturity, 504–506, **532, 537–542**
savings, 501, 503, 505, 507–508, 528, 529–530, 539, 552, 575, 588, 602, 603
serial, **545–546**
sinking-fund, **544–546**
tax-exempt, 137, 143, 148, 198, 252, 284, 411, 483, **532, 548–551**
Borrowing, government, **497–556**
economics, 3, 501, 524, 536, 541–542, 567, **575–576,** 586, **599–600**
limitations:
local, 88, 92, 381, 509–510, **515–516,** 521, 524, 539
state, **514–515,** 521, 539
purpose, **517–527**
Boston, finances, 19, 368
Bounties, 81
Budget Bureau (federal), 108, 111, 116, 122
Budgets, government, 91–94, 100, **104–124,** 523, 525
"cash-consolidated" and "conventional," 112
enactment, **115–121**
execution, **121–122**
federal, 105–124
formulation, 91, **108–115**
local, **93–94,** 105–124
scope, **105–108**
state, 105–124
Burden, tax, 180–191, **234–236, 244–248,** 333, 420
Bureau of Internal Revenue (see *Internal Revenue Service*)
Bureaus of municipal research, **102**
Business cycle:
as affected by fiscal matters, 587–588
effects on fiscal matters, 164, 465
Business taxes, 110, 205, 236, 237, **291–335,** 398, 571
administration, **327–328**
allocation, 150, **310–313,** 314, 326
federal, **292–308**
incidence, **177–178**
law, **325–327**
state, **308–325**
theory, 182–183
(see also under particular business taxes)
Butter substitutes tax, 133, 161, **200*n*,** 202

C

California:
expenditures, 19, 28, 39
taxes, 243, 344, 346, 382, 466
other subjects, 101, 514
Callable-term bonds, 504, 525, **538–539**
Cameras, taxes on, 238, 342
Capital expenditures (see *Expenditures, government*)
Capital gains tax:
corporation income tax, 293
personal income tax, **261–268,** 274, 573, 587, 599
Capital stock tax:
federal, 292–293
state, 144, **309–313,** 319, 330
Capitalization of taxes, **170–172,** 187, 245, 305, 329, **400–401,** 403, 405
Central control of local finances, **92–95**
Certificates of indebtedness, 540
Chain-store tax, 133, 147, 201, 202, **323,** 328
Charges:
enterprise, 72, 181, **432–436,** 439–440
license, 133, 244, 343, **447–449**
Charitable exemptions (see *Exemptions, tax*)
Chicago, finances, 19
Child labor tax, 201
Cigarette tax (see *Tobacco products tax*)
Cincinnati, taxes, 251
City finances:
debt, 509–512
enterprises, **32, 441**
expenditures, 30, **31, 32–33,** 90, 473–475
special assessments, **449–452**
taxes, 205, 377–379, 382
City manager government, **90,** 97
Civil service, 56, 86, **95–101,** 223–224, 375–376
Civil Service Commission, 376
Classified property tax, 318, **394–396**
Club dues tax, 204, 238, 342
Coinage receipts, 454
Collection, tax (see *Administration, tax,* and under particular taxes)
Collectivist doctrine, **54–55**
Colleges, government support, **40–41**
Colorado:
taxes, 151, 251, 376
other subjects, 50, 95*n*
Columbus (O.), taxes, 251
Commodity taxes, **337–355**
incidence, **156–167, 177, 350–351**
(see also under *Customs duties* and *Sales taxes*)
Community property:
and death taxes, 411*n*, **413–414**
and income taxes, **276–277,** 482
Comparative-social-benefit doctrine, **59–62, 70–73**
Compensatory doctrine of taxation, 194
Competition and tax shifting, **156–160**

Compliance costs, 215, **217–218,** 313, 327–328, 477, 480
Comptroller, government, 91, 92, 121–123, 419
Condemnation, excess, **452–453**
Conference of State Governors, 581
Confiscatory taxes (see *Taxation*)
Congressional action:
  budgets, 111–112, **115–120**
  taxes, **207–209,** 589, **597–598**
Connecticut:
  expenditures, 18
  taxes, 324, 343, 344, 373
Consciousness, tax (see *Tax consciousness*)
Consolidated returns, 201, 299
Constitutional limitations on taxation (see *Limitations*)
Consumption spending, fiscal effects on, 166–167, **200,** 350, 352, 403–405, 569, **571–572,** 575–577, 595
Conversion, debt, 500, 502, 504–505, 525–526
Cooperatives, taxation of, 193
Corporate excess tax, 309, 384*n*
Corporation income tax, 91, 235, **292–305,** 463, 571, 574, 597
  administration, 91, 221, 225
  basis, **293–300**
  consolidated returns, 201, 299
  federal, 235, 237–240, 246, 250, **292–305,** 329–330, 402, 431, 477, 482, 483, 487
  incidence, 171–172, 245, **329–330**
  law, 136, 149
  rates, 250, **300–301,** 486
  state, 221, 235, **241–243, 310–313,** 402, 464, 477
  theory, **173–176,** 186, 196
Corporation organization and entrance taxes, **308–309,** 326, 477
Corporation undistributed profits tax (see *Undistributed profits tax*)
Corporations, government, **436–437**
Cost-of-service doctrine, **180,** 188, 358, 363, 402
Council of Economic Advisors, 593
"Counterweight" theory, 581, **592–594**
Counties:
  control of local finances, **93–95**
  expenditure, 19, 30, **31, 33–35, 88,** 90
  taxes, 244, 374–375, 388
Credit, federal-state tax, 47, 307, 407–408, 409, **417–418,** 419, 481, 483, **486–487**
Crown tax, 348
Currency-privilege bonds, **453–454,** 526, 538*n*
Customs duties, 134, 138, 201, 219, 235, 237, 238, 241, **337–340,** 483*n*
Cyclical budget, 205, 579, 594–595

D

Dayton (O.), 251
Death taxes, **407–425,** 427–428, 492, 571
  administration, 215–216, **418–420**
  basis, **411–414,** 482
  estate tax, 407–409, 415
  exemptions, 193, 409, **414–415,** 422
  federal, 215–216, 235, 237–239, 246, **407–408,** 411–425, 427–428, 482, 483, 487, 552
  gifts in contemplation, 411–412
  inheritance tax, 408–410, 415–416, 419
  law, 136–137, 141, 143, 145, 146, 147, **410–411,** 478
  nonresidents, **410,** 418
  rates, 196, 408–409, **416–418,** 486
  state, 235, **241–242, 408–411,** 411–425, 419, 463*n*, 464, 480–481, 484, 487
  theory, 155, 182, **420–425**
Debt, government, **497–556**
  conversion, 500, 502, 504–505, 525–526
  default, 509, 510, **542–543,** 547
  economic effects, 3, 501, 524, 536, 541–542, 567, **575–578, 599–600**
  federal, **499–508,** 518–520, 525–530, 535–536, 537–556
  interest rates, 501–507, 516, **530–534,** 547, **553–555,** 580
  limitations:
    local, 88, 92, 381, 391, 509–510, **515–516,** 521, 524, 539
    state, **514–515,** 521, 539
  local, 500, **509–512,** 515–517, 520–526, 528–529, 534, 537–556
  management, 2, 500–508, **537–556, 579–580,** 599–600
  "moneyness," 526, **541–542,** 554, 575*n*, **576,** 599
  redemption, 106, 499, 504, **542–546,** 556, **576–577,** 587
  service, 20, 23, **26, 29,** 31–32, 34, 523
  short-term, 499, 501, 502, 505, 525, 534, **540–541**
  state, 500, **508–512,** 514–515, 520–526, 528–529, 534, 537–556
  tax delinquency notes, 101
  war loans, 499, **502–504, 518–520**
Defense spending (see *Expenditure, government: military*)
Deficit financing, 2, **578–579,** 584, 599, 601
Delaware:
  expenditure, 18, 28
  other subjects, 39, 310

Delinquency, tax, **393–394**
Depletion, 201, **297,** 333*n*
Depreciation, **293–296,** 599
Detroit, expenditure, 474
District of Columbia, taxes, 251, 344
"Direct" and "indirect" taxes:
  economic, 154*n*
  legal, **139–140**
Distribution theories of taxation, **179–191,** 218, **286–287, 331–332, 351–353, 402–403, 422–424,** 606
  ability-to-pay doctrine, **183–184,** 188, 191–192, 195, 253, 269, 286, 352, 402, 416, 423
  benefit doctrine, 72, **180–182,** 194, 253, 332, 358, 363, 402–403, 416, 423
  compensatory doctrine, 194
  neutrality doctrine, **185–186,** 424
  sacrifice doctrine, 60–62, **184–185,** 191–192, 195
  state partnership doctrine, 183
Diversity of revenue sources, **206–207**
Dividends:
  corporation income tax, 299, 303–304, 571
  personal income tax, **258,** 303–304, 477, 573
Domain (see *Public domain*)
Double taxation (see *Taxation*)
"Due process of law" limitation, **140–141, 143–146,** 326, 387

E

Earmarked revenues, 107, 138, 151, 366, 390, 464, 546
Economic effects of fiscal operations (see *Debt, government; Expenditure, government; Fiscal policy;* and *Taxation*)
Economic growth:
  fiscal effects of, **12–14, 73–75,** 233–234
  fiscal effects on, **585–586**
Economics and Public Finance, **3–4, 56–83, 153–178,** 255–257, 261–268, **286–288,** 561–604, 608
Economy in government, 26, **84–103**
Educational finance (see *School finance*)
Efficiency, government, 23, **84–103, 471–472**
  enterprises, 2, **431–433**
Elasticity, revenue, **205–206**
Elected fiscal officials, **92, 95–96, 223–224,** 228, 375
Electric light and power companies, 313–315
Eminent domain, 453
Employment, fiscal effects on, 2, 580, **583–584,** 586, 608
Enterprises, government, 29, 32, 107, 180, **429–442**
  borrowing, **521, 547–548**
  charges, 72, 181, **432–436,** 439–440
  city, **32, 441**
  federal, 436, **437–440**
  incorporation, **436–437**
  state, **29, 440–441**
Equalization:
  grants-in-aid, 38–39, **469–471,** 489, 491–492
  property tax, **388–389,** 470, 471*n*, 516
Equalization doctrines, **189–191,** 195, **424–425**
"Equal protection of law" limitation, **147,** 325, 383
Equity capital and taxation, 186
Equitable taxation (see *Taxation: distribution*)
Escheat, 453–454
Estate tax (see *Death taxes*)
Estimated tax, **279,** 598
Evasion, tax, 141, 198, 210*n*, **211–212,** 217, 218, 274–275, 279, **283–286,** 289, 303, 327, 349
Excess condemnation, **452–453**
Excess profits tax, 237–240, 292–293, **302–303,** 530*n*, 574
Excises, federal, 200, 235, 238, 239, 337, **341–343,** 348
Exemptions, tax, 143, 151, **191–194,** 204–205, 211, 347, 351, **369–372**
  charitable, 193, 198, 201, 202, 261, 299, 345, 370, 413, 422
  death taxes, 193, 409, **414–415,** 422
  federal instrumentalities, **147–149,** 252, 318, 345, 361, 369, 411, 548
  homestead, 196, 372
  minimum, **191–193,** 269–270, 415
  personal income tax, 46, 172, 191, 192, 205, 217, 239, 250, 261, **269–270,** 548–552
  property tax, 148, 151, 193, 196, 200, **369–372**
  social, 193–194
  state instrumentalities, 140, 252, 411, 431, 548
  tax-exempt bonds, 140, 143, 198, 252, 284, 411, 483, 532, **548–551**
Expenditure, government, **9–129**
  capital, 12, **29, 30, 31–33, 34,** 74, 106, 521–525, 591–595
  city, 30, **31, 32–33,** 90, 473–475
  county, 19, 30, **31, 33–35, 88,** 90
  debt service, 20, 23, **26, 29,** 31–32, 34, 523
  economic effects, 3, **566–567, 569–570,** 576, 578, **591–595**

Expenditures, government (*cont.*)
federal, **11–26,** 35–50, 89, 487–492, 582, 591–595
fire protection, 26
health and sanitation, 26, **29, 32, 34,** 35, **49–50,** 63, 75, 94
highway, 13, 17, 20, 28, **29,** 30, **31–32,** 33, **34,** 35, **42–45,** 54, 75, 94, 460–461, 488, 489, 594
housing development, 26, **31, 50**
law, **21–22**
local, **11–21, 30–35,** 35–50, 90, 592
military, 2, **12,** 18, **20–21, 22–24,** 59, 86, 595*n*
relief, 15, 16, **25–26,** 30, 33, 34–35, **45–50,** 58, 59, 63, 181, 482, 488–489, 510, 582, 594
research, 22, 25, 55, 74, 81
school, 13, 15, 17, 18, **19–21,** 28–30, **31–32, 34, 35–41,** 54, 63, 74, 82, 87, 94, 461, 488
social, 13, 15, 20–21, 23, **25–26, 29, 31–32, 34, 45–50,** 54, 488, 569, 584
special districts, 13, 19, **31, 35, 88,** 392
state, **11–21, 28–30,** 35–50, 43, 89–90, 592
transfer, **59,** 65, **76–78,** 569
veterans' aid, 12, **23–24,** 59, 82, 181, 512, 526, 569
Expenditure, personal, fiscal effects on (see *Consumption spending*)
Export taxes, 138–139, 142
Express companies, 313–315
Expropriatory power, 453

F

Farm aid, **25,** 39, 54, 59, 181, 370, 488, 569
Federal aid (see *Federal finance: aid*)
Federal Deposit Insurance Corporation, 79*n*
Federal Employment Stabilization Board, 581
Federal farm credit system, 436
Federal finance:
aid, 26, **39–40, 43–44, 48,** 342, 461, 482, 483, **487–492,** 594
debt, **499–508,** 518–520, 525–530, 535–536, 537–556
enterprises, 436, **437–440**
expenditure, **11–26,** 35–50, 89, 487–492, 582, 591–595
taxation, 30, 134, **137–141,** 200, 207–209, 215, 219–220, 228, **232–241,** 249–250, **292–308,** 325–326, **337–343, 407–408, 425–426,** 482–487
(see also under particular taxes and *Administration, tax* and *Law*)
Federal Housing Administration, 78–79
Federal instrumentalities limitation, **147–149,** 252, 318, 345, 361, 369, 411, 548
Federal National Mortgage Association, 79*n*
Federal-state relationships, **481–493**
grants-in-aid, 26, 39–40, **43–44,** 48, 342, 461, 482, 483, **487–492,** 594
separation of revenues, **483–484**
shared taxes, 483, **484–485**
supplementary state taxes, 483, **486**
tax credit, 47, 307, 407–408, 409, **417–418,** 419, 481, 483, **486–487**
Federal Reserve System and federal debt, 454, 506–508, 519, 528, 533, 535, 554, 576, 577, 580, 590, 599
Federal Trade Commission, 14, 54
Federation of Tax Administrators, 228
Fees, 72, 181, 244, **445–449**
Fifth Amendment, 137, 325
Fines, 453–455
Fire protection expenditure, 26
Firearms tax, 138, 206, 342
Fiscal Policy, 2, 7, 62, 205, 247, 270, 403–405, 524, 536, **559–604,** 608
Flood control, 25, 35
Florida, taxes, 221, 273, 315, 372, 417, 481
Foreign aid, 12, 22, **23–24,** 54, 570
Forest taxation, **320–321, 384**
Forfeitures, 453–455
Fourteenth Amendment, **143–147,** 326, 383
Franchise tax (see *Capital stock tax,* and *Corporation income tax: state*)
Fuel tax (see *Motor vehicle fuel tax*)
Funding debt (see *Debt: conversion*)

G

Gambling, taxes on, 322–323, 342
Gasoline tax (see *Motor vehicle fuel tax*)
General Accounting Office, 121, 123
General property tax (see *Property tax*)
General sales tax (see *Sales taxes*)
Georgia:
local accounts, 93
taxes, 243, 323, 382
Gift tax, 193, 235, **425–428**
Gifts to governments, 455
"Gold clause" bonds, **546**
Government ownership (see *Enterprises, government*)
Graduation, tax rate (see *Taxation: progressive*)
Grants-in-aid:
equalization, 38–39, **469–471,** 489, 491–492

Grants-in-aid (*cont.*)
federal, 26, 39–40, **43–44**, **48**, 342, 461, 482, 483, **487–492**, 594
state, 28, 38–39, 43, 64, 110, 381, 465, **466–472**, 475
Gross income (or gross profits) tax, 149, 204, 313, **314**, 319, 321, 326, 345, 348, 350–351, 359, 472
Gross sales tax, 344

H

Health and sanitation, **29–32**, **34**, 35, **49–50**, 63, 75, 94
Highway expenditure, 13, 17, 20, 28, **29**, 30, **31–32**, 33, **34**, 35, **42–45**, 54, 75, 94, 460–461, 488, 489, 594
(see also *Motor vehicle fuel tax* and *Motor vehicle license tax*)
History of Public Finance, 3, **605–608**
Home Loan banks, 79*n*
Home Owners' Loan Corporation, 444, 502
Homestead exemption, 196, 372
Hoover Commission, 89, 98
Hotel taxation, 472
Housing development, 26, **31**, 35, **50**, 371, 430, 445, 548
Houston (Tex.) taxes, 399*n*

I

Idaho, budget, 121
Illinois:
expenditure, 18
taxes, 243, 344, 346, 382, 384*n*, 466
Incentives:
expenditure and, **81**
taxes and, 186, 196, 199, 288, 303, 335, 350, 352, 421–422, **573–574**
Incidence, tax (see *Shifting, tax*)
Income tax (see *Corporation income tax* and *Personal income tax*)
Increment tax, 452
Incremental cost of taxation theory, 358–359
Indiana:
control of local finances, **95**
taxes, 221, 346
"Indirect" and "direct" taxes:
economic, 154*n*
legal, **139–140**
Individualistic doctrine, **53–54**
Inflation:
as affected by fiscal matters, 2, 12, **519–520**, 552, 554–555, **568–569**, 580, **583–585**
effects on fiscal matters, 12, **15–16**, 50, 197, 233, 298, 546–547, 586

Inheritance tax (see *Death taxes*)
Inland Waterways Corporation, 437
In lieu taxes, 137, 149*n*, 151, 291*n*, **314–316**, 320, 326, 368, 384, 463
Insurance company taxes, 237, 238, 241, **319–320**, 326, 331
Intangibles (see *Property tax*)
Interest:
payments, **26**, **29**, 30, **31–32**, 34, 59, 76, 112
rates on government bonds, 26, 500, 502–507, 516, **530–534**, 547, **553–555**, 580
receipts, 444–445
taxation, 176, 573
Intermediate-term debt issues, 504–506, **532**, **537–542**
Internal Revenue Service, 113, 213, 214, **219–220**, 224, 226*n*, 227, 280–282, 610
International Association of Chiefs of Police, 102
International City Managers Association, 102
International fiscal relationships, **493–495**
Interstate Commerce Commission, 14, 54, 311, 315, 326, 343
Interstate commerce limitation, **149–150**, 361, 372, 481
Interstate fiscal relationships, **476–481**, 486–487
reciprocity, 254, 360, 410, **478–479**
uniformity of tax laws, **479–480**
Investment:
fiscal effects on, 169, 174–175, 288, 301, 303–304, 329, 336, 403–405, 421, **573**, 584, 596
government, **444–445**
Iowa:
taxes, 217*n*, 221, 265, 343, 382
other subjects, 95, 510
Irrigation projects, 15, 25, 35

J

Jewelry taxes, 238, 342
Joint Committee on Internal Revenue Taxation, 208, 209
Joint Federal-State Action Committee, 484*n*
Justice in taxation (see *Taxation: distribution*)

K

Kansas, taxes, 382, 409, 412
Kentucky, taxes, 133, 322, 362, 395

L

Laissez-faire doctrine, **53–54,** 73
Land, taxation (see *Property tax: realty*)
Land value tax, **398–400**
Lands, public:
  federal, 442–443
  state, 443, 467
Law of taxation, 3–4, 21, 35, **132–151, 325–327, 372–373**
  subject-measure doctrine, **135–137,** 142, 252, 319*n*
  (see also *Limitations* and under particular taxes)
League of Women Voters, 103
Libraries, 35, **41–42**
License charges, 133, 244, 343, **447–449**
License taxes, 133, 243, **321–322,** 328, 356–361, 447–448
Liens, tax, **227–228**
Limitations:
  on federal tax power, **137–141,** 252, 325–326, 341, 548
  on state and local borrowing power, 88, 92, 381, 391, 509–510, **514–516,** 521, 524, 539
  on state and local tax power:
    federal constitution, **142–150,** 241, 252, 311, 315, 318, 326–327, 345, 387, **410–411,** 483*n,* 548
    state constitutions, **150–151,** 252, 326, 381, 387, 394
Limits of government spending, **64–66**
Liquor license charge, 133, 321, 328, 343
Liquor monopolies, 430, 433, 440–441
Liquor tax:
  federal, 200, 235, 238, 239, 337, **341–342,** 348, 482
  local, 235, 321, 472
  state, 149*n,* 221, 235, 241–243, 328, 343, 347, 348, 349, 463*n,* 464, 482
Local finance, 205, 600, 608
  debt, 500, **509–512,** 515–517, 520–526, 528–529, 534, 537–556
  expenditure, **11–21, 30–35,** 35–50, 90, 592
  taxation, 134, 136–137, 176–178, 205, 233–237, **244,** 251, 288, 321–322, 337, **367–368,** 397, **466, 472–473**
  (see also *Administration, tax* and under particular taxes)
Los Angeles, revenues, 445, 448, 474
Louisiana:
  taxes, 150, 269, 370*n,* 394
  other subjects, 18, 440*n*
Louisville (Ky.), 251
Luxury taxes, 352

M

Maine:
  debt, 543
  taxes, 310, 316, 409
Manufacturers' excise (see *Sales tax*)
Marginal doctrine, 60–61, 196, 431, 435, 607
Marihuana tax, 138, 200, 342
Married couples, income tax on, **271,** 276–277
Maryland:
  expenditure, 30
  taxes, 251, 265, 323, 344, 376, 379, 391, 395
Massachusetts:
  taxes, 243, 251, 283, 309, 311, 312, 384*n*
  other subjects, 30, 43, 97, 543
Mercantilism, 4, 73, 605–606
Merit system, **96–97**
Michigan, taxes, 151, 221, 243, 323, 325, 345, 393
Mileage tax, 313–315, **385**
Military expenditure (see *Expenditure*)
Mines, taxation of, 201, 297, **320–321,** 326, **384**
Minimization, tax (see *Avoidance, tax*)
Minnesota:
  domain, 343
  taxes, 311, 381, 382, 391, 395, 409, 427
Mississippi, taxes, 344, 345–346, 370*n,* 372, 399*n*
Missouri, expenditure, 18
Monetary Policy and Fiscal Policy, **579–580,** 584–585, **590,** 601, 608
Money-and-deposits tax, 395, 598
Monopolies, government, 430, 431, 433, 440–441
Monopoly and tax shifting, **160–161,** 175–176
Montana:
  domain, 443
  taxes, 382, 395
Mortgages, taxation, 146, 369, 373, 396, 463
Motor vehicle fuel tax, 42, 72, 91, 181, 204, 221, 235, **241–243, 361–366,** 464–465, 483, 484
  administration, 91, 217, **361–362**
  economics, **362–363**
  federal, 235, **238–240,** 341–342, 356, 361, 483, 484
  local, 235, 244, 466
Motor vehicle license charge, 42, 72, 91, 181, 221, 235, **241–243, 356–361,** 362–366, 463–465
  administration, 360–361
  law, 136, 147

Motor vehicle license charge (*cont.*)
local, 235, 357
federal, 357, 361
Multiple taxation (see *Taxation: double*)
"Multiplier," the, **563**, 564–565, 569, 592, 604
Municipal Bankruptcy Law, 543
Municipal Finance Officers Association, 102, 114*n*
Musical instruments tax, 238, 342
Mutual Security Program, 24
National Association of Manufacturers, 102, 103

N

National Association of Purchasing Agents, 102
National Association of Real Estate Boards, 103
National banks, (see *Bank taxes*)
National Committee on Governmental Accounting, 125, 128
National Conference of Commissioners of Uniform State Laws, 312*n*
National defense (see *Expenditure, government: military*)
National income:
fiscal effects on, **561–604**, 608
measure of expenditure, 11, 14
measure of tax burden, 233–236
National Labor Relations Board, 14
National Municipal League, 94
National Resources Board, 320
National Tax Association, 101*n*, 312, 314, 328, 611
National Youth Administration, 40
NATO, 12
Nebraska:
expenditure, 18, 30, 39
taxes, 243, 320, 390
Neutrality doctrine, **185–186**, 424
Nevada:
expenditure, 18
taxes, 273, 409, 417, 481
New Hampshire, taxes, 251, 409
New Jersey:
expenditure, 18, 46
taxes, 243, 322, 418
other subjects, 43, 97, 543
New Mexico, finances, 30, 39, 344
New Orleans, 344
New York:
expenditure, 30, 39, 46
taxes, 221, 243, 272*n*, 322, 343, 344, 358, 370*n*, 371, 374*n*, 379, 382, 398*n*, 472
other subjects, 105, 468
New York City:
budget, 101, 111, 114*n*, 119*n*
enterprises, 437*n*, 441
expenditure, 19, 33, 474
taxes, 215*n*, 324, 344, 345, 346, 368*n*, 375, 379, 382
other subjects, 101, 111, 114*n*, 445, 570
Nonresidents, taxes on:
death, **410**, 418
personal income, 252, 270
North Carolina:
control of local finances, 95*n*, 517
taxes, 323, 345–346
other subjects, 39, 543
North Dakota:
enterprises, 440*n*
taxes, 252, 372, 409

O

Ohio, taxes, 309, 391, 395, 472
Oil wells, taxation of, 201, 297, 321, 333*n*
Oklahoma, taxes, 372, 396
Old Age and Survivors Insurance (see *Social Security*)
Oleomargarine tax, 133, 161, **200*n***, 202
Opium tax, 200, 342
Oregon, taxes, 252, 375, 415, 427
Organization (corporation) tax, **308–309**, 326, 477

P

Panama Canal, 436, 437, 499, 520
Pari-mutuel tax, 322–323
"Pay-as-you-go":
capital outlay financing, **523–525**, 527, 540
taxation, 215, 239, **278–279**, 283, 287, 597, 598
Payroll tax:
federal, 30, 46, 112, 138, 172–173, 182, 201, 235, 239, 246, 293, **305–307**, 487, 571, 597
local, 223, 244
state, 107, 235, 241, **242**, 307, 487, 599
Penalties, tax, 227, 283, 453
Pennsylvania:
expenditures, 18, 46
taxes, 243, 251, 254, 309, 310, 382, 472
Pensions:
government employee, **48**, 97
military (see *Veterans' aid*)
Perpetual loans, 538–539
Personal exemptions (see *Exemptions: minimum*)
Personal income tax, 110, 172–176, 235, 236, **249–288**, 301, 354, 398, 433, 492, 571, 597

Personal income tax (*cont.*)
  administration, 215, 216, 217, 221, 225, 226, 269–270, **278–286**
  basis, 204, 251, **252–254**
  capital gains, **261–268**, 274, 573, 587, 599
  dividends, **258**, 303–304, 477, 573
  estimated tax, **279**
  exemptions, 46, 172, 191, 192, 205, 217, 239, 250, 261, **269–270, 548–552**
  federal, 215, 226, 235, 237–240, 246, **249–250,** 256, 262, 266–267, 269, 272–273, 278–282, 292, 303, 351, 402, 417–478, 483, 484, 487
  incidence, **172–176**
  information-at-source, 225, **280**
  law, 139, 144, 151, **252–254**
  local, 235, 244, **251,** 252, 460, 466, 472
  married couples, **271,** 276–277
  nonresidents, 252, 270
  psychic income, 255, **256–257**
  rates, 196–198, 205, 251, **269–278**
  return forms, **279–280**
  state, 221, 235, **241–243, 250–252,** 262, 267, 269, 273, 278, 282–283, 351, 402, 464, 477–478, 480–481, 597
  theory, 186, 254–257, 261–268
  withholding, 215, 239, **278–279,** 283, 287, 597, 598
Personalty taxation (see *Property tax: tangibles* and *intangibles*)
Personnel management, government, 56, **86, 95–99,** 100, 223–224
Philadelphia:
  rents, 445
  taxes, 251, 254*n*
Physiocrats, 4, 154*n*, 172, 606
Pittsburgh, taxes, 251, 399
"Police power," **133**
Political doctrine and Public Finance, **3–4, 52–56,** 607, 608
Poll tax, 136, 139, 151, 155, 184, 241, **288–289**
Port of New York Authority, 477*n*
Postal system, 107, 239, 437, **438–439,** 521
Premiums tax (insurance), 319–320, 331
President and fiscal action:
  budget, 108, 117, 122, 207, 209, 589, **597–598**
  taxes, 207, 209
Pressure groups, **6–7, 16–17,** 50, 68, 151, 209, 340
Prices (see *Inflation*)
Privilege doctrine, **182–183**
Probate duties (see *Death taxes*)
Processing taxes, 138
Progressive taxation (see *Taxation*)
Property tax, 43, 136, 204, 235, 237, 244, 246, 313, **367–405,** 462–463, 483*n*, 571, 597
  assessment, 95, 144, 146, 221, 223, 225, **374–386**
  basis, **368–374**
  capitalization, 245, **400–401,** 403, 405
  classified property tax, 318, **394–396**
  collection, 216, **392–394**
  delinquency, **393–394**
  equalization, **388–389,** 470, 471*n*, 516
  exempt property, 148, 151, 193, 196, 200, **369–372**
  intangibles, 146, **368–369,** 372–373, **380–381, 395–398**
  law, 139, 142, 143, 146
  rate limitation, 88, 92, 151, 206, 381, **391–392**
  rates, 385, **389–392**
  realty, 146, **368,** 372, **376–379, 394–395**
  review, 144, 223, **387–388**
  shifting, **167–172**
  state, 241, **242**
  tangibles, 146, **368,** 372, 373, **379–380, 395, 397–398**
Protective tariff, 138, 199, 201, **338–339**
Psychic income, 255, **256–257**
Public domain, 394, **442–444**
Public ownership (see *Enterprises, government*)
Public Roads Administration, 11
Public schools (see *School finance*)
Public utilities, taxation, **313–316,** 326, 331, 332, 359, **384–386**
Public works expenditure, 12, **29, 30, 31–33, 34,** 74, 106, 521–525, 591–595
"Pump-priming," **581–582**
Purchasing, government, 100

R

Racing, taxes on, **322–323,** 344
Railroad taxes, 147, 241, 313–316, 331, 342, 364–365, **384–385**
Railroads, government operation, 353, 376, 437
Realty (see *Property tax*)
Reciprocity:
  interstate, 254, 360, 410, **478–479**
  tariff, 340
Reconstruction Finance Corporation, 46, 79*n*, 502
Recording taxes, 396
Redemption, debt (see *Debt*)
Refunding, debt (see *Debt: conversion*)
Regulatory taxation (see *Taxation*)
Relief expenditure (see *Expenditure, government*)

Rents:
revenue, 443
taxation, **176,** 187
Reorganization, government, **87–92**
Retail sales tax, 165, 205, 216, 217, 344, **345–346,** 347, 350, 571
administration, 216, 217, 223, **348–349,** 484
Retirement, debt (see *Debt: redemption*)
Retroactive taxes, 146
Revenues, non-tax, **428–455**
Review, tax:
general, 221
property tax, 144, 223, **387–388**
Rhode Island:
expenditure, 30
taxes, 382, 384*n,* 415

S

"Sacrifice" doctrine, 60–62, **184–185,** 191–192, 195
Sales taxes, 110, **165–167,** 188, 200, 204, 235, 236, **241–243, 344–355,** 464–465, 482, 484, 587, 597
administration, **346–349,** 354, 480, 484
gross sales (turnover) tax, 344, 348
law, 148, 149*n*
local, 223, 235, 244, 460, 466, 472
manufacturers' excise, 165, 344–345, 346, 348, 350–351, 484
retail sales tax, 165, 205, 216, 217, 344, **345–346,** 347, 350, 571
theory, **351–353**
Saving, fiscal effects on, 166, 274, 288, 302, 329, 352, 403–405, **571–573,** 575–576, 584, 596
Savings, taxes on, 573, 584, 598
Savings bonds (see *Bonds, government*)
School finance:
expenditure, 13, 15, 17, 18, **19–21,** 28–30, **31–32, 34, 35–41,** 54, 63, 74, 82, 87, 94, 461, 488
federal aid, **39**
school districts, **31,** 33, **38,** 374–375
state aid, 34, **467–470**
Scranton (Pa.), taxes, 251, 399*n*
Securities Exchange Commission, 14, 54
Seignorage, 454
Senate Finance Committee, 208–209, 612
Separation of revenue sources:
federal-state, **483–484**
state-local, 458, 462–463
Serial bonds (see *Bonds, government*)
Severance taxes, 320–322, 463
Shared taxes:
federal, 483, **484–485**
state, 110, **463–465,** 475
Shifting, tax (see *Taxation*)
Shipping Board, U.S., 437
Short-term debt (see *Debt, government*)
Single tax, 206, 399, 606
Sinking funds, 500, 516, 523, **544–546**
Situs, tax, 135, **144–146, 372–373,** 410, 478
Sixteenth Amendment, 139, **250,** 252
Small Business Administration, 79
Social effects of taxation (see *Taxation*)
Social expenditure (see *Expenditure, government*)
Social Security:
benefit payments, 14–15, 21, 23, **30, 46–47,** 48–49, 54, 59, 60, 82, 94, 99, 107, 112, 138, 489, 569, 595
reserve fund, 444–445, 502, 527, 536, 554
taxes, **46–47,** 107, 112, 138, 172–173, 182, 238–240, 245, 246, 293, **305–308,** 530*n*
Sociology and Public Finance, 3–4
Soft drinks tax, **343–344,** 348
South Carolina, taxes, 344, 370*n,* 379, 382
South Dakota, finances, 372, 440*n*
Sovereign revenues, **453–455**
Special assessments, 181, **449–452**
Special districts:
debt, 515
expenditure, 13, 19, **31, 35,** 88, 392
Spending, fiscal effects on (see *Consumption spending*)
Spendings tax, 186, 239, 353–354, 599
Sporting goods tax, 238, 342
Springfield (Ill.), taxes, 251
Stability, revenue, **205**
Stamp tax, 205, 216, 238, **348**
State aid, 28, 38–39, 43, 64, 110, 381, 465, **466–472,** 475
State control of local finances, **92–95,** 375–376, 467–468, **517,** 547
State finances, 134, 209–210, 600, 608
debt, 500, **508–512,** 514–515, 520–526, 528–529, 534, 537–556
enterprises, **440–441**
expenditure, **11–21, 28–30,** 35–50, 53, 89–90, 592
taxation, 134, 136–137, 176–178, 205, 209–210, 217, **220–224, 233–238, 241–244,** 250–252, 288, 330–331, **343–346, 356–362, 408–411, 426–427,** 482–487
(see also *Administration, tax, Law of Taxation,* and under particular taxes)
"State instrumentalities" limitation, **140,** 252, 411, 431, 548
State-local fiscal relationships, 28, 38–39, 43, 64, 92–95, 110, 375–376, 381, **458–475, 517,** 547

State-partnership doctrine, 183
State tax commissions, 91, 92, 95, 134, 213, **221,** 360, 362, 384, 419
Statistics and Public Finance, 3–4
St. Louis, taxes, 251, 254*n*
Stock dividends, taxation of, 139
Stock transfer tax, 342, 343
"Subject and measure" doctrine, **135–137,** 142, 252, 319*n*
Subsidies, 25, **63–64,** 75, 76, **79–81,** 453, 606
Suburbs, fiscal problems, **473–475**
Sumptuary taxes, 200, 344, 353
Supplementary state taxes, 483, **486**
Surplus, budget, 500, 544, 556
Surplus financing, 2, **579,** 599, 601, 607

T

Tangible personalty (see *Property tax*)
Tariff, 134, 138, 201, 219, 235, 237, 238, 241, **337–340,** 483*n*
Tax barriers, 481
Tax commissions (see *State tax commissions*)
Tax consciousness, 91, 92, 95, 134, 213, **218,** 270, 360, 362, 384, 419
Tax Court, 213, **220,** 222, 282
Tax-exempt bonds (see *Bonds, government*)
Tax ferrets, 226
Taxation, **132–428**
  burden, 180–191, **234–236,** 244–248, 333, 420
  confiscatory, 141, 144, 145–146, 185, 195, 198, 207, 272–275
  counties, 244, 374–375, 388
  distribution, 3, **179–191,** 218, **286–287, 331–332, 351–353, 402–403, 422–424,** 606
  double, **144–146,** 254, 303, 373, 410–411, **477–479**
  economic effects, 3, 153–178, 262–266, 270, 274, 287–288, 296, 301, 303–304, 319, **332–336,** 343*n*, 401, 420–422, **566–567, 570–575, 595–599**
  federal, 32, 134, **137–141,** 200, 207–209, 215, 219–220, 228, **232–241,** 249–250, **292–308,** 325–326, **337–343, 407–408, 425–426,** 482–487
  law, 3, 4, 21, 35, **132–151, 325–327, 372–373**
  local, 134, 136–137, 176–178, 205, **233–238, 244,** 251, 288, 321–322, 337, **367–368,** 397, **466, 472–473**
  productivity, **204–207**
  progressive, 185, 190, **194–199,** 237, **245–247, 270–275,** 287, 315, 331–332, 417–418, 551
  regulatory, 133, 134, 138, 141, **199–202,** 206, 322, 323, 328, 331–332, 338–339, 342, **352–353,** 417–418
  shifting and incidence, 3, **153–178,** 218, 245, 289, 315, 324, **329–331,** 339, **362–363, 400–405,** 420, 606
  social effects, 244–248, 251, 287, 306–307, 354, **400–405,** 420, 607
  state, 134, 136–137, 176–178, 205, 209–210, 217, **220–224, 233–238, 241–244,** 250–252, 288, **308–327,** 330–331, **343–346, 356–362, 408–411, 426–427,** 482–487
  (see also *Administration, tax, Exemptions,* and under particular taxes)
Taxpayers associations, **101–102**
Telegraph and telephone tax, 313–315, 342, 350, 484*n*
Tennessee, taxes, 251
Tennessee Valley Authority, 15, 25, 54, 64, 74, 370, 439, 440*n*
Tenth Amendment, **141**
Texas:
  taxes, 243, 323, 344
  other subjects, 105, 443
Theory (see *Debt, government, Expenditure, government, Taxation,* and under particular taxes)
Theatre taxes, 205, 238, 322, 343, **344,** 472, 484
Tobacco products tax:
  federal, 200, 204, 235, 238, 337, **341–342,** 348, 571
  state, 204, **241–242,** 343, **344,** 347, 348, 349, 480, 484
Toledo (O.), taxes, 251
Toll roads, 72, 181, 365, **441–442,** 548
Tonnage tax, 142, 241
Townships, 30, **31, 33, 81,** 374–375
"Transfer" expenditures, **59,** 65, **76–78,** 569
Treasurer, government, **91,** 92, 419
Treasury Department, 112, 207, 213, 214, **219–220,** 224, 226*n*, 227, 280–282, 295, 301, 307, 500–508, 519–520, 527*n*, **528,** 554
Tribute, 453*n*
Trust funds, government, 32, 107, 444–445, 502, 527, 536, 554
Trusts:
  death tax, 412–413, **422**
  property tax, 146, 373, 380
  tax avoidance, 285, 412–413
Turnover tax (see *Sales taxes: gross sales tax*)

U

Undistributed profits tax, 201, 285*n*, 292, 293, **301–302**, 304, 573, 584, 598
Unemployment:
  and Fiscal Policy, 2, 580, **583–584**, 608
  insurance, 26, 30, **47–48**, 54, 241, **306–307**, 489, 586, 595, 599
Uniform tax laws, **479–480**
Unincorporated business tax, **324**
Unit rule, 313, **385**
United States Chamber of Commerce, 103
Use tax, 149, 345, 349, 361*n*, 362
Utah, taxes, 409, 411, 415

V

Value-added tax, **324–325**, 345
Value-of-service doctrine, **180–182**, 358, 363
Vermont, taxes, 243, 269
Veterans' aid:
  expenditure, 12, **23–24**, 59, 82, 181, 512, 526, 569
  tax privilege, 372
Virginia, taxes, 243, 315, 395

W

War finance, **518–520**, **529–530**
  Civil War, 6, 12, 237, 249, 292, 407, 499, 509
  Korean War, 7–8, 22, 240, 293, 504
  World War I, 6, 12, 237, 250, 499
  World War II, 7–8, 12, 22, 65, 219, 232, 239, 270, 293, 302–303, 502–503
  (see also *Expenditure, government: military*)
Washington (state):
  budget, 105
  taxes, 243, 345–346, 373
Waste, government, 2, 23, 26, 58, **84–103**, 491
Water supply systems, 35, 74
Ways and Means Committee, 207–208, 612
West Virginia:
  budget, 129
  taxes, 346, 395
Wisconsin:
  debt, 514
  taxes, 221, 251, 256, 310, 320, 373, 426
Withholding:
  personal income tax, 215, 239, **278–279**, 283, 287, 597, 598
  payroll tax, 306
Wyoming:
  taxes, 289, 371
  other subjects, 39, 105

Y

Yield, government bonds, 26, 500, 502–507, 516, **530–534**

Index of Authors

A

Abbott, C. C., 613
Adams, H. C., 607
Alderfer, H. F., 244*n*
Allen, E. D., 612
Allen, H. K., 40*n*
Allix, E., 607
American Enterprise Association, 612
Aristotle, 605

B

Backman, J., 295*n*, 434*n*
Bastable, C. F., 606
Birch, A. H., 613
Bird, F. L., 516*n*
Blakey, R. G., 613
Bloom, C. C., 334*n*
Blough, R., 207*n*, 613
Blum, W. J., 194*n*
Bodin, J., 184, 605
Boisguillebert, 606
Bollens, J. C., 35*n*
Bowen, H. R., 64*n*
Brazer, H. E., 13*n*
Break, G. F., 574*n*
Brown, E. C., 613, 614
Brownlee, O. H., 356*n*, 612
Buchanon, J. M., 534*n*
Bullock, C. J., 613
Burkhead, J., 104*n*, 613
Burns, A. F., 559*n*
Burns, E. M., 613
Butters, J. K., 293*n*, 559*n*, 613, 614

C

Caine, M. R., 613
Cameralists, 606, 607
Campbell, A. K., 334*n*
Campbell, C. D., 507*n*
Carafa, D., 605
Cary, W. L., 207*n*, 614
Casner, A. J., 413*n*
Collier, R. P., 154*n*
Colm, G., 613
Committee for Economic Development, 559*n*, 612
Cooley, T. M., 143, 144*n*
Cornick, P. H., 380*n*
Coughlin, R., 614
Council of State Government, 90*n*
Crockett, J. P., 219*n*

D

Dahl, R. A., 55*n*
Daland, R. T., 101*n*
Davenant, C., 606
DePodwin, H. J., 614
Due, J. F., 156*n*, 337*n*, 356*n*, 442*n*, 612, 614
Duesenberry, J. S., 559*n*

E

Ely, R. T., 607

F

Fabricant, S., 11*n*
Fagan, E. D., 189*n*, 194*n*
Federation of Tax Administrators, 222*n*
Fisher, I., 255*n*
Fitch, L. C., 383*n*, 548*n*
Floyd, J. S., 334*n*
Freeman, R. A., 41*n*
Friedman, M., 165*n*
Funk, R. L., 244*n*

G

Garwood, J. D., 382*n*
Gemmill, R. F., 262*n*
George, H., 399
Gerloff, W., 607
Gillin, M. H., 173*n*
Glaser, M. G., 440*n*
Goode, R., 173*n*, 293*n*, 304*n*, 614
Graziani, A., 607
Gronouski, S. A., 376*n*
Groves, H. M., 304*n*, 612, 613, 614
Guicciardini, 189, 605

H

Haig, R. M., 255*n*, 363*n*
Hall, C. A., 308*n*, 614
Hall, J. K., 301*n*, 382*n*
Han, P. B., 329*n*
Hansen, A. H., 559*n*, 614
Hansen, B., 614
Harberger, A. C., 297*n*, 522*n*
Harbeson, R. W., 64*n*
Harriss, C. L., 10*n*, 67*n*, 424*n*, 425*n*
Hart, A. G., 614
Hegeland, H., 563*n*
Heller, W. W., 283*n*, 356*n*
Hellerstein, J. R., 150*n*
Hellmuth, W. F., 297*n*
Herman, R. S., 110*n*
Hershey, R. L., 335
Hicks, U. K., 606
Holland, D. N., 308*n*, 331*n*
Holshouser, E. C., 358*n*
House Committee on Government Operations, 490*n*
Houthakker, H. S., 356*n*

I

Institut International de Finances Publiques, 247*n*
International City Managers Association, 103*n*
Isard, W., 614

J

Jeze, G., 607
Johnson, R. H., 243*n*
Johnson, V., 613
Joint Committee on Internal Revenue Taxation, 274, 612
Joint Economic Committee, 237*n*, 559*n*, 612
Justi, 606

K

Kaldor, N., 187*n*, 614
Kalven, H., 194*n*
Keith, E. G., 304*n*
Kendrick, M. S., 11*n*, 612
Kernow, E., 434*n*
Keynes, J. M., 563, 572, 582, 608
Kimmel, L. H., 104*n*, 614
Kroos, H. E., 618

L

Leland, S. E., 394*n*
Lent, G. E., 302*n*, 303*n*, 348*n*
Leroy Beaulieu, P., 606
Lindblom, C. E., 55*n*
Lindholm, R. W., 309*n*
Lintner, J., 293*n*, 613
Lockyer, C. R., 358*n*
Lutz, H. L., 614
Lynn, A. D., 397*n*

M

Macy, C. W., 189*n*, 376*n*
Martin, J. W., 358*n*, 385*n*
Maxwell, J. A., 483*n*, 559*n*
McCulloch, J. F., 606
McKean, R. N., 84*n*
McKenna, J. P., 559*n*
Mercantilists, 605–606
Mikesell, R. M., 614
Mill, J. S., 184, 606
Millikan, M. F., 559*n*
Minnesota Tax Study Committee, 334*n*
Mirabeau, 606
Montesquieu, 606
Montgomery, R. E., 614
Morrow, G. D., 150*n*
Morton, W. A., 404*n*
Mosher, F. C., 104*n*
Municipal Finance Officers Association, 100*n*, 449*n*
Murphy, H. C., 502*n*
Murray, W. G., 389*n*
Musgrove, R. H., 154*n*, 246, 613
Mushkin, S., 492*n*
Myers, E. A., 600*n*

N

National Association of Assessing Officers, 374*n*, 377*n*, 387*n*
National Association of Manufacturers, 612
National Bureau of Economic Research, 612
National Committee on Governmental Accounting, 125*n*, 126*n*
National Industrial Conference Board, 20, 233, 500, 610, 612
National Planning Association, 612
Neumark, F., 607
Newcomer, M., 367*n*

O

Oster, C. V., 615
Owen, W., 356*n*

P

Parnell, H., 53*n*
Paul, R. E., 615
Peacock, A. T., 618
Pechman, J. A., 287*n*
Penniman, C., 283*n*
Perry, J. H., 615
Petty, W., 606

Phillips, J. C., 254*n*
Physiocrats, 606
Pigou, A. C., 606, 615
Plank, E. H., 612
Plato, 605
Poole, K. E., 613

Q

Quesnay, 606

R

Ratchford, B. U., 329*n*, 508*n*, 545*n*
Ratner, S., 613
Rau, K. H., 607
Reck, D., 615
Ricardo, D., 606, 607
Roberts, W. A., 615
Rolph, E. R., 72*n*, 153*n*, 615
Ross, W. D., 358*n*, 371*n*
Royer, C. A., 194*n*
Rozental, A. A., 354*n*

S

Sanders, T. H., 615
Sause, G. H., 288*n*
Schaffle, A., 607
Schaller, H. G., 482*n*
Schanz, G., 607
Scheffer, W. F., 360*n*
Schmoller, G., 607
Seligman, R. A., 189*n*, 607
Seltzer, L. H., 261*n*
Shelton, J. P., 599*n*
Shoup, C. S., 264*n*, 383*n*, 613
Shultz, W. J., 408*n*, 613
Sigafoos, R. A., 254*n*
Simons, H. C., 55*n*, 190, 255*n*, 538*n*, 615
Smith, Adam, 4, 53, 154*n*, 183–184, 212, 339, **606**, 607
Smith, B. B., 615
Smith, D. T., 293*n*, 615
Smithies, A., 104*n*, 559*n*, 613
Soloway, A. M., 11*n*
Spengler, E. H., 402*n*
Spenser, Herbert, 14
Steger, W. A., 278*n*
Stein, L. von, 607
Steuart, J., 606
Stocker, F. D., 405*n*, 615
Stockfish, J. S., 448*n*
Stourm, R., 607
Stout, R. S., 600*n*
Strayer, P. J., 615
Strifling, L. B., 448*n*
Studenski, P., 183*n*, 500, 613
Surrey, S. S., 286*n*

T

Tax Foundation, 10, 107*n*, 275, 514*n*, 610
Tax Institute, 10, 35*n*, 302*n*, 356*n*, 371*n*, 380*n*, 458*n*, 473*n*, 574*n*, 609, 610, 612
Temple, W., 606
Temporary National Economic Committee, 202n
Tenner, I., 125*n*
Ture, N. B., 237*n*
Turgot, 606
Twentieth Century Fund, 612

U

United Nations, 67*n*, 104*n*
U. S. Bureau of the Budget, 235
U. S. Bureau of the Census, 10, 20, 29, 31, 32, 34, 233, 235, 242, 243, 463, 511, 610
U. S. Chamber of Commerce, 612
U. S. Department of Commerce, 242
U. S. Office of Education, 38
U. S. Treasury Department, 10, 23, 238, 304*n*, 412, 483*n*, 500, 505, 506, 610, 612

V

Vauban, 606
Vickrey, W. S., 255*n*, 425*n*, 615
Vitti de Marco, A. de, 607

W

Wagner, A., 189, 607
Walker, F. A., 194*n*
Weidenbaum, N. L., 615
Welch, R. B., 217*n*, 616
Wells, D. A., 607
Wertheimer, R. G., 335*n*
White, M. I., 259*n*
Wickham, R., 101*n*
Willis, J., 616

X

Xenophon, 605